ANNALS OF THE NEW YORK ACADEMY OF SCIENCES

VOLUME 252

MEDICAL CONSEQUENCES OF ALCOHOLISM

Edited by

Frank A. Seixas, Kenneth Williams, and Suzie Eggleston

The New York Academy of Sciences
New York, New York
1975

Library of Congress Cataloging in Publication Data

Main entry under title:

Medical consequences of alcoholism.

   (Annals of the New York Academy of Sciences ;
v. 252)
   Papers from a conference held by the National
Council on Alcoholism, Apr. 28-30, 1974 in Denver,
Colo.
   1. Alcoholism--Congresses. I. Seixas, Frank A.
II. Williams, Kenneth, 1937-   III. Eggleston,
Suzie. IV. National Council on Alcoholism.
V. Series. New York Academy of Sciences. Annals ;
v. 252.   [DNLM: 1. Alcoholism--Complications--
Congresses. WI NE538 v.252 / WM274 M489 1974]
Q11.N5 vol. 252 [RC565]   508'.1s [615'.7]
ISBN 0-89072-006-1   75-11691

ACS
Printed in the United States of America

ISBN 0-89072-006-1

ANNALS OF THE NEW YORK ACADEMY OF SCIENCES

VOLUME 252

April 25, 1975

MEDICAL CONSEQUENCES OF ALCOHOLISM*

Editors

Frank A. Seixas, Kenneth Williams, and Suzie Eggleston

Conference Chairman

Frank A. Seixas

◆

CONTENTS

*This series of papers is the result of a conference entitled The Medical Consequences of Alcoholism, held by the National Council on Alcoholism on April 28, 29, and 30, 1974.

302725

Part VI. Infectious Disease

Part VII. Cancer

Part VIII. The Place of Sedatives in Treatment

NATIONAL COUNCIL ON ALCOHOLISM COMMITTEE ON MEDICAL AFFAIRS

PREFACE

Frank A. Seixas

National Council on Alcoholism
New York, New York 10016

The tendency in the United States has been not only for the people in the health sciences to neglect alcoholism as contributing to physical pathology, but for the people treating alcoholism to neglect the alcohol-related physical pathologies as something separate, too late or trivial in the face of the major change in life style necessary to produce a contented abstinent individual from a discontented heavy drinker.

These tendencies have been so marked as to almost come to a point where the alcoholism treatment machinery would be completely divorced from other health treatment facilities and issues, using medical and scientific personnel as subsidiary and ancillary services such as are needed in any case by the general population. Whether this trend is salubrious and efficient could even be left unquestioned, if each group were to pursue its course without the question's being asked. But the question will not lie still, given man's incessant desire for holistic explanations and the efforts of involved people to make strides in the understanding of alcohol's effect on the brain and body of man.

The schism has historical roots in the United States. Here we had 80 years of a growing campaign against alcohol as an immoral and unhealthy, evil drug. This campaign, waged by the WCTU and later its more politically effective offshoot, the Anti-Saloon League, stressed both the evil nature of drinking and its fatal physical consequences. The culmination of this campaign in the 19th Amendment, prohibiting the sale and distribution of alcoholic beverages, brought to the United States a "noble experiment" for which it was not prepared and would not tolerate.

In the wake of repeal, not only was alcohol exonerated from the charge of being immoral, but is was conceived of as an innocuous drug in the physical sphere. Curiously enough, medical science, having just awakened to the importance of vitamins, was prepared to go along and elaborately prove that cirrhosis was caused by malnutrition, not by a poisonous effect of alcohol.

This conference marks a year in which a turning point has been achieved. Thirty-two years after Patek's study,[1] which seemed to demonstrate the effect of malnutrition in producing cirrhosis, Dr. Charles Lieber has been successful in producing cirrhosis in primates (baboons) given a fully nutritious diet.[2] Thus, alcohol has again become incriminated as in itself producing specific toxic effects with pathological organ changes. These results could not be obtained when alcohol represented 30% of the calories, but only if 50% of the calories came from alcohol over 4 years' time. The results neatly correlate with Lelbach's epidemiological study of cirrhosis in men described in his paper, where again the duration of large quantities of ethanol was associated with the development of cirrhosis.

The conclusions related to cirrhosis, however, do not stand alone. Lundquist, in his tone-setting paper on alcohol and the cell, differentiates between physiological doses and pharmacological doses of alcohol. It is in the pharmacological (large) dose that the permanent consequences to the cell come about. This theme then extends to the entire conference. The pancreas, gastrointestinal tract, muscle, bone, blood, heart, and even the lungs are seen to be affected pathologically by these large doses over long periods of time.

Without adaptive mechanisms in the brain, the primary organ affected physiologically by alcohol, one would be unable to withstand physiologically the onslaught of these quantities of alcohol. This is where tolerance[3] comes in and makes possible the accumulation of the quantities needed to produce the pathological physical effects.

It was only by making the assumption that alcoholism is a disease, a concept basic to Alcoholics Anonymous and consistently championed by the National Council on Alcoholism, that the men and women engaged in this task were given the impetus to work on the solutions to the problem. These solutions provide groundwork for other solutions to other problems. As the impact of these ideas begins to be assimilated, it is possible that a clear-cut differentiation of something we can call the disease of alcoholism will be made.

Cahalan and Room[4] in *Problem Drinking in American Men* buttress their contention that many people drift in and out of heavy drinking and of heavy drinking with associated societal problems. The societal problems vary according to the view of drinking that obtains in the community. There are a surprising number of people who suffer in only 1 of the problem areas. Thus, we wonder whether such persons should be considered alcoholics even during the height of their alcohol problem.

As we see last year's (1973) deaths from heart disease decreasing by 15% while deaths from cirrhosis climbed 67.1%,[5] we begin to see the strength of our mandate to delimit the person with progressive alcoholism from those with more incidental problems with the drug, as well as those whose flamboyant use of alcohol is an overlay upon another serious problem, psychiatric in nature.[6]

If studies show "the highest rates of problem drinking occurring in the census tracts with the highest proportions of low-income families coupled with high proportions of persons not living in families,"[5] can we not ask ourselves whether these people arrived at or stayed at these census tracts as a result of their alcoholism (a situation well documented in individual cases) rather than that poverty itself or aloneness itself caused the condition?

When we consider "the general stubborness of drinking problems among institutionalized persons,"[5] we must look at some of the results achieved by speakers at this conference, including the 50% abstinence rate achieved by Dr. Marshall Orloff's team, and prove, not hypothesize, that "reinforcements which the institutionalized person gets from evading the realities of outside existence" would really be operative in institutions that addressed concerted efforts towards obtaining abstinence in patients who can be said to be alcoholics.

A corner is being turned in the United States without great fanfare. Two surveys of members of Alcoholics Anonymous showed that in 3 years the number who had started that program as a result of the instructions of a physician increased 50%. The American Medical Society on Alcoholism has grown from a membership of 30 to a membership of over 700 physicians. Medical schools are beginning to see the wisdom of teaching their students about alcoholism.

This conference report is an attempt to help fill the information needs of such students and physicians. This year, several other volumes devoted to such needs have been published. *Medical Complications of Alcohol Abuse*,[7] sponsored by the Committee on Alcoholism and Drug Dependence of the American

Medical Association, provides a terse and authorative text. *Alcohol As a Drug*, by Charles Becker, Robert Roe, and Robert Scott,[8] provides a curriculum on pharmacology, neurology, and toxicology of alcohol. Volume III of Kissin and Begletier's *Biology of Alcoholism*[9] contains a vast amount of information on these topics. The Cecil-Loeb *Textbook of Medicine* will have in Vol. III[10] an extended section on alcoholism. Lastly, but perhaps most influential of all, the NIAAA Second Special Report to the U.S. Congress, "Alcohol and Health,"[11] dwells at length on the physical consequences of alcoholism.

The volume that follows this preface takes off with a discussion of what we now know about the cellular response to alcohol in pharmacological doses. Not only every cell, but the modifications that occur by virtue of the differentiation of function and structure in the cells of various organ systems are discussed. It continues with a section on the pathophysiology of the various diseases that occur in these systems, and in the final section speaks to the treatment directed towards these cells and the overriding necessity for these patients in the achievement of complete abstinence. If one looks for a thorough appraisal of alcohol's effect on the brain, it would have to be found in the previous volume, *Alcoholism and the Central Nervous System*.[12] But in this volume, it seemed appropriate to discuss the special indirect effect of alcohol on the brain that occurs after the liver has been compromised sufficiently to produce hepatic coma. The elucidation of the intimate effect of ammonia on the cellular metabolism of the brain may lead to more effective ways to deal with the disastrous problem of hepatic encephalopathy, resulting from the alcohol-damaged liver. The possibility of attacking advanced liver disease by a further means, transplantation of a healthier liver, is a real one, and the pioneering efforts of Dr. Thomas Starzl give us this hope.

Finally, in the exploration of methods of dealing with alcoholism before irreversible physical lesions develop, or in the course of their treatment (a subject covered in *The Person with Alcoholism*[13]), 1 particular issue of prime importance to the practicing internist or family physician is the question of long-term administration of other sedatives. This subject is addressed by 3 physicians with somewhat different points of view, all of which converge on the great hazard of indiscriminate long-term ambulatory use of such drugs in patients with alcoholism.

Our thanks for the success of the conference go to the National Council on Alcoholism Medical Affairs Committee of the Board, the Conference Planning Committee, the superb speakers, and the enthusiastic note-taking conference attendees. Our thanks also to the conference cosponsors—the International Council on Alcohol and Addictions, for whom it was a regional meeting, and to Mr. Archer Tongue, its Director, for his assistance in developing the international panel; to the University of Colorado Medical Center, also a cosponsor, its Dean, Dr. Harry P. Ward, Associate Dean, Dr. John W. Singleton, and Dr. Thomas A. Witten, who made many gracious local arrangements. Also our thanks to Rear Admiral William Lukash, White House physician, whose luncheon address on medicine in the People's Republic of China will be long remembered. The American Academy of Family Physicians, which granted credit for conference attendance, and the Department of Mental Health of the American Medical Association, which did likewise, receive our thanks. Most particularly, those who made the conference possible through their financial support get our deep appreciation. These cosponsors include the Commonwealth Fund, the United States Brewers Association, the Licensed Beverage Industries (now DISCUS), Pfizer

8 Annals New York Academy of Sciences

Inc. Laboratories Division, Wyeth Laboratories, and Hoffmann-LaRoche, Inc. The National Institute on Alcohol Abuse and Alcoholism also gave us their welcome blessing.

For again including us as a conference whose Proceedings are published as the Annals of The New York Academy of Sciences, we thank that august body. Particularly we wish to thank again, our own Mrs. Suzie Eggleston, whose assiduous work on the manuscripts brought this publication into being, and this year's coeditor, Dr. Kenneth Williams, who has devoted much labor and attention to the design and content of the book.

REFERENCES

1. PATEK, A. J. & O. D. RATNOFF. 1942. The natural history of Laennec's cirrhosis of the liver. Medicine 21: 207.
2. LIEBER, C. S., L. M. DECARLI, H. GANG, G. WALKER, & E. RUBIN. 1972. Hepatic effects of long-term ethanol consumption in primates. Medical Primatology, part III, 27–278.
3. CRITERIA COMMITTEE, NATIONAL COUNCIL ON ALCOHOLISM. 1972. Criteria for the diagnosis of alcoholism. Amer. J. Psychiat. and Ann. Intern. Med. August issues.
4. CAHALAN, D. & R. ROOM. 1974. Problem drinking in American men. Monograph No. 7. Rutgers Center of Alcohol Studies. New Brunswick, N.J.
5. CAHALAN, D., I. H. CISIN & H. M. CROSSLEY. 1969. American drinking practices: a national study of drinking behavior and attitudes. Monograph No. 6 Rutgers Center of Alcohol Studies. New Brunswick, N.J.
6. SEIXAS, F. A., R. CADORET & S. EGGLESTON, Eds. 1974. The Person with Alcoholism. Ann. N.Y. Acad. Sci. 233.
7. SUMMARY OF 1973 A.M.A. WASHINGTON CONFERENCE. Sponsored by the Committee on Alcohol and Drug Dependence of the American Medical Association. 1974. Medical Complications of Alcohol Abuse. American Medical Association. Chicago, Ill.
8. BECKER, C. E., R. L. ROE & R. A. SCOTT. 1974. Alcohol as a drug: a curriculum on pharmacology, neurology and toxicology. Medcom Press. New York, N.Y.
9. KISSIN, B. & H. BEGLEITER. 1974. Biology of Alcoholism. Vol. III. Plenum Press. New York, N.Y.
10. CECIL-LOEB TEXTBOOK OF MEDICINE. (In print) P. B. Beeson & W. McDermott, Eds.: Vol. III. W. B. Saunders Co., Philadelphia-London.
11. Alcohol & Health from the Secretary of HEW. June 1974. Second special report to the U.S. Congress. DHEW Publication No. (ADM)74-124.
12. SEIXAS, F. A. & S. EGGLESTON, Eds. 1973. Alcoholism and the Central Nervous System. Ann. N.Y. Acad. Sci. 215.
13. SEIXAS, F. A., R. CADORET & S. EGGLESTON, Eds. 1974. The Person with Alcoholism. Ann. N.Y. Acad. Sci. 233.

INTRODUCTORY REMARKS

Archer Tongue

International Council on Alcohol and Addictions
Lausanne, Switzerland

The Annual Medical Scientific Sessions of the National Council on Alcoholism have been valuable occasions for the exchange of scientific information in the field of alcoholism. It has been with much satisfaction, therefore, that the International Council on Alcohol and Addictions has cooperated with NCA in the sponsoring of an international symposium in the fifth medical scientific session.

It is important for national voluntary bodies in the field of alcoholism to keep in close touch with the scientific research and medical knowledge in their field. This is indeed indispensable if the work of our organizations is to have impact in their areas of operation. Moreover, the voluntary bodies can play a particular role in stimulating the exchange of scientific experience and information across the various disciplines involved.

The Denver Symposium was significant for presenting aspects of the effects of excessive alcohol use that are often not given sufficient attention. The high level of papers presented by a distinguished group of scientists resulted in a symposium, the proceedings of which will be a valuable source for all concerned with alcohol and alcoholism problems.

9

INTRODUCTION

Kenneth Williams

University of Pittsburgh School of Medicine
Pittsburgh, Pennsylvania 15261

Medical complications related to the ingestion of large amounts of alcoholic beverages are being identified with increasing frequency. The prevalence of these various diseases in the alcoholic population have generally not been established; rates seem to vary according to the subpopulation under study and the sensitivity of the techniques used to detect pathology. Frequently, however, the medical consequences are the reason for the drinker's seeking help.

Thus, an alcoholic will seek a doctor or the hospital emergency room because of physical or emotional complaints caused by his excessive ingestion of alcohol more readily than he might seek help for a "drinking problem." If the doctor is able to properly diagnose the problem as a manifestation of alcoholism, he has taken an important step in bringing his patient to recovery. Unfortunately, in this country at the present time, few physicians have been adequately trained to recognize the medical consequences of alcoholism or to diagnose the underlying disease. While programs have been initiated in the medical schools to correct this deficiency, the present publication should assist the currently active medical practitioner in this task.

The medical complications of alcohol abuse are frequently cited as criteria for diagnosis of alcoholism. In the N.C.A. Criteria for the Diagnosis of Alcoholism, there are 10 major criteria with a diagnostic level of "1." Six of these 10 are related to medical consequences of excessive alcohol ingestion. The medical complications can provide objective and reliable means of diagnosing alcoholism.

Compared with other psychoactive drugs, the ethyl alcohol molecule is very small. It is, under usual conditions, rapidly absorbed through the mucosal membranes of the gastrointestinal tract (especially the duodenum and jejunum) and enters the portal circulation. Distributed throughout the body in the arterial blood, the molecule diffuses rapidly across capillary membranes. It moves across tissue membranes by a process of simple diffusion. Within a few minutes after oral ingestion, it has been circulated to every tissue in the body. It is not blocked by the "blood-brain barrier" or the "placental barrier."

As it passes through the individual cell membranes, the alcohol molecule effects the stabilization of the membrane. Inside the cell, the molecule also affects the membrane's permeability and its transport mechanisms. In the cytoplasm, changes are effected in the intracellular enzyme systems, mitochondrion and endoplasmic reticulum.

In view of such wide distribution throughout the body organs and even into the individual cell, one can readily appreciate that a wide range of cellular functioning is affected by alcohol. It is probably true that ethyl alcohol is metabolically the most active drug known to affect the human body.

Dr. Lundquist's paper outlines the range of cellular functioning altered by alcohol.

INTERFERENCE OF ETHANOL IN CELLULAR METABOLISM

Frank Lundquist

Department of Biochemistry
University of Copenhagen
2200, Copenhagen, Denmark

Alcohol is both a rapidly metabolized nutrient and a dangerous drug, depending on the amount consumed and the duration of the exposure to the substance. This ambiguity is the cause of many difficulties in the interpretation of the results of alcohol consumption.

It appears to be a useful assumption that the physiological and biochemical actions of ethanol on the tissues and cells of the organism can be separated into 2 quite distinct groups. One group includes the direct and indirect consequences of ethanol metabolism, which are seen already at very low ethanol concentrations. The other group may be summarized as the pharmacological actions of alcohol. These are much less specific and are independent of the metabolism of ethanol itself. They become manifest only at high concentrations and are indeed similar to the actions of a large number of substances, chemically only remotely related to ethanol.

Inevitably there is a considerable concentration range in which both types of action are observed, but one may suggest that at concentrations that produce no measurable changes in the physiological (or psychological) parameters the effects caused by alcohol metabolism are predominant, while at concentrations in the range above 50 mM (200 mg/100 ml blood) the pharmacological actions are clearly manifest.

As the specific reactions of a number of organs and tissues are considered in the following lectures by experts in these fields, I shall restrict my contribution to more general remarks, though of course specific examples will be given.

DIRECT METABOLIC EFFECTS OF ETHANOL AT "PHYSIOLOGICAL" CONCENTRATIONS

Direct metabolic effects are restricted to the organs that metabolize ethanol. These are the liver and, only to a small degree, the kidney and possibly other organs as well. The physiological mechanism for alcohol metabolism starts functioning at very low concentrations and approaches its full velocity already at concentrations about 10 mM (40 mg/100 ml blood). The biochemistry of this mechanism is shown in TABLE 1.[19]

In man the intermediary product, acetaldehyde, is very effectively removed by aldehyde dehydrogenases, which are present in much higher activity in human liver than, for example, in the rat,[28] so the concentration of this substance in the circulating blood is only about 10 μM, widely independent of the alcohol concentration. The same is true in the pig, while in the rat the concentration appears to be somewhat higher. The acetate formed is released into the hepatic venous blood and builds up a concentration in the circulation of about 1 mM, again independent of the alcohol concentration. Some acetate is activated in the liver and transformed into lipids and other substances. Only a small part is oxidized to CO_2 in the liver (TABLE 2).

Apart from the presence of metabolites formed directly from ethanol, another important metabolic change is observed in the liver, *viz.* an increase in the con-

11

TABLE 1

Metabolism of Ethanol at Low Concentrations

CYTOSOL	Ethanol + NAD$^+$ $\longrightarrow$ Acetaldehyde + NADH + H$^+$
MITOCHONDRIA + CYTOSOL	Acetaldehyde + NAD$^+$ $\longrightarrow$ Acetate + NADH + H$^+$

Cytoplasmic free NADH/free NAD$^+$ increases 3–4 times.
Mitochondrial free NADH/free NAD$^+$ increases 2–3 times.
Concentration of acetate in blood increases to about 1 mM.
Concentration of acetaldehyde in blood increases to about 10 μM.
Concentration of AMP in liver is approximately doubled.

centration of reduced nicotinamide coenzymes. This can be followed by measuring certain substrate pairs in the liver or the hepatic venous blood. The lactate/pyruvate ratio and the hydroxybutyrate/acetoacetate ratio mirror the cytosolic and mitochondrial NADH concentration, respectively, and both are significantly increased (TABLE 1). Other redox couples may be used to determine the NADPH/NADP ratio, which is also elevated.

The cause of the increase in cytosolic NADH/NAD appears to be that alcohol dehydrogenase (ADH) produces NADH at a rate that balances the rate of its utilization (i.e., oxidation) in the following way. When the NADH produced can no longer be oxidized, its concentration increases, and this inhibits the ADH-reaction—as may be calculated from the kinetic results of Theorell and Chance.[26] In this way a balance at a new and higher NADH concentration is established. A consequence of such a mechanism is that ADH is not normally working at its maximal speed, even when the ethanol concentration is high enough to saturate the enzyme. Measurements of enzyme activities in liver tissue and other evidence have confirmed that this is the case, though to a different extent in different species.

The pathways by which NADH produced in the cytosol is reoxidized to NAD$^+$ has been the subject of much discussion. Some NADH may be reoxidized in the cytosolic compartment itself by reduction of intermediary metabolites to substances, which either leave the liver or accumulate continuously. Pyruvate, for

TABLE 2

Fate of Ethanol Carbon in the Liver

	CO$_2$	Acetate	Lipid
		(Percent of total metabolized)	
Pig liver perfused nonfasted	3	62	35
Rat liver perfused nonfasted	12	75	⁻13
fasted 48 h	10	83	7
Man nonfasted		75	
fasted		100*	

*Havel.[10]

example, is reduced by NADH to lactate, which leaves the liver, and dihydroxy-acetone phosphate is reduced to glycerol phosphate, which, at least initially, accumulates in the liver. Normally such reactions will account for only a very small proportion of the NADH oxidized. One mechanism, however, permits continuous accumulation of reduced substances: synthesis of fatty acids, which requires NADPH. A link between this coenzyme and NADH could be the energy-requiring cycle of reactions shown in TABLE 3. The evidence for the role of this cycle in alcohol metabolism is admittedly still rather indirect.[28] The major pathway of reoxidation of NADH is, however, the respiratory chain, but this encounters the problem how the reducing equivalents are transferred into the mitochondria, where this process takes place. Isolated mitochondria cannot oxidize added NADH, so it has been necessary to assume the existence of some mechanism that circumvents the direct transport of NADH through the mitochondrial membrane. A number of carriers have been suggested to take up hydrogen from cytosolic NADH and deliver it again inside the mitochondria, to be oxidized to water in the respiratory chain. The most widely accepted candidates for such carrier function are malate and glycerol phosphate which are oxidized intramitochondrially to oxaloacetate and dihydroxyacetone phosphate, respectively. These substances in turn are returned to the cytosol, though in the case of oxaloacetate through a series of intermediary steps.[8,19] The intramitochondrial glycerol phosphate de-

TABLE 3

Conversion of NADH to NADPH

1. $NADH + H^+ + Oxaloacetate \longrightarrow Malate + NAD^+$
2. $Malate + NADP^+ \longrightarrow Pyruvate + NADPH + H^+$
3. $Pyruvate + CO_2 + ATP \longrightarrow Oxaloacetate + ADP + P_i$
$NADH + NADP^+ + ATP \longrightarrow NADPH + NAD^+ + ADP + P_i$

hydrogenase (a flavoprotein) seems to have a rather high K_m, but as the concentration of glycerol phosphate in the liver cell during alcohol metabolism increases considerably, this shuttle is believed by some authors[32] to be important. Other mechanisms for the transfer of reducing equivalents into mitochondria have been seriously considered.[6]

The oxidation of acetaldehyde may apparently take place both in the cytosol and in mitochondria.[30] In the rat, some 80% of the activity is located in the mitochondria. The enzyme has a K_m below 0.1 μM, suitable for the effective removal of acetaldehyde.[7]

The efficient intramitochondrial oxidation of acetaldehyde is compatible with the increased hydroxybutyrate/acetoacetate ratio. The increased NADH concentration in the liver cell causes a number of metabolic changes involving carbohydrates, lipids, proteins, and other substances as well. The main effects may be summarized as follows:

The most remarkable effect is perhaps the strong inhibition of the citric acid cycle, which is evident from the single fact that the oxygen uptake required for ethanol oxidation in the rat liver is only slightly less than the measured oxygen uptake, leaving little room for other oxidative processes. Probably several steps in the citric acid cycle are inhibited simultaneously by the increased intramitochondrial NADH and ATP.[32] This inhibition may affect the anaplerotic pathways by which a number of substances are synthesized from intermediates of the cycle. A quantitative analysis of this consequence of ethanol metabolism has, however, not been performed.

The influence of increased NADH concentrations on carbohydrate metabolism is complex. Effects are observed both on glycogen metabolism and on gluconeogenesis, depending on the nutritional state of the organism.[20] In the well-fed organism, when glycogen is present in the liver a dose of alcohol seems to provoke glycogenolysis as the blood glucose concentration shows a transient increase. This effect is also observed in the perfused liver, so hormonal factors can at most be a partial explanation. The same is true of a possible glucose-sparing action in peripheral tissues of the increased acetate concentration. The increased concentration of AMP in the liver (TABLE 1) may interfere in glycogen synthesis or breakdown, and a directly activating effect on ATP-cyclase cannot be excluded, but at present no clear-cut explanation is available.

TABLE 4

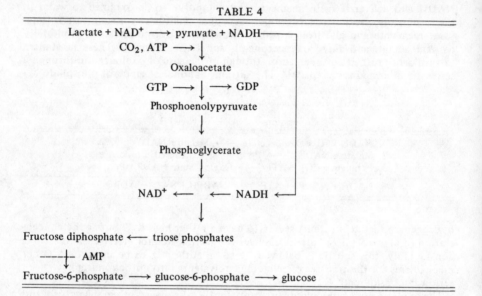

In the glycogen-depleted fasting state, blood glucose concentration is dependent on gluconeogenesis from a number of precursors, especially lactate, alanine, and glycerol. In human subjects a drastic fall in blood glucose concentration may be seen, when ethanol is consumed after prolonged fasting. Lactate is assumed to be a major precursor of glucose under these conditions through the series of reactions shown in TABLE 4. When ethanol is metabolized, the ratio between lactate and pyruvate increases, which means that the pyruvate concentration decreases to about one third of the previous value. As the rate-limiting carboxylation of pyruvate to oxaloacetate is strongly dependent on the pyruvate concentration (high K_m), this reaction will be inhibited, and thereby so will the whole series of reactions leading to glucose. Further inhibition is to be expected from the lowered oxaloacetate/malate ratio. This explanation of the inhibition of gluconeogenesis by alcohol was advanced by Krebs,[16] and it should hold also for other glucose precursors, which enter the gluconeogenic pathway at the level of pyruvate, e.g. serine and proline. Under conditions of fasting and malnutrition the effect of alcohol on gluconeogenesis may be dramatic.[20] As the lactate concentration in the circulating blood of the intact organism builds up, the pyruvate concentration should again approach normal levels in spite of the increased lactate/pyruvate concentration ratio, so normal gluconeogenesis may gradually be restored.

Glycerol metabolism is also changed by ethanol. Phosphorylation is inhibited presumably by the increased AMP concentration and the accumulating concentration of glycerophosphate, both known to inhibit glycerokinase. The primary cause of the increased glycerophosphate is again believed to be the elevated NADH/NAD ratio, which inhibits the conversion of glycerol phosphate to dihydroxyacetone phosphate by displacing the equilibrium. The consequence is a decrease in the uptake of glycerol and decreased glucose formation from glycerol. At the same time, the increase in glycerol phosphate may facilitate formation of triglycerides.

Conversion of other sugars to glucose is also changed by alcohol. Thus, galactose metabolism in the liver is primarily inhibited by the increased NADH concentration, which inhibits the conversion of UDP-gal to UDP-glu. The result is accumulation of galactose-1-phosphate, which in turn inhibits the phosphorylation of galactose about 50%. Also, the metabolism of fructose is changed. Here both NADH and acetaldehyde may play a role. The uptake of fructose is not changed significantly, but the fraction converted to glucose is increased and that converted to lactate and pyruvate is decreased, at least during fasting.

The influence of low concentrations of alcohol on the protein metabolism of the liver is more uncertain. Some proteins, e.g. albumin, seem to be synthesized at a reduced rate when ethanol is given, but ingestion of a mixture of amino acids or tryptophan[13] appears to restore the rate of synthesis. Also, the rate of transferrin synthesis is inhibited, while that of fibrinogen apparently is unaffected.[13] With regard to the synthesis of apolipoprotein, there appears to be no inhibition of the synthesis per se, nor of the release of the lipoprotein from the liver. A number of enzymes in the liver have been shown not to change in amount during prolonged alcohol treatment; this is true also of alcohol dehydrogenase itself.

The cause of the changes in protein synthesis in the liver in those cases where they have been established is unknown. Changes in the availability of some amino acids in the metabolic pool through interference with transport processes and transamination are possibilities that deserve further study.

Lipid metabolism in the liver may also be influenced by the changes of NADH. The high level of glycerol phosphate has been claimed to further triglyceride synthesis and the transhydrogenation to NADPH could directly activate fatty acid synthesis. A significant increase in the incorporation of FFA into liver triglycerides in intact rats has been observed at ethanol concentrations of 10 mM.[14]

The metabolism of other classes of substances in the liver may also be altered. Increased uric acid formation may be a consequence of the increased steady-state concentration of AMP.[27] This substance may be directly broken down to uric acid, as seen more markedly during metabolism of large loads of fructose. Moreover, the increased lactate concentration in the blood is known to compete with uric acid for the excretory mechanism in the kidney, resulting in an increased blood uric acid concentration. The pattern of products formed in the breakdown of some biogenic amines is also changed during ethanol metabolism. The formation of carboxylic acids such as 5-hydroxyindole acetic acid (from serotonin) and vanillylmandelic acid (from norepinephrine) and other similar substances is curtailed and the production of the corresponding reduced (alcoholic) products favored. At present the most likely explanation for this change appears to be competitive inhibition of aldehyde dehydrogenase by acetaldehyde, though the increased NADH/NAD ratio has also been made responsible for these changes. Both mechanisms may, in fact, be active.

INDIRECT EFFECTS OF "PHYSIOLOGICAL" ETHANOL METABOLISM

The large capacity of the liver as a biochemical factory causes the composition of the circulating blood to be changed significantly during alcohol metabolism. We have already seen some of the changes in the hepatic venous blood: The concentration of acetate increases to about 1 mM, that of acetaldehyde to $10 \mu M$. The lactate concentration also increased (because of decreased utilization), and a number of other more or less reproducible alterations, including those seen in the blood glucose concentration, take place. Acetate is apparently a good energy source for many tissues. It is metabolized by heart and skeletal muscles and probably by other cells as well. In the heart, acetate apparently replaces fatty acids as a fuel.[18] Acetate has the interesting property of decreasing lipolysis in adipose tissue. This is evidenced by the decline in the concentration of FFA to about half even when very small amounts of ethanol are consumed. There is a direct effect of acetate on the adipose cells,[4] but an insulin effect is not excluded in addition, in the situation when blood glucose is increased. A parallel fall in the concentration of FFA and glycerol is seen, as observed by Feinman and Lieber.[3]

Acetaldehyde production in the liver has been suggested to be the cause of alcoholic intoxication, but the fact that the concentration of this substance is virtually independent of the alcohol concentration would seem to exclude this possibility.

However, acetaldehyde is a chemically reactive substance, which could be imagined to interfere in metabolic reactions in the central nervous system, even at the low concentration of $10 \mu M$. Davis and Walsh[1,2] have suggested such interference in which acetaldehyde condenses with dopamine to form an alkaloid salsolinol and have verified the formation of this substance in brain and liver preparations. A similar condensation reaction involves dopamine and its oxidized product (dihydroxyphenylacetaldehyde) with formation of tetrahydropapaverolin, a substance with considerable similarity to the morphine family of alkaloids. The reaction has been demonstrated in liver and brain and seems to be enhanced by the presence of acetaldehyde, albeit in quite large concentrations. The mechanism is believed to be competitive inhibition of the oxidation of dihydroxy phenylacetaldehyde by aldehyde dehydrogenase, an enzyme that is also present in nervous tissue. These findings have formed the basis for interesting speculations on the mechanism of alcohol addiction and were discussed in considerable detail at the Symposium in 1972.[1]

EFFECTS OF HIGH ETHANOL CONCENTRATIONS

Elevated concentrations of ethanol have quite separate actions from those of physiological concentrations both in the liver and in other tissues. As alcohol in itself even at the highest concentrations compatible with life of mammalian cells has no effect on the activity of individual enzymes, i.e. ordinary soluble enzymes, the operative mechanism is likely to be concerned with the structural aspects of cell biochemistry. Already in the beginning of this century, interest was focused on cellular membranes as the target of pharmacologically active substances such as ethanol, ether, chloroform, and many others.[11] Their biological activity was found to be closely related to the distribution ratio of the substances between an aqueous solution and a lipid phase. This concept has since been refined and gives a remarkably good fit between physicochemical properties and pharmacological activity. However, the structure of simple membranes, as measured, for instance, through permeability properties, is not deteriorated measurably at the ethanol concentrations encountered in a biological setting; indeed, a stabilization, if anything, occurs. In preliminary experiments we examined the susceptibility of lysosomal membranes to ethanol by exposing isolated hepatocytes to 100 mM alcohol and measuring the acid phosphatase liberated into the supernatant of a homogenate. No increase was seen after 2 hours at $37°C$.

On the other hand, membrane structures of a more refined character, such as those involving active transport mechanisms or hormone receptor devices, have been shown to react significantly to concentrations of 100 mM ethanol or less. Among membrane systems of mammalian cells there are at least 2 that display definite changes in the presence of ethanol: the cell (plasma) membrane and the mitochondrial membrane.[22]

Cell membranes have been studied with advantage in erythrocytes, because these cells contain no other membranes. As early as 20 years ago Streeten and Solomon[24] clearly demonstrated a significant inhibition of the sodium pump in human erythrocytes at concentrations of ethanol as low as 70 mM. Similar effects were later observed in many other tissues, such as frog skin, kidney slices, and, above all, nervous tissues, including brain.[11] As the activity of the ion pump in the brain requires a considerable expenditure of energy, the effect of ethanol on this process may well explain the decrease in oxygen uptake of the brain observed *in vivo* in the presence of high alcohol concentrations.

The mechanisms at work in the liberation and action of some hormones comprise another point of pharmacological activity involving the plasma membrane for which there is some evidence.[23] An increased liberation of epinephrine by large alcohol doses has thus been reported by many authors. Similarly, an action on the hypothalamic-pituitary-adrenocortical endocrine system is well established, but it is not known with certainty whether any of these actions are directly caused by alcohol or are indirect consequences of changes in the brain, caused by the effect on the sodium pump. However, there are a few indications that ethanol may directly activate or facilitate the activation of the ATP cyclase system in some cells. Thus, the effect of glucagon on a liver cyclase preparation is increased by ethanol and other alcohols, although at concentrations above 1%.[5] Similar experiments in preparations from pancreatic islets showed an appreciable effect on the cyclase activity even at very low ethanol concentrations.[17] Alcohol has been claimed to sensitize the effect of glucose on the liberation of insulin from pancreas, but this effect has not been confirmed on isolated islets.[9]

Returning now to the effect of high ethanol concentrations on the liver, we may regard this as a special case insofar as ethanol, like many other substances foreign to the body, causes development of detoxication mechanisms predominantly located in the smooth endoplasmic reticulum. Prolonged treatment with large amounts of ethanol causes an increased capacity for ethanol elimination, and so does treatment with a number of other drugs in various species. At the same time, a significant proliferation of the smooth endoplasmic membrane system is observable. The magnitude of the extra alcohol-metabolizing capacity is not so easy to establish, but a conservative estimate is 50% of the normal rate.

The character of the extra system for ethanol metabolism has been the subject of much and heated discussion. In TABLE 5, 3 possibilities are listed. One school, building on an observation by Orme-Johnson and Ziegler,[21] has demonstrated the occurrence of a hydroxylation system involving cytochrome P_{450} and apparently similar to the systems causing hydroxylation of many other substances. Enzyme preparations have been made in which this reaction is separated from other alternative pathways and a requirement for NADPH and oxygen has been demonstrated.[25] Another group of investigators also implicate the endoplasmic reticulum but claim that its only role in alcohol metabolism is the production of hydrogen peroxide through oxidation of NADPH by molecular oxygen.[29] Hydrogen peroxide in turn can oxidize ethanol in the presence of catalase, as already demonstrated by Keilin and Hartree.[15] The peroxidation of alcohol seems normally to be limited by the rate of H_2O_2 formation, whereas catalase is present in excess. In all probability, both systems exist. The issue that is very difficult to decide is the relative quantitative role of these two pathways alternative to the ADH pathway. Both may in fact be considered as means employed by the organism to cope with pharmacological doses of ethanol. The mechanism by which the induction of these pathways takes place seems not to be specific for

TABLE 5

Pharmacological Mechanisms of Alcohol Metabolism

(a) Ethanol + H_2O_2 $\xrightarrow{\text{cat.}}$ Acetaldehyde + H_2O

NADPH + H^+ + O_2 $\longrightarrow$ H_2O_2 + $NADP^+$

(Ethanol + NADPH + O_2 $\longrightarrow$ acetaldehyde + $NADP^+$ + H_2O)

(b) Ethanol + NADPH + O_2 + H^+ $\xrightarrow{\text{cyt.}P_{450}}$ acetaldehyde + $NADP^+$ + H_2O

(c) Increased $(Na^+ - K^+)$ ATPase $\longrightarrow$
Increased NADH oxidation in respiratory chain $\longrightarrow$
Increased ethanol oxidation via ADH.

ethanol, but the details are still unknown. A third mechanism has been suggested by Israel et al.[31] to be responsible for part of the increased alcohol oxidation in the liver of rats fed large doses of alcohol for several weeks. They claim that the (Na + K)-requiring membrane ATPase functions at an increased rate under these conditions. This means that the cell has an increased need for ATP production. This need is met by utilization of the surplus capacity of the ADH pathway previously mentioned, through increased oxidation of NADH by mitochondria made possible by an increased level of ADP caused by the increased ATPase activity in a way reminicent of uncoupling of oxidative phosphorylation.

It may be relevant to point out here that the extra ethanol oxidation in the "induced" state at high alcohol concentrations in contrast to the "physiological" situation described above does not produce useful energy in any of the 3 cases, emphasizing again the pharmacological character of these mechanisms. No ATP is formed in the hydroxylation or peroxidation reactions, and the ATP production in the case of Israel's mechanism is used to drive the inefficient sodium pump.

The fact, already emphasized, that the pharmacological action of ethanol is rather unspecific makes it desirable to pinpoint a cellular lesion, which is found also with other drugs, which could give rise to tolerance and also to dependence. If such a lesion could be demonstrated it might explain a number of pathological processes as secondary results of the primary biochemical lesions. Now, though it may be wishful thinking at the present time, one could point to the inhibitory effect on the membrane-bound ion-transport mechanisms as the key process, as in fact Israel et al. have done.[12] Ion transport is so vital to all cells, and especially to those of the central nervous system, that we might have here a common source of the many and varied functional and morphological changes observed during chronic alcohol ingestion. Regarding the question of tolerance, the experiments of Israel et al. point to the possibility of compensatory development of the ATP-requiring ion pumps during prolonged alcohol treatment. This might simulate the normal state of the cell if alcohol is present—in other words provide tolerance.

What happens in the alcoholic central nervous system in the absence of alcohol is difficult to predict, but it may not be unreasonable to expect that symptoms of abstinence and addiction may ultimately be related to changes in the ionic environment of the cells.

REFERENCES

1. DAVIS, V. E. 1973. Neuroamine-derived alkaloids: A possible common denominator in alcoholism and related drug dependencies. Ann. New York Acad. Sci. **215:** 111–115.
2. DAVIS, V. E. & M. J. WALSH. 1970. Alcohol, amines and alkaloids; a possible biochemical basis for alcohol addiction. Science **167:** 1005–1007.
3. FEINMAN, L. & C. S. LIEBER. 1967. Effect of ethanol on plasma glycerol in man. Amer. J. Clin. Nutr. **20:** 400–403.
4. GLIEMAN, J. & O. SONNE. 1974. Unpublished observation.
5. GORMAN, R. E. & M. W. BITENSKY. 1970. Selective activation by short chain alcohols of glucagon responsive adenyl cyclase in liver. Endocrinology **87:** 1075–1081.
6. GRUNNET, N. 1970. Oxidation of extramitochondrial NADH by rat liver mitochondria. Possible role of acyl-SCoA elongation enzymes. Biochem. Biophys. Res. Comm. **41:** 909–917.
7. GRUNNET, N. 1973. Oxidation of acetaldehyde by rat liver mitochondria in relation to ethanol oxidation and the transport of reducing equivalents across the mitochondrial membrane. Eur. J. Biochem. **35:** 236–243.
8. GRUNNET, N., B. QUISTORFF & H. I. D. THIEDEN. 1973. Rate-limiting factors in ethanol oxidation by isolated rat liver parenchymal cells. Eur. J. Biochem. **40:** 275–282.
9. HEDESKOV, C. J. & K. CAPITO. 1974. Unpublished observation.
10. HAVEL, R. J. 1974. *In* Regulation of Hepatic Metabolism. Alfred Benzon Symposium VI. F. Lundquist and N. Tygestrup, Eds.: 189. Academic Press, New York, N.Y.
11. ISRAEL, Y. 1970. Cellular effects of alcohol. Quart. J. Stud. Alcohol **31:** 293–316.
12. ISRAEL, Y., H. KALANT, E. LEBLANC, J. C. BERNSTEIN & I. SALAZAR. 1970. Changes in cation transport and (Na + K)-activated adenosine trophosphatase produced by chronic administration of ethanol. J. Pharm. Exp. Therap. **174:** 330–336.
13. JEEJEEBHOY, K. N., M. J. PHILLIPS, A. BRUCE-ROBERTSON, J. HO & U. SODTKE. 1972. The acute effect of ethanol on albumin, fibrinogen and transferrin synthesis in the rat. Biochem. J. **126:** 1111–1126.
14. JOHNSON, O. 1974. Influence of the blood ethanol concentration on the acute ethanol induced liver triglyceride accumulation in rats. Scand. J. Clin. Lab. Invest. **33:** 207–213.
15. KEILIN, D. & E. F. HARTREE. 1936. Coupled oxidation of alcohol. Proc. Roy. Soc. (London). Ser. B. **119:** 141–159.
16. KREBS, H. A., R. A. FREEDLAND, R. HEMS & M. STUBBS. 1969. Inhibition of hepatic gluconeogenesis by ethanol. Biochem. J. **112:** 117–124.

17. KUO, W.-N., D. S. HODGINS & I. F. KUO. 1973. Adenylate cyclase in islets of Langerhans. J. Biol. Chem. **248**: 2705–2711.
18. LINDENEG, O., K. MELLEMGAARD, J. FABRICIUS & F. LUNDQUIST. 1964. Myocardial utilization of acetate, lactate and free fatty acids after ingestion of ethanol. Clin. Sci. **27**: 427–435.
19. LUNDQUIST, F. 1971. The metabolism of alcohol. *In* The biological basis of alcoholism. Y. Israel and J. Mardones, Eds.: 1–53. John Wiley & Sons. New York, N.Y.
20. LUNDQUIST, F. 1971. Influence of ethanol on carbohydrate metabolism. Quart. J. Stud. Alcohol. **32**: 1–12.
21. ORME-JOHNSON, W. H. & D. M. ZIEGLER. 1965. Alcohol mixed function oxidase activity of mammalian liver microsomes. Biochem. Biophys. Res. Comm. **21**: 78–82.
22. RUBIN, E., D. S. BEATTIE, A. TOTH & C. S. LIEBER. 1972. Structure and functional effects of ethanol on hepatic mitochondria. Fed. Proc. **31**: 131–140.
23. STOKES, P. E. 1971. Alcohol-endocrine interrelationships. *In* The Biology of Alcoholism *1*. B. Kissin and H. Begleiter, Eds.: 397–436. Plenum Press. New York, N.Y.
24. STREETEN, D. H. P. & A. K. SOLOMON. 1954. The effect of ACTH and adrenal steroids on K transport in human erythrocytes. J. Gen. Physiol. **37**: 643–661.
25. TESCHKE, R., Y. HASAMURA, J.-G. JOLY, H. ISHII & C. S. LIEBER. 1972. Microsomal ethanol-oxidizing system (MEOS): Purification and properties of a rat liver system free of catalase and alcohol dehydrogenase. Biochem. Biophys. Res. Comm. **49**: 1187–1193.
26. THEORELL, H. & B. CHANCE. 1951. Studies on liver alcohol dehydrogenase. II. The kinetics of the compound of horse liver alcohol dehydrogenase and reduced diphosphopyridine nucleotide. Acta Chem. Scand. **5**: 1127–1144.
27. THIEDEN, H. I. D. 1968. The effect of ethanol on the concentrations of adenine nucleotides in rat liver. FEBS Letter **2**: 121–123.
28. THIEDEN, H. I. D., N. GRUNNET, S. E. DAMGAARD & L. SESTOFT. 1972. Effect of fructose and glyceraldehyde on ethanol metabolism in human liver and in rat liver. Eur. J. Biochem. **30**: 250–261.
29. THURMAN, R. G., H.-G. LEY & R. SCHOLZ. 1972. Hepatic microsomal ethanol oxidation. Hydrogen peroxide formation and the role of catalase. Eur. J. Biochem. **25**: 420–430.
30. TOTTMAR, S. O. C., H. PETTERSON & K.-H. KIESSLING. 1973. The subcellular distribution and properties of aldehyde dehydrogenase in rat liver. Biochem. J. **135**: 577–586.
31. VIDELA, L., J. BERNSTEIN & Y. ISRAEL. 1973. Metabolic alterations produced in the liver by chronic ethanol administration. Increased oxidative capacity. Biochem. J. **134**: 507–514.
32. WILLIAMSON, J. R., C. M. SMITH & J. BRYLA. 1974. Feedback control between phosphate potential and citric acid cycle activity in rat and guinea pig liver mitochondria. *In* Regulation of Hepatic Metabolism. Alfred Benzon Symposium VI. F. Lundquist and N. Tygstrup, Eds.: 620–638. Academic Press. New York, N.Y.

PART II. THE GASTROINTESTINAL SYSTEM

A. The Liver

INTRODUCTION

Kenneth Williams

Of all the medical complications of alcoholism, none has been studied more extensively than alcoholic liver disease. The association between excessive drinking and liver disease has been recognized in the medical literature for over 100 years, and is now the best known consequence of heavy drinking by the medical profession as well as the lay public. The incidence of liver cirrhosis has even been widely used to calculate the prevalence of the disease of alcoholism (Jellinek Estimation Formula, W.H.O., 1951). Some may question whether alcoholic liver disease has received an emphasis out of proportion to its importance in the general area of alcoholism. As the papers that follow indicate, however, the massive research effort can now be seen to have paid off in increased understanding of the pathologic processes involved.

As the organ primarily responsible for metabolizing alcohol, the liver may also be the organ affected most frequently. Dr. Leevy's study in 1967 found that 20% of 3000 randomly selected alcoholics had cirrhosis. Other liver biopsy studies (Edmondson et al., Medicine **46**: 119, 1967) have found that 90% of chronic alcoholics had a fatty liver. Dr. Lieber's studies have shown the development of fatty livers in 100% of his volunteers, given sufficient amounts of alcohol. The incidence of cirrhosis and its associated mortality has been increasing in this country over the past 60 years. Cirrhosis of the liver has recently been reported to be the third leading cause of death in the age group 25–45 in New York City.

Until recently, it was widely taught in medical schools that poor nutrition was an invariable accompaniment of the development of Laennec's cirrhosis and that by attention to proper dietary habits, a drinker might avoid developing liver disease. The controversy over the relative importance of the causal role of malnutrition and ethanol continues today. However, the work of Dr. Lieber's group has accumulated evidence that, independent of dietary deficiencies, alcohol itself can be a sufficient cause for liver damage. His paper in this section reviews his recent studies in which for the first time, cirrhosis was produced in an experimental animal. His baboons developed the range of alcoholic liver disease from fatty liver to cirrhosis after 2–4 years of alcohol consumption while on a nutritionally adequate diet. Dr. Leevy's paper provides added knowledge about the mechanism whereby alcoholic hepatitis evolves to cirrhosis, implicating the role of hyaline-induced lymphocytic hyperactivity.

Dr. Lelbach's studies provide new insights into one of the questions frequently confronting the physician, "How much alcohol consumed over what time period is necessary for one to develop cirrhosis?" Dr. Lelbach's investigations show a close correlation between the incidence of precirrhotic or cirrhotic lesions and the total volume of alcohol ingested over the years of drinking. Biochemical individuality appears to play a role however, as some individuals are known to develop cirrhosis with relatively modest average daily alcohol consumption while others consuming large amounts of alcohol daily appear to be spared.

21

LIVER DISEASE, ALCOHOL, AND MALNUTRITION:
INTRODUCTORY REMARKS

Charles S. Davidson

Clinical Research Center
Department of Nutrition and Food Science
Massachusetts Institute of Technology
Cambridge, Massachusetts 03139

When I was a medical student, my professor of pathology was of the strong opinion that alcohol itself had little if anything to do with liver disease in man. He enjoyed his Scotch whisky. Some 33 years ago, when I first came to the Boston City Hospital, it was customary to call the liver disease in heavy drinkers so commonly seen there "alcoholic cirrhosis." I protested as I felt that we were not sure of the cause and particularly of the contribution of mal-nutrition. The interest in nutrition followed the experiments of Allen et al.[1] and Best et al.[2,3] and subsequently many others[4-6] producing cirrhosis in animals on a low-protein and choline-deficient diet. We had in 1947, the superb lectures[7] of Sir Harold Himsworth in Boston, which added fuel to the nutrition argument. He clearly pointed out the essential contribution of malnutrition in experimental animals. My colleagues at the Boston City then coined the phrase "nutritional cirrhosis." Moreover, a classification of liver diseases made at that time listed that in the alcoholic under the rubric "malnutrition." I again pro-tested, as I felt that we still were unable to assess the relative importance of alcohol and of malnutrition in the pathogenesis of this liver disease in man. I preferred to call the disease cirrhosis (or hepatitis) of the liver in an alcoholic, and I still prefer this.[8]

Some few years after this, Dr. Charles Lieber came to the Thorndike to work with our group and undertook the study of the relative contributions of alcohol and malnutrition to liver disease in experimental animals and man. His studies, begun there and continued many years since at Cornell and Mount Sinai, have been monumental. He and his colleagues have clearly shown that fatty liver can be produced in experimental animals and in man by alcohol while the diet is maintained at at least an adequate level of all nutrients. Finally, Dr. Rubin and Dr. Lieber have been able to produce in baboons not only fatty liver but also so-called alcoholic hepatitis and cirrhosis from alcohol while the baboons were consuming presumably a nutritious or at least adequate diet.[9] Some questions might be raised as to the adequacy of the choline and possibly some other nutrients in the diet, but as the baboons did not lose weight this may be of little significance. On the other hand, the large calorie intake (up to 8000 calories) may have prevented weight loss.

Another question must be considered in these baboons and in alcoholics: that of the influence of alcohol on the absorption of nutrients. Even though the intake of food may be sufficient, impaired absorption may result from the effect of alcohol on the mucosa of the gastrointestinal tract. Here again the failure of Rubin and Lieber's animals to lose weight or to appear malnourished may be against this hypothesis.

Finally comes the problem of putting these beautiful experiments of Lieber and his colleagues into perspective of the treatment of human alcoholics.

Alcoholic individuals frequently have nutritional deficiencies, as we know full well. Wernicke's encephalopathy, Korsakoff's syndrome, beriberi, pellagra, and scurvy are still seen in alcoholics. Moreover, a number of other conditions both of the nervous system and of the peripheral and heart muscles may be related to nutritional deficiency. With regard to the liver disease itself in man, malnutrition may be also an important contributing factor in its pathogenesis.

Thus, to put all this in perspective, we must continue to treat alcoholics with and without liver disease as if they were malnourished, as most of them are or will be.[10] The last word on pathogenesis of liver disease in man has not been spoken, I suspect.

REFERENCES

1. ALLEN, F. N., D. J. BOWIE, J. MacLEOD, Jr. & W. L. ROBINSON. 1924. Behavior of depancreatized dogs kept alive with insulin. Brit. J. Exp. Path. 5: 75–83.
2. BEST, C. H., J. M. HERSHEY & M. E. HUNTSMAN. 1932. The effects of the components of lecithine upon deposition of fat in the liver. J. Physiol. 75: 405–412.
3. BEST, C. H., W. S. HARTROFT, C. C. LUCUS & J. H. RIDOUT. 1949. Liver damage produced by feeding alcohol or sugar and its prevention by choline. Brit. Med. J. 2: 1001–1017.
4. GYORGY, P. & H. GOLDBLATT. 1942. Observations on the conditions of dietary hepatic injury (necrosis, cirrhosis) in rats. J. Exp. Med. 75: 335–368.
5. HARTROFT, W. S. 1954. The sequence of pathologic events in the development of experimental fatty liver and cirrhosis. Ann. N.Y. Acad. Sci. 57: 633–645.
6. TODHUNTER, E. N. 1971. Evolution of present concepts concerning the action of lipotropic agents. (Nutrition Society Symposium). Ed. Fed. Proc. 30: 130–176.
7. HIMSWORTH, H. P. 1950. Lectures on the Liver and its Diseases. Harvard Univ. Press. Cambridge, Mass.
8. DAVIDSON, C. S. 1970. Liver Pathophysiology; Its Relevance to Human Disease. Little, Brown. Boston, Mass.
9. RUBIN, E. & C. S. LIEBER. 1974. Fatty liver, alcoholic hepatitis and cirrhosis produced by alcohol in primates. New Eng. J. Med. 290: 128–135.
10. DAVIDSON, C. S. 1973. Dietary treatment of hepatic diseases. J. Amer. Diet. Ass. 62: 515–519.

INTERFERENCE OF ETHANOL IN HEPATIC
CELLULAR METABOLISM*

Charles S. Lieber

Section and Laboratory of Liver Disease and Nutrition
Veterans Administration Hospital
Bronx, New York 10468

and

Department of Medicine
Mount Sinai School of Medicine of the City University
of New York
New York, New York 10029

A question that is often raised is "in which way does an alcoholic differ from a nonalcoholic?" Inquiries have focused on psychological make-up, behavioral differences, and socioeconomic factors. More recently, however, physical differences have been delineated. Concerning the liver, it has been shown that prior to the development of liver disease, chronic ethanol exposure results in profound biochemical and morphologic changes. Consequently, the liver of an alcoholic does not respond normally to alcohol or to other drugs or even other toxic agents. Some of these persistent biochemical and morphologic changes are the consequences of the injurious effects of ethanol, whereas others may represent the possible adaptive responses to the profound changes in intermediary metabolism that are a direct and immediate consequence of the oxidation of ethanol itself. The latter—that is, the immediate effects of the oxidation of ethanol on intermediary metabolism—will be reviewed first, to be followed by an analysis of some persistent and in part adaptive changes following chronic ethanol consumption. Liver disease associated with alcoholism will be discussed in another paper in this monograph.

OXIDATION OF ETHANOL AND ITS DIRECT EFFECTS ON HEPATIC AND EXTRAHEPATIC INTERMEDIARY METABOLISM

Pathways of Ethanol Oxidation

Ethanol can be synthesized endogenously in trace amounts, but it is primarily an exogenous compound that is readily absorbed from the gastrointestinal tract. Only 2 to 10% of that absorbed is eliminated through the kidneys and lungs; the rest must be oxidized in the body, principally in the liver. This relative organ specificity probably explains why, despite the existence of intracellular mechanisms responsible for redox homeostasis, ethanol oxidation produces striking metabolic imbalances in the liver. These effects are aggravated by the lack of feedback mechanism to adjust the rate of ethanol oxidation to the metabolic state of the hepatocyte, and the inability of ethanol, unlike other major sources of calories, to be stored or metabolized to a marked degree in peripheral tissues (TABLE 1). The main hepatic pathway for ethanol disposition involves alcohol

*These studies were supported, in part, by grants from the National Institute of Alcohol Abuse and Alcoholism and the National Institute of Arthritis, Metabolism, and Digestive Diseases, and projects of the Veterans Administration.

TABLE 1

Characteristics of Ethanol Metabolism

1. Large caloric load, sometimes in excess of all other nutrients
2. Almost no renal or pulmonary excretion
3. No storage mechanism in the body
4. Oxidation predominantly in the liver
5. No feedback control of rates of ethanol oxidation

dehydrogenase, an enzyme of the cell sap (cytosol) that catalyzes the conversion of ethanol to acetaldehyde. Hydrogen is transferred from ethanol to the cofactor nicotinamide adenine dinucleotide (NAD), which is converted to its reduced form (NADH) (FIGURE 1A). The acetaldehyde produced again loses hydrogen and is converted to acetate, most of which is released into the blood stream. As a net result, ethanol oxidation generates an excess of reducing equivalents in the liver, primarily as NADH. In addition, ethanol can also be metabolized by an accessory pathway that requires NADPH as a cofactor and is localized in the endoplasmic reticulum, which is gathered in the microsomal fraction upon subcellular fractionation and ultracentrifugation (FIGURE 1B). There is also a debate on a possible role of catalase (FIGURE 1C and D). The various metabolic effects of ethanol can be attributed either to the NADH generation by the ADH path-

A.
$$CH_3CH_2OH + NAD^+ \xrightarrow[ADH]{} CH_3CHO + NADH + H^+$$

B.
$$CH_3CH_2OH + NADPH + H^+ + O_2 \xrightarrow[MEOS]{} CH_3CHO + NADP^+ + 2H_2O$$

C.
$$NADPH + H^+ + O_2 \xrightarrow[\substack{NADPH \\ Oxidase}]{} NADP^+ + H_2O_2$$
$$+$$
$$H_2O_2 + CH_3CH_2OH \xrightarrow[Catalase]{} 2H_2O + CH_3CHO$$

D.
$$HYPOXANTHINE + H_2O + O_2 \xrightarrow[\substack{Xanthine \\ Oxidase}]{} XANTHINE + H_2O_2$$
$$+$$
$$H_2O_2 + CH_3CH_2OH \xrightarrow[Catalase]{} 2H_2O + CH_3CHO$$

FIGURE 1. Ethanol oxidation by A, alcohol dehydrogenase (ADH); nicotinamide adenine dinucleotide (NAD), nicotinamide adenine dinucleotide, reduced form (NADH). B, the hepatic microsomal ethanol-oxidizing system (MEOS); nicotinamide adenine dinucleotide phosphate, reduced form (NADPH), nicotinamide adenine dinucleotide phosphate (NADP). C, a combination of NADPH oxidase and catalase; or D, xanthine oxidase and catalase.

TABLE 2

Metabolic Effects Linked to the Oxidation of Ethanol

Hyperlactacidemia and hyperuricemia
Enhanced production of lipids and lipoproteins
Decreased lipid oxidation and steatosis
Reduced glyconeogenesis and hypoglycemia
Inhibition of drug metabolism
Decreased FFA turnover

way or to the interaction with other microsomal functions in association with metabolism by the microsomal ethanol oxidizing system (MEOS) (TABLE 2). Some of the effects are also due to the metabolites of ethanol, acetaldehyde and acetate.

Effects of Excessive Hepatic NADH Generation

As shown in FIGURE 2, the oxidation of ethanol results in the transfer of hydrogen to NAD. The resulting enhanced NADH-NAD ratio, in turn, produces a change in the ratio of those metabolites that are dependent for reduction on the NADH-NAD couple. It was therefore proposed that the altered NADH–NAD

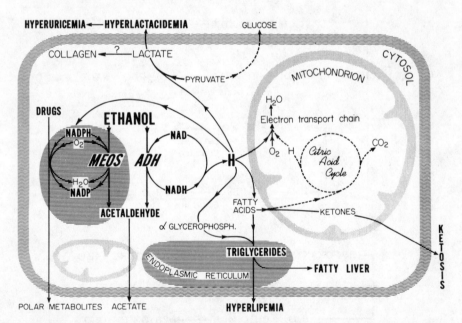

FIGURE 2. Metabolism of ethanol in the hepatocyte and schematic representation of its link to fatty liver, hyperlipemia, hyperuricemia, hyperlactacidemia, ketosis, and hypoglycemia. Pathways that are decreased by ethanol are represented by dashed lines. ADH, alcohol dehydrogenase: MEOS, microsomal ethanol-oxidizing system; NAD, nicotinamide adenine dinucleotide; NADH, nicotinamide adenine dinucleotide, reduced form; NADP, nicotinamide adenine dinucleotide phosphate; NADPH, nicotinamide adenine dinucleotide phosphate, reduced form.

ratio is responsible for a number of metabolic abnormalities associated with alcohol abuse.[1]

Hyperlactacidemia, Hyperuricemia, Acidosis

The enhanced NADH-NAD ratio reflects itself in an increased lactate-pyruvate ratio that results in hyperlactacidemia[2,3] because of both decreased utilization and enhanced production of lactate by the liver. The hyperlactacidemia contributes to acidosis and also reduces the capacity of the kidney to excrete uric acid, leading to secondary hyperuricemia.[3] Alcohol-induced ketosis (*vide infra*) may also promote the hyperuricemia. The latter may be related to the common

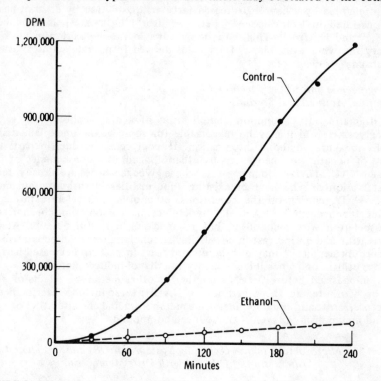

FIGURE 3. Effect of alcohol on total $^{14}CO_2$ production from [^{14}C]labeled chylomicrons in a pair of isolated perfused rat livers.[9]

clinical observation that excessive consumption of alcoholic beverages frequently aggravates or precipitates gouty attacks.[4] Alcoholic hyperuricemia can be readily distinguished from the primary variety by its reversibility upon discontinuation of ethanol abuse.[3] A fascinating but as yet hypothetical consequence of the increased availability of lactate may be the stimulation of collagen production, to be discussed subsequently.

Enhanced Lipogenesis and Depressed Lipid Oxidation

The increased NADH-NAD ratio also raises the concentration of α-glycerophosphate[5] that favors hepatic triglyceride accumulation by trapping fatty acids. In addition, excess NADH promotes fatty acid synthesis[6,7] possibly by the elongation pathway or transhydrogenation to nicotinamide adenine dinucleotide phosphate (NADP). Theoretically, enhanced lipogenesis can be considered a means for disposing of the excess hydrogen. Some hydrogen equivalents can be transferred into the mitochondria by various "shuttle" mechanisms. Since the activity of the citric acid cycle is depressed,[8,9] partly because of a slowing of the reactions of the cycle that require NAD, the mitochondria will use the hydrogen equivalents originating from ethanol, rather than from the oxidation through the citric acid cycle of two carbon fragments derived from fatty acids. Thus, fatty acids that normally serve as the main energy source of the liver are supplanted by ethanol. Decreased fatty acid oxidation by ethanol has been demonstrated in liver slices,[6,10] perfused liver[9] (FIGURE 3), isolated hepatocytes,[11] and *in vivo*.[12] This reduction results in the deposition in the liver of dietary fat, when available, or fatty acids derived from endogenous synthesis in the absence of dietary fat.[13-16]

Hypoglycemia and Hyperglycemia, Changes in the Metabolism of Galactose, Amines, and Steroids

A dramatic but uncommon complication of acute alcohol abuse is severe hypoglycemia, which may be responsible for some of the unexplained sudden deaths in acute alcoholic intoxication. Hypoglycemia is due, in part, to the block of hepatic gluconeogenesis by ethanol, again as a consequence of the increased NADH-NAD ratio in subjects whose glycogen stores are already depleted by starvation or who have preexisting abnormalities in carbohydrate metabolism.[17,18] Depending on the conditions, ethanol may accelerate rather than inhibit gluconeogenesis.[19] Actually, hyperglycemia has sometimes been described in association with alcoholism, but its mechanism is still obscure. Alcoholic pancreatitis and an increase in circulating catecholamines could be contributory. Glucose intolerance[20] may also be due, at least in part, to decreased peripheral glucose utilization,[21] possible secondary to ethanol-induced ketosis.[22]

As emphasized before,[1,23,24] a number of other metabolic effects of alcohol can be attributed to the generation of NADH; these include interference with galactose, serotonin, and norepinephrine metabolism and the alteration of hepatic steroid metabolism in favor of the reduced compounds.[25]

The Microsomal Ethanol-Oxidizing System (MEOS) and Associated Interaction of Ethanol with Drug Metabolism

Nature of the Non-ADH Pathways

The first indication of an interaction of ethanol with the microsomal fraction of the hepatocyte was provided by the morphologic observation that in rats, ethanol feeding results in a proliferation of the smooth endoplasmic reticulum (SER), to be discussed subsequently. This increase in SER resembles that seen after the administration of a wide variety of xenobiotic compounds including known hepatotoxins,[26] numerous therapeutic agents,[27] and food additives.[28] Most of these substances which induce a proliferation of the SER are metabolized, at least in part, in the microsomal fraction of the hepatocyte that comprises the SER. The observation that ethanol also produces proliferation of the SER raised the possibility that, in addition to its oxidation by ADH in the cytosol, ethanol may also be metabolized by the microsomes. A microsomal system capable of methanol oxidation has been described,[29] but its capacity for ethanol oxidation was extremely low. Subsequently, a microsomal ethanol-oxidizing system with a rate of ethanol oxidation 10 times higher than reported by Orme-Johnson and Ziegler[29] was described.[30,31] Differentiation from alcohol dehydrogenase was achieved by subcellular localization, pH optimum *in vitro*, cofactor requirements (FIGURE 1), and effects of inhibitors such as pyrazole.[32,33]

As early as 1945, Keilin and Hartree[34] showed that in the presence of a H_2O_2-generating system, catalase is capable of oxidizing ethanol. Some H_2O_2-generating systems, such as hypoxanthine-xanthine oxidase (FIGURE 1D), are present in the cytosol. In addition, hepatic microsomes also contain a H_2O_2-generating system, namely NADPH oxidase (FIGURE 1C). It was indeed found that the addition of catalase to this system allows it to oxidize methanol.[35] Catalase resides primarily in the microbodies, which, upon ultracentrifugation, are separated with the mitochondrial fraction. Other organelles, however, including the microsomes, contain traces of catalase activity. Therefore, the question arose as to what extent a combination of NADPH-oxidase-catalase (FIGURE 1C) could account for MEOS activity (FIGURE 1B). It has been reported that microsomes of acatalasemic mice fail to oxidize ethanol,[36] but this claim was found not to be the case.[37] Differentiation of MEOS from catalase was achieved by utilizing various inhibitors,[30-33] but these studies became the subject of controversy.[38] Actually, inhibitor studies are not relevant any more now that MEOS has been clearly differentiated and separated from ADH[39,40] and from catalase[39] by column chromatography (FIGURE 4).

The absence of catalase in the purified MEOS preparation was verified by the lack of catalatic activity (O_2 appearance) in the presence of a H_2O_2-generating system or the failure of H_2O_2 to disappear.[39] To rule out the possibility that the peroxidatic activity of catalase may still be present though catalatic activity may not be detectable, the effect of various H_2O_2-generating systems on the capacity of the purified fraction to oxidize ethanol was studied. The purified MEOS that actively oxidized ethanol in the presence of a NADPH–generating system had no activity with the H_2O_2–generating systems unless exogenous catalase was added.[41] This has been confirmed in a recent joint experiment carried out in microsomes of ethanol-treated rats (TABLE 3). Moreover, no radioactive catalase could be traced to the smooth membranes of the microsomes,[43] the fraction that exhibits an inductive response to chronic ethanol treatment (*vide infra*).

Respective Roles of the Various Ethanol-Oxidizing Systems

Even in the presence of pyrazole (a potent ADH inhibitor), ethanol metabolism was found to persist, both *in vivo*[44] and *in vitro*, in isolated perfused liver,[45] liver slices,[31] and isolated liver cells.[46,47] Furthermore, in the presence of pyrazole, glucose labeling from (1R-^{3}H) ethanol was nearly abolished, while H^3HO production was inhibited less than 50%. In view of the stereospecificity of ADH for (1R-^{3}H) ethanol, these findings again suggest "the presence of a significant pathway not mediated by cytosolic ADH."[48] The rate of this non-ADH-mediated oxidation varied depending on the concentrations of ethanol used, from 20 to 25%[31,44,45] to half or more[46,47] of the total ethanol metabolism. Additional evidence that this pyrazole-insensitive residual ethanol metabolism is not ADH-mediated was derived from the fact that the cytosolic redox state was unaffected.[49] The striking increase in the non-ADH fraction of ethanol metabolism with increasing ethanol concentrations[46,47] is consistent with the known K_m for ADH and MEOS: whereas the former has a K_m varying from 0.5 to 2 mM,[50,51] the latter has a value of 8 to 9 mM.[31] It has been estimated that the

H_2O_2-dependent catalase-mediated ethanol oxidation has a K_m of the same order of magnitude as that of MEOS.[38] This raises the question of the respective roles of these two systems for the non-ADH-mediated ethanol oxidation. An indirect answer to this question can be derived from the generally accepted view that rates of H_2O_2-mediated peroxidation are limited by the amount of H_2O_2 generated rather than the amount of catalase itself. In perfused livers, the total capacity of the organ to generate H_2O_2 is very low and has been estimated at 40–70 nmoles/min/g of liver[52] in the presence of physiological substrates. This is only $\frac{1}{10}$ or even less than the estimated rates of non-ADH-mediated ethanol oxidation.[44] Moreover, ethanol was found to inhibit the activity of NADPH oxidase.[41] Even in the presence of unusual substrates for H_2O_2 generation, this pathway still would account for only a minor fraction of the non-ADH-mediated ethanol oxidation in control rats. This interpretation is consistent with the results of Thurman and Scholz,[53] who found that menadione, although it strikingly

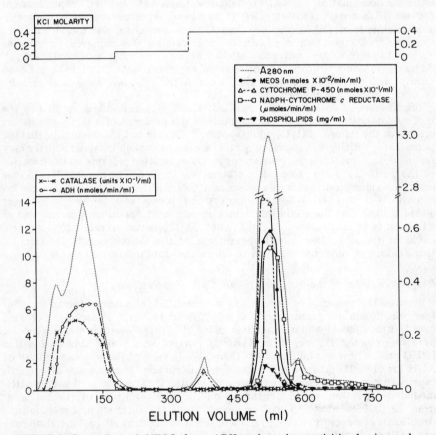

FIGURE 4. Separation of MEOS from ADH and catalase activities by ion-exchange column chromatography on DEAE-cellulose. Sonicated microsomes from rats fed laboratory chow were further solubilized by treatment with sodium deoxycholate and put onto a DEAE-cellulose column (2.5 × 45 cm). The separation of the enzyme activities was achieved by a stepwise increase of the salt gradient.[41]

TABLE 3

Isolation of a MEOS Fraction Obtained from Hepatic Microsomes of Female
Rats Fed an Alcohol-Containing Liquid Diet for 5 Weeks*

Incubation Medium	Purified MEOS fraction	
	Pool 1	Pool 2
	nmoles acetaldehyde/ min/flask	
NADPH	104.2	44.5
NADPH-generating system	105.0	40.5
H_2O_2-generating system	0	0
H_2O_2-generating system and catalase	52.7	48.7

*Collaborative study of Teschke, Thurman, Hasumura, Hesse, and Lieber in New York, December, 1973. MEOS activity was determined with ethanol (50 mM), NADPH (0.4 mM) or a NADPH-generating system consisting of 0.4 mM $NADP^+$, 8 mM sodium isocitrate and 2 mg per ml of isocitrate dehydrogenase. Peroxidatic activity of catalase was measured with an H_2O_2-generating system consisting of 10 mM glucose and 1.0 μg glucose oxidase. Bovine liver catalase (Sigma Chemical Company, St. Louis, Mo.) (300 units/flask) was added to some of the flasks. All incubation media (final volume 3.0 ml) contained 1 mM EDTA and 5 mM $MgCl_2$. The protein concentration per flask was 3.0 and 2.0 mg for pool 1 and 2, respectively. Absence of catalatic activity in the MEOS fraction was verified by measurement of the H_2O_2 disappearance of 240 nm.[42]

increased H_2O_2 generation and ethanol oxidation by microsomes *in vitro*, nevertheless failed to affect the alcohol dehydrogenase-independent rates of ethanol utilization by perfused livers. By contrast, the MEOS could account for the bulk of the non-ADH-mediated ethanol oxidation.[44]

Interaction of Ethanol with Drug Metabolism

Interactions of the effects of ethanol and various drugs have been widely recognized.[54] Intoxicated individuals are more susceptible to several medications.[55] These various effects are usually attributed to additive or synergistic effects of alcohol and various drugs on the central nervous system. However, the existence of an at least partially common microsomal system for ethanol and drug metabolism sheds new light on the interaction of ethanol and drug metabolism. The increased susceptibility of the inebriated individual could be explained, at least in part, by the effect of ethanol on microsomal drug-detoxifying enzymes. It has indeed been found that ethanol inhibits the metabolism of a variety of drugs *in vitro*[56-59]. With some systems, such as aniline hydroxylase, this inhibition is of a competitive nature.[57,60] These *in vitro* effects may explain the observation that *in vivo*, simultaneous administration of ethanol and drugs slows the rate of drug metabolism.[57,59] Conversely, in the presence of drugs, there is inhibition of ethanol metabolism.[44] Drugs also inhibit ethanol oxidation by microsomes *in vitro* in a way that has been considered strong evidence for the catalase-independent nature of MEOS.[61] In addition, some drugs inhibit alcohol dehydrogenase.[62] The interaction of ethanol with drug metabolism may have some important practical consequences. Indeed, in the United States, more than 50% of all lethal road accidents are associated with an elevated blood alcohol level.[53] One may wonder to what extent the loss of control on the road may be due not only to ethanol itself, but to an ethanol-drug interaction considering that a large segment of the population is given sedatives and tranquilizers.

Effects of the Metabolites of Ethanol: Acetaldehyde and Acetate

Acetaldehyde is the first major "specific" oxidation product of ethanol, whether the latter is oxidized by the classic alcohol dehydrogenase of the cytosol or by the more recently described microsomal system. Except after Antabuse® administration, acetaldehyde concentrations after alcohol ingestion are small, but it has long been speculated that they may contribute to the complications of alcoholism.[64] Moreover, it has been found recently that at high ethanol blood levels, blood acetaldehyde is higher in alcoholics than in nonalcoholics. This

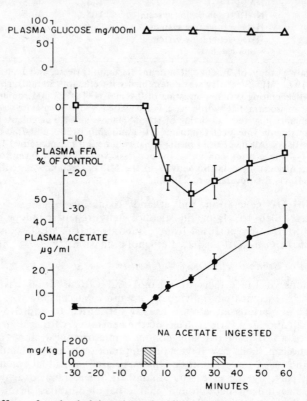

FIGURE 5. Effect of oral administration of sodium acetate on plasma glucose, FFA, and acetate. Points represent average values for 5 volunteers. Variation is expressed as SEM. Plasma FFA at zero time averaged $572 \pm 91 \mu eq/liter.$[84]

possibly reflects enhanced MEOS activity, since the blood acetaldehyde concentration drops precipitously at ethanol levels that correspond to MEOS desaturation.[65] Although the exact pathway of its metabolism is still unknown, it is generally accepted that aldehyde oxidation proceeds by means of aldehyde dehydrogenase, 80% of the activity of which is located in the mitochondria.[66,67] Whether ethanol consumption alters the activity of acetaldehyde dehydrogenase is the subject of debate, with both increases[68,69] and no changes[70,71] reported. Since metabolism of acetaldehyde via aldehyde dehydrogenase results in the generation of NADH, some of the acetaldehyde effects could be attributed to the NADH generation, as discussed before in the case of ethanol. Acetaldehyde, however, is a very reactive compound that may exert some toxic effects of its own, such as the reduction of the activity of the shuttles for the transport of reducing equivalents into the mitochondria[72,73] and inhibition of site I of oxidative phosphorylation.[73] In addition, acetaldehyde could produce its effects through catecholamine release,[74] whose excretion is reported to be increased after ethanol.[75] Several ethanol effects upon the brain have been attributed to acetaldehyde.[76,77] As reviewed before,[78] ethanol exerts various cardiovascular effects, including increased splanchnic blood flow and cardiac output;[79] a number of these could be secondary to the action of acetaldehyde. In addition, acetaldehyde was shown to interfere with myocardial protein synthesis,[80] which may relate to the cardiotoxicity of ethanol.

The exact fate of acetaldehyde is still the subject of debate. That acetylCoA is formed from ethanol is indicated by the observation that [^{14}C]ethanol can be traced to a variety of metabolites of which acetylCoA is a precursor, such as fatty acids and cholesterol, as reviewed elsewhere.[78] It is noteworthy that a large fraction of the carbon skeleton of ethanol is incorporated in hepatic lipids after ethanol administration.[81,82] The acetaldehyde that results from the oxidation of ethanol could be converted to acetylCoA via acetate. The reverse possibility, namely that ethanol is converted directly to acetylCoA, which in turn could be either incorporated into various metabolites or yield acetate, has not been ruled out. In any event, acetate has been found to markedly increase in the blood after ethanol administration.[83,84]

Although *in vitro*, the liver can readily utilize acetate, *in vivo* most of the acetate is metabolized in peripheral tissues.[85] The effects of a rise of circulating acetate on intermediary metabolism in various tissues have not been defined, except for adipose tissue, where it was found to be responsible, at least in part, for the decreased release of free fatty acids (FFA) and the fall of circulating FFA.[84] It is noteworthy that within minutes of imbibing an acetate-containing drink, a significant fall of circulating free fatty acids can be observed in man (FIGURE 5). A fall in FFA, a major fuel for peripheral tissues, may have significant metabolic consequences.

ADAPTIVE METABOLIC CHANGES FOLLOWING PROLONGED ETHANOL INTAKE

It is common knowledge that chronic alcohol consumption produces increased tolerance to ethanol. This is generally attributed to central nervous system adaptation. In addition, recent studies have shown the development of metabolic adaptation—that is, an accelerated clearance of alcohol from the blood. Furthermore, there is an associated increased capacity to metabolize other drugs as well. Moreover, the liver acquires an enhanced capacity to rid itself of lipids through lipoprotein secretion into the blood stream. It is noteworthy that these functions, which adaptively increase after chronic ethanol feeding (TABLE 4) involve to a large extent the activity of the hepatic smooth endoplasmic reticulum, which undergoes significant change after chronic alcohol consumption. It was indeed observed 10 years ago that ethanol feeding results in a proliferation of the smooth membranes of the hepatic endoplasmic reticulum.[86,87] This ultramicroscopic finding was subsequently confirmed[88-90] and established on a biochemical basis by the demonstration of an increase in both phospholipids and total protein content of the smooth membranes.[91] Its functional counterparts include accelerated metabolism of drugs (including ethanol) and lipoprotein production.

Accelerated Ethanol Metabolism After Chronic Ethanol Consumption

Regular drinkers tolerate large amounts of alcoholic beverages mainly because of central nervous system adaptation. In addition, alcoholics develop increased rates of blood ethanol clearance, so-called metabolic tolerance.[92,93] Experimental ethanol administration also results in an increased rate of ethanol metabolism.[31,94,95] The mechanism of this acceleration is the subject of debate.

Increase of Ethanol Metabolism Related to the ADH Pathway

There is a controversy over whether ethanol consumption affects activities of hepatic ADH, with most investigators reporting no change, or even decreases.[96] In alcoholics, liver ADH was found to be lowered even in the absence of liver damage.[97] Extrahepatic ADH, particularly the gastric one, has been reported to increase after alcohol feeding,[98] but this has not been confirmed either after acute or chronic ethanol administration.[99]

Actually, the question whether there is a moderate change in hepatic ADH activity may not have direct bearing on the problem of rates of alcohol metabolism, since it is generally recognized that ADH activity is usually not the rate-limiting factor in that pathway. There are numerous examples of the lack of correlation between rates of ethanol oxidation and hepatic ADH activity. For instance, the increase in ADH activity after propylthiouracil was associated with a slowing of ethanol metabolism.[100] ADH was found to be heterogeneous, and several isoenzymes have been described in human liver.[101,102] In addition, an atypical ADH has been isolated[103] that, in vitro, has a much higher activity at physiological pH than does the normal variety. Although those individuals with "atypical" ADH have enzyme activities several times higher than normal in vitro, this is not accompanied by an acceleration of the metabolism of ethanol in vivo.[104] This discrepancy supports the view that in the process of ADH-mediated ethanol oxidation, ADH itself is not rate-limiting but that velocities may depend on availability of the cofactor NAD, especially the speed of the reoxidation of the ADH-NADH complex. As an example of an accelerator of ethanol metabolism that may involve the ADH pathway, fructose can be cited.[105] Its action[106,107] may be due to a speeding up of the reoxidation of NADH,[108] although this mechanism has recently been questioned.[109] In any event, in view of the moderate nature of the fructose effect and the potential hepatotoxicity of the compound, its use is presently not recommended.

The mechanism that could contribute to the acceleration of ADH–dependent ethanol metabolism after ethanol consumption is based on increased NADH reoxidation, for instance because of enhanced ATPase activity.[110] Mitochondrial mechanisms that have been postulated include enhanced shuttling of the H^+ equivalent from the cytosol to the mitochondria after chronic ethanol feeding. We failed to find evidence in favor of this possibility.[72] In general, it must be pointed out that if, following chronic ethanol consumption, changes affecting the ADH pathway (such as ATPase activity) were exclusively responsible for the acceleration of ethanol metabolism, the latter should be fully abolished by pyrazole treatment, but this was not the case.[31,44] This raises the possibility of the involvement of non-ADH pathways.

Non-ADH-Related Acceleration of Ethanol Metabolism

Calculations show that when corrected for microsomal losses during the preparative procedure, the rise in MEOS activity can account for $\frac{1}{2}$ to $\frac{2}{3}$ of the increase in blood ethanol clearance.[44] The unaccounted-for difference may actually result from a secondary increase in oxidation via ADH, a pathway limited by the rate of NADH reoxidation. This indeed could be accelerated by an increase in MEOS activity, since the latter is associated with enhanced NADPH utilization, and the NADPH–NADP and NADH–NAD systems are linked.[111] Moreover, evidence is accumulating that NADH may serve as partial electron donor for microsomal drug-detoxifying systems.[112] Interestingly, upon addition of ethanol to microsomes, a modified type-II binding spectrum appears, the magnitude of which is tripled by ethanol treatment.[113]

Indirect evidence that MEOS activity may play a role *in vivo* can be derived from the fact that other drugs (such as barbiturates) that increase total hepatic MEOS activity[114] were also found to enhance rates of blood ethanol clearance.[44,115,116] Some other studies failed to verify this effect.[117,118] In the latter investigations, however, long-acting barbiturates were used and ethanol clearance was tested in close association with barbiturate administration, at a time when blood barbiturate levels were probably elevated. Under these conditions, it was found that barbiturates interfere with blood ethanol clearance.[44] Interestingly, asthmatics were recently found to exhibit an accelerated clearance of ethanol from the blood, possibly as a result of long-standing drug consumption.[119]

There is also some debate over whether ethanol feeding enhances catalase activity in rats. Both an increase[120] and no change[31,121,122] have been reported. In man there was no increase.[93] This question, however, may not be fully relevant to the rate of ethanol metabolism, since peroxidative metabolism of ethanol in the liver is probably limited by the rate of hydrogen peroxide formation rather than by the amount of available catalase.[123] Ethanol consumption does, however, enhance the activity of hepatic NADPH oxidase,[120,124,125] which, as illustrated in FIGURE 1C, can participate in H_2O_2 generation. It is conceivable that this mechanism contributes to ethanol metabolism *in vivo* (and to its increase after chronic ethanol consumption) by furnishing the H_2O_2 needed for peroxidative oxidation of ethanol. As discussed before, however, the amount of H_2O_2 generated by the liver is small[52,123] and even when increased by ethanol consumption could not account for the rate of ethanol clearance observed.[96,126] Moreover, ethanol was found recently to inhibit NADPH oxidase activity.[41] Catalase appears to participate primarily in the oxidation of methanol, at least in the rat, whereas in the monkey alcohol dehydrogenase may play a greater role in that respect.[127]

Stimulation of the Microsomal Drug-Metabolizing Enzymes

Enhanced Drug Metabolism (Drug Tolerance)

The proliferation of hepatic SER induced by ethanol has a functional counterpart: an increased activity of a variety of microsomal drug-detoxifying enzymes.[56,58,90,95,128] Ethanol also increases the content of microsomal cytochrome P-450 and the activity of NADPH-cytochrome P-450 reductase.[88,128] These increases occur in the smooth membranes.[91,128] Furthermore, ethanol feeding raises the hepatic phospholipid content,[129] including that of the smooth microsomal membranes.[91] Moreover, it has been shown that microsomal cytochrome P-450, a reductase, and phospholipids play a key role in the microsomal hydroxylation of various drugs.[130] Therefore, the increase in the activity of hepatic microsomal drug-detoxifying enzymes and in the content of cytochrome P-450 induced by ethanol ingestion offers a likely explanation for the recent observation that ethanol consumption enhances the rate of drug clearance *in vivo*. The tolerance of the alcoholic to various drugs has been generally attributed to central nervous system adaptation.[131] However, there is sometimes a dissociation in the time course of the decreased drug sensitivity of the animal and the occurrence of central nervous system tolerance: the decreased drug sensitivity was found to precede the central nervous system tolerance.[132] Thus, in addition to central nervous system adaptation, metabolic adaptation must be considered. Indeed, it has been shown recently that the rate of drug clearance from the blood is enhanced in alcoholics.[133] Of course this could be due to a variety of factors other than ethanol, such as the congeners and the use of other drugs so commonly associated with alcoholism. Our studies showed, however, that administration of pure ethanol with nondeficient diets under metabolic ward conditions resulted in a striking increase in the rate of blood clearance of meprobamate (FIGURE 6) and pentobarbital.[95] Similarly, an increase in the metabolism of aminopyrine[134] and tolbutamide[90] was found. Furthermore, the capacity of liver slices from animals fed ethanol to metabolize meprobamate was also increased,[95] which clearly shows that ethanol consumption affects drug metabolism in the liver itself, independently of drug excretion or distribution.

Increased CCl₄ Toxicity in Alcoholics

The stimulation of microsomal enzyme activities also applies to those which convert exogenous substrates to toxic compounds. For instance CCl_4 exerts its toxicity only after conversion in the microsomes. Alcohol pretreatment remarkably stimulates the toxicity of CCl_4.[135] These experiments were carried out at a time when the ethanol had disappeared from the blood to rule out the increase

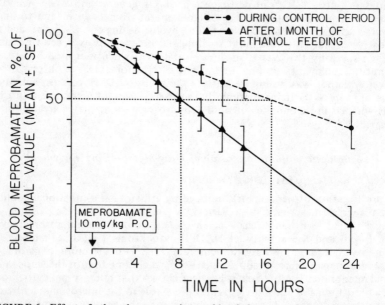

FIGURE 6. Effect of ethanol consumption on blood clearance of meprobamate in man.[95] Four alcoholic volunteers were tested before and after 1 month of ethanol ingestion; half-lives are shown by the dotted lines on *x* and *y* axes.

TABLE 4

Adaptive Changes Following Chronic Ethanol Consumption

Accelerated ethanol metabolism
Accelerated drug metabolism
Increased lipoprotein production
Side Effects:
Increased susceptibility to some hepatotoxic agents
Energy wastage
Ethanol dependence

of the toxicity of CCl_4 due to the presence of ethanol.[136] The potentiation of the CCl_4 toxicity by ethanol pretreatment may account for the clinical observation of the enhanced susceptibility of alcoholics to the hepatotoxic effects of CCl_4.[137] Thus, these studies demonstrate that chronic alcohol consumption is associated with enhanced toxicity of some noxious compounds, and it is likely that a larger number of toxic agents will be found to display a selective injurious action in the alcoholic. This side effect is possibly an undesirable consequence of the "adaptive" response to chronic ethanol consumption (TABLE 4).

Energy Cost of Microsomal Oxidations

Administration of either ethanol or other drugs enhances oxygen consumption of drug-pretreated animals over that of untreated controls.[138] This could result from the increased activity of the microsomal enzymes and the associated oxygen utilization. Furthermore, in these microsomal oxidations there is no coupling of oxidation to phosphorylation. Thus, heat is produced without conservation of chemical energy. This could conceivably be responsible for the fact that ethanol has a greater specific dynamic action in alcoholics than in normal persons,[139] since microsomal ethanol oxidation might be induced in the former but not in the latter. Moreover, this effect may also cause the lesser growth[129] in animals fed ethanol than in those given isocaloric carbohydrate, since heat produced in excess of the needs for temperature homeostasis represents energy wastage. A similar mechanism may explain, at least in part, the weight loss of subjects upon isocaloric substitution of food by ethanol and the relative lack of weight gain upon addition of ethanol to the diet compared to the effect of addition of other calories (FIGURE 7). Besides the energy-wasteful pathway of ethanol metabolism, there are, of course, a number of mechanisms whereby ethanol might affect the efficient disposal of ingested calories, such as interference with digestion and absorption (discussed in other papers in this monograph), but this was not the case under conditions of the study shown in FIGURE 7. Ethanol might also enhance other catabolic pathways that are not effectively coupled with the formation of high-energy phosphate bonds, such as the initial steps in amino acid degradation and the so-called futile metabolic cycles. Moreover, acetaldehyde may uncouple oxidative phosphorylation in mitochondria.[73] In any event, as shown in FIGURE 7, concerning body weight, ethanol calories do not fully "count," at least at a relatively high ethanol intake, and especially in alcoholics. This energy wastage conceivably represents another undesirable side effect of chronic ethanol consumption (TABLE 4). Similarly, as discussed elsewhere,[141] some aspects of physical dependence might also be linked to the increase in microsomal enzyme activities.

Increase in Microsomal Functions Related to Lipid Metabolism

Cholesterol Metabolism

The many functions of the endoplasmic reticulum include cholesterol synthesis. Increased cholesterol synthesis after ethanol[142] may have a microsomal basis akin to that after barbiturates and may explain, in part, the accumulation of cholesterol ester observed in the liver after feeding of alcohol,[142,143] especially with a cholesterol-free diet. When ethanol is given with cholesterol-containing diets, decreased cholesterol catabolism, evidenced by a reduction in bile-acid production and turnover after alcohol feeding, plays a major part (FIGURE 8).

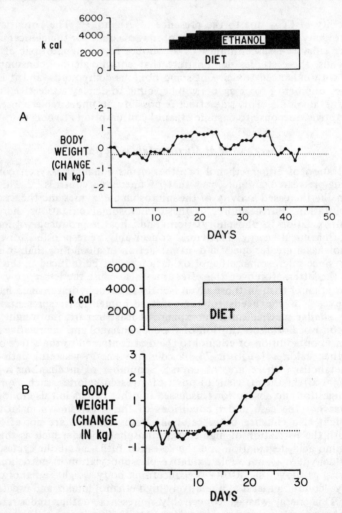

FIGURE 7. Effect on body weight of the addition of 2000 Kcal daily as ethanol (A) or chocolate (B) to the diet of the same subject.[140] The dotted line represents the mean change during the control period.

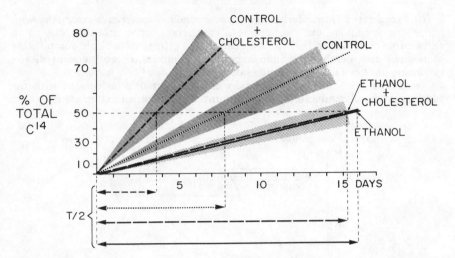

FIGURE 8. Cumulative excretion in feces of labeled bile acids following an intraperitoneal injection of [^{14}C]cholic acid. Shaded areas represent SEM.[142]

Alcoholic Hyperlipemia

In both man[144] and the rat[145] ethanol administration produces mild hyperlipemia, involving especially the very low-density lipoproteins. Incorporation into lipoprotein of intragastrically administered [^{3}H]palmitate (FIGURE 9) and intravenously injected [^{14}C]lysine (FIGURE 10) is increased,[145] suggesting enhanced lipoprotein production. Fatty acids are esterified, and lipoproteins are formed in the endoplasmic reticulum. Furthermore, chronic feeding of ethanol increases hepatic lipoprotein production, even when ethanol is not present at the time of testing, which reveals an increased capacity for lipoprotein synthesis[146] (FIGURE 11). Moreover, ethanol consumption enhances the activity of hepatic microsomal L-α-glycerophosphate acyltransferase.[148] The mechanism of the alterations of these microsomal functions produced by ethanol has not been clarified. It could be linked directly to the fact that ethanol can be oxidized at this key metabolic site. Ethanol could also induce hepatic production of lipoproteins indirectly by enhancing the availability of fatty acids either by decreasing their oxidation or by enhancing synthesis, as alluded to before. Increased glycerolipid production has indeed been found after ethanol feeding.[149] Ethanol feeding was observed to enhance the activity of glycosyltransferase in the Golgi apparatus[150] and to increase the synthesis of the protein moiety of lipoproteins.[145] In some individuals, the response is markedly exaggerated because of a fatty diet[151-155] or because of some underlying abnormality of lipid or carbohydrate metabolism, such as a forme fruste of essential hyperlipemia,[144,156,157] pancreatitis,[158] diabetes, or prediabetes[144,159] or an increased susceptibility to ethanol itself.[155]

After a single very large dose of ethanol, there is a moderate increase in circulating lipids to which the intestines may contribute.[160] The more pronounced hyperlipemia found after chronic ethanol consumption, however, seems to be primarily of hepatic origin, whereas the intestine plays little, if any, role in the increase of the lipemia.[146,161]

The exaggerated form of alcoholic hyperlipemia is sometimes associated with hemolytic anemia (Zieve's syndrome). The hemolysis is probably due to an extracorpuscular factor[162,163] and the associated change in the lipid composition of the red cell membrane.[164] An experimental model for an incipient Zieve's syndrome has been described in the rat.[165]

Contrasting with the hyperlipemia, which is commonly associated with the administration of moderate to large amounts of ethanol, an extremely high dose

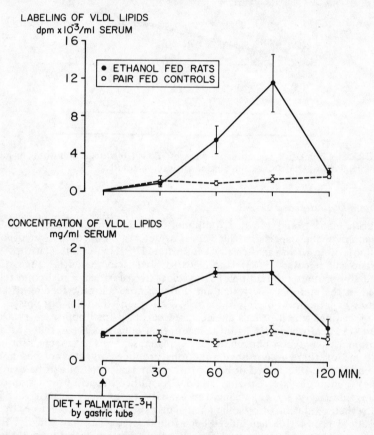

FIGURE 9. Concentration and labeling of the lipid moiety of serum very low-density lipoproteins (VLDL; d < 1.019) at different times after administration (by gastric tube) of ethanol or isocaloric control diets labeled with [³H]palmitic acid. Both groups of rats were fed the corresponding diets for 24 days before the experiments.[145]

has been reported to decrease serum triglycerides,[166] very low-density lipo-proteins,[167] high-density lipoproteins[168] and the incorporation of glucosamine into the carbohydrate moiety of serum lipoproteins[169] in the rat. These inhibi-tory effects can be related to the observation that the administration of an acute large dose of ethanol or addition of ethanol to isolated perfused livers depresses protein synthesis[170,171] and lipid secretion.[172] This may be due to the high ethanol concentration used. Indeed, more recently, when livers were per-

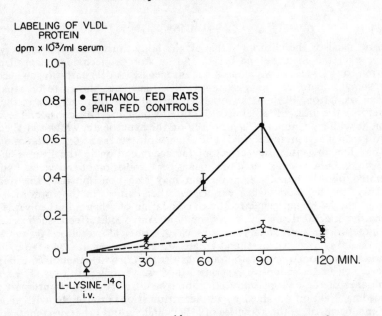

FIGURE 10. Incorporation of L-lysine-^{14}C into the protein moiety of serum very low density lipoproteins (VLDL; d < 1.019) at different times after intravenous injection.[145]

fused with ethanol in concentrations more in keeping with *in vivo* conditions, no inhibition of lipoprotein secretion was found.[7] The depressive effects of high concentrations of ethanol compared to the adaptive response to the lower may be a reflection of the hepatotoxic effect of ethanol.

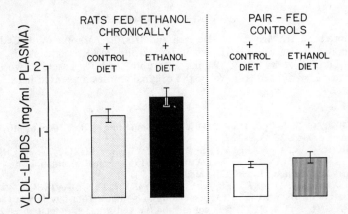

FIGURE 11. Comparison between acute and chronic ethanol administration on post-prandial lipemia in the rat. Animals were pair-fed liquid diets containing either ethanol (36% of total calories) or isocaloric carbohydrates (controls) for 3–4 weeks. Alcohol-fed rats developed hyperlipemia in response to a load of diet with or without ethanol; by contrast, control fed rats did not develop hyperlipemia in response to an acute administration of ethanol containing diet (3 g ethanol per kg body weight).[147]

SUMMARY

To rid itself of the absorbed ethanol, the body must burn it, since very little can be excreted in urine and breath and no storage mechanism is available. In addition to the well-known alcohol dehydrogenase (ADH) pathway, an accessory microsomal ethanol-oxidizing system (MEOS) has been shown to be capable of ethanol oxidation. Both pathways have the bulk of their activity in the liver. Therefore, the task of ethanol oxidation, which may be considerable in the alcoholic with high intake, falls primarily on the hepatocyte, which switches from fat to ethanol as a preferred fuel. This change promotes the oxidation of ethanol but has the unwanted side effect of fat accumulation in the liver. Enhanced lipogenesis could be considered as a means for disposition of the excess hydrogen generated upon ethanol oxidation and may also contribute to the steatosis. Similarly, the hepatocyte can export to other tissues (in the form of lactate) some of the hydrogen generated by the oxidation of ethanol in the liver. The resulting hyperlactacidemia produces some unwanted side effects, such as acidosis and hyperuricemia secondary to a block of uric acid excretion. To the extent that ethanol is oxidized by the alternate MEOS pathway, it slows the oxidation of other microsomal substrates, such as drugs. Chronic ethanol consumption, however, engenders adaptive responses in these various pathways. The smooth membranes of the endoplasmic reticulum (the ultrastructural counterpart of the microsomal fraction obtained by ultracentrifugation) proliferate, with an associated enhancement of the activities of MEOS and various other drug-metabolizing enzymes. As a consequence, rates of drug metabolism (including alcohol metabolism) are accelerated after chronic ethanol consumption. Similarly, the capacity of the liver microsomes to form and export lipids (as lipoproteins secreted into the blood stream) is enhanced in the alcoholic, at least in the adaptive stage that precedes the phase of liver injury. Clearing of the fat from the liver is promoted by ketosis and hyperlipemia, but the latter may be detrimental, especially in individuals with preexisting blood lipid abnormalities.

ACKNOWLEDGMENTS

I am indebted to Miss L. M. DeCarli and Drs. E. Baraona, A. I. Cederbaum, L. Feinman, Y. Hasumura, H. Ishii, J.-G. Joly, M. Korsten, A. F. Lefevre, S. Matsuzaki, P. Misra, R. C. Pirola, E. Rubin, and R. Teschke, who, among many others contributed to most of the original studies presented here.

REFERENCES

1. LIEBER, C. S. & C. S. DAVIDSON. 1962. Some metabolic effects of ethyl alcohol. Amer. J. Med. **33**: 319–327.
2. LIEBER, C. S., C. M. LEEVY, S. W. STEIN, W. S. GEORGE, G. R. CHERRICK, W. H. ABELMANN & C. S. DAVIDSON. 1962. Effect of ethanol on plasma free fatty acids in man. J. Lab. Clin. Med. **59**: 826–832.
3. LIEBER, C. S., D. P. JONES, M. S. LOSOWSKY & C. S. DAVIDSON. 1962. Interrelation of uric acid and ethanol metabolism in man. J. Clin. Invest. **41**: 1863–1870.
4. NEWCOMBE, D. S. 1972. Ethanol metabolism and uric acid. Metabolism **21**: 1193–1203.
5. NIKKILA, E. A. & K. OJALA. 1963. Role of hepatic L-α-glycerophosphate and triglyceride synthesis in production of fatty liver by ethanol. Proc. Soc. Exp. Biol. Med. **113**: 814–817.
6. LIEBER, C. S. & R. SCHMID. 1961. The effect of ethanol on fatty acid metabolism: Stimulation of hepatic fatty acid synthesis in vitro. J. Clin. Invest. **40**: 394–399.

7. GORDON, E. R. 1972. Effect of an intoxicating dose of ethanol on lipid metabolism in an isolated perfused rat liver. Biochem. Pharmacol. **21:** 2991–3004.

8. FORSANDER, O. A., P. H. MAENPAA & M. P. SALASPURO. 1965. Influence of ethanol on the lactate/pyruvate and β-hydroxybutyrate/acetoacetate ratios in rat liver experiments. Acta Chem. Scand. **19:** 1770–1771.

9. LIEBER, C. S., A. LEFEVRE, N. SPRITZ, L. FEINMAN & L. M. DeCARLI. 1967. Difference in hepatic metabolism of long- and medium-chained fatty acids: The role of fatty acid chain length in the production of the alcoholic fatty liver. J. Clin. Invest. **46:** 1451–1460.

10. BLOMSTRAND, R., L. KAGER & O. LANTTO. 1973. Studies on the ethanol-induced decrease of fatty acid oxidation in rat and human liver slices. Life Sci. **13:** 1131–1141.

11. ONTKO, J. A. 1973. Effects of ethanol on the metabolism of free fatty acids in isolated liver cells. J. Lipid Res. **14:** 78–86.

12. BLOMSTRAND, R. & L. KAGER. 1973. The combustion of triolein-1-^{14}C and its inhibition by alcohol in man. Life Sci. **13:** 113–123.

13. LIEBER, C. S., N. SPRITZ & L. M. DeCARLI. 1966. Role of dietary, adipose and endogenously synthesized fatty acids in the pathogenesis of the alcoholic fatty liver. J. Clin. Invest. **45:** 51–62.

14. LIEBER, C. S. & N. SPRITZ. 1966. Effects of prolonged ethanol intake in man: Role of dietary, adipose and endogenously synthesized fatty acids in the pathogenesis of the alcoholic fatty liver. J. Clin. Invest. **45:** 1400–1411.

15. LIEBER, C. S., N. SPRITZ & L. M. DeCARLI. 1969. Fatty liver produced by dietary deficiencies: Its pathogenesis and potentiation by ethanol. J. Lipid Res. **10:** 283–287.

16. MENDENHALL, C. L. 1972. Origin of hepatic triglyceride fatty acids: Quantitative estimation of the relative contributions of linoleic acid by diet and adipose tissue in normal and ethanol-fed rats. J. Lipid Res. **13:** 177–183.

17. FREINKEL, N. & R. A. ARKY. 1966. Effects of alcohol on carbohydrate metabolism in man. Psychosom. Med. **28:** 551–563.

18. LUMENG, L. & E. J. DAVIS. 1970. Mechanism of ethanol suppression of gluconeo-genesis. J. Biol. Chem. **25:** 3179–3185.

19. KREBS, H. A., R. HEMS, & P. LUND. 1973. Accumulation of amino acids by the perfused rat liver in the presence of ethanol. Biochem. J. **134:** 697–705.

20. PHILLIPS, G. B. & H. F. SAFRIT. 1971. Alcoholic diabetes. Induction of glucose intolerance with alcohol. J.A.M.A. **217:** 1513–1519.

21. LOCHNER, A., J. WULFF & L. L. MADISON. 1967. Ethanol-induced hypoglycemia. 1. The acute effects of ethanol on hepatic glucose output and peripheral glucose utilization in fasted dogs. Metabolism **16:** 1–18.

22. LEFEVRE, A., H. ADLER & C. S. LIEBER. 1970. Effect of ethanol on ketone metabolism. J. Clin. Invest. **49:** 1775–1782.

23. LIEBER, C. S. 1968. Metabolic effects produced by alcohol in the liver and other tissues. Advances Intern. Med. **14:** 151–199.

24. LIEBER, C. S. 1969. Alcohol and the liver. *In* The Biological Basis of Medicine. E. E. Bittar, Ed.: 317–344. Academic Press. New York, N.Y.

25. ADMIRAND, W. H., T. CRONHOLM & J. SJOVALL. 1970. Reduction of dehydro-epiandrosterone sulfate in the liver during ethanol metabolism. Biochim. Biophys. Acta **202:** 343–348.

26. MELDOLESI, J. 1967. On the significance of the hypertrophy of the smooth endo-plasmic reticulum in liver cells after administration of drugs. Biochem. Pharmacol. **16:** 125–129.

27. CONNEY, A. H. 1967. Pharmacological implications of microsomal enzyme induction. Pharmacol. Rev. **19:** 317–366.

28. LANE, B. P. & C. S. LIEBER. 1967. Effects of butylated hydroxytoluene on the ultrastructure of rat hepatocytes. Lab. Invest. **16:** 342–348.

29. ORME-JOHNSON, W. H. & D. M. ZIEGLER. 1965. Alcohol mixed function oxidase activity of mammalian liver microsomes. Biochem. Biophys. Res. Commun. **21:** 78–82.

30. LIEBER, C. S. & L. M. DeCARLI. 1968. Ethanol oxidation by hepatic microsomes: Adaptive increase after ethanol feeding. Science 162: 917–918.
31. LIEBER, C. S. & L. M. DeCARLI. 1970. Hepatic microsomal ethanol oxidizing system: In vitro characteristics and adaptive properties in vivo. J. Biol. Chem. 245: 2505–2512.
32. LIEBER, C. S., E. RUBIN & L. M. DeCARLI. 1970. Hepatic microsomal ethanol oxidizing system (MEOS): Differentiation from alcohol dehydrogenase and NADPH oxidase. Biochem. Biophys. Res. Commun. 40: 858–865.
33. LIEBER, C. S. & L. M. DeCARLI. 1973. The significance and characterization of hepatic microsomal ethanol oxidation in the liver. Drug Metab. Dispos. 1: 428–440.
34. KEILIN, D. & E. F. HARTREE. 1945. Properties of catalase: Catalysis of coupled oxidation of alcohols. Biochem. J. 39: 293–301.
35. GILLETTE, J. R., B. B. BRODIE & B. N. LA DU. 1957. The oxidation of drugs by liver microsomes: On the role of TPNH and oxygen. J. Pharmacol. Exp. Ther. 119: 532–540.
36. VATSIS, K. P. & M. P. SCHULMAN. 1973. Absence of ethanol metabolism in 'acatalatic' hepatic microsomes that oxidize drugs. Biochem. Biophys. Res. Commun. 52: 588–594.
37. LIEBER, C. S. & L. M. DeCARLI. 1974. Oxidation of ethanol by hepatic microsomes of acatalasemic mice. Biochem. Biophys. Res. Commun. 60: 1187–1192.
38. THURMAN, R. G., H. G. LEY & R. SCHOLZ. 1972. Hepatic microsomal ethanol oxidation. Hydrogen peroxide formation and the role of catalase. Eur. J. Biochem. 25: 420–430.
39. TESCHKE, R., Y. HASUMURA, J.-G. JOLY, H. ISHII & C. S. LIEBER. 1972. Microsomal ethanol-oxidizing system (MEOS): Purification and properties of a rat liver system free of catalase and alcohol dehydrogenase. Biochem. Biophys. Res. Commun. 49: 1187–1193.
40. MEZEY, E., J. J. POTTER & W. D. REED. 1973. Ethanol oxidation by a component of liver microsomes rich in cytochrome P-450. J. Biol. Chem. 248: 1183–1187.
41. TESCHKE, R., Y. HASUMURA & C. S. LIEBER. 1974. Hepatic microsomal ethanol oxidizing system: Solubilization, isolation and characterization. Arch. Biochem. Biophys. 163: 404–415.
42. LÜCK, H. 1963. Catalase. In Methods of Enzymatic Analysis. H. U. Bergmeyer, Ed.: 885–888, Academic Press. New York, N.Y.
43. REDMAN, C. M., D. J. GRAB & R. IRUKULLA. 1972. The intracellular pathway of newly formed rat liver catalase. Arch. Biochem. Biophys. 152: 496–501.
44. LIEBER, C. S. & L. M. DeCARLI. 1972. The role of hepatic microsomal ethanol oxidizing system (MEOS) for ethanol metabolism in vivo. J. Pharmacol. Exp. Ther. 181: 279–287.
45. PAPENBERG, J., J. P. VON WARTBURG & H. AEBI. 1970. Metabolism of ethanol and fructose in the perfused rat liver. Enzym. Biol. Clin. 11: 237–250.
46. THIEDEN, H. I. D. 1971. The effect of ethanol concentration on ethanol oxidation rate in rat liver slices. Acta Chem. Scand. 25: 3421–3427.
47. GRUNNET, N., B. QUISTORF & H. I. D. THIEDEN. 1973. Rate-limiting factors in ethanol oxidation by isolated rat-liver parenchymal cells. Eur. J. Biochem. 40: 275–282.
48. ROGNSTAD, R. & D. G. CLARK. 1974. Tritium as a tracer for reducing equivalents in isolated liver cells. Eur. J. Biochem. 42: 51–60.
49. GRUNNET, N. & H. I. D. THIEDEN. 1972. The effect of ethanol concentration upon in vivo metabolite levels of rat liver. Life Sci. (II) 11: 983–993.
50. REYNIER, M. 1969. Pyrazole inhibition and kinetic studies of ethanol and retinol oxidation catalyzed by rat liver alcohol dehydrogenase. Acta Chem. Scand. 23: 1119–1129.
51. MAKAR, A. B. & G. J. MANNERING. 1970. Kinetics of ethanol metabolism in the intact rat and monkey. Biochem. Pharmacol. 19: 2017–2022.
52. OSHINO, N., B. CHANCE, H. SIES & T. BUCHER. 1973. The role of H_2O_2 genera-

tion in perfused rat liver and the reaction of catalase compound I and hydrogen donors. Arch. Biochem. Biophys. **154**: 117–131.

53. THURMAN, R. G. & R. SCHOLZ. 1973. The role of hydrogen peroxide and catalase in hepatic microsomal ethanol oxidation. Drug Metab. Dispos. **1**: 441–448.

54. FORNEY, R. B. & F. W. HUGHES. 1968. Combined effects of alcohol and other drugs. C. C. Thomas. Springfield, Ill.

55. SOEHRING, K. & R. SCHUPPEL. 1966. Wechselwirkungen zwisehen Alkohol und Arzneimitteln. Deutsch. Med. Wschr. **91**: 1892–1898.

56. RUBIN, E. & C. S. LIEBER. 1968. Hepatic microsomal enzymes in man and rat: Induction and inhibition by ethanol. Science **162**: 690–691.

57. RUBIN, E., H. GANG, P. S. MISRA & C. S. LIEBER. 1970. Inhibition of drug metabolism by acute ethanol intoxication. A hepatic microsomal mechanism. Amer. J. Med. **49**: 801–806.

58. ARIYOSHI, T., E. TAKABATAKE & H. REMMER. 1970. Drug metabolism in ethanol induced fatty liver. Life Sci. **9**: 361–369.

59. SCHÜPPEL, R. 1971. Wirkungen von Alkohol auf den Arzneistoffwechsel. *In* Alcohol and the Liver. W. Gerok, K. Sickinger & H. H. Hennekeuser, Eds.: 227–242, Schattauer Verlag. New York, N.Y.

60. COHEN, G. M. & G. J. MANNERING. 1973. Involvement of a hydrophobic site in the inhibition of the microsomal p-hydroxylation of aniline by alcohols. Molec. Pharmacol. **9**: 383–397.

61. HILDEBRANDT, A. G., M. SPECK & I. ROOTS. 1974. The effects of substrates of mixed function oxidase on ethanol oxidation in rat liver microsomes. Naunyn Schmiedeberg Arch. Pharmacol. **281**: 371–382.

62. SUTHERLAND, V. C., T. N. BURBRIDGE, J. E. ADAMS & A. SIMON. 1960. Cerebral metabolism in problem drinkers under the influence of alcohol and chlorpromazine hydrochloride. J. Appl. Physiol. **15**: 189–196.

63. VOAS, R. B. 1973. Alcohol as an underlying factor in behavior leading to fatal highway crashes. *In* Proc. First Annual Alcoholism Conference of the National Institute on Alcohol Abuse and Alcoholism. M. E. Chafetz, Ed.: 324–331. DHEW (NIH) 74–675, U.S. Government Printing Office. Washington, D.C.

64. TRUITT, E. B., JR. & G. DURITZ. 1966. The role of acetaldehyde in the actions of ethanol. *In* Biochemical Factors in Alcoholism. P. P. Maickel, Ed.: 61–69, Pergamon Press. New York, N.Y.

65. KORSTEN, M., S. MATSUZAKI, L. FEINMAN & C. S. LIEBER. 1975. High blood acetaldehyde levels following ethanol administration: Differences between alcoholic and non-alcoholic subjects. New Eng. J. Med. In press.

66. MARJANEN, L. 1972. Intracellular localization of aldehyde dehydrogenase in rat liver. Biochem. J. **127**: 633–639.

67. GRUNNET, N. 1973. Oxidation of acetaldehyde by rat-liver mitochondria in relation to ethanol oxidation and the transport of reducing equivalents across the mitochondrial membrane. Eur. J. Biochem. **35**: 236–243.

68. DAJANI, R. M., J. DANIELSKI & J. M. ORTEN. 1963. The utilization of ethanol II. The alcohol-acetaldehyde dehydrogenase systems in the livers of alcohol-treated rats. J. Nutr. **80**: 196–204.

69. HORTON, A. A. 1971. Induction of aldehyde dehydrogenase in a mitochondrial fraction. Biochim. Biophys. Acta **253**: 514–517.

70. RASKIN, N. H. & L. SOKOLOFF. 1972. Ethanol-induced adaptation of alcohol dehydrogenase activity in rat brain. Nature **236**: 138–140.

71. REDMOND, G. & G. COHEN. 1971. Induction of liver acetaldehyde dehydrogenase: Possible role in ethanol tolerance after exposure to barbiturates. Science **171**: 387–389.

72. CEDERBAUM, A. I., C. S. LIEBER, A. TOTH, D. S. BEATTIE & E. RUBIN. 1973. Effects of ethanol and fat on the transport of reducing equivalents into rat liver mitochondria. J. Biol. Chem. **248**: 4977–4986.

73. CEDERBAUM, A. I., C. S. LIEBER & E. RUBIN. 1974. The effect of acetaldehyde on mitochondrial function. Arch. Biochem. Biophys. **161**: 26–39.

74. EADE, N. R. 1959. Mechanism of sympathomimetic action of aldehydes. J. Pharmacol. Exp. Ther. **127:** 29–34.
75. PERMAN, E. S. 1958. The effect of ethyl alcohol on the secretion from the adrenal medulla in man. Acta Physiol. Scand. **44:** 241–247.
76. DAVIS, V. E. & M. J. WALSH. 1970. Alcohol, amines and alkaloids: A possible biochemical basis for alcohol addiction. Science **167:** 1005–1007.
77. TRUITT, E. B., Jr. & M. J. WALSH. 1973. The role of biogenic amines in the mechanism of action of anti-alcohol drugs. *In* Proc. First Annual Alcoholism Conference of the National Institute on Alcohol Abuse and Alcoholism. M. E. Chafetz, Ed.: 100–111. DHEW (NIH) 74–675. U.S. Government Printing Office. Washington, D.C.
78. LIEBER, C. S. 1967. Metabolic derangement induced by alcohol. Ann. Rev. Med. **18:** 35–54.
79. STEIN, S., C. S. LIEBER, G. R. CHERRICK, C. M. LEEVY & W. H. ABELMANN. 1963. The effect of ethanol on systemic and hepatic blood flow in man. Amer. J. Clin. Nutr. **13:** 68–74.
80. SCHREIBER, S. S., K. BRIDEN, M. ORATZ & M. A. ROTHSCHILD. 1972. Ethanol, acetaldehyde, and myocardial protein synthesis. J. Clin. Invest. **51:** 2820–2826.
81. SCHEIG, R. 1971. Lipid synthesis from ethanol in liver. Gastroenterology **60:** 751.
82. BRUNENGRABER, H., M. BOUTRY, L. LOWENSTEIN & J. M. LOWENSTEIN. 1974. The effect of ethanol on lipogenesis by the perfused liver. *In* Alcohol and Aldehyde Metabolizing Systems. R. G. Thurman, T. Yonetani, J. R. Williamson & B. Chance, Eds.: 329–357. Academic Press. New York, N.Y.
83. LUNDQUIST, F., N. TYGSTRUP, K. WINKLER, K. MELLEMGAARD & S. MUNCK-PETERSEN. 1962. Ethanol metabolism and production of free acetate in the human liver. J. Clin. Invest. **41:** 955–961.
84. CROUSE, J. R., C. D. GERSON, L. M. DeCARLI & C. S. LIEBER. 1968. Role of acetate in the reduction of plasma free fatty acids produced by ethanol in man. J. Lipid Res. **9:** 509–512.
85. KATZ, J. & I. L. CHAIKOFF. 1955. Synthesis via the Kreb's cycle in the utilization of acetate by rat liver slices. Biochim. Biophys. Acta **18:** 87–101.
86. ISERI, O. A., L. S. GOTTLIEB & C. S. LIEBER. 1964. The ultrastructure of ethanol-induced fatty liver. Fed. Proc. **23:** 579.
87. ISERI, O. A., C. S. LIEBER & L. S. GOTTLIEB. 1966. The ultrastructure of fatty liver induced by prolonged ethanol ingestion. Amer. J. Path. **48:** 535–555.
88. RUBIN, E., F. HUTTERER & C. S. LIEBER. 1968. Ethanol increases hepatic smooth endoplasmic reticulum and drug-metabolizing enzymes. Science **159:** 1469–1470.
89. LIEBER, C. S. & E. RUBIN. 1968. Alcoholic fatty liver in man on a high protein and low fat diet. Amer. J. Med. **44:** 200–207.
90. CARULLI, N., F. MANENTI, M. GALLO & G. F. SALVIOLI. 1971. Alcohol-drugs interaction in man: Alcohol and tolbutamide. Eur. J. Clin. Invest. **1:** 421–424.
91. ISHII, H., J.-G. JOLY & C. S. LIEBER. 1973. Effect of ethanol on the amount and enzyme activities of hepatic rough and smooth microsomal membranes. Biochim. Biophys. Acta **291:** 411–420.
92. KATER, R. M. H., N. CARULLI & F. L. IBER. 1969. Differences in the rate of ethanol metabolism in recently drinking alcoholic and nondrinking subjects. Amer. J. Clin. Nutr. **22:** 1608–1617.
93. UGARTE, G., T. PEREDA, M. E. PINO & H. ITURRIAGA. 1972. Influence of alcohol intake, length of abstinence and meprobamate on the rate of ethanol metabolism in man. Quart. J. Stud. Alcohol **33:** 698–705.
94. TOBON, F. & E. MEZEY. 1971. Effect of ethanol administration on hepatic ethanol and drug-metabolizing enzymes and on rates of ethanol degradation. J. Lab. Clin. Med. **77:** 110–121.
95. MISRA, P. S., A. LEFEVRE, H. ISHII, E. RUBIN & C. S. LIEBER. 1971. Increase of ethanol, meprobamate and pentobarbital metabolism after chronic ethanol administration in man and in rats. Amer. J. Med. **51:** 346–351.

96. LIEBER, C. S. 1973. Hepatic and metabolic effects of alcohol (1966–1973). Gastro-enterology **65:** 821–846.
97. UGARTE, G., M. E. PINO & I. INSUNZA. 1967. Hepatic alcohol dehydrogenase in alcoholic addicts with and without hepatic damage. Amer. J. Dig. Dis. **12:** 589–592.
98. MISTILIS, S. P. & A. GARSKE. 1969. Induction of alcohol dehydrogenase in liver and gastrointestinal tract. Aust. Ann. Med. **18:** 227–231.
99. DE SAINT-BLANQUAT, G., P. FRITSCH & R. DERACHE. 1972. Activite alcool-deshydrogenasique de la muqueuse gastrique sous l'effet de différents traitements éthanoliques chez le rat. Path. Biol. **20:** 249–254.
100. HILLBOM, M. E. 1971. Regulation of hepatic elimination of ethanol in vivo. FEBS Letters **17:** 303–305.
101. SCHENKER, T. M., L. J. TEEPLE & J. P. VON WARTBURG. 1971. Heterogeneity and polymorphism of human liver alcohol dehydrogenase. Eur. J. Biochem. **24:** 271–279.
102. PIETRUSZKO, R., H. THEORELL & C. DeZALENSKI. 1972. Heterogeneity of alcohol dehydrogenase from human liver. Arch. Biochem. Biophys. **153:** 279–293.
103. VON WARTBURG, J. P., J. PAPENBERG & H. AEBI. 1965. An atypical human alcohol dehydrogenase. Canad. J. Biochem. **43:** 889–898.
104. EDWARDS, J. A. & D. A. PRICE EVANS. 1972. Ethanol metabolism in subjects possessing typical and atypical liver alcohol dehydrogenase. Clin. Pharmacol. Ther. **8:** 824–829.
105. LUNDQUIST, F. & H. WOLTHERS. 1958. The influence of fructose on the kinetics of alcohol elimination in man. Acta Pharmacol. **14:** 290–294.
106. THIEDEN, H. I. D. & F. LUNDQUIST. 1967. The influence of fructose and its metabolism on ethanol metabolism in vitro. Biochem. J. **102:** 177–180.
107. LOWENSTEIN, L. M., R. SIMONE, P. BOULTER & P. NATHAN. 1970. Effect of fructose on alcohol concentration in the blood in man. J.A.M.A. **213:** 1899–1901.
108. HOLZER, H. & S. SCHNEIDER. 1955. Zum Mechanismus der Beeinflussung der Alkoholoxydation in der Leber durch Fructose. Klin. Wschr. **33:** 1006–1009.
109. THIEDEN, H. I. D., N. GRUNNET, S. E. DAMGAARD & L. SESTOFT. 1972. Effect of fructose and glyceraldehyde on ethanol metabolism in human liver and in rat liver. Eur. J. Biochem. **30:** 250–261.
110. BERNSTEIN, J., L. VIDELA & Y. ISRAEL. 1973. Metabolic alterations produced in the liver by chronic ethanol administration. II. Changes related to energetic parameters of the cell. Biochem. J. **134:** 515–522.
111. VEECH, R. L., L. V. EGGLESTON & H. A. KREBS. 1969. The redox state of free nicotinamide-adenine dinucleotide phosphate in the cytoplasm of rat liver. Biochem. J. **115:** 609–619.
112. COHEN, B. S. & R. W. ESTABROOK. 1971. Microsomal electron transport reactions. III. Cooperative interactions between reduced diphosphopyridine nucleotide and reduced triphosphopyridine nucleotide linked reaction. Arch. Biochem. Biophys. **143:** 54–65.
113. RUBIN, E., C. S. LIEBER, A. P. ALVARES, W. LEVIN & R. KUNTZMAN. 1971. Ethanol binding to hepatic microsomes: Its increase by ethanol consumption. Biochem. Pharmacol. **20:** 229–231.
114. LIEBER, C. S. & L. M. DeCARLI. 1970. Effect of drug administration on the activity of the hepatic microsomal ethanol oxidizing system. Life Sci. **9:** 267–276.
115. FISCHER, H.-D. 1962. Der Einfluss von Barbituraten auf die Entgiftungsgeschwindig-keit des Athanols. Biochem. Pharmacol. **11:** 307–314.
116. MEZEY, E. & E. A. ROBLES. 1974. Effect of phenobarbital administration on ethanol metabolism and on ethanol metabolizing enzymes in man. Gastroenterology **66:** 248–253.
117. TEPHLY, T. R., F. TINELLI & W. D. WATKINS. 1969. Alcohol metabolism: role of microsomal oxidation in vivo. Science **166:** 627–628.
118. KLAASSEN, C. D. 1969. Ethanol metabolism in rats after microsomal metabolizing enzyme induction. Proc. Soc. Exp. Biol. Med. **132:** 1099–1102.
119. SOTANIEMI, E., R. ISOACHO, E. HUHTI, M. HUIKKO & O. KOIVISTO. 1972.

Increased clearance of ethanol from the blood of asthmatic patients. Ann. Allerg. **30:** 254–257.

120. CARTER, E. A. & K. J. ISSELBACHER. 1971. The role of microsomes in the hepatic metabolism of ethanol. Ann. N.Y. Acad. Sci. **179:** 282–294.

121. HAWKINS, R. D., H. KALANT & J. M. KHANNA. 1966. Effects of chronic intake of ethanol on rate of ethanol metabolism. Canad. J. Physiol. Pharmacol. **44:** 241–257.

122. VON WARTBURG, J. P. & M. ROTHLISBERGER. 1961. Enzymatische Veränderungen in der Leber nach langdürnder Belastrung mit Aethanol und Methanol bei der Ratte. Helv. Physiol. Acta **19:** 30–41.

123. BOVERIS, A., N. OSHINO & B. CHANCE. 1972. The cellular production of hydrogen peroxide. Biochem. J. **128:** 617–630.

124. LIEBER, C. S. & L. M. DeCARLI. 1970. Reduced nicotinamide-adenine dinucleotide phosphate oxidase: Activity enhanced by ethanol consumption. Science **170:** 78–79.

125. THURMAN, R. G. 1973. Induction of hepatic microsomal reduced nicotinamide adenine dinucleotide phosphate-dependent production of hydrogen peroxide by chronic prior treatment with ethanol. Molec. Pharmacol. **9:** 670–675.

126. VIDELA, L., J. BERNSTEIN & Y. ISRAEL. 1973. Metabolic alterations produced in the liver by chronic ethanol administration. I. Increased oxidative capacity. Biochem. J. **134:** 507–514.

127. MAKAR, A. B., T. R. TEPHLY & G. J. MANNERING. 1968. Methanol metabolism in the monkey. Molec. Pharmacol. **4:** 471–483.

128. JOLY, J.-G., H. ISHII, R. TESCHKE, Y. HASUMURA & C. S. LIEBER. 1973. Effect of chronic ethanol feeding on the activities and submicrosomal distribution of reduced nicotinamide adenine dinucleotide phosphate (NADPH)-cytochrome P-450 reductase and the demethylases for aminopyrine and ethylmorphine. Biochem. Pharmacol. **22:** 1532–1535.

129. LIEBER, C. S., D. P. JONES & L. M. DeCARLI. 1965. Effects of prolonged ethanol intake: Production of fatty liver despite adequate diets. J. Clin. Invest. **44:** 1009–1021.

130. LU, A. Y. H., H. W. STROBEL & M. J. COON. 1969. Hydroxylation of benzphetamine and other drugs by a solubilized form of cytochrome P-450 from liver microsomes: Lipid requirement for drug demethylation. Biochem. Biophys. Res. Commun. **36:** 545–551.

131. KALANT, H., J. M. KHANNA & J. MARSHMAN. 1970. Effect of chronic intake of ethanol on pentobarbital metabolism. J. Pharmacol. Exp. Ther. **175:** 318–324.

132. RATCLIFFE, F. 1969. The effect of chronic ethanol administration on the responses to amylobarbitone sodium in the rat. Life Sci. **8:** 1051–1061.

133. KATER, R. M. H., G. ROGGIN, F. TOBON, P. ZIEVE & F. L. IBER. 1969. Increased rate of clearance of drugs from the circulation of alcoholics. Amer. J. Med. Sci. **258:** 35–39.

134. VESELL, E. S., J. G. PAGE & G. T. PASSANANTI. 1971. Genetic and environmental factors affecting ethanol metabolism in man. Clin. Pharmacol. Ther. **12:** 192–201.

135. HASUMURA, Y., R. TESCHKE & C. S. LIEBER. 1974. Increased carbon tetrachloride hepatotoxicity following chronic ethanol consumption and its mechanism. Gastroenterology **66:** 415–422.

136. TRAIGER, G. J. & PLAA, G. L. 1972. Relationship of alcohol metabolism to the potentiation of CCl_4 hepatotoxicity induced by aliphatic alcohols. J. Pharmacol. Exp. Ther. **183:** 481–488.

137. MOON, H. D. 1950. The pathology of fatal carbon tetrachloride poisoning with special reference to the histogenesis of the hepatic and renal lesions. Amer. J. Path. **26:** 1041–1057.

138. PIROLA, R. C. & C. S. LIEBER. 1973. Energy cost of ethanol metabolism. Clin. Res. **21:** 719.

139. TREMOLIERES, J. & L. CARRE. 1961. Études sur les modalités d'oxydation de l'alcool chez l'homme normal et alcoolique. Rev. de l'Alcoolisme **7:** 202–227.

140. PIROLA, R. C. & C. S. LIEBER. 1972. The energy cost of the metabolism of drugs, including ethanol. Pharmacology **7:** 185–196.

141. LIEBER, C. S. 1972. Ethanol metabolism and biochemical aspects of alcohol tolerance and dependence. *In* Chemical and Biological Aspects of Drug Dependence. S. J. Mule & H. Brill, Eds.: 135–161. CRC Press. Cleveland, Ohio.

142. LEFEVRE, A. F., L. M. DeCARLI & C. S. LIEBER. 1972. Effect of ethanol on cholesterol and bile acid metabolism. J. Lipid Res. **13:** 48–55.

143. LIEBER, C. S., D. P. JONES, J. MENDELSON & L. M. DeCARLI. 1963. Fatty liver, hyperlipemia and hyperuricemia produced by prolonged alcohol consumption, despite adequate dietary intake. Trans. Ass. Amer. Physicians **76:** 289–300.

144. LOSOWSKY, M. S., D. P. JONES, C. S. DAVIDSON & C. S. LIEBER. 1963. Studies of alcoholic hyperlipemia and its mechanism. Amer. J. Med. **35:** 794–803.

145. BARAONA, E. & C. S. LIEBER. 1970. Effects of chronic ethanol feeding on serum lipoprotein metabolism in the rat. J. Clin. Invest. **49:** 769–778.

146. BARAONA, E., R. C. PIROLA & C. S. LIEBER. 1973. The pathogenesis of post-prandial hyperlipemia in rats fed ethanol-containing diets. J. Clin. Invest. **52:** 296–303.

147. BARAONA, E. & C. S. LIEBER. 1975. Alcoholic hyperlipemia. *In* Handbuch der inneren Medizin. G. Schettler, H. Greten, G. Schlierf & D. Seidel, Eds. Springer-Verlag, New York.

148. JOLY, J.-G., L. FEINMAN, H. ISHII & C. S. LIEBER. 1973. Effect of chronic ethanol feeding on hepatic microsomal glycerophosphate acyltransferase activity. J. Lipid Res. **14:** 337–343.

149. MENDENHALL, C. L., R. H. BRADFORD & R. FURMAN. 1969. Effect of ethanol on glycerolipid metabolism in rat liver. Biochim. Biophys. Acta **187:** 501–509.

150. GANG, H., C. S. LIEBER & E. RUBIN. 1973. Ethanol increases glycosyl transferase activity in the hepatic Golgi apparatus. Nature (New Biology) **243:** 123–125.

151. BREWSTER, A. C., H. G. LANKFORD, M. G. SCHWARTZ & J. F. SULLIVAN. 1966. Ethanol and alimentary lipemia. Amer. J. Clin. Nutr. **19:** 255–259.

152. VERDY, M. & A. GATTEREAU. 1967. Ethanol, lipase activity, and serum-lipid level. Amer. J. Clin. Nutr. **20:** 997–1004.

153. BARBORIAK, J. J. & R. C. MEADE. 1968. Enhancement of alimentary lipemia by preprandial alcohol. Amer. J. Med. Sci. **255:** 245–251.

154. WILSON, D. E., P. H. SCHREIBMAN, A. C. BREWSTER and R. A. ARKY. 1970. The enhancement of alimentary lipemia by ethanol in man. J. Lab. Clin. Med. **75:** 264–274.

155. KUDZMA, D. J. & G. SCHONFELD. 1971. Alcoholic hyperlipidemia: Induction by alcohol but not by carbohydrate. J. Lab. Clin. Med. **77:** 384–395.

156. MENDELSON, J. H. & N. K. MELLO. 1973. Alcohol-induced hyperlipidemia and β-lipoproteins. Science **180:** 1372–1374.

157. GINSBERG, H., J. OLEFSKY, J. W. FARQUHAR & G. M. REAVEN. 1974. Moderate ethanol ingestion and plasma triglyceride levels. Ann. Intern. Med. **80:** 143–149.

158. KESSLER, J. I., M. MILLER, D. BARZA & S. MISHKIN. 1967. Hyperlipemia in acute pancreatitis. Metabolic studies in a patient and demonstration of abnormal lipoprotein-triglyceride complexes resistant to the action of lipoprotein lipase. Amer. J. Med. **42:** 968–977.

159. CHAIT, A., A. W. FEBRUARY, M. MANCINI & B. L. LEWIS. 1972. Clinical and metabolic study of alcoholic hyperlipidaemia. Lancet **2:** 62–64.

160. MISTILIS, S. P. & R. K. OCKNER. 1972. Effects of ethanol on endogenous lipid and lipoprotein metabolism in small intestine. J. Lab. Clin. Med. **80:** 34–46.

161. HERNELL, O. & O. JOHNSON. 1973. Effect of ethanol on plasma triglycerides in male and female rats. Lipids **8:** 503–508.

162. BALCERZAK, S. P., M. P. WESTERMAN & E. W. HEINLE. 1968. Mechanism of anemia in Zieve's syndrome. Amer. J. Med. Sci. **255:** 277–287.

163. POWELL, L. W., H. P. ROESER & J. W. HALIDAY. 1972. Transient intravascular haemolysis associated with alcoholic liver disease and hyperlipidaemia. Aust. N. Z. J. Med. **1:** 39–43.

164. WESTERMAN, M. P., S. P. BALCERZAK & E. W. HEINLE. 1968. Red cell lipids in

Zieve's syndrome: Their relation to hemolysis and to red cell osmotic fragility. J. Lab. Clin. Med. **72:** 663–670.

165. BARAONA, E. & C. S. LIEBER. 1969. Fatty liver, hyperlipemia and erythrocyte alterations produced by ethanol feeding in the rat. Amer. J. Clin. Nutr. **20:** 356–357.

166. DAJANI, R. M. & C. S. KOUYOUMJIAN. 1967. A probable direct role of ethanol in the pathogenesis of fat infiltration in the rat. J. Nutr. **91:** 535–539.

167. MADSEN, N. P. 1969. Reduced serum very low-density lipoprotein levels after acute ethanol administration. Biochem. Pharmacol. **18:** 261–262.

168. KOGA, S. & C. HIRAYAMA. 1968. Disturbed release of lipoprotein from ethanol induced fatty liver. Experientia **24:** 438–439.

169. MOOKERJEA, S. & A. CHOW. 1969. Impairment of glycoprotein synthesis in acute ethanol intoxication in rats. Biochim. Biophys. Acta **184:** 83–92.

170. ROTHSCHILD, M., M. ORTAZ, J. MONGELLI & S. S. SCHREIBER. 1971. Alcohol-induced depression of albumin synthesis: reversal by tryptophan. J. Clin. Invest. **50:** 1812–1818.

171. JEEJEEBHOY, K. N., M. J. PHILLIPS, A. BRUCE-ROBERTSON, J. HO & U. SODTKE. 1972. The acute effect of ethanol on albumin, fibrinogen and transferrin synthesis in the rat. Biochem. J. **126:** 1111–1126.

172. SCHAPIRO, R. H., G. D. DRUMMEY, Y. SHIMIZU & K. J. ISSELBACHER. 1964. Studies on the pathogenesis of the ethanol-induced fatty liver. II. Effect of ethanol on palmitate-1-C^{14} metabolism by the isolated perfused rat liver. J. Clin. Invest. **43:** 1338–1347.

PROTEIN SYNTHESIS IN THE HEPATOCYTE*

Murray Oratz,† ‡ Marcus A. Rothschild,† § and
Sidney S. Schreiber † §

†*Radioisotope Service*
Veterans Administration Hospital
New York, New York 10010

‡*Department of Biochemistry*
New York University College of Dentistry
New York, New York 10010

§*Department of Medicine*
New York University School of Medicine
New York, New York 10016

The level of serum albumin has often been relied upon to reflect the status of the liver in health and disease. It is well known that, while the concentration of serum albumin is decreased in alcohol-induced cirrhosis, data are available indicating that in many cases the exchangeable albumin pool is not depressed;[1] further, when alcohol is removed and adequate nutrition supplied, the albumin-synthesizing potential is restored.[2] The question whether the removal of alcohol or the institution of adequate nutrition was responsible for the liver's recovery has been the subject of much debate. *In vivo* the level of albumin is the net result of synthesis, degradation, and distribution, and in the whole animal albumin synthesis is influenced by the interplay of the nutritional status of the animal, environment,[3] hormones, oncotic equilibrium,[4] and toxins, as well as the state of health. Thus, *in vivo*, it is difficult to study the effect of one isolated factor in albumin synthesis, and for this reason the isolated perfused liver was employed. The advantages are obvious: (a) the perfusion medium can be altered in a particular manner with any substance with the knowledge that the substance perfusing the liver has not been altered by prior passage through any tissue: (b) the effects of pretreatment of the inact animal on the liver's ability to synthesize albumin can be studied by removal of the liver after pretreatment; and (c) subcellular systems can be isolated following perfusion and correlative evidence of altered microstructure with altered liver function may be obtained.

In the present study the isolated perfused liver was used to study the effects of altered nutrition, in the absence and presence of ethyl alcohol, on the liver's ability to synthesize albumin as well as the correlative effect on the endoplasmic reticulum-bound polysome, the organelle responsible for the synthesis of albumin.

The results indicated that a short term fast of 24 hours was sufficient to decrease albumin synthesis to one-half that found in livers from fed donors. The decrease in albumin synthesis was coincident with a disaggregation of the bound polysome. However, this effect could be readily reversed by the presence

*Supported in part by United States Public Health Service grant HL 09562 and the Louise and Bernard Palitz Fund.

51

of high concentrations of specific amino acids. Perfusion of livers from fed donors with alcohol induced the same effect, which could be reversed to some degree by specific amino acids. But if the liver was derived from a fasted donor the effects could not be reversed by these amino acids. The effect of alcohol and fasting on the endoplasmic reticulum-bound polysome was the same but the mechanism appears different.

METHODS

Donors: Fed or 24-hour fasted 1.2–1.4-kg rabbits were used in all studies. The standard rabbit chow (Wayne Rabbit Ration, Allied Mills, Inc., Chicago, Ill.) consisted of 17% protein, 2% fat, and 15% fiber, and the average intake was 80–120 g/day.

Perfusate: The perfusate consisted of washed rabbit red cells made up to a final hematocrit value of 25–27% with Krebs-Henseleit bicarbonate buffer containing 3 g% rabbit or bovine albumin, 0.08% glucose and amino acids at levels equivalent to that found in fed rabbit serum. The perfusate was gassed with 95% O_2–5% CO_2 and pH maintained at 7.4.

In the alcohol studies, ethyl alcohol was added to the perfusate at an initial concentration of 0.22%, and this level was maintained by the constant infusion of ethanol during the experimental period.

Perfusion: The techniques for removal of the liver and its perfusion have been previously described in detail.[5]

Perfusion was directed into the portal vein at a rate of 1.0–1.4 ml/g of liver per min. The perfusion volume of 140–170 ml was recirculated and oxygenated by a disc oxygenator that received the output from the inferior vena cava. Bile was collected from the cannulated biliary duct.

Albumin Synthesis: The carbonate-^{14}C technique was used to label the hepatic-arginine intracellular pool. Since arginine is the immediate precursor not only of the arginine residue in albumin but also of urea, a direct product precursor relationship exists.[6-8] After 60 min. of perfusion (control and experimental) 100 μCi of carbonate-[14]C (specific activity 5 m Ci/mmole) was injected directly into the inflow tube to the portal vein and the perfusion continued for 2.5 hrs.

Albumin synthesis was determined by the following formula:

$$\text{Albumin Synthesis} = \frac{\text{Albumin guanidino C-specific activity}}{\text{Synthesized Urea C-specific activity}} \times \text{perfusate albumin}$$

Synthesized urea carbon-specific activity is presumed to equal the precursor arginine guanidino carbon-specific activity.

ANALYTICAL METHODS

The total protein in the perfusate was measured by a biuret method[9] and albumin partition by a Kern microelectrophoresis unit.[10] RNA was measured by the method of Fleck and Begg[11] and DNA by the method of Keck.[12] Albumin was isolated from the perfusate by preparative acrylamide gel electrophoresis.[5]

The perfusate albumin from the pooled fractions was hydrolyzed with 6 N HCl and the hydrolyzate neutralized. After the effluent was reacted with arginase, a portion was incubated with urease according to the method of Conway and Bryne[13] and the ammonia released by 45% K_2CO_3 was trapped in 2 N H_2SO_4 and assayed with Nessler's reagent. An identical portion was incubated with urease and treated with H_3PO_4, and the CO_2 released was trapped in phenethylamine, which was then dissolved in 15 ml of 0.7% butyl-PBD in toluene-methanol (1:1); the ^{14}C was assayed in an ambient-temperature liquid scintillation counter. The urea carbon-specific activity of the perfusate was determined in the same way with use of the supernatant from a heated tungstic acid precipitated sample.

In those perfusions where bovine albumin was employed, albumin was isolated by 2 alcohol-trichloracetic acid separations with intervening dialyses. These techniques have been shown to result in clean albumin preparations that have the same ^{14}C guanidino carbon-specific activity as do those isolated by immunochemical or acrylamide gel methods.[14]

Lactate, pyruvate, and alcohol levels were obtained by employing Sigma Chemical Co. kits 846, 726, and 331. Samples of perfused blood were obtained at 30-min intervals and the concentrations of lactate and pyruvate determined on each sample.

In order for the carbonate-^{14}C method to be valid, the rates of synthesis of albumin and urea should remain constant during the experimental period. Otherwise situations may arise wherein the major portion of urea is synthesized when the specific activity of the arginine precursor pool is high while the major portion of albumin is synthesized when the specific activity of this precursor pool is low. This would lead to a calculated albumin synthesis rate that is falsely low. The reverse situation would result in falsely high calculated values for albumin production. In the isolated perfused liver system after the introduction of [^{14}C] CO_2, the total urea radioactivity peaks by 5–10 min of perfusion or earlier. Thereafter, there is no increase in the count rate due to [^{14}C] urea, indicating that the amount of labeled arginine is insignificant. Thus, the formation of radioactive albumin (from the same [^{14}C] arginine from which the urea was derived) by the incorporation of radioactive arginine into albumin must occur in that early period, and it is this event that determines the specific activity of the guanidino carbon in the isolated albumin. Any subsequent alteration in the synthesis of albumin would have an undetectable effect on the albumin-specific activity because of the large mass of perfusate albumin (4000 mg). On the other hand, any alteration in urea synthesis would alter the specific activity of the synthesized urea, resulting in false values for albumin synthesis. Urea synthesis was monitored at 10–15-minute intervals during the perfusion, and perfusions that did not have a stable urea synthetic rate were not used. Further verification of the method was carried out in at least one study in all groups, by measuring albumin synthesis with an immunochemical method along with the [^{14}C] CO_2 method using high-titer monospecific antibody against rabbit albumin.

Immunochemical quantitation of the newly synthesized albumin was determined by the method of Mancini et al.[15] All batches of antiserum were tested against various dilutions of rabbit serum to assure the presence of only a monospecific antibody. Also, the antiserum was tested against bovine albumin to determine the absence of cross-reaction. The data in a prior study[16] and the present study derived by the 2 independent methods agreed quantitatively in 24 of 32 combined studies and were in the same direction in the other 8 studies.

Since alcohol might inhibit the release of newly synthesized albumin, the rate of release of labeled albumin has been studied in both alcohol and control perfusates. Labeled albumin was detected in the alcohol and control perfusates by at least 35 min after the [^{14}C] carbonate injection. The peak specific activity occurred by 100–120 min, as it did in the nonalcohol perfused control studies, indicating essentially the same release of the labeled albumin in control and alcohol studies. If release were delayed by alcohol, the peak specific activity of the released albumin would have occurred later.

POLYSOMAL ISOLATION

Polysomes were isolated from the whole liver, after the 2.5–3-hr perfusion employing the techniques described by Blobel and Potter[17] as modified below. Following homogenization in 2 volumes of 0.25 M sucrose-TKM buffer, nuclei, debris, and mitochondria were separated by a 10-min spin at 15 000 g and supernatant was layered over a 1.38–2 M sucrose discontinuous gradient in TKM-containing cell sap as an RNase inhibitor, as suggested by Blobel and Potter.[18] After a 20-hr spin at 105 000 g (No. 40 rotor, Spinco Model L ultracentrifuge) the bound polysomes sedimenting into the 1.38 M sucrose layer were removed, treated with $\frac{1}{4}$ vol of 20% Triton $^-$5% sodium deoxycholate solution, and recentrifuged through 2 M sucrose in TKM-cell sap for 20 hrs, as above. The pellet obtained from this interface was considered to represent the polysomes that had been bound to the endoplasmic reticulum. The unbound or free polysomes sedimented through the 2 M sucrose and were harvested as a pellet following the initial 20-hr spin. The pellet was frozen at $-20°$ and treated identically with the bound pellet obtained 24 hours later.

In livers from fed donors the large quantity of glycogen present prevents effective isolation of the free polysomes. Thus, in these livers, amylase was added to the postmitochondrial supernatant at a final concentration of 70 units/ml. After 30 min at 4° with gentle stirring, the same amount of amylase was added, and stirring at 4° continued for another 30 min. No effect of this amylase treatment was noted on polysomal aggregation.

Polysome Analysis: The polysomes obtained from the endoplasmic membranes were suspended in 1 ml of cold distilled water and 16–20 absorbance units (260 nm) was layered over a 34-ml linear sucrose gradient (0.3–1.1M in TKM over a 2-ml cushion of 60% sucrose). These gradients were spun at 25,000 rpm in an SW 27.1 at 4°C for 2 hrs and the resultant gradient was analyzed in a ISCO ultraviolet analyzer at 254 nm model UA-4 (Instrumentation Specialties Co.)

POLYSOMAL LABELING

The pattern and extent of labeling of polysomal RNA was determined by the addition of [^{3}H] uridine; 1.5 m Ci (26 Ci/mmole) in the perfusate during the 2.5-hour perfusion. The isolated factions (bound and free) were analyzed as above in an ISCO ultraviolet analyzer and 1 ml fractions collected, and 0.1 ml was plated on Whatman 3-mm discs. The discs were treated sequentially with ice-cold 7% trichloroacetic acid containing nonradioactive uridine for 10 min, washed with ice-cold 7% trichloroacetic acid, cold ethanol, ethanol-ether (1:1 v/v), and ether, then air-dried. The dried discs were suspended in 5 ml 0.7% butyl-PBD in toluene and counted in a liquid scintillation counter, appropriate corrections being made for ^{14}C contamination in the ^{3}H channel.

RESULTS

In order to study the interrelationship between nutrition and alcohol on the liver's ability to synthesize albumin it was necessary to first establish the effects of altered nutrition on albumin production. In TABLE 1 is a summary of the effects of a prior fast as well as the effects of specific amino acids on albumin synthesis. Following a 24-hour fast, albumin synthesis declined to 8 mg/hr/100 g wet liver wt, as against 16 mg in control donors fed up to the time of operation. When the perfusate was augmented with either tryptophan, arginine, ornithine, lysine, or phenylalanine at a final concentration of 10 mM, albumin synthesis was stimulated to levels equivalent to that observed in the fed liver preparation. In every case the increased albumin synthesis was accompanied by an increased production of urea. When the liver was derived from a fed donor, the addition of tryptophan, arginine, or ornithine to the perfusate did not cause an increase in albumin synthesis above that obtained with the control perfusate. Perfusion of the fasted preparation with the essential amino acids leucine, valine, methionine, and histidine failed to stimulate albumin synthesis and coincidently did not increase urea production.[5]

TABLE 1

The Effects of Amino Acids on Albumin and Urea Synthesis

Donor	Perfusate	n	Albumin Synthesis mg/hr/100 g*	Urea Synthesis mg/hr/100 g*
Fed	Control	6	16 ± 1	34 ± 6
Fasted	Control	6	8 ± 1	42 ± 4
Fasted	Tryptophan	5	18 ± 4	55 ± 3
Fasted	Arginine	8	19 ± 2	122 ± 10
Fasted	Ornithine	5	17 ± 2	60 ± 6
Fasted	Lysine	4	20 ± 2	63 ± 5
Fasted	Phenylalanine	5	20 ± 3	93 ± 7

*Values are means ± S.E.M.

Further, here as in prior studies,[19,20] a 24-hour fast resulted in a decrease in the RNA/DNA ratio of the liver from 2.45 ± 0.13 in the fed preparation to 1.80 ± 0.10 in the fasted preparation. Likewise, the protein/DNA ratio also decreased from 69 ± to 53 ± 2. Following supplementation of the perfusate with the stimulating amino acids, the RNA/DNA ratio in the fasted preparation increased to 2.05 ± 0.06. The total DNA content in all these preparations remained essentially constant at 100–120 mg per liver.

No difference in the viability of the stimulated and nonstimulated livers was observed. The parameters of oxygen extraction, bile production, lactate/pyruvate ratios, and perfusate pH were essentially the same.

THE EFFECT OF ALCOHOL ON ALBUMIN SYNTHESIS

In these studies, the perfusate contained 220 mg% ethanol and the livers were preperfused for 60 min prior to the addition of [14C]carbonate. The concentration of ethanol was maintained by the constant infusion of ethanol. The effects of alcohol on albumin synthesis are shown in TABLE 2. When the liver was derived from a fed animal, albumin synthesis was lowered from 16 mg to 6 mg, a value observed in fasted preparations. It had previously been reported

TABLE 2

The Effect of Alcohol on Albumin and Urea Synthesis

Donor	Perfusate	n	Albumin Synthesis mg/hr/100 g*	Urea Synthesis mg/hr/100 g*
Fed	Alcohol	8	6 ± 1	11 ± 2
Fed	Alcohol + Ornithine or Tryptophan or Arginine	15	10 ± 1	15 – 28
Fasted	Alcohol	7	5 ± 1	18 – 23
Fasted	Alcohol + Ornithine or Tryptophan or Arginine	10	4 ± 1	20 ± 4

*Values are means ± S.E.M.

that the presence of tryptophan in the alcohol-containing perfusate restored the liver's ability to synthesize albumin provided the liver was derived from a well-nourished donor.[19] Since tryptophan was one of those amino acids that stimulated a fasted preparation, would the other amino acids that proved effective with a fasted preparation be effective with the fed preparation perfused with alcohol? Of all the amino acids, only arginine and ornithine were capable of increasing albumin synthesis to values between 9 and 12 mg, and, again, this increase was accompanied by an increase in urea production.

Alcohol did not significantly affect the RNA/DNA in these livers. The value of 2.34 ± 0.19 was essentially the same as in the fed preparations; similarly the protein/DNA ratio was essentially unchanged at 62 ± 4.

When the liver was derived from a fasted donor and perfused with alcohol, albumin synthesis was 5 mg/hr/100 g wet liver wt, essentially the same as in the liver from a fed donor. However, an excess of tryptophan, arginine or onithine was ineffective in stimulating albumin synthesis.

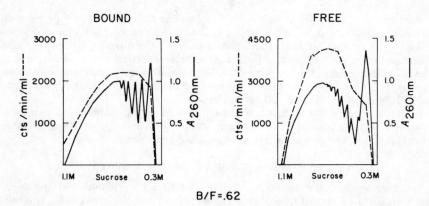

FIGURE 1. Sucrose gradient patterns of free and membrane-bound polysomes prepared from postmitochondrial supernatants of livers derived from fed donors. Livers were perfused with control perfusate. The ratio B/F is the ratio of the radioactivity to absorbance in the bound polysomes to that in the free polysomes.

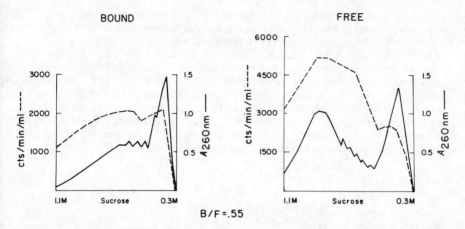

FIGURE 2. Sucrose gradient patterns of free and membrane-bound polysomes prepared from postmitochondrial supernatants of livers derived from fasted donors. Livers were perfused with control perfusate. B/F ratio is described in FIGURE 1.

Polysomes and Ribosome Turnover: At the end of the perfusion period, free and endoplasmic-reticulum-bound polysomes were isolated and examined by centrifugation through linear sucrose gradients. When the liver was derived from fed donors, both classes of polysomes were considerably aggregated and both contained a greater proportion of heavy polysomes (FIGURE 1). The radio-activity paralleled the absorbance curve, and when the RNA was isolated from these polysomes and analyzed on sucrose gradients it was found that the radioactivity was indeed associated with the RNA of the ribosomes. The relative specific activity—i.e. counts, per absorbance unit of the bound polysomes—was 60% that of the specific activity of the free polysome. It has been suggested that

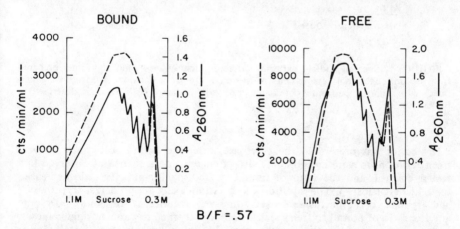

FIGURE 3. Sucrose gradient patterns of free and membrane-bound polysomes prepared from postmitochondrial supernatants of livers derived from fasted donors. Livers were perfused with control perfusate augmented with the stimulating amino acids indicated in the text. B/F ratio is described in FIGURE 1.

the bound ribosomal subunits are derived from the free subunits[21] and this ratio may represent the extent of equilibration between these two classes of ribosomes in the hepatocyte in the experimental period.

When polysomes were isolated from livers of fasted donors, only the free polysome was aggregated while the bound polysome was disaggregated with an increase in the proportion of small polysomes (FIGURE 2). But the ratio of specific activity of the bound to the free was the same as in the fed preparation. Augmenting the perfusate to these livers from fasted donors with some of the stimulating amino acids reaggregated the bound polysomes, and the ratio of the relative specific activity of bound polysome to free polysome did not change. It was the same as in the fed or fasted livers (FIGURE 3).

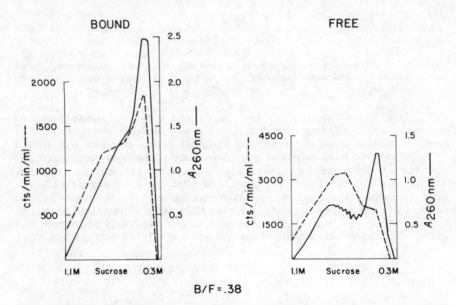

FIGURE 4. Sucrose gradient patterns of free and membrane-bound polysomes prepared from postmitochondrial supernatants of livers derived from fed donors. Livers were perfused with control perfusate containing 220 mg% ethanol. B/F ratio is described in FIGURE 1.

If alcohol was present in the perfusate, then the bound polysomes of livers from fed donors were considerably disaggregated, more than that observed in a fasted control, and the ratio of bound to free specific activity ratio decreased to 0.42 (FIGURE 4). The addition of the stimulating amino acids, tryptophan, and arginine to the perfusate caused some reaggregation of the bound polysome and the ratio of bound to free specific activity returned towards normal values.

The presence of alcohol in the perfusate of a liver from a fasted donor disaggregated both free and bound polysomes, and the addition of arginine, tryptophan, ornithine or phenylalanine was totally ineffective in causing any degree of reaggregation.

DISCUSSION

The use of the isolated perfused liver as an investigative tool has many advantages: (a) the effect on albumin production by the animal's nutritional status can be determined at any time; (b) altered nutrition can be imposed and its immediate effect on albumin synthesis ascertained, and (c) the effects of alcohol on protein synthesis can be delineated in the absence or presence of altered nutrition.

When donor rabbits were fasted for 24 hours, albumin production was 50% less than fed controls. Perfusing these fasted livers with either tryptophan, arginine, ornithine or phenylalanine restored the production of albumin, while the essential amino acids leucine, valine, methionine, or histidine were without effect, as has been noted.[5] Furthermore, tryptophan, arginine, or ornithine did not increase albumin production when the liver was derived from a fed donor.

We looked for some correlation between the increased albumin synthesis and the amino acids responsible for the increase. Protein synthesis in different isolated organs is diminished when the amino acid level in the perfusate is low and stimulated when the amino acid level is high,[22,23] but our levels of amino acids were kept constant except for the specific acid being tested. Albumin synthesis may be sensitive to the presence of a single amino acid. In the liver, tryptophan has been singled out as the rate-limiting acid for protein synthesis, since tryptophan is the least abundant amino acid in mixed liver protein as well as the free amino acid pool.[24] Albumin contains one tryptophan residue per molecule,[25] and with the constant turnover of protein within the hepatocyte it appears unlikely that the required one tryptophan/albumin molecule would not be available. A more likely candidate for the rate-limiting amino acid for albumin synthesis is arginine. In the intact hepatocyte the high level of arginase activity and intracellular protein synthesis results in a very low concentration of intracellular arginine.[26] A consistent finding in our studies was that the augmented synthesis of albumin was often accompanied by an increase in urea production and any increase in urea production must, in part, be due to an increased level of arginine. There are 26 residues of arginine in albumin,[25] and it is suggested that albumin synthesis occurs when there is more than enough arginine to supply the needs of priority protein synthesis, such as that of intracellular enzymes, and that consumed in the synthesis of urea. A second observation was the stimulation of albumin synthesis by ornithine, an amino acid that is not found in protein. This effect can be explained by the fact that ornithine is the precursor of arginine in the urea cycle, and an alternate mechanism should also be considered. The synthesis of urea by the action of arginase on arginine also produces ornithine. Excess ornithine can be metabolized by a pathway leading to putrescine, the decarboxylation product of ornithine catalyzed by ornithine decarboxylase. Putrescine is the precursor of spermidine and spermine. These polyamines have been implicated in the binding of the large ribosomal subunit to the endoplasmic reticulum to produce the intracellular organelle responsible for albumin synthesis, the endoplasmic reticulum-bound polysome.[27] Those amino acids that failed to stimulate albumin synthesis likewise failed to increase urea production or increase the degree of aggregation of the bound polysome.

When livers were derived from fed donors, a short exposure to alcohol decreased albumin synthesis to levels seen in fasted controls and resulted in a shift of the bound polysome population from aggregated to disaggregated.[19] But unlike the case of the fasted preparation there were fewer radioactive ribosomes associated with the bound RNA. The addition of tryptophan, ornithine, or arginine to the alcoholic perfusate effected a partial recovery by the liver. Albumin synthesis as well as urea production increased, and a partial reaggregation of the bound polysome with an increase in the associated radioactivity occurred. However, these stimulating amino acids were ineffective when the liver came from a fasted animal and was perfused with alcohol.

Both fasting and perfusing livers from fed donors with alcohol caused a disaggregation of the bound polysomes, but the different effect on the ratios of bound to free polysome specific activity suggested that a different mechanism was operative. In the fasted preparation the hepatic content of RNA decreased, and since 90% of intracellular RNA is ribosomal it is not unlikely that this would result in a decrease in the number of ribosomes available for binding to messenger RNA. Since the bound ribosomes are derived from the free ribosome pool and the free ribosomes were considerably aggregated, there would then be less ribosomes available for the bound pool, resulting in the formation of lightly aggregated bound polysomes. Since the specific activity ratio of the bound to the free polysomes was similar to that in the fed preparation, this would suggest that rates of initiation, i.e., the attachment of the first ribosome to mRNA, and transit times, i.e., movement of the ribosome along mRNA and, thus, the rate of synthesis of the polypeptide chain, were not markedly affected. Thus, the decreased protein synthesis was related to the fewer number of participating ribosomes. The reaggregation of the bound polysome that occurs with the stimulating amino acids was coincident with the increase in hepatic RNA.

Contrariwise, when fed preparations were perfused with alcohol, no significant decrease in hepatic RNA was observed. However, the disaggregated bound polysome, unlike the fasted preparation, had a lower level of radioactivity relative to the free polysome. This state could result if alcohol or its metabolite interfered with initiation, as well as slowing down the transit time of the ribosome along the mRNA. This would result in a polysome that is disaggregated and populated with older ribosomes, ribosomes that had become attached to mRNA before the pool became labeled. When albumin synthesis was stimulated there was some reaggregation as well as an increase in the ratio of bound to free specific activity indicating an increase in the rate of initiation of bound ribosomes with mRNA.

The lack of effect on the free polysomes during fasting or in the "fed alcohol" state suggests that the state of aggregation, rates of initiation, and transit times of the bound polysome may be interrelated with the binding of the large ribosomal subunit to the endoplasmic reticulum. The effect being on the subunit itself or on the integrity of the membrane at the sites of binding.

Alcohol and fasting both inhibit albumin synthesis, and both stresses can be altered by excess amino acids while the combination of fasting and alcohol prevents recovery from either. Since protein synthesis is the ultimate event requiring all other metabolic processes, these findings indicate a definite interdependence of amino acids and alcohol in moderating or mediating the pathologic effects of either stress. Excess specific amino acids are capable of preventing the alcohol-induced depression of albumin synthesis as long as the liver is not subjected to a fasting background.

REFERENCES

1. BERSON, S. A. & R. S. YALOW. 1954. The distribution of ^{131}I-labeled human serum albumin introduced into ascitic fluid. Analysis of the kinetics of a three compartment

catenary transfer system in man and speculations on possible sites of degradation. J. Clin. Invest. **33**: 377.

2. ROTHSCHILD, M. A., M. ORATZ, D. ZIMMON, S. S. SCHREIBER, I. WEINER & A. VAN CANEGHEM. 1969. Albumin synthesis in cirrhotic subjects with ascites studies with carbonate-^{14}C. J. Clin. Invest. **48**: 344.

3. ORATZ, M., C. WALKER, S. S. SCHREIBER, S. GROSS & M. A. ROTHSCHILD. 1967. Albumin and fibrinogen metabolism in heat and cold stressed rabbits. Amer. J. Physiol. **213**: 1341.

4. ORATZ, M. 1970. Plasma Protein Metabolism. Academic Press. New York, N.Y.

5. ROTHSCHILD, M. A., M. ORATZ, J. MONGELLI, L. FISHMAN & S. S. SCHREIBER. 1969. Amino Acid regulation of albumin synthesis. J. Nutr. **98**: 395.

6. SWICK, R. W. 1958. Measurement of protein turnover in rat liver. J. Clin. Invest. **231**: 751.

7. REEVE, E. B., J. R. PEARSON & D. C. MARTZ. 1963. Plasma protein synthesis in the rat liver: method for measurement of albumin formation in vivo. Science **139**: 914.

8. McFARLANE, A. S. 1963. Measurement of synthesis rates of liver produced plasma proteins. Biochem. J. **89**: 277.

9. GORNALL, A. G., C. J. BARDAWILL & N. M. DAVID. 1949. Determination of serum proteins by means of the biuret reaction. J. Biol. Chem. **177**: 751.

10. ROTHSCHILD, M. A., S. S. SCHREIBER, M. ORATZ & H. L. McGEE. 1958. The effects of adrenocortical hormones on albumin metabolism studied with albumin ^{131}I. J. Clin. Invest. **37**: 1229.

11. FLECK, A. & D. BEGG. 1965. The estimation of ribonucleic acid using ultraviolet absorption measurements. Biochim. Biophys. Acta. **108**: 333.

12. KECK, K. 1956. An ultramicro technique for the determination of deoxypentose nucleic acid. Arch. Biochem. Biophys. **63**: 446.

13. CONWAY, E. J. & A. BYRNE. 1933. Absorption apparatus for micro determination of certain volatile substances: micro determination of ammonia. Biochem. J. **27**: 419.

14. ROTHSCHILD, M. A., M. ORATZ, J. MONGELLI & S. S. SCHREIBER. 1968. Effects of a short term fast on albumin synthesis in vivo, in the perfused liver and on amino acid incorporation by hepatic microsomes. J. Clin Invest. **47**: 2591.

15. MANCINI, G., A. O. CARBONARA & J. F. HEREMANS. 1965. Immuno chemical quantitation of antigens by single radial immuno diffusion. Immunochemistry. **2**: 235.

16. ORATZ, M., S. S. SCHREIBER & M. A. ROTHSCHILD. 1973. Study of albumin synthesis in relation to urea synthesis. Gastroenterology **65**: 647.

17. BLOBEL, G. & V. R. POTTER. 1967. Studies of free and membrane bound ribosomes in rat liver. 1. Distribution as related to total cellular RNA. J. Molec. Biol. **26**: 279.

18. BLOBEL, G. & V. R. POTTER. 1967. Ribosomes in rat liver: An estimate of the percentage of free and membrane bound ribosomes interacting with messenger RNA in vivo. J. Molec. Biol. **28**: 539.

19. ROTHSCHILD, M. A., M. ORATZ, J. MONGELLI & S. S. SCHREIBER. 1971. Alcohol induced depression of albumin synthesis: Reversal by tryptophan. J. Clin. Invest. **50**: 1812.

20. ORATZ, M., M. A. ROTHSCHILD, A. BURKS, J. MONGELLI & S. S. SCHREIBER. 1973. Protein Turnover: 131. Ciba Foundation Symposium 9 (new series). Elsevier. Amsterdam, The Netherlands.

21. HULSE, J. L. & F. O. WETTSTEIN. 1972. Two seperable cytoplasmic pools of native ribosomal subunits in chick embryo tissue culture cells. Biochem. Biophys. Acta. **269**: 265.

22. MORGAN, H. E., D. C. N. EARL, A. BROADUS, E. B. WOLPERT, K. E. GIGER & L. S. JEFFERSON. 1971. Regulation of protein synthesis in heart muscle. I. Effect of amino acid levels on protein synthesis. J. Biol. Chem. **246**: 2152.

23. McGOWN, E., A. G. RICHARDSON, L. M. HENDERSON & P. B. SWAN. 1973. Effect of amino acids on ribosome aggregation and protein synthesis in perfused rat liver. J. Nutr. **103**: 109.

24. PRONCZUK, A. W., B. S. BALIGA, J. W. TRIANT & H. N. MUNRO. 1968. Comparison of the effect of amino acid supply on hepatic polysome profiles in vivo and in vitro. Biochim. Biophys. Acta. **157**: 204.
25. JACOBS, S. & A. KOJ. 1969. Amino acid composition of rabbit plasma albumin and fibrin. Anal. Biochem. **27**: 178.
26. ROGERS, Q. R., R. A. FREEDLAND & R. A. SYMMONS. 1972. In vivo synthesis and utilization of arginine in the rat. Amer. J. Physiol. **223**: 236.
27. KHAWAJA, J. A. 1971. Interaction of ribosomes and ribosomal subparticles with endoplasmic reticulum membranes in vitro: Effect of spermine and magnesium. Biochem. Biophys. Acta. **254**: 117.

LIVER DISEASE AND ALCOHOL: FATTY LIVER, ALCOHOLIC HEPATITIS, CIRRHOSIS, AND THEIR INTERRELATIONSHIPS*

Charles S. Lieber

Section and Laboratory of Liver Disease and Nutrition
Veterans Administration Hospital
Bronx, New York 10468
and
Department of Medicine
Mount Sinai School of Medicine of the City University of New York
New York, New York 10029

INTRODUCTION

In its milder form, alcoholic liver disease is characterized by accumulation of excess fat in the liver, so-called *fatty liver*. This is a very common complication of alcoholism, usually benign and fully reversible, though, recently, increasing numbers of unexplained deaths have been described in alcoholics whose sole finding at autopsy was a massive fatty liver.[1] When a number of liver cells die and this necrosis causes inflammation, one is dealing with *alcoholic hepatitis*, a more severe form of alcoholic liver injury associated with a mortality ranging from 10 to 30%, depending on the series. Eventually, scarring by fibrous tissue occurs and its excess distorts the normal architecture of the liver; fibrous bands dissect the liver and alter its function. The term *cirrhosis* characterizes this more severe, irreversible form of alcoholic liver injury. Cirrhosis is a serious disease that afflicts the patient with numerous disorders, especially those derived from the interference of blood flow by the scarred liver and the resulting portal hypertension with formation of ascites, collateral circulation (esophageal varices), and gastrointestinal bleeding. Bleeding and other complications, such as hepatic coma, often lead to a fatal outcome. With the steadily increasing incidence of alcoholism, death rates from cirrhosis had a parallel rise to the point that in U.S. urban areas, cirrhosis of the liver is the third or fourth cause of death between the ages of 25–65.

Though not all subjects with cirrhosis are alcoholics, the majority admit to excessive drinking. The relationship between alcoholism and the development of cirrhosis, however, has remained the subject of intense debate. Since not all alcoholics develop cirrhosis, the concept has prevailed that excessive alcohol drinking by itself is not sufficient to produce cirrhosis and that other factors must play a key role. One of the most hotly debated issues of the last 50 years dealt with the question whether liver disease in the alcoholic is due to *alcohol itself* or solely to the *malnutrition* so commonly associated with alcoholism. This and related questions are listed in TABLE 1.

ALCOHOLIC FATTY LIVER

Fatty liver (the early stage of alcoholic liver injury) occurs very commonly among alcoholics: in a liver biopsy study of chronic alcoholics, 90% had a fatty

*Work supported in part by grants from the National Institute of Alcohol Abuse and Alcoholism and the National Institute of Arthritis, Metabolism, and Digestive Diseases, and projects of the Veterans Administration.

63

TABLE 1
Possible Etiologic Factors in Alcoholic Liver Injury

1. Malnutrition alone
2. Ethanol itself
3. Congeners
4. A combination of the above

liver.[2] Moreover, in recent years, the incidence of fatty liver has been increasing both in Europe and the U.S., with an associated enhanced mortality.[1,3] Studies aimed at elucidating the pathogenesis of the steatosis may ultimately result in a better understanding, treatment, and perhaps prevention of this disorder. Investigative efforts have largely been aimed at defining the origin and mechanism of fat deposition, including the respective role of alcohol per se and that of nutritional deficiencies so commonly associated with alcoholism.

Pathogenesis of the Alcoholic Fatty Liver

Origin and Mechanisms of Fat Deposition in the Liver

FIGURE 1 illustrates the main mechanisms whereby fatty liver can develop, namely excessive supply of lipids to the liver or interference with lipid deposition. As illustrated in FIGURE 1, lipids that accumulate in the liver can originate from 3 main sources: dietary lipids, which reach the bloodstream as chylomicrons, adipose tissue lipids, which are transported to the liver as free fatty acids (FFA), and lipids synthesized in the liver itself. These fatty acids of various sources can accumulate in the liver because of a large number of metabolic disturbances, discussed in detail elsewhere[4,5] and represented schematically in FIGURE 1. The 4 major disturbances that have been proposed are (a) increased peripheral fat mobilization, (b) decreased hepatic lipoprotein release,

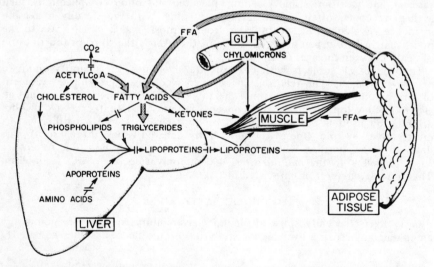

FIGURE 1. Possible mechanisms of fatty liver production through either increase or decrease of lipid transport and metabolism.

(c) decreased lipid oxidation in the liver, and (d) enhanced hepatic lipogenesis. Depending on the experimental conditions, any of the 3 sources and the 4 mechanisms can be implicated. The main event leading to the development of the alcoholic fatty liver, however, can be summarized as follows: ethanol, which has an almost "obligatory" hepatic metabolism, replaces the fatty acids as a normal fuel for the hepatic mitochondria. This results in fatty acid accumulation, directly because of decreased lipid oxidation and indirectly because 1 way for the liver to dispose of excess hydrogen generated by ethanol oxidation is to synthesize more lipids. Fatty acids derived from adipose tissue accumulate in the liver only when very large amounts of ethanol are given.[6,7] The lipids increase in the liver despite the fact that the transport mechanisms via release of lipoproteins from the liver into the bloodstream are stimulated by ethanol, at least during the initial state of intoxication.

Alcohol as a Direct Cause of the Fatty Liver

Each gram of ethanol provides 7.1 calories, which means that 20 ounces of 86-proof beverage represents about 1500 calories, or $\frac{1}{2}$ to $\frac{2}{3}$ of the normal daily caloric requirement. Therefore, the alcoholic has a much reduced demand for food to fulfill his caloric needs. Since alcoholic beverages do not contain significant amounts of protein, vitamins, and minerals, the intake of these nutrients may readily become borderline or insufficient. Economic factors may also reduce the consumption of nutrient-rich food by the alcoholic. In addition to acting as "empty calories," alcohol can result in malnutrition by interfering with the normal processes of food digestion and absorption.[8] For all these reasons, deficiency diseases readily develop in the alcoholic. In rodents, severely deficient diets result in liver damage even in the absence of alcohol. Extrapolation from these animal results to man led to the belief that in alcoholics, the liver disease is due not to ethanol but solely to the nutritional deficiencies and that, given an adequate diet, alcohol is merely acting by its caloric contribution and is not more toxic than a similar caloric load derived from fats or starches.[9] This opinion prevailed, despite some statistical evidence gathered both in France[10] and in Germany[11] indicating that the incidence of liver disease correlated with the amount of alcohol consumed rather than with deficiencies in the diet. A major challenge to the concept of the exclusively nutritional origin of alcoholic liver disease arose from an improvement in the method of alcohol feeding to experimental animals. Indeed, when the conventional alcohol feeding procedure is used, namely when ethanol is given as part of the drinking water, rats usually refuse to take a sufficient amount of ethanol to develop liver injury, if the diet is adequate. This aversion of rats to ethanol was counteracted by the introduction of the new technique of feeding of ethanol as part of a nutritionally adequate totally liquid diet.[12-14] With this procedure, ethanol intake was sufficient to produce a fatty liver despite an adequate diet. This technique is now widely adopted for the study of the pathogenesis of the fatty liver in the rat. In addition to the fatty liver, ethanol dependence developed in these rats, as witnessed by typical withdrawal seizures after cessation of alcohol intake.[15]

Having established an etiologic role for ethanol in the pathogenesis of the experimental fatty liver, the question of its importance for the development of human pathology remained. To determine whether ingestion of alcohol, in amounts comparable to those consumed by chronic alcoholics, is capable of injuring the liver, even in the absence of dietary deficiencies, volunteers (with or without a history of alcoholism) were given a variety of nondeficient diets under metabolic ward conditions, with ethanol either as a supplement to the diet or as an isocaloric substitution for carbohydrates.[12,13,16] In all these individuals, ethanol administration resulted in fatty liver development that was evident both on morphologic examination and by direct measurement of the lipid content of the liver biopsies, which revealed a rise in triglyceride concentration up to 25-fold.

The Influence of Dietary Factors

Role of Dietary Fat. As discussed before, alcohol ingestion leads to deposition in the liver of dietary fat. This observation prompted an investigation into the role of the amount and kind of dietary fat in the pathogenesis of alcohol-induced liver injury. Rats were given liquid diets containing a normal amount of protein for rodents (18% of total calories), with varying amounts of fat. Reduction in dietary fat to a level of 25% (or less) of total calories was accompanied by a significant decrease in the steatosis induced by ethanol[17] (FIGURE 2). The importance of dietary fat was confirmed in volunteers: for a given alcohol intake, much more steatosis developed with diets of normal fat content than with a low-fat diet.[18] In addition to the amount, the chain length of the dietary fatty acid is also important for the degree of fat deposition in the liver after alcohol feeding. Replacement of dietary triglycerides containing long-chain fatty acids (LCT) by fat-containing medium-chain fatty acids (MCT) markedly reduced the capacity of alcohol to produce a fatty liver in rats.[19] The pro-

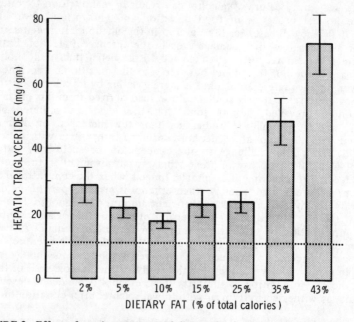

FIGURE 2. Effect of varying amounts of dietary fat on the degree of alcoholic steatosis. Hepatic triglycerides in 7 groups of rats given ethanol (36% of calories) with a diet of normal protein (18% of calories). Average hepatic triglyceride concentration in the control animals is indicated by a dotted line. (From Lieber and DeCarli.[17] By permission of *Amer. J. Clin. Nutr.*)

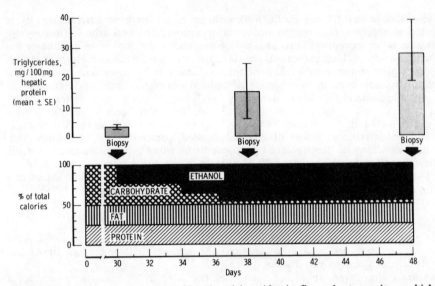

FIGURE 3. Effect of ethanol on hepatic triglycerides in five volunteers given a high-protein, low-fat diet. (From Lieber.[29])

pensity of medium-chain fatty acids to oxidation rather than to esterification most likely explains the reduction in alcoholic steatosis upon replacement of dietary long-chain fatty acids by medium-chain fatty acids.

Role of Protein and Lipotropic Factors (Choline and Methionine). Although deficiencies in dietary protein and lipotropic factors (choline and methionine) can produce fatty liver in growing rats,[9] primates are far less susceptible to protein and lipotrope deficiency than rodents.[20] Clinically, treatment with choline of patients suffering from alcoholic liver injury has been found to be ineffective in the face of continued alcohol abuse and, experimentally, massive supplementation with choline failed to prevent the fatty liver produced by alcohol in volunteer subjects.[21] This is not surprising, since there is no evidence that a diet deficient in choline is deleterious to adult man. Unlike rat liver, human liver contains very little choline oxidase activity, which may explain the species difference with regard to choline deficiency. The phospholipid content of the liver represents another key difference between the ethanol- and choline-deficient fatty liver. After the administration of ethanol, hepatic phospholipids increase,[13] whereas in the fatty liver produced by choline deficiency they decrease.[22] Thus, hepatic injury induced by choline deficiency appears to be primarily an experimental disease of rats with little, if any, relevance to human alcoholic liver injury. Even in the rats, massive choline supplementation failed to prevent fully the ethanol-induced lesion, whether alcohol was administered acutely[23] or chronically.[24] Alcohol has been reported to either aggravate[25] or attenuate[26] choline-induced liver injury.

Protein deficiency undoubtedly may affect the liver, but this has not yet been clearly delineated in human adults. In children, protein deficiency leads to steatosis, one of the manifestations of kwashiorkor. In adolescent baboons, however, protein restriction to 7% of total calories (as part of a low-fat diet,

14% of calories) did not result in liver injury on either biochemical analysis or light and electron microscopic examination even after 19 months.[27] Conversely, an excess of protein was not capable of preventing ethanol from producing fat accumulation in human volunteers, as illustrated in FIGURE 3. In that study, dietary protein represented 25% of total calories, or $2\frac{1}{2}$ times the recommended amount. Thus, even in the absence of protein deficiency, ethanol is capable, in man, of producing striking changes in the liver. Severe protein deficiency (4% of total calories) did also produce steatosis in the baboon.[27] Similar lesions were reported in the rhesus monkey.[28] When protein deficiency is present, it could potentiate the effect of ethanol. Indeed, administration of ethanol with a diet deficient in protein and lipotropic factors had more pronounced effects than that of either factor alone,[30,31] at least in rodents.

In addition to the fat accumulation, alcohol abuse results in marked ultrastructural changes of both mitochondria and rough endoplasmic reticulum.[4,16,21]

Prevention and Treatment of the Alcoholic Fatty Liver

Various chemicals and procedures to reduce or prevent the alcoholic fatty liver have been reviewed before,[32] and the role of dietary fat and lipotropic factors have already been discussed.

Among the drugs capable of decreasing the capacity of ethanol to produce a fatty liver, one must list the barbiturates[33,34] and antihistamine derivatives.[35] Asparagine, previously reported as protective,[36] has now been found ineffective after acute[37] and prolonged[24] ethanol intake. To the list of measures previously reported to prevent the fatty liver produced by 1 large dose of ethanol,[32] one can add the β-sympathicolytic agents,[38] pyridyncarbinol,[39] and cold exposure.[40] In rats, hyperbaric oxygen was found to be protective.[41]

Adenosine triphosphate has previously been reported to protect against acute ethanol-induced fatty liver.[42] However, when given in moderate amounts, it restored liver adenosine triphosphate levels to normal without protecting against the ethanol-induced fatty liver;[43] the partial protection afforded by much larger doses[42] can possibly be attributed to nonspecific effects. Chlorpromazine, which inhibits ADH activity, failed to prevent the fatty liver produced by an acute large ethanol dose.[44] There is a controversy over whether pyrazole, another ADH inhibitor, prevents the fatty liver produced by a single large dose of ethanol: some found no reduction,[45] whereas others found prevention.[46,47] The difference is perhaps due to the dose of the drug[48] or the sex of the animal[49] used. Although some acute effects of ethanol on lipid metabolism were prevented by pyrazole,[50] the effects of pyrazole on the consequences of chronic ethanol ingestion were inconclusive,[51] a not unexpected result in view of the hepatotoxicity of pyrazole.[52] A derivative of pyrazole, 3, 5-dimethyl pyrazole, was shown to reduce the fatty liver resulting from a single large dose of ethanol by blocking free-fatty-acid mobilization from adipose tissue.[53]

Anabolic steroids were reported to be ineffective by some[54] (but not by others[55,56]) in accelerating the disappearance of fat from the alcoholic fatty liver.

DEVELOPMENT OF MITOCHONDRIAL INJURY

The first indication that ethanol interferes with mitochondrial function was derived from the observation that addition of ethanol to liver slices significantly depressed fatty acid oxidation.[57] This observation, subsequently confirmed in isolated perfused liver,[19] was explained on the basis of the altered NADH:NAD ratio concomitant with the ethanol oxidation, as discussed before. It became apparent, however, that in addition to the changes in intermediary metabolism directly linked to the oxidation of ethanol through the shift in NADH:NAD ratio, chronic ethanol ingestion results in more lasting changes in both the function and the structure of various hepatic subcellular organelles, including the mitochondria.

Alcoholics are known to have profound mitochondrial changes in their liver,[58,59] including the swelling and disfiguration of mitochondria, disorientation of the cristae, and intramitochondrial crystalline inclusions. Increased serum activity of the intramitochondrial enzyme glutamate dehydrogenase was also reported in alcoholics.[60] From these clinical observations, however, it was impossible to determine whether the mitochondrial changes were a direct result of chronic ethanol intake or were secondary to other factors, such as dietary deficiencies. This question was resolved by the observation of Iseri et al.,[61] who showed that, in the rat, isocaloric substitution of ethanol for carbohydrate in otherwise adequate diets leads to enlargement and alterations of the configuration of the mitochondria. Mitochondrial changes similar to those seen in chronic alcoholics were also produced by isocaloric substitution of ethanol for carbohydrate in baboons[27] and in man, both in alcoholics[16,62] and in nonalcoholics.[21] Mitochondrial alterations occurred under a variety of conditions, which included high-protein, low-fat, and choline-supplemented diets.[16,21] Degenerated mitochondria were conspicuous, and the debris of these degraded organelles was also found within autophagic vacuoles and residual vacuolated bodies.[63] These ultrastructural changes in the mitochondria are associated with increased fragility and permeability[64-66] and decreased phospholipid content.[67] The mechanism of this alteration of mitochondrial membranes is unknown but may be linked to depression of mitochondrial protein synthesis by ethanol consumption.[65] These altered mitochondria have a reduction in cytochrome a and b content[65] and in succinic dehydrogenase activity,[65,68] although in one study[69] succinic dehydrogenase activity measured in total liver homogenates was reported to be increased in ethanol-fed rats. The striking structural changes of the mitochondria are associated with corresponding functional abnormalities. Indeed, the respiratory capacity of the mitochondria was found to be depressed[70,71] when pyruvate and succinate were used as substrates. Other substrates were also found to have reduced oxidation by the mitochondria of ethanol-fed rats, except for α-glycerophosphate, the oxidation of which was reported by some to be increased[72] or unchanged,[73] whereas others found it to be decreased.[71] Oxidative phosphorylation was found to be selectively altered at site I.[74] Since the structural changes of the mitochondria persist, the question arose whether these in turn could be responsible for some alterations in lipid metabolism beyond those attributed to the altered redox change.[75] The first indication that ethanol consumption may result in more persistent metabolic changes arose from the observation that alcohol ingestion is associated with a progressive increase in *ketonemia and ketonuria*, which was most pronounced in the fasting state (FIGURE 4).[76] The ketonemia may aggravate the acidosis of the hyperlactacidemia[12] and, on occasion, may lead to severe alcoholic ketoacidosis.[77] The capacity for ethanol to produce ketonemia was found to be greater than that of fat itself—provided, however, that fat was present in the diet. Thus, fat seems to play a permissive role.[76] Preliminary observations indicated that mitochondria obtained from ethanol-fed rats, when incubated *in vitro*, even in the absence

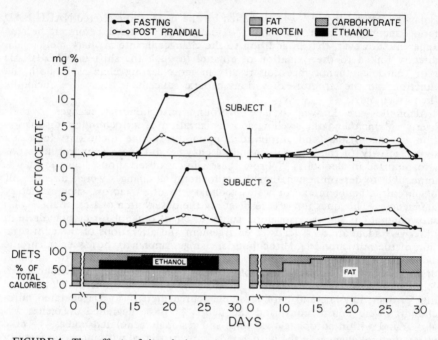

FIGURE 4. The effect of isocaloric replacement of dietary carbohydrate (by either alcohol or fat) on blood acetoacetate concentration in two subjects, both in the fasting and postprandial states. (From Lefevre et al.[76] By permission of J. Clin. Invest.)

of ethanol, displays decreased capacity to oxidize fatty acid but enhanced β-oxidation, which may be responsible for the increased ketogenesis.[78] Decreased fatty acid oxidation, whether as a function of the reduced citric acid-cycle activity (secondary to the altered redox potential) or as a consequence of permanent changes in mitochondrial structure, offers the most likely explanation for the deposition of fat in the liver after chronic alcohol ingestion, especially fat derived from the diet.[7,18,79] It is noteworthy that high concentrations of acetaldehyde, the product of ethanol metabolism, mimic the defects produced by chronic ethanol consumption on oxidative phosphorylation of site I.[80] One may wonder to what extent chronic exposure to acetaldehyde is the cause for the defect observed after chronic ethanol consumption.

In addition to the striking mitochondrial alteration, the membranes of the rough endoplasmic reticulum appear decreased on electron microscopy, and this reduction has now been substantiated by chemical fractionation.[81] One of the main functions of the rough endoplasmic reticulum is *protein synthesis*. This subject has not been extensively studied after chronic ethanol consumption, but acute ethanol administration or addition of ethanol to perfused isolated livers was found to depress protein synthesis.[82,83] It is also of special interest that the ultrastructural changes found in the early stages of the alcoholic fatty liver are identical to those seen in more severe stages of alcoholic liver disease, namely alcoholic hepatitis, which raises the question of the possible role of the fatty liver as a precursor to the hepatitis.

TRANSITION OF FATTY LIVER TO ALCOHOLIC HEPATITIS AND CIRRHOSIS

It has been known for a long time that alcoholics may display liver complications of a varying degree of severity ranging from the still reversible fatty liver to the alcoholic hepatitis and, finally, irreversible cirrhosis. The relationship between alcoholic fatty liver and alcoholic hepatitis and cirrhosis (FIGURE 5) has been the subject of much debate. It is usually accepted that cirrhosis (characterized by extensive scarring or fibrosis) may be, at least in part, a consequence of the necrosis and inflammation associated with the alcoholic hepatitis. The idea that the fatty liver is a precursor of the hepatitis has been less well accepted. It must be pointed out, however, that although hepatic fat accumulation by itself may be harmless, it reflects a severe metabolic disturbance in the liver. It is possible that this disturbance, when exaggerated, may eventually engender irreversible damage of the hepatocyte. Necrosis in turn could lead to inflammation, resulting in "alcoholic hepatitis." Indeed, comparable electron microscopic changes of the mitochondria accompany alcoholic hepatitis[58] and the fatty liver produced experimentally by the administration of alcohol.[16,62,63,84] Alteration of the rough endoplasmic reticulum was also found in patients with alcoholic hepatitis.[58] This corresponds to the reduction in rough endoplasmic reticulum seen by electron microscopy after ethanol consumption.[61-63] Although the alcoholic fatty liver is not an inflammatory condition and is distinguishable from alcoholic hepatitis by light microscopy, the remarkable similarity of the ultrastructural features in the hepatocytes suggests that the former may be the precursor of the latter.

Rats fed alcohol in liquid diets, although they get a fatty liver, do not develop the more severe forms of liver injury seen in alcoholics, namely hepatitis and cirrhosis. We wondered whether this failure might be due to the fact that in the rat, even when alcohol is given as part of a liquid diet, its intake does not exceed 36% of total calories, which corresponds to moderate consumption in man. Also of potential importance was the fact that whereas, development of cirrhosis in man requires 5 to 20 years of steady drinking, the rat lives only about 2 years. To overcome this difficulty, we turned to the baboon, a species that is long-lived and phylogenetically closer to man than the rat. Baboons were housed at the Laboratory for Experimental Medicine and Surgery in Primates, (New York). First, baboons were given a dose of ethanol similar to that given the rat (that is, 36% of total calories) and again a fatty liver developed (FIGURE 6) but no hepatitis or cirrhosis.[27] We then increased the dose of alcohol to 50% of the total calories, taking advantage of the liquid diet technique first developed

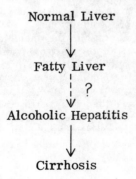

FIGURE 5. Possible link between the three types of liver injury in the alcoholic.

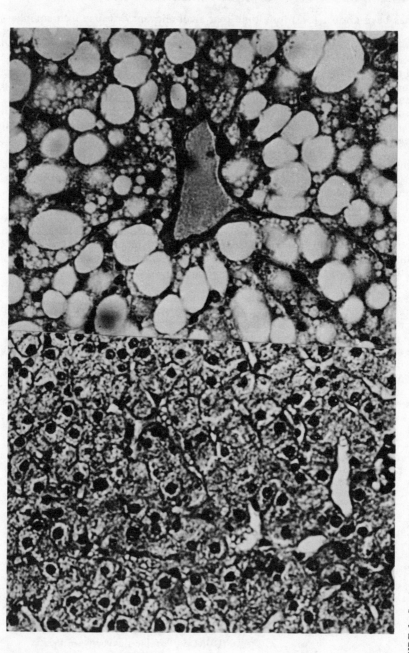

FIGURE 6. Section of baboon liver shows normal hepatic architecture during control period (left) and conspicuous fatty metamorphosis after 15 months of administration of ethanol with a high-protein diet (right). (H & E × 300. From Lieber et al.[27] By permission of Karger.)

in the rat and now applied to the baboon.[85] The overall composition of the diet is shown in FIGURE 7.[85] With this diet, alcohol intake was sufficient to result in periods of obvious inebriation. One intoxicated baboon is shown in FIGURE 8. Upon interruption of alcohol administration, some withdrawal symptoms (such as seizures) were observed. These experiments are still in progress, but at the writing of this report the following results have been observed: 15 baboons fed the isocaloric control diet maintained normal livers, whereas all the animals given ethanol developed excessive fat accumulation. In addition, 5 showed typical alcoholic hepatitis and cirrhosis evolved in 6 baboons studied for 2–4 years, (FIGURE 9). The features of alcoholic hepatitis were comparable to the human variety. These included hyaline sclerosis in the central zones of the lobules, inflammation, necrosis, and hyaline bodies. In man, alcoholic hepatitis can occur with all degrees of steatosis.[86] It is characterized by extensive necrosis and inflammation with, as a hallmark, alcoholic hyaline, an irregular, often paranuclear inclusion with a clumped appearance.[87,88] These

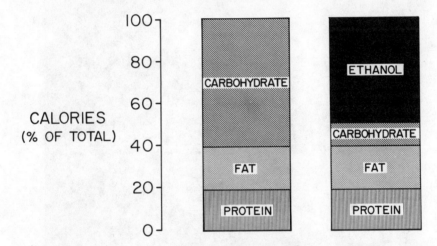

FIGURE 7. Composition in percentage of total calories of the two liquid diets fed to the baboons. (From Lieber and DeCarli.[85] By permission of *J. Med. Primatology.*)

hyaline bodies are distinguishable from giant mitochondria by both light and electron microscopy. Seen through the light microscope, giant mitochondria, which are common in alcoholic liver disease, appear as round regular cytoplasmic bodies that stain red with eosin. By electron microscopy, giant mitochondria have been observed both in the rat[61,84,89] and in man,[21,62,63] but Mallory's alcoholic hyaline has been noted only in primates. The alcoholic hyaline appears on electron-microscopic examination as fibrillar material in random orientation without specific organelles discernable.[86,88,90,91] Because of its fibrillar nature, the origin has been suggested by some to be the endoplasmic reticulum, whereas others believe it to result from *de novo* formation.[92] Indeed, morphologic[93] and chemical[94] studies have suggested that hyaline represents an accumulation of a naturally occurring protein of the microfilament system.

Although alcoholic hyaline is highly characteristic of alcoholic hepatitis, it is also found in Indian childhood cirrhosis,[95] hepatoma,[96-98] primary biliary

FIGURE 8. Inebriated baboon in his cage.

cirrhosis,[99] and Wilson's disease.[100] In a Scandinavian population, alcoholic hyaline was found in approximately 6% of consecutive liver biopsies[101] or in 10% of consecutive biopsies of alcoholics.[102] In 82% of cases in which Mallory bodies were found, the remaining pathological lesions associated with alcoholic hepatitis (necrosis and inflammation) were also present, and in almost all the cases with Mallory bodies there was some degree of fatty liver.[101,102] Alcoholic hyaline was present in more than $\frac{1}{3}$ of a consecutive biopsy series of patients

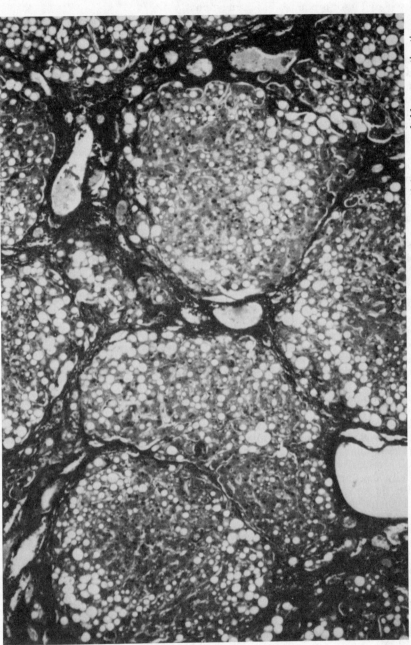

FIGURE 9. Cirrhosis in a baboon fed alcohol for four years. Fat is regularly distributed through nodules surrounded by connective tissue septa. (Chromotrope-aniline blue; ×60. From Lieber and DeCarli.[85] By permission of J. Med. Primatology.)

with cirrhosis.[102] The natural history has been well described,[103-106] and the associated poor prognosis has been emphasized.[107]

It has been widely postulated that hepatitis, through the necrosis and inflammation, may in turn initiate scarring (or fibrosis) and, eventually cirrhosis. The earliest deposition of fibrous tissue appears to occur in the central zones of the hepatic lobule, leading to what has been called "central hyaline sclerosis," a lesion commonly associated with alcoholic hepatitis.[2] The appearance of this lesion appears to bridge the gap between alcoholic hepatitis and cirrhosis and supports the theory that one is a precursor of the other. Similar lesions were present in the baboons fed alcohol. It is noteworthy that no experimental production of hepatitis has been reported in primates before: fibrosis or cirrhosis only has been produced after the feeding of severely deficient diets, lacking in protein and/or choline.[20, 108, 109] Thus, for the first time an experimental model has now been developed[85] that reproduces all the liver lesions observed in the alcoholic, namely fatty liver, hepatitis, and cirrhosis.[110, 111] This model will now hopefully serve for a better understanding of the mechanism whereby alcohol produces its lesions thereby enabling the development of rational forms of prophylaxis and therapy. The preliminary data gathered thus far already bring an answer to some questions that have been the subject of long-standing debate. The most important one is the demonstration that severe liver injury can be produced by prolonged alcohol ingestion, even in the absence of a deficient diet. This is not to downgrade the importance of good nutrition in the alcoholic. Adequate nutrition is essential for the normal functioning of all organs, including the liver.

CONTRIBUTORY FACTORS

The importance of a good *diet* should be particularly stressed in the alcoholic, who has a propensity to poor intake. Furthermore, alcohol has a direct corrosive effect on the gut, part of which is concentration-dependent.[112] Alcoholics have been shown to display *malabsorption* for a number of essential nutrients, including vitamins B_1[113] and B_{12};[114] combining malnutrition with alcoholism is obviously adding insult to injury. As discussed before, we have shown how nutritional factors affect the severity and degree of alcoholic fatty liver development. We now plan to analyze to what extent these as well as other nutritional factors determine the severity of the hepatitis and the cirrhosis secondary to alcohol abuse. We are also seeking to determine whether the baboons will eventually develop not only the morphologic lesions of hepatitis and cirrhosis but also the secondary complications associated clinically with the full-blown disease, including hypoalbuminemia, portal hypertension, ascites, and sequelae of the collateral circulation.

The fact that not all baboons fed ethanol developed either hepatitis or cirrhosis raises the challenging question of the cause for the enhanced susceptibility to alcohol that exists in some animals. In man too, *individual predisposition* must play a major role since not all heavy drinkers develop cirrhosis. It would be of obvious clinical importance to learn to recognize this enhanced susceptibility at an early stage of the disease. The hallmark of cirrhosis is the development of bands of fibrotic tissue, characterized, biochemically, by collagen accumulation. It is noteworthy that both rats and baboons fed ethanol display enhanced hepatic *collagen formation* and increased hepatic collagen proline hydroxylase activity, which conceivably play a role in the collagen accumulation.[115] It may be significant that this increased enzyme activity can be detected at the early fatty liver stage and thus precedes most of the manifestation of persistent alcoholic liver injury listed in TABLE 2.

Reports of the association of appetite for alcohol, and cirrhosis with color-vision disturbances,[116-118] although questioned by some,[119,120] have nevertheless brought up important unsolved problems concerning the possible role of *genetic factors* in the pathogenesis of alcoholism and cirrhosis. Although no group is immune to alcoholic cirrhosis, various segments of our society are affected differently. For instance, it is generally recognized that American Jews are relatively spared whereas American Indians seem to be more prone to develop alcoholic cirrhosis. These differences are commonly attributed to cultural factors leading to alcoholism, although genetic influences favoring either alcoholism, cirrhosis, or both, have not been ruled out. Individual differences in rates of ethanol metabolism appear, in part, genetically controlled,[121] and the possible role of heredity for the development of alcoholism in man has recently been emphasized.[122] Differences in rates of ethanol metabolism[123] and sensitivity to alcohol[124] according to racial background were also reported. Fenna et al.[123] found that blood ethanol clearance is significantly faster in Caucasians than in Eskimos and Indians, whereas Indians have a greater capacity for acceleration of blood ethanol clearance after ethanol consumption. The differences could not be correlated with previous ethanol intake or dietary habits, suggesting that a genetic mechanism may be implicated, although the influence of environmental factors was not fully excluded.

TABLE 2

Persistent Injurious Effects After Chronic Ethanol Consumption

Altered mitochondrial functions and structure
Necrosis and inflammation
Central sclerosis
Septal fibrosis
Cirrhosis

TREATMENT OF CIRRHOSIS

Because the pathogenesis of cirrhosis remains unknown, it is not surprising that, except for improved symptomatic management, no convincing therapeutic progress has been made in the treatment of patients with either alcoholic hepatitis or cirrhosis. Trials with adrenocorticosteroid therapy for alcoholic hepatitis have yielded conflicting results. Helman et al.[125] described improved survival with prednisolone, 40 mg per day, in a very severely ill group of patients, but not in those with milder illness. Campra et al.[126] found no benefit from prednisone, and Porter et al.[127] could not demonstrate the utility of 6-methyl prednisolone (40 mg per day). Since steroid therapy has significant associated morbidity, its use is not currently recommended, especially in view of the fact that it has been shown to adversely affect patients with alcoholic cirrhosis.[128]

SUMMARY

The first gross manifestation of alcoholism in the liver is fat accumulation. That the steatosis can be attributed to ethanol itself rather than to the malnutrition so commonly associated with alcoholism was demonstrated in human volunteers, in baboons, and in rats fed alcohol as part of a nutritionally adequate diet. The fat that accumulates in the liver was found to derive primarily from dietary lipid (when available) and from endogenously synthesized lipids, when ethanol was given as part of a low-fat diet. The steatosis was also decreased by reducing the fat content of the diet or by substituting medium chain for long-chain triglycerides. Low-protein diet potentiated but high-protein diet did not prevent fat accumulation. The more severe complications, namely inflammation (alcoholic hepatitis) and cirrhosis, were observed when the dose of alcohol was increased to 50% of total calories in a study conducted in baboons given alcohol as part of a totally liquid nutritionally adequate diet. Signs of inebriation as well as withdrawal symptoms (seizures) were observed. Despite the lack of dietary deficiency, all animals fed ethanol developed fatty liver. In addition, hepatitis was observed in some and the lesion progressed to incomplete and complete cirrhosis in 6 of 15 baboons after 2–4 years of ethanol consumption.

This study demonstrates that alcohol itself, independently of dietary deficiencies, is a cause for the liver damage, and this new experimental model for alcoholic liver injury in the nonhuman primate illustrates the relationship of the fatty liver to the more severe stages of the disease. Indeed, it is noteworthy that already at the fatty liver stage, mitochondrial lesions identical with those seen in alcoholic hepatitis occur. Moreover, collagen accumulation, the hallmark of cirrhosis, is already detectable at the early stages of fat accumulation, suggesting that the fatty liver can be considered a precursor of the more severe complications of alcoholism.

ACKNOWLEDGMENTS

I am indebted to Miss L. M. DeCarli and Drs. E. Baraona, A. I. Cederbaum, L. Feinman, Y. Hasumura, H. Ishii, J.-G. Joly, A. F. Lefevre, S. Matsuszaki, J. Moor-Jankowski, E. Muchmore, R. C. Pirola, E. Rubin, and R. Teschke, who among many others contributed to most of the original studies presented here.

REFERENCES

1. KRAMER, K., L. KULLER & R. FISHER. 1968. The increasing mortality attributed to cirrhosis and fatty liver, in Baltimore (1957–1966). Ann. Intern. Med. 69: 273–282.
2. EDMONDSON, H. A., R. L. PETERS, H. H. FRANKEL & S. BOROWSKY. 1967. The early stage of liver injury in the alcoholic. Medicine 46: 119–129.
3. BÖHLE, E., W. ERB & W. SIEDE. 1972. Alkohol und Fettleber. Internist 9: 247–255.
4. LIEBER, C. S. 1969. Alcohol and the liver. In The Biological Basis of Medicine. E. E. Bittar, Ed. 5 (9): 317–344. Academic Press, New York., N.Y.
5. LIEBER, C. S. 1974. Effects of ethanol upon lipid metabolism. Lipids 9: 103–116.
6. BRODIE, B. B., W. M. BUTLER, M. G. HORNING, R. P. MAICKEL & H. M. MALING. 1961. Alcohol-induced triglyceride deposition in liver through derangement of fat transport. Amer. J. Clin. Nutr. 9: 432–435.
7. LIEBER, C. S., N. SPRITZ & L. M. DeCARLI. 1966. Role of dietary, adipose and endogenously synthesized fatty acids in the pathogenesis of the alcoholic fatty liver. J. Clin. Invest. 45: 51–62.
8. LINDENBAUM, J. & C. S. LIEBER. 1971. Effects of ethanol on the blood, bone marrow, and small intestine of man. In Proceedings of the Symposium on Biological Aspects of Alcohol. M. K. Roach, W. M. McIsaac & P. J. Creaven, Eds. 3: 27–45. University of Texas Press. Austin, Tex.
9. BEST, C. H., W. S. HARTROFT, C. C. LUCAS & J. H. RIDOUT. 1949. Liver damage produced by feeding alcohol or sugar and its prevention by choline. Brit. Med. J. 2: 1001–1007.

10. PEQUIGNOT, G. 1962. Die Rolle des Alkohols bei der Atiologie von Leberzirrhosen in Frankreich. Munchen. Med. Wschr. **103**: 1464–1468.
11. LELBACH, W. K. 1967. Leberschaden bei chronischem Alkoholismus. Acta Hepatosplen. **14**: 9–39.
12. LIEBER, C. S., D. P. JONES, J. MENDELSON & L. M. DeCARLI. 1963. Fatty liver, hyperlipemia, and hyperuricemia produced by prolonged alcohol consumption, despite adequate dietary intake. Trans. Ass. Amer. Physicians **76**: 289–300.
13. LIEBER, C. S., D. P. JONES & L. M. DeCARLI. 1965. Effects of prolonged ethanol intake: Production of fatty liver despite adequate diets. J. Clin. Invest. **44**: 1009–1021.
14. DeCARLI, L. M. & C. S. LIEBER. 1967. Fatty liver in the rat after prolonged intake of ethanol with a nutritionally adequate new liquid diet. J. Nutr. **91**: 331–336.
15. LIEBER, C. S. & L. M. DeCARLI. 1973. Ethanol dependence and tolerance: A nutritionally controlled experimental model in the rat. Res. Commun. Pathol. Pharmacol. **6**: 983–991.
16. LIEBER, C. S. & E. RUBIN. 1968. Alcoholic fatty liver in man on a high protein and low fat diet. Amer. J. Med. **44**: 200–206.
17. LIEBER, C. S. & L. M. DeCARLI. 1970. Quantitative relationship between the amount of dietary fat and the severity of the alcoholic fatty liver. Amer. J. Clin. Nutr. **23**: 474–478.
18. LIEBER, C. S. & N. SPRITZ. 1966. Effects of prolonged ethanol intake in man: Role of dietary, adipose and endogenously synthesized fatty acids in the pathogenesis of the alcoholic fatty liver. J. Clin. Invest. **45**: 1400–1411.
19. LIEBER, C. S., A. LEFEVRE, N. SPRITZ, L. FEINMAN & L. M. DeCARLI. 1967. Difference in hepatic metabolism of long- and medium-chained fatty acids: The role of fatty acid chain length in the production of the alcoholic fatty liver. J. Clin. Invest. **46**: 1451–1460.
20. HOFFBAUER, F. W. & F. G. ZAKI. 1965. Choline deficiency in baboon and rat compared. Arch. Path. **79**: 364–369.
21. RUBIN, E. & C. S. LIEBER. 1968. Alcohol-induced hepatic injury in non-alcoholic volunteers. New Eng. J. Med. **278**: 869–876.
22. ASHWORTH, C. T., F. WRIGHTMAN & V. BUTTRAM. 1961. Hepatic lipids. Arch. Path. **72**: 620–624.
23. DiLUZIO, N. R. 1958. Effect of acute ethanol intoxication on liver and plasma lipid fractions of the rat. Amer. J. Physiol. **194**: 453–456.
24. LIEBER, C. S. & L. M. DeCARLI. 1966. Study of agents for the prevention of the fatty liver produced by prolonged alcohol intake. Gastroenterology **50**: 316–322.
25. TAKEUCHI, J., A. TAKADA, Y. HASUMURA, Y. MATSUDA & F. IKEGAMI. 1972. Acute alcoholic liver injury and choline deficiency. Meth. Achievm. Exp. Path. **6**: 81–110.
26. PATEK, A. J., S. C. BOWRY & S. ANURAS. 1973. Alcohol and sucrose in choline deficiency cirrhosis in the rat. Arch. Pathol. **96**: 377–382.
27. LIEBER, C. S., L. M. DeCARLI, H. GANG, G. WALKER & E. RUBIN. 1972. Hepatic effects of long-term ethanol consumption in primates. Medical Primatology. E. I. Goldsmith & J. Moor-Jankowski, Eds. Part III: 270–278. Karger. Basel, Switzerland.
28. KUMAR, V. & V. RAMALINGASWAMI. 1972. Mechanism of fatty liver in protein deficiency: An experimental study in the rhesus monkey. Gastroenterology **62**: 445–451.
29. LIEBER, C. S. 1967. Chronic alcoholic hepatic injury in experimental animals and man: Biochemical pathways and nutritional factors. Fed. Proc. **26**: 1443–1448.
30. KLATSKIN, G., W. A. KREHL & H. O. CONN. 1954. The effect of alcohol on the choline requirement. I. Changes in the rat's liver following prolonged ingestion of alcohol. J. Exp. Med. **100**: 605–614.
31. LIEBER, C. S., N. SPRITZ & L. M. DeCARLI. 1969. Fatty liver produced by dietary deficiencies: Its pathogenesis and potentiation by ethanol. J. Lipid Res. **10**: 283–287.
32. LIEBER, C. S. 1966. Hepatic and metabolic effects of alcohol. Gastroenterology **50**: 119–133.

33. VINCENZI, L., J. MELDOLESI, M. T. MORINI & P. BUSSAN. 1967. Protective effect of phenobarbital and SKF 525a on the acute ethanol-induced fatty liver. Biochem. Pharmacol. **16:** 2431-2432.

34. KOFF, R. S., E. A. CARTER, S. LUI & K. J. ISSELBACHER. 1970. Prevention of the ethanol-induced fatty liver in the rat by phenobarbital. Gastroenterology **59:** 50–61.

35. WOOLES, W. R. & R. J. WEYMOUTH. 1968. Prevention of the ethanol induced fatty liver by chlorcyclizine-induced maintenance of hepatic lipid oxidation. Lab. Invest. **18:** 709–714.

36. LANSFORD, E. M., I. D. HILL & W. SHIVE. 1962. Effects of asparagine and other related nutritional supplements upon alcohol-induced rat liver triglyceride elevation. J. Nutr. **78:** 219–222.

37. CHEW, B. K., N. M. ALEXANDER, R. SCHEIG & G. KLATSKIN. 1968. Fatty liver, adenosine triphosphate and asparagine. Biochem. Pharmacol. **17:** 2463–2469.

38. ESTLER, C. J. & H. P. T. AMMON. 1967. The influence of beta adrenergic blockade on the ethanol-induced derangement of lipid transport. Arch. Int. Pharmacodyn. **166:** 333–341.

39. AMMON, H. P. T. & W. ZELLER. 1965. Der Einfluss von α-Pyridylcarbinol auf die durch Alcohol erzeugte Fettleber der Ratte. Arzneimittelforschung **15:** 1369–1371.

40. RADOMSKI, M. W. & J. D. WOOD. 1964. The lipotropic action of cold. I. The influence of cold and choline deficiency on liver lipids of rats at different intakes of dietary methionine. Can. J. Physiol. Pharmacol. **42:** 769–777.

41. L'HUILLER, J. R., R. ROUDIER & J. THUILLER. 1967. Evidence histologique de l'éfficacité et de l'innocuité de l'oxygène hyperbare dans le traitement de l'intoxication éthylique expérimentale. Med. Pharmacol. Exp. **16:** 513–519.

42. HYAMS, D. E. & K. J. ISSELBACHER. 1964. Prevention of fatty liver by administration of adenosine triphosphate. Nature **204:** 1196–1197.

43. MARCHETTI, M., V. OTTANI, P. ZANETTI & P. PUDDU. 1968. Aspects of lipid metabolism in ethanol-induced fatty liver. J. Nutr. **95:** 607–611.

44. KOFF, R. S. & J. J. FITTS. 1972. Chlorpromazine inhibition of ethanol metabolism without prevention of fatty liver. Biochem. Med. **6:** 77–81.

45. BUSTOS, G. O., H. KALANT, J. M. KHANNA & J. LOTH. 1970. Pyrazole and induction of fatty liver by a single dose of ethanol. Science **168:** 1598–1599.

46. MORGAN, J. C. & N. R. DiLUZIO. 1970. Inhibition of the acute ethanol-induced fatty liver by pyrazole. Proc. Soc. Exp. Biol. Med. **134:** 462–466.

47. BLOMSTRAND, R. & L. FORSELL. 1971. Prevention of the acute ethanol-induced fatty liver by 4-methypyrazole. Life Sci. **10** (Part II): 523–530.

48. NORDMANN, R., C. RIBIERE, H. ROUACH & J. NORDMANN. 1972. Paradoxical effects of pyrazole on acute ethanol-induced fatty liver. Rev. Eur. Etud. Clin. Biol. **17:** 592–596.

49. DOMANSKI, R., D. RIFENBERICK, F. STEARNS, R. M. SCORPIO & S. A. NARROD. 1971. Ethanol-induced fatty liver in rats: effects of pyrazole and glucose. Proc. Soc. Exp. Biol. Med. **138:** 18–20.

50. PRANCAN, A. V. & J. NAKANO. 1972. Effect of pyrazole on conversion of ethanol and acetate into lipids in rat liver. Res. Commun. Chem. Pathol. Pharmacol. **4:** 181–191.

51. KALANT, H., J. M. KHANNA & G. O. BUSTOS. 1972. Effect of pyrazole on the induction of fatty liver by chronic administration of ethanol. Biochem. Pharmacol. **21:** 811–819.

52. LIEBER, C. S., E. RUBIN, L. M. DeCARLI, P. S. MISRA & H. GANG. 1970. Effects of pyrazole on hepatic function and structure. Lab. Invest. **22:** 615–621.

53. BIZZI, A., M. T. TACCONI, E. VENERONI & S. GARATTINI. 1966. Triglyceride accumulation in liver. Nature **209:** 1025–1026.

54. FENSTER, L. F. 1966. The nonefficacy of short-term anabolic steroid therapy in alcoholic liver disease. Ann. Intern. Med. **65:** 738–744.

55. JABBARI, M. & C. M. LEEVY. 1967. Protein anabolism and fatty liver of the alcoholic. Medicine **46:** 131–139.

56. MENDENHALL, C. L. 1968. Anabolic steroid therapy as an adjunct to diet in alcoholic hepatic steatosis. Amer. J. Dig. Dis. **13**: 783–791.
57. LIEBER, C. S. & R. SCHMID. 1961. The effect of ethanol on fatty acid metabolism: Stimulation of hepatic fatty acid synthesis in vitro. J. Clin. Invest. **40**: 394–399.
58. SVOBODA, D. J. & R. T. MANNING. 1964. Chronic alcoholism with fatty metamorphosis of the liver. Mitochondrial alterations in hepatic cells. Amer. J. Pathol. **44**: 645–662.
59. KIESSLING, K. H. & L. PILSTROM. 1971. Ethanol and the human liver. Structural and metabolic changes in liver mitochondria. Cytobiologie **4**: 339–348.
60. KONTTINEN, A., G. HARTEL & A. LOUHIJA. 1970. Multiple serum enzyme analyses in chronic alcoholics. Acta Med. Scand. **188**: 257–264.
61. ISERI, O. A., C. S. LIEBER & L. S. GOTTLIEB. 1966. The ultrastructure of fatty liver induced by prolonged ethanol ingestion. Amer. J. Path. **48**: 535–555.
62. LANE, B. P. & C. S. LIEBER. 1966. Ultrastructural alterations in human hepatocytes following ingestion of ethanol with adequate diets. Amer. J. Path. **49**: 593–603.
63. RUBIN, E. & C. S. LIEBER. 1967. Early fine structural changes in the human liver induced by alcohol. Gastroenterology **52**: 1–13.
64. FRENCH, S. W. 1968. Fragility of liver mitochondria in ethanol-fed rats. Gastroenterology **54**: 1106–1114.
65. RUBIN, E., D. S. BEATTIE & C. S. LIEBER. 1970. Effects of ethanol on the biogenesis of mitochondrial membranes and associated mitochondrial functions. Lab. Invest. **23**: 620–627.
66. FRENCH, S. W. & T. TODOROFF. 1970. Hepatic mitochondrial fragility and permeability. Arch. Path. **89**: 329–336.
67. FRENCH, S. W., T. J. IHRIG & R. J. MORIN. 1970. Lipid composition of RBC ghosts, liver mitochondria and microsomes of ethanol-fed rats. Quart. J. Stud. Alcohol **31**: 801–809.
68. OUDEA, M. C., A. N. LAUNAY, S. QUENEHERVE & P. OUDEA. 1970. The hepatic lesions produced in the rat by chronic alcoholic intoxication. Histological, ultrastructural and biochemical observations. Rev. Europ. Études Clin. et Biol. **15**: 748–764.
69. VIDELA, L. & Y. ISRAEL. 1970. Factors that modify the metabolism of ethanol in rat liver and adaptive changes produced by its chronic administration. Biochem. J. **118**: 275–281.
70. KIESSLING, K. H. & L. PILSTROM. 1968. Effect of ethanol on rat liver. V. Morphological and functional changes after prolonged consumption of various alcoholic beverages. Quart. J. Stud. Alcohol **29**: 819–827.
71. RUBIN, E., D. S. BEATTIE, A. TOTH & C. S. LIEBER. 1972. Structural and functional effects of ethanol on hepatic mitochondria. Fed. Proc. **31**: 131–140.
72. KIESSLING, K. H. 1968. Effect of ethanol on rat liver. VI. A possible correlation between α-glycerophosphate oxidase activity and mitochondrial size in male and female rats fed ethanol. Acta Pharmacol. **26**: 245–252.
73. PILSTROM, L. & K. H. KIESSLING. 1972. A possible localization of α-glycerophosphate dehydrogenase to the inner boundary membrane of mitochondria in livers from rats fed with ethanol. Histochemie **32**: 329–334.
74. CEDERBAUM, A. I., C. S. LIEBER & E. RUBIN. 1974. Effect of chronic ethanol treatment on mitochondrial functions. Arch. Biochem. Biophys. **165**: 560–569.
75. GORDON, E. R. 1972. The effect of chronic consumption of ethanol on the redox state of the rat liver. Canad. J. Biochem. **50**: 949–957.
76. LEFEVRE, A., H. ADLER & C. S. LIEBER. 1970. Effect of ethanol on ketone metabolism. J. Clin. Invest. **49**: 1775–1782.
77. JENKINS, D. W., R. W. ECKEL & J. W. CRAIG. 1971. Alcoholic ketoacidosis. J.A.M.A. **217**: 177–183.
78. TOTH, A., C. S. LIEBER, A. I. CEDERBAUM, D. S. BEATTIE & E. RUBIN. 1973. Effects of ethanol and diet on fatty acid oxidation by hepatic mitochondria. Gastroenterology **64**: 198.
79. MENDENHALL, C. L. 1972. Origin of hepatic triglyceride fatty acids: Quantitative

estimation of the relative contributions of linoleic acid by diet and adipose tissue in normal and ethanol-fed rats. J. Lipid Res. **13**: 177–183.

80. CEDERBAUM, A. I., C. S. LIEBER & E. RUBIN. 1974. Effect of acetaldehyde on mitochondrial function. Arch. Biochem. Biophys. **161**: 26–39.

81. ISHII, H., J.-G. JOLY & C. S. LIEBER. 1973. Effect of ethanol on the amount and enzyme activities of hepatic rough and smooth microsomal membranes. Biochim. Biophys. Acta **291**: 411–420.

82. ROTHSCHILD, M., M. ORATZ, J. MONGELLI & S. S. SCHREIBER. 1971. Alcohol-induced depression of albumin synthesis: reversal by tryptophan. J. Clin. Invest. **50**: 1812–1818.

83. JEEJEEBHOY, K. N., M. J. PHILLIPS, A. BRUCE-ROBERTSON, J. HO & U. SODTKE. 1972. The acute effect of ethanol on albumin, fibrinogen and trans-ferrin synthesis in the rat. Biochem. J. **126**: 1111–1126.

84. ISERI, O. A., L. S. GOTTLIEB & C. S. LIEBER. 1964. The ultrastructure of ethanol-induced fatty liver. Fed. Proc. **23**: 579.

85. LIEBER, C. S. & L. M. DeCARLI. 1974. An experimental model of alcohol feeding and liver injury in the baboon. J. Med. Primatology. **3**: 153–163.

86. REPPART, J. T., R. L. PETERS, H. A. EDMONDSON & R. F. BAKER. 1963. Electron and light microscopy of sclerosing hyaline necrosis of the liver. The de-velopment of alcoholic hyaline bodies. Lab. Invest. **12**: 1138–1153.

87. CHRISTOFFERSEN, P. & E. JUHL. 1971. Mallory bodies in liver biopsies with fatty changes but no cirrhosis. Acta. Pathol. Microbiol. Scand. (A) **79**: 201–207.

88. ISERI, O. A. & L. S. GOTTLIEB. 1971. Alcoholic hyalin and megamitochondria as separate and distinct entities in liver disease associated with alcoholism. Gastro-enterology **60**: 1027–1035.

89. RUBIN, E., F. HUTTERER & C. S. LIEBER. 1968. Ethanol increases hepatic smooth endoplasmic reticulum and drug-metabolizing enzymes. Science **159**: 1469–1470.

90. BIAVA, C. 1964. Mallory alcoholic hyalin: a heretofore unique lesion of hepato-cellular ergastoplasm. Lab. Invest. **13**: 301–320.

91. SMUCKLER, E. S. 1968. The ultrastructure of human alcoholic hyaline. Amer. J. Clin. Pathol. **49**: 790–797.

92. ALBUKERK, J. & J. L. DUFFY. 1972. Origin of alcoholic hyaline. An electron microscopic study. Arch. Pathol. **93**: 510–517.

93. YOKOO, H., O. T. MINNICK, F. BUTTI & G. KENT. 1972. Morphologic variants of alcoholic hyaline. Amer. J. Pathol. **69**: 25–40.

94. WIGGERS, K. D., S. W. FRENCH, B. S. FRENCH & B. N. CARR. 1973. The ultra-structure of Mallory body filaments. Lab. Invest. **29**: 652–658.

95. ROY, S., V. RAMALINGASWAMI & N. D. NAYAK. 1971. An ultrastructural study of the liver in Indian childhood cirrhosis with particular reference to the structure of alcoholic hyaline. Gut **12**: 693–701.

96. EDMONDSON, H. A. 1958. Tumors of the liver and intrahepatic bile ducts. *In* Atlas of Tumor Pathology. Armed Forces Institute of Pathology, sect. 7, fascicle **25**: 49.

97. NORKIN, S. A. & D. CAMPAGNA-PINTO. 1968. Cytoplasmic hyaline inclusions in hepatoma. Histochemical study. Arch. Pathol. **86**: 25–32.

98. KEELEY, A. F., O. A. ISERI & L. S. GOTTLIEB. 1972. Ultrastructure of hyaline cytoplasmic inclusions in a human hepatoma: relationship to Mallory's alcoholic hyalin. Gastroenterology **62**: 280–293.

99. GERBER, M. A., W. ORR, H. DENK, F. SCHAFFNER & H. POPPER. 1973. Hepato-cellular hyaline in cholestasis and cirrhosis: its diagnostic significance. Gastroenter-ology **64**: 89–98.

100. SCHAFFNER, F., I. STERNLIEB, T. BARKER & H. POPPER. 1962. Hepatocellular changes in Wilson's disease. Histochemical and electron microscopic studies. Amer. J. Pathol. **41**: 315–327.

101. CHRISTOFFERSEN, P. 1970. The incidence and frequency of Mallory bodies in 1,100 consecutive liver biopsies. Acta Pathol. Microbiol. Scand. (A) **78**: 395–400.

102. CHRISTOFFERSEN, P. & K. MIELSEN. 1971. The frequency of Mallory bodies in liver biopsies from chronic alcoholics. Acta Pathol. Microbiol. Scand. (A) 79: 274–278.

103. LISCHNER, M. W., J. F. ALEXANDER & J. T. GALAMBOS. 1971. Natural history of alcoholic hepatitis. I. The acute disease. Amer. J. Dig. Dis. 16: 481–494.

104. ALEXANDER, J. F., M. W. LISCHNER & J. T. GALAMBOS. 1971. Natural history of alcoholic hepatitis. II. The long-term prognosis. Amer. J. Gastroenterol. 56: 515–525.

105. GALAMBOS, J. T. 1972. Natural history of alcoholic hepatitis. III. Histological changes. Gastroenterology 63: 1026–1035.

106. HARINASUTA, U., B. CHOMET, K. ISHAK & H. J. ZIMMERMAN. 1967. Steatonecrosis—Mallory body type. Medicine 46: 141–162.

107. KERN, W. H., W. P. MIKKELSEN & F. L. TURRILL. 1969. The significance of hyaline necrosis in liver biopsies. Surg. Gynecol. Obstet. 129: 749–754.

108. RUEBNER, B. H., J. MOORE, R. B. RUTHERFORD, A. M. SELIGMAN & G. D. ZUIDEMA. 1969. Nutritional cirrhosis in rhesus monkeys: Electron microscopy and histochemistry. Exper. Molec. Path. 11: 53–70.

109. WILGRAM, G. F. 1959. Experimental Laënnec type of cirrhosis in monkeys. Ann. Intern. Med. 51: 1134–1158.

110. LIEBER, C. S., L. M. DeCARLI & E. RUBIN. 1975. Sequential production of fatty liver, hepatitis and cirrhosis in sub-human primates fed ethanol with adequate diets. Proc. Nat. Acad. Sci. USA. 72: 2.

111. RUBIN, E. & C. S. LIEBER. 1974. Fatty liver, alcoholic hepatitis and cirrhosis produced by alcohol in primates. New Eng. J. Med. 290: 128–135.

112. BARAONA, E., R. C. PIROLA & C. S. LIEBER. 1974. Small intestinal damage and changes in cell population produced by ethanol ingestion in the rat. Gastroenterology 66: 226–234.

113. TOMASULO, P. A., R. M. H. KATER & F. L. IBER. 1968. Impairment of thiamine absorption in alcoholism. Amer. J. Clin. Nutr. 21: 1340–1344.

114. LINDENBAUM, J. & C. S. LIEBER. 1969. Alcohol-induced malabsorption of vitamin B_{12} in man. Nature 224: 806.

115. FEINMAN, L. & C. S. LIEBER. 1972. Hepatic collagen metabolism: Effect of alcohol consumption in rats and baboons. Science 176: 795.

116. CRUZ-COKE, R. & A. VARELA. 1966. Inheritance of alcoholism. Lancet 2: 1282–1284.

117. UGARTE, G. R., R. CRUZ-COKE, L. RIVERA & H. ALTSCHILLER. 1970. Relationship of color blindness to alcoholic liver damage. Pharmacology 4: 297–308.

118. CRUZ-COKE, R., L. RIVERA, A. VARELA & J. MARDONES. 1972. Correlation between colour vision disturbance and appetite for alcohol. Clin. Genet. 3: 404–410.

119. FIALKOW, P. J., H. C. THULINE & L. F. FENSTER. 1966. Lack of association between cirrhosis and the common types of color blindness. New Eng. J. Med. 275: 584–587.

120. RIFFENBURGH, R. S. & J. F. SHEA. 1970. Lack of association between color blindness and alcoholism. Eye Ear Nose Throat Monthly 49: 240–242.

121. VESELL, E. S., J. G. PAGE & G. T. PASSANANTI. 1971. Genetic and environmental factors affecting ethanol metabolism in man. Clin. Pharmacol. Ther. 12: 192–201.

122. GOODWIN, D. W. 1971. Is alcoholism hereditary? Arch. Gen Psychiat. 25: 545–549.

123. FENNA, D., L. MIX, O. SCHAEFER & J. A. L. GILBERT. 1971. Ethanol metabolism in various racial groups. Can. Med. Assoc. J. 105: 472–475.

124. WOLFF, P. H. 1972. Ethnic differences in alcohol sensitivity. Science 175: 449–450.

125. HELMAN, R. A., M. H. TEMKO, S. W. NYE, W. SYLVANUS & H. J. FALLON. 1971. Alcoholic hepatitis. Natural history and evaluation of prednisolone therapy. Ann. Intern. Med. 74: 311–321.

126. CAMPRA, J. L., E. M. HAMLIN, R. J. KIRSHBAUM, M. OLIVER, A. G. REDEKER

     & T. B. REYNOLDS. 1973. Prednisone therapy of acute alcoholic hepatitis: Report of a controlled trial. Ann. Intern. Med. **79:** 625–631.

127. PORTER, H. P., F. R. SIMON, C. E. POPE, W. VOLWILER & L. F. FENSTER. 1971. Corticosteroid therapy in severe alcoholic hepatitis. New Eng. J. Med. **284:** 1350–1355.

128. ANDERSEN, S. B., T. BALSLEV, M. BJORNEBOE, V. FABER, S. GJORUP, B. HARVALD, K. IVERSEN, O. JESSEN, E. JOHL & H. E. JORGENSEN. 1969. Effect of predisone on the survival of patients with cirrhosis of the liver. Lancet **1:** 119–121.

CIRRHOSIS IN THE ALCOHOLIC AND ITS RELATION TO THE VOLUME OF ALCOHOL ABUSE

Werner K. Lelbach

Department of Internal Medicine
University Clinics of Bonn
Bonn-Venusberg, Federal Republic of Germany

At first sight, it is puzzling to find that cirrhosis of the liver apparently develops only in a minor proportion of heavy drinkers and alcoholics, which seems to contradict the well-established association[1] between alcoholism and cirrhosis. A statistic based on 10 series of autopsy records (TABLE 1) shows that the incidence of cirrhosis in alcoholics ranged from as low as 2.4% to a maximum figure of about 28%. This statistic is a partly corrected extension of original data from Jolliffe and Jellinek,[54] who calculated an average incidence of only 8% as against an estimated 1.2% in the general nonalcoholic population. Varying diagnostic standards in a number of these older autopsy series may have contributed to an underrepresentation. The modified statistic presented here yields a higher average incidence, of 18%, which is largely due to the inclusion of Wilen's selected sample. This sample is outstanding in that it takes account of the potential length of drinking history and of minimum levels of daily alcohol intake.

In more recent series where liver biopsies were performed during life (TABLE 2), the incidence of cirrhosis among defined alcoholics, though definitely higher, still reaches only 30%, which is close to Wilen's percentage. According to cross-sectional studies of this kind, it can be safely assumed that cirrhosis will develop only in roughly $\frac{1}{4}$ to $\frac{1}{3}$ of those who heavily indulge in alcohol abuse during a lengthy period of their lives. In my own series of 320 biopsy cases, well-established cirrhosis was seen in 12%.

This proportion, however, seems to contrast strikingly with the high incidence of alcoholism in cirrhosis of the liver in all those regions of the world where the sale and consumption of alcoholic beverages is an integral part of social and economic life (TABLE 3). For North and South America the average incidence of alcoholism in cirrhosis is now 66%, for Europe 42%. A small number of series from Asia, where alcohol consumption is low or nonexistent, shows an average incidence of only 11% (TABLE 4). A calculation based on 80 clinical and autopsy series comprising a total of 20,000 cases shows that in the Western World an alcohol etiology in cirrhosis of the liver is found in 50% of the cases (TABLE 5). Even in the United Kingdom, where, owing to high taxes imposed on alcoholic beverages since 1914,[128,133] an alcohol etiology had previously played a laudably minor role, alcohol is now of about equal importance with other causes[126] or in some areas even the predominant one.[34,52,53]

If one endeavors to resolve this apparent discrepancy and to study the association between alcohol abuse and cirrhosis, 3 essential points should be kept in mind:

(1) Ethanol is an ambivalent molecule that possesses a metabolic and a pharmacologic side. An intake per time unit up to a certain magnitude can effectively be dealt with by several metabolic degradation systems. However, an intake that exceeds the capacity of these systems will result in an elevation of the blood alcohol level, bringing out the pharmacologic or toxic properties of this central nervous

85

TABLE 1

Incidence of Cirrhosis in Alcoholics at Autopsy[75]

Author and Year of Publication		Size of Sample N	Cirrhosis		Comment
			No. of Cases	Percent of Sample	
Formad	1886	250	6	2.4%	sudden death due to alcohol
Klopstock	1906	25	1	4.0%	
v. Baumgarten	1908	?	?	5–6%	
Barbier & Jaquis	1939	231	17	7.4%	
Delore & Devant	1939	140	14	10.0%	
Fahr	1909/11	309	32	10.4%	(13 cases of Laennec's cirrhosis; 19 cases of "fatty liver plus secondary induration")
Kayser	1888	155	21	13.5%	death in delirium tremens
Jagić	1906	151	22	14.6%	alcohol psychosis
Kern	1913	170	28	16.5%	advanced Laennec's + fatty cirrhosis
			48	28.2%	incipient Laennec's + fatty cirrhosis
Boles & Clark	1936	228	58	25.4%	
Wilens	1947	519	145	27.9%	35 years and older; more than 1 pint of whiskey or equivalent per day for many years
		(600)	(40)	(6.7%)	(nonalcoholic control group)

TABLE 2

Incidence of Cirrhosis in Alcoholics

Incidence of Cirrhosis in Alcoholics at Autopsy

(period covered: 1886–1947)

Lelbach[75]: 10 series; 2178 cases
        range: 2.4–27.9% of cases

Average: 18%

Incidence of Cirrhosis in Alcoholics as Evidenced by Liver Biopsy During Life

(period covered: 1944–1962)

von Oldershausen[93,94]: 11 series; 778 cases

Average: 30.8%

(period covered: 1950–1966)

Leevy[66–68]: 1 series; 3000 cases

Average: 29%

Incidence of Cirrhosis in Alcoholics of the Present Series as Evidenced by Liver Biopsies

Lelbach[70]: 1 series; 320 cases

Average: 12%

TABLE 3

Alcohol Etiology in Cirrhosis of the Liver (Clinical and Autopsy Series)

Author	Country	Region	Period	Size of Sample	No. of Alcoholics	Percent Alcohol Etiology	Comment
Europe							
Caroli et al.[14]	France	Paris	1954–57	505	420	83.2	all types
Fauvert et al.[30]	France	Paris	1952–58	295	192	65.1	all types
Heimann et al.[47]	Belgium	Brussels	1949–63	100	40	40.0	all types
Riva & Weiner[110]	Switzerland	Bern	1946–56	68	60	88.2	PC**
Baumberger[6]	Switzerland	Zurich	1961–65	521	451	86.6	all types
Constam[19]	Switzerland	Zurich	1937–40	142	115	81.0	PC
Roch & Fehr[112]	Switzerland	Geneva	1931–40	230	182	79.0	PC
Moeschlin & Righetti[84]	Switzerland	Solothurn	1959–68	185	132	71.3	PC and PNC‡
Roch & Wohlers[111]	Switzerland	Geneva	1900–30	431	241	56.0	PC
Ruf-Bächtiger[118]	Switzerland	Chur	1942–64	132	73	55.3	all types
Rilliet & Keil[109]	Switzerland	Geneva	1941–48	227	112	49.1	all types
Heer[46]	Switzerland	Zurich	1949–67	390	118	30.2	all types
Mussini et al.[86]	Italy	Bologna	1960	124	86	69.4	all types
Pinto Correia et al.[102]	Portugal	Lisbon	1961–67	274	140	51.0	all types
Forshaw[34]	U.K.	Liverpool	1961–72	67	42	62.7	all types
Jain et al.[52]	U.K.	Birmingham	1965–72	181	93	51.4	all types (adults)
Lee[64]	U.K.	East London	1914–63	182	84	46.1	all types
Stone et al.[128]	U.K.	Birmingham	1959–64	155	52	33.5	all types
Sherlock[125]	U.K.	London	1959–65	561	134	23.9	all types
Schubert[121]	Germany	Hamburg	1939	84	63	75.0	PC
Gigglberger[39]	Germany	Regensburg	1960–66	200	115	57.5	PC
Naunyn[88]	Germany	Strassburg	1904	170	90	52.9	all types
Gros[40]	Germany	Mainz	1949–55	260	115	44.2	PC
Piesbergen et al.[101]	Germany	Hamburg	1958–65	327	121	37.0	all types
Kaeding[55]	Germany	Rostock	1955	56	20	35.7	all types
Popp[103]	Germany	Hamburg	1934–39	326	115	35.3	all types

TABLE 3 (Continued)

Author	Country	Region	Period	Size of Sample	No. of Alcoholics	Percent Alcohol Etiology	Comment
Gigglberger[38]	Germany	Regensburg	1953–58	200	68	34.0	PC
Creutzfeldt & Beck[20]	Germany	Freiburg	1942–62	560	185	33.0	all types
Falck et al.[29]	Germany	Berlin	1953–62	200	60	30.0	all types
Müting et al.[84a]	Germany	Homburg	1958–65	140	38	27.1	all types
Falck & Horn[28]	Germany	Berlin	1947–56	100	26	26.0	all types
Selmair et al.[123]	Germany	Kassel	1963–68	212	55	25.9	all types
Hartmann & Kottke[45]	Germany	Göttingen	1946–56	62	14	22.6	all types
Franken & Mohr[36]	Germany	Düsseldorf	1954–62	276	49	17.7	types not stated
v. Oldershausen[90,91]	Germany	Tüb./Marb./Berlin	1946–59	669	91	13.6	all types
Kühn & Tilse[63]	Germany	Lübeck	not stated	143	17	11.9	all types
Allert[2]	Germany	Bonn	1950–55	106	11	10.4	all types
Kalk[57]	Germany	Kassel	1949–56	542	46	8.5	PC, PNC, Hemochr.
Börner[9]	Germany	Bonn	1955–59	142	12	8.4	all types
Südhof[129]	Germany	Göttingen	1946–52	123	7	5.7	all types
Schneiderbaur[120]	Austria	Vienna	1935–64	560	439	78.4	all types
Eppinger[24]	Austria	Vienna	1925	327	159	42.7	all types
Frank & Leodolter[35]	Austria	Vienna	1963–67	271	96	35.4	all types
Seifert & Dittrich[122]	Austria	Vienna	1961–65	381	116	30.4	all types
Holzner et al.[49]	Austria	Vienna	1944–53	439	69	15.7	all types
Čerlek[15]	Yugoslavia	Zagreb	1950–60	137	41	29.9	PC and PNC
Halonen & Saksela[44]	Finland	Helsinki	1920–45	100	29	29.0	PC
Sundberg & Adlercr.[131]	Finland	Helsinki	1945–57	226	65	28.8	all types
Hällén & Linné[41]	Sweden	Malmö	1951–68	768	353	46.0	all types
Wadman et al.[135]	Sweden	Uppsala	1951–68	125	38	30.4	all types (only ♂)
		Dalecarlia	1951–64	97	24	24.7	all types (only ♂)

North and South America

Conn et al.[18]	U.S.A.	West Haven	1965-66	225	213	94.7	types not stated
Powell & Klatskin[104]	U.S.A.	New Haven	1951-63	283	268	94.7	PC
Patek & Post[95]	U.S.A.	New York	1937-41	54	47	87.0	PC
Bloomfield[8]	U.S.A.	San Francisco	1935-38	42	36	85.7	PC
Reid et al.[107]	U.S.A.	Baltimore	1968	100	84	84.0	all types
Garceau et al.[37]	U.S.A.	Boston	1959-61	471	390	82.8	all types
Kimball et al.[60]	U.S.A.	Buffalo	1936-45	143	115	80.4	decompensated PC
Hall & Morgan[42]	U.S.A.	Los Angeles	1939	68	54	79.4	PC
Hall et al.[43]	U.S.A.	Los Angeles	1933-46	782	618	79.0	PC
Fagin & Thompson[26]	U.S.A.	Detroit	1944	71	56	78.9	all types
Patek et al.[96]	U.S.A.	New York	1938-48	124	95	76.6	PC and PNC
Ricketts et al.[108]	U.S.A.	Chicago	1945-49	50	38	76.0	PC
Brick & Palmer[13]	U.S.A.	Several regions	1955-59	1000	745	74.5	PC and PNC
Nissen[89]	U.S.A.	New York	1920	117	85	72.6	PC
Daoud et al.[21]	U.S.A.	Albany	1962	220	150	68.2	PC and PNC
Hoffman & Lisa[48]	U.S.A.	New York	1920-45	93	61	65.6	PC
Douglas & Snell[23]	U.S.A.	Rochester	1940-44	444	284	64.0	PC
Rubin et al.[117]	U.S.A.	New York etc.	1962	342	209	61.1	PC and PNC
Ratnoff & Patek[106]	U.S.A.	New York	1922-42	386	207	53.6	PC
Fleming & Snell[32]	U.S.A.	Rochester	1942	200	102	51.0	PC
Mallory[77]	U.S.A.	Boston	1897-1931	550	269	48.9	PNC
Kirshbaum & Shure[61]	U.S.A.	Chicago	1943	356	149	41.9	PC
Boles et al.[11]	U.S.A.	Philadelphia	1942-46	142	50	35.2	PC
Boles & Clark[10]	U.S.A.	Philadelphia	1933-35	243	84	34.6	all types
Howard & Watson[50]	U.S.A.	Minneapolis	1935-44	100	25	25.0	all types
Evans & Gray[25]	U.S.A.	Los Angeles	-1938	217	49	22.1	PC
Sepúlveda et al.[124]	Mexico	Mexico	1956	119	98	82.4	PC
Armas-Cruz et al.[4]	Chile	Santiago	1946-50	202	138	68.3	PC

Far and Near East, Soviet Union

Wang[136]	China (Manch.)	Mukden	1936	54	16	31.0	PC
Chün et al.[17]	China	Canton	1950-59	69	8	11.6	PC

TABLE 3 (Continued)

[P'an Cy et al.94: Incidence of alcoholism in Chinese cirrhotics: 5–41.5%]

Author	Country	Region	Period	Size of Sample	No. of Alcoholics	Percent Alcohol Etiology	Comment
Fernando et al.31	Ceylon	Colombo	1941–47	43	12	27.9	PC
Nakamura et al.87	Japan	Sendai	1920–57	61	10	16.4	all types
Yoshida142	Japan	Several regions	1962	882	124	14.0+	all types
Munzer85	Syria	Damascus	1968	210	12	6.0	all types
Sutherland132	India	Vizagapatam	1905	?	?	3.0	PC
Rao105	India	Vizagapatam	1933	64	2	3.1	PC
Sağlam119	Turkey	Istambul	1934	321	8	2.5	mostly PC
Borhanmanesh12	Iran	Fars	1966–68	66	1	1.5	all types
Yenikomshian141	Lebanon	Beirut	1926–31	70	insignificant		all types
Mnushkin & Poljak83	Soviet Union	Moskva	1953–57	70	10	14.3	all types
Australia							
Chapman16	Austral.	Newcastle	1950–61	98	27	27.6	all types
Africa							
Anthony et al.3	Uganda	Kampala	1972	91	17	18.7	all types
				(11)	(8)	(72.7)	(PC)
Steiner et al.127	Senegal	Dakar	1947–57	239	–	0.0	all types

+Drinkers of 650 ml pure alcohol per week for 10 or more years.

** = Percentage valid only for cases of Laennec's cirrhosis with known etiology.

‡PC = Portal cirrhosis; PNC = Postnecrotic cirrhosis.

TABLE 4

Incidence of Alcoholism in Cirrhosis of the Liver Throughout the World
(Based on Data Contained in Table 3)

(Clinical and autopsy series)
North and South America (Time covered: 1897–1968) 28 series; 7144 cases Range: 22.1–94.7% Average: 66%
Europe (Time covered: 1900–1972) 51 series; 13 099 cases Range: 5.7–90.7% Average: 42%
Far and Near East, Soviet Union (Time covered: 1933–1968) 10 series; 1840 cases Range: 1.5–31.0% Average: 11%

depressant. This ambivalent nature clearly distinguishes alcohol from the group of classic hepatotoxic agents, such as carbon tetrachloride. Any discussion of the question whether ethanol should be regarded as a hepatotoxic agent—and considerable evidence in favor of this has been accumulated during the past decade[76,76a,114]—has to start from an appreciation of this dual nature. In addition, some of the metabolizing systems seem to be capable of adaptation under the condition of a continuous saturation. All this rules out any simple kind of dose dependancy in alcohol-induced organic damage.

(2) An increase in hepatic fat content, easily reversible by abstinence alone,[71,139] can be brought about within days to weeks by ingestion of appropriate amounts of alcohol.[113] This seems to be a purely metabolic problem. The development of more serious damage ultimately leading to cirrhosis, however, requires considerably longer periods of time in the range of 10–20 years, as clinical observation has shown. Thus, in addition to dosage, the dimension of time or the chronicity and persistence of alcohol abuse becomes an essential element.

(3) For the individual alcoholic, the risk of cirrhosis will finally be determined by his disposition or individual susceptibility. The specific factors predisposing an alcoholic are biologically still an enigma, and susceptibility is not measurable in quantitative terms. But we may suspect with some assurance that biochemical individuality constitutes an essential part of this somewhat mythical concept of susceptibility. In the present context, the term "biochemical individuality" is meant to designate the individual's genetically determined capacity to metabolize alcohol and the metabolic adaptability to an increasing intake. A genetically determined aberration of lipid metabolism in alcoholic subjects with hyperlipemia was recently described by Mendelson and Mello[82]; its manifestation proved to be

TABLE 5

Incidence of an Alcohol Etiology in Cirrhosis of the Liver in the Western World

(Period: 1897–1972. Clinical and autopsy series— North and South America; Australia; Europe) 80 series—20 243 cases Average: 50.4%

dose-dependent, i.e., blood alcohol levels had to be maintained above 50 mg/100 ml for prolonged periods. Immunological problems may also play a role in alcoholic hepatitis, which seems to be the precursor of cirrhosis.[69]

Clinical investigation of the quantitative aspects of alcohol abuse in cirrhosis of the liver should take cognizance of this complex interrelationship between dosage of alcohol intake, length of time during which this intake is maintained, and individual susceptibility. It becomes clear that for clinical purposes neither mean daily intake nor duration of heavy drinking alone but only the combined appreciation of at least these two variables is necessary if the relation between cirrhosis and the volume of alcohol abuse is to be examined.

With the aim of investigating particularly this relation, a fairly homogenous group of 526 male alcoholics, consecutively admitted to a special sanitarium in West Germany for voluntary withdrawal treatment, was examined for clinical, biochemical, and histologic symptoms and signs of liver disease.[70] A detailed interrogation of each one of these patients was carried out by the same interviewer in order to collect data on individual drinking habits, especially duration of alcohol abuse and daily minimum and maximum intake. These data were processed before independently collected results of biochemical tests and liver biopsies became known. For confirmation of the reliability of these data a second interview was carried out at a later date by the psychiatrist in charge of the institution. Furthermore, each patient's social agency record as well as records on all episodes of prior hospital treatment was screened for quantitative data contained therein. Also, information from physicians consulted in the past and from next of kin were registered. In view of the tendency to minimize rather than to exaggerate the actual volume of consumption, the final computation was based on the highest figures admitted for duration and mean daily or weekly intake. With all due caution, imperative in this kind of retrospective assessment of drinking habits, it was thought that this mode of procedure might yield relative figures of sufficient reliability to permit statistical evaluation, even if the actual absolute values had been higher.

The relevant data for the total group are given in TABLE 6. It can be seen that for the overwhelming majority of these cases it was the first withdrawal treatment, and alcohol was the only etiologic factor. Less than 10% had in the past experienced episodes of alcoholic psychosis. Most of the cases did not present features compatible with the picture of the end-stage drunkard, which is in keeping with the noncompulsory character of treatment in this institution. It should also be pointed out that, owing to lack of facilities, manifest internal disease requiring hospital treatment precludes admission to this sanitarium. About 80% of the patients were daily imbibers. The average daily alcohol intake of roughly 180 g ethanol in this group compares well with figures reported from other groups of alcoholics of different nationality.[74]

In 320 alcoholics, liver biopsies could be performed during withdrawal; in an additional 14 cases previous or present clinical examination had shown well-established, in some of them temporarily decompensated, cirrhosis of the liver. These 334 cases were arranged in 4 groups according to the length of drinking history, and the percentage of cases with normal histology, fatty infiltration, potentially precirrhotic lesions, and cirrhosis was assessed (FIGURE 1).

It becomes evident that the incidence of cirrhosis and precirrhotic lesions rose steadily with increasing length of drinking history. Conversely, the percentage of uncomplicated fatty infiltration as well as of cases with normal histology decreased to finally 13.5 or 4%, respectively. The calculated mean daily alcohol consumption in these 4 groups, however, also rose with increasing duration of alcohol abuse, indicating that the influence of these 2 variables could not be determined separately. Therefore, two subgroups (A and B) of 108 alcoholics each with a daily consumption of either less or more than 160 g ethanol were selected, who were strictly comparable with respect to duration of alcohol abuse (mean 7.9 ± 4 years), age, and body weight. The average daily intake for group A was 126 g (100–152 g), for group B 227 g (188–266 g) of ethanol. Histology showed that the percentage of precirrhotic lesions was more than twice as high in group B (32%) as in group A (14%). Cirrhosis morbidity was nil in group A and 14% in group B, a difference of high statistical significance. This suggested that in the absence of other cirrhogenic factors alcohol abuse led to cirrhosis in some of the subjects only if their mean daily alcohol intake had been sufficiently high.

The reason why a threshold dose of 160 g of ethanol per day was chosen for

TABLE 6

Synopsis of Relevant Data for a Group of 526 German Alcoholics Examined During Voluntary Withdrawal Treatment

Mean Age:	40.0 ± 10.5 years
(range: 19–64 years)	
Somatic History:	
Infectious hepatitis:	
(average: 20.4 years prior to present examination)	62 cases (=12%)
Alcohol as sole etiologic factor:	325 cases (=62%)
First withdrawal treatment:	455 cases (=86%)
Previous episodes of DT:	45 cases (=8.6%)
Mean Duration of Alcohol Abuse:	9.1 ± 5.8 years
(range: 1–36 years)	
Subgroups: I) 158 cases:	1–5 y. (3.5 ± 1.3 years)
II) 191 cases:	6–10 y. (7.8 ± 1.4 years)
III) 120 cases:	11–15 y. (12.8 ± 1.5 years)
IV) 57 cases:	>15 y. (21.1 ± 5.4 years)
Daily Alcohol Consumption:	
(reliable data in 417 cases)	
Mean daily intake:	178.5 g ethanol/day
(range: 27–468 g/day)	
Average of minimum admitted:	145 g ethanol/day
Average of maximum admitted:	212 g ethanol/day
Subgroups: <160 g/day:	168 cases (=40%)
160–240 g/day:	186 cases (=45%)
>240 g/day:	63 cases (=15%)

differentiation between these 2 groups was a suggestion made by Péquignot.[97–99] Up to 1970, Péquignot[100] had collected a total of 381 case reports of cirrhosis from hospitals of 7 French towns and an equal number of noncirrhotic controls, closely matched as to sex, age, body weight, and nutritional habits (TABLE 7). Although careful nutritional histories revealed no significant difference in caloric or protein intake between patients and controls, mean daily alcohol consumption had been more than twice as high in the patients with cirrhosis as in the controls. About 60% of the cirrhotics had admitted an average daily consumption exceeding 160 g for roughly 20 to 25 years.

A biochemical explanation for choosing this threshold dosage may be seen in the fact that the rate at which the average human being can metabolize alcohol has been estimated to range between 100 and—as an absolute maximum—200 mg per

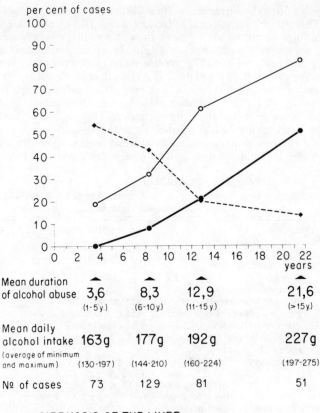

per cent of cases

FIGURE 1. Relative frequency of cirrhosis and precirrhotic lesions and its relation to the volume of alcohol abuse among 334 drinkers.

kg body weight per hour;[137] the lower value would account for the complete disposal of 160 to 180 g of ethanol per day for a person weighing between 65 and 75 kg. Provided that this intake is evenly spaced over the 24 hours of the day, it would not entail an elevation of the blood alcohol concentration. The alcoholic, however, is interested in an intake per time unit that exceeds his total capacity for disposal and produces intoxication. Maximum possibly daily alcohol consumption will usually be self-limiting by virtue of the narcotic action of alcohol. If, on the other hand, an alcoholic has become sufficiently dependent he may experience partial withdrawal phenomena during a drinking episode if his blood alcohol level drops, even though this fall may be relatively small.[78] An addicted alcoholic will therefore try to maintain a more or less continuous intake of alcohol higher than his capacity for disposal. This means that the total amount of alcohol consumed during his drinking life is largely dependent on the length of his drinking history and thus becomes a function of time.

In order to introduce a quantifiable element of individuality, mean daily alcohol intake was expressed as mg/kg body weight/hour. FIGURE 2 shows that the mean figures for duration of abuse as well as intake per kg body weight rose steadily from normal histology to cirrhosis of the liver, indicating that there may be a quantifiable correlation. Theoretical averages of this kind are, of course, not applicable to real-life drinking habits, since considerable day-to-day fluctuation of intake has been demonstrated in free-choice drinking experiments.[78,79] If we assume that the intake is spaced over the 16 waking hours of the day, the figures for mean intake would have been 120, 145, 169, 167, and 186 mg/kg/h, respectively. A mean intake of 186 mg/kg per 16 hours over 17 years, as recorded in cirrhosis, would correspond well with figures for the absolute maximum rate of disposal (180 mg/kg/h) reported by Thompson,[134] which would be accompanied by a more or less continuous elevation of blood alcohol levels during waking hours. Beyond that, any reduction of caloric or protein intake would have resulted in an additional increase in blood alcohol levels at sustained or even decreased volumes of intake.[65,78-81]

Preliminary rough calculations based on several subgroups within the total 526 cases had suggested that the total amounts of alcohol consumed per kg of body weight during drinking life correlated positively with the incidence of cirrhosis. Therefore, all histologically examined cases with presumably reliable data on duration of alcohol abuse and average daily intake were included in a subsample comprising 265 alcoholics, 239 of whom had been steady daily drinkers; only in 24 cases had there been so-called weekend-drinking, and 2 patients had reported a pattern of periodic drinking. The subsample contained 108 subjects with severe liver damage, histologically defined as exceeding in degree uncomplicated fatty liver, and 39 with cirrhosis. For each patient the dose-by-time product was computed on a body-weight basis. The individual product values were then grouped according to rank into 13 classes and within each class plotted against the percentage of severe liver damage and the incidence of cirrhosis of the liver.

TABLE 7

Alcohol Consumption in 381 French Patients with Cirrhosis of the Liver
as Compared to an Equal Number of Noncirrhotic Controls[100]

	Cirrhosis of "alcoholic" or cryptogenic etiology (n = 381)		Noncirrhotic controls (n = 381)	
Mean daily intake in g ethanol	196		82	
Frequency distribution of alcohol consumption	No. of cases	%	No. of cases	%
<80 g/day	13	4	198	52
80–160 g/day	142	37	146	38
>160 g/day	226	59	37	10
	381	100	381	100

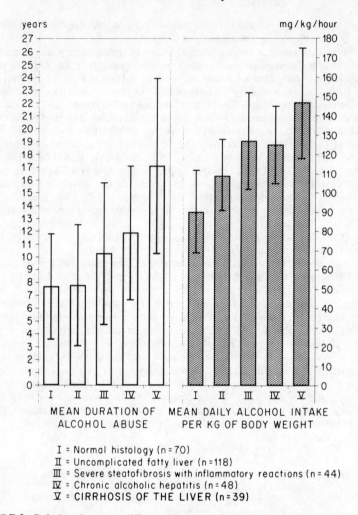

FIGURE 2. Relation between different stages of alcoholic liver disease and volume of alcohol abuse in 320 histologically examined cases (mean ± standard deviation of length of drinking history and of alcohol intake calculated per kg body weight and hour).

Considering the doubtful reliability even of cross-checked data on past consumption habits, it was expected to find at best only a loose correlation. However, for this fairly homogeneous group of mostly steady daily drinkers, analysis of regression showed a remarkably significant relation between total amounts of alcohol ingested per kg body weight and relative frequency of cirrhosis as well as of liver lesions of more than merely metabolic origin, e.g. simple fatty liver (FIGURES 3 and 4). Since in the majority of these cases the clinical histories had not revealed any etiologic factor other than alcohol abuse, this strongly suggests a cause-effect relationship but also gives evidence of the importance of individual susceptibility. If one follows Péquignot's estimate[98] that a daily intake of 180 g of ethanol maintained for roughly 25 years could be considered as an "average cirrhogenic dose," this would correspond to a total intake of about 4200 liters of 100-proof U.S. whiskey at a body weight of 70 kg. For the group of German alcoholics presented here, an intake of this size and duration would have been connected with a 50% risk of suffering from cirrhosis of the liver at the end of this period. In an additional 30% of the cases in this class, potentially precirrhotic lesions were present (FIGURE 4). A hypothetical calculation of this kind would, in a strict sense, be applicable only to this group of alcoholics, and reflections of this nature should not be misused to construe, for instance, some sort of "formula" that most certainly would be an unwarranted oversimplification of biological interdependencies.

An experimental counterpart for this clinical experience was recently described by Rubin et al.[115,116] They succeeded for the first time in producing the whole range of alcohol-induced liver lesions as seen in human pathology, including cirrhosis of the liver, in nonhuman primates after only 4 years of feeding them

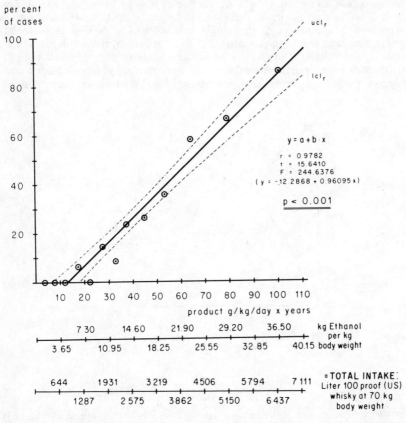

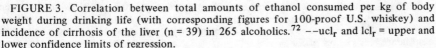

FIGURE 3. Correlation between total amounts of ethanol consumed per kg of body weight during drinking life (with corresponding figures for 100-proof U.S. whiskey) and incidence of cirrhosis of the liver (n = 39) in 265 alcoholics.[72] --ucl_r and lcl_r = upper and lower confidence limits of regression.

nutritionally adequate diets in which alcohol replaced 50% of total calories as isocaloric substitute for carbohydrates. The daily alcohol intake in these baboons
ranged between 4.5 and 8.3 g of ethanol per kg body weight, which corresponds
to an hourly influx of 186 to 346 mg of ethanol per kg body weight. This influx
lies well above the maximum figures for alcohol disposal in the human and permits alcohol to continuously exert its pharmacologic effect during the whole
length of the experiment.

It was attempted to draw a rough summary sketch of the pattern of alcohol
consumption that, in view of the heterogeneity of drinking patterns, is probably
the most hazardous one for a primarily healthy subject in promoting alcoholic
liver disease up to the final stage of cirrhosis, irrespective of the influence of additional enhancing factors (FIGURE 5). For the individual drinker who has passed
the prodromal stage of alcoholism the danger will probably be greatest if for an
uninterrupted prolonged stretch of time (months? years?) the rate of alcohol intake is kept high enough to maintain a more or less persistently elevated blood
alcohol level. The rate of influx will have to be raised accordingly with increasing
tissue tolerance due to metabolic adaptation or may be lowered if metabolism is
slowed down as a result of, for instance, inadequate nutrition. As compared with
this pattern, a succession of drinking bouts, even if they lead to severe acute
intoxication, is in the long run probably less dangerous, if these bouts are interrupted by intermittent abstinence of sufficient length during which the excep-
tionally high regenerative potential of the liver parenchyma will have a chance
for repair of damage. In the absence of additional cirrhogenic factors, it seems

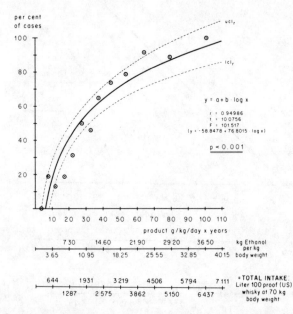

FIGURE 4. Correlation between total amounts of ethanol consumed per kg of body
weight during drinking life (with corresponding figures for 100-proof U.S. whiskey) and
incidence of severe liver damage (n = 108; severe steatofibrosis with inflammatory reactions;
chronic alcoholic hepatitis; cirrhosis) in 265 alcoholics.[72] --ucl$_r$ and lcl$_r$ = upper and lower
confidence limits of regression.

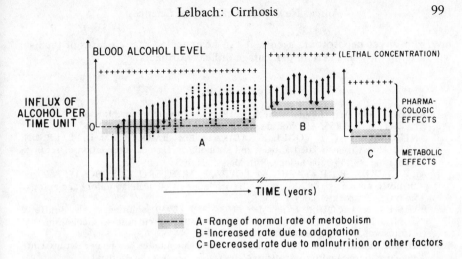

FIGURE 5. Pattern of drinking that is probably most hazardous as regards development of cirrhosis in the alcoholic.

that only a certain percentage of heavy drinkers will live long enough and be able to drink hard enough to develop alcoholic cirrhosis. What is meant by "hard enough" will be individually determined within a wide range of biological variability.

SUMMARY

The obvious and so far unresolved discrepancy between the notoriously high rate of alcoholism in cirrhosis of the liver throughout the Western world and the apparently low incidence of cirrhosis in chronic alcoholics is still a challenge for clinical investigation. There is no doubt that alcohol ingested in large doses for prolonged periods, among other undesirable consequences, has a deleterious effect on the liver, the organ that is the predominant site of alcohol metabolism. If it seems reasonable to postulate that alcohol per se can be a noxious agent for the liver—for which concept circumstantial evidence is increasing—then the dual nature of this substance must be taken into consideration. Up to a certain intake per time unit, alcohol is readily metabolized and completely disposed of by several physiologic mechanisms. However, if the ingestion of alcohol exceeds the capacity of these systems, the pharmacologic or toxic aspect of this molecule becomes manifest. This precludes any simple or straight dose-response relationship as regards alcohol-induced liver damage of more than mere metabolic importance, such as alcoholic fatty liver. In order to elucidate the essential factors in the relationship between the volume of alcohol abuse and the development of cirrhosis in alcoholics, a large body of clinical and histologic data as well as of cross-checked information on drinking habits was collected in a total of 526 male alcoholics undergoing voluntary withdrawal treatment in a special institution in West Germany. In spite of the drawbacks of a retrospective study of this kind, it could be demonstrated that for this sample a close correlation existed between the incidence of cirrhosis of the liver or of precirrhotic lesions, respectively, and the total volume of alcohol ingested over the years of drinking. It was also shown that individual susceptibility—whatever its biological counterpart may be—plays an equally important role. Owing to the peculiar properties that distinguish alcohol from direct hepatotoxic agents, it can be expected that cirrhosis of the liver will develop only in a certain percentage of heavy drinkers.

REFERENCES

1. ALCOHOLISM AND LIVER DISEASE. 1960. Gastroenterology 39: 643.
2. ALLERT, M. L. 1955. Alkoholismus und Leberzirrhose. Med. Klin.: 1815.
3. ANTHONY, P. P., C. L. VOGEL, F. SADIKALI, L. F. BARKER & M. R. PETERSON. 1972. Hepatitis-associated antigen and antibody in Uganda: correlation of serological testing with histopathology. Brit. Med. J. 1: 403.
4. ARMAS-CRUZ, R., R. YAZIGI, O. LOPEZ, E. MONTERO, G. LOBO. 1951. Portal cirrhosis. An analysis of 208 cases with correlation of clinical, laboratory and autopsy findings. Gastroenterology 17: 327.
5. BARBIER & JACQUIS. Lyon Med. 163: 719 (1939), quoted by N. Joliffe & E. M. Jellinek. 1941. Vitamin deficiencies and liver cirrhosis in alcoholism. VII. Cirrhosis of the liver. Quart. J. Stud. Alcohol 2: 544.
6. BAUMBERGER, N. 1967. Alkoholische Leberschäden unter besonderer Berücksichtigung des Zieve-Syndroms. Inaugural-Dissertation. Zürich, Switzerland.
7. VON BAUMGARTEN, P. 1907. Über die durch Alkohol hervorzurufenden pathologisch-histologischen Veränderungen. Berlin. Klin. Wschr. 44: 1331.
8. BLOOMFIELD, A. L. 1938. The natural history of chronic hepatitis (cirrhosis of the liver). Amer. J. Med. Sci. 195: 429.
9. BÖRNER, P. 1961. Ätiologie und Todesursachen der verschiedenen Formen der Leberzirrhose in den Jahren 1955–1959. Deutsch. Med. Wschr. 86: 43.
10. BOLES, R. S. & J. F. CLARK. 1936. The role of alcohol in cirrhosis of the liver. A clinical and pathologic study based on four thousand autopsies. J.A.M.A. 107: 1200.
11. BOLES, R. S., R. S. CREW & L. W. DUNBAR. 1947. Alcoholic cirrhosis. J.A.M.A. 134: 670.
12. BORHANMANESH, F., A. GHAVAMI, W. DUTZ & S. BAGHERI. 1971. Cirrhosis of the liver in Iran. A prospective study on 66 cases. J. Chron. Dis. 23: 891–905.
13. BRICK, I. B. & E. D. PALMER. 1964. One thousand cases of portal cirrhosis of the liver. Arch. Int. Med. 113: 501.
14. CAROLI, J., P. MAINGUET, P. RICORDEAU & A. FOURES. 1959. De l'importance de la laparoscopie et de la laparoscopie en couleurs dans la classification anatomo-clinique des cirrhoses du foie. Cirrhose alcoolique et nutritionelle. Rapports présenté au XXXIIe Congrès Francais de Médécine, Lausanne 1959. Masson. Paris, France.
15. ČERLEK, S. 1964. Comparative analysis of clinical symptoms and of findings at autopsy in cirrhosis of the liver. Acta hepatosplen. (Stuttgart) 11: 74.
16. CHAPMAN, B. L. 1966. Cirrhosis of the liver, Newcastle, N.S.W.: a study of 98 cases. Med. J. Aust. 1: 51.
17. CHÜN, T., Ch. KUO-HAO & H. SHUANG-FENG. 1964. A study on the morphology and etiology of Laennec's cirrhosis. Chin. Med. J. (Peking) 83: 142.
18. CONN, H. O., W. SCHREIBER, ST. G. ELKINGTON & TH. R. JOHNSON. 1969. Cirrhosis and diabetes. I. Increased incidence of diabetes in patients with Laeenec's cirrhosis. Amer. J. Digest. Dis. 14: 837.
19. CONSTAM, CH. 1943. Über Laennecsche Lebercirrhose. Klinische Auswertung von 160 autoptisch bestätigten Lebercirrhosen der Medizinischen Universitätsklinik Zürich aus den Jahren 1937–1940. Helv. Med. Acta 10: 507.
20. CREUTZFELDT, W. & K. BECK. 1966. Erhebungen über Ätiologie, Pathogenese, Therapieerfolge und Überlebenszeit an einem unausgewählten Krankengut von 560 Patienten mit Leberzirrhose. Deutsch. Med. Wschr. 91: 682.
21. DAOUD, A. S., L. G. JAGOVIC & R. A. FLORENTIN. 1962. Interrelationship of cirrhosis of the liver, alcohol intake, coronary arteriosclerosis and myocardial infarct. Circulation 26: 650.
22. DELORE, B. & M. DEVANT. 1939. Sur la proportion des cas d'alcoolisme chez les malades d'un service hospitalier. Communication à la société médicale des Hôpitaux de Lyon. Lyon Méd. 162: 713.

23. DOUGLAS, B. E. & A. M. SNELL. 1950. Portal cirrhosis: an analysis of 444 cases with notes on modern methods of treatment. Gastroenterology 15: 407.
24. EPPINGER, H. 1937. Die Leberkrankheiten. Allgemeine und spezielle Pathologie und Therapie der Leber. J. Springer. Vienna, Austria.
25. EVANS, N. & P. A. GRAY. 1938. Laennec's cirrhosis. Report of 217 cases. J. A.M.A. 110: 1159.
26. FAGIN, I. D. & F. M. THOMPSON. 1944. Cirrhosis of the liver. An analysis of seventy-one cases. Ann. Intern. Med. 21: 285.
27. FAHR, TH. 1909. Zur Frage des chronischen Alkoholismus. Verhandl. Deutsch. Patholog. Gesellschaft: 13. Tagung. 162.
28. FALCK, I. & G. HORN. 1957. Klinische Studien zur Leberzirrhose. IV. Zur Ätiologie der Leberzirrhose. Z. Ges. Inn. Med. 12: 610.
29. FALCK, I., H. G. HEINRICH, E. JUTZI, W. KÖHLER, G. MOHNICKE & K. VETTER. 1962. Laboratoriumsuntersuchungen bei Leberkrankheiten. II. Mitteilung: Leberzirrhose. Deutsch. Z. Verdau.- u. Stoffwechselkr. 22: 137.
30. FAUVERT, R., J. P. BENHAMOU, P. BOIVIN, F. DARNIS & L. HARTMANN. 1959. Biologie des cirrhoses alcooliques. Cirrhose alcoolique et nutritionelle, rapports présentés au XXXIIe Congrès Français de Médecine. Lausanne 1959. Masson. Paris, France.
31. FERNANDO, P. B., O. R. MENDOZA & P. K. AJASURIYA. 1948. Cirrhosis of the liver in Ceylon and its relation to diet. Lancet 2: 205.
32. FLEMING, G. R. & A. M. SNELL. 1942. Portal cirrhosis with ascites: An analysis of 200 cases, with special reference to prognosis and treatment. Amer. J. Dig. Dis. 9: 115.
33. FORMAD, H. F. 1886. The "pig-backed" or alcoholic kidney of drunkards. Trans. Ass. Amer. Physicians 1: 225.
34. FORSHAW, J. 1972. Alcoholic cirrhosis of the liver. Brit. Med. J. 4: 608.
35. FRANK H. & I. LEODOLTER. 1971. Leberzirrhose. Klinisch-statistische Untersuchungen mit besonderer Berücksichtigung der Prognose. Deutsch. Med. Wschr. 96: 1291.
36. FRANKEN, F. H. & D. MOHR. 1969. Katamnestische und klinische Untersuchungen zur Prognose der Leberzirrhose. Acta Hepatosplen. 16: 185.
37. GARCEAU, A. J., T. C. CHALMERS & THE BOSTON INTER-HOSPITAL LIVER GROUP. 1963. The natural history of cirrhosis. I. Survival with esophageal varices. New Eng. J. Med. 268: 469.
38. GIGGLBERGER, H. 1959. Zur Ätiologie der Laennec'schen Cirrhose. Münch. Med. Wschr. 101: 858.
39. GIGGLBERGER, H. 1968. Zur Ätiologie der Lebercirrhose. Klinisch-statistische Untersuchungen an 400 Kranken. Acta Hepatosplen. 15: 415.
40. GROS, H. 1956. Zur Ätiologie der Laennec'schen Leberzirrhose. Medizinische 1: 686.
41. HÄLLEN, J. & I. LINNE. 1970. Cirrhosis of the liver in one community. A study of liver cirrhosis from a city with one hospital: incidence, etiology, and prognosis. In Alcoholic Cirrhosis and Other Toxic Hepatopathias. A. Engel & T. Larsson, Eds.: 336. Nordiska Bokhandelns. Förlag. Stockholm, Sweden.
42. HALL, E. M. & W. A. MORGAN. 1939. Progressive alcoholic cirrhosis. A clinical and pathological study of sixty-eight cases. Arch. Pathol. 27: 672.
43. HALL, E. M., A. Y. OLSEN & F. D. DAVIS. 1953. Portal cirrhosis. Clinical and pathologic review of 782 cases from 16,600 necropsies. Amer. J. Pathol. 29: 993.
44. HALONEN, P. & N. SAKSELA. 1946. Liver cirrhosis in Finland. Ann. Med. Intern. Fenn. 35: 7.
45. HARTMANN, F. & S. KOTTKE. 1958. Beobachtungen zur Differentialdiagnose von Hepatitis, Cholangitis und Leberzirrhose. Münch. Med. Wschr. 100: 705.
46. HEER, H. R. 1969. Die Leberzirrhosen und die primären Leberkarzinome im Sektionsgut des Histopathologischen Instituts der Universität Zürich 1949–1967. Europäische Hochschulschriften, Reihe VII, Medizin 2. Verlag H. Lang & Cie. AG, Bern, Switzerland.
47. HEIMANN, R. & D. ARDICHVILI. 1968. Étude d'une centaine de cirrhoses bruxelloises. I. Aspects sociologiques. Acta Gastroent. Belg. 31: 107.

48. HOFFMAN, J. & J. R. LISA. 1947. Significance of clinical findings in cirrhosis of the liver. A study of 93 autopsied cases. Amer. J. Med. Sci. 214: 525.
49. HOLZNER, H., E. RISSEL & K. SPRINGER. 1956. Zur Ätiologie und Todesursache der verschiedenen Formen der Leberzirrhose. Deutsch. Med. Wschr. 81: 264.
50. HOWARD, R. C. & J. WATSON. 1947. Antecedent jaundice in cirrhosis of the liver. Arch. Intern. Med. 80: 1.
51. JAGIC, N. 1906. Klinische Beiträge zur Ätiologie und Pathogenese der Leberzirrhosen. Wien. Klin. Wschr. 19: 1058.
52. JAIN, S., A. PATON & M. H. WANSBROUGH-JONES. 1973. Cirrhosis in Birmingham. Midl. Med. Rev. 9: 13.
53. JAIN, S., A. PATON & M. H. WANSBROUGH-JONES. 1973. Alcoholic cirrhosis of the liver. Brit. Med. J. 1: 116.
54. JOLLIFFE, N. & E. M. JELLINEK. 1941. Vitamin deficiencies and liver cirrhosis in alcoholism. VII. Cirrhosis of the liver. Quart. J. Stud. Alcohol 2: 544.
55. KAEDING, A. 1955. Ätiologische Faktoren der Leberzirrhose. Ärztl. Wschr. 10: 497.
56. KALK, H. 1954. Cirrhose und Narbenleber. 1. Aufl. F. Enke. Stuttgart, Germany.
57. KALK, H. 1957. Cirrhose und Narbenleber. 2. Aufl. F. Enke. Stuttgart, Germany.
58. KAYSER, O. 1888. Ein Beitrag zur Alkoholfrage. Inaugural-Dissertation. Kiel, Germany.
59. KERN, W. 1913. Über Leberveränderungen bei chronischem Alkoholismus. Z. Hyg. Infektionskr. 73: 143. (Leipzig).
60. KIMBALL, S., W. H. CHAPPKE & S. SANES. 1947. Jaundice in relation to cirrhosis of the liver. J.A.M.A. 134: 662.
61. KIRSHBAUM, J. D. & N. SHURE. 1943. Alcoholic cirrhosis of the liver: a clinical and pathologic study of 356 cases selected from 12,267 autopsy cases. J. Lab. Clin. Med. 28: 721.
62. KLOPSTOCK, F. 1906. Alkoholismus und Lebercirrhose. Virchows Archiv 184: 304.
63. KÜHN, H. A. & H. TILSE. 1961. From H. A. Kühn, Die Ätiologie der Zirrhose vom klinischen Standpunkt. Deutsch. Ges. Verd.-u. Stoffwechselkrankh. 20. Tagung, Kassel, Oktober 1959. Gastroenterologia (Basel). Suppl. 95: S. 53.
64. LEE, F. I. 1966. Cirrhosis and hepatoma in alcoholics. Gut. 7: 77.
65. LEEVY, C. M. 1973. The influence of alcohol and malnutrition on drug metabolism. International Symposium on Hepatotoxicity. Tel Aviv, Israel, March 1973.
66. LEEVY, C. M. & W. TEN HOVE. 1967. Pathogenesis and sequelae of liver disease in alcoholic man. In Biochemical Factors in Alcoholism. R. P. Maickel, Ed.: 151. Pergamon Press. Oxford, England.
67. LEEVY, C. M. 1967. Clinical diagnosis, evaluation and treatment of liver disease in alcoholics. Fed. Proc. 26: 1445.
68. LEEVY, C. M. 1968. Cirrhosis in alcoholics. Med. Clin. N. Amer. 52: 1445.
69. LEEVY, C. M. 1975. The lymphocyte in alcohol liver disease. In Alcoholic Liver Pathology. Y. Israel, J. Khanna & H. Kalant, Eds., Addiction Research Foundation. Toronto, Canada.
70. LELBACH, W. K. 1966, 1967. Leberschäden bei chronischem Alkoholismus. Ergebnisse einer klinischen, klinisch-chemischen und bioptisch-histologischen Untersuchung an 526 Alkoholkranken während der Entziehungskur in einer offenen Trinkerheilstätte. Acta Hepatosplen. 13: 321; 14: 9.
71. LELBACH, W. K. 1971. Die alkoholische Fettleber—ihre Rückbildung durch Alkohol-Abstinenz. Münch. Med. Wschr. 113: 1549.
72. LELBACH, W. K. 1972. Dosis-Wirkungs-Beziehung bei Alkohol-Leberschäden. Deutsch. Med. Wschr. 97: 1435.
73. LELBACH, W. K. 1971. Alkoholischer Leberschaden und Alkoholentwöhnung. In Alcohol and the Liver. W. Gerok, K. Sickinger & H. H. Hennekeuser Eds.: 537. F. K. Schattauer-Verlag. New York, N.Y.
74. LELBACH, W. K. 1974. Organic pathology related to volume and pattern of alcohol use. In Research Advances in Alcohol and Drug Problems. Y. Israel, Ed.: John Wiley & Sons. New York, N.Y.

75. LELBACH, W. K. 1975. Quantitative aspects of drinking in alcoholic liver cirrhosis. *In* Alcoholic Liver Pathology. Y. Israel, J. Khanna & H. Kalant, Eds.: Addiction Research Foundation, Toronto.
76. LIEBER, C. S. & E. RUBIN. 1968. Ethanol—A hepatotoxic drug. Gastroenterology 54: 642.
76a. LIEBER, C. S. 1973. Hepatic and metabolic effects of alcohol (1966–1973). Gastroenterology 65: 821.
77. MALLORY, F. B. 1932. New Eng. J. Med. 206: 1231. From Stone, W. D., N. R. Kitslam & A. Paton. 1968. The natural history of cirrhosis. Quart. J. Med. 37: 119 No. 128.
78. MELLO, N. K. & J. H. MENDELSON. 1970. Experimentally induced intoxication in alcoholics: a comparison between programed and spontaneous drinking. J. Pharmacol. Exp. Ther. 173: 101.
79. MELLO, N. K. & J. H. MENDELSON. 1971. A quantitative analysis of drinking patterns in alcoholics. Arch. Gen. Psychiat. 25: 527.
80. MELLO, N. K. & J. H. MENDELSON. 1972. Drinking patterns during work-contingent and noncontingent alcohol acquisition. Psychosom. Med. 34: 139.
81. MENDELSON, J. H. 1970. Biologic concomitants of alcoholism. I and II. New Eng. J. Med. 283: 24–32; 71–81.
82. MENDELSON, J. H. & N. K. MELLO. 1973. Alcohol-induced hyperlipidemia and beta lipoprotein. Science 180: 1372.
83. MNUSHKIN, A. S. & E. I. POLYAK. 1959. Njekatoryje osobennosti etiologii i kliniki tsirrosov pečeni. (Certain features specific to the etiology and clinic of liver cirrhosis). Klin. Med. (Moskva) 37: 84.
84. MOESCHLIN, S. & P. RIGHETTI. 1970. Wine and cirrhosis. *In* Alcoholic Cirrhosis and Other Hepatopathias. A. Engel and T. Larsson, Eds. Nordiska Bokhandelns Förlag. Stockholm, Sweden.
84a. MÜTING, D., N. LACKAS, H. REIKOWSKI & S. RICHMOND. 1966. Leberzirrhose und Diabetes mellitus. Deutsch. Med. Wschr. 91: 1433.
85. MUNZER, D. 1968. The pathogenesis of cirrhosis of the liver in the Middle East. A study of 210 cases. Amer. J. Gastroenterol. 49: 241.
86. MUSSINI, H. & C. CHIERICI. 1960. Sulla etiopatogenesi della cirrosi epatica. Clinica (Bologna) 20: 25.
87. NAKAMURA, T., S. NAKAMURA & T. KIMURA. 1959. Studies on cirrhosis of the liver. V. Etiology. Tohoku J. Exp. Med. 69: 225.
88. NAUNYN, B. Lebercirrhose. 1904. Verh. Deutsch. Ges. Path., 8. Tagung, 1904, Heft No. 2: 59. Strassburg, Germany.
89. NISSEN, A. H. 1920. Cirrhosis of the liver showing jaundice and ascites. An analytic study of 117 cases. Med. Clin. N. Amer. 4: 555.
90. VON OLDERSHAUSEN, H. F. 1962. Zur Klinik und Pathogenese der alkoholischen Leberschäden. Eine Studie über funktionelle und morphologische Leberveränderungen nach akuter und chronischer Einwirkung von Alkohol und deren Abgrenzung von Leberschäden anderer Ätiologie. Habilitationsschrift. Berlin, Germany.
91. VON OLDERSHAUSEN, H. F. 1962. Klinische und experimentelle Beiträge zur Frage der Leberschädigung durch Äthylalkohol. Deutsch. Ges. f. Verd.-u. Stoffwechselkrankh. 21. Tagung. Gastroenterologia (Basel). Suppl. to 97: 215.
92. VON OLDERSHAUSEN, H. F. 1964. Über die Pathogenese alkoholischer Leberschäden. Deutsch. Med. Wschr. 89: 867.
93. VON OLDERSHAUSEN, H. F. 1970. Alkoholische Leberschäden. Therapiewoche 20: 59.
94. P'AN CY et al., Achievements in the research on hepatic diseases in the period of 10 years since the foundation of the People's Republic of China. Zhong Neike Z. 7: 1027 (1959) from: Chün, T., Ch. Kuo-Hao & H. Shuang Feng. 1964. A study on the morphology and etiology of Laennec's cirrhosis. Chin. Med. J. (Peking) 83: 142 No. 17.
95. PATEK, A. J. & J. POST. 1941. Treatment of cirrhosis of the liver by a nutritious diet and supplement rich in vitamin B complex. J. Clin. Invest. 20: 481.

96. PATEK, A. J., J. POST, O. D. RATNOFF, H. MANKIN & R. W. HILLMAN. 1948. Dietary treatment of cirrhosis of the liver. J.A.M.A. **138:** 543.
97. PÉQUIGNOT, G. 1958. Enquête par interrogatoire sur les circonstances diététiques de la cirrhose alcoolique en France. Bull. Inst. Nat. Hyg. **13:** 719.
98. PÉQUIGNOT, G. 1961. Die Rolle des Alkohols bei der Aetiologie von Lebercirrhosen in Frankreich. Münch. Med. Wschr. **103:** 1464.
99. PÉQUIGNOT, G. 1963. Les enquêtes par interrogatoire permettent-elles de déterminer la fréquence de l'étiologie alcoolique des cirrhoses du foie? Bull. Acad. Nat. Méd. (Paris) **147:** 90.
100. PÉQUIGNOT, G. 1971. About the geographical aspects of cirrhosis. *In* Alcohol and the Liver. W. Gerok, K. Sickinger & H. H. Hennekeuser, Eds.: New York, N.Y.
101. PIESBERGEN, H. & J. JUNGERMANN. 1966. Zur Ätiologie und Pathogenese der Leberzirrhose. Z. Gastroenterol. **4:** 345.
102. PINTO CORREIA, J., M. E. AREIAS, E. MONTEIRO, M. GARNEL & F. MADEIRA. 1971. Liver Cirrhosis. Clinical experience with 274 unselected cases. Digestion **4:** 223.
103. POPP, L. 1943. Statistischer Beitrag zur Frage der Ätiologie der Leberzirrhose. Z. Klin. Med. **142:** 106.
104. POWELL, W. J., JR. & G. KLATSKIN. 1968. Duration of survival in patients with Laennec's cirrhosis. Influence of alcohol withdrawal, and possible effects of recent changes in general management of the disease. Amer. J. Med. **44:** 406.
105. RADHAKRISHNA RAO, M. V. 1933. An investigation into "decompensated" portal cirrhosis. Indian J. Med. Res. **21:** 389.
106. RATNOFF, O. D. & A. J. PATEK. 1942. The natural history of Laennec's cirrhosis of the liver; analysis of 386 cases. Medicine **21:** 207.
107. REID, N. C. R. W., P. W. BRUNT, W. B. BIAS, W. C. MADDREY, B. A. ALONSO & F. L. IBER. 1968. Genetic characteristics and cirrhosis: a controlled study of 200 patients. Brit. Med. J. **2:** 463.
108. RICKETTS, W. E., J. B. KIRSNER & W. L. PALMER. 1950. Clinical observations on the severity of liver failure in portal cirrhosis. Gastroenterology **15:** 245.
109. RILLIET, B. & CH. KEIL. 1950. Étude de la cirrhose hépatique pendant les années de guerre. Considérations sur les variations de la fréquence. Helv. Med. Acta Ser. A **17:** 532.
110. RIVA, G. & D. M. WEINER. 1960. Zur Ätiologie der Lebercirrhose. Bull. Schweiz. Akad. Med. Wiss. **16:** 65.
111. ROCH, M. & H. WOHLERS. 1931. Données statistiques concernant 431 cas de cirrhose. Presse méd. **39:** 1341.
112. ROCH, M. J. & J. FEHR. 1942. Les cirrhoses à la clinique médicale de Genève de 1931 à 1940. Rev. Méd. Suisse Rom. **62:** 81.
113. RUBIN, E. & C. S. LIEBER. 1968. Alcohol-induced hepatic injury in nonalcoholic volunteers. New Eng. J. Med. **278:** 869.
114. RUBIN, E. & C. S. LIEBER. 1968. Malnutrition and liver disease—an overemphasized relationship. Amer. J. Med. **45:** 1.
115. RUBIN, E. & C. S. LIEBER. 1973. Experimental alcoholic hepatitis: a new primate model. Science **182:** 712.
116. RUBIN, E. & C. S. LIEBER. 1974. Fatty liver, alcoholic hepatitis and cirrhosis produced by alcohol in primates. New Eng. J. Med. **290:** 128.
117. RUBIN, E., S. KRUS & H. POPPER. 1962. Pathogenesis of postnecrotic cirrhosis in alcoholics. Arch. Path. **73:** 288.
118. RUF-BÄCHTIGER, L. 1967. Zur Prognose der Lebercirrhose. Schweiz. Med. Wschr. **97:** 124.
119. SAĞLAM, T. 1949. Sur le traitement de la cirrhose hépatique. Schweiz. Med. Wschr. **79:** 497.
120. SCHNEIDERBAUR, A. 1964. Zur Frage der Häufigkeit der Zunahme und der Ätiologie der Leberzirrhose. Wien. Med. Wschr. **114:** 738.
121. SCHUBERT, R. 1940. Klinische Auswertung autoptisch bestätigter atrophischer Leberzirrhosen. Z. Klin. Med. **137:** 328.

122. SEIFERT, E. & H. DITTRICH. 1967. Zur Entwicklungsdauer chronischer posthepatischer Lebererkrankungen. Acta Hepatosplen. **14:** 341.
123. SELMAIR, H., V. ILIC & K. RADDATZ. 1970. Die Lebenserwartung der dekompensierten Leberzirrhose. Münch. Med. Wschr. **112:** 1241.
124. SEPÚLVEDA, B., E. ROJAS & L. LANDA. 1956. Los factores etiologicos en la cirrosis del higado. Rev. Invest. Clin. **8:** 189.
125. SHERLOCK, S. 1966. Waldenström's chronic active hepatitis. Acta Med. Scand. **179** Suppl 445: 426.
126. SHERLOCK, S., P. BRUNT & P. J. SCHEUER. 1971. Clinical and pathological aspects of alcoholic liver disease. *In* Alcohol and the Liver. W. Gerok, K. Sickinger & H. H. Hennekeuser, Eds. F. K. Schattauer Verlag. New York, N.Y.
127. STEINER, P. E., R. CAMAIN & J. NETIK. 1959. Observations on cirrhosis and liver cancer at Dakar, French West Africa. Cancer Res. **19:** 567.
128. STONE, W. D., N. R. K. ISLAM & A. PATON. 1968. The natural history of cirrhosis. Experience with an unselected group of patients. Quart. J. Med. **37:** 119.
129. SÜDHOF, H. 1954. Vergleichende Untersuchungen über die Häufigkeit chologener Zirrhosen, Beobachtungen am Krankengut der Göttinger Klinik in den Jahren 1946–1952. Münch. Med. Wschr. **96:** 607.
130. SUMMERSKILL, W. H. J., C. S. DAVIDSON, J. H. DIBLE, G. K. MALLORY, S. SHERLOCK, M. D. TURNER & ST. J. WOLFE. 1960. Cirrhosis of the liver. A study of alcoholic and non-alcoholic patients in Boston and London. New Eng. J. Med. **262:** 1.
131. SUNDBERG, M. & E. ADLERCREUTZ. 1959. Zur Kenntnis der Ätiologie der Lebercirrhose in Finnland. Acta Hepatosplen. **6:** 17.
132. SUTHERLAND, D. W. 1905. The pathology of cirrhosis of the liver. Indian Med. Gaz. **40:** 121.
133. TERRIS, M. 1967. Epidemiology of cirrhosis of the liver: national mortality data. Amer. J. Public Health **57:** 2076.
134. THOMPSON, G. N. Alcoholism. 1956. C. C Thomas. Springfield, Ill.
135. WADMAN, B., E. S. SPENCER & I. WERNER. 1971. Liver cirrhosis in three Scandinavian communities. Acta Med. Scand. **189:** 221.
136. WANG, CH'ENG FA. 1936. Cirrhosis of the liver. I. Etiology, symptomatology, liver function tests, and gastric juice findings. Chin. Med. J. (Peking) **30:** 891.
137. WESTERFELD, W. W. & M. P. SHULMAN. 1959. Metabolism and caloric value of alcohol. J.A.M.A. **170:** 197.
138. WILDHIRT, E. 1955. Klinische und bioptische Beobachtungen über die Ätiologie der Leberzirrhose. Med. Klin. **50:** 1093.
139. WILDHIRT, E. 1971. Über die Rolle des Alkoholentzugs in der Therapie der alkoholischen Leberschäden. *In* Alcohol and the Liver. W. Gerok, K. Sickinger & H. H. Hennekeuser, Eds. F. K. Schattauer Verlag. New York, N.Y.
140. WILENS, S. L. 1947. The relationship of chronic alcoholism to atherosclerosis. J. A.M.A. **135:** 1136.
141. YENIKOMSHIAN, H. A. 1934. Nonalcoholic cirrhosis of the liver in the Lebanon and Syria. J.A.M.A. **103:** 660.
142. YOSHIDA, T., H. KAWATA, O. FUKUI, T. KOIZUMI, M. ASADA & M. WADA. 1965. Cirrhosis of the liver in Japan. Acta Hepatosplen. **12:** 268.

ALCOHOLIC HEPATITIS, CIRRHOSIS, AND IMMUNOLOGIC REACTIVITY

Carroll M. Leevy, Thomas Chen, and Rowen Zetterman

Division of Hepatology and Nutrition
Department of Medicine
New Jersey Medical School
College of Medicine and Dentistry of New Jersey
Newark, New Jersey 07103

Serial observations in over 40 alcoholics reveal there is a marked variation in the time required for transformation of alcoholic hepatitis to cirrhosis. Some exhibited morphologic evidence of cirrhosis in less than a year, while others took as long as 12 years before its appearance. No relationship could be established between the amount and type of alcoholic beverages and the dietary intake in patients who developed cirrhosis.[1]

These findings have led to the consideration that altered immunologic reactivity might be responsible for the conversion of alcoholic hepatitis to cirrhosis (FIGURE 1). This thesis is supported by the progressive shortening of the interval required for recurrence of alcoholic hepatitis with healing and subsequent resumption of alcoholism. An immunologic role in pathogenesis is also suggested by occasional hypersensitivity reactions following ingestion of alcoholic beverages; the ability of acetaldehyde to depolymerize protein, which could then serve as an antigen; and the morphologic findings in alcoholic hepatitis, which simulate an Arthus-like reaction and/or delayed hypersensitivity reaction.

BACKGROUND AND METHODOLOGY

Theoretically, either bursal dependent ("B" cell) hyperreactivity with the production of nonspecific antibodies and specific antibodies, or thymus dependent ("T" cell) hyperreactivity with the development of chemotactic, cytotoxic, and/or fibrogenic factors could be responsible for progressive necrosis and fibrosis in chronic liver disease. Recent studies indicate that both of these cell types produce blastogenic and migration inhibition factors and that their hyperreactivity overlaps in most autoimmune processes.

Patients with alcoholic hepatitis have a normal number of "B" cells when assayed by immunoglobulin labeling. An investigation of serum immunoglobulin patterns in patients with alcoholic hepatitis and cirrhosis reveals a nonspecific increase in IgG, IgA, and IgM. Although a relatively greater increase in IgA or IgM has been found, such increments are characteristic of individual reactivity and severity rather than causative factors. Immunofluorescent techniques show IgA separated and purified from cirrhotic sera binds to hyaline in alcoholic hepatitis, and it is postulated that this fraction may contain an antibody.[3] Antinuclear activity is suggested by nuclear staining by cirrhotic IgM. Moreover, enhancement of antibody titers to bacterial and dietary proteins is often present in the patient with alcoholic cirrhosis. These findings suggest that specific autoantibodies that contribute to tissue injury may be present in alcoholic liver disease. On the other hand, unlike other chronic liver diseases, such as biliary cirrhosis and chronic active hepatitis, which progress spontaneously, there is a lack of non-organ-specific antibodies in most patients with alcoholic hepatitis or cirrhosis (TABLE 1).

106

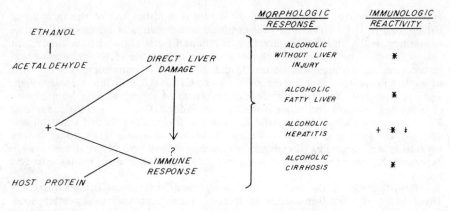

FIGURE 1. Role of immunologic reactivity in pathogenesis of liver disease of the alcoholic.

Nutrient depletion may have a profound influence on antibody production, so that in the malnourished alcoholic, special attention should be focused on nutrient balance in assessing humoral reactivity. Marked impairment of circulating antibody response to antigenic stimuli has been documented in pyridoxine deficiency. There is a qualitative difference in the type of antibody formed as well as a diminution in total quantity of antibody produced. This is not specifically related to inanition, since there is little correlation between growth and antibody response,[4] and pyridoxine antagonists will also inhibit antibody production.

CELL-MEDIATED LYMPHOCYTE REACTIVITY

Although histologic lesions of alcoholic hepatitis simulate the Arthus phenomenon, perhaps representing an antigen-antibody reaction, we have concentrated our efforts on studies of cell-mediated immunity in alcoholic hepatitis, since there is equal histologic evidence of host graft type of rejection reaction. Theoretically, skin tests should provide the best index to delayed sensitivity; however, the multiplicity of other exogenous and endogenous factors in the alcoholic have prevented interpretation of results of skin tests using the usual antigens. A higher incidence of sensitivity reactions is encountered, but this may be due to mechanisms other than liver injury.

Cell-mediated immunologic reactivity in alcoholic liver disease was first determined in our laboratory by addition of autologous liver to cultured lympho-

TABLE 1
Non-Organ-Specific Immune Markers in Sera of Chronic Liver Disease

	Percent of Antibodies to:		
	Mitochondria	Smooth Muscle	Nuclei
Chronic Active Hepatitis	20%	70%	35%
Primary Biliary Cirrhosis	90%	10%	5%
Alcoholic Cirrhosis	0%	5%	0%

cytes. Lymphocytes were cultured by use of a modification of the method of Hirschhorn et al.[5] Fifty ml of venous blood was drawn into a disposable syringe containing 1000 units of preservative-free heparin and allowed to sediment for 1 to 2 hours. The leukocyte-rich plasma was removed and the cells were harvested, washed 3 times, and counted, and 2 times 10^6 lymphocytes was added to each culture tube containing media-199 (GIBCO), penicillin, streptomycin, 1-glutamine, and 20% autologous human serum. Autologous liver homogenate (1.0 mg per culture) and other materials were added. Cultures were incubated at 37°C under 5% carbon dioxide and harvested at 3 or 5 days. Transformation was assessed by adding 2 mc of tritiated thymidine to cultures 24 hours before harvesting and assessing the degree of incorporation into DNA. Results were expressed by the stimulation index derived by dividing control values into test values.

A modification of the method of Soborg[6] and of Glade et al.[7] was used for direct assay of migration-inhibiting factor. Lymphocytes were harvested as described above and lymphocyte suspension was resuspended in 1.5 ml of "complete media." Heparin-free capillary tubes were filled with the cell suspension and sealed with Plasteline. The capillary tube was centrifuged in a micro-hematocrit centrifuge for 1 minute at 250 g. The tubes were then cut beneath the cell fluid interface and placed in a Lexy culture chamber sealed with silicone grease and cover slips. Studies were done in triplicate. Control chambers were filled with "complete media" only, and experimental chambers were filled with "complete media" plus autologous liver homogenate (1.0 mg per ml media) or other test agents. The cells were allowed to migrate for 18 hours at 37°C under 5% carbon dioxide atmosphere. The chambers were placed in an Omega D-2 enlarger and the projected image was traced, and areas of migration were determined by planimetry. The results were expressed as percent inhibition migration by test substances as compared to controls.

AUTOLOGOUS LIVER AND ETHANOL EFFECTS

Addition of autologous liver to cultured lymphocytes obtained from patients with alcoholic hepatitis evokes a significant increase in the stimulation index and a decrease in migration inhibition equivalent to that encountered in chronic active hepatitis and biliary cirrhosis (FIGURE 2). This does not occur in uncomplicated fatty liver or inactive cirrhosis of alcoholics. These findings have been interpreted as evidence that alcoholic hepatitis represents a delayed hypersensitivity reaction.

Absolute ethyl alcohol in amounts less than 4 mg per culture, or acetaldehyde in amounts less than 10 μg per culture added to cultured lymphocytes from patients with alcoholic hepatitis also evoked a significant increase in stimulation index (FIGURE 3). Acetaldehyde added to lymphocytes from patients with chronic active hepatitis also produced an increase in the stimulation index, suggesting encountered responses are nonspecific reactions on the part of injured lymphocytes. Lymphocyte reactivity to autologous liver and ethanol, noted originally, is no longer present when clinical and laboratory evidence of alcoholic hepatitis disappears. In contrast, when both of these test substances are added together, lymphocyte hyperreactivity reoccurs.[8] A combination of ethanol and autologous liver also produces a greater response during the period of active alcoholic hepatitis.

The specificity of lymphocyte reactivity to ethanol and acetaldehyde has been investigated. A molecule of ethanol, unlike acetaldehyde, does not display

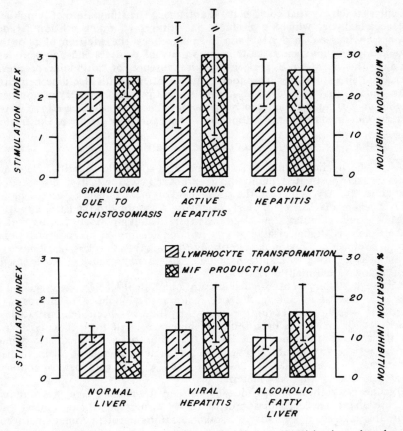

FIGURE 2. Influence of autologous liver on lymphocyte reactivity in various hepatic disorders.

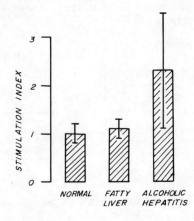

FIGURE 3. Influence of ethanol (4 mg) or acetaldehyde (10 μg) on lymphocyte stimulation index in liver disease of the alcoholic.

chemical reactivity that could make it antigenic. The stimulation of lymphocytes by acetaldehyde, which is produced in cultures to which ethanol is added, evokes an increase in 5 AMP and is enhanced by the addition of phosphodiesterase inhibitors such as caffeine. A variety of peptides and polypeptides including the hepatitis B antigen (despite absence of antibodies or previous hepatitis) also stimulates lymphocytes from patients with alcoholic hepatitis. It thus appears that acetaldehyde, hepatitis B antigen, and a variety of nonspecific agents may stimulate damaged lymphocytes. These nonspecific effects have, as yet, an undefined role in the pathogenesis of chronic liver disease of the alcoholic.

ALCOHOLIC HYALINE

Alcoholic hyaline, which is characteristic of alcoholic hepatitis, plays a key role in any postulated immunologic process in chronic liver disease of the alcoholic. It may represent the progenitor or morphologic effect of humoral and/or cell-mediated immunologic reactivity. According to the latter hypothesis, hyaline could stimulate sensitized cells to release lymphocyte factors that produce a delayed hypersensitivity-type reaction leading to necrosis and fibrosis; alternatively, it could stimulate antibody-forming cells to release antibodies that, in turn, by reacting with antigen, could be of key importance in development of morphologic abnormalities (FIGURE 4).

Although Mallory in his original description of alcoholic hyaline suggested that this material was noxious and a key factor in development of cirrhosis,[9] this postulate was not tested until recently. Hyaline has been demonstrated with macrophages, and it has been shown to be chemotactic for leukocytes.[10] There are three types of hyaline: type I with filaments that are 14.1 mm in diameter and run parallel to each other; type II whose filaments average 15.2 mm in diameter and are randomly oriented (FIGURE 6); and type III, composed of granular or homogenous electron-dense material.[11]

Hyaline is synthesized by ribosomes either attached or free; it accumulates because of increased production or decreased dispersal.[12] Histochemical studies show this material is a relatively insoluble, actinlike protein containing carbohydrate, lipid, and a large number of basic groups with arginine, tyrosine, and

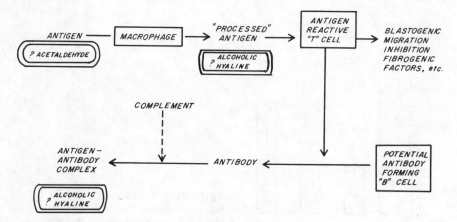

FIGURE 4. Possible role of alcoholic hyaline in immunologic reactivity in liver disease.

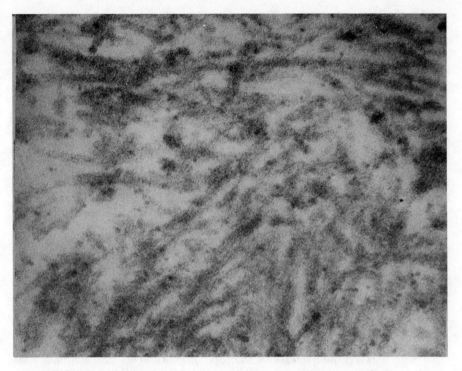

FIGURE 5. Electron micrograph of isolated and purified alcoholic hyaline.

sulfhydroxyl groups. Hyaline has been demonstrated in a large number of hepatic disorders, including alcoholic hepatitis, Indian childhood cirrhosis, Wilson's disease, and chronic active hepatitis. The histochemical reactivity of hyaline in these conditions differs, either because of contamination with microsomes, mitochondria, or cell sap, or because of chemical differences in hyaline associated with various hepatic disorders. This actinlike protein may now be isolated and purified by layering liver, which contains it over a discontinuous sucrose gradient, centrifuging at 99,000 *g*, incubating with deoxycholate, and extracting with guanidine.[13]

The availability of a purified extract of alcoholic hyaline permits in-depth studies of immunologic events. Addition of this material (10 μg protein per culture) to cultured lymphocytes from patients with alcoholic hepatitis causes a significant increase in production of stimulation and migration-inhibition factors (FIGURE 5). If both purified alcoholic hyaline and acetaldehyde are added to sensitized lymphocytes, a significant further increase in the stimulation index occurs. An assay of immunologic response of purified alcoholic hyaline shows that it exhibits a different behavior in lymphocytes obtained from patients with hyaline associated with alcoholic hepatitis, chronic active hepatitis, or cholestasis.[14] These observations prompted us to examine the possibility that an alcoholic hyaline produces transfer factor. Preliminary data indicate that it does;[15] this is compatible with the suggestion that alcoholic hyaline serves as a neoantigen to evoke a series of reactions leading to chronic liver disease.

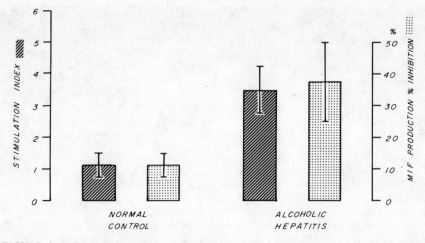

FIGURE 6. Influence of purified hyaline on immunologic reactivity in alcoholic hepatitis.

PHYTOHEMAGGLUTININ (PHA) RESPONSIVENESS

A major problem in a consideration of immunologic hyperactivity in the pathogenesis of alcoholic liver injury is the fact that many alcoholics exhibit an overall decrease in immunocompetence, as reflected in the reduction in lymphocyte response to the mitogen PHA (FIGURE 7). In our experience, this is associated with a reversible decrease in the total quantity of "T" cells although the number of "B" cells remains within normal limits. PHA responsiveness is regularly reduced in patients with severe degrees of alcoholic hepatitis.[16] This lack of response could be due to lymphocyte injury, nutrient deficiency, which interferes with DNA synthesis, or the presence of a circulating antagonist. Our investigations indicate that each of these factors may contribute to the lack of responsiveness of lymphocytes from patients with alcoholic hepatitis.

The capacity of malnutrition to alter production of cell-mediated immunity has been well documented. Patients with marked deficiency of folic acid,

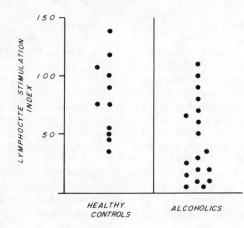

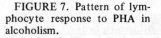

FIGURE 7. Pattern of lymphocyte response to PHA in alcoholism.

vitamin B_6, vitamin B_{12}, or zinc exhibit decreased responsiveness, which returns to normal with corrective therapy.[17] The ability of pyridoxine deficiency to depress delayed hypersensitivity has led to the suggestion that this vitamin or its coenzyme is an essential component in the sequence of reactions between sensitized cell and allergin-producing pathologic sequelae.[4] Pyridoxine deficiency interferes with incorporation of amino acids into protein and impairs nucleic acid synthesis, with subsequent deleterious effects on cell replication and protein biosynthesis, thus accounting for its adverse effects on immune response. Similar effects occur with a deficiency of other nucleogenic vitamins: folic acid and vitamin B_{12}.

A deficit of specific nutrients interferes with the stimulation index when alcoholic hyaline is added to lymphocytes; however, it has no influence on production of migration-inhibition index. Patients with severe terminal-phase alcoholic hepatitis preserve the MIF response to alcoholic hyaline, although there is a quantitative decrease in total "T" cells.[18] These observations are made more complicated by the fact that nutrient deficiency per se may be responsible for the accumulation of hyaline. Hyaline has been demonstrated following surgically constructed jejunoileal and jejunocolic bypass for obesity;[19] this has been attributed to specific nutrient deficits[20] and to changes in microflora of the intestine.[21]

FIBROGENESIS AND IMMUNE MECHANISM

Efforts have been made to link fibrogenesis and fibroplasia to immune mechanisms in a variety of hepatic disorders. Immunologic hyperreactivity could contribute to fibrosis by evoking cell necrosis, releasing fibrogenic factors during antigen-antibody reactions, or elaborating fibrogenic factors from stimulated lymphocytes. The key to this process is the proliferation of the mesenchymal cell in response to liver injury.[22] Studies of *in vitro* hepatic DNA synthesis first showed the importance of these cells in human liver injury and demonstrated factors that control their activity.[23] These cells subserve a variety of functions: phagocytosis, gammaglobulin production, and fiber formation.[24]

Investigations have been undertaken to explore the possibility that sensitized lymphocytes release factors that contribute to fibrosis. This avenue of research was prompted by the finding that when lymphocytes from patients with schistosomiasis are stimulated with cercarial antigen and those from chronic active hepatitis are stimulated with hepatitis B antigen will release a factor that increases the incorporation of tritiated proline into collagen.[25] The fibrogenic factor is assessed by harvesting the supernatant of lymphocyte cultures and adding it along with tritiated proline to a culture of L-929 fibroblasts (FIGURE 8).

A significant increase is noted in the amount of radioactive hydroxyproline in collagen secreted by the fibroblasts when the supernatant from lymphocytes stimulated by purified alcoholic hyaline is added to the cultured fibroblasts. Lymphocytes from patients with alcoholic hepatitis and a decrease in PHA responsiveness exhibit the same response to alcoholic hyaline as those that have normal response to this mitogen. It thus appears that migration-inhibition factor and fibrogenic factor are elaborated despite a decrease in overall immunocompetence.

These observations have led us to postulate that alcoholic hyaline, which may accumulate because of ethanol toxicity, nutritional deficiency, or, more probably, a combination of these factors, stimulates both "B" and "T" lymphocytes. "T" cell stimulation causes a release of a fibrogenic factor that, in combination

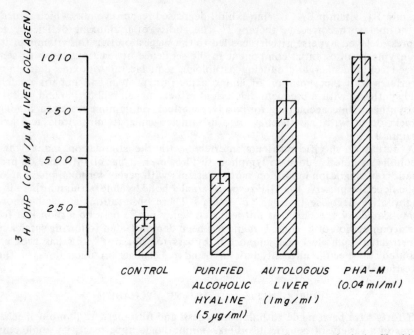

FIGURE 8. Influence of lymphocyte supernatant on collagen synthesis in fibroblast culture.

with ethanol toxicity, may play an important role in the development of fibrosis and eventual appearance of cirrhosis. According to this hypothesis, the damaged liver cell, through immunologic mechanisms, becomes the important factor in perpetuating liver injury in the alcoholic.

SUMMARY AND CONCLUSIONS

1. Alcoholic hyaline, a key component of alcoholic hepatitis, which is the recognized precursor of cirrhosis in alcoholics, has been isolated and purified to determine its role in immunologic reactivity. This actin-like protein accumulates because of its increased production or reduced dispersal in the presence of liver damage induced by ethanol and/or nutrient deficits. Hyaline added to lymphocytes from patients with alcoholic hepatitis causes a significant increase in stimulation index and production of migration-inhibition factor. The supernatant of alcoholic hyaline-stimulated lymphocytes evokes a significant increase in the incorporation of tritiated proline into collagen by cultured fibroblasts.

2. These data demonstrate a causal relationship between alcoholic hyaline, immunologic hyperactivity, and fibrogenesis, and support the hypothesis that hyaline-induced lymphocyte hyperactivity plays a central role in conversion of alcoholic hepatitis to cirrhosis. It thus appears that accumulated hyaline serves as a neoantigen; an effort should be made to identify hyaline and decrease its production or facilitate its dispersal in prophylaxis and treatment of alcoholic hepatitis and cirrhosis. Elucidation of the precise composition of alcoholic hyaline is now desirable to further assess immunopathologic factors in chronic liver disease in alcoholics.

REFERENCES

1. LEEVY, C. M. 1970. Hard liquor and cirrhosis. *In* Skandia International Symposia on Alcoholic Cirrhosis and Other Toxic Hepatopathias. A. Engel & T. Larsson, Eds.: 283, Nordiska Bokhandelns Forlag, Stockholm, Sweden.
2. McDERMOTT, R. P., R. E. ROCKLIN, L. CHASS, J. R. DAVID & S. F. SCHLOSS-MAN. 1974. Re-evaluation of *in vitro* cellular immunity using purified human T and B cells: some unexpected findings, J. Clin. Invest. June, 1974.
3. ZIMMERMAN, H. H. & D. F. LEVI. 1969. Separate autoimmune mechanisms for 7s and 19s globulins in Laennec's cirrhosis, Arch. Int. Med. **124:** 153.
4. AXELROD, A. E. & A. C. TRAKATELLIS. Relationship of pyridoxine to immunologic phenomena. *In* Vitamins and Hormones 2. Academic Press. New York, N.Y.
5. HIRSCHHORN, K., F. H. BACH, R. L. KOLODNY, I. L. FIRSCHEIN & N. HASHEM. 1963. Immune response and mitosis of human peripheral blood lymphocytes *in vitro.* Science **142:** 1185.
6. SOBORG, M. 1967. *In vitro* detection of cellular hypersensitivity in man. Specific migration inhibition of white blood cells from brucella-positive persons, Acta Med. Scand. **182:** 167.
7. GLADE, P. R., S. W. BRODER, H. GROTSKY & K. HIRSCHHORN. 1971. The use of cultured lymphoid cells as target cells for the detection of migration inhibitory factors. *In In Vitro* Methods in Cell-Mediated Immunity. B. R. Bloom & P. R. Glade, Eds.: Academic Press. New York, N.Y.
8. SORRELL, M. & C. M. LEEVY. 1972. Lymphocyte transformation and alcoholic liver injury. Gastroenterology **63:** 1020.
9. MALLORY, F. B. 1911. Cirrhosis of the liver. Five different types of lesions from which it may arise. Bull. Johns Hopkins Hosp. **22:** 69.
10. SCHAFFNER, F. & H. POPPER. 1970. Alcoholic hepatitis in the spectrum of ethanol-induced liver injury. Scand. J. Gastroenterol. Suppl. **7:** 69.
11. YOKOV, H., O. T. MIMICK, F. BATTI & G. KENT. 1972. Morphologic variants of alcoholic hyaline. Amer. J. Path. **69:** 25.
12. FRENCH, S. W. & P. L. DAVIES. 1973. The Mallory body in the pathogenesis of alcoholic liver disease. *In* Proc. Symposium Alcoholic Liver Pathology. Toronto, Canada.
13. FRENCH, S. W., T. J. IRIG & B. A. NORAM. 1972. A method of isolation of a purified fraction. Lab. Invest. **26:** 240.
14. ZETTERMAN, R., A. LUISADA OPPER & C. M. LEEVY. Alcoholic hepatitis—cell-mediated immunologic response to alcoholic hyaline. J. Clin. Invest. In press.
15. SUNDARAM, M., R. ZETTERMAN & C. M. LEEVY. 1974. Unpublished data.
16. ZETTERMAN, R. & C. M. LEEVY. 1974. Immunologic reactivity and alcoholic liver disease. Bull. New York Acad. Med. In press.
17. LEEVY, C. M. & F. SMITH. 1974. Nutritional factors in alcoholic liver disease in man. *In* The Liver and Its Diseases. F. Schaffner, S. Sherlock & C. M. Leevy, Eds.: Intercontinental Medical Book Corp. New York, N.Y.
18. ZETTERMAN, R. K., T. CHEN & C. M. LEEVY. 1974. Autoimmunity in alcoholic hepatitis. Proc. Vth Meeting International Assoc. Study Liver.
19. PETERS, R. L. & T. B. REYNOLDS. 1973. Hepatic changes simulating alcoholic liver disease, post ileo jejunal bypass. Gastroenterology **65:** 564.
20. MOXLEY, R. T., III, T. POZEFSKY & D. H. LOCKWOOD. 1974. Protein nutrition and liver disease after jejunoileal bypass for morbid obesity. New Eng. J. Med. **290:** 921.
21. O'LEARY, J. P., J. W. MAHER, J. L. HOLLENBECK & E. R. WOODWARD. 1974. Pathogenesis of hepatic failure following jejunoileal bypass. Gastroenterology **66:** 859.
22. LEEVY, C. M. 1963. *In vitro* studies of hepatic DNA synthesis in percutaneous liver biopsy specimens from man. J. Lab. Clin. Med. **61:** 761.
23. LEEVY, C. M. 1973. Liver Regeneration in Man. Charles C Thomas, Springfield, Ill.
24. LEEVY, C. M. 1966. Abnormalities of hepatic DNA synthesis in man. Medicine **45:** 423.
25. CHEN, T. & C. M. LEEVY. 1973. Collagen biosynthesis in hepatic fibrosis. Gastroenterology **64:** 178.

ON MECHANISMS IN HYPERAMMONEMIC COMA–WITH PARTICULAR REFERENCE TO HEPATIC ENCEPHALOPATHY

Bengt Hindfelt

Department of Neurology
University Hospital
Lund, Sweden

During the last two decades the pathogenesis of hepatic encephalopathy has been the subject of intense investigation and a matter of controversy.[11,24,28,36] The subject is extremely complex, and it is not surprising that to date no unifying hypothesis covering all aspects of hepatic coma has been presented. Summarizing the available information, it seems reasonable to conclude that most evidence favors the role of ammonia and its metabolism in the pathogenesis of hepatic coma. It is well documented that increased dietary protein, ammonia-releasing resins, and ammonium salts may induce precoma or coma in a susceptible individual with compromised liver function.[28] Furthermore, hyperammonemia is a prominent laboratory finding in most patients with hepatic encephalopathy,[27] and temporal fluctuations in the blood ammonia concentration are generally reflected in the neuropsychiatric state of the patient.[24] There is also some biochemical evidence incriminating ammonia. The brain has a low capacity for synthesizing urea, if any at all,[25] and ammonia "detoxification" occurs mainly by glutamine formation.[39] Since glutamine is diffusable, it occurs in the extracellular fluid and its concentration in the cerebrospinal fluid (CSF) relates to the severity of the cerebral dysfunction.[14] The same is true for α-ketoglutaramate in CSF, a metabolite involved in the ammonia-glutamine metabolism.[36]

The neuropathological paradigm of hepatic encephalopathy is the abnormal protoplasmatic astrocyte–the Alzheimer type II–with its enlarged nucleus, devoid of chromatine and with intranuclear inclusion bodies.[1,21] Similar astrocytic changes occur in the hyperammonemic animal with a portacaval shunt,[7] and have also been reported in monkeys subjected to long-term i.v. infusions of ammonium salt.[8] Accordingly, the neuropathological hallmark in congenital hyperammonemia is an abundant Alzheimer type II glia.[6] No hypothesis fulfills all requirements for a general acceptance, but the effects of hyperammonemia explain many of the features of hepatic coma. Furthermore, ammonia as the toxic agent is the rationale for the few effective therapeutic means in the treatment of this condition (restriction of dietary protein, oral broad-spectrum antibiotics, cleansing enemas, colonic exclusion, lactulose and so on).

PATHOPHYSIOLOGY

Coma, irrespective of its genesis, is always associated with a fall in oxidative metabolism of the brain.[16,23] Hepatic encephalopathy and coma are no exceptions. The oxygen consumption of the brain (CMR_{O_2}) is reduced and the fall in oxygen uptake parallels clinical deterioration.[10,29] In deep coma the oxygen consumption is reduced to roughly half the normal.[29] The interpretation of the fall in CMR_{O_2} is dual. Either it may indicate a primary interference with the energy metabolism of the brain, causing neuronal dysfunction and coma, or it may reflect an all-over lowered neuronal activity secondary to a disturbance of function or excitability of the tissue.

EXPERIMENTAL HYPERAMMONEMIA—BEHAVIORAL ASPECTS

Acute hyperammonemia, induced by i.p. injection of ammonium acetate[17,18] may produce short-lasting coma or convulsions in a normal rat. The response is dose-dependent, and with amounts close to the LD-50 dose (0.78 mM/100 g b.w.) tonic-clonic convulsions usually follow within 15 min after the injection. The convulsions are preceeded by myoclonic jerks and intense startle response to tactile and acoustic stimulation. A lower dose (0.52 mM) will frequently cause a brief precoma or coma, lasting for 30–45 min, followed by complete recovery. The coma, with onset 10–15 min after the injection, is also preceeded by neuronal facilitation, myoclonic movements, and startle response. During coma, respiration slows down and painful stimulation does not elicit any response. The animal is flaccid and the rightening reflex is lost. The corneal reflex, however, is always retained. In protacaval-shunted rats, 3–8 weeks after the operation[43] an i.p. injection of 0.52 mM of ammonium acetate/100 g b.w. likewise induces an anesthetic coma, lasting for 3–5 hours or ending fatally. The coma usually follows within minutes after the injection. Myoclonus and startle response are seen before the onset of coma. Respiration decreases gradually, becoming irregular and gasping. Pain evokes no response and the animal is completely flaccid. Convulsions do not occur. In fatal cases the corneal reflex disappears early. In surviving animals, hind-limb paralysis and ataxia are seen, but these clear during the subsequent 24 hours.

Normalization of the blood ammonia level occurs within a couple of hours. The peak arterial ammonia concentrations are not significantly different from those encountered in unshunted rats given the same does of ammonium acetate.[18] Thus, it seems as if the brain that has been exposed to ammonia for some time is more sensitive to acute ammonia loads than normally. This may lend support to the hypothesis that the brain in chronic liver disease is more vulnerable, "sensitized" to metabolic disturbances.

AMMONIA AND ENERGY METABOLISM

The brain, lacking capacity for urea synthesis,[25] "detoxifies" ammonia by means of glutamine formation.[39] The metabolic pathway consists of two reactions:

$$\alpha\text{-ketoglutarate} + \text{ammonia} + \text{NADH} + \text{H}^+ \xrightleftharpoons{\text{(GDH)}} \text{glutamate} + \text{NAD}^+ \quad (1)$$

$$\text{glutamate} + \text{ammonia} + \text{ATP} \xrightarrow{\text{(GS)}} \text{glutamine} + \text{ADP} + \text{P}_i \quad (2)$$

The first step is a reductive amination of α-ketoglutarate from the TCA cycle to glutamate, a reaction catalyzed by glutamic acid dehydrogenase (GDH). The second sequence is an ATP-requiring amidation of glutamate to glutamine. In this reaction glutamine synthetase (GS) is the active enzyme. An accelerated glutamine formation, due to an increased ammonia load, may theoretically interfere with brain energy metabolism by various mechanisms: (1) α-ketoglutarate may be diverted from the TCA cycle at such a rate that substrate depletion occurs within the cycle, causing a slower rate of oxidation,[5] (2) the reductive amination of α-ketoglutarate is associated with NAD^+ production[42] that may decrease the amount of NADH available for oxidation in the electron transport chain, thereby decreasing oxygen consumption and energy production, (3) the amidation of glutamate to glutamine is ATP-consuming, increasing the energy demands of the tissue.

With this as a background it seems reasonable to expect that increased brain ammonia concentrations are associated with changes in the energy metabolism. However, unequivocal evidence indicating an interference of ammonia with oxygen consumption is lacking. Ammonia in pathophysiological concentrations, occuring clinically in patients with hepatic coma, does not interfere with the oxygen consumption of cerebral tissue *in vitro*.[38] A significant reduction in oxygen uptake is observed only with excessively high ammonia concentrations.[26] Experimental *in vivo* data on the effect of hyperammonemia on cerebral oxygen consumption are sparse and inconsistent. In anesthetized dogs, with moderate elevation of the blood ammonia concentration, a significant fall in CMR_{O_2} occurs with ammonium acetate or chloride infusions but not with ammonium hydroxide.[22] The interpretation has to await confirmation of these results.

The energy state of the brain, i.e., the content of high-energy phosphates (phosphocreatine–PCr, ATP, ADP, and AMP) has been analyzed regionally in experimental animals during acute hyperammonemic coma.[18,33] In this situation there is a moderate fall in the PCr content in all regions, probably indicating a pH-induced shift in the creatinephosphokinase equilibrium due to lactate accumulation. With a high dose of ammonium acetate (0.78 mM/100 g b.w.) minor changes occur in the adenylate pool 30 min after injection. A slight fall in ATP and minor rises in the ADP and AMP contents are encountered, especially in the brainstem, which seems to be particularly sensitive to acute ammonia loads.[18,33]

Thus, the brain in hyperammonemic coma is not depleted of energy, though the changes are compatible with some dysbalance between energy production and consumption. α-ketoglutarate is not depleted but, rather, increased,[18,34] indicating that the glutamine formation does not take place at a rate causing substrate depletion of the TCA cycle. Glycolysis is increased, as evidenced by increased pyruvate and lactate content, and provides more substrate for oxidation, compensating for the α-ketoglutarate drainage.[18] Not only are lactate and pyruvate contents increased but the lactate/pyruvate ratio is also raised, indicating a change in the cytoplasmatic redox state. Knowing the intracellular pH makes it possible to calculate from the lactate dehydrogenase equilibrium the $NADH/NAD^+$ ratio,[19] which is elevated in acute hyperammonemia.[18]

$$\frac{NADH}{NAD^+} = \frac{lactate}{pyruvate} \times \frac{K}{H^+} \quad (K = 1, 11 \times 10^{-11} M)$$

Thus there is some evidence that ammonia affects the energy state of the brain, but it can be questioned whether these changes are primary events or secondary to alterations in neuronal activity. During the induction of coma, 15 min after the injection of the ammonium acetate (0.52 or 0.78 mM/100 g b.w.), the cerebral adenylate pools are normal and changes are observed only at 30 min with the higher dose. These changes in the energy state may be secondary to unobserved convulsive activity, since the animals are paralyzed and artifically ventilated during the procedure.

It should also be added that the energy state changes are not directly related to the intracellular ammonia concentration *per se*,[17] which indicates that the changes are probably secondary to alterations induced by the metabolism of ammonia.

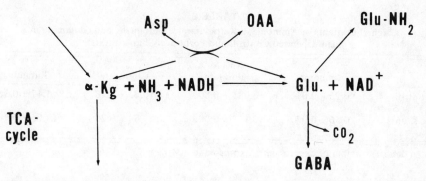

FIGURE 1. Ammonia and amino acid metabolism. The abbreviations used are α-kg (α-ketoglutarate), glu (glutamate), glu-NH$_2$ (glutamine), GABA (α-aminobutyric acid), Asp (aspartate), and OAA (oxaloacetate).

AMMONIA AND AMINO ACID METABOLISM

Ammonia is intimately involved in the formation of amino acids (FIGURE 1), glutamic, aspartic, and α-aminobutyric acids (GABA), substances with presumed transmitter functions.[9] Thus, it is conceivable that ammonia may affect neuronal activity and CMR_{0_2} by affecting the pools of these acids, either by changing the availability of transmitters or by changing the relation between excitatory and inhibitory transmitter material.

In acute ammonia intoxication, glutamine formation is accelerated and the content in brain tissue increased.[35] The ammonia and α-ketoglutarate concentrations are increased, as is also the cytoplasmatic $NADH/NAD^+$ ratio (TABLE 1).[18] The glutamate content is significantly decreased (TABLE I).

A similar metabolic pattern is observed in the rats with a portacaval shunt, 3 weeks after the shunting procedure (TABLE 2). The brain tissue ammonia is increased, approximately doubled. Alpha-ketoglutarate is unchanged or slightly increased, and the glutamine content shows a very marked rise. Glutamate, how-

TABLE 1
Cerebral Contents of Ammonia, α-Ketoglutarate, and Glutamate
in Acute Hyperammonemia[18]*

	Ammonia	α-Ketoglutarate	Cytoplasmatic $NADH/NAD^+$	Glutamate
Controls n = 11	0.30 ± 0.04	0.131 ± 0.005	$2.6 \cdot 10^{-3}$	11.82 ± 0.18
0.52 mM NH$_4$Ac/ 100 g b.w. n = 6	1.75 ± 0.40	0.151 ± 0.007	$4.7 \cdot 10^{-3}$	11.41 ± 0.23
0.78 mM NH$_4$Ac/ 100 g b.w. n = 7	3.20 ± 0.25	0.155 ± 0.009	$5.9 \cdot 10^{-3}$	10.99 ± 0.18

*The cytoplasmatic redox state is calculated from the LDH equilibrium (see text). Expressed in mM/kg w.t.

TABLE 2

Cerebral Contents of Ammonia, α-Ketoglutarate, Glutamate, and Glutamine in
Sham-Operated Controls and Portacaval-Shunted Rats*

	Ammonia	α-Keto-glutarate	Glutamate	Glutamine
Controls n* = 5	0.25 ± 0.04	0.095 ± 0.009	10.83 ± 0.18	4.47 ± 0.38
pc-shunts n = 11	0.56 ± 0.03	0.112 ± 0.006	9.64 ± 0.26	14.06 ± 0.78

*n denotes number of experiments. Expressed in mM/kg w.t.

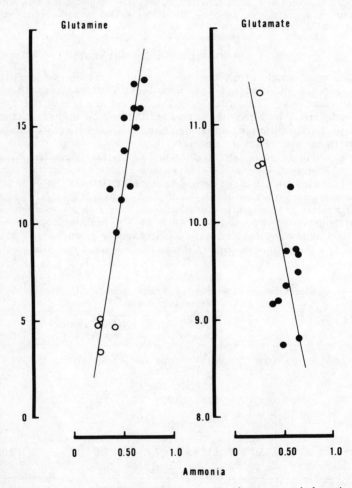

FIGURE 2. The correlation between brain ammonia, glutamate, and glutamine contents in portacaval-shunted rats (3-week group). Expressed in mM/kg w.t.

ever, is decreased by 1.2 mM/kg w.t. or 11%, while aspartate is unchanged (2.56 ± 0.10 in controls, 2.66 ± 0.06 mM/kg w.t. in the pc-shunted group). The brain tissue ammonia content shows a linear relationship to the rise in glutamine and an inverse correlation with the glutamate content (FIGURE 2).[43]

The induction of hyperammonemic coma in the pc-shunted animals[43] is associated with changes in glutamate and especially in aspartate. The brain ammonia concentration is increased to about 3 times the baseline level, and glutamine is not significantly changed during this early phase. At least, there is no rise in glutamine content. Glutamate is significantly ($p < 0.05$), though moderately, lowered and aspartate is reduced by more than 1/3. Alpha-ketoglutarate remains essentially unchanged. The metabolic pattern is slightly different at 45 min after the induction of coma.[43] At that point glutamine is increased, while aspartate remains at the same low level. However, there is a further fall in glutamate content, of about 1 mM/kg w.t.

COMMENT

The decrease in brain glutamate (and aspartate) in hyperammonemia is unexpected, considering the metabolic pathway (reaction 1, FIGURE 1). The enzyme, GDH, participating in the reductive amination of α-ketoglutarate to glutamate, is primarily confined to the mitochondria.[31] If the cytoplasmatic redox state and the total contents of ammonia and α-ketoglutarate in any way reflect the intramitochondrial state, the glutamate pool would expand by mass action. The opposite is the case, and there are various possible interpretations.

A disequilibrium of the GDH reaction seems unlikely, at least in the pc-shunted animals with sustained and low-grade hyperammonemia. The GDH activity in the normal brain is high (900 M/g w.t./hr),[41] and its activity increases steeply with minor increases in the ammonia concentration.[2]

Glutamine formation can not exceed glutamate production if the outlined metabolic pathway is the main or only one. The activity of glutamine synthetase in brain (reaction 2) is lower than that of GDH,[3] and the enzyme is saturated with ammonia at quite lower ammonia concentrations than is GDH.[32] Furthermore, L-methionine DL-sulfoximine (MSO), which irreversibly inactivates glutamine synthetase[30,44] does not prevent the fall in glutamate in either acute or sustained hyperammonemia,[17,43] although the activity of glutamine synthetase may drop to 30–50% of normal.[30]

Studies on the incorporation of ^{15}N into glutamate and glutamine have revealed that the metabolism of these substances and related amino acids (aspartate, GABA) is compartmented.[3] Thus, there are separate pools of glutamate that are probably functionally different. The data indicate that only a minor part of the total glutamate is operative in glutamine formation and that the major pool is in close contact with the α-ketoglutarate of the TCA cycle. ^{15}N from ammonium salt is preferentially incorporated into the small pool that is converted into glutamine.

If the total contents of ammonia and α-ketoglutarate are qualitatively representative for the intramitochondrial state, the glutamate content would be expected to be increased with a normal or more reduced redox state (reaction 1). In portacaval-shunted rats the cytoplasmatic $NADH/NAD^+$ ratio is normal or slightly raised.[20,43] Despite this, the total brain glutamate is significantly decreased. This may indicate that some other pool or pools of glutamate, not participating in glutamine formation, may be drastically reduced or even depleted. Since glutamate (and aspartate) probably have important functions as transmitters,[9] it is tempting to suggest that hyperammonemic coma reflects transmission failure due to depletion of certain critical pools of these amino acids. The increased sensitivity of the brain to acute hyperammonemia in pc-shunted rats may be the consequence of reduced glutamate pools, which may also explain the absence of convulsive activity. The metabolic mechanisms by which the glutamate and aspartate contents are being reduced are unknown.

REFERENCES

1. ADAMS, R. D. & J. M. FOLEY. 1953. The neurological disorder associated with liver disease. *In* Metabolic and Toxic Diseases of the Nervous System. H. H. Merritt and C. C. Hare, Eds.: 198–237.
2. VAN DEN BERG, C. J. 1970. Glutamate and glutamine. *In* Handbook of Neurochemistry. 3: 355–379. Plenum Press. New York, N.Y.
3. BERL, S. 1966. Glutamine synthetase. Determination of its distribution in brain during development. Biochemistry 5: 916.
4. BERL, S., G. TAKAGAKI, D. D. CLARKE & H. WAELSCH. 1962. Metabolic compartments in vivo. J. Biol. Chem. 237: 2562.
5. BESSMAN, S. P. & A. N. BESSMAN. 1955. Cerebral and peripheral uptake of ammonia in liver disease with an hypothesis for mechanism of hepatic coma. J. Clin. Invest. 34: 622.
6. BRUTON, C. J., J. A. N. CORSELLIS & A. RUSSELL. 1970. Hereditary hyperammonemia. Brain 93: 423.
7. CAVANAGH, J. B. & MA HTA KUY. 1971. Type II Alzheimer change experimentally produced in astrocytes in the rat. J. Neurol. Sci. 12: 63–75.
8. COLE, M., R. B. RUTHERFORD & F. O. SMITH. 1972. Experimental ammonia encephalopathy in the primate. Arch. Neurol. 26: 130.
9. CURTIS, D. R. & G. A. R. JOHNSTON. 1968. Amino acid transmittors. *In* Handbook of Neurochemistry. A. Lajtha, Ed. 4: 115–134. Plenum Press, New York, N.Y.
10. FAZEKAS, J. E., E. T. HOWARD, W. R. EHRMANSTRAUT & R. M. ALMAN. 1956. Cerebral metabolism in hepatic insufficiency. Amer. J. Med. 21: 843.
11. FISCHER, J. F. & R. J. BALDERASSINI. 1971. False neurotransmittors and hepatic failure. Lancet 2: 75.
12. FOLBERGROVA, J., V. MACMILLAN & B. K. SIESJÖ. 1972. The effects of hypercapnic acidosis upon some glycolytic and Krebs' cycle associated intermediates in the rat brain. J. Neurochem. 19: 2507.
13. FOLBERGROVA, J., J. V. PASSONEAU, O. H. LOWRY & D. W. SCHULTZ. 1969. Glycogen, ammonia and related metabolites in the brain during seizures evoked by methionine sulphoximine. J. Neurochem. 16: 191–203.
14. GILON, E., A. SZEINBERG, G. TRUMAN & E. BODENZI. 1959. Glutamine estimation in cerebrospinal fluid in cases of liver cirrhosis and hepatic coma. J. Lab. Clin. Med. 53: 714.
15. GOLDBERG, N. D., J. V. PASSONEAU & O. H. LOWRY. 1966. Effects of changes in brain metabolism on the levels of citric acid cycle intermediates. J. Biol. Chem. 10: 3997.
16. HEYMAN, A., J. L. PATTERSON & R. W. JONES. 1951. Cerebral circulation and metabolism in uremia. Circulation 3: 558–563.
17. HINDFELT, B. 1973. The effect of acute ammonia intoxication upon the energy state of the brain in rats pretreated with L-methionine D-L-sulphoximine (MSO). Scand. J. Clin. Lab. Invest. 31: 289.
18. HINDFELT, B. & B. K. SIESJÖ. 1971. Cerebral effects of acute ammonia intoxication. II. The effect upon energy metabolism. Scand. J. Clin. Lab. Invest. 28: 365.
19. HOHORST, H. J. 1960. Der Reduktionszustand des Diphohphopyridin-Nukleotidsystems in lebendem Gewebe. Ph.D. Dissertation, Phil. Fakultät. Marburg, Germany.
20. HOLMIN, T. & B. K. SIESJÖ. 1974. The effect of portacaval anastomosis upon the energy state and upon acid-base parameters of the rat brain. J. Biochem. To be published.

21. VON HÖSSLIN, C. & A. ALZHEIMER. 1912. Ein Beitrag zur Klinik und patologischen Anatomie der Westphal-Strümpellschen Pseudosklerose. Z. Ges. Neurol. Psychiatr. 8: 183.
22. JAMES, J. M., M. GARASSINI & E. LARBI. 1971. The effect of ammonium salts on cerebral and hind-limb consumption of oxygen and glucose in the ventilated dog. Clin. Sci. 41: 403.
23. KETY, S. S., B. D. POLIS, C. S. NADLER & C. F. SCHMIDT. 1948. The blood flow and oxygen consumption of the human brain in diabetic acidosis and coma. J. Clin. Invest. 27: 500.
24. McDERMOTT, W. V. & R. D. ADAMS. 1954. Episodic stupor associated with Eck fistula in human with particular reference to metabolism of ammonia. J. Clin. Invest. 33: 1.
25. McILWAIN, H. & H. BACHELARD. 1971. Biochemistry and the Central Nervous System. 4th edit.: 197–199. Williams & Wilkins. Baltimore, Maryland.
26. McKHANN, G. M. & D. B. TOWER. 1961. Ammonia toxicity and cerebral oxidative metabolism. Amer. J. Physiol. 200: 420.
27. PHEAR, E. A., S. SHERLOCK & W. H. J. SUMMERSKILL. 1955. Blood ammonia levels in liver disease and hepatic coma. Lancet 1: 836.
28. PHILLIPS, G. B., R. SCHWARTZ, G. J. GABUZDA & C. S. DAVIDSON. 1952. The syndrome of impending hepatic coma in patients with cirrhosis of the liver, given certain nitrogenous substances. New Eng. J. Med. 247: 239.
29. POSNER, J. B. & F. PLUM. 1960. Toxic effects of carbon dioxide and azetazolamide in hepatic encephalopathy. J. Clin. Invest. 39: 1246.
30. RAO, S. I. N. & A. MEISTER. 1972. In vivo formation of methionine sulphoximine phosphate, a protein-bound metabolite of methionine sulphoximine. Biochemistry 11: 1123.
31. SALGANICOFF, L. & E. DE ROBERTIS. 1965. Subcellular distribution of the enzymes of the glutamic acid, glutamine and α-aminobutyric acid cycles in rat brain. J. Neurochem. 12: 287.
32. SCHNACKERZ, K. & L. JAENICKE. 1966. Reinigung and Eigenschaften der Glutamine aus Schweinehirn. Z. Physiol. Chem. 347: 127.
33. SCHENKER, S., D. W. McCANDLESS, E. BROPHY & M. LEWIS. 1967. Studies on the intracerebral toxicity of ammonia. J. Clin. Invest. 46: 838.
34. SHOREY, J., D. W. McCANDLESS & S. SCHENKER. 1967. Cerebral α-ketoglutarate in ammonia intoxication. Gastroenterology 53: 706.
35. TEWS, J. K. & W. E. STONE. 1965. Free amino acids and related compounds in brain and other tissues: Effects of convulsant drugs. Prog. Brain. Res. 16: 135.
36. VERGARA, F., F. PLUM & T. DUFFY. 1974. Alpha-ketoglutaramate: Increased concentrations in the cerebrospinal fluid of patients in hepatic coma. Science 183: 81.
37. WAELSCH, H. 1961. Compartmentalized biosynthetic reactions in the central nervous system. In Regional Neurochemistry. S. S. Kety & J. Elkes, Eds.: 57–64.
38. WALSHE, J. M., L. DE CARLI & C. S. DAVIDSON. 1958. Some factors influencing cerebral oxidation in relation to hepatic coma. Clin. Sci. 17: 11.
39. WEIL-MALHERBE, H. 1962. Ammonia metabolism in the brain. In Neurochemistry. K. A. C. Elliott, I. H. Page & J. H. Quastel, Eds.: 321–330. Charles C Thomas. Springfield, Ill.
40. WILLIAMSON, I. R. & B. E. CORKEY. 1969. Assay of intermediates of the citric acid cycle and related compounds by fluorometric enzyme methods. In Methods in Enzymology. Vol. 13. Citric Acid Cycle. J. M. Lowenstein, Ed.: 412–513. Academic Press. N.Y.
41. WILLIAMSON, D. H., P. LUND & H. A. KREBS. 1967. The redox state of free nicotine-amide-adenine dinucleotide in the cytoplasm and mitochondria of rat liver. Biochem. J. 103: 514.
42. WORCEL, A. & M. ERECINSKA. 1962. Mechanism of inhibitory action of ammonia on the respiration of rat liver mitochondria. Biochim. Biophys. Acta 65: 27.
43. HINDFELT, B., F. PLUM & T. DUFFY. 1975. To be published.
44. PACE, L. & E. E. McDERMOTT. 1952. Methionine sulphoximine and some enzyme systems involving glutamine. Nature 169: 415.

THE ROLE OF ALCOHOLISM IN HEPATIC IRON STORAGE DISEASE*

Lawrie W. Powell

Department of Medicine
Division of Gastroenterology
University of Queensland
Royal Brisbane Hospital
Brisbane, 4029
Queensland, Australia

Following the publication of Sheldon's classic monograph[1] on hemochromatosis in 1935 and the extensive review of 787 cases by Finch and Finch[2] in 1955, the disorder known as idiopathic hemochromatosis was widely regarded as a specific disease entity resulting from an inherited defect in iron metabolism. The clinical diagnosis at that time rested largely on the characteristic triad of diffuse skin pigmentation, hepatomegaly, and diabetes mellitus. The introduction of percutaneous needle biopsy of the liver added precision to the diagnosis. Unfortunately it has also led to considerable confusion, since histologically stainable iron deposits are common in cirrhotic livers,[3,4] especially in alcoholic subjects, and some investigators have equated even mild to moderate siderosis in cirrhosis with hemochromatosis. This confusion is aggravated by the high prevalence of alcoholism in patients with hemochromatosis.[2,5,6]

The purpose of this presentation is to attempt to clarify the difference between hemochromatosis and alcoholic cirrhosis with mild to moderate hemosiderin deposits in the liver and to discuss the role of alcoholism in the pathophysiology and symptomatology of hemochromatosis.

DEFINITION AND DIAGNOSIS

Hemochromatosis can be defined simply as a disease of iron storage in the parenchymal cells of the liver and other organs, with eventual fibrosis and functional inefficiency of the organs involved. The pathological diagnosis is usually made on the basis of cirrhosis or fibrosis of the liver in association with gross hemosiderin deposits in the parenchymal and other cells, and with parenchymal iron deposits in such other organs as the pancreas and the heart.[1,2] However, if the diagnosis is based solely on histological criteria, difficulty can arise in distinguishing hemochromatosis from alcoholic cirrhosis with increased stainable tissue iron because, as stated above, mild to moderate degrees of siderosis are common in alcoholic cirrhosis and because the degree of stainable iron does not always parallel the actual tissue iron concentration.[4,16] The distinction can usually be achieved if some assessment is made of the *degree* of iron excess, since this is the major distinguishing feature between hemochromatosis and the majority of cases of alcoholic cirrhosis with secondary iron overload. *Body iron stores in symptomatic patients with idiopathic hemochromatosis usually exceed 10 grams,*

*This work was supported in part by the National Health and Medical Research Council of Australia.

124

whereas they rarely do so in alcoholic cirrhosis. An assessment of total body iron stores can be made by one or more of the following procedures:

(a) Measurement of the amount of iron removed by *repeated venesection*,[7] i.e., a retrospective assessment.

(b) Quantitative tests in which the *urinary iron excretion* is measured following the injection of an iron chelating agent.[8-13] Either diethylenetriamine penta-acetic acid (DTPA) or desferrioxamine may be used. For practical purposes the desferrioxamine-induced urinary iron excretion provides a good semiquantitative measure of body iron stores, although more complex techniques have been used and probably allow more accurate quantitation of the degree of iron overload.[9,13] A 24-hour urinary excretion of iron in excess of 2.0 mg following the intramuscular injection of 500 mg desferrioxamine is indicative of excessive parenchymal iron deposits.[11] In patients with untreated idiopathic hemochromatosis the amount usually exceeds 10 mg in 24 hours, whereas in the majority of patients with alcoholic cirrhosis the desferrioxamine-induced urinary iron excretion is usually less than this.[12]

(c) *Chemical estimation of tissue iron concentration* in biopsy samples, which provides a more direct method of estimating storage iron, and relatively simple techniques are now available to achieve this.[13,14] Several workers in different centers have now demonstrated a good correlation between liver iron concentration and estimates of total body iron stores based on chelation tests or venesection measurements in control subjects and in patients with various forms of iron overload.[14-16] The study of Barry[16] included patients with cirrhosis and stainable hepatic iron as well as patients with idiopathic hemochromatosis, and that author confirmed that estimation of liver iron concentration usually enabled one to distinguish between the 2 conditions. In patients with untreated hemochromatosis he found the liver iron concentration in the range 1.8 to 5.0 g/100 g dry weight, whereas in patients with cirrhosis, values in excess of 1 g/100 g dry weight were exceptional. In control normal subjects, liver iron concentration averaged 0.07 to 0.1 g/100 g dry weight and seldom exceeded 0.15 g/100 g. Barry concluded that when liver iron concentration is less than 1.5 g/100 g dry weight the iron is unlikely to be the cause of the cirrhosis.

(d) *Measurement of serum ferritin concentration.* Recently published studies[17,18] have confirmed that ferritin is present in serum in relatively small amounts (normal range approximately 10–100 ng/ml) and can be quantitated accurately by radioimmunoassay. Moreover, the serum ferritin level closely parallels body iron stores. Further work is required to establish the nature and significance of ferritin in serum, but the actual levels show promise of being at least as useful in assessing body iron stores as the chelation tests or perhaps even liver iron concentration.

Suggested criteria for the clinician and pathologist for the diagnosis of hemochromatosis along the lines outlined above are summarized in TABLE 1. As defined in this way, with emphasis on the degree of parenchymal iron overload, the distinction between hemochromatosis and alcoholic cirrhosis is usually straightforward. However, it should be emphasized that in a minority of patients with alcoholic cirrhosis, secondary iron accumulation may occur to such a degree that the clinical and pathological appearances and tissue iron concentrations are virtually indistinguishable from those in patients with idiopathic hemochromatosis.[19-21] Furthermore, prolonged exposure to a high dietary intake of iron and alcohol can result in hemochromatosis, as has been established conclusively in the Bantu of South Africa.[21,22] Therefore, implicit in the diagnosis of primary

TABLE 1

Suggested Criteria for the Diagnosis of Hemochromatosis

Clinical:	Evidence of fibrosis or cirrhosis of the liver
	plus
	grossly increased body iron stores (assessed by response to repeated vene-section, injection of an iron-chelating agent, hepatic iron concentration, or serum ferritin level (see text).
Pathological:	Cirrhosis or fibrosis of the liver
	plus
	grossly increased iron concentration in liver and other organs (preferably assessed by chemical analysis—e.g. concentrations of iron in excess of 1.0 g/100 g dry weight in liver[1]).

or idiopathic hemochromatosis is the exclusion of possible causes of secondary iron overload (TABLE 2).

Helps in distinguishing between idiopathic hemochromatosis and hemochromatosis resulting from gross iron accumulation in a cirrhotic patient are a positive family history of iron storage disease, a history of abstinence from alcohol, and previous histological evidence of cirrhosis without siderosis. In addition, in the experience of the present writer, when gross iron deposition does follow pre-existing cirrhosis, a cause is often apparent, such as portacaval anastomosis, hemolysis, or prolonged iron administration.

ALCOHOLISM AND IDIOPATHIC HEMOCHROMATOSIS

Even if one accepts that most patients with hemochromatosis are suffering from the genetic or inherited variety of the disease, as now seems to be widely believed,[16,23,24] any theory of its pathogenesis must account for the fact that at least 30% of patients with idiopathic hemochromatosis drink excessive amounts of alcohol.[2,5,25] In Australia, approximately 40% of patients with hemochromatosis consume the equivalent of more than 100 g of ethyl alcohol per day,[25,26] whereas control levels of alcohol consumption in this population are considerably less than this.[27] In an attempt to analyze the role of alcoholism in idiopathic hemochromatosis and to determine whether idiopathic hemochromatosis in alcoholic subjects differs from this disease in nonalcoholic subjects, we have reviewed the clinical and pathological features and prevalence of familial iron storage disease in 110 patients with hemochromatosis treated in Brisbane over the past 18

TABLE 2

Classification of Hemochromatosis

1. Primary or Idiopathic Hemochromatosis
   (a) latent or precirrhotic stage
   (b) cirrhotic stage
2. Secondary Hemochromatosis
   (a) hepatic cirrhosis with secondary iron accumulation
   (b) hepatic cirrhosis and iron overload associated with certain anemias—especially those with ineffective erythropoiesis
   (c) liver disease resulting from chronic alcohol ingestion associated with excess dietary iron ("Bantu-type hemochromatosis")

years. The criteria for diagnosis of hemochromatosis were those stated previously and included an estimate of total body iron stores greater than 10 g on the basis of chelation tests or response to venesection therapy. Forty-five of these patients, or 41%, were classed as "alcoholic" on the basis of a daily alcohol consumption equivalent to 100 g of ethyl alcohol or more, and these patients were compared with the remaining 65 as regards the above details. In view of claims that hemochromatosis is virtually always secondary to alcoholism and exogenous iron ingestion,[28,29] it is noteworthy that, despite detailed interrogation of the patients and their close relatives, 23% of the patients were regarded as total abstainers and their socioeconomic background and dietary habits were very similar to those of the alcoholic group except for alcoholic ingestion. A preliminary report of these details has been published in abstract form.[30] The results are summarized in TABLES 3–7, and in each instance the corresponding figures are quoted from the review of Finch and Finch[2] for comparison.

TABLE 3

Hemochromatosis
Symptoms Present at Time of Presentation

	% Positive		
	Present Series		Finch and Finch (1955)
	Alcoholic	Nonalcoholic	
Symptoms			
Polyuria (diabetes)	30.0	33.8	47.5
Lethargy	71.1	61.5	46.0
Skin pigmentation	62.2	72.3	32.5
Abdominal pain	30.0	33.8	28.0
Edema	15.5	9.2	17.0
Loss of libido	73.3	64.4	14.0
Nausea/vomiting	31.1	18.4	8.0
Jaundice	15.5	0	–
Peripheral neuritis	11.1	0	15

Clinical Features

The symptoms present at the time of presentation are listed in TABLE 3. It can be seen that the presenting symptoms in the alcoholic and nonalcoholic patients were very similar except for jaundice, symptoms of peripheral neuritis, and edema, which were significantly more common in the alcoholic group. In contrast to the findings of Finch and Finch in their retrospective review of 787 cases of hemochromatosis,[2] skin pigmentation was noted in about $\frac{2}{3}$ of the patients in the present series and loss of libido in a similar proportion.

The physical signs present at the time of diagnosis were also similar in the alcoholic and the nonalcoholic patients (TABLE 4). However, as might be expected, ascites, jaundice, spider nevi, and Dupuytren's contractures were more common in the alcoholic group. Thus, the presenting symptoms and signs were very similar in the 2 groups of patients except for the greater prevalence of evidence of hepatocellular disease in the alcoholic group. The major difference in physical signs between the present series and that reviewed by Finch and Finch was the prevalence of testicular atrophy (78.8% versus 18%). Presumably this was

TABLE 4

Hemochromatosis

Signs at Time of Presentation

	% Positive		
	Present Series		Finch and Finch
Signs	Alcoholic	Nonalcoholic	(1955)
Pigmentation	100	95.4	85
Hepatomegaly	100	92.3	94
Testicular atrophy	82.2	75.4	18
Splenomegaly	35.5	20.0	50
Ascites	15.5	0	35
Jaundice	15.5	0	10
Dupuytren's contracture	31.0	7.7	−
Spider nevi	35.5	6.1	60
Arthritis (pseudogout)	26.6	29.2	−

often not recorded in the patients reviewed by Finch and Finch, since subsequent studies have shown this to be a very common feature of hemochromatosis.[25,26,31] The laboratory investigations were also very similar in the alcoholic and nonalcoholic groups except for evidence of more frequent hepatocellular damage in the alcoholic group (serum transaminase elevation in 35.5% of the alcoholic patients as against 15.4% of the nonalcoholic group).

Complications

The complications that developed during the course of the illness are shown in TABLE 5. The figures were almost identical in the alcoholic and nonalcoholic groups except for hepatic failure, which developed in 11% of alcoholic subjects but was not encountered in nonalcoholic patients. Cardiac failure was much less common in this series than in that of Finch and Finch. The causes of death were again very similar in the 2 groups except that hepatic failure or bleeding from esophageal varices did not account for any deaths in the nonalcoholic patients in contrast to 3 (27.2%) of the alcoholic group (TABLE 6). The latter was comparable to the figure quoted by Finch and Finch[2] (30%). The major differences

TABLE 5

Hemochromatosis

Complications Developing During Illness

	% Positive		
	Present Series		Finch and Finch
Complication	Alcoholic	Nonalcoholic	(1955)
Hepatic failure	11.1	0	−
Diabetes mellitus	73.3	72.3	82
(requiring insulin)	44.4	46.1	72
Abdominal pain	35.5	33.8	35 to 40
Cardiac disease	7.8	4.6	30
Malignant hepatoma	13.3	12.3	14

in cause of death between this series and the cases reviewed by Finch and Finch was the higher occurrence of malignant hepatoma in the present series (36.9%, as against 14%). This probably reflects the less frequent death rate from cardiac complications and diabetes mellitus in the present series and the possibly greater longevity currently achieved by phlebotomy therapy.[5,32]

Pathology

A characteristic pattern of fibrosis and lobular disruption of the liver was seen in nonalcoholic patients with idiopathic hemochromatosis. It differed from the pattern seen in alcoholic cirrhosis and it showed some similarity to the lesion resulting from chronic biliary obstruction (FIGURES 1 and 2). In particular there were areas in which the lobular architecture was partially preserved and central veins were still identifiable in a fairly normal position. The changes are described in detail elsewhere.[38] In approximately $\frac{3}{4}$ of the patients with *familial* hemo-

TABLE 6

Hemochromatosis
Causes of Death

	% of Deaths*		
	Present Series (19)		Finch and Finch (1955)
	Alcoholic (11)	Nonalcoholic (8)	
Cardiac failure	18.1 (2)	12.5 (1)	30
Hepatic failure or GI bleeding	27.2 (3)	0	30
Malignant hepatoma	36.4 (4)	37.5 (3)	14
Infection	9.1 (1)	12.5 (1)	12
Diabetic coma	0	0	4
Cerebral vascular disease	9.1 (1)	25 (2)	–
Other	0	12.5 (1)	10

*Numbers in parentheses refer to numbers of patients.

chromatosis who drank more than the equivalent of 100 g of ethyl alcohol per day, the histological appearance of the liver resembled that found in patients with the idiopathic disease who were abstainers. In the remaining quarter the appearances were those of micronodular alcoholic cirrhosis, the iron distribution in the nodules being very irregular.[38] On review, these latter patients were found to drink very heavily, most in excess of the equivalent of 200 g ethanol per day. However, since these patients had a family history of iron storage disease in 1 or more 1st-degree relatives who were abstainers, it was concluded that these patients had idiopathic hemochromatosis and that their liver damage had been markedly aggravated by alcoholic disease.[38]

Prognosis

As can be seen from TABLE 6, there were 11 deaths among the 45 alcoholics during the period of study and 8 deaths among the 65 nonalcoholics. Although this difference is not statistically significant, there were more deaths from hepatic failure and gastrointestinal bleeding in the alcoholic group. The incidence of

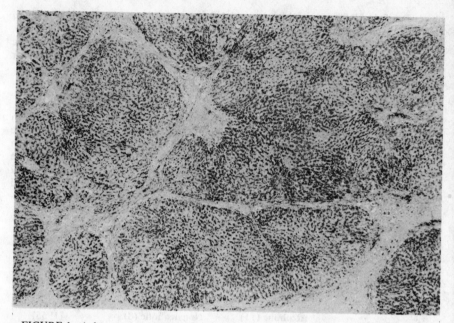

FIGURE 1. A low-power section of liver obtained at autopsy from a patient with untreated idiopathic familial hemochromatosis. It shows the combination of discrete parenchymal nodules and partially preserved lobules characteristic of the untreated idiopathic disease (iron stain).

malignant hepatoma was comparable in the 2 groups. When the groups were analyzed with respect to the effect of venesection therapy, the nonalcoholic patients showed a significant response (42 of 45 who had received venesection therapy were still alive and without serious complications, as against 12 of 20 in the nonvenesected group ($\chi^2 = 7.19$, $P < 0.01$). The corresponding figures for the alcoholic patients were $\frac{16}{23}$ among those venesected and $\frac{10}{22}$ for those not venesected ($\chi^2 = 1.52$; $P > 0.2$). Although in these studies the decision for treatment by phlebotomy was not made on a strictly random basis according to a controlled trial, the patients were under the care of different physicians whose opinions varied with respect to the value and advisability of phlebotomy therapy; furthermore, more alcoholic than nonalcoholic patients did not consent to therapy. These results are similar to those of the smaller analysis published previously,[5] which indicated that venesection therapy probably prolongs life in nonalcoholic subjects but that a beneficial effect in alcoholic patients was not obvious. Further statistical analysis of the data to analyze the independent effects of alcoholism and removal of iron[33] confirmed the detrimental effect of alcoholism on the outcome of the disease ($\chi^2 = 3.26$, $P < 0.05$), and the beneficial effect of iron removal in nonalcoholic subjects ($\chi^2 = 7.22$, $P < 0.01$), and there was no evidence of interaction between the 2 factors. In other words, iron and alcohol appeared to be acting as 2 independent factors in this disease.

Family Studies

Perhaps the most convincing evidence that alcoholic patients with hemochromatosis are suffering from the same basic disease as their nonalcoholic counterparts

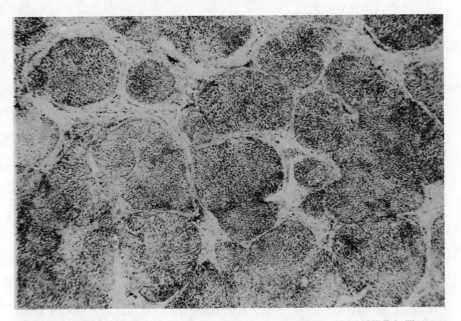

FIGURE 2. An autopsy section of liver from the same patient as in FIGURE 1. There are multiple small discrete parenchymal nodules embedded in fibrous tissue. However, in contrast to the pattern seen in alcoholic cirrhosis, the parenchymal cells show little or no disturbance except for the iron accumulation, and in some areas partially preserved lobules are still present.

TABLE 7
Prevalence of Abnormalities in Iron Metabolism in 1st-Degree Relatives

	Patients with Hemochromatosis			Patients with Alcoholic Cirrhosis and Hemosiderosis
	Present Series		Finch & Finch (1955)	
	Alcoholic	Nonalcoholic		Present Series
No. of families	11	12	12	9
No. of relatives	37	39	50	34
Test	% Abnormal			
Serum iron	29.7	32	20	0
Response to chelating agent	27	37.2	–	2.9
Increased hepatic iron	13.5	22.8	–	–
Full syndrome of hemochromatosis	5.7	13	–	0

lies in the study of 1st-degree relatives. Family studies in the present series (similar to those reported in detail by Powell[25]) showed no significant difference in the prevalence of abnormalities of iron metabolism between the relatives of alcoholic patients and the relatives of nonalcoholic patients (TABLE 7). Moreover, of 34 relatives of 9 patients with alcoholic cirrhosis and mild hemosiderosis, only 1 had a detectable abnormality of iron metabolism (TABLE 7). This subject also suffered from diabetes mellitus, but, unfortunately, further investigation of the case was not possible.

The above findings strongly suggest that the majority of patients with hemochromatosis have the genetic form of the disease, whether or not they consume alcohol. Why then the high percentage of patients with this disease who drink heavily? Sheinberg[34] recently postulated that clinically manifest hemochromatosis develops in those patients who are homozygous for a pair of abnormal autosomal genes, whereas heterozygotes do not develop overt disease unless they suffer superimposed liver disease, especially from alcoholism. This hypothesis could explain the observations reported above. Nonalcoholic probands with hemochromatosis (possibly homozygotes) have a higher proportion of 1st-degree relatives with overt disease than alcoholic probands (TABLE 7). Alcoholism could result in overt disease in heterozygotes by accelerating the already increased intestinal iron absorption[36,37] or by adding superimposed liver disease. In Australia, the estimated prevalence of overt hemochromatosis is about 1 in 10 000 and the gene frequency approximately 1 in 150.[37] A relatively high prevalence of heterozygotes in the population and the precipitation of overt disease in some of them by alcoholism could thus explain the high proportion of alcoholic patients with hemochromatosis. However, the validity of this concept must await the detection of the specific genetic abnormality in idiopathic hemochromatosis.

SUMMARY AND CONCLUSIONS

1. An increase in stainable iron in the liver is common in patients with hepatic cirrhosis, but in the majority of patients the degree of iron overload is considerably less than in hemochromatosis. Thus, the 2 diseases can usually be distinguished if an attempt is made to quantitate total body iron stores.

2. Uncommonly, the degree of iron accumulation in patients with preexisting cirrhosis may be large enough to produce the clinical and pathological appearances of hemochromatosis. However, the majority of patients with hemochromatosis have the genetic form of the disease (i.e., primary or idiopathic hemochromatosis).

3. The high prevalence of alcoholism in patients with hemochromatosis may be due to the fact that heterozygous subjects, who would not normally manifest symptoms, develop overt disease because of the superimposed effects of alcoholism.

REFERENCES

1. SHELDON, J. H. 1935. Haemochromatosis. Oxford University Press. London, England.
2. FINCH, S. C. & C. A. FINCH. 1955. Idiopathic hemochromatosis: an iron storage disease. Medicine 34: 381–430.
3. BELL, E. T. 1955. Relation of portal cirrhosis to hemochromatosis and to diabetes mellitus. Diabetes 4: 435–446.

4. CONRAD, M. E., A. BERMAN & W. H. CROSBY. 1962. Iron kinetics in Laennec's cirrhosis. Gastroenterology **43**: 385–390.
5. POWELL, L. W. 1970. Changing concepts in haemochromatosis. Postgrad. Med. J. **46**: 200–209.
6. MacDONALD, R. A. 1963. Idiopathic hemochromatosis: genetic or applied? Ann. Intern. Med. **112**: 184–193.
7. HASKINS, D., A. R. STEVENS, S. C. FINCH & C. A. FINCH. 1952. Iron metabolism. Iron stores in man as measured by phlebotomy. J. Clin. Invest. **31**: 543–547.
8. WALSH, R. J., K. W. PERKINS, C. R. B. BLACKBURN, R. SANDFORD & S. CANTRILL. 1963. The use of DTPA in the diagnosis and management of idiopathic haemochromatosis. Aust. Ann. Med. **12**: 192–196.
9. FIELDING, J. 1965. Differential ferrioxamine test for measuring chelatable body iron. J. Clin. Path. **18**: 88–97.
10. POWELL, L. W. & M. J. THOMAS. 1967. The use of diethylene triamine penta-acetic (D.T.P.A.) in the clinical assessment of total body iron stores. J. Clin. Path. **20**: 896–904.
11. HARKER, L. A., O. D. FUNK & C. A. FINCH. 1968. Evaluation of storage iron by chelates. Amer. J. Med. **45**: 105–115.
12. BARRY, M., G. C. CARTEI & S. SHERLOCK. 1969. Differential ferrioxamine test in haemochromatosis and liver disease. Gut **10**: 697–704.
13. BARRY, M., G. C. CARTEI & S. SHERLOCK. 1970. Quantitative measure of iron stores with diethylenetriamine penta-acetic acid. Gut **11**: 899–904.
14. LUNDVALL, O., A. WEINFELD & P. LUNDIN. 1969. Iron stores in alcoholic abusers. I. Liver Iron. Acta Med. Scand. **185**: 259–269.
15. WALKER, A. J., J. P. G. MILLER, I. W. DYMOCK, K. B. SHILKIN & A. WILLIAMS. 1971. Relationship of hepatic iron concentration to total chelatable body iron in conditions associated with iron overload. Gut **12**: 1011–1014.
16. BARRY, M. 1973. Iron and chronic liver disease. J. Roy. Coll. Phycns. Lond. **8**: 52–62.
17. JACOBS, A., F. MILLER, M. WORWOOD, M. R. BEAMISH & C. A. WARDROP. 1972. Ferritin in the serum of normal subjects and patients with iron deficiency and iron overload. Brit. Med. J. **4**: 206–208.
18. WALTERS, G. O., E. M. MILLER & M. WORWOOD. 1973. Serum ferritin concentration and iron stores in normal subjects. J. Clin. Path. **26**: 770–772.
19. SABESIN, S. M. & L. B. THOMAS. 1964. Parenchymal siderosis in preexisting portal cirrhosis. A pathologic entity simulating idiopathic and transfusional hemochromatosis. Gastroenterology **46**: 477–485.
20. TYRER, J. H., L. W. POWELL & W. BURNETT. 1966. Hémochromatose primitive constitutionnelle ou hémochromatose secondaire à une cirrhose alcoolique? Observation d'un cas compliqué d'hépatome malin et de thrombose de la viene porte. Presse Méd. **74**: 1135.
21. CHARLTON, R. W. & T. H. BOTHWELL. 1966. Hemochromatosis: dietary and genetic aspects. *In* Progress in Hematology. E. B. Brown & C. V. Moore, Eds.: 298. Grune & Stratton. New York, N.Y.
22. ISAACSON, C., H. C. SEFTEL, K. J. KEELEY & T. H. BOTHWELL. 1961. Siderosis in the Bantu: the relationship between iron overload and cirrhosis. J. Lab. Clin. Med. **58**: 845.
23. FINCH, C. A. 1972. Hemochromatosis. *In* Hematology. P. K. Schneider & S. D. Boynton, Eds. McGraw-Hill Book Co. New York, N.Y.
24. GRACE, N. D. & L. W. POWELL. 1974. Iron storage disorders of the liver. Gastroenterology. **67**: 1257.
25. POWELL, L. W. 1965. Iron storage in relatives of patients with haemochromatosis and in relatives of patients with alcoholic cirrhosis and haemosiderosis. Quart. J. Med. **34**: 427–442.
26. POWELL, L. W., R. MORTIMER & O. D. HARRIS. 1971. Cirrhosis of the liver: A comparative study of the four major aetiological groups. Med. J. Aust. **1**: 941–950.
27. WILKINSON, P., J. M. SANTAMARIA & J. G. RANKIN. 1969. Epidemiology of alcoholic cirrhosis. Aust. Ann. Med. **18**: 222–226.

28. MacDONALD, R. A. 1964. Hemochromatosis and hemosiderosis. C. T. Thomas. Springfield, Ill.
29. MacDONALD, R. A. 1973. Hemochromatosis and Wilson's disease. *In* The Liver. E. A. Gall & F. K. Mostofi, Eds.: 466–479. Williams & Wilkins Co. Baltimore, Md.
30. POWELL, L. W. 1970. Tissue damage in haemochromatosis: an analysis of the roles of iron and alcoholism. Aust. Ann. Med. **19**: 424.
31. WILLIAMS, R., P. J. SCHEUER & S. SHERLOCK. 1962. The inheritance of idiopathic haemochromatosis. Quart. J. Med. **31**: 249–265.
32. WILLIAMS, R., P. M. SMITH, E. J. F. SPICER, M. BARRY & S. SHERLOCK. 1969. Venesection therapy in idiopathic haemochromatosis. Quart. J. Med. **38**: 1–16.
33. RAO, C. R. 1952. Advanced statistical methods in biometric research. John Wiley & Sons Inc. New York, N.Y.
34. SCHEINBERG, H. 1973. The genetics of hemochromatosis. Arch. Int. Med. **132**: 126–128.
35. CHARLTON, R. W., P. JACOBS, H. SEFTEL & T. H. BOTHWELL. 1964. Effect of alcohol on iron absorption. Brit. Med. J. **2**: 1427–1429.
36. WILLIAMS, R., C. S. PITCHER, A. PARSONSON & H. S. WILLIAMS. 1965. Iron adsorption in the relatives of patients with idiopathic haemochromatosis. Lancet **1**: 1243–1248.
37. WALSH, R. J., K. W. PERKINS & C. R. B. BLACKBURN. 1964. A genetic study of haemochromatosis. Abstracts, 10th Congress of International Society of Haematology. F. 16.
38. POWELL, L. W. & J. F. R. KERR. 1975. The pathology of the liver in hemochromatosis. *In* Pathobiology Annual. H. L. Ioachim, Ed. Appleton-Century-Crofts. New York, N.Y.

NEWER APPROACHES TO TREATMENT OF LIVER DISEASE IN THE ALCOHOLIC

Carroll M. Leevy, Rowen Zetterman, and Frank Smith

Division of Hepatology and Nutrition
Department of Medicine
New Jersey Medical School
College of Medicine and Dentistry of New Jersey
Newark, New Jersey 07103

It is desirable to routinely focus attention on liver function and structure in control of alcoholism and prevention of liver disease in the chronic alcoholic. Recognition of liver injury in alcoholics has been greatly facilitated by standardization of measurements of liver size and introduction of simple screening techniques; ear densitometry to determine hepatic dye clearance; and wide acceptance of percutaneous liver biopsy as necessary to assess the nature, severity, and activity of a liver lesion.[1,2]

Despite absence of overt evidence of liver disease, at least $\frac{2}{3}$ of alcoholics hospitalized with delirium tremens exhibit significant alterations in liver function and morphology.[3] Approximately $\frac{1}{3}$ have normal liver histology; however, studies of selected members of this group reveal a significant increase in microsomal enzymes associated with enlarged mitochondria and hyperplasia of the endoplasmic reticulum. A second $\frac{1}{3}$ exhibit fatty metamorphosis, focal inflammation, and/or alcoholic hepatitis, with or without clinical and laboratory abnormalities. The final $\frac{1}{3}$ have fibrosis and/or cirrhosis accompanied by iron deposition in many instances, and occasionally by hepatoma (FIGURE 1).

Prospective studies indicate most chronic alcoholics initially develop fatty metamorphosis, which disappears despite continued alcoholism, attributed to an adaptive response.[4] In contrast, 80% of patients with alcoholic hepatitis who continue alcoholism, in our experience, develop cirrhosis (FIGURE 1). In reducing morbidity and mortality from alcoholic liver disease, it is, therefore, essential to recognize and treat early reversible hepatic lesions to forestall cirrhosis. This is achieved in 70% of patients by a multidisciplinary program that interrupts alcoholism by focusing attention on psychological, social, and dietary factors and supportive measures for tissue damage.[5] It is essential to improve further the outlook for the alcoholic by developing better methods to detect, treat, and cure early phases of liver injury.

RECOGNITION AND TREATMENT OF NUTRIENT DEFICITS

Toxic or metabolic effects of ethanol and nutrient deficits are of equal importance in the production of changes in intermediary metabolism that lead to subcellular alterations, fatty liver, alcoholic hepatitis, and cirrhosis (FIGURE 2). In therapy, a multidisciplinary approach should be used, with equal attention given to control of ethanol intake and provision of nutrients demonstrated to contribute to development of hepatic changes. Patients should be informed of encountered biochemical and morphologic abnormalities and allowed to serially follow the influence of abstinence for their correction. For those who are refractory to this regimen, some success may be achieved by a program designed to maintain food intake despite continued consumption of alcoholic beverages.[6]

135

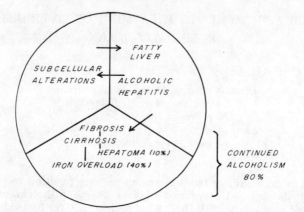

FIGURE 1. Morphologic findings on liver biopsy in 108 alcoholics hospitalized with delirium tremens.

Clinical stigmata of nutrient deficiency, including glossitis, anemia, and neuropathy, are often present in the alcoholic with established liver disease and are usually due to a decrease in intake of essential nutrients. Protein, vitamin, mineral, and lipid abnormalities are quite frequent in both those with and those without overt evidence of liver injury (FIGURE 3). All patients with alcoholic hepatitis or cirrhosis exhibit a deficit of one or more vitamins if sensitive and specific laboratory methods are used to detect circulating levels of these micronutrients.[7] The most common deficiencies are of folic acid, thiamine, and vitamin B_6, which have profound influence on nucleic acid, carbohydrate, and protein metabolism. These nutrients should be replaced by provision of a nutritious diet with appropriate supplements. An attempt should be made to provide a balanced diet; even so, as yet unidentified deficits may persist and contribute to progressive liver injury. This is illustrated by the recent recognition of phosphate depletion in the malnourished alcoholic with liver disease.[8] Low serum phosphate is often associated with a decrease in red blood cell 2, 3-DPG, necessary for oxygen transport to tissue. This is accompanied by mental ab-

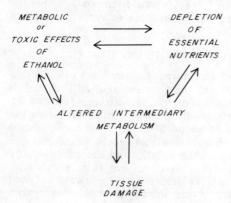

FIGURE 2. Interrelationship of factors that contribute to tissue injury in the alcoholic.

normalities, which disappear only with phosphate repletion and a return of the oxygen dissociation curve to normal (FIGURE 3).

It has been emphasized that liver lesions may occur in alcoholics despite a normal diet. In actual practice, the typical alcoholic with liver disease ingests a grossly inadequate diet; moreover, normal nutrient requirements in the face of

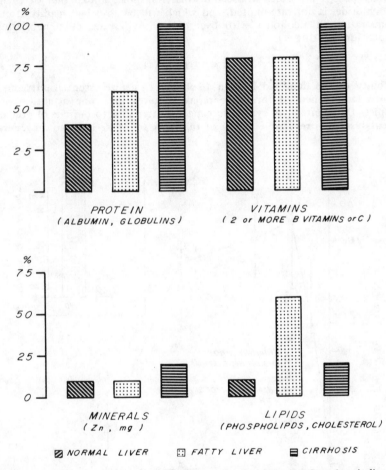

FIGURE 3. Incidence of nutrient deficits in randomly selected patients hospitalized with medical complications of alcoholism.

a high intake of alcoholic beverages have not been defined. An ideal diet to prevent malnutrition must take into account the fact alcohol may interfere with intestinal transport and utilization of essential nutrients.

INCREASING NUTRIENT ABSORPTION

Investigations of the absorption of thiamine hydrochloride whose intestinal transport is rate-limited indicate that either nutrient depletion or nutrient depletion plus ethanol causes a significant decrease in blood and tissue levels attained after a 50-mg dose of the vitamin is given orally.[9,10] Nutrient repletion is accompanied by a restoration of normal absorptive capacity; it is possible, however, to also protect the host under these circumstances by either giving thiamine parenterally or administering a molecular form of thiamine such as thiamine propyl disulfide, whose intestinal transport, unlike that of thiamine hydrochloride, is not rate-limited, and which will be absorbed readily after oral administration in alcoholics with liver disease,[11] despite acute inebriation or malnutrition (FIGURE 4).

NUTRIENT UTILIZATION

Inability of the damaged liver in alcoholics to utilize essential nutrients and produce factors needed for tissue repair requires the same attention of the therapist. Deficient DNA synthetic capacity attendant to deficits of precursors and catalysts or irreversible injury of the DNA template leads to aregenerative

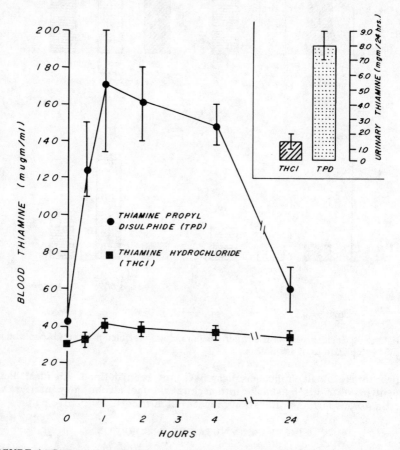

FIGURE 4. Comparative effectiveness of 50 mg of thiamine hydrochloride and thiamine propyl disulfide in correcting deficits of blood thiamine.

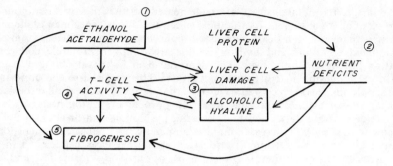

FIGURE 5. Therapeutic approaches to prophylaxis of cirrhosis in alcoholics.

phases of liver injury.[12] A significant increase in *in vitro* hepatic DNA synthesis occurs in the folate-repleted patient with alcoholic hepatitis. In contrast, hepatic DNA synthesis is markedly diminished in the presence of folate depletion or following large ethanol intake (FIGURE 5).

Aregenerative phases of liver injury are characterized by depletion of enzymes required for ethanol metabolism.[13] Ethanol evokes a significant increase in microsomal pentobarbital hydroxylase in a folate-repleted alcoholic, whereas this effect is diminished or may not occur in folate-depleted persons with deficient nucleic acid synthesis. It is vitally important to improve hepatic ethanol oxidative capacity in alcoholics if alcoholism is not interrupted. A decrease in hepatic activity of alcohol dehydrogenase and pentobarbital hydroxylase may be corrected by nutrient repletion. Deficiency of folic acid, vitamin B_6, vitamin B_{12}, zinc, and protein, which are necessary for normal nucleic acid synthesis, should be corrected to restore normal ethanol metabolism.

TREATMENT OF IMMUNOLOGIC ABNORMALITIES

Alcoholic hepatitis is the most important liver lesion in the alcoholic because of its propensity to lead to cirrhosis.[13] Despite interruption of alcohol intake and provision of an adequate diet, some of these patients progress to cirrhosis,[14] and the possibility that an autoimmune mechanism, perhaps amenable to therapy, is responsible has been considered. It is assumed that ethanol and nutritional deficiency lead to liver cell damage and increased production or decreased disposal of alcoholic hyaline, an actinlike protein. This insoluble protein serves as a neoantigen and evokes lymphocyte hyperreactivity.[15]

Alcoholic hyaline, which is a foreign protein, evokes reactions leading to necrosis, inflammation, and fibrosis. This schema offers the possibility of preventing transformation of alcoholic hepatitis to cirrhosis and development of its sequelae: first, interruption of alcohol intake—which, however, may not interrupt the development of cirrhosis; second, replacement of deficits of essential nutrients to repair liver damage, decrease hyaline formation, increase immunologic reactivity, and increase collagenase activity; third, directly suppressing formation or reactivity of alcoholic hyaline; fourth, suppressing lymphocyte reactivity and liberation of various noxious factors; and finally, directly decreasing deposition of collagen or increasing its absorption (FIGURE 5).

Attention must be first focused on interrupting ethanol intake, since alcohol both produces hepatocyte injury and evokes fibrosis. In the presence of active liver damage, its metabolism is often decreased, so that injury is compounded when alcohol is consumed. If ethanol is added to a biopsy specimen of alcoholic hepatitis, there is a significant increase in collagen synthesis.[16] Greater amounts of radioactive proline and hydroxyproline are found in insoluble collagen in hepatitis but not in fatty liver. The damaged liver in the alcoholic also has a significant reduction in collagenase activity.[17] This emphasizes the importance of ethanol-induced liver cell damage in accumulation of collagen synthesis and the need to stop alcohol intake in interrupting progressive fibrogenesis.

In subjects with a deficiency of folic acid, pyridoxine and/or vitamin B_{12} replacement therapy will increase immunocompetence and hepatic regeneration.[18] A deficiency of these vitamins is associated with a decrease in nucleic acid and protein synthesis, resulting in impairment of antibody formation and cell-mediated hyperactivity (FIGURE 6). Altered immunologic reactivity both increases susceptibility to infection and prevents normal immunologic events that may be necessary to interrupt progressive or chronic liver injury. Nutrient repletion should also receive priority because of the need to initiate repair of liver damage, which is necessary to forestall accumulation of hyaline and production of collagen.

Several controlled studies have been conducted to determine the influence of

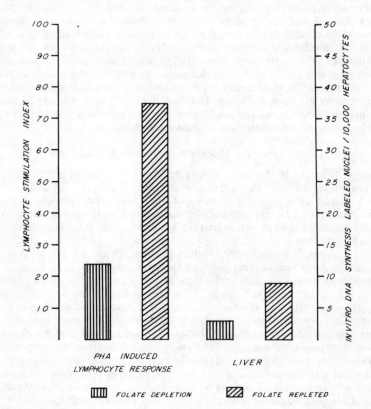

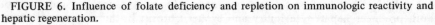

FIGURE 6. Influence of folate deficiency and repletion on immunologic reactivity and hepatic regeneration.

                    PREDNISONE   COLCHICINE   PENICILLAMINE

LYMPHOCYTE
REACTIVITY   ↓   —   —

FIBROGENESIS:
  PROLINE HYDROXYLASE   ↓
  COLLAGEN SECRETION   ↓
  CROSS LINKAGE   ↓

FIBROCLASIA
  COLLAGENASE   ↑

FIGURE 7. Influence of pharmacologic agents on collagen deposition and resorption.

corticosteroids on clinical features and prognosis in alcoholic hepatitis.[19-22] There is a decrease in mortality in selected patients; however, 3 studies have not shown any change in morbidity or mortality. Moreover, in 1 study, corticosteroids were found to increase the mortality from cirrhosis in alcoholics.[23] Nevertheless, since corticosteroids alter immunologic reactivity in alcoholic hepatitis, it is reasonable to explore further their usefulness in accelerating hyaline resorption and interruption of fibrogenesis.

Corticosteroids will also decrease proline hydroxylase, which is necessary for conversion of proline into hydroxyproline, and increase collagenase, which hastens its reabsorption (FIGURE 7). Two other agents have been utilized in efforts to directly influence fibrogenesis: colchicine, which, by direct action in the microtubular apparatus of fibroblasts, inhibits secretion of collagen;[24] and penicillamine, which interferes with the crosslinkage needed for formation of the collagen molecule.[25] Preliminary studies in our laboratory demonstrate that *in vivo* colchicine prevents the *in vitro* fibrogenic activity of the supernatant of lymphocytes stimulated by purified alcoholic hyaline. This and other molecules may, therefore, be of value in interrupting fibrogenesis in alcoholic hepatitis.

SYMPTOMATIC THERAPY

Alcoholics in whom cirrhosis is already present require symptomatic and supportive measures in addition to efforts to interrupt ethanol intake, repair nutrient deficits, and prevent untoward effects of immunologic hyperreactivity. Complications that require special therapy include portal hypertension with ascites or bleeding esophageal varices; liver failure with sensorial changes, bleeding tendency, or the hepatorenal syndrome; and extrahepatic complications, such as infections, pancreatitis, or peripheral neuropathy. Flow sheets should be used to follow serially the influence of available therapeutic regimens: (1) Ascites responds to diuretics and sodium restrictions;[26] however, in the alcoholic, special consideration should be given to nutrient depletion, which may alter response to diuretics and make it necessary to provide vitamin and mineral supplements. Salt-poor albumin may be valuable in selected patients refractory to these measures. (2) Bleeding esophageal varices require replacement of blood loss and measures to control bleeding with a consideration of balloon tamponade,[27] local vasopressin,[28] and shunt surgery.[29] (3) Hepatic encephalopathy is usually controlled by protein restriction and broad-spectrum antibiotics or lactulose[30] and correction of deficits of potassium or phosphate. (4) Generalized bleeding tendency and the hepatorenal syndrome in alcoholics with cirrhosis are usually not responsive, but it is desirable to give supportive therapy for the liver disease and coagulation disturbances or renal dysfunction. Infections, pancreatitis, cardiomyopathy, peripheral neuropathy, delirium tremens, and trauma should be promptly recognized and treated.

Special consideration should be given to all forms of drug therapy in alcoholics with cirrhosis. The patient with overt liver disease frequently exhibits a decrease in hepatocyte uptake capacity as well as conversion of therapeutic agents into

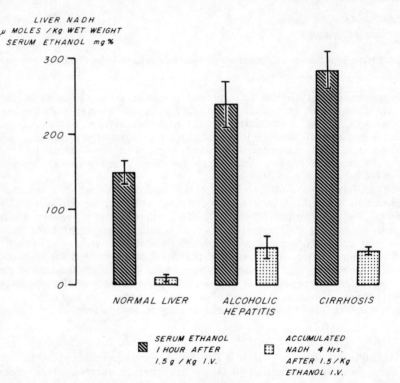

FIGURE 8. Accumulation of ethanol in alcoholic patients with liver disease due to a reduction in its clearance rate attendant to hepatic damage.

active metabolites or excretory products.[31-33] With mild liver injury, there is often increased removal rate of drugs due to ethanol-induced hyperplasia and hyperfunction of drug metabolism microsomes. In contrast, in alcoholics with severe, acute, or chronic hepatic damage, a decrease in drug-metabolizing capacity occurs and leads to accumulation of administered pharmacologic agents (FIGURE 8). This makes it necessary for the clinician to withhold or modify the dosage of certain drugs. Antibuse, tranquilizers, and sedatives whose half life is prolonged in severe liver injury should be used only under carefully controlled circumstances in the alcoholic with cirrhosis; wherever possible they should be avoided, and in all instances their relative merits must be weighed against potential danger attendant to disordered metabolism in alcoholics with overt liver disease.

Summary and Conclusions

1. The chronic alcoholic regularly exhibits alterations in liver function and morphology. Currently available screening techniques should be used routinely in all alcoholics to recognize subcellular alterations, fatty metamorphosis, and alcoholic hepatitis. Primary attention should be focused on proper treatment of these reversible phases of liver injury to forestall development of cirrhosis and its complications, including portal hypertension, liver failure, and hepatoma, which are largely responsible for escalating morbidity and mortality from chronic alcoholism.

2. Investigations of the mechanism of cirrhosis indicate hepatic fibrosis develops because of ethanol-induced increments in collagen synthesis, reduced activity of liver collagenase, and/or hyaline-induced immunologic hyperactivity. Abstinence, correction of nutrient deficits, avoidance of hepatotoxic drugs other than ethanol, and symptomatic measures for features of liver failure are necessary to preserve life and interrupt progression of hepatic fibrosis. Pharmacologic agents that suppress immunologic response and reduce fibrogenesis may be valuable therapeutic adjuncts in selected patients.

References

1. LEEVY, C. M. 1973. Liver Regeneration in Man. Charles C Thomas. Springfield, Ill. 1973.
2. LEEVY, C. M. 1974. Evaluation of Liver Function in Clinical Practice. Lilly Research Laboratories. Indianapolis, Ind.
3. LEEVY, C. M., C. TAMBURRO, M. KIRKLAND & C. CABANSAG. 1969. Biochemical alterations in delirium tremens. *In* Biochemical and Clinical Aspects of Alcohol Metabolism. V. Sardesai, Ed.: 241. Charles C Thomas. Springfield, Ill.
4. LEEVY, C. M. 1967. Clinical diagnosis, evaluation and treatment of liver disease in alcoholics. Fed. Proc. 26: 1474.
5. LEEVY, C. M., C. L. CUNNIFF, D. WALTON & M. HEALEY. 1954. Organization and function of a clinic for the alcoholic patient with liver disease. Quart. J. Stud. Alcohol. 15: 537.
6. LEEVY, C. M. 1972. Physiological and nutritional interrelationships in alcoholism, *In* Proc. Western Hemisphere Nutrition Congress III: 210.
7. BAKER, H. & O. FRANK. 1968. Clinical Vitaminology: Methods and Interpretation. Interscience Pub. New York, N. Y.
8. RAJAN, K. S., R. LEVINSON & C. M. LEEVY. 1973. Abnormalities in RBC 2, 3-DPG in hepatic encephalopathy. Gastroen terology 64: 191.
9. THOMSON, A. D., H. BAKER & C. M. LEEVY. 1970. Patterns of ^{35}S-thiamine hydrochloride absorption in the malnourished alcoholic. J. Lab. Clin. Med. 76: 34.
10. THOMSON, A. D. & C. M. LEEVY. 1972. Observations on the mechanism of thiamine hydrochloride absorption in man. Clin. Sci. 43: 153.
11. THOMSON, A. D., O. FRANK, H. BAKER & C. M. LEEVY. 1971. Thiamine propyl disulfide: Absorption and utilization. Ann. Int. Med. 74: 529.
12. LEEVY, C. M. 1966. Abnormalities of hepatic DNA synthesis in man. Medicine 45: 423.
13. LEEVY, C. M. 1974. Drug metabolism in liver disease. Proc. International Symp on Hepatotoxicity. Israel J. Med. Sci.
14. GALAMBOS, J. T. 1974. Alcoholic hepatitis. *In* The Liver and Its Diseases. F. Schaffner, S. Sherlock & C. M. Leevy, Eds.: 255. Intercontinental Medical Book Pub. New York, N. Y.

15. ZETTERMAN, R. K., T. CHEN & C. M. LEEVY. 1974. Autoimmunity in alcoholic hepatitis. Proc. 5th Meeting International Assoc. Study Liver.
16. CHEN, T. S. N. & C. M. LEEVY. 1974. Collagen biosynthesis in liver disease of the alcoholic. J. Lab. Clin. Med.
17. CHEN, T. 1974. Unpublished data.
18. LEEVY, C. M. & F. SMITH. 1974. Nutritional factors in alcoholic liver disease in man. In The Liver and Its Diseases. F. Schaffner, S. Sherlock and C. M. Leevy, Eds. Intercontinental Medical Book Pub. New York, N. Y.
19. CAMPRA, J. L., E. M. HAMLIN, R. J. KIRSHBAUM, M. OLIVIER, A. G. REDEKER & T. B. REYNOLDS. 1973. Prednisone therapy of acute alcoholic hepatitis. Report of a controlled trial. Ann. Int. Med. 79: 625.
20. HELMAN, R. A., M. H. TEMKO, S. W. NYE & H. J. FALLON. 1971. Alcoholic hepatitis. Natural history and evaluation of prednisolone therapy. Ann. Int. Med. 74: 311.
21. PORTER, H. P., F. R. SIMON, C. E. POPE, W. VOLWILER & L. F. FENSTER. 1971. Corticosteroid therapy in severe alcoholic hepatitis. A double-blind drug trial. New Eng. J. Med. 284: 1350.
22. BLITZER, B. L., M. G. MUTCHNICK, P. H. JOSHI, M. M. PHILLIPS, J. M. FESSEL & H. O. CONN. 1973. Adrenocorticosteroid therapy in alcoholic hepatitis; a prospective double-blind randomized study. Gastroenterology 64: 880.
23. COPENHAGEN STUDY GROUP FOR LIVER DISEASES. 1969. Effect of Prednisone on the survival of patients with cirrhosis of the liver. Lancet 1: 119.
24. WILSON, L., J. R. BAMBURG, S. B. MIZEL, L. M. GRISHAM & K. M. CRESSWELL. 1974. Interaction of drugs with microtube proteins. Fed. Proc. 33: 158.
25. KLEIN, L. & C. NOWACEK. 1969. Effect of penicillamine on new and pre-existing (^{3}H) collagen in vivo. Biochem. Biophys. Acta 194: 504.
26. HOFMAN, F., Ed. 1968. Diuretics in clinical medicine. Proc. Peter Bent Brigham Symposium, Excerpta Medica. New York, N. Y.
27. MERIGAN, T. C., R. M. HOLLISTER, P. F. GRYSKA, G. W. B. STARKEY & C. S. DAVIDSON. 1960. Gastrointestinal bleeding with cirrhosis, a study of 172 episodes in 158 patients. New Eng. J. Med. 263: 579.
28. SCHWARTZ, S. I. 1970. Influence of vasoactive drugs on portal circulation. Ann. N. Y. Acad. Sci. 170: 296.
29. MUTCHNICK, M. G., E. LERNER & H. O. CONN. 1974. Portal-systemic encephalopathy and portacaval anastomosis: a prospective controlled investigation, Gastroenterology 66: 1005.
30. SCHENKER, S., K. J. BREEN & A. M. HOYUMPA. 1974. Hepatic encephalopathy: Current status. Gastroenterology 66: 121.
31. KALANT, H., J. M. KHANNA & J. MARSHMAN. 1970. Effect of chronic intake of ethanol on pentobarbital metabolism. J. Pharmacol. Exp. Ther. 175: 318.
32. ESHCHAR, J. & M. ELIAKIM, Eds. 1974. International Symposium on Hepatotoxicity. Israel. 1974.
33. GEROK, W., K. SICKINGER & H. H. HENNEKEUSER, Eds. 1971. International Conference on Alcohol and the Liver. Freiburg, Germany.

CURRENT POLICIES IN HEPATIC TRANSPLANTATION: CANDIDACY OF PATIENTS WITH ALCOHOLIC LIVER DISEASE OR PREFORMED ANTIDONOR ANTI-BODIES AND A REAPPRAISAL OF BILIARY DUCT RECONSTRUCTION*

Thomas E. Starzl, Charles W. Putnam, Makoto Ishikawa,
Reginaldo Picache, Bo Husberg, Charles G. Halgrimson,
and Gerhard Schroter

Departments of Surgery and Pediatrics
University of Colorado Medical Center
Denver, Colorado 80220
Veterans Administration Hospital
Denver, Colorado

K. A. Porter

Department of Pathology
St. Mary's Hospital and Medical School
London, England

INTRODUCTION

During the 10 years since the first orthotopic hepatic transplantation was performed in Denver, over 200 patients have had liver replacement throughout the world, according to the American College of Surgeons Registry.[6] We have contributed 82 cases to this total, at a rate of about 10 per year since 1967, when the first long-term survivor was treated.[14]

In this communication, the survivals for these 82 recipients will be recorded. In addition, current policy will be reexamined in 3 areas on the basis of recently acquired or summarized data. Two of the questions pertain to candidacy for liver transplantation with particular reference to patients with alcoholic liver disease and to recipients who possess performed antidonor antibodies. Finally, a reappraisal of our experience with biliary reconstruction has led to modifications in the approach to this major area of technical failure.

SURVIVAL STATISTICS

The 1- and 2-year survivors from our 82 consecutive cases have been 18 and 9, respectively (TABLE 1). Our longest survivor of the 13 still alive is now nearly 5 years posttransplantation, another is $4\frac{1}{2}$ years, and 2 others have passed the 3-year mark.

The 10 late deaths, the causes for which are given in TABLE 2, have occurred from 12 to 41 months postoperatively. The latest mortality (OT 19), at $3\frac{1}{2}$ years,

*This work was supported by research grants from the Veterans Administration; by grants AI-AM-08898 and AM-07772 from the National Institutes of Health; by grants RR-00051 and RR-00069 from the General Clinical Research Centers Program of the Division of Research Resources, National Institutes of Health.

145

TABLE 1

Cases of Orthotopic Liver Transplantation Treated in Denver

		Lived		
	Number	1 Year	2 Years	Alive Now
1963–1966	6	0	0	0
1967	6	1	0	0
1968	12	5	2	0
1969	6	2	1	1
1970	10	2	1	1
1971	11	2	2	2
1972	11	5	3	3
1973	13	1	0	3
1974 (to April 1)	7	0	0	3
Total	82	18	9	13

followed a bout of *Hemophilus* septicemia. At autopsy, the homograft arteries had occlusive lesions similar to those seen in renal transplants.[13]

The most important causes of the high acute failure rate have been technical, of which complications of biliary duct reconstruction are the most common. The important contribution of faulty biliary drainage to mortality and morbidity, including cholangitis, will be discussed in a later section. After technical failures, rejection and systemic infection lead the list.

TRANSPLANTATION FOR ALCOHOLIC LIVER DISEASE

Early in our experience it was suggested that patients with alcoholic liver disease presented an especially poor candidacy for hepatic transplantation.[14] The reasons for this opinion were twofold. First, cirrhotic patients have a predictably

TABLE 2

The Present Status of 18 1-Year Survivors After Orthotopic Liver Transplantation. Eight Are Still Alive from 14 to 58 Months. The Other 10 Eventually Died from the Causes Listed Below.

OT NO.	Time of Death (Months)	Cause of Death
15	12	Recurrent cancer
29	12	Serum hepatitis and liver failure
8	13	Recurrent cancer
58	$13\frac{1}{2}$	? Chronic rejection ? Recurrent hepatitis
16	$13\frac{1}{2}$	Rejection and liver failure
14	14	Recurrent cancer
54	19	Multiple liver abscesses necessitating retransplantation
36	20	Systemic *Nocardia* infection and chronic aggressive hepatitis
13	30	Rejection and liver failure following retransplantation
19	41	*Hemophilus* septicemia and secondary liver and renal failure

TABLE 3

Alcoholic vs Nonalcoholic Liver Disease Treated by Orthotopic Hepatic Transplantation

	Alcoholic	Nonalcoholic	Total
No. of Patients	10	72	82
Alive	1*	12	13
Dead	9	60	69
Mean Survival of those who died	29 days	136 days	122 days

*3 weeks posttransplantation.

higher operative risk, in part due to the frequency of pulmonary and other infectious complications. Secondly, for all but those patients with clearly terminal esophageal variceal hemorrhage, hepatic coma or advanced secondary renal failure, uncertainty about the natural course of the disease usually leads to a decision against transplantation until such time as the patient's condition becomes patently hopeless. Many then die before a suitable liver becomes available; the few who are given transplants enter the operating room in a moribund state.

Of the 82 consecutive recipients of hepatic homografts, 1 was treated for alcoholic hepatitis and 9 carried the diagnosis of Laennec's cirrhosis without concurrent hepatoma (TABLE 3). Nine of the 10 patients have died, from 3 to 121 (mean 29) days posttransplantation; the only surviving recipient is in good condition 4 weeks postoperatively. In contrast, 12 of the 72 patients with transplants for nonalcoholic liver disease are still alive from a few weeks to nearly 5 years later. The mean survival of the patients in the nonalcoholic group who have died is more than 4 times that of the alcoholic recipients (TABLE 3).

The causes of death for the alcoholic patients are given in TABLE 4. Two deaths were the result of complications of biliary reconstruction (see later), and 3 were related to homograft rejection. Of the remaining 4 patients, 2 died in

TABLE 4

Duration of Survival and Cause of Death in 10 Alcoholic Recipients of Hepatic Homografts

OT No.	Age (Years)	Survival (Days)	Cause of Death
22	33	10	Biliary obstruction
28	39	13	Disruption of choledochoduodenostomy, bile peritonitis
32	46	3	Unexplained coma
39	47	26	Unrelieved preexisting coma
40	44	32	Rejection, pneumonitis, petechial hemorrhages of CNS
62	44	121	Rejection and liver failure, pulmonary emboli
70	40	34	Pneumonitis
75	48	8	Rejection and liver failure
81	47	15	*Aspergillus* pneumonitis with dissemination
82	37	Alive (4 weeks)	—

coma, which was unrelieved by transplantation or which evolved immediately postoperatively, and 2 succumbed to pulmonary infectious complications.

CURRENT POLICY

If liver transplantation is to succeed in patients with alcoholic cirrhosis, potential recipients must be selected earlier, treated aggressively to prevent or correct infectious, pulmonary, and other complications, and given transplants before their condition has markedly deteriorated. The latest patient (OT 82) in the alcoholic group met these criteria, and his early postoperative convalescence has been untroubled. Despite the otherwise poor results to date, we will continue to consider the occasional patient with alcoholic liver disease with a hopeless prognosis, but who is not moribund and does not have potentially lethal infectious or other complications, as an acceptable candidate for liver transplantation.

CANDIDACY OF RECIPIENTS WITH PREFORMED ANTIDONOR ANTIBODIES

Hyperacute Rejection of Hepatic Homografts

The pathophysiology of hyperacute rejection has been well worked out in recent years. The initiating event is apparently fixation of preformed antidonor antibody to the transplant. This was first noted in kidneys (which contain blood-group antigens) transplanted to ABO-incompatible recipients.[11] In more recent years, the predominant cause of hyperacute rejection has been the presence in the serum of the recipient of antigraft cytotoxic antibodies, as was first described by Terasaki[15] and confirmed by Kissmeyer-Nielsen[7] and others.[12,17]

In the laboratory, a form of hyperacute rejection can be produced by transplanting organs between widely disparate species, as for example from pigs to dogs.[4] Canine serum contains heterospecific antiporcine cytotoxic antibodies that rapidly affix to the graft, setting into motion a chain of events that destroys it in minutes.

With either heterografts or homografts transplanted to recipients that possess preformed antigraft antibodies, the actual destruction of the organ is a complex process in which formed blood elements and clotting factors are entrapped by the graft.[5,10,12] The resulting occlusion of the major vessels causes ischemic necrosis, which gives a characteristic purple or mottled appearance to the tissue.

Because of the special filtering properties of the renal microvasculature, the kidney is unusually prone to the irreversible consequences of hyperacute rejection. In contrast, there is evidence that the liver may be unusually resistant to this process. For example, pig livers continue to perform rudimentary functions for a number of hours while being perfused with human blood.[3] Even in the difficult pig-to-dog heterograft model, in which kidneys are grossly rejected in a few seconds, the liver often does not suffer this fate until more than an hour has elapsed after revascularization.[5]

If the resistance of the liver to hyperacute rejection proves to be sufficiently great to permit its transplantation under conditions that would be categorically unacceptable for kidneys, an important limitation to the practicality of the procedure may be eased. Patients dying of liver disease, particularly those with alcoholic liver disease, as discussed above, usually cannot wait long for their homografts. If liver transplantation can be carried out despite preformed antibody states, some patients who would otherwise be deprived of treatment might no longer be arbitrarily excluded. In this connection, our experience with 6 patients given transplants despite preformed antibodies—of the antiblood group or the lymphocytotoxic varieties—will be discussed.

TABLE 5

Three Cases of Orthotopic Transplantation of ABO-Incompatible Livers

OT Number	Age (Years)	Diagnosis	Donor Recipient ABO Types	Preoperative Isoagglutinin Titer	Survival	Cause of Death	Pathologic Changes in Liver
59	11/12	Biliary atresia	AB ⟶ A	1:4 (anti-B)	173 days	Septicemia (from liver?)	Arterial and arteriolar narrowing (past rejection)
60	46	Primary biliary cirrhosis	AB ⟶ A	1:32 (anti-B)	61 days	Septicemia (from liver?) Pulmonary emboli	Mild cytomegaloviral infection No rejection
61	42	Postnecrotic cirrhosis	A ⟶ O	1:512 (anti-A)	41 days	Disseminated Herpes and cytomegalovirus Pulmonary emboli Brain infarction	Cytomegalovirus infection No rejection

ABO Incompatibility

In 1972, 3 patients with ABO-mismatched livers were donors to recipients whose condition was considered sufficiently grave that they could not wait for a compatible organ (TABLE 5). Hyperacute rejection did not occur, and no other obvious adverse consequences were seen. The titers of antigraft isoagglutinins were variable, but at least in 1 case (OT 61) reached prodigious levels (TABLE 6). The 3 patients all eventually died but the pathologic findings in the homografts were remarkably minor. The homograft biliary system of one of the patients (OT 60) became partially obstructed by the mechanism of cystic duct stenosis shown in FIGURE 1B; following biliary reconstruction, the recipient died of pulmonary and septic complications. The other 2 patients had almost no abnormalities in their liver when they died of infectious complications.

TABLE 6

Serial Antigraft Isoagglutinin Titers in the 3 Recipients of ABO-Incompatible Livers Described in TABLE 4

Posttransplantation Day	OT 59	OT 60	OT 61
	(ANTI-B)	(ANTI-B)	(ANTI-A)
0	1:4	1:32	1:512
1	1:4	1:16	
3	1:1	1:4	1:64
5	1:1	1:2	1:64
7	1:1	1:8	1:2048
9	1:4	1:64	1:8192
11	1:4	1:64	1:8192
13	1:4	1:32	1:4096
15	1:4	1:16	1:2048
17	—	1:8	1:1024
19	1:2	1:4	1:1024
21	1:1	1:4	1:512
28	1:1	1:2	1:256
35	1:2	1:2	1:128
42	1:2	1:2	
49	1:2	1:1	
56	1:2	1:8	
63	1:2		
70	1:2		
77	1:8		
84	1:4		

Cytotoxic Antibodies

The ability of the ABO-incompatible liver to remain healthy under conditions that would be predictably harmful to most kidneys is a feature we have also seen in another kind of preformed-antibody situation. During the last 2 years, 3 potential liver recipients were found to have in their serum cytotoxins against most of the lymphocyte donors of an indifferent screening panel. Thus, the prospect of finding a liver donor without a positive cytotoxic antibody crossmatch was considered nil. Consequently, the decision was made to proceed with the transplantations, in the face of positive crossmatches, despite the potentially adverse prognostic implications.

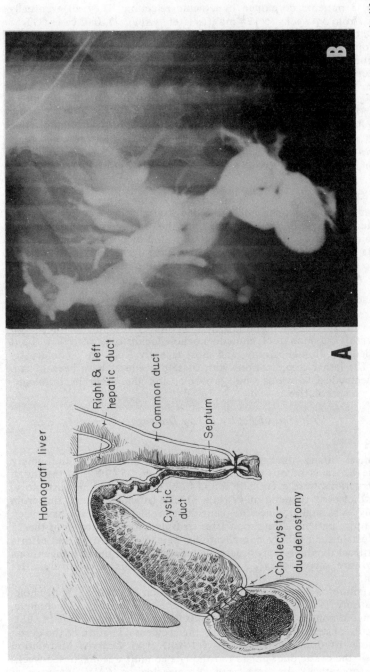

FIGURE 1. Two kinds of biliary duct obstruction after cholecystoduodenostomy. (A) The anatomic basis for a technical error that cost the life of 3 patients. Distal ligation of the double-barreled extrahepatic duct system resulted in total biliary obstruction. This recurrent accident has caused us to perform cholangiography on all liver homografts before transplantation. (B) The kind of biliary obstruction caused by stenosis of the cystic duct. Martineau reported that cytomegalovirus infection of the duct could be responsible for this development,[8] but frequently no obvious etiologic factor can be found.

None of the 3 patients developed hyperacute rejection. They all eventually died, however, from $3\frac{1}{2}$ weeks to $13\frac{1}{2}$ months later (TABLE 7). In 2 cases (OT 58 and 63), the homograft livers had only minor histopathologic changes at late biopsy or autopsy. In the third (OT 71), the homograft functioned poorly from the start. Although this could have been a manifestation of acute antibody-mediated rejection, the organ appeared to be severely damaged by ischemia, as well as cellular rejection, when removed 10 days after its transplantation. The homograft was replaced with a chimpanzee heterograft, against which the recipient also had cytotoxins. The chimpanzee liver functioned for most of the 14 subsequent days of the patient's life. Upon pathologic examination the heterograft was well preserved, with little evidence of rejection. Centrilobular cholestasis was a prominent feature. This was our third trial of chimpanzee-to-man transplantation, the other two having been previously reported.[4,14]

Current Policy

Preformed antibody states should be avoided if at all possible. However, the experience cited above with recipients having either anti-red cells or cytotoxic antibodies against their donors suggests that this kind of positive crossmatch is not an absolute but only a *relative contraindication* for liver transplantation.

A Reappraisal of Biliary Reconstruction

As mentioned earlier, complications of biliary reconstruction have claimed many of the early posttransplantation casualties. Biliary drainage has been reconstituted with several techniques, including cholecystoduodenostomy after ligation of the graft common duct, choledochocholedochostomy with or without a T-tube, choledochoduodenostomy, and most recently Roux-en-Y cholecystojejunostomy. The lethal complications with these procedures have been of two kinds, one mechanical, obvious, and provable, and the other bacteriologic, subtle, and as yet speculative.

Problems of Faulty Biliary Drainage

Mechanical Problems

The mechanical biliary duct problems have been obstruction and biliary fistulae. In the 82 cases of orthotopic transplantation, 25 (30%) of the initial biliary reconstructions were eventually found to be mechanically unsatisfactory, leading to death or early reoperation (TABLE 8). The true incidence of this problem is probably even higher, since incipient duct problems may not have been recognized in those patients dying soon after transplantation. Thirteen of the 25 patients with established biliary complications were reoperated on and efforts made to reconstruct the duct. Only 4 patients recovered from the reinterventions and only two are alive today, 3 months and 2 years respectively after transplantation.

There were failures with each kind of reconstruction (TABLE 8). With cholecystoduodenostomy (FIGURE 2A), the most frequently employed technique, fistulae were uncommon but 25% of the patients had proved obstruction (TABLE 8). In a few, acute obstruction was caused by the accidental ligation of the cystic duct at the time of donor hepatectomy (FIGURE 1A). *Delayed* obstruction (FIGURE 1B) of the cystic duct portion of the bile conduit was diagnosed weeks to months postoperatively. In some cases, cytomegalovirus (CMV) infection of the duct was implicated,[8] but in most instances no obvious etiologic factor ac-

TABLE 7

Three Cases of Orthotopic Hepatic Transplantation in Which the Recipients Had Antidonor Cytotoxic Antibodies

OT Number	Age (Years)	Diagnosis	Preoperative Cytotoxicity Titer	Survival	Cause of Death	Pathologic Changes in Liver
58	34	Chronic aggressive hepatitis	1:2	407 days	Stopped immunosuppression Hepatic insufficiency	Resolution of previous obstructive changes at 8½-month biopsy. (No autopsy)
63	49	Primary biliary cirrhosis	1:64	26 days	Gastrointestinal hemorrhage	Normal liver
71	1 11/12	Biliary atresia	1:16 (Homograft) 1:16 (Heterograft)	(Removal of the graft at 10 days) 14 days after retransplantation	Pulmonary edema, bronchial hemorrhage	Acute rejection, cellular and humoral No evidence of cellular rejection. Centrilobular cholestasis.

TABLE 8

Kind of Primary Bile Duct Reconstruction used in 82 Consecutive Cases of Orthotopic Liver Transplantation

	Cholecysto-duodenostomy	Choledocho-choledochostomy	Roux-en-Y Cholecysto-jejunostomy	Choledocho-duodenostomy	Cholecysto-Loop Jejunostomy	Total
Number	59	9	8	4	2	82
Obstruction	15	0	2	0	0	17*
Fistula	2	5	0	1	0	8*

*In these 25 cases, reoperation(s) was performed in 13 patients with attempt at duct reconstruction. A satisfactory recovery followed in only 4 of the recipients. Two later died after 6 and 13½ months posttransplantation survival. The other 2 are alive after 3 months and 2 years, respectively. Both survivors now have the final biliary duct reconstruction shown in FIGURE 2C.

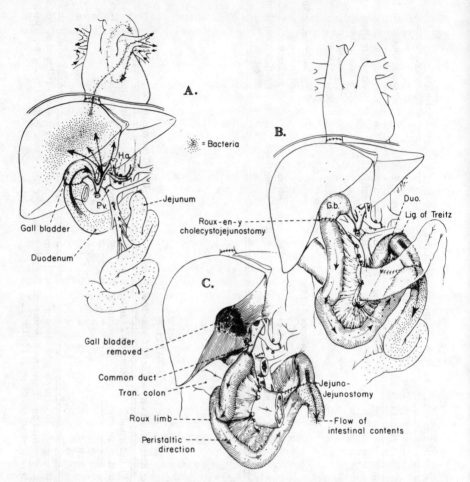

FIGURE 2. Schematic representation of the bacterial contamination or lack thereof in 3 different kinds of biliary reconstruction. (A) Cholecystoduodenostomy. This extremely simple operation probably carries the greatest risk of graft infection. (B) Roux-en-Y cholecystojejunostomy. This operation protects from hepatic sepsis by placing the new liver at a distance from the main gastrointestinal stream by virtue of an isoperistaltic limb of jejunum at least 18 inches long. (C) Roux-en-Y choledochojejunostomy. The end-to-end duct-to-bowel anastomosis is simple if the duct is dilated (FIGURE 3B), as would be the case if a conversion became necessary from B to C.

counted for the partial obstruction. With anastomosis of the graft common duct to the host duct or duodenum, biliary fistulae developed in about half the recipients. Obstruction has not been documented after these kinds of reconstruction.

Eight primary reconstructions with Roux-en-Y cholecystojejunostomy (FIGURE 2B) have been performed. One acute obstruction was caused by the technical accident shown in FIGURE 1A. A second patient had a delayed partial obstruction of the cystic duct diagnosed by transhepatic cholangiography (FIGURE 3B). He was reexplored and the drainage converted to Roux-en-Y choledochojejunostomy (FIGURE 2C).

Bacteriologic Complications

With the technical problems discussed above, clinical (and usually histopathologic) evidence of cholangitis was frequently documented.

Another kind of infectious complication, as yet hypothetical, may occur despite a technically satisfactory biliary reconstruction and no morphologic evidence of cholangitis. It has been documented that systemic infections and even asymptomatic bacteremia are common after hepatic transplantation.[14] For years, it has been suspected that the transplanted liver itself was the portal by which the microorganisms gained access to the blood stream, since no other foci of infection could be identified and because the kinds of bacteria detected by blood cultures in these patients were strikingly similar to those found in dogs and pigs subjected to liver injury or hepatic transplantation.[1] Theoretically, at least, the bacteria could have entered the homograft by either of 2 routes, the portal vein or the biliary duct system. The latter now seems to be the far more important source.

The reason for this view lies in the exposed position of the biliary duct system in relation to the gastrointestinal flora, as depicted schematically for a cholecystoduodenostomy in FIGURE 2A. Once bacteria gain access to the liver by this route, they may then escape through a bacteriologically porous liver without producing any histopathologically significant cholangitis on the way. If bacteria do indeed gain access to the liver and then the circulation via the biliary system, then a logical approach would be to place the homograft ducts as far removed from the mainstream of the gastrointestinal tract as possible, as in FIGURES 2B and 2C.

Current Policy

With these technical and bacteriologic considerations in mind, we have evolved and are attempting to follow 6 principles in establishing and assessing biliary drainage: (1) preservation of maximum homograft extrahepatic biliary duct tissue; (2) performance of cholangiography in all homografts prior to transplantation; (3) placement of the liver in a relatively bacteria-free relation to the mainstream gastrointestinal continuity; (4) avoidance of stents and drains; (5) intensification of diagnostic efforts to differentiate between obstruction and rejection in the recipient with abnormal liver function; and (6) early reoperation for suspicion of obstruction. None of the currently available methods of reconstruction completely meets all of these objectives, so that considerable individualization of care is necessary.

A Roux-en-Y cholecystojejunostomy (FIGURE 2B), our present procedure of choice, does at least partially meet all of the above objectives. If biliary obstruction later develops, the Roux limb can be detached, the gallbladder removed, and an anastomosis performed to the now dilated common duct (FIGURE 2C).

The most important objection to this approach is that creation of the Roux-en-Y jejunal limb can be extremely difficult in liver recipients, adding 3–6 hours of operating time and considerable additional blood loss to the already lengthy and bloody procedure. The reason for this is that in the adult recipient dying of hepatic failure, the small-bowel mesentery usually is quite edematous and laced with massive collaterals. Under these adverse conditions, it may be the better part of valor to perform a simple cholecystoduodenostomy with the objective of

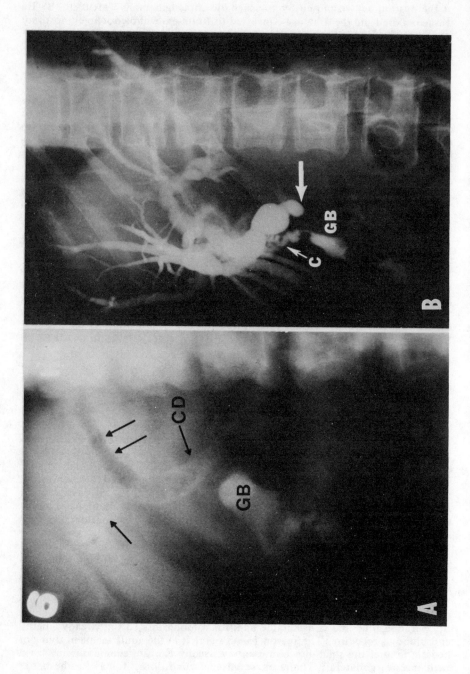

reexploring at a later time if the biliary drainage is suspected of being inadequate. If at the time of transplantation the gallbladder is found to be defective, we would now make a choice between choledochocholedochostomy with T-tube stenting and a Roux-en-Y choledochojejunostomy.

No matter what the initial procedure, an intense suspicion about and investigation of the cause for postoperative jaundice is the basic principle of postoperative management. A simple precaution is to routinely perform intravenous cholangiography early in the postoperative period (FIGURE 3A) in order to establish baseline delineation of the biliary anatomy. In almost all of our patients who do develop jaundice, transhepatic cholangiography (FIGURE 3B) and percutaneous needle biopsy are part of the work-up. Percutaneous transhepatic cholangiography has been greatly expedited by using the Chiba needle, introduced in Japan[9,16] and now being employed in several American centers. These thin-walled, small-caliber, flexible needles permit the diagnostic studies to be done with greater safety.

It is not yet established that these changes in policy will improve the results of liver transplantation. Our approach is fundamentally different from that proposed by Calne, who believes that duct-to-duct reconstruction over a T-tube and preservation of the Sphincter of Oddi when possible, will be the better solution to the technical and infectious complications of biliary drainage.[2] The fact that different methods are being tried to solve a generally recognized set of problems should be an advantage in evolving solutions that can be eventually agreed upon and applied by all.

Summary

Eighty-two patients have been treated by orthotopic hepatic transplantation in Denver since 1963. Eighteen and nine patients have lived for 1 year and 2 years posttransplantation, respectively. Thirteen recipients are still alive from 3 weeks to almost 5 years postoperatively.

Current policy has been reexamined in 3 areas in light of this experience. First, only the occasional potential recipient with alcoholic liver disease, free of infectious or other complications, is an acceptable candidate for this procedure. Second, the presence in the recipient's serum of preformed anti-red cell or lymphocytotoxic antibodies to his donor is a *relative*, but not an absolute, contraindication to hepatic transplantation, since the liver appears to be more resistant to hyperacute rejection than the kidney. Finally, a 6-point program has been outlined for establishing and evaluating bile drainage, in order to prevent or

FIGURE 3. Posttransplantation cholangiographic studies. (A) Intravenous cholangiogram in a 47-year-old recipient of a hepatic homograft, the biliary drainage for which was with Roux-en-Y cholecystojejunostomy (FIGURE 2B). The patient's liver function studies were normal at the time of the examination. However, the findings of a very slightly dilated common duct and air in the biliary system (*arrows*) are suspicious for low-grade obstruction. (B) A percutaneous transhepatic cholangiogram performed 4 weeks posttransplantation because of persistent elevations of the serum bilirubin (8–10 mg%). At the time of transplantation, biliary drainage had been established with a Roux-en-Y cholecystojejunostomy (FIGURE 2B). After obtaining this study, the patient was reexplored, the gallbladder removed, and the Roux limb anastomosed to the dilated common duct (*large arrow*), as shown in FIGURE 2C. The patient's jaundice rapidly cleared, and he now has normal liver function, 3 months posttransplantation. GB—gallbladder; CD—common bile duct; C—cystic duct.

remedy both the technical and bacteriologic complications associated with faulty biliary reconstruction.

REFERENCES

1. BRETTSCHNEIDER, L., J. L. TONG, D. S. BOOSE, P. M. DALOZE, G. V. SMITH, C. HUGUET, H. BLANCHARD, C. G. GROTH & T. E. STARZL. 1968. Specific bacteriologic problems with canine orthotopic liver transplantation. Arch. Surg. 97: 313.
2. CALNE, R. Y. & R. WILLIAMS. 1968. Liver transplantation in man. I. Observations on technique and organization in five cases. Brit. Med. J. 4: 535.
3. EISEMAN, B., D. S. LIEM & F. RAFFUCCI. 1965. Heterologous liver perfusion in treatment of hepatic failure. Ann. Surg. 162: 329.
4. GILES, G. R., H. J. BOEHMIG, H. AMEMIYA, C. G. HALGRIMSON & T. E. STARZL. 1970. Clinical heterotransplantation of the liver. Transplant. Proc. 2(4): 506.
5. GILES, G. R., H. J. BOEHMIG, J. LILLY, H. AMEMIYA, H. TAKAGI, A. J. COBURG, W. E. HATHAWAY, C. B. WILSON, F. J. DIXON & T. E. STARZL. 1971. The mechanism and modification of rejection of heterografts between divergent species. Transplant. Proc. 2(4): 522.
6. GROTH, C. G. 1974. Personal communication.
7. KISSMEYER-NIELSEN, F., S. OLSEN, V. P. PETERSON & O. FJELDBORG. 1966. Hyperacute rejection of kidney allografts, associated with pre-existing humoral antibodies against donor cells. Lancet 2: 662.
8. MARTINEAU, G., K. A. PORTER, J. CORMAN, B. LAUNOIS, G. SCHROTER, W. PALMER, C. W. PUTNAM, C. G. GROTH, C. G. HALGRIMSON, I. PENN & T. E. STARZL. 1972. Delayed biliary duct obstruction after orthotopic liver transplantation. Surgery, 72: 604.
9. OKUDA, K., K. TAMIKAWA, T. EMURA, S. KURATOMI, S. JINNOUCHI, K. URABE, T. SUNIKOSHI, Y. KANDA, Y. KUKUYAMA, H. MUSHA, H. MORI, Y. SHIMOKAWA, F. YA-USHIJI & Y. MATSUURA. 1974. Nonsurgical, percutaneous transhepatic cholangiography—diagnostic significance in medical problems of the liver. Amer. J. Dig. Dis., 19: 21.
10. SIMPSON, K. M., D. L. BUNCH, H. AMEMIYA, H. J. OBEHMIG, C. B. WILSON, F. J. DIXON, A. J. COBURG, W. E. HATHAWAY, G. R. GILES & T. E. STARZL. 1970. Humoral antibodies and coagulation mechanisms in the accelerated or hyperacute rejection of renal homografts in sensitized canine recipients. Surgery, 68: 77.
11. STARZL, T. E. 1964. Experience in Renal Transplantation. W. B. Saunders Co. Philadelphia, Pa.
12. STARZL, T. E., H. J. BOEHMIG, H. AMEMIYA, C. B. WILSON, F. J. DIXON, G. R. GILES, K. M. SIMPSON & C. G. HALGRIMSON. 1970. Clotting changes including disseminated intravascular coagulation during rapid renal homograft rejection. New Eng. J. Med., 283: 383.
13. STARZL, T. E., K. A. PORTER, G. SCHROTER, J. CORMAN, C. G. GROTH & H. L. SHARP. 1973. Autopsy findings in a long-surviving liver recipient. New Eng. J. Med., 289: 82.
14. STARZL, T. E. & C. W. PUTNAM. 1969. Experience in Hepatic Transplantation. Philadelphia, W. B. Saunders Co.
15. TERASAKI, P. I., T. L. MARCHIORO & T. E. STARZL. 1965. Sero-typing of human lymphocyte antigens: Preliminary trials on long-term kidney homograft survivors. In Histocompatibility Testing. J. J. van Rood & D. B. Amos, Eds.: 83. National Academy of Sciences, National Research Council, Washington, D.C.
16. TSUCHIYA, Y. 1969. A new, safer method of precutaneous transhepatic cholangiography. Jap. J. Gastroenterol. 66: 438.
17. WILLIAMS, G. M., D. M. HUME, R. P. HUDSON, JR., P. J. MORRIS, K. KANO & F. MILGROM. 1968. "Hyperacute" renal homograft rejection in man. New Eng. J. Med. 279: 611.

SURGICAL CONSEQUENCES OF ALCOHOLISM

Marshall J. Orloff

Department of Surgery
School of Medicine
University of California, San Diego
La Jolla, California 92103

Those involved in the therapy of alcohol abuse do not usually associate the field of surgery with considerations of alcoholism or its treatment. There is no surgical operation that can cure chronic alcoholism with the exception, perhaps, of Pavlov's operation of cervical esophagostomy, a simple procedure that diverts all material taken orally out through an opening in the neck but is socially and physiologically unacceptable. Nevertheless, it is accurate to state that day in and day out surgeons must care for large numbers of patients who are suffering from the ravages of alcoholism and who have surgical illnesses that are a direct result of or are coincidental to alcohol abuse. Somewhere between 8 and 17% of patients admitted to general hospitals are alcoholics, and more than a fair share of these are cared for on the surgical service. Therefore, alcoholism is an illness of major concern and importance to surgical specialists, and an understanding of manifestations of alcoholism and their management is essential to the proper practice of surgery.

GENERAL PROBLEMS ASSOCIATED WITH SURGERY IN ALCOHOLICS

There are certain general problems that are regularly encountered in alcoholic patients who develop surgical diseases of any kind (TABLE 1). In patients with acute alcoholic intoxication, the diagnosis of an acute surgical illness may be extraordinarily difficult because of altered consciousness. It is often impossible to obtain a meaningful history of the disease from the patient. Physical signs are often blunted and the recognition of pain is frequently lost in an alcoholic stupor. Symptoms such as vomiting, nausea, and anorexia may be erroneously attributed to the alcoholism rather than to the underlying acute appendicitis or ruptured viscus. As a result, there may be serious delays in definitive treatment with disastrous consequences.

A second problem concerns the inability of the acutely intoxicated patient to cooperate with or even passively accept necessary therapy. Irrational behavior that involves pulling out nasogastric tubes, intravenous catheters, and indwelling bladder catheters, disrupting skeletal traction, and refusing to cough or to ambulate impedes recovery from an operation and sometimes results in self-inflicted bodily harm.

The development of delerium tremens after an operation of any kind is a frequent occurrence among chronic alcoholics and adds greatly to the mortality and morbidity of the illness on which this serious complication is superimposed. We have observed postoperative delerium tremens in alcoholic patients who have abstained from alcohol for weeks and sometimes months. The mortality from delerium tremens by itself is about 10%, and when added to the metabolic demands imposed by a major operation, the rate is considerably higher.

Pulmonary complications are inordinately frequent following operations on patients with alcoholism. Next to liver disease, chronic lung disease is the most

TABLE 1

General Problems Associated with Surgery in Alcoholic Patients

1. Difficulties in diagnosis due to altered consciousness
2. Inability to cooperate with therapy
3. Postoperative delerium tremens
4. High incidence of pulmonary complications
5. Malnutrition and delayed healing
6. Liver insufficiency
7. Difficulties in anesthesia

frequent disorder found in alcoholics. The reasons are several. Approximately 60% of alcoholics smoke more than 1 pack of cigarettes per day. Furthermore, considerable evidence indicates that chronic alcoholism retards the rate of leukocyte mobilization and is associated with an increased susceptibility to infection. The incidence of tuberculosis is much higher in alcoholics than in the general population. In acute intoxication, the cough reflex is depressed so that aspiration pneumonia, atelectasis, and lung abscess are trademarks of the alcoholic. When an operation is performed on any patient with chronic lung disease and the effects of anesthesia, immobilization, and incisional pain associated with coughing are added to the underlying pulmonary disorder, the development of serious pulmonary infection during the postoperative period is difficult to prevent.

Chronic alcoholics, particularly those with advanced liver disease, sometimes have trouble with wound healing as a result of malnutrition and vitamin deficiencies.

The most serious problem encountered in chronic alcoholics who require surgery is the development of progressive liver dysfunction and failure. It is not unusual for a patient with compensated alcoholic liver disease to decompensate following an operation of only moderate magnitude. We have observed the development of full-blown hepatic coma after such simple operations as herniorrhaphy or hemorrhoidectomy. There is no question that alcoholic liver disease significantly increases the risk of any operation.

Finally, anesthesia in patients with alcoholism is associated with a variety of special problems. In acutely intoxicated patients requiring emergency surgery there is the danger of aspiration pneumonia due to a full stomach and a depressed cough reflex. In individuals with alcoholic liver disease, the halogenated anesthetic agents may be dangerous. Resistance to anesthesia is sometimes observed in chronic alcoholics, so that the usual doses of anesthetic agents are not effective and the control of anesthesia may be difficult. Prolonged respiratory depression following anesthesia sometimes occurs as a result of delayed hepatic metabolism of anesthetic agents and muscle relaxants.

SURGICAL DISEASES ASSOCIATED WITH ALCOHOLISM

In addition to general problems encountered in alcoholic patients who require surgery, there is a sizable number of specific surgical diseases that are a consequence of alcoholism (TABLE 2). The most common and serious of these is cirrhosis of the liver, which is discussed in detail below. The second most frequent category of disease caused by alcoholism is traumatic injury. One-half of all fatal automobile accidents occur in people who are under the influence of alcohol. Similarly, over 50% of home accidents are related to alcoholism. One-third of head injuries in adults are caused by alcoholic intoxication, and these are particularly difficult to diagnose and treat because of the clouding of important symptoms and signs by the effects of alcohol on the central nervous system.

A third condition often related to alcoholism is the body surface burn. Fully $\frac{1}{3}$ of thermal injuries occur as a result of carelessness in patients who are intoxicated with alcohol.

Of the several causes of acute pancreatitis, the most frequent is chronic alcoholism. The current hypothesis is that alcohol produces pancreatitis by stimulating pancreatic secretion while at the same time obstructing the pancreatic duct by causing duodenitis and spasm of the sphincter of Oddi. Chronic pancreatitis, the relentless form of this disease, is almost always associated with alcoholism. It is a particularly difficult condition to treat and is associated with a significant mortality.

Alcohol stimulates gastric acid secretion and irritates the gastric mucosa. These qualities are responsible for several digestive disorders that sometimes require surgical therapy. The most common of these is alcoholic gastritis with bleeding that occasionally is of such magnitude as to require an emergency operation to control hemorrhage. Another condition is the Mallory-Weiss syndrome, a tear in the mucosa at the gastroesophageal junction that results from forceful vomiting after the ingestion of large quantities of alcohol and often produces massive hemorrhage. The frequency of peptic ulcer has been reported to be increased in chronic alcoholics, although the exact incidence is a matter of controversy. Lastly, spontaneous rupture of the lower esophagus, an often lethal condition that Boerhaave first described in 1724 in an alcoholic Dutch admiral, is a surgical emergency that almost always results from violent vomiting during alcoholic intoxication.

Several types of cancer are particularly prevalent in chronic alcoholics. The incidence of carcinoma of the oropharynx and the larynx is considerably higher

TABLE 2
Surgical Diseases Associated with Alcoholism

1. Cirrhosis of the liver
2. Injuries
3. Burns of body surface
4. Pancreatitis
5. Gastritis with bleeding
6. Mallory-Weiss syndrome
7. ? Peptic ulcer
8. Spontaneous rupture of esophagus
9. Cancer
   a. Oropharynx
   b. Larynx
   c. Esophagus
   d. Hepatoma
10. Lesions of the extremities
    a. Dupuytrens' contracture
    b. Saturday night palsy
    c. Venous leg ulcers
    d. Civilian frostbite
    e. Restraint injuries

among alcoholics than in the general population. Between 60 and 80% of patients who develop carcinoma of the esophagus give a history of chronic alcoholism. In the United States, cancer of the liver in adults is found mainly in patients with cirrhosis of the liver, some of whom have alcoholic cirrhosis.

Finally, a number of lesions of the extremities are seen frequently or mainly in patients with chronic alcoholism. An intriguing but unexplained relationship exists between Dupuytren's contracture of the hand and alcoholism. "Saturday night palsy" is a wrist drop that results from lying on the radial nerve during an alcoholic stupor. Venous leg ulcers, sometimes called "wine sores," are frequent in alcoholics. Frostbite in civilians is almost confined to derelict alcoholics who are exposed to cold while intoxicated. Lastly, a variety of neurologic and vascular injuries are seen in alcoholic patients who have been placed in restraints in jails, psychiatric facilities, and hospitals.

ALCOHOLIC CIRRHOSIS, PORTAL HYPERTENSION, AND BLEEDING ESOPHAGEAL VARICES

The most frequent condition that demands surgical treatment in alcoholic patients is portal hypertension due to cirrhosis of the liver. In the United States, a substantial majority of the cases of cirrhosis are due to chronic alcohol abuse. Cirrhosis is reported to be the ninth leading cause of death among people of all ages, and the fourth leading cause of death in those over the age of 40.[11] During the past 15 years, the death rate from cirrhosis is reported to have increased more than that from any other cause of mortality. The social cost of alcoholic cirrhosis has been estimated to be 3 billion dollars per year.

There are a number of important clinical manifestations of cirrhosis and portal hypertension that require the attention of surgeons. The most frequent ones are bleeding esophageal varices, hepatic coma, and ascites. Less frequent but significant manifestations are the hyperdynamic cardiovascular state, hypersplenism, and renal failure. Limitations of space preclude a discussion of all of these, but some remarks about bleeding esophageal varices are in order. This complication is responsible for $\frac{1}{3}$ of the deaths of cirrhotic patients, and is the one most amenable to surgical therapy.

The lethality of alcoholic cirrhosis is shown in TABLE 3, which presents survival rates of patients admitted to general hospitals because of cirrhosis. The study at the top of the table is the classic work of Ratnoff and Patek, who examined in retrospect the case histories of 386 patients admitted to 5 New York hospitals between 1916 and 1938.[12] Only $\frac{1}{3}$ of those with ascites were alive 1 year after

TABLE 3
Natural History of Alcoholic Cirrhosis

Authors	Cases	Complications	Survival in %		
			1 Year	2 Years	5 Years
Ratnoff and Patek (5	296	Ascites	32	17	7
New York Hospitals,	245	Jaundice	26	23	5
1916–1938)[12]	106	Hematemesis	28	25	20
Boston Inter-Hospital	467	Varices	34	21	$5\frac{1}{2}$
Liver Group (7 Boston	288	Varices without bleeding	43	25	8
Hospitals, 1959–1961)[3]	179	Varices with bleeding	21	14	$1\frac{1}{2}$

TABLE 4

Mortality of First Variceal Hemorrhage in Cirrhosis

Authors	Reported	Type of Hospital	No. of Patients	Mortality—%
Ratnoff & Patek[12]	1942	Five private-teaching	106	40
Higgins[4]	1947	City indigent	45	76
Atik & Simeone[1]	1954	City indigent	59	83
Nachlas et al.[7]	1955	City indigent	102	59
Cohn & Blaisdell[2]	1958	City indigent	456	74
Taylor & Jontz[13]	1959	Veterans	102	45
Merigan et al.[5]	1960	City indigent	74	76
Orloff	1962	City indigent	87	84
		Total	1031	Mean 73

hospitalization, and little over a handful survived 5 years. The survival rates in patients with jaundice and hematemesis were quite similar.

The study in the lower portion of the Table is the more recent prospective study of the 7-hospital Boston Inter-Hospital Liver Group.[3] Of the patients who bled from esophageal varices, 79% were dead within 1 year. In the entire group of 467 patients, only 26 lived for 5 years. The results of these studies indicate that once a patient has entered a hospital for treatment of cirrhosis, his chances of living for 1 year have been about the same as those of patients with acute lymphocytic leukemia, and the chances of his surviving 5 years have been similar to those observed in most untreated cancers.

The cirrhotic patient who enters the hospital with his first episode of bleeding esophageal varices has had less than a 50–50 chance of leaving the hospital alive (TABLE 4). The immediate mortality of the first bleeding episode has averaged 70% or more during each decade since 1940. From these statistics, it is apparent that the emergency treatment of bleeding esophageal varices is the most important problem in the therapy of portal hypertension. The prompt and definitive control of the initial bleeding episode is where our efforts must be directed if the survival rate of patients with varix hemorrhage is to be improved. For this compelling reason, we have focused our attention on emergency therapy and have conducted prospective studies in unselected patients of the various methods of emergency treatment.

During the past quarter century a variety of nonoperative emergency measures have been used to control bleeding from esophageal varices. The most widely used nonoperative modalities have been esophageal balloon tamponade, systemic intravenous administration of pituitrin, regional administration of pituitrin by selective catheterization of the mesenteric arteries, and gastroesophageal hypothermia. All of these are nondefinitive forms of treatment that have as their objective the temporary control of bleeding so that the patient can be deliberately prepared for a definitive operation. All of them have been successful in stopping hemorrhage, but, unfortunately, they have failed to affect the overall mortality of the underlying disease because of the frequent recurrence of bleeding or the development of hepatic failure before definitive treatment could be applied.

Two forms of emergency surgical treatment have been used to control bleeding varices in patients with alcoholic cirrhosis. These are emergency transesophageal ligation of varices and emergency portacaval shunt. Transesophageal varix ligation is not a definitive procedure, since varices invariably recur and bleed if nothing is done subsequently to relieve the portal hypertension. The only definitive form of therapy currently available is emergency portacaval shunt. The main question about emergency surgical treatment has concerned the tolerance of critically ill patients for major operations that are performed in the face of bleeding.

Fifteen years ago we initiated a series of prospective studies of the various methods of emergency treatment of bleeding varices in unselected patients with alcoholic cirrhosis.[8-10] The 3 treatment programs that we have compared are: (1) medical therapy with esophageal balloon tamponade, followed, when possible, by elective portacaval shunt; (2) emergency transesophageal ligation of varices, followed, when possible, by elective portacaval shunt; and (3) emergency portacaval shunt. The diagnosis was made in all of our patients within 7 hours of admission to the Emergency Room by use of an organized diagnostic plan that we have reported previously.[9,10] Emergency operation was undertaken within 8 hours of admission, and rigorous lifelong follow-up has been conducted in our Portal Hypertension Clinic such that the current status of 98.3% of the patients is known.

TABLE 5 and FIGURE 1 summarize the results of our prospective studies. Early survival rates associated with the 2 forms of surgical therapy were about 3 times greater than the survival rate resulting from medical treatment alone ($P = <0.001$). Seven-year survival, both actual and predicted by the life-table method, was significantly greater following emergency portacaval shunt than after either of the two other types of emergency treatment ($P = <0.001$). From these data we have concluded that emergency portacaval shunt is the most effective treatment of bleeding esophageal varices in patients with alcoholic cirrhosis.

What about the patients who recover from an episode of bleeding esophageal varices as a result of nondefinitive emergency treatment? Abundant data indicate that almost all such patients will bleed again unless their portal hypertension is corrected by an elective portal systemic shunt. Despite this established consequence and the absence of any other form of effective treatment, there has been considerable controversy about the value of elective portacaval shunt, largely as a result of the lack of any valid data from prospective clinical trials. However, the preliminary results of such a prospective study have been reported recently by Mikkelsen and are summarized in FIGURE 2.[6] In selected "good risk" cirrhotic patients, randomized into medical and surgical treatment groups, the 5-year survival rate was 60% for the patients treated by elective portacaval

TABLE 5

Comparison of Three Types of Emergency Treatment of Bleeding Esophageal Varices in Unselected Patients with Cirrhosis

	Medical Therapy*	Varix Ligation*	Emergency Portacaval Shunt
Number of patients	59	28	115
Jaundice on admission—%	42	57	46
Ascites on admission—%	41	50	55
Encephalopathy on admission—%	25	25	21
Mean liver index on admission	2.8	2.8	2.5
Early survival—%	17	54	48
Seven year survival—%	0	18	30

*Followed by elective portacaval shunt when possible.

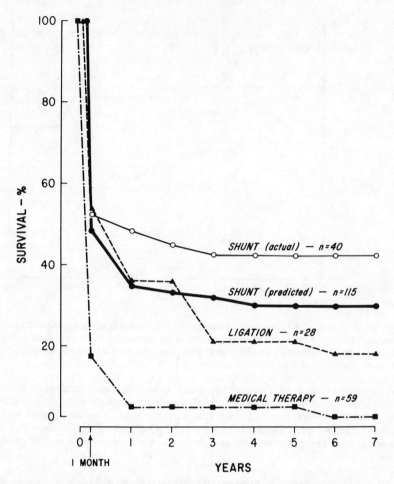

FIGURE 1. Cumulative survival rates associated with 3 forms of emergency treatment of bleeding esophageal varices calculated by the life-table method. Actual survival of 40 patients who were operated on 7 or more years ago is also shown. (From Orloff *et al.*[10] By permission of *Archives of Surgery*.)

shunt and only 10% for the patients treated medically. These results provide strong support for the use of elective portacaval shunt in patients who are fortunate enough to recover from an episode of varix hemorrhage.

In the course of conducting our prospective clinical trials of emergency therapy of bleeding varices, we have accumulated a substantial long-term experience with chronic alcoholic patients and have obtained some interesting data. TABLE 6 shows the influence of the pattern of alcoholism on the survival of bleeding cirrhotic patients who underwent emergency portacaval shunt. Seventy-eight percent of the patients in our study admitted to chronic alcoholism for more than 10 years, and only 12% reported drinking heavily for less than 5 years. However, the survival rates were not significantly different between the 2 groups.

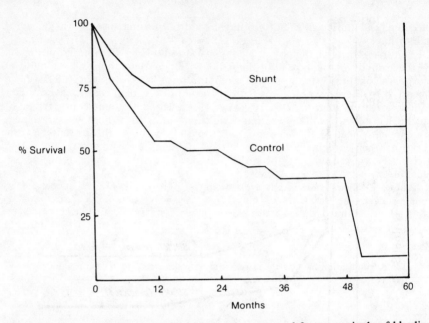

FIGURE 2. Survival of "good risk" patients who recovered from an episode of bleeding varices and then were randomized into an elective portacaval-shunt group (37 patients) and a control-medical treatment group (38 patients) as calculated by the life-table method. (From Mikkelsen.[6] By permission of *Archives of Surgery*.)

Seventy-three percent of the patients drank heavily during the week preceding the onset of bleeding and, in fact, $\frac{1}{3}$ of the patients drank after they vomited blood. On the other hand, 7% of the patients bled from esophageal varices despite abstention from alcohol for over a year. There was a significant difference in survival between patients who had abstained for more than a month prior to

TABLE 6
Influence of Pattern of Alcoholism on Survival After
Emergency Portacaval Shunt for Bleeding Varices

	Percent of Patients	Survival %	Influence on Survival
Years of Alcoholism Preoperatively			
>10	78	40	None
5–10	10	40	
<5	12	62	
Last Ingestion of Alcohol Before Bleeding			
<2 days	61 ⎫		
3–7 days	12 ⎬	39	P = <0.02
8–30 days	7 ⎭		
>1 month	21	71	
Postoperative Alcoholism (2–10 years)			
Resumption	47	70	P = <0.02
Abstinence	53	88	

bleeding, and those who had continued to drink during the month preceding hemorrhage.

Extensive efforts at therapy of alcoholic cirrhotics have often been questioned on the grounds that almost all of the patients will continue their suicidal habit of chronic alcoholism after discharge from the hospital. Nothing is further from the truth. A little over $\frac{1}{2}$ of our patients have not returned to drinking during a follow-up period of from 2 to 10 years. Those who did resume consumption of alcohol had a significantly lower long-term survival rate than those who abstained. We are convinced that the unique relationship between the patient and the surgeon, when combined with frequent and lifelong follow-up visits, can be used effectively to prevent a substantial number of patients from returning to alcoholism.

TABLE 7 shows the extent to which our efforts have been successful in rehabilitating the survivors of emergency portacaval shunt. On the basis of clinical and laboratory examinations, the general status of our patients is excellent or good in 61%, fair in 18% and poor in 20%. All but one of the patients

TABLE 7

Rehabilitation of Alcoholic Cirrhotics After Emergency Portacaval Shunt

	Percent of Group		
	Males	Females	Total
General Status			
Excellent or good			61
Fair			18
Poor			20
Work Status			
Working	59	69	62
Not working	38	15	31
Insufficient data	3	15	6
Unchanged compared to 1 year preop.	84	64	79
Increased compared to 1 year preop.	16	18	17
Decreased compared to 1 year preop.	0	18	4

considered to be in poor condition have returned to alcoholism. Almost $\frac{2}{3}$ of the patients are working and leading productive lives. Ninety-six percent of the patients are doing either more work or the same amount of work as they were doing 1 year preoperatively. It should be noted that these results have been achieved without the aid of psychiatrists, social workers, and other professionals who have expertise in the treatment of alcoholism. There is reason to believe that greater success in rehabilitation could be obtained with the active participation and help of professional personnel who are trained in the care of alcoholic patients.

In concluding these comments on alcoholic cirrhosis, it should be emphasized that the surgeon is called upon to treat the life-threatening but tertiary manifestations of disease that occur at the end of the line. Surgical therapy often preserves life, but it does not directly affect either the primary disease, chronic alcoholism, or the secondary disease, cirrhosis of the liver. These underlying diseases frequently continue or progress following successful surgical therapy. How much better off the patients would be if chronic alcoholism could be arrested before producing cirrhosis and bleeding varices and, failing that, how much better off they would be if surgical therapy were combined with effective means of preventing a return to alcohol abuse.

SUMMARY

1. The problems of alcoholism are regularly and frequently encountered in the practice of surgery.

2. Alcoholics who require surgical treatment present a number of general problems that include difficulties in diagnosing disease, inability to cooperate with therapy, postoperative delerium tremens, frequent pulmonary infection, delayed wound healing, liver dysfunction, and difficulties with anesthesia.

3. Alcoholism causes several specific surgical diseases. These include cirrhosis of the liver, traumatic injuries, burns, pancreatitis, gastric bleeding, rupture of the esophagus, several types of cancer and a variety of lesions of the extremities.

4. Alcoholic cirrhosis and portal hypertension produce several surgical complications, the most important of which is bleeding esophageal varices. Varix hemorrhage is frequently lethal, and emergency treatment is of paramount importance. Our prospective evaluation of emergency therapy during the past 15 years has shown that *emergency portacaval shunt* is the most effective therapeutic measure.

5. In patients who recovered from an episode of varix hemorrhage following nondefinitive treatment, results of a recent prospective clinical trial indicate that subsequent *elective portacaval shunt* prolonged life significantly.

6. Surgical therapy of the complications of cirrhosis, unfortunately, does not affect the underlying alcoholism or liver disease. By frequent follow-up we have managed to keep $\frac{1}{2}$ of our patients from returning to alcohol and $\frac{2}{3}$ have resumed productive work. However, it is likely that these results could be improved by a program of rehabilitation that includes effective therapy of alcoholism. Our greatest efforts should be directed toward this objective.

REFERENCES

1. ATIK, M & F. SIMEONE. 1954. Massive gastrointestinal bleeding: A study of 296 patients at City Hospital of Cleveland. Arch. Surg. 69: 355–365.
2. COHN, R. & F. W. BLAISDELL. 1958. The natural history of the patient with cirrhosis of the liver with esophageal varices following the first massive hemorrhage. Surg. Gynec. Obstet. 106: 699–701.
3. GARCEAU, A. J., T. C. CHALMERS & THE BOSTON INTER-HOSPITAL LIVER GROUP. 1963. The natural history of cirrhosis: I. Survival with esophageal varices. New Eng. J. Med. 268: 469.
4. HIGGINS, W. H. JR. 1947. The esophageal varix: A report of 115 cases. Amer. J. Med. Sci. 214: 436–441.
5. MERIGAN, T. C. JR., R. M. HOLLISTER, P. F. GRYSKA, G. W. G. STARKEY & C. S. DAVIDSON. 1960. Gastrointestinal bleeding with cirrhosis: Study of 172 episodes in 158 patients. New Eng. J. Med. 263: 579–585.
6. MIKKELSEN, W. P. 1974. Therapeutic portacaval shunt. Preliminary data on controlled trial and morbid effects of acute hyaline necrosis. Arch. Surg. 108: 302.
7. NACHLAS, M. M., J. E. O'NEILL & A. J. A. CAMPBELL. 1955. The life history of patients with cirrhosis of the liver and bleeding esophageal varices. Ann. Surg. 141: 10–23.
8. ORLOFF, M. J. 1962. A comparative study of emergency transesophageal ligation and non-surgical treatment of bleeding esophageal varices in unselected patients with cirrhosis. Surgery 52: 103–116.
9. ORLOFF, M. J. 1967. Emergency portacaval shunt: A comparative study of shunt,

varix ligation and nonsurgical treatment of bleeding esophageal varices in unselected patients with cirrhosis. Ann. Surg. **166**: 456–478.

10. ORLOFF, M. J., J. G. CHANDLER, A. C. CHARTERS III, J. K. CONDON, D. E. GRAMBORT, T. R. MODAFFERI & S. E. LEVIN. 1974. Emergency portacaval shunt treatment for bleeding esophageal varices. Prospective study in unselected patients with alcoholic cirrhosis. Arch. Surg. **108**: 293.

11. ORLOFF, M. J. 1974. An appraisal of progress in the treatment of portal hypertension. Arch. Surg. **108**: 269.

12. RATNOFF, O. D. & A. J. PATEK, JR. 1942. Natural history of Laennec's cirrhosis of liver. Analyses of 386 cases. Medicine **21**: 207–268.

13. TAYLOR, F. W. & J. G. JONTZ. 1959. Cirrhosis with hemorrhage. Arch. Surg. **78**: 786–790.

B. The Pancreas

INTRODUCTION

Kenneth Williams

Pancreatitis is one of the more frequent causes for hospitalization in alcoholics following bouts of drinking. This does not so much speak to the frequency of this condition relative to other medical complications of alcoholism as to the painful severity of the acute attack. Individuals with acute alcoholic pancreatitis can be as uncomfortable as any patients in medicine. Superimposed on the abdominal pain is often copious vomiting and malodorous diarrhea.

This condition illustrates one of the hallmarks of alcoholism, for following full medical explanations, with apparent full realization of what they are doing, these patients will commonly continue to drink and precipitate repeated attacks of pancreatitis. I'm sure most physicians caring for alcoholics have seen some patients with this condition hospitalized 20 times or more.

Although pancreatitis has been recognized as an affliction of alcoholics for nearly 100 years, the sequence of events whereby alcohol produces the pathologic changes in the pancreas is today incompletely understood. However, the amount of newly acquired scientific information in *The Pancreas* section of this monograph is considerable. Progress in the understanding of alcoholic pancreatitis, especially its pathogenesis, has proceeded rapidly in recent years. The included papers present a careful delineation of our current knowledge in this area.

ALCOHOL AND THE PANCREAS

Henri Sarles

Unité de Recherches de Pathologie Digestives
Marseille, France

Howard and Jordan[1] were the first authors to show that gallstone pancreatitis and alcoholic pancreatitis had different clinical and pathological courses. It has been found in our laboratory that alcoholic chronic pancreatitis belongs to a particular form of chronic pancreatitis (CP) that has been described under the name of chronic calcifying pancreatitis (CCP). This disease is characterized by a peculiar group of pathological features.[2-4] A blind histological study of 100 cases of chronic pancreatitis made by two observers with the aid of a computer has shown that these features differentiate CCP from the other forms of CP. The first visible features of CCP is the precipitation, in ducts and acini, of protein plugs formed mainly by the normal pancreatic fluid proteins.[5] These protein precipitates can be washed out by the flow of fluid. When they remain in the ducts, they retract and calcify, forming pancreatic stones. The presence in the ducts of these protein plugs or stones seems to be the origin of all other lesions. They irritate the duct epithelium, which atrophies and then disappears, allowing the connective periductal tissue to proliferate and obstruct segments of ducts. In the obstructed areas, the pancreatic exocrine tissue disappears and is replaced by sclerosis; sometimes, when a certain quantity of secretory parenchyma persists, its progressive dilatation leads to the formation of cysts and pseudocysts. This describes the typical features of CCP, which are:

1. Lobular distribution of the lesions. At first one abnormal lobule is surrounded by large areas of normal tissue. In these lobular foci, one finds (a) a dilatation of some ducts or acini, forming rounded cavities, (b) the frequent presence of protein plugs or stones in these rounded cavities, (c) intra- and perilobular sclerosis.

2. Half of the cases are associated with cysts or pseudocysts.

3. The course of the disease is complicated by acute attacks, more often edema and fatty necrosis than hemorrhagic necrosis, which tend to diminish when the pancreatic tissue is largely destroyed.

This evolution is inevitable whatever the dietetic, medical, or surgical treatment, and therefore puts chronic calcifying pancreatitis into the group of chronic pancreatitis as defined by the Marseille Symposium.[6]

In Europe, in South America, and very probably in North America, the cause of CCP is mostly alcoholism.[3,7,8] Chronic alcoholic calcifying pancreatitis is generally observed in men drinking at least 2 years (generally 6 to 10 years) a mean quantity of 150 ml of alcohol per day. The nature of the alcoholic beverage seems to play no role. The usual diet of these patients, when known, was significantly richer in proteins and fats than the diet of normal controls. In fact, the association of alcoholism and malnutrition has never been proved to play a rôle in the disease. The first symptoms of the disease are generally observed at 38 years of age. Causes other than alcoholism are responsible for identical lesions: protein insufficiency during childhood in the Afro-Asiatic intertropical area is the most frequent. The idiopathic form is fairly rare; the form secondary to hyperparathyroidism, the congenital form, is also rare.

An identical or very similar disease exists spontaneously in the rat, and we found it twice among some hundred rabbits.[9] The pancreatic lithiasis of cattle is quite different: although the stones are identical the lesions are localized immediately around the main duct or some of its proximal branches.[10]

In our laboratory it has been found that the action of alcohol is different and often contrary, depending on whether the animal is or is not adapted to regular consumption of it. We therefore will examine acute and chronic experimental alcoholism separately.

ACUTE ALCOHOLISM

Acute alcoholism may be defined as the occasional introduction of ethanol through the digestive tract or the veins in men or animals not accustomed to regular consumption of it.

Dog

Sphincter of Oddi

Menguy et al.[11] and Walton et al.[12] have shown that ethanol consumption increases the resistance of the sphincter of Oddi to the flow of bile.

Release of Intestinal Hormones

The contact of ethanol with duodenojujenal mucosa does not seem to have a significant action on the release of secretin or pancreozymin in the waking animal.[13]

Release of Gastrin by the Antrum and Secretion of Hydrochloric Acid by the Stomach

It has been shown by Woodward et al.[14] and by Treffot et al.[15] that the contact of ethanol with the antral mucosa increases the release of gastrin. This action disappears after antrectomy. The action of intragastric ethanol on hydrochloric acid secretion reaches its maximum at an ethanol concentration of 16% (v/v).[16] Elwin considers this fact proof that the release of gastrin is decreased by higher concentrations. When the passage of gastric fluid into the duodenum is prevented, the pancreatic secretion of proteins induced by infusion of either 40% or 80% ethanol into the stomach is maximum with 80% ethanol. This secretion of pancreatic proteins is suppressed by antrectomy.[17] One can therefore conclude that the release of gastrin increases with increasing concentration of ethanol, at least until 80%, but that the gastric acid secretion is inhibited above 16%. In the dog, gastrin has a direct excitatory effect on the secretion of proteins by the pancreatic tissue.

After the consumption of ethanol, the release of gastrin and another mechanism, probably cholinergic,[14,19,20] leads to a secretion of H^+, which in turn will release secretin in the duodenum.

Direct Inhibitory Action of Ethanol on Pancreatic Secretion[13,21]

Since the inhibitory effect is normally more or less completely screened by the passage of H^+ ions from the stomach into the duodenum, it is necessary to prevent gastric fluid from entering the duodenum, for instance by opening the gastric Thomas cannula. In these conditions, the intravenous injection of 0.7 to 1.5 g/kg ethanol inhibits the pancreatic secretion of water and bicarbonate and, much more significantly, protein secretion. This inhibition is suppressed by intravenous infusion of 75 μg/kg/h atropine[21] or of 0.75 mg/kg/h pentonium and partially abolished by vagotomy.[22] On the other hand, previous reserpinization is ineffective.[23] This means that in the animals that are not adapted to alcohol consumption, alcohol excites a cholinergic inhibitory mechanism probably originating in the brain and passing through the vagus nerve. Interaction between ethanol and gastroduodenal hormones is evident: alcohol-induced pancreatic inhibition is more marked under infusion of pure secretin (1 CU/kg/h), less marked under infusion of secretin at the same dose +3 Crick Harper and Raper U CCK/kg/h. The existence of other cholinergic inhibitory nerves extending to the pancreas by other routes than the vagus nerve is suggested by the fact that in vagotomized animals this inhibition is only partially abolished. We must point out that Bayer et al.[24] did not find an inhibitory action of ethanol on protein secretion. The confirmation of our results in man[25] makes them probable in the dog, especially since they have been reproduced in another series of 5 dogs in the laboratory (unpublished results).

Gross Action on Pancreatic Secretion

The action of ethanol on pancreatic secretion is extremely complex, because it brings into play at the same time mechanisms that increase the secretion and others that decrease it. The final result in a dog receiving 1 g/kg ethanol into the stomach (the gastric Thomas cannula being closed to enable gastric secretion to enter the duodenum) is an increase of flow rate and bicarbonate output corresponding to 0.25 CU secretin and an increase of protein output corresponding to 0.33 Crick Harper and Raper U CCK-PZ,[26] which is a very weak stimulation of the gland. It must be added that nobody has been able to produce pancreatic lesions in the dog by acute administration of ethanol.[9]

Rat

Intragastric infusion of ethanol at doses up to 12 g/kg is able to kill the rat but not capable of producing pancreatic lesions.[9] De Saint-Blanquat and Derache[27] showed that the rat stomach isolated and incubated with diluted ethanol releases gastrin.

Rabbit

Electromyographic study on the rabbit showed that after ethanol infusion (1 g/kg) the sphincter of Oddi contracts more, with an increase of the number and the size of the spikes. Moreover, the biliary pressure rose from 2 to 10 cm water.[28]

Man

Sphincter of Oddi

It has been shown by Davis and Pirola[31] and by Capitaine and Sarles[32] that intraduodenal injection or intravenous infusion of ethanol increased the tone of the sphincter of Oddi. This increase is nevertheless moderate, and lower than during the course of benign vaterian stenosis (odditis), a disease that causes chronic pancreatitis, but never of the chronic calcifying type caused by chronic alcoholism.[3]

Release of Gastrointestinal Hormones

The contact of ethanol with the duodenal mucosa leads to a weak pancreatic secretion of water and bicarbonate but not of proteins, suggesting the release of a small quantity of secretin.[33,34] According to Korman et al.,[36] the release of gastrin due to alcohol ingestion is weak and lower than after a normal meal.

Direct Inhibitory Action on the Pancreas

It has been shown by Mott et al. that intragastric injection of 150 ml of 40% (v/v) ethanol gave rise to an inhibition of water and bicarbonate pancreatic secretion but gave a much stronger inhibition of enzyme secretion.[25] The peak is obtained 60 to 75 minutes after ethanol injection at the time of the peak alcohol blood level. Intravenous injection of 10% ethanol (0.60 g/kg) has the same inhibitory effect as soon as after the first minutes. These results have been confirmed by Marin et al.[37]

Gross Results in Pancreatic Secretion

As in the dog, pancreatic secretion in man induced by the consumption of 150 ml of 40% ethanol is weak (unpublished results). There is no proof that acute alcoholism (occasional consumption of alcohol in people not adapted to its regular consumption) might be a cause of acute pancreatitis. Acute pancreatitis is seen in chronic alcoholics.[1,38]

Summary

Acute oral consumption or intravenous injection of ethanol in men or animals not adapted to chronic alcohol consumption has a complex action on pancreatic secretion by means of varied and often antagonistic mechanisms. Compared with the action of a meal, the result is a weak pancreatic secretion and a relatively weak increase of the tone of the sphincter of Oddi. There is no evidence that this could be a cause of acute or chronic pancreatic lesions.

CHRONIC ALCOHOLISM

Dog

It has been shown by experiments in our laboratory that accustoming the animals to the daily consumption of 2g/kg ethanol leads to profound modifications of gastroduodenal hormone release, of pancreas parasympathetic tone, and of the effect of acute consumption of ethanol on the pancreas. These studies were made on a group of 6 dogs provided with gastric and pancreatic Thomas cannulae to allow the collection of juice in waking animals and to prevent gastric juice from entering the duodenum by opening the gastric cannula. One of these dogs had been previously vagotomized. In experiments on gastroduodenal hormone release, the gastric canulla was opened (normal gastroduodenal transit). These alcoholic dogs have been studied with a given experimental protocol before starting daily consumption of alcohol. The same protocol was repeated at different times from the 6th week to the 2nd year of chronic alcoholism. A group of 5 control dogs that did not receive daily doses of alcohol were subjected to the same experiments at the same time.

Basal Pancreatic Secretion (Pancreatic Juice Collected After 18 Hours Fasting)

Basal pancreatic secretion is not significantly different in chronic alcoholic and nonalcoholic animals (unpublished data).

Sensitivity of Acinar Cells to Gastroduodenal Hormones

The pancreatic response (protein output and, at a lesser degree, flow rate and bicarbonate output) to CCK-PZ infusion increases as early as the 6th week of chronic alcohol consumption to a maximum at the 14th week and finally diminishes to return to prealcoholic level at the 9th month. This reveals a transitory increase of the acinar cells sensitively by CCK-PZ. The same effect has been found on stomach (see below).

On the other hand, the response to secretin does not vary during the first 8 months. At the 12th month, protein concentration and output during a perfusion of secretin are significantly weaker than before chronic alcohol consumption. It is questionable if this functional decrease is not secondary to the development of chronic pancreatic lesions. This point will be resolved when the animals are sacrificed and the pathological study is performed.

CCK-PZ Release

Intraduodenal instillation of 20 ml oleic acid, after 14 months of chronic alcoholism, leads to a pancreatic protein secretion 6 times higher than during the prealcoholic period. Water and bicarbonate secretion is only slightly modified. This can be explained by a considerable increase of CCK-PZ release during chronic alcoholism.[39] If the response of duodenal mucosa to oleic acid is increased in chronic alcoholic dogs, the injection of ethanol into the duodenum is unable to modify the pancreatic secretion in those provided with a pancreatic cannula as in the prealcoholic period.

Gastrin Release

At the 14th month of chronic alcoholism, the response of the antral mucosa to a meat meal (150 g lean meat) is a gastrin release (radioimmunoassay) significantly higher and more prolonged than in nonalcoholic animals. The difference is still higher when 1 g/kg 50% ethanol is added to the meat.[15,40]

Gastric H^+ Secretion

According to Chey et al.[41] when dogs are given alcohol in large doses and high concentrations for a period of 6 months, the mean maximal acid output by stomach increases by 35% in response to histamine. Later it returns to control values.[42,43]

Direct Action of Ethanol on the Pancreas

The more surprising effect of chronic alcoholism concerns the direct action of ethanol on pancreatic secretion. As early as the 6th week, the inhibition secondary to an intravenous injection of 1.3 g/kg ethanol begins to decrease. At the 40th week, flow rate increases. At the 12th month, the inhibition is no longer observed, but there appears a strong increase of pancreatic secretion, especially of protein output and concentration.[5,44] Like the inhibitory action obtained during the prealcoholic period the excitatory effect of intravenous ethanol during chronic alcoholism is abolished by perfusion of 75 μg/kg/h atropine and 0.75 mg/kg/h of a ganglioplegic (penthonium). This inhibitory action was not abolished in the vagotomized animals. It was not modified by previous reserpinization.[23] At this stage, alcohol acts therefore through a cholinergic mechanism, probably at the level of the intrapancreatic vagal synapse. The reasons why chronic alcoholism reverses the direct effect of ethanol on the pancreas are not clear. The assumption of two types of cholinergic pathways, inhibitory and excitatory—the first one predominating and screening the second one in the nonalcoholic animal, but more sensitive to ethanol and destroyed by chronic alcohol consumption—would explain these discrepancies.

Gross Result on Pancreatic Secretion

The consequence of these different effects of chronic alcoholism is the secretion of a juice more concentrated in proteins. As soon as the 6th week of intoxication, protein precipitates rich in calcium carbonate and identical to human small pancreatic stones are visible in pancreatic juice. These protein plugs may temporarily obstruct the ducts. Secretion stops and resumes again precipitously when the plugs are excreted by the pancreatic cannula. The formation of these protein precipitates is not related to calcium concentration of pancreatic juice. The latter tends to diminish in the chronic alcoholic dog.[45]

It has been reported by Cueto et al.[46] that ethanol administration (5 g/kg/day, 5 days per week, through a gastrotomy) to dogs given a fat- and protein-rich diet leads as early as the 6th week to "chronic pancreatitis" lesions if the gastric content is not diverted from the duodenum. We were unable to produce pancreatic lesions in dogs fed with a well-balanced diet, not enriched in fat proteins, and associated with ethanol (5 g/kg/day).[9] It is questionable whether the difference between the work of Cueto et al. and ours is due to the different diets. It seems more difficult to produce a chronic pancreatitis in the dog than in the rat. Besides, in contrast to man and rat, the dog does not spontaneously develop lesions identical to the chronic calcifying pancreatitis.

Rat

The fact that the rat has neither gallblader nor sphincter of Oddi but nevertheless develops lesions very similar to human chronic pancreatitis must be considered when one is tempted to think that a conflict between hypersecretion of the pancreas and hypertony of the sphincter of Oddi explains the action of ethanol on the human pancreas.[9]

In the rat, spontaneous chronic pancreatitis and spontaneous protein precipitates in pancreatic juice are frequent. But the frequency of this spontaneous disease is significantly increased by the consumption of 20% ethanol over 2 years.

Secretion of Proteins

The pancreatic juice of these chronic alcoholic rats has a protein concentration almost twice as high as that of nonalcoholic control animals. The frequency of protein precipitates in the juice is correlated with the hyperconcentration of proteins in the juice.

The Level of Exportable Enzymes (Lipase, Trypsin, Chymotrypsin, Amylase) in Pancreatic Tissue is higher in the fasting chronic alcoholic rat than in a nonalcoholic matched control. This effect has been mentioned by Goslin et al.[47] and has been confirmed in our laboratory.[48] 124 male Wistar rats weighing 80 to 120 g at the beginning of the experiment were divided randomly into 2 groups, 1 receiving ad libitum 20% (v/v) ethanol, the other water. Each group was randomly divided into series of 8 to 12 rats that received 4 different types of diets combining different intakes of casein and fat. The experiment lasted from 2 to 21 months. Trypsinogen, amylase, lipase, total proteins and DNA were measured in pancreatic tissue at the end of the experiment. Indeed, the action of ethanol on pancreatic enzymes is determined by the dietary intake of proteins and fat. Associated with a moderately low protein diet (7% of total calories), alcohol diminishes the pancreatic gland content of exportable enzymes. But, associated with a 35% fat and 18% protein diet, it increases amylase, trypsinogen, and chymotrypsinogen. The number of zymogen granules is significantly diminished, their size not being modified. This suggests that enzyme concentration is increased in the zymogen granules.[49]

Radioautohistography[50]

The intracellular transport of newly synthetized pancreatic proteins was studied by autoradiography[51] in 2 groups of Wistar rats receiving a balanced diet: the first group was given 20% ethanol for 4 months and the control group water. The transit of proteins from the endoplasmic reticulum to the lumen of the acinus is accelerated in alcoholic rats from the zymogen granules to the lumen. This suggests the action of CCK-PZ or acetylcholine.

In Contrast to Protein Hypersecretion, Protein Biosynthesis Rate in the Alcoholic Pancreas has generally been found to be diminished. Sardesai and Orten[52] found in rats receiving 20% ethanol for almost 1 year a decrease of DL-14C-leucine incorporation in proteins. The rats received a commercial diet with probably a low lipid content but comprising 20% proteins. Orregomatte et al.,[53] giving an identical diet (protein 19.3%, fat 3.5%), and ethanol (4.8 g/kg/day) for 2 to 65 days found an important decrease of ^{32}P into pancreatic phospholipids. Dagorn et al.[54] recently studied this problem in rats receiving 2 types of diets ("normal diet": protein 18.5% of total calories, fat 10%; "fatty diet": protein 17% of total calories, fat 35%). Each group was divided into 2 subgroups 1 receiving water, the other 20% ethanol over 4 to 8 months. The protein biosynthesis rate was calculated by relating the level of radioactive proteins 10 minutes after injection of [^{14}C]leucine to the level of this amino acid in the gland, either in the fasting state or 1 hour after intragastric oleic acid injection into the stomach (endogenous CCK-PZ release). The biosynthesis rate of the fasting animal was not significantly decreased in the 2 alcoholic groups. But 1 hour after oleic acid intragastric injection, pancreatic protein biosynthesis rate was significantly decreased in the alcoholic rats receiving the "fatty diet" compared with that of nonalcoholic controls receiving the same diet. With the "normal diet," there is no difference between alcoholics and nonalcoholics. As in dog, this work focuses on the interaction between ethanol and gastroduodenal hormones: the difference between alcoholic and nonalcoholic rats is significant only when the animals are stimulated by oleic acid, whose action on CCK-PZ release is well known.[55,15] The fact that ethanol has a significant action only when the diet has a high fat content can be compared with the fact that the pancreatic content of exportable enzymes is increased when ethanol is associated with a high-fat, normal-protein diet and on the other hand with the fact that men with alcoholic chronic calcifying pancreatitis have a diet significantly richer in proteins and fats than normal controls. It has been shown that intraintestinal digestion products of fats and proteins are the specific stimulants of the release of CCK-PZ.

Numerous studies show therefore that the acinus pancreatic cell of alcoholic rats for a long time secretes (and therefore should synthetize, at least after a certain delay) more proteins than pancreatic cells of nonalcoholic rats: protein concentration of the juice is higher, as well as enzyme level, in the gland of the fasting animal; transit time of zymogen granules to the lumen of the acinus is decreased. Contrary to what should be expected, when ethanol consumption has a significant action on protein biosynthesis rate, this action is a decrease and not an increase. Two explanations are possible: (1) when pancreatic secretion begins, biosynthesis rate is diminished for the first hour and increases later. This dissociation has been found *in vitro* by Morisset[56] but not *in vivo* by Reggio.[57] It therefore will be useful to study the biosynthesis rate in alcoholic animals from 1 to 8 hours after a meal. (2) It is also possible to assume that intracellulary transit time is so accelerated after a fatty meal in alcoholic animals that 1 part of the radioactivity has left the gland at the time of the experiment and therefore that the method of calculating the biosynthesis rate is inadequate in this case.

In summary, although results in regard to biosynthesis rate are uncertain, the pancreatic acinar cell of chronic alcoholic rats is hyperfunctioning and producing a juice hyperconcentrated in proteins, which precipitate in the ducts. The action of chronic alcoholism on the acinar cell is very similar to the action of CCK-PZ and gastrin or cholinergic drugs, which is not surprising, since we have demonstrated in the dog that the release of CCK-PZ and gastrin is increased as well as parasympathetic tone of the gland.

Man

Man has been less studied than the rat and the dog. It is nevertheless reasonable to think that the consequence of chronic alcoholism on the human pancreas is the same as on animals.

Release of Gastrin

The release of gastrin after ingestion of ethanol is higher in patients with chronic alcoholic calcifying pancreatitis than in normal controls (unpublished results). It has been shown by Harvey et al.[58] that the level of radioimmunologically estimated CCK-PZ was considerably higher in patients with chronic pancreatic insufficiency than in controls. The interpretation of the author is that the hormone release is increased because its target cell is destroyed by the disease. But as we showed that CCK-PZ is increased in the chronic alcoholic dog before any manifestation of pancreatic insufficiency, we may assume that chronic alcoholism has a direct action on CCK release in man as in the dog.

A Morphometric Ultrastructural Study of the Exocrine Pancreatic Cells of Men with CCP

Only fragments of pancreas absolutely devoid of lesions at the beginning of the disease were studied. There was no difference in the ductal cells of chronic alcoholics from those of controls. The acinar cells of pancreas from patients with chronic alcoholic calcifying pancreatitis presented features showing a hyperfunctioning: larger cells, larger nucleus, larger nucleoli, increase of endoplasmic reticulum and of Golgi apparatus, and increased number of immature zymogen granules. These features are identical to those observed when the animal is chronically treated with gastrin or CCK-PZ.[59]

As described in the first part of this paper, the first pancreatic lesion seems to be, as in the rat, precipitation in the ducts of normal enzymatic proteins, which later on calcify, forming stones. In man, calcification of these protein plugs could be favored by an increased calcium concentration in the juice in contrast to the dog.[60,61] This increase is not specific for chronic calcifying pancreatitis, for it is also found in other pancreatic diseases (cancer, acute pancreatitis, chronic pancreatitis of different origin, diabetic pancreas).[60] But it could favor the calcification of pancreatic plugs. The mechanism by which the pathological pancreas increases the concentration of calcium in the juice above normal limits is not well established. Concentration of serum proteins in pancreatic juice is similarly increased.[62] This could be due to a transudation of plasma through the partially atrophied or destroyed epithelium of the ducts. Moreover, these serum proteins could play a role, favoring the formation of protein precipitates.

The problem in man is complicated because, as opposed to what happens in the rat, it has been possible to find in pancreatic juice of patients with alcoholic CCK an unusual protein, lactoferrin.[63,64] This protein has a molecular weight of 78,000. It is normally present in saliva but not in gastric juice nor in bile. In chronic calcifying pancreatitis, it is present in the pancreatic juice even when the lesions are very limited at the beginning of the disease. It has been found in approximately 5% of controls; it is therefore possible that lactoferrin preexists the lesions, representing a variation of the normal pancreatic secretion comparable to the salivary secretion of group A, B, O. Moreover, it is known that lactoferrin combines with other proteins to form complexes.[65] Lactoferrin could therefore favor the precipitation of normal hyperconcentrated proteins. This could explain on one hand the existence of idiopathic forms of chronic calcifying pancreatitis and, on the other, the fact that although many people drink, very few have chronic calcifying pancreatitis.

In conclusion, the relation between the action of ethanol on the pancreas and pancreatitis seems to have been established. Ethanol seems to be harmful to the pancreas only in men or animals adapted to its regular consumption. There is perhaps a definition of "chronic alcoholism." Psychiatrists call chronic alcoholism a poorly defined state of psychological dependence. The fact that above a certain duration of ethanol consumption for a certain dose of ethanol, the action of this product on one organ changes and is even reversed, could serve for a definition of chronic alcoholism.

Alcohol acts in chronic alcoholic people by increasing pancreatic secretion of proteins, this increase being not sufficiently compensated for by a parallel increase of the secretion of water and electrolytes. The cause of this secretory disorder is complex, but it is possible to summarize it in a single mechanism: the increase of parasympathetic tone could by itself explain the increased release of CCK-PZ and gastrin. Increased parasympathetic tone could also explain the fact that in patients with CCP, as in patients with mucoviscidosis, the excretion of Na^+ and Cl^- by perspiration is significantly increased. Hyperconcentrated proteins precipitate in the ducts, resulting in the formation of protein plugs and stones and for the chronic lesions of the ducts and later on the lobules. In man, it is possible that the presence of lactoferrin favors this precipitation.

The mechanism by which acute lesions are linked to chronic lesions is still not well understood. The conflict between hypertonia of the sphincter of Oddi and hypersecretion of pancreatic juice seems not to be responsible (see above). The assumption of a conflict between pancreatic hypersecretion and an intrapancreatic obstacle due to protein plugs and stones is more satisfactory. Acute pancreatic lesions certainly explain the possible occurrence of subcutaneous osteocuticular bone fatty necrosis. The recurrence of acute lesions probably explains the peripancreatic fibrosis that compresses the main bile duct and the splenic vein: a transudation in the peripancreatic tissue of toxic products responsible for inflammatory lesions has been demonstrated by Ohlsson[66] in the course of experimental acute pancreatitis.

REFERENCES

1. HOWARD, J. M. & G. JORDAN. 1968. Surgical Diseases of the Pancreas. J. P. Lippincott Co. Philadelphia, Pa.

2. SARLES, H., R. MURATORE & J. C. SARLES. 1961. Étude anatomique des pancréatites de l'adulte. Sem. Hop. Paris 37: 1507–1522.
3. SARLES, H., J. C. SARLES, R. BAMATTE, R. MURATORE, M. GAINI, C. GUIEN, J. PASTOR & F. LEROY. 1965. Observations on 205 confirmed cases of acute pancreatitis, recurring pancreatitis and chronic pancreatitis. Gut 6: 545–559.
4. PAYAN, H., H. SARLES, M. DEMIRDJIAN, A. P. GAUTIER, R. C. CROS & J. P. BURBEC. 1972. Study of the histological features of chronic pancreatitis by corresponding analysis. Identification of chronic calcifying pancreatitis as an entity. Rev. Eur. Et. Clin. Biol. 17(7): 663–670.
5. SARLES, H. 1971. Alcoholism and pancreatitis. Scand. J. Gastroent. 6(3): 193–198.
6. SARLES, H. 1963. Pancreatitis. Symposium of Marseille. Kager. Basel, Switzerland.
7. SARLES, H. 1974. Chronic calcifying pancreatitis. Chronic alcoholic pancreatitis. Gastroenterology (Progress Report) 66(4).
8. SARLES, H. 1973. An international survey on nutrition and pancreatitis. Digestion 9(5): 389–403.
9. SARLES, H., G. LEBREUIL, F. TASSO, C. FIGARELLA, F. CLEMENTE, M. A. DEVAUX, B. FAGONDE & H. PAYAN. 1971. A comparison of alcoholic pancreatitis in rat and man. Gut 12: 377–388.
10. VERINE, H. 1973. Recherches sur la lithogenèse pancréatique. Apports de la pathologie comparés et de la pathologie expérimentale. These de Doctorat en Biologie Humaine. Univ. of Lyon.
11. MENGUY, R. B., G. A. HALLENBECK, J. L. BOLLMAN & J. H. GRINDLAY. 1958. Intraductal pressures and sphincteric resistance in canine pancreatic biliary ducts after various stimuli. Surg. Gynec. Obstet. 106(3): 306.
12. WALTON, B. E., H. SHAPIRO, T. YEUNG & E. R. WOODWARD. 1965. Effect of alcohol on pancreatic duct pressure. Amer. Surg. 31: 142.
13. TISCORNIA, O., L. GULLO, H. SARLES, M. A. DEVAUX, G. MICHEL & R. GRIMAUD. 1973. The inhibition of canine exocrine pancreatic secretion by intravenous ethanol. Digestion 9: 231–240.
14. WOODWARD, E. R., C. ROBERTSON, H. D. RUTTENBERG & H. SHAPIRO. 1957. Alcohol as a gastric secretory stimulant. Gastroenterology 32: 727–737.
15. TREFFOT, M. J., O. M. TISCORNIA, G. PALASCIANO, G. HAGE & H. SARLES. 1975. Chronic alcoholism and endogenous gastrin. Am. J. Gastroenterol. In press.
16. ELWIN, C. E. 1969. Stimulation of gastric acid secretion by irrigation of the antrum with some aliphatic alcohols. Acta Physiol. Scand. 75: 1–11.
17. TISCORNIA, O., L. GULLO, C. B. MOTT, M. A. DEVAUX, H. SARLES, G. PALASCIANO & G. HAGE. 1973. The effects of intragastric ethanol upon canine exocrine pancreatic secretion. Digestion 9: 490–501.
18. SHAPIRO, H., L. D. WRUBLE, J. N. ESTES & L. G. BRITT. 1968. Pancreatic secretion stimulated by the action of alcohol on the gastric antrum. Amer. J. Digt. Dis. 13: 536–539.
19. DAVES, I. A., J. H. MILLER, B. A. F. LEHMI & J. C. THOMPSON. 1965. Mechanism and inhibition of alcohol stimulated gastric secretion. Surg. Forum 16: 305–307.
20. HIRSCHOWITZ, B. J., H. M. POLLARD, S. W. HARTWELL & J. LONDON. 1956. The action of ethyl alcohol on gastric acid secretion. Gastroenterology 38: 244–253.
21. TISCORNIA, O., L. GULLO, H. SARLES, M. A. DEVAUX, G. MICHEL & R. GRIMAUD. 1972. The inhibition of canine exocrine pancreatic secretion by intravenous ethanol. Gastroenterology 62(4): 866.
22. TISCORNIA, O., G. HAGE, G. PALASCIANO, A. BRASCA, M. A. DEVAUX & H. SARLES. 1973. The effects of pentolinium and vagotomy on the inhibition of canine exocrine pancreatic secretion by intravenous ethanol. Biomédecine 18(2): 159–163.
23. TISCORNIA, O., G. PALASCIANO, J. DZIENISZEWSKI & H. SARLES. 1975. Simultaneous changes in pancreatic and gastric secretion induced by acute intravenous ethanol infusion. Effects of atropine and reserpine. To be published.
24. BAYER, M., J. RUCICK & C. S. LIEBER. 1972. Inhibitory effect of ethanol on canine exocrine pancreatic secretion. Gastroenterology 63: 619–626.
25. MOTT, C. D., H. SARLES, O. TISCORNIA & L. GULLO. 1972. Inhibitory action of alcohol on human exocrine pancreatic secretion. Amer. J. Digt. Dis. 17(10): 902–910.

26. TISCORNIA, O., L. GULLO, H. SARLES, C. B. MOTT, A. BRASCA & M. A. DEVAUX. 1974. The effects of intragastric and intraduodenal ethanol on canine exocrine pancreatic secretion. Digestion 10: 52–60.
27. DE SAINT-BLANQUAT, G. & R. DERACHE. 1971. Effets de l'administration d'éthanol sur la teneur en gastrine de l'estomac de rat. J. Physiol. 63: 533–544.
28. SARLES, J. C. & A. MIDEJEAN. 1973. Electromyographic study of the action of alcohol upon the sphincter of Oddi. Digestion 9: 93–94.
29. SOLOMON, N., T. E. SOLOMON, E. D. JACOBSON & L. L. SHANBOUR. 1973. Inhibition of pancreatic secretion and metabolism by ethanol. Gastroenterology 64: 804.
30. SOLOMON, T. E., N. SOLOMON, L. L. SHANBOUR & E. D. JACOBSON. 1973. Mechanism of inhibition of pancreatic secretion by nicotine. Gastroenterology 64: 805.
31. DAVIS, A. E. & R. C. PIROLA. 1968. The relationship of alcohol to pancreatic disease. In Progress in Pancreatology. Proceedings of the 3rd Symposium of the European Pancreatic Club: 211–215. Czechoslovak Medical Press. Prague, Czechoslovakia.
32. CAPITAINE, Y. & H. SARLES. 1971. Action de l'éthanol sur le tonus du sphincter d'Oddi chez l'homme. Biol. Gastroent. 3: 231–236.
33. GALINDO, F. 1968. Alcoholismo y pancreatitis. Algunas consideraciones fisiopatogénicas. Presn. Med. Argent. 55: 1196.
34. CAPITAINE, Y., C. H. MOTT, L. GULLO & H. SARLES. 1971. Action de l'éthanol sur la sécrétion pancréatique chez l'homme. Biol. Gastroent. 3: 193–198.
35. PETERSEN, T. & H. E. BERSTAD. 1973. The interaction between pentagastrin and cholecystokinin on pancreatic secretion in man. Scand. J. Gastroent. 8(3): 257–263.
36. KORMAN, M. G., C. SOVENY & J. HANSKY. Effect of food on serum gastrin evaluated by radioimmunoassay. Gut 12: 619–624.
37. MARIN, G. A., N. L. WARD & R. FISCHER. 1973. Effect of ethanol on pancreatic and biliary secretions in humans. Amer. J. Digt. Dis. 18(10): 825–833.
38. KAGER, L., S. LINDBERG & G. AGREN. 1972. Alcohol consumption and acute pancreatitis in men. Scand. J. Gastroent. 7, suppl. 15: 3–38.
39. PALASCIANO, G., O. TISCORNIA, G. HAGE & H. SARLES. 1974. Chronic alcoholism and endogenous CCK-PZ. Biomédecine 21: 94–97.
40. HAGE, G., O. TISCORNIA, G. PALASCIANO & H. SARLES. 1974. Inhibition of pancreatic exocrine secretion by intracolonic oleic acid infusion in the dog. Biomédecine 21: 263–267.
41. CHEY, W. Y., S. KOSAY & S. H. LORBER. 1972. Effects of chronic administration of ethanol on gastric secretion in dogs. Amer. J. Dig. Dis. 17: 153–159.
42. YOSHIMORI, M., W. CHEY, R. ESCOFFERY & C. LILLIBRIDGE. 1972. Effects on gastric secretion of acid and parietal cells in dogs. Gastroenterology 62: 732.
43. LILLIBRIDGE, C. B., M. YOSHIMORI & W. Y. CHEY. 1973. Observations on the ultrastructure of oxyntic cells in alcohol-fed dogs. Amer. J. Dig. Dis. 18(5): 443–454.
44. TISCORNIA, O., G. PALASCIANO & H. SARLES. 1975. Canine exocrine pancreatic secretory changes induced by acute and chronic ethanol administration. To be published.
45. SARLES, H., O. TISCORNIA, G. PALASCIANO, A. BRASCA, G. HAGE & M. A. DEVAUX. 1972. Effects of chronic intragastric ethanol administration on canine exocrine pancreatic secretion. Scand. J. Gastroent. 8: 85–96.
46. CUETO, J., N. TAJEN & B. ZIMMERMAN. 1967. Studies of experimental alcoholic pancreatitis in the dog. Surgery 62: 159–166.
47. GOSLIN, J., S. S. HONG, D. F. MAGBE & T. T. WHITE. 1965. Relationship between diet, ethyl alcohol consumption and some activities of the exocrine pancreas in rats. Arch. Inst. Pharmadodyn. 157: 462–469.
48. SARLES, H., C. FIGARELLA & F. CLEMENTE. 1971. The interactions of ethanol, dietary lipids and proteins on the rat pancreas. 1. Pancreatic enzymes. Digestion 4(1): 13–22.
49. TASSO, F., J. CLOP & H. SARLES. 1971. The interaction of ethanol. dietary lipids and proteins on the rat pancreas. 2. Ultrastructural study. Digestion 4(1): 23–14.
50. LECHENE DE LA PORTE, P. & H. SARLES. 1975. Étude par autoradiographie du

transport et de l'excrétion des enzymes pancréatiques dans la cellule acineuse de rats alcooliques. Biol. Gastroent. To be published.

51. JAMIESON, J. D. & G. E. PALADE. 1967. Intracellular transport of secretory proteins in the pancreatic exocrine cell. 1. Role of the peripheral elements of the Golgi complex. J. Cell Biol. **34:** 577–598.

52. SARDESI, V. M. & J. M. ORTEN. 1968. Effect of prolonged alcohol consumption in rats on pancreatic protein synthesis. J. Nutr. **96:** 241–246.

53. ORREGO-MATTE, H., E. NAVIA, A. FERES & L. COSTAMAILLERE. 1968. Ethanol injection and incorporation of ^{32}P into phospholipids of pancreas in the rat. Gastroenterology **56:** 280–285.

54. DAGORN, J. C., R. MICHEL, C. FIGARELLA & H. SARLES. 1975. Effet de l'alcoolisme chronique sur la synthèse des enzymes pancréatiques chez le rat avant et après stimulation de la sécrétine. Biol. Gastroenterol. In press.

55. MEYER, T. H. & R. S. JOHN. 1972. Canine pancreatic response to intestinally perfused fatty acid. Gastroenterology **62:** 874.

56. MORISSET, J. A. & P. D. WEBSTER. 1971. In vitro and in vivo effects of pancreazymin urecholine and cyclic AMP on rat pancreas. Amer. J. Physiol. **228:** 202–208.

57. REGGIO, N., H. CAILLA DECKMYN & G. MARCHIS-MOUREM. 1971. Effect of pancreazymin on rat pancreatic enzyme biosynthesis. J. Cell. Biol. **50:** 338–343.

58. HARVEY, R. F., L. DOWSETT, M. HARTOG & A. E. READ. 1973. A radioimmunoassay for cholestokinin-pancreazymin. Lancet **2:** 826–827.

59. TASSO, F., N. STEMMELIN, J. CLOP, R. C. CROS, J. P. DURBEC & H. SARLES. 1973. Comparative morphometric study of the human pancreas in its normal state and in primary chronic calcifying pancreatitis. Biomedecine **18(2):** 134–144.

60. GULLO, L., H. SARLES, C. B. MOTT, O. TISCORNIA, A. M. PAULI & J. PASTOR. 1974. Pancreatic secretion of calcium in the normal man and in various diseases of the pancreas. Rendic. Gastroent. **6:** 35–44.

61. GOEBELL, H., CH. STEFFEN, CH. BODE & K. HUPE. 1970. Calcium ausscheidung im Pankreassaft von Hunden durch Pankreozymin. Klin. Wschr. **48:** 755–757.

62. CLEMENTE, F., T. RIBEIRO, E. COLOMB, C. FIGARELLA & H. SARLES. 1971. Comparaison des protéines de sucs pancréatiques humains normaux et pathologiques. Dosages des protéines sériques et mise en evidence d'une protéine particuliére dans la pancréatitite chronique calcifiante. Biochim. Biophys. Acta **251(3):** 456–466.

63. COLOMB, E., J. P. ESTEVENON, C. FIGARELLA, O. GUY & H. SARLES. 1974. Characterization of an additional protein in pancreatic juice of men with chronic calcifying pancreatitis. Identification of lactoferrin. Biochim. Biophys. Acta **342:** 306–312.

64. ESTEVENON, J. P., H. SARLES & C. FIGARELLA. 1975. Abnormal presence of lactoferrin in the duodenal juice of patients suffering from chronic calcifying pancreatitis. To be published.

65. HECKMAN, A. N. 1971. Association of lactoferrin with other proteins, as demonstrated by changes in electrophoretic mobility. Biochim. Biophys. Acta **251:** 380–387.

66. OHLSSON, E. G. 1971. Studies in liver circulation function and morphology during and after periods of extrahepatic biliary occlusion in the dog. Thèse de Doctorat en Médecine. Malmot 9.

SECRETORY AND METABOLIC EFFECTS
OF ALCOHOL ON THE PANCREAS

Paul D. Webster, III

Medical Service
Veterans Administration Hospital
Augusta, Georgia 30904

and

Department of Medicine
Medical College of Georgia
Augusta, Georgia 30902

This is a review of selected aspects and literature concerning the effects of alcohol on secretory and metabolic functions of the pancreas. Dr. Sarles, who presented the preceding paper, and coworkers have contributed greatly to our understanding of the effects of alcohol on the pancreas.

We are in the developmental phase in our understanding of the effects of alcohol on the pancreas. Hypotheses are in an early stage of formulation. Many reported observations have not been confirmed, while others need to be extended.

It is well established that chronic and heavy alcohol consumption is frequently associated with pancreatitis. Alcohol appears to be a factor in from 40 to 95% of patients. The wide range depends on the type of population under study; for example, reports originating from private hospitals indicate that only 30 to 50% of patients with pancreatitis are alcoholics, whereas studies originating from Veterans Administration Hospitals or large city hospitals indicate an association in from 90 to 95%. Alcoholic pancreatitis tends to be recurrent and progressive and to result in pancreatic exocrine insufficiency.

Three mechanisms have been postulated to explain how alcohol causes pancreatitis. These are: first, the suggestion that alcohol stimulates pancreatic secretion and at the same time in some manner produces partial obstruction of the ductal system; second, the suggestion that malnutrition, especially protein, in some way impairs pancreatic cellular function, leading to pancreatitis; and third, the suggestion that alcohol has a metabolic or cytotoxic effect on the pancreas. These postulates will be discussed in detail.

Early investigators suggested that alcohol stimulates pancreatic secretion and at the same time produces spasm of the sphincter of Oddi or causes other physiologic changes resulting in partial obstruction to stimulated flow. The "partial obstruction to stimulated flow" concept has been prevalent in the explanation of experimental pancreatitis. Secretory studies have not supported this hypothesis. In fact, studies published as early as 1952, by Dreiling and coworkers,[1] and later by Brooks and Thomas,[2] did not support the concept of stimulated secretion following alcohol administration. At present, the bulk of evidence is against such a postulated mechanism.

Malnutrition, particularly protein malnutrition, has been suggested as playing a prominent role in alcoholic pancreatitis. In certain populations, protein malnutrition is associated with a high incidence of pancreatitis. The high incidence of pancreatitis in black males who give a history of severe protein malnutrition and alcoholism support this hypothesis. Studies published by Dr. Sarles have not supported the etiologic role of malnutrition. It would seem that protein malnutrition or general malnutrition may aggravate or predispose to acinar cell injury. However, at this time, the precise role of malnutrition in acute pancreatitis has not been defined.

There seems to be increasing evidence that alcohol in itself is a cytotoxic agent and that in high concentrations it interferes with specific metabolic functions, resulting in altered secretion and impaired synthesis. Investigations on the liver support this contention. Much of the data I will present suggests a direct effect of alcohol on pancreatic cellular function.

I will review several variables that are important and must be considered when evaluating data concerning effects of alcohol on pancreatic secretion and metabolism.

1. *What is the duration of alcohol administration?* It seems quite possible that alcohol has different effects, depending on whether it is administered for a short or long period of time.

2. *What was the route of alcohol administration?* There appear to be differences in the effects of alcohol depending on whether it was administered orally, intravenously, or intraperitoneally. Oral administration was reported to increase pancreatic secretion, possibly by the release of gastrin. Studies from our own laboratory have shown that oral administration of alcohol to rats is associated with a brief and modest stimulation of pancreatic secretion.

Intravenous administration of alcohol appears to be the desired route to determine direct effects of alcohol on pancreatic cell function. Unfortunately, long-term studies cannot be carried out on intravenous administration. Secretory studies utilizing intravenous alcohol have been performed on large animals, such as men, dogs, and cats, while metabolic studies have been performed on small animals, such as rats or mice.

Intraperitoneal administration of alcohol has been used by some investigators. However, high concentrations result in inflammatory changes in the peritoneum and pancreas. The resulting inflammation with ascites may alter rates of pancreatic secretion and metabolism. I do not think that studies using the intraperitoneal route of administration can be accepted without sufficient documentation that the route of administration has not influenced the type of results obtained.

3. *What parameters of pancreatic secretion or metabolism were studied?* The pancreas secretes water, bicarbonate, and digestive enzymes. Some of the apparent discrepancies in the literature may relate to the parameter of secretion examined. For example, it is possible that alcohol may decrease ductal cell secretion but not alter acinar cell secretion. Such changes would be associated with decreases in secretion of water and bicarbonate but no change in amylase or lipase.

4. *What species of animal were employed?* There is no reason to believe that man, dog, cat, rat, pigeon, or rabbit will react in an identical fashion to either acute or chronic alcohol administered at different doses and by different routes. Nevertheless, I am impressed by the uniformity of reported results of alcohol on pancreatic secretion although a number of species of animals have been used.

5. *What was the diet?* It is known that pancreatic digestive enzyme secretion is sensitive to dietary influences, and dietary adaptation is well established. When one reports changes in protein or amylase synthesis or secretion, the possibility that diet may influence such results must be considered. This is especially true for studies lasting more than 3 to 4 days.

6. *What controls were employed?* It is obvious that pancreatic secretion is quite variable. Likewise, rates of protein synthesis, RNA synthesis, glucose oxidation, and other metabolic responses are variable. One should be sure that control animals were included in all groups under observation.

I would like to review selected papers that have reported effects of alcohol on pancreatic function.

Dreiling and coworkers reported 12 patients; 5 with and 7 without evidence of pancreatic disease.[1] Secretory studies were performed. The results indicate that following intravenous administration of alcohol to a point of inebriation, the external pancreatic secretion as measured by volume, bicarbonate, and amylase was not augmented. These investigators suggested that the role of alcohol in causing pancreatitis was not that of a direct stimulatory effect.

Brooks and Thomas examined effects of alcohol on canine external pancreatic secretion.[2] Five percent alcohol was administered to dogs with duodenal and gastric fistulae. The investigators concluded that dilute alcohol had little stimulating effect upon the external pancreatic secretion when given into the duodenum or intravenously to chronic fistulae dogs.

A number of publications followed in the 1950s and 1960s. Many of these studies demonstrated that alcohol was associated with decreased pancreatic secretion and challenged the thesis that alcoholic pancreatitis was a result of pancreatic secretory stimulation with partial obstruction to flow.

Solomon and coworkers have examined effects of intravenous infusions of alcohol in anesthetized rats.[3] They found that alcohol inhibited water and bicarbonate secretion but not protein secretion. Both *in vitro* and *in vivo* ethanol caused decreases in tissue ATP content but had no effect on cyclic AMP content. These results support the hypothesis of inhibition of pancreatic exocrine secretion by a direct effect of ethanol on the secretory cell.

Marin and coworkers reported on effects of ethanol on pancreatic and biliary secretion in humans.[4] Jejunal or intravenous alcohol administration in doses of 1 gm/kg body weight caused a marked reduction in volume and output of pancreatic enzymes, bicarbonate, and bile salts. These changes indicate that acute administration of large doses of ethanol causes rapid changes in the composition of duodenal aspirates in humans.

Mott and coworkers reported on the inhibitory action of alcohol on human exocrine secretion.[5] The effect of intragastric and intravenous ethanol administration on exocrine secretion of human pancreas was studied in 15 subjects. By either route, ethanol administration substantially reduced volume, concentration, and output of bicarbonate, lipase and chymotrypsin. They interpreted this effect as a direct inhibition of pancreas by ethanol.

Bayer and coworkers studied the effects of intravenous ethanol on steady-state secretin and pancreozymin-stimulated pancreatic secretion in dogs.[6] After administration of intravenous alcohol, prompt and marked inhibition of volume occurred. There was a reduction in concentration and output of bicarbonate and a rise in chloride concentration.

In summary, a number of investigators have reported that acute alcohol administration was associated with decreased pancreatic secretion. Decreased secretion involved centroacinar or ductal cells as well as acinar cells.

I would like to discuss studies directed toward examining metabolic effects of alcohol on pancreatic cell function.

Sardesai examined effects of prolonged alcohol consumption on biosynthesis of pancreatic proteins in rats.[7] A decrease in protein synthesis was observed, including specifically trypsin and ribonuclease, by pancreas of animals maintained on 20% ethanol. It was concluded that these effects resulted from a direct action of alcohol on pancreatic tissue rather than alterations in caloric or protein intake.

Orrego-Matte and coworkers examined effects of ethanol in rats on incorporation of ^{32}P into pancreatic phospholipids.[8] They found that rats under acute or chronic ethanol ingestion had significantly lower amounts of ^{32}P incorporated into pancreatic phospholipids. They suggested that ethanol might interfere with the cholinergic mechanism.

Mezey and coworkers examined pancreatic function and intestinal absorption in 37 chronic alcoholic patients without liver disease. Pancreatic response to secretin stimulation was abnormal in 44% of these patients. They suggested that subclinical protein malnutrition was one of the causes of protein dysfunction.[9]

In conclusion, there is considerable experimental evidence derived from a number of animal species to indicate that acute and chronic alcohol administration is associated with impaired pancreatic secretion of bicarbonate as well as protein. These effects may be direct toxicity of alcohol on the acinar or ductal cells. The precise mechanism operative at the molecular level has not been identified. In addition, therapy to prevent pancreatic damage in the chronic alcoholic has not been developed.

REFERENCES

1. DREILING, D. A., A. RICHMAN & N. F. FRADKIN. 1952. The role of alcohol in the etiology of pancreatitis. Gastroenterology 20: 636–646.
2. BROOKS, FRANK P. & J. EARL THOMAS. 1953. The effect of alcohol on canine external pancreatic secretion. Gastroenterology 23: 36–39.
3. SOLOMON, N., T. E. SOLOMON, E. D. JACOBSON & L. L. SHANBOUR. 1974. Direct effects of alcohol on in vivo and in vitro exocrine pancreatic secretion and metabolism. Am. J. Dig. Dis. 19: 253–260.
4. MARIN, G. A., N. L. WARD, A. B. FISCHER & M. E. ROBERT. 1973. Effect of ethanol on pancreatic and biliary secretions in humans, Amer. J. Dig. Dis. 18: 825–833.
5. MOTT, C., H. SARLES, O. TISCORNIA & L. GULLO. 1972. Inhibitory action of alcohol on human exocrine pancreatic secretion. Amer. J. Dig. Dis. 17: 902–910.
6. BAYER, M., J. RUDICK, C. S. LIEBER & H. D. JANOWITZ. 1972. Inhibitory effect of ethanol on canine exocrine pancreatic secretion. Gastroenterology 63: 619–626.
7. SARDESAI, V. M. & J. M. ORTEN. 1968. Effects of prolonged alcohol consumption in rats on pancreatic protein synthesis. J. Nutr. 96: 241–246.
8. ORREGO-MATTE, H., E. NAVIA, A. FERES & L. COSTAMAILLERE. 1969. Ethanol ingestion and ingestion and incorporation of ^{32}P into phospholipids of pancreas in the rat. Gastroenterology 56: 280–285.
9. MEZEY, E., E. JOW, R. E. SLAVIN & F. TOBON. 1970. Pancreatic function and intestinal absorption in chronic alcoholism. Gastroenterology 59: 657–664.

ALCOHOLISM, ALCOHOLIC PANCREATITIS, AND PANCREATIC SECRETION*

David A. Dreiling

Pancreatic Research Laboratory
Department of Surgery
Mount Siani School of Medicine
of the City University of New York 10029

In the 1950s, I took a very active role in developing and championing the mechanistic pathogenesis of alcoholic pancreatitis.[1] At that time, the role of ductal obstruction seemed to be required to elucidate experimental data and clinical observations discordant to the classical hypothesis of common-channel and biliary regurgitation.[2,3] Since the original studies had indicated that intravenously administered ethanol did not affect pancreatic secretion, it was postulated that the action of alcohol was local to the stomach and duodenum.[1] In the stomach, alcohol elicited a profuse secretion of HC1; in the duodenum, it produced mucosal edema, with swelling and obstruction to the papilla of Vater. The profuse secretion of acid upon entry into the duodenum incited the release of large amounts of secretin that, in turn, stimulated a brisk secretion of pancreatic juice against the obstruction present at the termination of the pancreatic duct. Increased intraductal pressures would then lead to rupture of the finer duct radicals, with permeation of the interstitial tissue by activated pancreatic enzymes, which would then induce chemical inflammation leading to edema, hemorrhage, and necrosis. Repair was effected by liquefaction, calcification, and fibrosis. The pathogenesis of alcoholic pancreatitis could, thus, be naively presumed to be the end result of a cycle of recurrent acute inflammations followed by attempts at repair so that the pancreas was reduced at last to a calcified fibrotic shrunken organ, with parenchymal and intraductal calcification producing a ductal system characterized by alternating stenosis and dilatation.

Paralleling these early simplistic pathophysiologic concepts were the classic investigations of pancreatic secretion with intravenous secretin, studies that rapidly defined the normal ranges for the discriminative parameters, i.e., (1) rate of flow, (2) bicarbonate concentration, and (3) rate of enzyme secretion and also delineated the patterns of secretion observed in pancreatic pathologies,[4-6] i.e., (1) quantitative deficiency in which the rate of flow was decreased with normal bicarbonate and normal enzyme (pancreatic cancer); (2) qualitative deficiency in which the flow and enzyme secretion were normal but the bicarbonate concentration was diminished (chronic pancreatitis); (3) total deficiency, in which all three parameters were reduced (end-stage pancreatic atrophy); (4) isolated enzyme deficiency, in which the flow and bicarbonate were normal but the enzyme secretion was diminished (nutritional pancreatic fibrosis); and (5) discordant secretion, in which the rate of flow was markedly increased with or without depression of bicarbonate (hemochromatosis).

Emphasis in these early studies with secretin was on the lower limits of the normal range, which for the standard test and an 80-minute postsecretin collection were as follows:[7] (1) for volume 2.0 ml/kg, (2) for bicarbonate 90 mEq/ liter, and (3) for amylase 6.0 U/kg.

*Supported in part by Grant NIAMD 03889, NIH.

The lower range was important, since deficient secretion was used to diagnose pancreatic pathology and to differentiate between pancreatic cancer and pancreatic inflammation. On these bases, it could be postulated and corroborated that the "quantitative" deficient secretion in pancreatic cancer depended on the site and degree of pancreatic duct obstruction, the reduction of flow being greatest for lesions of the head, lesser to marginal for lesions of the body, and minimal to nonexistent for lesions of the tail of the organ.[8] The "qualitative" secretory defect of chronic pancreatitis—i.e., decreased bicarbonate concentration—was more difficult to elucidate and required the development of the concept of ductal function by Dreiling et al.[9] According to this concept, water and bicarbonate were secreted in response to secretin by the proximal tubular cells; the secretion as it passed through the small and medium-sized collecting ducts underwent an equilibration and an exchange of bicarbonate for chloride, the measure of which depended on (1) the rate of secretion, (2) the rate of transit through the duct system, (3) the cross-sectional area of the collecting duct surface, and (4) the functional integrity of the ductal epithelium.[10]

Laboratory investigations in animals, including studies with ACTH,[11] and steroids,[12] alloxan,[13] ethionine,[14] ADH,[15] ductal ligation and reconstructions,[16,17] stop-flow analysis,[10] and duct perfusion experiments,[18] lent support to this concept, as did superficial analysis of secretory data of patients with chronic alcoholic pancreatitis. It seemed plausible to relate the low bicarbonate concentrations obtained in the duodenum after secretin administered to patient with alcoholic pancreatitis to the increased opportunity for bicarbonate-chloride interchange in a partially obstructed dilated duct system, which necessarily implied stasis and increased epithelial surface. In due time, however, the complacency of the pancreatic physiologist was disturbed by 3 factors:

(1) Spiro's observation that acute pancreatitis in the alcoholic did not occur during the inception of acute alcoholism but rather after 5–10 yrs. of excessive alcoholic intake.[19] The implication of this clinical observation was that acute pancreatitis developed on a substratum of chronic inflammation paralleling the pathogenesis of alcoholic cirrhosis in which previous fatty liver and acute alcoholic hepatitis mirror a cellular and metabolic damage. The question arose, "Did alcohol injure the pancreas by some cellular metabolic pathway and would this explain the development of acute pancreatitis in the alcoholic more satisfactorily than the mechanistic hypothesis?"

(2) Mounting evidence in the experimental animal and man that the pancreatic ductular system is capable of regeneration by hypertrophy and/or hyperplasia and that the pancreatic parenchyma is dynamic and responsive to trophic influences of hormones and "toxins".[17, 20–23]

(3) The elucidation of the secretory pattern, discordant secretion, as the response of the pancreas in pathologies that produce hypersecretory states, the demonstration that alcoholism per se induces pancreatic hypersecretion, and the hypothesis that this pancreatic hypersecretion is due to increased ductular cell mass.[24–26] This initial response to pancreatic injury is substantiated by secretory data and supported by the pancreatic secretory capacity studies in health and disease using "maximum" or augmented tests of pancreatic secretion.[26,27]

Some of the experimental and clinical evidence that had led to the changing concepts of pathophysiology of alcoholic pancreatitis, substituting metabolic pathogenetic mechanisms for pure mechanistic ones, can be summarized as follows.

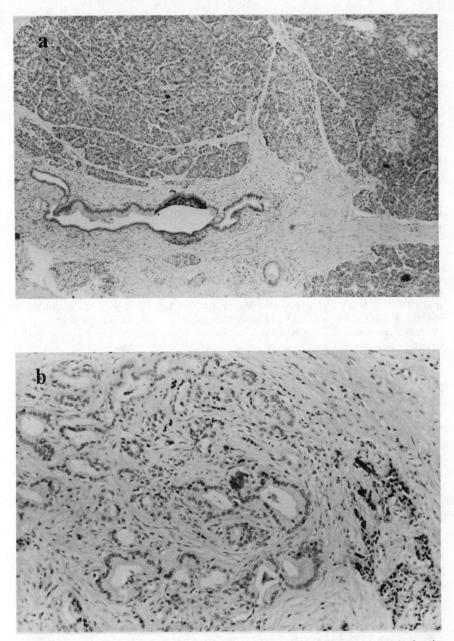

FIGURE 1. (a) Pancreatic secretion from resected gland in minimal pancreatitis showing minimal inflammation and minimal parenchymal disruption. (b) Pancreatic section showing interlobular fibrosis and ductular reduplication.

GROSS PATHOLOGIC FINDINGS

Resected surgical specimens in surgery performed for alcoholic pancreatitis do not uniformly demonstrate the classical calcification, duct stenoses, and ductular dilations. In my series of over 60 alcoholic patients undergoing 60–80% pancreatic resections, approximately $\frac{1}{3}$ of the cases disclosed grossly normal ducts without dilatation. While the incidence of this finding will vary depending on the locale and the specific indications for surgery, additional evidence from peroral fibrooptic endoscopy makes clear that grossly normal caliber ducts do occur in chronic alcoholic pancreatitis and that the obstructed duct is not a sine qua non in pathogenesis. Sarles et al. have produced carefully documented evidence to suggest that the earlier pathology in the increased secretion of a proteinaceous material causing plugs by precipitation in the smaller ductules.[28] My group has evolved a parallel concept from histologic study of resected pancreas in patients with minimal pathologies and short clinical histories. These glands reveal minimal inflammation and minimal parenchymal disruption. Rather there appears to be interlobular fibrosis and ductular reduplication (FIGURE 1).

EVIDENCE FOR PANCREATIC REGENERATION

That the pancreatic ductular mass can undergo dynamic change ranging from atrophy to regeneration by hypertrophy and/or hyperplasia can no longer be questioned. The affirmative evidence includes (1) data from patients with hypersecretory states, i.e., cirrhosis, hemochromatosis, and the Zollinger-Ellison syndrome alcoholism; (2) observed augmentation of pancreatic parenchyma in the experimental animal in response to administration of hormones trophic to the pancreas, i.e., growth hormone, gastrin, CCK-PZ; (3) observed histologic regeneration and functional recovery in animals and man after injury to the pancreatic parenchyma followed by withdrawal of the noxious agent; and (4) sequential studies of secretory capacity in man, specifically in alcoholics and following major pancreatic resection, indicating recovery and regeneration of pancreatic parenchyma.

In some of our earliest experimental studies, we showed that the pancreas could be extensively damaged by toxins such as alloxan and ethiomine or the parenchyma almost totally atrophied by ductal ligation for periods of months but that this damage histologically and functionally monitored by sequential biopsy and sequential secretory testing was reversible, with recovery of structure and function. We reported, moreover, but did not comprehend the significance of, the observation of recovery of secretory capacity beyond the control manipulative level. In man, similar data were obtained by annual sequential secretin testing of a group of alcoholics (FIGURE 2) with alcoholic pancreatitis. The data clearly showed that patients who continued to drink had almost linear deterioration of flow and bicarbonate concentration while those who ceased drinking showed a gradual recovery of secretory capacity.

EVIDENCES DEDUCED FROM ELUCIDATION OF THE HYPERSECRETORY STATES, THE DEFINITION OF THE PATTERN OF SECRETION IN EARLY ALCOHOLIC PANCREATITIS, AND THE DELINEATION OF THE AUGMENTED SECRETORY CAPACITY OF THE PANCREAS IN HEALTH AND DISEASE

Although in our earliest studies with secretin in the 1950s, we recognized that a few patients, notably those with hemochromatosis appeared to elaborate ex-

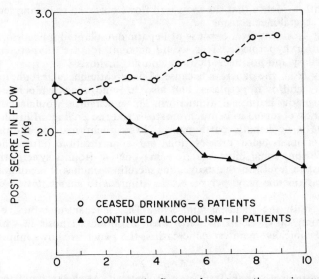

FIGURE 2. Sequential annual postsecretin flow and postsecretin maximum bicarbonate concentration in 6 alcoholic patients who stopped drinking and in 11 who continued to drink.

cessive quantities of pancreatic juice in response to secretin, attention was riveted on the lower limits of the secretory range and the deficiency patterns of secretion, which were of importance in pancreatic diagnosis. Periodic reports of "hypersecretion" in patients with cirrhosis received little attention until it became evident that patients with Zollinger-Ellison syndrome displayed enormous pancreatorrhea (TABLE 1). The matter of pancreatic hypersecretion has been

TABLE 1

Average Standard and Augmented Secretin Test Responses in Patients with
"Pancreatic Hypersecretion"

		Standard 80 min			Augmented 80 min	
	No.	Average Flow ml	Average HCO_3 Content mEq	No.	Average Flow ml	Average HCO_3 Content mEq
Biliary Cirrhosis	44	294	32.4	1	587	50.3
Nonalcoholic Cirrhosis	39	307	36.5	2	591	58.4
Alcoholic Cirrhosis	95	401	43.2	3	874	76.6
Zollinger-Ellison	11	483	48.5	5	911	97.9
Hemochromatosis	19	772	60.9	3	1249	118.5
Normal Average	257	259	26.8	22	438	44.7
Range		117–395	15.9–35.6		248–570	28.5–57.9

clarified with evidence that the increased flows observed following secretin to be derived by several mechanisms:

1. Mainly from the liver because of hepatic ductular reduplication, i.e., hypertrophy and/or hyperplasia. This would account for the "hypersecretion" observed in biliary and postnecrotic nonalcoholic cirrhosis.

2. Mainly from the pancreas because of pancreatic ductular reduplication, i.e., hypertrophy and/or hyperplasia, and also to endogenous endocrine augmentation of exogenous hormonal stimulation. This mechanism would account for the hypersecretion observed in hemochromatosis and the Zollinger-Ellison Syndrome where there is no hepatic participation. In hemochromatosis, the pathology is interstitial fibrosis with preservation and augmentation of parenchyma. In Zollinger-Ellison, some increased flow may derive from a synergistic effect of elevated gastrin levels on the exogenous secretin stimulus. It is possible also that the hypergastrinemia may, per se, be the stimulus to augmentation of secreting parenchyma.

3. From both the pancreas and liver. This mechanism would explain the hypersecretion observed in patients with alcoholic cirrhosis in which, in the absence of clinically manifest pancreatitis, the pancreas shows minimal pathol-

TABLE 2

Comparison of Secretin Test Data of Patients with Alcoholism but Without Cirrhosis or Pancreatitis with Secretin Test Data of Patients with "Pancreatic Hypersecretion"

	No.	Average 80' Flow ml/Kg	Average Max HCO_3 mEq/liter	Average 80' HCO_3 Secretion mEq
Alcoholism	28	4.9	95	30.6
Biliary Cirrhosis	44	4.4	108	32.4
Nonalcoholic Cirrhosis	39	4.5	106	36.5
Alcoholic Cirrhosis	95	6.2	94	43.2
Hemochromatosis	19	9.4	96	60.9

ogy. Ductular reduplication by hypertrophy and hyperplasia would thus occur in both organs.

Additional unexpected data were obtained from simultaneous clinical investigations in my laboratory and in the department of Orlando Bordalo, working in Portugal, namely, that chronic alcoholics without manifest cirrhosis or manifest pancreatitis also displayed pancreatic hypersecretion (TABLE 2). At first glance it would appear that hypersecretion in the alcoholic without clinically manifest pancreatitis would be incompatible with the observation of classical "normal flow–low bicarbonate" secretory pattern in clinically manifest alcoholic chronic pancreatitis. However, critical review of existing data clearly indicates that among the patients with alcoholic pancreatitis there are some with hypersecretion (TABLE 3). Moreover, when the flow and bicarbonate data are plotted on frequency-distribution charts it becomes evident that the data consist of 2 populations with regard to flow and 1 uniform population with regard to bicarbonate concentration (FIGURE 3). The hypersecreting group represents the early mild cases of alcoholic pancreatitis; the "lower flow–low bicarbonate" cases represent the more advanced cases of chronic alcoholic pancreatitis. The pathogenetic sequence would be initial injury and response in the patients with

TABLE 3

Postsecretin Data of Patients with Alcoholic and Biliary Tract Pancreatitis

	No.	Average Flow ml/kg/80 min	Average Max HCO$_3$ Conc. mEq/liter	Average HCO$_3$ Secretion mEq/80 min
Alcoholic Pancreatitis	204	2.6	56	6.4
% Above Lower Limit		67%	2%	12%
% Above Upper Limit		14%	0%	0%
Biliary Tract Pancreatitis	104	2.9	64	7.8
% Above Lower Limit		75%	2%	14%
% Above Upper Limit		21%	0%	0%
Alcoholism	28	4.9	95	30.6

alcoholism corresponding to hypersecretion, then progressive loss of flow and decrease in bicarbonate concentration, corresponding to the secretion pattern of early or minimal alcoholic pancreatitis, and finally extensive fibrosis and parenchymal replacement with further loss of flow and marked diminuation of bicarbonate concentration corresponding to end stage alcoholic pancreatic fibrosis and calcification.

The final link of evidence is afforded by clinical studies of secretory capacity in alcoholics before and following major pancreatic resections for symptomatic chronic alcoholic pancreatitis. Secretory mass or pancreatic secretory capacity can be defined by the use of augmented testing. In my laboratory, we have employed a protocol of in-tandem standard secretin tests (1.0 U/kg) followed by augmented testing (4.0 U/kg). Two sigma ranges developed with the augmented stimulus allow the interpretation of results in normal patients and patients with chronic pancreatitis along the classical patterns established for the standard test (TABLE 4), with the additional information that the augmented stimulus appears to increase the secretory defect characteristic of tumor and inflammation. Thus, comparison of standard and augmented data indicates (TABLE 5): (1) in pancreatic cancer there is a fixation of flow response (TABLE 5B); (2) in pancreatic inflammation, there is a fixation of bicarbonate concentration (TABLE 5C); and

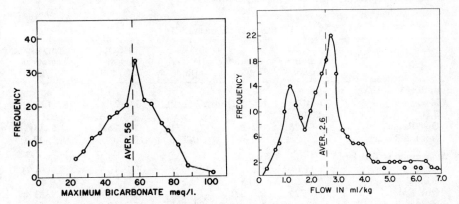

FIGURE 3. Frequency distribution plot of flow and bicarbonate response to secretin in patients with chronic alcoholic pancreatitis.

TABLE 4

Secretin Test Data "Standard and Augmented" of Patients Without Pancreatic Disease (A), Patients with Chronic Pancreatitis (B), and Patients with Pancreatic Cancer (C).

A. Normal Means and Ranges
123 Patients

	80' Flow		HCO_3	
	ml	ml/kg	mEq/L	mEq/80'
Standard (1.0 U/kg)				
Mean	200	3.2	108	20.8
Lower Limit	128	2.0	90	16.8
Upper Limit	272	4.0	130	24.9
Augmented (4.0 U/kg)				
Mean	390	6.3	117	40.7
Lower Limit	212	4.5	93	22.5
Upper Limit	614	8.1	141	58.9

B. Chronic Pancreatitis (91)

	Volume ml/80'	Volume ml/kg	[HCO_3] mEq/L	HCO_3 Secretion mEq/80'	Amylase Secretion U/kg
Standard (1.0 U/kg)					
Mean	170	2.8 (3.2)	62 (110)	12.7 (21.6)	13.3 (21.4)*
S.D.	74	1.4	14	4.6	14.6
Obs. Range	31–452	0.5–8.8	28–91	1.8–21.9	0.8–36.8
Normal Range		2.0–4.4	90–130	12.2–31.0	6.7–42.2
Augmented (4.0 U/kg)					
Mean	241	3.9 (6.3)	63 (117)	17.9 (40.7)	17.4 (36.7)
S.D.	108	1.4	17	5.9	15.4
Obs. Range	55–549	0.5–13.2	34–98	6.1–30.1	1.7–42.8
Normal Range		4.5–8.1	93–141	25.2–58.9	8.3–65.1

*Fig. in ( ) represents Corresponding Means Normals

C. Pancreatic Cancer (52)

	Volume ml/80'	Volume ml/kg	[HCO_3] mEq/L	HCO_3 Secretion mEq/80'	Amylase Secretion U/kg
Standard (1.0 U/kg)					
Mean	1 107	1.5 (3.2)	97 (110)	10.0 (21.6)	8.3 (21.4)*
S.D.	34	0.4	9	3.8	3.1
Obs. Range	39–175	0.2–2.7	74–131	1.3–25.3	1.6–14.3
Normal Range		2.0–4.4	90–130	12.2–31.0	6.7–42.2
Augmented (4.0 U/kg)					
Mean	125	1.7 (6.3)	109 (117)	12.7 (40.7)	11.2 (36.7)
S.D.	42	0.5	12	4.8	6.4
Obs. Range	41–229	0.8–3.2	79–137	1.4–29.4	1.9–21.4
Normal Range		4.5–8.1	93–141	25.2–58.9	8.3–65.1

*Fig. in ( ) represents Corresponding Means Normals

TABLE 5

Comparison of Standard and Augmented Secretin Response Data
in Normal Patients (A), Patients with Pancreatic Cancer (B),
and Patients wtih Chronic Pancreatitis (C)

A. Normal Series	Approximate Increase
Volume ml	100%
Volume ml/kg	100%
HCO_3 mEq	100%
$[HCO_3]$ mEq/liter	10%
Amylase U/kg	30%
B. Pancreatic Cancer	Approximate Increase
Volume ml	15%
Volume ml/kg	15%
HCO_3 mEq	15%
$[HCO_3]$ mEq/liter	10%
Amylase U/kg	30%
C. Chronic Pancreatitis	Approximate Increase
Volume ml	40%
Volume ml/kg	40%
HCO_3 mEq	40%
$[HCO_3]$ mEq/liter	Fixed or Decrease
Amylase U/kg	30%

(3) from a theoretic point of view, the standard stimulus is standard only for the normal patient. This fact becomes obvious when one compares standard and augmented responses to secretin following resection of 60–80% of the pancreas. The response data are identical and, thus, represent a true secretory capacity or ductal cell mass (TABLE 6).

Finally, we have had the opportunity of testing pancreatic secretion sequentially at 3-month intervals following major pancreatic resection in 17 patients with alcoholic pancreatitis. The data (FIGURE 4) clearly indicate an increasing responsiveness to secretin stimulation. That this augmentation of function represents pancreatic regeneration rather than mere restoration of function is implied by the observation that comparison of standard and augmented responses that, initially, present identical function, but with time, show divergence,

TABLE 6

Standard and Agumented Secretin Test Data of 8 Patients Studied
Within 1 Month of Subtotal (left) Pancreatectomy

	Volume ml/80'	Volume ml/kg	$[HCO_3]$ mEq/liter	HCO_3 Secretion mEq/80'	Amylase Secretion U/kg
Standard Mean	109	1.7	62	6.9	8.4
Augmented Mean	112	1.8	61	6.7	6.0

i.e., the pancreas begins to respond to the augmented stimulus with augmented secretion (FIGURE 5).

In summary, I should like to formulate a new hypothesis of pathophysiology of alcoholic pancreatitis and to construct from the evidence presented a new pathogenetic mechanism for alcoholic pancreatitis supplanting the classical mechanistic thesis. A strong parallelism exists between the pancreas and the liver. In the latter, it is clear that prolonged ingestion of excessive quantities of ethanol induces endoplasmic retication hyperplasia, causes specific and non-specific enzyme induction, and is associated with electron-microscopic aberrations of the mitochondria. The sum total alterations in metabolic pathways result almost invariably in the accumulation of fat in the liver, and this pathology appears to be associated with increased hepatic responsiveness to secretin, probably on the basis of increased hepatic ductular mass or function. In the pancreas of alcoholics, the metabolic alterations induced by ethanol have not been elucidated to date but the physiologic effects of injury are documented by increased secretions of proteinaceous material and by increased flows in response to secretin presumed to result from ductular reduplication induced by injury. In

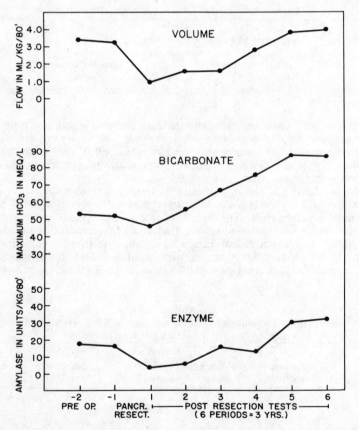

FIGURE 4. Average sequential secretin test data (6 patients) before and following major pancreatic resections (60–80% distal decompression procedures).

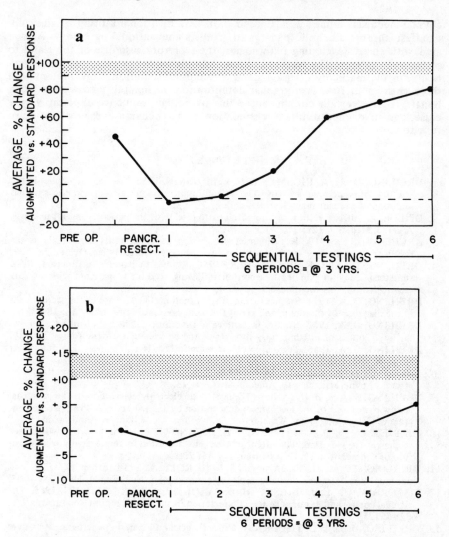

FIGURE 5. Sequential secretin test data before and following major pancreatic resections (60–80% distal decompression procedures). The data of 6 patients are analyzed in the comparison of augmented and standard responses for volume (a) and bicarbonate concentration (b). Studies were done at intervals of between 3 and 6 months.

the liver, the metabolic alterations proceed in some alcoholics to a point at which there is gross cellular damage, as indicated by alcoholic hepatitis, from which point continued alcoholism inexorably progresses to a cycle of liver cell necrosis, repair, and fibrosis, all characterizing cirrhosis. In the pancreas, this would correspond to the development of an attack of clinically manifest acute pancreatitis, again induced in a group of apparently susceptible alcoholics by factors incompletely understood. Here too, there commences a cycle of parenchymal necrosis, repair, and fibrosis, with calcification resulting in clinically manifest chronic alcoholic pancreatitis and its conventional pathology. Associated with these developing pathologies, the secretory response of the gland to secretin shifts from the hypersecretion state through normal flows and, eventually, in the markedly diseased gland to decreased secretion. Concomitant with these changes in flow is a gradual deterioration in the ability to secrete bicarbonate. Under certain circumstances this pathologic sequence apparently may cease, and there then results a regeneration of parenchyma and a restoration of function.

REFERENCES

1. DREILING, D. A., A. RICHMAN & N. F. FRADKIN. 1952. The role of alcohol in the etiology of acute pancreatitis. The effect of intravenous alcohol on the external secretion of the pancreas. Gastroenterology 20: 636.
2. OPIE, E. L. 1901. Relation of cholelithiasis to disease of the pancreas and fat necrosis. Amer. J. Med. Sci. 121: 27.
3. ARCHIBALD, E. 1919. Experimental production of pancreatitis in animals as the result of the resistance of the common duct sphincter. Surg. Gynec. Obstet. 28: 529.
4. DREILING, D. A. & F. HOLLANDER. 1950. Studies in pancreatic function. II. A statistical study of pancreatic secretion following secretin in patients without pancreatic disease. Gastroenterology 15: 620.
5. DREILING, D. A. 1951. Studies in pancreatic function. IV. The use of the secretin test in the diagnosis of tumors in and about the pancreas. Gastroenterology 18: 184.
6. DREILING, D. A. 1953. Studies in pancreatic function. V. The use of the secretin test in the diagnosis of inflammatory diseases of the pancreas. Gastroenterology 24: 540.
7. DREILING, D. A. 1955. Technique of the secretin test. Normal ranges. J. Mount Sinai Hosp. N.Y. 21: 363.
8. DREILING, D. A. & H. D. JANOWITZ. 1956. Exocrine pancreatic secretion. The effects of pancreatic disease. Amer. J. Med. 21: 98.
9. DREILING, D. A. & H. D. JANOWITZ. 1959. The electrolyte secretion of the pancreas. A new hypothesis of the mechanism of secretion by the pancreas. In Proc. World Congress of Gastroenterology, Washington, D.C. Williams & Wilkins. Baltimore, Md.
10. PERRIER, C. V., D. A. DREILING & H. D. JANOWITZ. 1946. A stop flow analysis of pancreatic secretion. The effect of transient occlusion in the electrolyte composition of pancreatic juice. Gastroenterology 46: 700.
11. DREILING, D. A., H. D. JANOWITZ & H. ROLBIN. 1958. Effect of ACTH and adrenocortical steroids on pancreatic secretion in man. New Eng. J. Med. 258: 603.
12. TISCORNIA, O. M., J. HAUSKY, H. D. JANOWITZ & D. A. DREILING. 1965. The adrenal cortex and external pancreatic secretion in the dog. J. Mount Sinai Hosp. N.Y. 32: 551.
13. DREILING, D. A. & O. TISCORNIA. 1965. Effect of alloxan on pancreatic electrolyte secretion. Physiologist 8: 156.
14. FELDMAN, M., D. A. DREILING, A. PAULINO, III, F. SCHAFFNER & H. D. JANOWITZ. 1963. Effect of DL-ethionine on electrolyte secretion of the dog pancreas. Amer. J. Physiol. 205: 878.
15. BANKS, P. A., J. RUDICK, D. A. DREILING & H. D. JANOWITZ. 1968. Effect of antidiuretic hormone on pancreatic exocrine secretion. Amer. J. Physiol. 215: 361.
16. PAULINO, A., III & D. A. DREILING. 1960. Chronic duodenal obstruction: A mechano-vascular etiology of pancreatitis. II. Experimental observations. Amer. J. Digest. Disease 5: 996.
17. TISCORNIA, O. M. & D. A. DREILING. 1966. Recovery of pancreatic exocrine secretory capacity following prolonged ductal obstruction. Bicarbonate and amylase response to hormonal stimulation. Ann. Surg. 164: 267.
18. WASTELL, C., J. RUDICK, & D. A. DREILING. 1969. Bicarbonate-chloride exchange across pancreatic duct epithelium. Amer. J. Gastroent. 52: 99.

19. STRUM, W. B. & H. S. SPIRO. 1971. Chronic pancreatitis. Ann. Int. Med. **74**: 264.
20. BOOTH, A. N. & J. J. ROCKLIS. 1964. Prolonged pancreatic hypertrophy and reversibility in rats fed raw soybean meal. Proc. Soc. Exp. Biol. Med. **116**: 1067.
21. POLYAK, R. I. 1966. Regenerative and compensatory phenomena in pancreas after resection. Biull. Eksp. Biol. Med. (Moscow) **62**: 95.
22. LEHV, M. & P. J. FITZGERALD. 1968. Pancreatic acinar regeneration. IV. Regeneration after surgical resection. Amer. J. Path. **53**: 513.
23. TISCORNIA, O. M. & D. A. DREILING. 1966. Does the pancreatic gland regenerate? Gastroenterology **51**: 267.
24. DREILING, D. A., A. GREENSTEIN & O. BORDALO. 1973. The hypersecretory states of the pancreas. Med. Chir. Dig. (Paris) **2**: 185.
25. DREILING, D. A. & O. BORDALO. 1973. Secretory patterns in minimal pancreatic inflammatory pathologies. Amer. J. Gastroent. **60**: 60.
26. DREILING, D. A., A. GREENSTEIN & O. BORDALO. 1973. Newer concepts of pancreatic secretory patterns, pancreatic secretory mass and pancreatic secretory capacity. J. Mount Sinai Hosp. N.Y. **40**: 666.
27. DREILING, D. A., A. GREENSTEIN & O. BORDALO. 1974. A comparison of standard and augmented secretin test responses in patients with and without pancreatic disease. Amer. J. Gastroent. In press.
28. SARLES, H. 1971. Alcoholism and pancreatitis. Scand. J. Gastroent. **6**: 193.

RELATIONSHIP BETWEEN ALCOHOLISM AND PANCREATIC INSUFFICIENCY

Eugene P. DiMagno, Juan R. Malagelada, and Vay L. W. Go

Mayo Clinic and Mayo Foundation
Rochester, Minnesota 55901

INTRODUCTION

Exocrine pancreatic insufficiency is the cause of steatorrhea[1] and creatorrhea[3] in chronic pancreatitis. Alcoholism is a major cause of chronic pancreatitis, and the relationships of the duration of alcoholism to steatorrhea, diabetes, and calcification have been determined in clinical studies.[5, 8, 12] However, in a recent study,[3] we found that steatorrhea and creatorrhea did not occur in patients who had chronic pancreatitis secondary to various pathologic conditions until the enzyme outputs were 10% or less of maximal values. Although pancreatic enzyme secretion may decline gradually as the years of alcoholism continue, there are no data to support this supposition.

Therefore, by using a previously validated technique,[6] we quantified pancreatic trypsin and lipase enzyme outputs in health and in patients with chronic alcoholic pancreatitis during basal periods and in response to the continuous intravenous infusion of the maximal stimulatory dose of cholecystokinin-pancreozymin (CCK-PZ). Relationships among duration of alcoholism, pancreatic enzyme outputs, malabsorption, and complications of pancreatitis were then investigated.

MATERIAL

Seventeen patients (11 men and 6 women, 35 to 71 years old) with chronic alcoholism (defined as a habit of the proportion to result in continuing or recurrent interference with a normal life mode) were studied. Before this study, all patients had either calcification of the pancreas (12 patients) or tissue diagnosis of chronic pancreatitis (8 patients); 3 patients had both. Fecal fat determinations were made in 16 and fecal nitrogen in 11. All 17 had CCK-PZ administered intravenously, and, in addition, 11 of the patients had measurements of basal pancreatic enzyme secretion. Control data were derived from 28 healthy nonalcoholic male volunteers, 21 to 56 years of age; 21 control subjects were studied with intravenous CCK-PZ infusions; and all 28 had basal measurements of pancreatic enzyme outputs.

METHODS

Total outputs of trypsin and lipase were measured by our method.[6] Briefly, this technique entails placement of a double-lumen duodenal tube and a separate gastric sump tube under fluoroscopic control so that the duodenal perfusion site is located in the second part of the duodenum, the duodenal aspirate site is 20 cm distally at the ligament of Trietz, and the gastric sump tube is in the gastric antrum. Gastric contents are continuously aspirated while a normal saline solution (warmed to 37°C, pH 6.0, isotonic, and containing a nonabsorbable marker—polyethylene glycol) is perfused through the duodenal loop at 10 ml/

min. Pooled 20-minute samples from the ligament of Treitz are collected, by siphonage, over ice.

Studies were divided into 2 parts. Initially, during the first hour, to measure basal secretion, the normal saline solution was perfused through the duodenum and normal saline infused intravenously. During the second hour, to test pancreatic function under direct maximal stimulatory conditions, exogenous CCK-PZ (supplied by Dr. V. Mutt, Karolinska Institutet) was given by vein at a rate of 0.25 CHR units/kg/minute while the duodenal isotonic saline perfusion was continued.

Concentrations of polyethylene glycol were measured in both gastric and duodenal samples.[9] Trypsin and lipase concentrations were determined by an automatic titration method employing TAME (*p*-toluenesulfonyl-2-arginine methyl ester) and fat emulsion (Lipomul®) as substrates for the respective enzyme activities.[11] The enzymes were then expressed as enzyme output in kilo units (kU) per hour, based on recovery in relation to polyethylene glycol.[10] The percentage of normal values was derived from the observed enzyme output as compared with the mean normal values obtained from the 28 healthy volunteers. Fecal fat[13] and nitrogen[2] outputs were measured during a 48-hour period while patients were on a standard diet containing 100 g of fat.

The rank-sum test was used to determine statistical significance.[4]

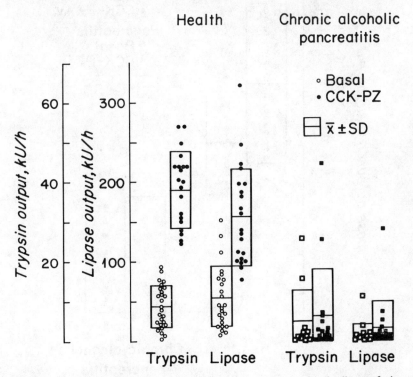

FIGURE 1. Trypsin and lipase outputs in response to intraduodenal saline perfusion and intravenous cholecystokinin-pancreozymin in health and chronic pancreatitis. Vertical columns represent mean ± 1 standard deviation.

RESULTS

Pancreatic Enzyme Outputs in Health and Chronic Pancreatitis

Hourly enzyme outputs in response to CCK-PZ administration were reduced in chronic alcoholic pancreatitis (FIGURE 1). Overlap between health and chronic pancreatitis was restricted to 2 patients who had chronic calcific pancreatitis. In health, with maximal CCK-PZ stimulation, there was a 3.5-fold increase of trypsin outputs and a 2.84-fold increase in lipase output over basal levels. By contrast, in chronic pancreatitis, no significant increase above basal enzyme outputs was observed. The ratio of lipase output to trypsin output in both the basal and stimulatory states was significantly higher ($P < 0.01$) in health as compared to that in chronic pancreatitis (FIGURE 2). However, no differences were noted between basal and stimulated (IV CCK-PZ) conditions within each group.

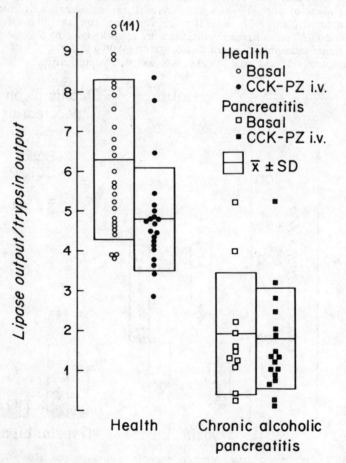

FIGURE 2. Ratio of lipase output to trypsin output in health and chronic alcoholic pancreatitis under basal and intravenous CCK-PZ stimulation.

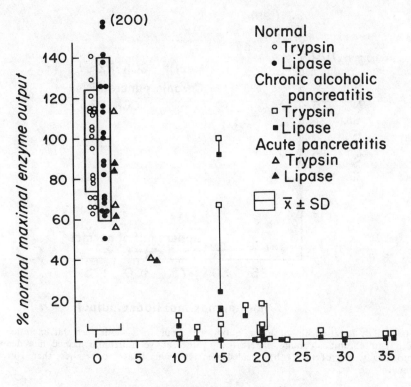

FIGURE 3. Relationship of trypsin and lipase to duration of alcoholism in health, acute pancreatitis, and chronic alcoholic pancreatitis.

Relationship of Duration of Alcoholism to Pancreatic Enzyme Output

Of the 17 patients with chronic alcoholic pancreatitis, all 5 with greater than 20 years of alcoholism had lipase and trypsin outputs of less than 10% of normal maximal values (FIGURE 3). Of the 12 patients with alcoholism of 10 to 20 years' duration, 11 had lipase outputs below normal. Patients with acute pancreatitis had subnormal trypsin and lipase outputs, but these were considerably higher than the outputs for the group with chronic pancreatitis (FIGURE 3).

When differences between trypsin and lipase secretion were observed in patients with chronic alcoholic pancreatitis, trypsin output was maintained to a greater degree of normalcy than was lipase output. In the 2 patients with lipase outputs of less than 10% and trypsin outputs of greater than 10%, steatorrhea was observed and creatorrhea was not.

Quantitative Relationships Between Malabsorption and Pancreatic Enzymes

Steatorrhea (>7 g of fat/24 h) was not observed until lipase outputs were less than 10% of the normal maximal output in response to CCK-PZ (<15 kU/h).

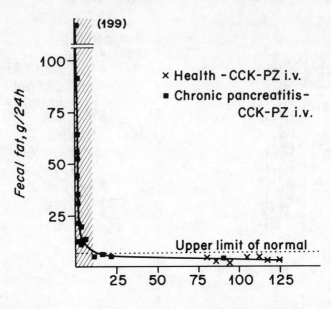

FIGURE 4. Relationship of lipase output per hour to 24-hour fecal fat excretion in health and chronic alcoholic pancreatitis. Values above horizontal dashed line denote steatorrhea (>7 g of fat/24 h). Shaded area represents lipase outputs less than 10% of normal.

All patients with steatorrhea had enzyme outputs below this level, and patients as well as healthy subjects without steatorrhea had enzyme outputs greater than 10% of normal value (FIGURE 4). Creatorrhea (>2.5 g of stool nitrogen/ 24 h) was related to reduced trypsin outputs because it occurred only when trypsin outputs were less than 10% of normal maximal trypsin output (<3.8 kU/h) (FIGURE 5).

TABLE 1

Distribution of Patients According to Lipase Output, Steatorrhea, Calcification, and Diabetes Mellitus in Relation to Duration of Alcoholism

| | Duration of Alcoholism | | |
	10–20 Yr	>20 Yr	Total
No. of patients	12	5	17
Subabnormal exocrine enzyme secretion	11	5	16
Steatorrhea	8	5	13
Pancreatic calcification	7	5	12
Diabetes	7	5	12

Relationship Between Duration of Alcoholism and Complications of
Chronic Alcoholic Pancreatitis

In all patients who had greater than 20 years of alcoholism, pancreatic calcification, steatorrhea, and diabetes were present (TABLE 1). Although 8 patients with 10 to 20 years of alcoholism had steatorrhea and 7 had diabetes

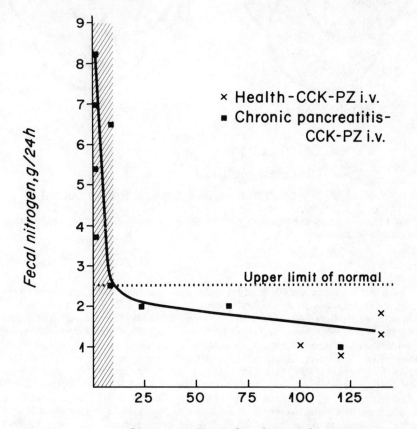

× Health-CCK-PZ i.v.
■ Chronic pancreatitis-
      CCK-PZ i.v.

FIGURE 5. Relationship of trypsin outputs per hour to 24-hour fecal nitrogen excretion in health and chronic alcoholic pancreatitis. Values above horizontal dashed line denote creatorrhea (>2.5 g of nitrogen/24 h). Shaded area represents trypsin outputs less than 10% of normal.

or steatorrhea, only 4 patients had all of these (FIGURE 6). In addition, 3 patients of this group had diminished lipase secretion above the 10% normal maximal value without steatorrhea (TABLE 1). When the 17 patients are considered as a group, pancreatic calcification and diabetes were seen in 12 (70%) and steatorrhea was present in 13 (76%). When calcification and steatorrhea occurred, diabetes was invariably present (FIGURE 6).

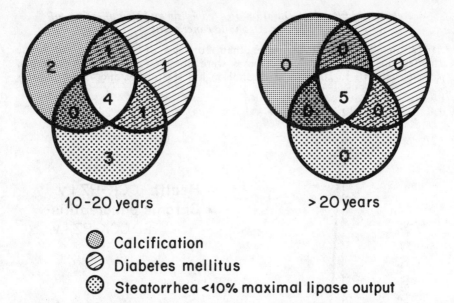

FIGURE 6. Relationships of pancreatic calcification, diabetes mellitus, and steatorrhea to duration of alcoholism.

DISCUSSION

As in our previous, similar study,[3] our group demonstrated diminished enzyme outputs in response to a maximal stimulatory dose of CCK-PZ in patients with chronic alcoholic pancreatitis. In the present study, we have further shown that even at basal conditions (perfusion of the duodenal loop with saline), patients with chronic alcoholic pancreatitis secrete at their maximal rate, and even after CCK-PZ stimulation, these patients cannot increase enzyme secretory rates for trypsin and lipase (FIGURE 1). However, under basal and maximal stimulatory conditions, patients with chronic alcoholic pancreatitis secreted relatively more trypsin than lipase (FIGURE 2). It appears that trypsin, which is secreted in an inactive form, is maintained to a greater degree than is lipase, which is secreted in an active form.[7] Since synthesis and secretory pathways for trypsin and lipase differ within the pancreatic acinar cell,[7] parallel secretory rates for health and chronic pancreatitis would not be expected if one pathway is damaged preferentially or to a greater degree than the other. These data support the clinical lack of protein malnutrition despite steatorrhea in some patients with pancreatic insufficiency. In our study, 2 patients had steatorrhea without creatorrhea. The relationship between the outputs of lipase and trypsin supports the findings of Minaire et al.,[10] who observed the same basic information while measuring qualitative enzyme concentrations in patients with chronic pancreatitis. Since lipase output decreases more rapidly than does trypsin output as alcoholism progresses (FIGURE 3), lipase secretion is a more reliable predictor of exocrine secretory reserve function than is trypsin secretion, and the level of lipase should be determined when pancreatic secretory studies are done.

The gradual, progressive decline of the pancreatic exocrine enzyme outputs in patients with increasing duration of chronic alcoholism (FIGURE 3) leads inevitably to steatorrhea. As has been noted by others,[8, 12] steatorrhea is a late sequel and is explained by the large exocrine reserve capacity for enzyme secretion that must be reduced to 10% of normal before malabsorption occurs (FIGURES 4 and 5). In the current study, all patients with more than 20 years of alcoholism had steatorrhea as well as diabetes and pancreatic calcification. However, 4 of the 12 patients with alcoholism from 10 to 20 years' duration had either diabetes mellitus or calcification, or both, without steatorrhea. Therefore, diabetes and calcification may appear before evidence of malabsorption, but if pancreatic secretion is measured, it usually will be diminished.

REFERENCES

1. BERNARD, C. 1856. Mémoire sur le Pancréas et sur le Rôle du Suc Pancréatique dans les Phénomènes Digestifs, Particulièrement dans la Digestion des Matières Grasses Neutres. J. B. Baillier. Paris, France.
2. CHIBNALL, A. C., M. W. REES & E. F. WILLIAMS. 1943. The total nitrogen content of egg albumin and other proteins. Biochem. J. **37:** 354–359.
3. DiMAGNO, E. P., V. L. W. GO & W. H. J. SUMMERSKILL. 1973. Relations between pancreatic enzyme outputs and malabsorption in severe pancreatic insufficiency. N. Eng. J. Med. **228:** 813–815.
4. DIXON, W. J. & F. J. MASSEY, JR. 1957. Introduction to Statistical Analysis. 2nd edit.: 289. McGraw-Hill Book Co., New York, N.Y.
5. GAMBILL, E. E. & D. G. PUGH. 1948. Pancreatic calcification: study of clinical and roentgenologic data on thirty-nine cases. Arch. Intern. Med. **81:** 301–315.
6. GO, V. L. W., A. F. HOFMANN & W. H. J. SUMMERSKILL. 1970. Simultaneous measurements of total pancreatic, biliary, and gastric outputs in man using a perfusion technique. Gastroenterology **58:** 321–328.
7. HOKIN, L. E. 1967. Metabolic aspects and energetics of pancreatic secretion. *In* Handbook of Physiology. Section 6: Alimentary Canal. Vol. 2. C. F. Code & W. Heidel, Eds.: 935–953. American Physiological Society. Washington, D.C.
8. HOWARD, J. M. & E. W. EHRLICH. 1960. The etiology of pancreatitis: a review of clinical experience. Ann. Surg. **152:** 135–146.
9. HYDEN, S. 1956. A turbidometric method for determination of higher polyethylene glycols in biologic materials. Kgl. Lantbrukuks-Högskal. Ann. **22:** 139–145.
10. MINAIRE, Y., L. DESCOS, J. P. DALY, M. B. BERERD & R. LAMBERT. 1973. The interrelationships of pancreatic enzymes in health and disease under cholecystokinin stimulation. Digestion **9:** 8–20.
11. PELOT, D. & M. I. GROSSMAN. 1962. Distribution and fate of pancreatic enzymes in small intestine of the rat. Amer. J. Physiol. **202:** 285–288.
12. SARLES, H. 1961. Discussion. *In* Ciba Foundation Symposium on the Endocrine Pancreas: Normal and Abnormal Functions. A. V. S. De Reuck & M. P. Cameron, Eds.: 255–256; 274. Little, Brown & Co., Boston, Mass.
13. VAN de KAMER, J. H., H. ten B. HUININK & H. A. WEYERS. 1949. Rapid method for the determination of fat in feces. J. Biol. Chem. **177:** 347–355.

MANAGEMENT OF MILD AND SEVERE
ALCOHOLIC PANCREATITIS

O. Dhodanand Kowlessar

Gastroenterology Division
Jefferson Medical College
Thomas Jefferson University
Philadelphia, Pennsylvania 19107

The mechanism by which the heavy consumption of ethanol leads to attacks of pancreatitis is not clear. The administration of ethanol to human subjects and experimental animals has been reported to produce the following physiologic, biochemical, and ultrastructural changes in the pancreas: (a) substantial inhibition of volume, concentration, and output of bicarbonate, lipase, and chymotrypsin; (b) a concomitant direct effect on the sphincter of Oddi that would increase sphincteric resistance with resultant increase in intrapancreatic ductal pressure; (c) ductal metaplasia; (d) decreased protein synthesis; (e) inhibition of uptake of ^{32}P into pancreatic phospholipids; (f) increased cellular autophagia; (g) accumulation of lipid droplets in acinar cells; (h) cytoplasmic degradation of acinar, centroacinar, and duct cells; (i) mitochrondrial swelling and reduction of their inner membranes; (j) impairment of Na^+-dependent uptake of lysine, proline, and methionine by pancreatic slices from alcohol-treated mice *in vitro*; and (k) precipitation of protein plugs in the pancreatic duct system.[1-3] In spite of these observations, many of them made in experimental animals, the mode of production of alcoholic pancreatitis is still debatable and requires further investigation.

Classically, alcohol-induced pancreatitis has been classified pathologically as interstitial (edematous) and hemorrhagic. Clinically, it may be classified as acute, or acute recurrent and chronic, or chronic recurrent with a varying spectrum of severity from mild to very severe. In general, mild pancreatitis is characterized by nausea, vomiting, abdominal pain, frequently gradual in onset and mild to moderate in severity, low-grade fever, and tachycardia. The majority of the patients are moderately heavy drinkers, and the clue to the alcohol etiology is provided by the characteristic time relationship between a night's overindulgence and the onset of pain some 24 to 48 hours later.[4] On the other hand, severe pancreatitis is a disease of multiple organ involvement. The characteristic findings in the severe form are: (a) presence of incipient or actual shock, (b) depressed serum calcium, (c) evidence of respiratory insufficiency, (d) pleural effusion, (e) significant hyperglycemia, (f) marked hemoconcentration, and (g) failure to respond to initial treatment.

TREATMENT

The primary management of mild pancreatitis is the reduction of pancreatic stimulation, the relief of abdominal pain, and frequent and careful monitoring of the patient's clinical status and vital signs.

INHIBITION OF PANCREATIC SECRETORY ACTIVITY

An important principle in the management of acute pancreatitis is the "splinting of the inflamed pancreas" by suppression of pancreatic secretion. Achievement of this therapeutic goal is accomplished by cessation of oral intake of food and continuous nasogastric suction since food and hydrochloric acid are powerful stimulants for the release of secretin and cholecystokinin-pancreozymin (CCK-PZ), which in turn promote the secretion of water, bicarbonate, and pancreatic enzymes.

In a recent study of 29 patients,[5] nasogastric suction provided no clear-cut therapeutic advantage over no-suction in the treatment of attacks of mild to moderately severe, uncomplicated, acute alcoholic pancreatitis. The authors concluded that nasogastric suction might be considered elective rather than mandatory for these patients. In a disease with such a diverse symptom complex and one in which a mild case can rapidly deteriorate into a severe and catastrophic illness, one needs a further study in which there is a clearer definition of the clinical picture and a larger group of patients. It is likely that until there is more convincing evidence, clinicians will continue to use nasogastric suction in pancreatitis while paying attention to the discomfort and potential complications of nasogastric suction.

The anticholinergics propantheline (Pro-Banthine®) bromide, 30 mg, or methantheline (Banthine®) bromide, 50 mg, given parenterally every 6 to 8 hours, have enjoyed wide popularity, although their efficacy remains in doubt. Their pharmacologic effects include suppression of gastric and pancreatic secretion, relaxation of the sphincter, partial inhibition of pancreatic enzyme production, and decreases in the rates of oxygen uptake and intermediary metabolism. However, it should be borne in mind that they aggravate paralytic ileus, worsen abdominal distention, and increase urinary retention and heart rate. In view of these untoward effects, anticholinergics should be withheld until the paralytic ileus has decreased and peristalsis has returned to normal.

Recently,[6] glucagon in an initial loading dose of 1 mg intravenously, followed in one-half hour by a second loading dose of 0.5 mg, to be followed by a continuous infusion of 1.0 to 1.5 mg in 5% dextrose or normal saline every 4 hours has been reported to result in rapid clinical improvement, with relief of pain associated with a fall of serum amylase. The mechanism of the beneficial effect is due to the inhibition of pancreatic secretion, thus suppressing the activity of the acutely inflamed gland. Of note, glucagon can increase splanchnic blood flow by both decreasing splanchnic resistance and increasing cardiac output.[7,8] This effect of glucagon as a vasodilator may deprive the pancreas of its needed blood supply, thereby increasing injury to the gland. In mild to moderate experimental pancreatitis,[9] glucagon therapy was associated with pancreatic hemorrhage. Although this has not been reported in the publications on glucagon therapy in clinical pancreatitis, careful monitoring of patients thus treated is necessary. Likewise, the serum calcium should be monitored frequently.

CONTROL OF PAIN

The pain is usually severe, and should be treated promptly with adequate doses of analgesics. Meperidine (Demerol®), which has less effect on the tone of the sphincter of Oddi than morphine, is probably the drug of choice and should be given parenterally in doses of 75 to 100 mg every 4 to 6 hours to assure prompt and adequate relief of pain. In mild cases, the patient obtains some relief from the nasogastric suction and in 72 to 96 hours is pain-free with the recommended doses of meperidine. Continuous epidural block with an inlying polyethylene catheter can partially control severe pain and spasm. It can decrease the metabolic and respiratory depression associated with large doses of analgesics and improve respiratory function by reducing abdominal and diphragmatic spasm.

FLUIDS AND ELECTROLYTES

The continued gastric suction and the abstinence from any oral intake make it necessary to replace body fluids and electrolytes carefully. The amount of normal saline with supplemental potassium chloride to be administered may vary between 3 and 6 liters daily and should be estimated by considering the insensible loss, the amount of sweating, the elevation of temperature, the volume of gastric suction, and the anticipated urinary output. Glucose must be administered cautiously, for it may aggravate a diabetic state that has been precipitated by acute pancreatitis. When hyperglycemia and glycosuria are marked and diabetic acidosis is imminent, small doses of insulin must be given.

Thus, the management of mild pancreatitis is managed easily using nasogastric suction, meperidine for pain, careful monitoring of intake and output, and electrolyte replacement. After the nasogastric suction is discontinued, the patient should be placed initially on clear liquids without fat and gradually given solid foods, preferably small frequent feeding with antacids one–half hour after each meal. There is no rationale for antimicrobial therapy in mild alcoholic pancreatitis.

SEVERE PANCREATITIS

The course of therapy for patients with severe pancreatitis must depend on the changing status of the patients' overall clinical condition on a daily or even an hourly basis. In view of present methods of patient monitoring, one can anticipate dire physiologic derangements before they occur and institute appropriate, aggressive measures to combat them. These patients should be admitted preferably to an intensive-care unit, where they can be carefully monitored and observed closely. After the passage of a nasogastric tube and a urinary catheter, with meperidine given for pain, a central venous pressure line or, preferably, a Swan-Ganz catheter should be inserted, and blood, plasma, low-molecular-weight dextran, or fluids should be given to maintain the venous pressure around 10 cm of water and a urinary output of 40 to 60 cc per hour. Sodium chloride or Ringer's solution with added calcium gluconate or calcium chloride may be used. In patients with significant hypoalbuminemia, albumin should be administered. If the patient continues to be hypotensive in spite of adequate fluid replacement, an infusion of 1 in 500,000 isoproterenol hydrochloride (Isuprel®) may be given, commencing with a dose rate of 0.5–4.0 µg/min with careful electrocardiographic monitoring.[10] Peritoneal dialysis should be attempted in those patients whose symptoms fail to improve after a period of conservative therapy and who appear to be dying of their disease. The dialysate recently used with some success consists of sodium, 141 mEq/liter; calcium, 3.5 mEq/liter; magnesium, 1.5 mEq/liter; chloride, 101 mEq/liter; and lactate, 4.5 mEq/liter, given via a standard peritoneal dialysis catheter. After a one-half hour delay, the fluid is removed by straight drainage, and the procedure is repeated. Dramatic improvement in shock, oliguria, and correction of electrolyte imbalance has occurred in many patients.[11]

ANTIMICROBIAL

The prophylactic use of antimicrobials for the prevention of infection in severe cases of acute pancreatitis is purely empirical and without controled studies. It has been proposed that the protein-rich exudate in edematous, poorly perfused tissues is favorable for bacterial growth. After appropriate cultures of blood, urine, sputum, and effusions and if one accepts the concept of prophylaxis, intramuscular ampicillin, 500 mg, and kanamycin, 200 mg, every 6 hours, may be initiated. Sustained or high spiking fevers (higher than 40°C) in patients with pancreatitis strongly suggests pancreatic abscess or cholangitis. Surgical drainage or relief of duct obstruction, followed by appropriate antimicrobials, is the treatment of choice.

Respiratory failure is one of the most insidious and dangerous complications of acute pancreatitis.[12-14] The respiratory complications include hypoxia, alkalosis secondary to hyperventilation, pulmonary edema, atelectasis, pleural effusion, bacterial and aspiration pneumonia, and pulmonary emboli.

The bedside determination of pulmonary wedge pressure and cardiac output with a balloon-tipped pulmonary artery catheter has resulted in improvement in the management of these patients.[14] The following measures have proved useful in one recent, well-studied group of patients: daily chest roentgenogram; arterial blood gas determinations in room air and at 40, 60, and 100% oxygen; endotracheal intubation with prolonged end expiratory pressure for a respiratory rate greater than 36 per minute; arterial PO_2 less than 65 mm Hg on 40 to 60% oxygen and alveolar-arterial oxygen differences of greater than 400 mm Hg; and digitalis and furosemide therapy if the pulmonary wedge pressure is elevated. Feller et al.[14] found that endotracheal intubation proved an excellent supportive measure in their patients. If impaired pulmonary function persists after 4 to 5 days of intubation, tracheostomy should be performed.

HYPERCATABOLIC STATE OF PANCREATITIS

Significant weight loss of 1.5 to 2.0 kg daily is a frequent observation in severe pancreatitis. Body reserves of protein and fat are rapidly depleted because of the nature of the underlying disease and the fact that many of these patients are taking nothing by mouth. In view of the recent observations by Dudrick[15] and others[16,17] that intravenous hyperalimentation is highly effective in many types of catabolic states, it is not surprising that a similar approach is recommended for patients with severe pancreatitis. Ideally, intravenous hyperalimentation should be started immediately. Attention should be directed to the care of the catheter, daily electrolytes, blood sugar, glycosuria, and the intake of vitamins, calcium, and phosphorous. Recently, Feller et al.[14] recommended that the patient be started on an elemental diet either through a fine nasogastric polyethylene tube or via a gastrostomy or jejunostomy feeding catheter as soon as bowel function has returned towards normal as evidenced by active peristaltic sounds. The elemental diets provide 1 cal/ml and are generally well tolerated in volumes up to 3 liters per day. It has been claimed that both intravenous hyperalimentation and elemental diets have little stimulatory effect on the pancreas.[18] In fact, instillation of elemental diet into the proximal jejunum of dogs results in a brisk pancreatic secretory response, but the fluid is watery and "enzyme-poor."[19] The failure of elemental diet to stimulate pancreatic enzyme secretion offers a theoretical advantage as a nutritional source during the convalescent phase of acute pancreatitis.

The indications for surgery in acute pancreatitis are: (a) difficulty in diagnosis, (b) deterioration of the clinical condition of the patient, and (c) suspected pseudocyst or pancreatic abscess.

In some medical centers the surgical approach to severe pancreatitis is to recommend routine operative intervention with insertion of drainage tubes. Some surgeons recommend an aggressive approach, including cholecystostomy, enterostomy, gastrostomy, and drainage of the lesser and greater peritoneal sacs. In a few instances, total or subtotal pancreatectomy has been performed, clearly influencing the survival of the acutely ill patient with hemorrhagic pancreatitis.

The early and follow-up usage of ultrasonic scanning will help to differentiate pancreatic pseudocysts from pancreatic abscesses and pancreatic phlegmon. The technique will alert both the internist and the surgeon as to whether operative drainage is indicated. In addition to drainage of the abscess and cholecystostomy, large sump tubes are placed across the posterior wall of the upper part of the abdomen for postoperative irrigation. Either a gastrostomy or jejunostomy tube is inserted for feeding purposes in the postoperative period. Acute pseudocysts may have to be drained if they are expanding, become secondarily infected, or precipitate massive gastrointestinal hemorrhage. The treatment of choice for acute pseudocyst is simple external drainage. Internal drainage into a neighboring hollow viscus should be performed on patients with chronic pseudocyst.

Thus, in severe pancreatitis, it is critical to anticipate problems by careful daily and/or hourly observations that can be readily monitored with our current, advanced technology. Careful attention must be directed to fluid and electrolyte balance, shock, respiratory failure, nutritional depletion, abscess and pseudocyst formation, pulmonary edema, and gastrointestinal hemorrhage. A broader approach and the recognition that severe pancreatitis is a multisystem disease will continue to lead to improved results in terms of decreased mortality.

REFERENCES

1. MOTT, C., H. SARLES, O. TISCORNIA & L. GULLO. 1972. Inhibitory action of alcohol on human exocrine pancreatic secretion. Amer. J. Dig. Dis. 17: 902–910.
2. SARLES, H. 1971. Alcoholism and pancreatitis. (A review). Scand. J. Gastroent. 6: 193–198.
3. GEOKAS, M. C. 1972. Acute pancreatitis (medical progress). Calif. Med. 117: 25–39.
4. MARKS, I. N., S. BANK & J. H. LOUW. 1971. Some current views on pancreatitis. S. Afr. Med. J. 45: 1138–1140.
5. LEVANT, J. A., D. M. SECRIST, H. RESIN, R. STURDEVANT & P. H. GUTH. 1974. Nasogastric suction in the treatment of alcoholic pancreatitis. A controlled study. J.A.M.A. 229: 51–52.
6. KNIGHT, M. J., J. R. CONDON & R. SMITH. 1971. Possible use of glucagon in treatment of pancreatitis. Brit. Med. J. 2: 440–442.
7. KOCK, N. G., S. TIBBLIN & W. G. SCHENK, JR. 1970. Hemodynamic responses to glucagon: an experimental study of central, visceral and peripheral effects. Ann. Surg. 171: 373–379.
8. PARMLEY, W. W., G. GLICK & E. H. SONNENBLICK. 1968. Cardiovascular effects of glucagon in man. New Eng. J. Med. 279: 12–17.
9. CONDON, R. E., J. H. WOODS, T. L. POULIN, W. G. WAGNER & C. A. PISSIOTIS. 1974. Experimental pancreatitis treated with glucagon or lactated Ringer solution. Arch. Surg. 109: 154–158.
10. LOUW, J. H., I. N. MARKS & S. BANK. 1967. The management of severe acute pancreatitis. Postgrad. Med. J. 43: 31–44.
11. BOLOOKI, H. & M. L. GLEIDMAN. 1968. Peritoneal dialysis in treatment of acute pancreatitis. Surgery 64: 466–471.
12. INTERIANO, B., I. D. STUARD & R. W. HYDE. 1972. Acute respiratory distress syndrome in pancreatitis. Ann. Int. Med. 77: 923–926.
13. RANSON, J. H. C., D. F. ROSES & S. D. FINK. 1973. Early respiratory insufficiency in acute pancreatitis. Ann. Surg. 178: 75–79.

14. FELLER, J. H., R. A. BROWN, G. P. MACLAREN TOUSSAINT & A. G. THOMPSON. 1974. Changing methods in treatment of severe pancreatitis. Amer. J. Surg. **127:** 196–201.
15. DUDRICK, S. & R. RUBERG. 1971. Principles and practice of parenteral nutrition. Gastroenterology **61:** 901–910.
16. VOGEL, C. M., R. J. KINGSBURY & A. E. BAUE. 1972. Intravenous hyperalimentation: a review of $2\frac{1}{2}$ years experience. Arch. Surg. **105:** 414–419.
17. WAY, C. N., H. C. MENG & H. H. SANDSTEAD. 1973. An assessment of the role of parenteral alimentation in the management of surgical patients. Ann. Surg. **177:** 103–111.
18. VOITK, A. J., R. A. BROWN, A. H. McARDLE, E. J. HINCHEY & F. N. GURD. 1972. Clinical uses of an elemental diet—preliminary studies. Canad. Med. Ass. J. **107:** 123–129.
19. CASSIM, M. M. & D. B. ALLARDYCE. 1974. Pancreatic secretion in response to jejunal feeding of elemental diet. Ann. Surg. **180:** 228–231.

C. The Small Intestine

INTRODUCTION

Kenneth Williams

The second part of the monograph ends with a consideration of the effect of alcohol on small-intestinal function. These papers are helpful in understanding the complex interplay between alcohol consumption and malnutrition, for it can be now shown that even if the alcoholic consumes a nutritionally adequate diet, the effect of large amounts of alcohol on intestinal absorption of nutrients can produce malnutrition.

Dr. Mezey's paper outlines the importance of alcohol and dietary deficiency in malabsorption, although large amounts of alcohol could be demonstrated to produce pathologic histological changes in the mucosa, deranged motility, and defective absorption.

Dr. Lindenbaum reports his experiments in which ingestion of large amounts of alcohol (representing approximately 50% of total caloric intake) produced malabsorption of vitamin B_{12} in spite of a fully nutritious diet supplemented with vitamins.

This second section of the monograph, *The Gastrointestinal System,* does not consider the medical complications of alcoholism affecting the stomach, except for consideration given to cancer in this area (see Part VII, *Cancer*). Alcohol is known to be capable of producing acute superficial, hemorrhagic gastritis. Clinically this condition is considered to be common in alcoholics following a prolonged drinking bout. Whether or not the ingestion of large amounts of alcohol can be implicated in producing peptic ulcer disease appears not to be resolved at the present time.

The only lesion of the lower gastrointestinal tract known to be related to alcoholism is hemorrhoids. This condition frequently accompanies the portal hypertension found in patients with Laennec's cirrhosis.

INTESTINAL FUNCTION IN CHRONIC ALCOHOLISM*

Esteban Mezey

Department of Medicine
Baltimore City Hospitals
and
The Johns Hopkins University School of Medicine
Baltimore, Maryland 21224

Chronic alcoholism is a frequent cause of malnutrition and vitamin deficiencies. While it is well recognized that chronic alcoholism can lead to malnutrition due to poor dietary intake, disturbances in digestion and absorption of nutrients that may contribute to malnutrition have also been shown to occur. Intestinal malabsorption and pancreatic dysfunction were initially demonstrated in alcoholic patients with cirrhosis of the liver.[1-3] Similar abnormalities were later documented in chronic alcoholic patients with minimal or no liver disease.[4-10] The substances that have been shown to be malabsorbed are: D-xylose,[4-6] thiamine,[7-8] folic acid,[9,10] and fat[5,6] (TABLE 1). The alcoholic patients in whom these abnormalities have been detected had no overt clinical evidence of malabsorption. However, a history of symptoms of epigastric pain and diarrhea was obtained at admission in 15 and 22 percent respectively of 56 patients studied in the metabolic unit at Baltimore City Hospitals. The malabsorption is detected after alcohol binges, and in most cases is corrected to normal when an adequate diet is given with or without the continuation of moderate alcohol intake.[6,10] A direct toxic effect of ethanol and malnutrition have both been considered as causes of the absorption abnormalities.

EFFECTS OF ETHANOL ON THE INTESTINE

Ethanol, besides being absorbed by the intestine, has been shown to be metabolized by the intestinal mucosa and to have a variety of effects on the metabolism of the intestine and on its capacity to absorb a number of substances.

Absorption of Ethanol

Ethanol is rapidly absorbed by the gastrointestinal tract. The absorption starts in the stomach and continues in the upper small intestine. The high concentrations of ethanol reached in the jejunum immediately after ingestion of a dose of 0.8 g ethanol/kg body weight (FIGURE 1) decreases rapidly reaching levels that are in equilibrium with the vascular space by 120 minutes after ingestion[11]. The absorbed ethanol is distributed throughout the body water and appears in the urine, pulmonary alveolar air, spinal fluid, and the remainder of the intestine. The appearance and increase of ethanol in the ileum parallels the levels in the vascular space, suggesting that ethanol enters the ileum from the vascular space rather than by traveling down the length of the intestine.

Ethanol administered by the intravenous route in a similar dose of 0.8 g/kg body weight (FIGURE 2) also is distributed throughout the gastrointestinal tract at concentrations paralleling those found in the vascular space.[11]

*This work was supported in part by Grant No. MH 14251 from the National Institute on Alcohol Abuse and Alcoholism and by the United States Brewer's Association, Inc.

TABLE 1
Malabsorption in Chronic Alcoholism

Substance	Method	No. of Pts. Studied	No. Abnormal	Percent Abnormal	References
D-xylose	Oral dose	55	9	18	Small et al[4]
		25	19	76	Roggin et al[5]
		37	9	24	Mezey et al[6]
Thiamine	Oral dose	20	$p < 0.005$*		Tomasulo et al[7]
		34	$p < 0.001$*		Thomson et al[8]
Folic Acid	Oral dose	24	$p < 0.01$*		Halsted et al[9]
	Jejunal Perfusion	11	8	73	Halsted et al[10]
Vitamin A	Oral dose	37	3	8	Small et al[4]
Vitamin B_{12}	Schilling Test	17	8	47	Roggin et al[5]
Fat	Stool determination	27	15	56	Roggin et al[5]
		37	13	55	Mezey et al[6]

*Significantly different from corresponding values in control subjects.

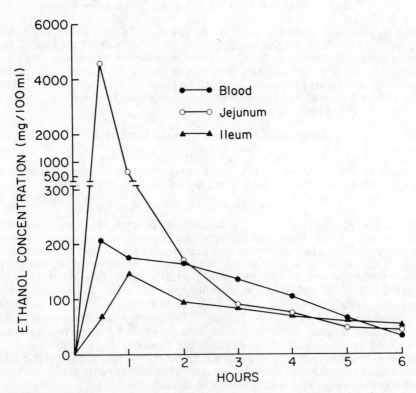

FIGURE 1. Distribution of ethanol in the blood, jejunum, and ileum after the acute oral ingestion of ethanol, 0.8 g/kg body weight, in one patient. (From Halsted et al.[11] By permission of *American Journal of Clinical Nutrition*.)

Metabolism of Ethanol

Alcohol dehydrogenase, an enzyme present in the supernatant fraction of tissue homogenates, which is the principal enzyme catalyzing the oxidation of ethanol in the liver,[12] has been found to be distributed in a number of tissues including the intestine in both the rat[13-15] and man.[13] The alcohol dehydrogenase activities obtained in various rat tissues in our laboratory are shown in TABLE 2. In the gastrointestinal tract the activity of alcohol dehydrogenase was found to be highest in the mucosa of the stomach and upper jejunum and lower

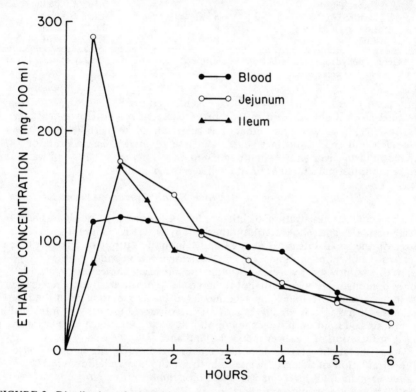

FIGURE 2. Distribution of ethanol in the blood, jejunum, and ileum after the intravenous administration of ethanol, 0.8 g/kg body weight, in one patient. (From Halsted et al.[11] By permission of *American Journal of Clinical Nutrition*.)

in the ileum. The activity of alcohol dehydrogenase in the upper intestine was about $\frac{1}{5}$ of the activity found in the liver. Other investigators have found similar activities of alcohol dehydrogenase in the upper small intestine of the rat;[13-15] however they obtained lower comparative liver alcohol dehydrogenase activities, so that in their reports the activity of alcohol dehydrogenase in the intestine calculates to be between $\frac{1}{2}$ and $1\frac{1}{2}$ times that found in the liver. The discrepancies in the activities of rat liver alcohol dehydrogenase may be related to differences in assay methodology. Intestinal alcohol dehydrogenase has been found to have at least 2 isoenzymes on agar gel electrophoresis in the rhesus monkey[17] but has

TABLE 2

Tissue Distribution of Alcohol Dehydrogenase Activity in the Rat

Tissue	Animals (No.)	Alcohol Dehydrogenase* (μmoles/mg protein/hr)
Liver	34	0.821 ± 0.260
Retina	6	0.256 ± 0.106
Gastric Mucosa	8	0.203 ± 0.038
Intestinal Mucosa		
Upper Third	8	0.155 ± 0.067
Middle Third	8	0.108 ± 0.061
Lower Third	8	0.033 ± 0.025
Kidney	8	0.112 ± 0.074

*Alcohol dehydrogenase activity was determined as described by Mezey et al.[16] The values are expressed as means ± S.D.

not been characterized further. Krebs and Perkins[18] have suggested that intestinal alcohol dehydrogenase may be of bacterial origin. However, Carter and Isselbacher[14] showed that ethanol is metabolized to carbon dioxide by rat stomach and small-intestinal slices. The rate of metabolism was about 68% of that found by liver slices when compared on a wet-weight basis and was not different in intestinal slices obtained from germ-free animals.

Effects of Ethanol on Intestinal Metabolism and Absorption

The acute administration of ethanol has been shown to result in increases in triglyceride[19] and cholesterol synthesis[20] by intestinal slices, triglyceride content of the small intestinal mucosa and lymphatic output of triglycerides, cholesterol, and phospholipids[21]. The increased triglyceride synthesis could be partially suppressed by pyrazole, while the increased cholesterol synthesis[19] was only demonstrable when ethanol remained in the intestinal lumen,[20] suggesting that the effects of ethanol may be mediated by its metabolism in the intestinal mucosa. It has also been suggested that the observed increases in intestinal lipid synthesis and lipid output by the lymph may contribute to the hyperlipemia and fatty infiltration of the liver induced by ethanol.[21]

Other metabolic effects demonstrated for ethanol on the intestine have been the stimulation of adenyl cyclase in both rat and human jejunum in vitro,[22] and a decrease in ATP levels in the small intestine in rat in vitro and in vivo after both acute and chronic administration.[23]

Ethanol has been shown to inhibit small-intestinal transport of amino acids and glucose in the rat in vitro and after its acute administration in vivo.[13,24,25] It has been suggested that the inhibitory effect of ethanol in intestinal transport could be related either to the effect of ethanol in lowering ATP content[23] or to the inhibitory effect of ethanol, demonstrated in other tissues,[26] on the activity of Na-, K-, and Mg-stimulated ATPase, which has been observed to be associated with active transport.[25]

Recently Baraona et al.[27] showed that the acute administration of ethanol to rats resulted in hemorrhagic erosions of the tips of the intestinal villi, decreases in the enzymatic activities of lactase and thimidine kinase, located principally in the villus and crypt cells respectively, and decreased oxygen consumption. On the other hand, chronic administration with an adequate diet resulted in shortening of the intestinal villi, decreases in the number of epithelial cells lining the villi, and decreases in the activities of the villus enzymes lactase, sucrase, and alkaline phosphatase, but increases in the crypt enzyme thimidine kinase and in the incorporation of thimidine into DNA. However, unlike the findings of decreased intestinal transport after the acute administration of ethanol, the chronic administration with an adequate diet has not resulted in decreases in the absorption of D-xylose[28] or folic acid.[29]

Effect of Ethanol Administration on Intestinal Absorption in Man

In man the direct addition of ethanol to intestinal perfusates in a concentration of 2% has been shown to inhibit the intestinal uptake of L-methionine.[30] However, the oral administration of ethanol has been shown to inhibit the absorption of thiamine[8] and folic acid[9] in only a small number of the patients tested (TABLE 3).

We studied the effect of acute and intravenous administration of ethanol on the absorption of D-xylose in 7 chronic alcoholic patients admitted to the metabolic unit at Baltimore City Hospitals. None of the patients had clinical or laboratory evidence of significant liver disease. Liver biopsy in 3 of the 7 patients revealed mild to moderate fatty infiltration of the liver. D-xylose absorption was tested after 12 hours of fasting by giving a 25-g oral dose. The tests were done at 2-day intervals with and without the addition of oral or intravenous ethanol in a dose of 0.8 g/kg of body weight. In the case of ethanol administration by the oral route, $\frac{1}{2}$ of the ethanol dose was given with the D-xylose mixed in 250 ml of tap water and the remaining $\frac{1}{2}$ given immediately thereafter mixed in another 250 ml of water. Ethanol was administered by the intravenous route as a 20% (v/v) solution in normal saline, and the D-xylose given immediately after ending the infusion. Samples of blood obtained every hour for 5 hours, and a 5-hour urine collection was analyzed for pentose by the method of Roe and Rice.[31] The oral administration of ethanol resulted in a decrease in the urinary excretion of D-xylose in all 7 patients (FIGURE 3). The mean 5-hour urinary excretion of D-xylose after oral ethanol was 3.86 ± 0.89 ($\pm$SD) g, which is significantly lower than the mean excretion of 6.70 ± 1.81 g obtained without ethanol ($p < 0.01$). On the other hand, ethanol administration by the intravenous route had no significant effect on urinary D-xylose excretion. A mean excretion of D-xylose of 6.34 ± 2.30 g was obtained, which is similar to the control value. The concentration of D-xylose in the blood was decreased by oral ethanol only at 1 hour after

TABLE 3

Effect of Acute Ethanol Administration on Intestinal Absorption in Man

Substance	Method	Dose of Ethanol	No. of Patients Studied	No. with Decreased Absorption	References
L-Methionine	Intestinal perfusion	2% in perfusate	10	55% mean inhibition	Israel et al[30]
Thiamine	Oral dose	144 g orally	9	3	Thomson et al[8]
		1.5 g/kg i.v.	3	1	
Folic Acid	Oral dose	4.5 oz whiskey	5	1	Halsted et al[9]
D-xylose	Oral dose	0.8 g/kg orally	7	7	Mezey, present study
		0.8 g/kg i.v.	7	0	

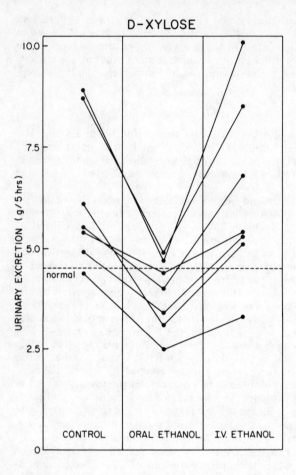

D-XYLOSE

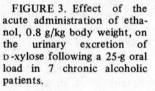

FIGURE 3. Effect of the acute administration of ethanol, 0.8 g/kg body weight, on the urinary excretion of D-xylose following a 25-g oral load in 7 chronic alcoholic patients.

its administration (FIGURE 4) to a mean value of 26.6 ± 10.5 mg/100 ml blood, as against a control mean value of 40.5 ± 10.1 mg/100 ml blood (p < 0.05). Ethanol administered intravenously had no significant effect on the concentration of D-xylose obtained in the blood at any time. It was initially thought that the decrease in early blood concentrations of D-xylose after oral ethanol administration could have been due to an effect of ethanol in delaying gastric emptying.[32] However, this mechanism was discounted by showing no significant gastric residual in 3 patients 1 hour after the ingestion of the ethanol and D-xylose. The administration of a hyperosmolar solution of glycine and alanine of osmolarity equivalent to the ethanol solution to 2 subjects resulted in no changes in the urinary excretion of D-xylose in the urine. The hyperosmolar amino acid solution behaved like the ethanol solution in lowering the blood concentration of D-xylose at 1 hour (FIGURE 5). But by 3 hours there was a fall in D-xylose concentration following the ethanol solution, whereas with the hypertonic amino acid solution the levels of D-xylose remained elevated throughout the 5 hours. These observations suggest that hyperosmolarity delays absorption but that ethanol in addition to its hyperosmolar effect also has an inhibitory effect on the absorptive capacity itself.

The acute administration of ethanol by either the oral or intravenous route in a dose of 0.8 g/kg body weight was shown to alter the motility of the small intestine.[33] In the jejunum there was inhibition of type I waves, which are mixing waves and impede the forward progress of intestinal contents, while in the ileum there was an enhancement of type III waves, which represent a change in tonus of the intestine and are associated with propulsion of intestinal contents. These effects of ethanol on the small intestine may contribute to the diarrhea seen in binge-drinking alcoholics.

The chronic administration of ethanol in man together with an adequate dietary intake has been shown to result in a decrease in vitamin B_{12} absorption in all the patients studied,[34] but in a decreased folate absorption in only a few,[9,10] (TABLE 4). Furthermore, the administration of ethanol to 11 subjects in doses ranging between 148 and 256 g/day for 2 to 3 weeks did not result in a decrease in D-xylose absorption. The mean 5-hour urinary D-xylose excretion was 7.70 ± 0.169 g before and 8.13 ± 1.39 g after the feeding of ethanol. Jejunal biopsies were performed in 7 of the 11 subjects and no abnormalities were found in the jejunal mucosa when examined by light microscopy. However, ultrastructural changes consisting of abnormalities of the mitochondria, endoplasmic reticulum, and Golgi apparatus have been described by Rubin et al.[35] in chronic alcoholic patients fed ethanol with an adequate diet.

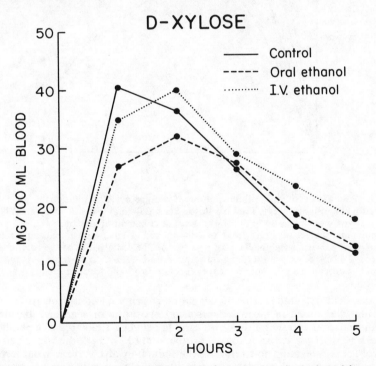

FIGURE 4. Effect of the acute administration of ethanol, 0.8 g/kg body weight, on mean blood concentrations of D-xylose following a 25-g oral load in 7 chronic alcoholic patients.

MALNUTRITION AND MALABSORPTION

The occurrence of intestinal malabsorption has been well documented in malnourished populations.[36,37] Among alcoholics, abnormalities of absorption have been found most frequently in patients with a history of poor dietary intake and folate deficiency.[9,10,38] Recovery from malabsorption of D-xylose (FIGURE 6)

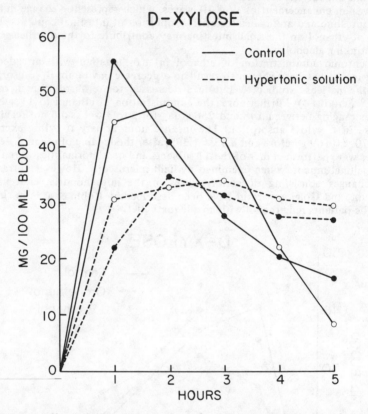

FIGURE 5. Effect of the administration of a hyperosmolar solution of glycine and alanine on the urinary excretion of D-xylose after a 25-g oral load in 2 subjects. The solutions ingested were made up in 500 ml of water and contained glycine, 49 g, and alanine, 58.1 g for one subject weighing 75 kg (●--●--●), and glycine, 46.5 g, and alanine, 55.2 g, for the other subject, weighing 71.5 kg (o--o--o). The osmolarities of the solutions were 2.61 and 2.48 osmoles per liter, respectively, and are equivalent to those obtained when ethanol in a dose of 0.8 g/kg body weight is dissolved in 500 ml for each subject.

and folic acid detected in chronic alcoholic patients on admission to the metabolic unit was found in most patients after institution of a normal diet despite the continuation of ethanol in doses carying between 190 and 256 g per day for 2 weeks.[6,10] However, feeding a low-protein diet (25 g) with the continuation of ethanol for 2 weeks did not result in the induction of D-xylose malabsorption. Also, while neither a low-folate diet nor ethanol alone resulted in malabsorption in 1 patient each, their combination in 2 patients studied resulted in decreased

TABLE 4

Effect of Chronic Ethanol Administration on Intestinal Absorption in Man

| | | Dose of Ethanol | | Results | | |
| | | Daily Amount (g) | Duration | No. of Patients Studied | No. with Decreased Absorption | |
Substance	Method					References
Folic Acid	Oral dose	80–96	10 days	1	1	Halsted et al[9]
	Intestinal perfusion	192	2 weeks	7	2	Halsted et al[10]
Vitamin B$_{12}$	Schilling test	158–235	3–8 weeks	4	4	Lindenbaum et al[34]
D-xylose	Oral dose	148–256	2–4 weeks	11	0	Mezey, present study

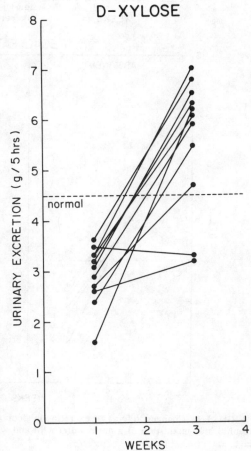

FIGURE 6. Changes in D-xylose absorption in chronic alcoholic patients following admission to the hospital and institution of a normal diet with ethanol in doses varying between 190 and 256 g per day.

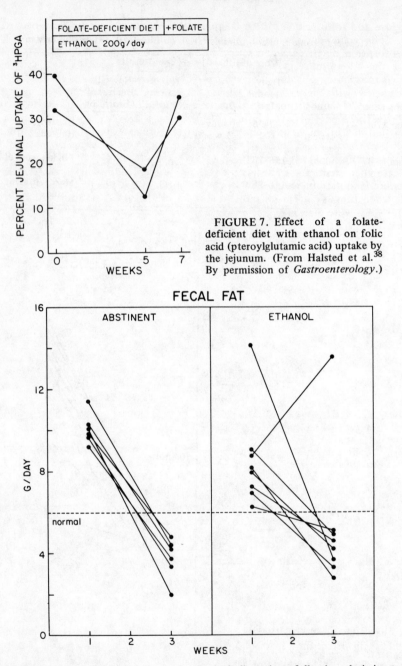

FIGURE 7. Effect of a folate-deficient diet with ethanol on folic acid (pteroylglutamic acid) uptake by the jejunum. (From Halsted et al.[38] By permission of *Gastroenterology*.)

FIGURE 8. Changes in fecal fat excretion in alcoholic patients following admission to the hospital and institution of a normal diet with and without ethanol in a dose of 256 g per day.

D-xylose and folic acid (FIGURE 7) absorption in both, with recovery occurring after folic acid administration despite continuation of ethanol intake.[38] The malabsorption occurred when serum folate levels in the patients had decreased to 1.0 and 1.9 ng/ml respectively (normal > 5 ng/ml). Intestinal biopsies revealed normal morphology by light microscopy. Other investigators have described abnormalities with more severe folate deficiency and bone marrow megaloblastosis.[39,40] Unfortunately, no determinations of intestinal absorption were made in these patients. Our studies suggest that dietary folate deficiency is an important factor in the development of malabsorption in chronic alcoholic patients and that this occurs prior to the detection of morphological abnormalities of the intestine by light microscopy.

Steatorrhea (fecal fat excretion > 6 g/day) was a finding in 14, or 33%, of 42 chronic alcoholics on admission to the hospital. It disappeared in all but 1 patient when they were placed on an adequate diet in the metabolic unit whether or not they were also receiving ethanol in a dose of 256 g/day (FIGURE 8). The patient who continued to have steatorrhea had radiological evidence of pancreatic calcification. The presence of steatorrhea in the chronic alcoholic patients corre-

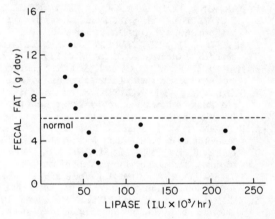

FIGURE 9. Relationship between fecal fat excretion and pancreatic output of lipase following cholecystokinin-pancreozymin-secretin stimulation.

lated best with decreased pancreatic function, in particular with a low lipase output of the pancreas following cholecystokinin-pancreozymin-secretin stimulation (FIGURE 9). This agrees with the observations of Roggin et al.,[41] who found decreases in pancreatic lipase output following stimulation by test meal in a group of alcoholic patients at admission to the hospital with recovery to normal values when retested 4–6 weeks after hospitalization.

SUMMARY AND CONCLUSIONS

These studies show that malabsorption of a number of substances is a common occurrence in chronic alcoholic patients who came to the hospital because of acute and chronic alcoholism. The group of patients studied is obviously a selected group of severely ill alcoholics, and the studies therefore give no information as to what the general incidence of malabsorption may be in the larger alcoholic population. Both ethanol and dietary deficiency have been shown to have effects on the intestine. Effects of ethanol in producing histological abnormalities of the intestinal mucosa, decreasing absorptive capacity, and altering intestinal motility were demonstrated after the acute administration of single large doses. On the other hand, the ingestion of smaller doses of ethanol with an adequate diet for a prolonged period in man, with the exception of producing consistent decreases in vitamin B_{12} absorption and ultrastructural changes in the intestinal mucosa, did only on occasion result in malabsorption of other substances.

The importance of dietary deficiencies as a factor in malabsorption and maldigestion was demonstrated by the recovery to normal of D-xylose and folic acid malabsorption and the disappearance of steatorrhea, the last-mentioned correlating with abnormal pancreatic function, after institution of an adequate diet despite ethanol feeding. Also, while the feeding of neither ethanol nor a folate-deficient diet alone induced malabsorption, the combination of the two factors did. These findings suggest that malabsorption occurs principally in alcoholic patients who have dietary insufficiencies.

REFERENCES

1. BARAONA, E., H. ORREGO, O. FERNANDEZ, E. AMENABAR, E. MALDONADO, F. TAG & A. SALINAS. 1962. Absorptive function of the small intestine in liver cirrhosis. Amer. J. Dig. Dis. 7: 318–330.
2. SUN, D. C. H., R. A. ALBACETE & J. K. CHEN. 1967. Malabsorption studies in cirrhosis of the liver. Arch. Int. Med. 119: 567–572.
3. MARIN, G. A., M. L. CLARK & J. R. SENIOR. 1969. Studies of malabsorption occurring in patients with Laënnec's cirrhosis. Gastroenterology 56: 727–736.
4. SMALL, M., A. LONGARINI & N. ZAMCHECK. 1959. Disturbances of digestive physiology following acute drinking episodes in "skid-row" alcoholics. Amer. J. Med. 27: 575–585.
5. ROGGIN, G. M., F. L. IBER, R. M. H. KATER & F. TOBON. 1959. Malabsorption in the chronic alcoholic. Johns Hopkins Med. J. 125: 321–330.
6. MEZEY, E., E. JOW, R. E. SLAVIN & F. TOBON. 1970. Pancreatic function and intestinal absorption in chronic alcoholism. Gastroenterology 59: 657–664.
7. TOMASULO, P. A., R. M. H. KATER & F. L. IBER. 1968. Impairment of thiamine absorption in alcoholism. Amer. J. Clin. Nutr. 21: 1340–1344.
8. THOMSON, A. L., H. BAKER & C. M. LEEVY. 1970. Patterns of ^{35}S-thiamine hydrochloride absorption in the malnourished alcoholic patient. J. Lab. Clin. Med. 76: 34–45.
9. HALSTED, C. H., R. C. GRIGGS & J. W. HARRIS. 1967. The effect of alcoholism on the absorption of folic acid (H^3-PGA) evaluated by plasma levels and urine excretion. J. Lab. Clin. Med. 69: 116–131.
10. HALSTED, C. H., E. A. ROBLES & E. MEZEY. 1971. Decreased jejunal uptake of labelled folic acid (^{3}H-PGA) in alcoholic patients: roles of alcohol and nutrition. N. Eng. J. Med. 285: 701–706.
11. HALSTED, C. H., E. A. ROBLES & E. MEZEY. 1973. Distribution of ethanol in the human gastrointestinal tract. Amer. J. Clin. Nutr. 26: 831–834.
12. ISSELBACHER, K. J. & N. J. GREENBERGER. 1964. Metabolic effects of alcohol on the liver. N. Eng. J. Med. 270: 351–356, 402–410.
13. SPENCER, R. P., K. R. BRODY & B. M. LUTTERS. 1964. Some effects of ethanol on the gastrointestinal tract. Amer. J. Dig. Dis. 9: 599–604.
14. CARTER, E. A. & K. J. ISSELBACHER. 1971. The metabolism of ethanol to carbon dioxide by stomach and small intestinal slices. Proc. Soc. Exp. Biol. Med. 138: 817–819.
15. MISTILIS, S. P. & A. GARSKE. 1969. Induction of alcohol dehydrogenase in liver and gastrointestinal tract. Aust. Ann. Med. 18: 227–231.
16. MEZEY, E., G. R. CHERRICK & P. R. HOLT. 1968. Biliary excretion of alcohol dehydrogenase. J. Lab. Clin. Med. 71: 798–806.

17. VON WARTBURG, J. P. & J. PAPENBERG. 1966. Alcohol dehydrogenase and ethanol metabolism. Psychosom. Med. 28 (II): 405–413.
18. KREBS, H. A. & J. R. PERKINS. 1970. The physiological role of liver alcohol dehydrogenase. Biochem. J. 118: 635–644.
19. CARTER, E. A., G. D. DRUMMEY & K. J. ISSELBACHER. 1971. Ethanol stimulates triglyceride synthesis by the intestine. Science 174: 1245–1247.
20. MIDDLETON, W. R. J., E. A. CARTER, G. D. DRUMMEY & K. J. ISSELBACHER. 1971. Effect of oral ethanol administration on intestinal cholesterogenesis in the rat. Gastroenterology 60: 880–887.
21. MISTILIS, S. P. & R. K. OCKNER. 1972. Effects of ethanol on endogenous lipid and lipoprotein metabolism in small intestine. J. Lab. Clin. Med. 80: 34–46.
22. GREENE, H. L., R. H. HERMAN & S. KRAEMER. 1971. Stimulation of jejunal adenyl cyclase by ethanol. J. Lab. Clin. Med. 78: 336–342.
23. CARTER, E. A. & K. J. ISSELBACHER. 1973. Effect of ethanol on intestinal adenosine triphosphate (ATP) content. Proc. Soc. Exp. Biol. Med. 142: 1171–1173.
24. CHANG, T., J. LEWIS & A. J. GLAZKO. 1967. Effect of ethanol and other alcohols on the transport of amino acids and glucose by everted sacs of rat small intestine. Biochem. Biophys. Acta 135: 1000–1007.
25. ISRAEL, Y., I. SALAZAR & E. ROSENMANN. 1968. Inhibitory effects of alcohol on intestinal amino acid transport in vivo and in vitro. J. Nutr. 96: 499–504.
26. ISRAEL, Y., H. KALANT & I. LAUFER. 1965. Effect of ethanol on Na, K, Mg-stimulated microsomal ATPase activity. Biochem. Pharmacol. 14: 1803–1914.
27. BARAONA, E., R. C. PIROLA & C. S. LIEBER. 1974. Small intestinal damage and changes in cell population produced by ethanol ingestion in the rat. Gastroenterology 66: 226–234.
28. BROITMAN, S. A., M. D. SMALL, J. J. VITALE & N. ZAMCHECK. 1961. Intestinal absorption and urinary excretion of xylose in rats fed reduced protein and thyroxine or alcohol. Gastroenterology 41: 21–28.
29. HALSTED, C. H., K. BHANTHUMNAVIN & E. MEZEY. Jejunal uptake of tritiated folic acid (^{3}H-PGA) in the rat studied by in vivo perfusion. Submitted for publication.
30. ISRAEL, Y., J. E. VALENZUELA, I. SALAZAR & G. UGARTE. 1969. Alcohol and amino acid transport in the human small intestine. J. Nutr. 98: 222–224.
31. ROE, J. H. & E. W. RICE. 1948. A photometric method for the determination of free pentoses in animal tissues. J. Biol. Chem. 173: 507–512.
32. BARBORIAK, J. J. & R. C. MEADE. 1970. Effect of alcohol on gastric emptying in man. Amer. J. Clin. Nutr. 23: 1151–1153.
33. ROBLES, E. A., E. MEZEY, C. H. HALSTED & M. M. SCHUSTER. 1972. Effect of ethanol on intestinal motility in man. (abst.) Gastroenterology 67: 799.
34. LINDENBAUM, J. & C. S. LIEBER. 1969. Alcohol induced malabsorption of vitamin B_{12} in man. Nature 224: 806.
35. RUBIN, E., B. J. RYBAK, J. LINDENBAUM, C. D. GERSON, G. WALKER & C. S. LIEBER. 1972. Ultrastructural changes in the small intestine induced by ethanol. Gastroenterology 63: 801–814.
36. HERSKOVIC, T. 1969. Protein malnutrition and the small intestine. Amer. J. Clin. Nutr. 22: 300–304.
37. MAYORAL, L. G., K. TRIPATHY, O. BOLAÑOS, H. LOTERO, E. DUQUE, F. T. GARCIA & J. GHITIS. 1972. Intestinal, functional, and morphologic abnormalities in severely protein malnourished adults. Amer. J. Clin. Nutr. 25: 1084–1091.
38. HALSTED, C. H., E. A. ROBLES & E. MEZEY. 1973. Intestinal malabsorption in folate-deficient alcoholics. Gastroenterology 64: 526–532.
39. BIANCHI, A., D. W. CHIPMAN, A. DRESKIN & N. S. ROSENSWEIG. 1970. Nutritional folic acid deficiency with megaloblastic changes in the small bowel epithelium. N. Eng. J. Med. 282: 859–861.
40. HERMOS, J. A., W. H. ADAMS, Y. K. LIU, L. W. SULLIVAN & J. S. TRIER. 1972. Mucosa of the small intestine in folate-deficient alcoholics. Ann. Int. Med. 76: 957–965.
41. ROGGIN, G. M., F. L. IBER & W. G. LINSCHEER. 1972. Intraluminal fat digestion in the chronic alcoholic. Gut 13: 107–111.

EFFECTS OF CHRONIC ETHANOL ADMINISTRATION ON INTESTINAL ABSORPTION IN MAN IN THE ABSENCE OF NUTRITIONAL DEFICIENCY*

John Lindenbaum

Medical Service, Harlem Hospital Center
New York, New York 10037
and College of Physicians and Surgeons
Columbia University
New York, New York 10032

Charles S. Lieber

Department of Medicine
Mount Sinai School of Medicine
New York, New York 10029
and Section of Liver Disease and Nutrition
Bronx Veterans Administration Hospital
Bronx, New York 10468

INTRODUCTION

Chronic alcoholism is frequently associated with impaired intestinal absorption.[1-6] A high incidence of malabsorption of xylose, fat, vitamin B_{12}, folic acid, and thiamine has been documented in malnourished chronic alcoholics, with recovery of absorptive function after withdrawal of alcohol and ingestion of a nutritious diet.[1-6] Acute ethanol administration has been reported to cause impairment in intestinal absorption in rats,[7,8] hamsters,[9] and man,[10] and chronic ethanol feeding in rats results in malabsorption of vitamin B_{12}[11] and carbohydrates,[12] and decreased jejunal enzyme activities[13] despite adequate vitamin and protein intake. Chronic ethanol administration in man with a nutritious diet causes ultrastructural abnormalities in intestinal villous cells.[14]

Since malnutrition alone may result in malabsorption,[15,16] the relative importance of ethanol ingestion and depletion of nutrients in causing malabsorption in chronic alcoholic patients has been uncertain. To determine whether ethanol alone, in the absence of associated nutritional deficiency, causes impairment of small bowel function in man, we studied the effects of chronic alcohol administration under controlled metabolic ward conditions on intestinal absorption in human volunteers.

SUBJECTS AND METHODS

The experimental design was similar to that used in several previous studies.[17,18] Eight adult male volunteers, ages 43–56, with a history of chronic alcoholism, participated after giving informed consent. They had been hospitalized for 1 month or more before the study began and had been maintained on a hospital diet with vitamin supplements. At the time of study each subject

*This work was supported in part by grants AA 00249, AA00224, and AM 12511 from the U.S. Public Health Service, and VA Project Number 5251-04.

TABLE 1

Percent Urinary Excretion of [57Co] Vitamin B_{12} During Control Periods and Ethanol Administration in Human Volunteers

| Subject | % Urinary [57Co] B_{12} Excretion | | | | Number of Days on Ethanol When Tested | Maximum Ethanol Dose % Total Caloric Intake |
| | Control (Pre- and/or Postethanol) | | Ethanol | | | |
	24 hr	48 hr	24 hr	48 hr		
1	42.4	51.4	27.4	33.0	13	46
	40.7*	50.6	11.9	20.6	26	
2	12.1	16.2	5.9	9.1	21	60
	12.1*	16.8	6.7	11.0	31	
	11.2*	17.5				
3	17.0	21.0	13.1	17.4	21	60
4	10.5	15.4	5.9	10.2	34	66
5	18.3	18.8	3.1	3.9	21	46
	14.7*	19.4	6.1†	7.9	28	
6	20.9	30.0	14.5	22.7	23	46
	15.4	25.3	10.2	10.5	37	
7	10.2	14.4	17.3	23.1	25	46
			17.8	25.5	33	
8	7.4	10.6	8.8	11.0	25	46

*Postethanol period, 8–22 days after cessation of alcohol administration.
†[57Co] B_{12} given with 9 g pancreatin (Viokase®).

was asymptomatic and had a normal hemogram, liver function tests and biopsy morphology, serum folate and B_{12} concentrations, and xylose and B_{12} absorption test.

Throughout each of 3 study periods on a metabolic ward, (preethanol control, ethanol, and postethanol control) they received daily vitamin supplements.[18] The daily dose of supplemental folic acid was 200 μg, except in subjects 1 through 4, who took 1200 μg of pteroylglutamic acid by mouth daily. In addition, subjects 2, 3, 5, 6 and 7 received 30 mg of folic acid parenterally during the control and ethanol periods.

Protein intake comprised 12.5% of total calories (76–86 g/d) in 6 subjects and 25% in 2 (150 g/d, subjects 3 and 5). Fat intake in the subjects in whom lipid balance studies were performed is shown in TABLE 4. During the alcohol period, ethanol was substituted isocalorically for carbohydrate as in previously reported studies,[17, 18] and comprised 46–66% of total caloric intake (TABLE 1) or 173–253 g/day. Absorption studies were performed after 11–38 days of ethanol administration.

Absorption Studies

Vitamin B_{12} absorption was studied by the urinary excretion method of Schilling[19] after ^{57}Co-cyanocobalamin (0.75 μg; specific activity 0.6–1.0 μCi/μg) was given orally with intrinsic factor concentrate. Two 1-mg "flushing" doses of nonradioactive B_{12} were given at 2 and 24 hours and urine collected for 48 hours. Five-hour urinary xylose excretion and 2-hour serum xylose concentrations were measured by the method of Roe and Rice[20] after the oral administration of 25 g of D-xylose in the fasting state. Three subjects also received 20 g of pyrogen-free xylose as a 10% solution intravenously over a 30-minute period on other occasions; serum xylose was measured at 30-minute intervals for 3 hours and urinary xylose excretion for 5 and 24 hours after the infusion. Fecal fat excretion was determined by the method of van de Kamer[21] in continuous 72-hour specimens obtained throughout the ethanol and control periods.

TABLE 2

Urinary Xylose Excretion After an Oral Dose During Control Periods
and Ethanol Administration in Human Volunteers*

Subject	Preethanol Period	Ethanol Period	Postethanol Period
1	5.6	8.2(21)	6.3
2	7.1	9.9(24), 11.5(30)	6.0
3	6.4	8.7(24)	
5	8.5	14.4(11), 12.0*(14), 11.1*(16)	8.5
6	6.4	8.0(14), 10.6*, 8.0*(32)	6.0
7	5.1	5.1*(16), 8.5(20), 8.0*(32)	6.1

*The urinary excretion of xylose in grams over a 5-hour collection period after the oral administration of 25 grams is shown before, during, and after chronic ethanol ingestion. Numbers in parenthesis indicate days on alcohol. Asterisks denote occasions on which ethanol was withheld during the 5 hours of the test. Postethanol studies were done 5–12 days after cessation of alcohol administration.

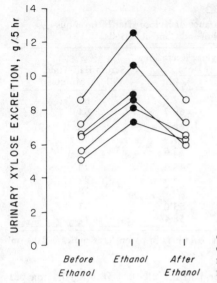

FIGURE 1. Urinary xylose excretion after an oral 25-g dose in 6 subjects during control and ethanol periods. In 4 subjects who were tested more than once during the ethanol period, mean values are shown.

RESULTS

Vitamin B_{12} Absorption

The 24- and 48-hour urinary excretion of ^{57}Co-cyanocobalamin is shown in TABLE 1. The data from the first 4 subjects have been previously reported.[22] B_{12} excretion during the period of ethanol administration was less than control values in subjects 1–6 (p $<$ 0.05 at both 24 and 48 hours). In 3 subjects the 24-hour excretion during the ethanol period fell below the lower limit of normal for the test in our laboratory (7.5%). In 2 subjects (nos. 7 and 8), both on the lowest daily ethanol dose, no depression of vitamin B_{12} absorption was seen during alcohol administration. Thus, a decrease in B_{12} absorption was seen in each of the 3 subjects ingesting ethanol as 60–66% of caloric intake but only in 3 of the 5 receiving alcohol as 46% of intake. There was no significant difference in 24-hour urine volumes between ethanol and control periods (mean ± 1 SD, control periods 1837 ± 720 ml, ethanol 2146 ± 929 ml, p $>$ 0.5).

The concomitant administration of a pancreatic extract did not result in normal vitamin B_{12} absorption during the alcohol period (subject 5, TABLE 1).

Xylose

Urinary xylose excretion after the oral dose was measured in alcohol and control periods in 6 of the subjects (TABLE 2).   In each subject urinary xylose excretion was increased during ethanol administration (FIGURE 1) over control values (mean of control periods 6.7 ± 1.1 g, alcohol 9.4 ± 1.9 g, p $<$ 0.005). The increase in xylose excretion was noted regardless of whether ethanol was withheld during the 5-hour period of the test. Serum xylose concentrations at 2 hours after the dose were higher during the ethanol period

232 Annals New York Academy of Sciences

TABLE 3
Urinary Excretion and Serum Disappearance of Xylose after Intravenous
Administration During Alcohol and Control Periods

Subject	Period	Urinary Xylose Excretion, % of Dose 5 hr	24 hr	Serum Half-Time, (T1/2), Minutes
5	control	58.0	62.5	83
	ethanol (29)	64.7	69.7	64
7	control	41.7	48.4	88
	ethanol (25)	51.7	57.9	76
	ethanol* (31)	44.3	53.6	83
8	control	43.6	48.2	79
	ethanol (21)	41.6	48.4	97
	ethanol* (24)	44.6	50.7	78
Mean	control	47.8	53.0	83
	ethanol	51.9	58.4	77

*Ethanol withheld during first 5 hours of test. Numbers in parenthesis indicate days on ethanol.

(mean of control periods 41 ± 5.4 mg per 100 ml, alcohol 56.5 ± 10.1 mg per 100 ml, p < 0.05).

To determine whether differences in the metabolism or excretion of xylose might account for the increased serum and urinary xylose levels during ethanol administration, the serum disappearance and urinary excretion of xylose given intravenously was studied in 3 subjects (TABLE 3). No significant differences were noted between control and ethanol periods.

Fat

Fecal fat excretion during ethanol and control periods was studied in 5 of the subjects (TABLE 4). Fat absorption appeared to improve slightly while on ethanol in 4 of the 5 subjects.

DISCUSSION

These studies extend our original observation[27] that chronic ethanol administration results in impairment of vitamin B_{12} absorption in man despite adequate

TABLE 4
Fecal Fat Excretion During Ethanol and Control Periods
in Human Volunteers*

Subject	Fat Intake, g/day	Fecal Fat Excretion, % of Intake/Day Preethanol	Ethanol	Postethanol
1	67	2.24†	1.61 ± 0.33	1.85 ± 0.67
5	100	3.06 ± 0.35	1.74 ± 0.90	1.77 ± 0.42
6	67	3.96 ± 1.99	2.30 ± 0.31	2.54 ± 0.42
7	79	3.42 ± 0.53	3.54 ± 1.29	3.36 ± 1.33
8	78	5.23 ± 1.54	3.15 ± 1.71	4.68 ± 0.95

*Mean (± 1 SD) values are shown. Fat intake was constant for each subject throughout the 3 periods. Normal, less than 7%/day.
†Mean of 2 72-hr stool collections.

nutrient intake. The failure of 2 subjects receiving the lowest dose of ethanol to develop B_{12} malabsorption suggests that the effect may be, in part, dose-related. The block in B_{12} assimilation presumably existed at the level of ileal uptake, or transport through or out of the ileal cell, since the malabsorption occurred despite the concomitant administration of gastric intrinsic factor and, in 1 subject, of pancreatin. The precise mechanism of disturbance of ileal function induced by alcohol remains to be established. The B_{12} malabsorption that occurs in rats chronically fed ethanol has been recently shown to be associated with impairment in the ileal uptake step with decreased binding of the B_{12}-intrinsic factor complex by the villous cell.[11]

In view of the demonstrated malabsorption of vitamin B_{12} in several subjects, it is somewhat surprising that the same subjects absorbed xylose and fat so well. Mezey et al.[3] and Halsted et al.[4,23] have also found that the administration of ethanol (in daily doses of 134–300 g) for 2–4 weeks along with adequate diet did not cause steatorrhea or xylose malabsorption in human volunteers. It may be relevant that at the doses administered in the performance of the absorption tests, B_{12} is absorbed by a specialized active transport mechanism, and xylose and fatty acids (predominantly or completely) by "passive diffusion." In everted jejunal segments of rats, it has recently been reported that single doses of ethanol interfere with active transport of low doses of thiamine, but not with passive diffusion at high vitamin concentrations.[24]

Significant *increases* in the serum and urinary xylose levels attained after oral administration were noted with chronic ethanol ingestion in our subjects. The studies of the disposition of the pentose given intravenously indicate that these findings cannot be explained by an alteration in the clearance of xylose from the blood stream or in its urinary excretion. It has been shown that xylose absorption increases when the rate of delivery of the sugar to the small bowel is decreased or when intestinal motility is inhibited.[25] Single doses of ethanol in man have been reported to delay gastric emptying[26,27] or inhibit jejunal motility.[28] It is possible that ethanol administration resulted in an increase in xylose absorption (and possibly fat absorption as well) via one of these mechanisms.

SUMMARY

The administration of 173–253 g of ethanol daily along with a nutritious diet and vitamin supplements for 13–37 days resulted in impairment of vitamin B_{12} absorption in 6 of 8 volunteer subjects. The B_{12} malabsorption was not corrected by giving intrinsic factor or pancreatin. The absorption of xylose and fat was not inhibited by alcohol administration. Serum and urinary xylose levels were increased over control values during periods of ethanol ingestion.

ACKNOWLEDGMENTS

Ms. Nancy Shea and Mr. Jnan R. Saha provided valuable technical assistance.

REFERENCES

1. LINDENBAUM, J. & C. S. LIEBER. 1971. Effects of ethanol on the blood, bone marrow, and small intestine of man. *In* Biological Aspects of Alcohol. M. K. Roach, W. M. McIsaac & P. J. Creaven, Eds.: 27. University of Texas Press. Austin, Tex.
2. ROGGIN, G. M., F. L. IBER, R. M. H. KATER & F. TABON. 1969. Malabsorption in the chronic alcoholic. Johns Hopkins Med. J. **125:** 321.

3. MEZY, E., E. JOW, R. E. SLAVIN & F. TABON. 1970. Pancreatic function and intestinal absorption in chronic alcoholism. Gastroenterology 59: 657.
4. HALSTED, C. H., E. A. ROBLES & E. MEZEY. 1971. Decreased jejunal uptake of labeled folic acid (H^3-PGA) in alcoholic patients. Roles of alcohol and nutrition. New Eng. J. Med. 285: 701.
5. TOMASULO, P. A., R. M. H. KATER & F. L. IBER. 1968. Impairment of thiamine absorption in alcoholism. Amer. J. Clin. Nutr. 21: 1341.
6. THOMSON, A. D., H. BAKER & C. M. LEEVY. 1970. Patterns of ^{35}S-thiamine hydrochloride absorption in the malnourished alcoholic patient. J. Lab. Clin. Med. 76: 34.
7. ISRAEL, Y., I. SALAZAR & E. ROSENMANN. 1968. Inhibitory effects of alcohol on intestinal amino acid transport in vivo and in vitro. J. Nutr. 96: 499.
8. CHANG, T., J. LEWIS & A. J. GLAZKO. 1967. Effect of ethanol and other alcohols on the transport of amino acids and glucose by everted sacs of rat small intestine. Biochem. Biophys. Acta 135: 1000.
9. SPENCER, R. P., K. R. BRODY & B. M. LUTTERS. 1964. Some effects of ethanol on the gastrointestinal tract. Amer. J. Dig. Dis. 9: 599.
10. ISRAEL, Y., J. E. VALENZUELA, J. SALAZAR & G. UGARTE. 1969. Alcohol and amino acid transport in the human small intestine. J. Nutr. 98: 222.
11. LINDENBAUM, J., N. SHEA, J. R. SAHA & C. S. LIEBER. 1973. Mechanism of alcohol-induced malabsorption of vitamin B_{12}. Gastroenterology 64: 762.
12. LINDENBAUM, J., N. SHEA, J. R. SAHA & C. S. LIEBER. 1972. Alcohol-induced impairment of carbohydrate absorption. Clin. Res. 20: 459.
13. BARAONA, E., R. C. PIROLA & C. S. LIEBER. 1974. Small intestinal damage and changes in cell population produced by ethanol ingestion in the rat. Gastroenterology 66: 801.
14. RUBIN, E., B. J. RYBAK, J. LINDENBAUM, C. D. GERSON, G. WALKER & C. S. LIEBER. 1972. Ultrastructural changes in the small intestine induced by ethanol. Gastroenterology 63: 801.
15. KLIPSTEIN, F. A. 1970. Recent advances in tropical malabsorption. Scand. J. Gastroenterol. Suppl. 6: 93.
16. LINDENBAUM, J., J. F. PEZZIMENTI & N. SHEA. 1974. Small intestinal function in vitamin B_{12} deficiency. Ann. Internal Med. 80: 326.
17. LIEBER, C. S. & E. RUBIN. 1968. Alcoholic fatty liver in man on high protein and low fat diet. Amer. J. Med. 44: 200.
18. LINDENBAUM, J. & C. S. LIEBER. 1969. Hematologic effects of alcohol in man in the absence of nutritional deficiency. New. Eng. J. Med. 281: 333.
19. SCHILLING, R. F. 1953. Intrinsic factor studies. II. The effect of gastric juice on the urinary excretion of radioactivity after the oral administration of radioactive vitamin B_{12}. J. Lab. Clin. Med. 42: 860.
20. ROE, J. H. & E. W. RICE. 1949. Photometric method for determination of free pentoses in animal tissues. J. Biol. Chem. 173: 347.
21. van de KAMER, J. H., H. HUININK TEN BOKKEL & H. A. WEYERS. 1949. Rapid method for the determination of fat in feces. J. Biol. Chem. 177: 347.
22. LINDENBAUM, J. & C. S. LIEBER. 1969. Alcohol-induced malabsorption of vitamin B_{12} in man. Nature 224: 806.
23. HALSTED, C. H., E. A. ROBLES & E. MEZEY. 1973. Intestinal malabsorption in folate-deficient alcoholics. Gastroenterology 64: 526.
24. HOYUMPA, A., H. MIDDLETON, F. WILSON & S. SCHENKER. 1974. Dual system of thiamine transport: Characteristics and effect of ethanol. Gastroenterology 66: 714.
25. FORDTRAN, J. S., K. H. SOERGEL & F. J. INGELFINGER. 1962. Intestinal absorption of d-xylose in man. New Eng. J. Med. 267: 274.
26. BARBORIAK, J. J. & R. C. MEADE. 1970. Effect of alcohol on gastric emptying in man. Amer. J. Clin. Nutr. 23: 1151.
27. COOKE, A. R. 1972. Ethanol and gastric function. Gastroenterology 62: 501.
28. ROBLES, E. A., C. H. MEZEY, C. H. HALSTED & M. M. SCHUSTER. 1972. Effects of ethanol on intestinal motility in man. Gastroenterology 62: 799.

INTRODUCTION

Kenneth Williams

A few years ago it was taught that the only significant cardiac disease found in alcoholics was a type of alcoholic cardiomyopathy thought to be related to beri-beri heart disease and thiamine deficiency. While this illness is still observed in skid-row alcoholics, whose diets are considered to be notoriously inadequate, it is now appreciated that this is the least important and least frequently seen category of patient with heart disease related primarily to alcohol consumption. Within the past 15 years considerable work has been done to resolve the confusion surrounding whether the heart problems seen are due to alcohol itself ("alcoholic cardiomyopathy") or attributable to nutritional deficiency, nutritional imbalance, or trace metal contamination.

The prolonged ingestion of moderate or large amounts of alcohol (probably 8 oz or more daily) is now recognized to produce a well-defined clinical syndrome referred to as "alcoholic cardiomyopathy" (or, in Dr. Talbott's paper, "toxic primary alcoholic heart disease"; in Dr. Gunnar's paper, "alcoholic heart disease"); the entity appears to develop after several years of heavy alcohol consumption independently of nutritional deficiencies and appears to be attributable to the direct toxic effect of alcohol on the heart muscle. Dr. Gunnar's paper outlines the clinical features and course of this disease, in which cardiomegaly and congestive heart failure with pulmonary vascular congestion are found. Pathological examination usually shows diffuse myocardial fibrosis and hypertrophy with glycoprotein infiltration. Early detection and abstinence from alcohol appear to be therapeutically most important.

While most investigators believe this type of heart disease to be the most important clinically, the incidence is unknown, primarily because of the failure of physicians to take an accurate history regarding alcohol consumption and because of a general lack of knowledge regarding this disease entity. Certainly the disease occurs much more frequently than is appreciated. Previous work by Dr. Gunnar has shown that the daily consumption of 3 ounces of alcohol over a period of 5 years can alter normal cardiac structure. This would certainly put a large number of people in this country at risk of developing alcoholic cardiomyopathy for consumption of this amount of alcohol is common. However, most patients with alcoholic cardiomyopathy reported in the literature have consumed quantities in excess of this amount for longer than 5 years. Biochemical individuality would also appear to play a role in the development of this disease, since some individuals are more susceptible than others to this cardiotoxic effect of alcohol.

In addition, the alcoholic is a risk to develop conductive heart disturbances with arrhythmias related to mineral and electrolyte imbalance. The low tissue levels of potassium, magnesium, and zinc found in the alcoholic appear to play an etiologic role here. Dr. Talbott's paper outlines his clinical categorization of heart disease seen in alcoholics in the Baltimore Public Inebriate Program and presents his experience with this ("conductive") type of heart disease.

There is a prevalent belief that alcohol has a beneficial effect on cardiac function. For instance, many doctors suggest to their patients with coronary artery disease that they take alcohol as a coronary vasodilator. The American Heart Association has even recently stated publically that alcohol is beneficial in coronary artery disease. The authors of the following papers have disagreed, citing recent studies that have shown the effects of acute alcohol ingestion to be deleterious to cardiac function, especially to patients with preexisting heart disease. Alcohol does not act as a coronary artery vasodilator, and it has an inconsistent effect on coronary artery blood flow. Any possible increase in coronary circulation is probably functionally insignificant. It seems highly unlikely that there would be an actual increase in blood flow to ischemic areas. In addition, there is a consistently demonstrated decrease in left ventricular contractility caused by the acute ingestion of alcohol, with a decrease in mechanical efficiency of the left ventricle. The first part of Dr. Regan's paper details these acute responses of the heart to ethanol.

Dr. Regan's paper continues by outlining his findings in dogs maintained in a normal nutritional state except for ingesting a quantity of alcohol approximately equivalent to that commonly ingested by alcoholics. In 18 months, left ventricular performance was impaired, with a "stiffness" being demonstrated in the ventricular walls.

PRIMARY ALCOHOLIC HEART DISEASE*

G. Douglas Talbott†

Baltimore Public Inebriate Program
Baltimore, Maryland 21203

Three major organ systems are greatly affected by ethyl alcohol: the gastro-intestinal tract, the central nervous system, and the cardiovascular system. Present evidence indicates that the heart may be the organ most dangerously affected.

It has long been known that the excessive consumption of alcohol has deleterious effect on the abnormal heart,[1-3] resulting in what we choose to term secondary alcoholic heart disease. In this context, ingestion of alcohol has been reported as the direct cause of sudden and unexpected death by cardiac arrest.[4,5] Now it has also been established that alcohol, taken in excess over a period of years, is capable of damaging a normal heart and causing a condition which we call primary alcoholic heart disease (PAHD).

A study of the literature and clinical observations made by the author in his capacity of Medical Director of the Baltimore Public Inebriate Program (BPIP), where more than 1500 alcoholics were seen during the first year of the Program's operation, has lead to the belief that PAHD consists of three separate clinical entities, each the result of a different etiological mechanism, and each responding best to treatment based on consideration of that specific mechanism. These clinical entities are: (1) Nutritional type, (2) Toxic type, and (3) Conductive type of PAHD.

It is our purpose to describe and differentiate these three types and to suggest for each a plan of treatment which, in our hands, has proved successful.

BACKGROUND

A disease characterized chiefly by cardiomegaly and congestive failure among habitual drinkers, in the absence of any recognizable abnormality of either the coronary artery, the valves, the septum, or the myocardial wall, began to be reported in the literature, near the middle of the 19th century, under the general term "alcoholic cardiomyopathy." Additional signs and symptoms, as well as response to treatment, varied rather widely.[6-8]

As advances in science brought electronic microscopy, and increasingly sophisticated invasive techniques to the aid of cardiovascular study, it became possible to identify and to document previously unsuspected alterations in both structure and function of the normal heart in its response to various agents, including ethyl alcohol.[9] It became evident that the ingestion of alcohol can affect the heart through either of three separate mechanisms. Clinical experience by various workers demonstrated that early recognition of any of these types of PAHD, if followed by appropriate therapy and future abstinence from alcohol, can halt, and sometimes reverse, the course of the disease.

Only recently has PAHD become chemically and histologically identifiable. Confusion still delays recognition, defies differentiation, prevents effective

*This work was supported, in part, by Grant AA-00596-03.

†Present address: Dekalb County Health Department, 500 Winn Way, Decatur, Georgia 30030.

therapy, and thus contributes to the high mortality from heart disease that is known to exist among alcoholics.[10] Further investigation of the effects of alcohol on the heart, by use of the most sophisticated techniques, is greatly needed. But in the meantime, much can be accomplished, by the meticulous application of simple diagnostic techniques.

SIGNS AND SYMPTOMS OF PAHD

We suspect some type of PAHD whenever we find irregular pulse, dyspnea, or other indication of cardiac failure in the absence of any discernable abnormality of cardiac valves or retinal vessels, especially in a known alcoholic who has had no previous cardiac complaints.

Since the BPIP is not funded to permit the use of elaborate laboratory procedures, we were forced to discover that, in most instances, a reliable diagnosis can be based on a combination of commonly available diagnostic procedures: an accurate history, with special attention to nutritional intake, consumption of alcohol, and onset of symptoms; a careful physical examination; and such simple laboratory procedures as chest X-ray, ECG, and determination of circulation time by the Decholin arm-to-tongue technique.

NUTRITIONAL PAHD

Nutritional or beri-beri heart disease was first recognized in the Orient, where it was common in a population subsisting almost entirely on husked rice, with consequently severe lack of thiamine. Later the condition was recognized among Europeans whose excessive consumption of alcohol, at the expense of a balanced diet, led to the same nutritional deficiency. Nutritional heart disease appeared in the United States during the Depression but was generally more common and of greater severity among alcoholics. Since it has become customary to add nutritional supplements to many of our staple foods, nutritional heart disease has almost disappeared from our population; even skid-row alcoholics, who seldom present a history of normal diet, show comparatively slight incidence of this condition, and we have found it in no more than 10% of our PAHD patients.

The presenting complaints are of dyspnea, orthopnea, paroxysmal nocturnal palpitations, and, occasionally, angina. At later stages of the disease, peripheral neuritis may develop, as may mental aberrations. The condition can be fatal.[11]

Physical examination reveals fast pulse, small pulse pressure (usually without hypertension), and fluctuating accumulations of extracellular fluid at various sites. Circulation time is accelerated. One investigator has reported evidence of cardiac insufficiency, primarily right-sided,[12] and another has noted high output failure.[11] The heart is enlarged, and the ECG may show fugitive T-wave inversion at times[13] but reverts to normal after massive doses of thiamine. Enzyme determinations, clotting time, and all routine blood and urine analyses are within normal limits. Diagnosis is facilitated by an accurate history, particularly with respect to dietary habits and intake of alcohol.

This condition makes poor response to standard treatment for cardiac failure: digitalis and diuretics provide little relief. But response to thiamine is dramatic. We prefer to give oral doses of 50 mg, 3 times a day, during the hospital stay. If more rapid action seems imperative, thiamine may be given intramuscularly, 10 mg every 8 to 12 hours for a period of 48 hours. Intravenous thiamine is to be avoided because of the danger of intravascular flooding.

Dietary therapy is useful. The patient is discharged on vitamin supplements, with emphasis on B complex and C. It is stressed that abstinence from alcohol is essential to recovery.

Toxic PAHD

This is by far the most common of the 3 types of PAHD and accounts for at least 80% of the PAHD patients we see at BPIP.

It has been demonstrated that even 1 generous dose of ethyl alcohol produces immediate effect on cardiac function,[14] and that the frequent consumption of as little as 3 ounces, over a period of 5 years or longer, can appreciably alter normal cardiac structure.[15] Myofibers are fragmented and destroyed;[16] contractile elements are altered or lost[17] and replaced by swollen mitochondria and edema fluid. Glycogen is irregularly accumulated and deposited.[18] The permeability of the cell membrane is altered.[16,20] The structure of the cell itself is modified, for the nuclei become more widely spaced, sometimes enlarged or changed in shape.[16,17] Lipid deposition is increased.[21] Vacuolinization, with hydrophic fatty and hyalin degeneration, can usually be seen, and often focal areas of inflammatory cell response can be detected.[8] The resultant fibrous scarring is accompanied by at least a partial loss of compliance in the ventricle, particularly on the left side.

Such structural alterations may become profound and of tremendous hemodynamic importance before clinical symptoms become apparent. The first symptoms are limited to the pulmonary circuit. Dyspnea appears, precipitated and aggravated by exercise, or sometimes occurring as a nocturnal paroxysm. Labored breathing is accompanied by wet rales as fluid accumulates in the thorax. Pulse and blood pressure become elevated. Gradually and sequentially the signs of right failure appear: edema, ascites, the pulsations of an enlarged liver, venous distention in the neck. Unfortunately, this constellation of signs and symptoms lends itself to misinterpretation as a "silent" coronary, a constrictive pericarditis,[22] or even beri-beri heart disease[21] if no dependable dietary history is available and alcoholic history is not admitted. But in toxic PAHD there is neither angina nor abnormality of the retinal vessels to suggest atherosclerosis; there is no hematological indication of infection or cardiac toxins to suggest pericarditis; furthermore, the condition is not improved by either the classic regimen for cardiac failure or by massive doses of thiamine.

Since diagnosis by means of invasive techniques frequently is impractical, because of either unavailability or high cost, often the suspicious clinician must rely on the patient's history, careful physical examination, and a few basic laboratory procedures to confirm his diagnostic impression.

It may be difficult to elicit a reasonably accurate history of drinking habits, since a patient may be quite reluctant, outside skid row, to risk the label of "alcoholic." But in the absence of other reasons for the patient's symptoms, toxic PAHD should be suspected if any 2 or 3 of the following physical signs of alcoholism are present: an enlarged liver with a sharp, tender edge, and no history of previous cardiac failure; spider angiomata; a red thenar eminence; rhinophyma; caput medusae; palpable and symptomatic internal hemorrhoids; radiologically demonstrable esophageal varices.

History of a reasonable nutritional intake during the preceding several months, in addition to the failure of thiamine to alleviate the cardiac symptoms, will rule out nutritional heart disease. Absence of arrhythmia will rule out conductive PAHD. Toxic PAHD is then indicated.

Noninvasive techniques are useful in confirming a clinical impression of toxic PAHD. The ECG shows a characteristic alteration: Q waves may be absent in leads II, III, and AVF; tall, peaked T waves appear in V2 and V3. When phonocardiogram can be combined with ECG, the prolonged left ventricular time thus revealed reflects the decreased ventricular compliance resulting from structural change.[23] In contrast to nutritional PAHD, circulation time is normal. Chest X-rays are not especially helpful until late in the course of the disease, when ventricular hypertrophy has had time to develop, or after the activity of the ventricular wall has appreciably decreased.

Where resources permit, catheter studies will verify ventricular wall involvement compatible with collagen deposition and fibrosis, by demonstrating increased diastolic ventricular filling, decreased left-sided cardiac output, and increased wedge pressure.

In treating toxic PAHD we have found the regimen recommended by Burch to be most effective. This consists of (1) complete abstinence from alcohol, (2) prolonged bed rest, sometimes extending over a period of several months, and (3) standard therapy for a failing heart—a digitalis preparation and a diuretic. A high-protein diet may also be helpful. The prognosis for toxic PAHD is often poor because diagnosis has not been made until after irreversible structural damage has been done. When the condition is recognized in its early stages, bed rest and abstinence may prevent the onset of overt cardiac failure.

CONDUCTIVE PAHD

It has long been recognized that the habitual intake of alcohol destroys the normal balance of electrolytes.[24-27] Disturbance of the electrolyte balance affects the conductivity of the heart and results in arrhythmias. For example, Singer[28] demonstrated that 7 oz of vodka produces premature ventricular contractions in the healthy heart within 30 minutes. This type of reaction appears to be primary within the conductive system, since no abnormalities of the ventricular wall, competence, contractility, or ejection time appear, except as they may relate to the alcohol-induced arrhythmia.

The arrhythmias most commonly reported in the literature of alcoholic heart disease are auricular fibrillation, supraventricular tachycardia, ventricular premature beat, and nodal rhythm, roughly in that order of incidence.[22,29] Patients with severe arrhythmias sometimes develop seizures that have Wolff-Parkinson-White characteristics.[30,31] In our experiences, the administration of magnesium usually controls such seizures, which are of cardiac rather than cerebral origin, but many of these patients would benefit from the care available in an established coronary ward.

Though we are not equipped to do real-time monitoring in the detoxification ward at BPIP, we have devised a system of ECG monitoring of the patient during his first 24 hours on the ward, by use of a Holter rig. This has provided us with ample evidence of arrhythmias. In our observation, sinus tachycardia, accompanied by true cardiovascular hypertension, is almost always present when the patient is admitted for detoxification. In diminishing order of incidence we have also noted ventricular premature contractions, auricular premature contractions, a combination of both types of premature contractions, nodal tachycardia, varying degrees of intra- and sinoventricular block, and ventricular tachycardia. The prolonged, and often progressive, fatigue that accompanies the detoxification process tends to produce cardiovascular events that are potentially catastrophic, such as cardiogenic shock, ventricular fibrillation or flutter, cardiac standstill, and abrupt, predominantly left-sided, failure. Any of these could result in sudden death.

We have found that we can usually control and often prevent arrhythmias by administering an oral alcoholism treatment solution called OATS‡. This solution combines relatively high doses of magnesium and potassium in a fructose base. Its use enables us to avoid the parenteral administration of fluids while minimizing the incidence of arrhythmias. When ECG monitoring indicates ventricular flutter or tachycardia, the patient is immediately transferred to a coronary ward. For control of vomiting and/or convulsions we prefer oral diazepam. When necessary, this medication is given intravenously, but at a very slow rate.

Conductive PAHD is of especial interest because it seems probable that the chief pathological mechanism is the same as that which causes the high mortality sometimes reported for the withdrawal syndrome. Uncontrolled arrhythmias are clinically predominant in both situations.

REFERENCES

1. GOULD, L., F. JAYNAL, M. ZAHIR & R. F. GOMPRECHT. 1972. Effects of alcohol on the systolic time intervals. Quart. J. Stud. Alcohol 33: 451–463.
2. CONWAY, N. 1968. Hemodynamic effects of ethyl alcohol in patients with coronary heart disease. Brit. Heart J. 30: 638–644.
3. WILSON, D. E., P. H. SCHREIBMAN, A. C. BREWSTER & R. A. ARBY. 1970. The enhancement of alimentary lipemia by ethanol in man. J. Lab. Clin. Med. 75: 264–274.
4. LAURIE, W. 1971. Alcohol as a cause of sudden unexpected death. Med. J. Aust. 1: 1224–1227.
5. NEVINS, M. A. & L. J. LYON. 1972. Sudden death and metabolic derangement in alcoholism with malnutrition. J. Med. Soc. N.J. 69: 155–157.
6. FERRANS, V. J., J. C. RIOS, A. S. GOOCH, D. NUTTER, V. T. DeVITA & D. W. DATLOW. 1966. Alcoholic cardiomyopathy. Amer. J. Med. Sci. 252: 123–136.
7. MASSUMI, R. A. 1965. Primary myocardial disease. Report of fifty cases and review of the subject. Circulation 31: 19–41.
8. BURCH, G. E. & T. D. GILES. 1971. Alcoholic cardiomyopathy. Concept of the disease and its treatment. Amer. J. Med. 50: 141–145.
9. AHMED, S. S., G. E. LEVINSON & T. J. REGAN. 1973. Depression of myocardial contractility with low doses of ethanol in normal man. Circulation 48: 378–385.
10. SCHMIDT, W. & J. DeLINT. 1973. The mortality of alcoholic people. Alcohol Health and Research World (NIAAA), experimental issue, Summer 1973: 16–20.
11. KING, J. F., R. EASTON & M. DUNN. 1972. Acute pernicious beri-beri heart disease. Chest 61: 512–514.
12. AMELUNG, D. 1971. Alcoholic cardiomyopathy. (abst.). Quart. J. Stud. Alcohol 32: 245.
13. EVANS, W. 1961. Alcoholic cardiomyopathy. Amer. Heart J. 61: 556–567.
14. REGAN, T. J., G. E. LEVINSON, H. A. OLDEWURTEL, M. J. FRANK, A. B. WEISSE & C. B. MOSCHOS. 1969. Ventricular function in noncardiacs with alcoholic fatty liver: role of ethanol in the production of cardiomyopathy. J. Clin. Invest. 48: 397–407.
15. GUNNAR, R. M. & G. C. SUTTON. 1971. Alcoholic cardiomyopathy. D. M. Sept. 1971.

‡Oral Alcoholism Treatment Solution contains varying specified concentrations of calcium, magnesium, potassium, sodium, and zinc, with a fructose base. It is especially prepared for Baltimore Public Inebriate Program by Custom Laboratories, 930 West Baltimore Street, Baltimore, Md. 21223.

16. ALEXANDER, C. S. 1966. Idiopathic heart disease. II. Electron microscopic examination of myocardial biopsy specimens in alcoholic heart disease. Amer. J. Med. **41:** 229–234.
17. SHANOFF, H. M. 1972. Alcoholic cardiomyopathy: an introductory review. Canad. Med. Assoc. J. **106:** 55–62.
18. SCHMALBRUCH, H. & T. DUME. 1969. Klinisch inapperente Alkoholschädigung der menschlichen Herzmuskelzelle. Arch. Kreislaufforsch **58:** 202–227.
19. SEBENY, G. 1971. Effects of alcohol on the electrocardiogram. Circulation **44:** 558–564.
20. WENDT, V. E., C. WU, R. BALCONE, G. DOTY & R. J. BING. 1965. Hemodynamic and metabolic effects of chronic alcoholism in man. Amer. J. Cardiol. **15:** 175–183.
21. SANDERS, M. G. 1970. Alcoholic cardiomyopathy: a critical review. Quart. J. Stud. Alcohol **31:** 324–368.
22. BRIGDEN, W. & J. ROBINSON. 1964. Alcoholic heart disease. Brit. Med. J. **2:** 1283–1289.
23. SPODICK, D. H., V. M. PIGOTT & R. T. CHIRIFE. 1972. Preclinical cardiac malfunction in chronic alcoholism. New Eng. J. Med. **287:** 677–680.
24. HARTEL, G., A. LOUHIJA & A. KONTTINEN. 1969. Cardiovascular study of 100 chronic alcoholics. Acta Med. Scand. **185:** 507–513.
25. KALBFLEISCH, J. M., R. D. LINDEMAN, H. E. GINN & W. O. SMITH. 1963. Effects of ethanol administration on urinary excretion of magnesium and other electrolytes in alcoholic and normal subjects. J. Clin. Invest. **42:** 1471–1475.
26. McCOLLISTER, R. J., E. B. FLINK & R. P. DOE. 1960. Magnesium balance studies in chronic alcoholism. J. Lab. Clin. Med. **55:** 98–104.
27. SEELIG, M. S. 1969. Electrographic patterns of magnesium depletion appearing in alcoholic heart disease. Ann. N.Y. Acad. Sci. **162:** 906–917.
28. SINGER, K. & W. B. LUNDBERG. 1972. Ventricular arrhythmias associated with the ingestion of alcohol. Ann. Intern. Med. **77:** 247–248.
29. PIZA, E. J. & S. L. BURSTIN. 1967. Cardiopatía alcohólica. II. Estudio de 36 autopsies de alcohólicos crónicos: revisión anatomaptológica. Arch. Inst. Cardiol. Méx. **37:** 711–728.
30. SATALINE, L. 1973. Cardiac standstill simulating seizures. J.A.M.A. **225:** 747.
31. TALBOTT, G. D. & O. F. GANDER. 1974. Convulsive seizures in the alcoholic: a clinical appraisal. Maryland Med. J. In press.

METABOLIC EFFECTS OF ALCOHOL ON THE HEART*

Richard J. Bing, Harald Tillmanns, and Shigeaki Ikeda

Huntington Memorial Hospital
Pasadena, California 91105
and
The University of Southern California
Los Angeles, California 90024

The relationship between heart disease and alcoholism was apparently first described by Walshe in 1873.[1] The expression "alcoholic cardiomyopathy" was coined by Mackenzie in 1902.[2] Prior to this, in 1884, Bollinger described the Munich beer heart (cardiac hypertrophy existing in beer drinkers).[3] The statistics presented by Bollinger are interesting: In 1884, he found in Munich a beer consumption of 432 liters per head of population; this included newborns. In 1929, Wenckebach first described beri-beri heart disease,[4] and since that time many of the effects of alcohol on the heart have been thought to be the result of nutritional deficiencies. This is not the case, as demonstrated recently by Robin and Goldschlager,[5] who reported a patient with alcoholic noncirrhotic beri-beri heart disease, developing low cardiac output failure shortly after successful treatment with thiamine. In 1966, Wendt and associates published a paper on the acute effect of alcohol on the human myocardium,[6] followed by another study on the effect of chronic alcoholism on cardiac metabolism in man.[7] Wendt was able to observe the release of intramyocardial enzymes into coronary vein blood and proposed that alcohol might alter membrane permeability and impair the activity of metabolic pathways.[7] This assumption has been supported by autopsy determination of the activities of several enzymes in the left ventricle of patients who died of alcoholic cardiomyopathy.[8] Analysis of the specimens demonstrated a marked reduction in cellular activity of certain oxidative enzymes, such as NAD-dependent isocitrate dehydrogenase (NAD-ICDH), and a significant increase in the activity of some glycolytic enzymes, particularly glyceraldehydephosphate dehydrogenase, the enzyme responsible for the glycolytic substrate phosphorylation. An accumulation of triglycerides in the heart muscle of animals exposed to alcohol was demonstrated by Regan et al. in 1966.[9] This observation has been confirmed by Marciniak et al.[10]

Alcohol may affect both cardiac contractility and metabolism. Despite marked changes in cardiac metabolism, ethanol results in clear-cut changes in myocardial contractility only after many years of exposure.

Before entering into a discussion of effects of ethanol on heart muscle, it is necessary to discuss briefly some of the possible mechanisms that can result in disturbance of myocardial contractility. This subject has developed into a very active field of investigation because of its possible clinical implications. In discussing this field, the possible actions of ethanol on subcellular organelles, such as the sarcoplasmic reticulum, the mitochondria, and the contractile proteins, must be considered.

*Supported by grants from the National Institutes of Health (No. 5 R01 AA00304-02) and the Council for Tobacco Research—U.S.A., Inc.

243

Function of the Sarcoplasmic Reticulum

Excellent reviews of this subject have been published by Hasselbach[11] and by Ebashi.[12] These workers demonstrated that the relaxing activity of the muscle was an inherent property of a particulate fraction of the muscle, the sarcoplasmic reticulum (SR). The clue to the function of the SR system was the ability to induce relaxation by means of decreasing the concentration of Ca^{++}. It was established that the SR system can store Ca^{++} in the presence of ATP and an intravesicular precipitating agent (oxalate).[11,12]

When the contractile protein actomyosin is made to contract with ATP, inability to relax (syneresis) occurs. The relaxing factor that can abolish syneresis has been identified as SR and possibly, on the basis of more recent work, also as mitochondria. The findings suggested that some ion was involved in the contraction-relaxation cycle, and this ion was identified as Ca^{++}. Weber suggested that the relaxing granules of the SR may remove Ca^{++} and thus induce relaxation.[13] The main role of the sarcoplasmic reticulum is therefore consistent with that of Ca^{++} pumping, the Ca^{++} being pumped out of the membrane of the SR granules, in order to permit Ca^{++} combination with contractile elements of the muscle. During relaxation the Ca^{++} returns to the SR granules or the mitochondria. Thus, there occurs a rapid binding and subsequent release or a rapid accumulation with no release. The former process occurs in the absence of inorganic phosphate or oxalate, the latter in the presence of either oxalate or phosphate. It became apparent that the accumulation of Ca^{++} in the presence of either oxalate or phosphate is the result of movement of Ca^{++} across the vesicular grana with subsequent precipitation to calcium phosphate or calcium oxalate within the vesicle.[14] The accumulation process in the absence of precipitating ion is referred to as binding, and the accumulation in the presence of precipitating anion is referred to as uptake.[15] It is likely that the first step in Ca^{++} uptake entails ATP-induced changes of the membrane before any splitting of ATP occurs.

Role of Mitochondria

Mitochondria apparently are not only the site of formation of high-energy phosphates, and therefore the prime site for production of ATP, but also, according to Carafoli, concentrate Ca^{++} in the mitochondria as the SR fraction does.[16] This represents an active process, as shown by the fact that the mucopolysaccharide stain ruthenium red completely blocks the uptake of Ca^{++} at very low concentrations.[16] Carafoli furnishes convincing proof of the ability of mitochondria to relax myofibrils.

Contractile Proteins

Alcohol may also have a direct effect on contractile proteins, although this has never been adequately demonstrated. However, as will be shown later, a change in binding and attachment of calcium to the regulatory protein, troponin-A, may be operative in diminished contractility of animals or man exposed to alcohol for long periods of time. The evidence available so far indicates only that this regulatory system, composed of troponin-A and -B and tropomyosin, is in part associated with actin in the I-filaments, where, in a manner not yet understood, it regulates the ATPase activity of the myosin and its response to the intracellular Ca^{++}.[17] Originally considered as a single protein, troponin has been shown to consist of at least 3 different distinct proteins, some of them not sufficiently identified.

The action of calcium is probably due to its binding to a high-affinity Ca^{++} binding site on troponin-A, one of the constituents of troponin. Thus, Ca^{++}, in effecting excitation-contraction coupling, acts to reverse the inhibition of the primary interaction between actin and myosin by the tropomyosin-troponin complex. Tropomyosin and troponin in the absence of Ca^{++} act as repressors, while Ca^{++} serves as a depressor.[17]

These general considerations are of considerable importance in elucidating myocardial failure. For example, there seems to be a definite relationship between intracellular Ca^{++} overload and high-energy phosphate deficiency as a factor in the production of myocardial fiber necrosis.[18] Isoproterenol is one of those compounds which apparently, by inhibiting calcium binding and uptake, cause an excessive concentration of Ca^{++} in the heart muscle. This mechanism may be responsible for the lesions in heart muscle induced by isoproterenol first described by Rona.[19] This hypothesis is gaining in importance because of the finding that Ca^{++} antagonists such as verapamil are capable of protecting animals against structural damage induced by isoproterenol. Even in the hamster with hereditary myocardial degeneration and cardiomyopathy, verapamil is able to prevent myocardial degeneration, possibly by inhibiting transmembrane Ca^{++} transference.[20]

MYOCARDIAL EFFECTS OF ALCOHOL

Alcohol has been rated as an effective coronary vasodilator.[21-24] The effect on the coronary circulation, however, has remained controversial; some investigators finding an increase,[25-27] some a diminution in coronary blood flow.[9, 28-30] Sulzer[28] and Wakim,[31] in dogs and turtles, respectively, reported a progressive dilatation of the heart. Depression of myocardial contractility in isolated heart preparations is a result of alcoholic toxicity; this was also reported by Haggard,[32] Loomis,[33] and Lochner.[27] Other workers found, in contrast, that alcohol has an acute stimulating effect on the mammalian heart.[34-36]

It is likely that the acute effects of alcohol are dose-dependent. When alcohol is infused into patients to blood levels below 50 mg/100 cc of blood, effective coronary blood flow rises.[37] The change, however, is not significant. The cardiac index remains unchanged. At this blood concentration, slight changes were noted in stroke volume, heart rate, and peripheral vascular resistance. There was no change in mean arterial pressure, but there was a slight nonsignificant fall in coronary vascular resistance.[37]

In animals in which much higher doses of blood levels of alcohol could be attained (about 200 mg/100 cc of blood), the effective coronary blood flow increased significantly with a fall in coronary vascular resistance.[37] Different results were obtained by Gilbert and Fenn,[38] Webb,[30] Lasker,[25] and Schmitthener.[39] In the closed-chest dog, Ganz[26] found an increase in coronary flow at dosages of alcohol comparable to the experiments reported here. In those animals, cardiac output rose progressively and in proportion to the blood concentration of alcohol.[37] Of particular significance was the effect of high concentrations of alcohol (above 200 mg/100 cc of blood) on cardiac contractility. While alcohol had no effect on the velocity of contraction at low concentration, a significant depression was noted at ethanol levels of about 200 mg%.[37] These results were in agreement with the studies reported by others, such as Ganz,[26] Webb,[30] Sulzer,[28] and Wakim.[31] The cause of diminished myocardial contractility is not clear, but it may be the result of acute biochemical changes similar to those observed in animals and in man when exposed to small concentrations of alcohol in the blood over long periods of time.

Our laboratory has been engaged for the last 2 years in an investigation of prolonged administration of ethanol on cardiac metabolism and performance in the dog[40] and in the effect of prolonged alcohol administration on calcium transport in heart muscle of the dog.[41] The animals were divided into 2 groups, a control group and a group receiving alcohol. In the experimental series, dogs received 400 ml of a 25% solution of alcohol added to food and drinking water. In these dogs, total myocardial blood flow, cardiac output, and myocardial oxygen consumption remained at control values. After 3 to 6 months of exposure to alcohol, no significant changes in cardiac contractility, using the maximal rate of left ventricular pressure rise dp/dt max were detected.[40,41] When the afterload of the heart was increased with angiotensin, a slight but significant decline in cardiac contractility was observed. Significant changes in mitochondrial function were found.[40,41] They can be summarized: (a) there occurred a diminution in mitochondrial NAD-dependent isocitrate dehydrogenase (NAD-ICDH), (b) a fall in mitochondrial oxygen consumption and in the respiratory control indices, and (c) a diminution in myocardial ATP content. It is likely that these changes are the result of a direct toxic effect of ethanol itself.

The finding of relatively undisturbed hemodynamics or contractility was not surprising in the light of Regan's observation that alcohol administration of over several years is necessary to produce myocardial failure.[42] He speculated that 10–15 years of exposure to alcohol may be necessary to produce changes in contractility. The finding of normal contractility after 3 months of alcohol ingestion in the presence of serious biochemical alterations in mitochondria suggests that myocardial contractility is not dependent on the integrity of mitochondrial function.

Calcium binding and uptake in dogs exposed to prolonged periods of alcohol ingestion proved interesting. Similarities were discovered in calcium transport in animals exposed to alcohol and those with myocardial failure. In both groups, disturbances in calcium binding and uptake of both sarcoplasmic reticulum and mitochondria were discovered. Because hearts of animals exposed to alcohol have diminished calcium binding and uptake by sarcoplasmic reticulum and mitochondria,[41] one might expect disturbances in cardiac relaxation. Calculations based on the method of Cohn et al., using negative peak dp/dt as an index of relaxation process,[43] furnish a trend indicating diminished relaxation during angiotensin infusion; however, because of considerable scatter, these values are not statistically significant. Disturbed respiratory function of the mitochondria could be a contributory factor, since deficient ability of mitochondria to take up calcium has been found in failing hearts of animals by Sordahl.[44]

To return to the question why it takes so long to develop changes in myocardial contractility in both animals and man exposed to alcohol, several reasons may be adduced. In the first place, the changes in calcium transport are not as severe as those found after myocardial infarction, congestive heart failure or cardiomyopathy.[44–49] Secondly, in both acute myocardial ischemia and hereditary cardiomyopathy of the hamster, the contractile elements themselves are morphologically involved, and the mitochondrial lesions are only part of general process of myocardial reaction. The latter explanation appears to be the most reasonable. We are currently studying the effective of alcohol on the contractile elements in animals exposed to alcohol for a period of almost 2 years. It could well be that diminished contractility is dependent on direct involvement of the contractile elements of the heart.

REFERENCES

1. WALSHE, W. H. 1873. Diseases of the Heart and Great Vessels. 4th edit. London, England.
2. MACKENZIE, J. 1902. The study of the pulse: 237. Edinburgh and London.
3. BOLLINGER, O. 1884. Über die Häufigkeit und Ursachen der idiopathischen Herzhypertrophie in München. Deutsche med. Wchr. 10: 180.
4. AALSMER, W. C. & K. R. WENCKEBACH. 1929. Herz und Kreislauf bei der Beri-Beri-Krankheit. Wien. Arch. inn. Med. 16: 193.
5. ROBIN, E. and N. GOLDSCHLAGER. 1970. Persistence of low cardiac output after relief of high output by thiamine in a case of alcoholic beri-beri and cardiac myopathy. Amer. Heart J. 80: 103.
6. WENDT, V. E., R. AJLUNI, T. A. BRUCE, A. S. PRASAD & R. J. BING. 1966. Acute effects of alcohol on the human myocardium. Amer. J. Cardiol. 17: 804.
7. WENDT, V. E., C. WU, R. BALCON, G. DOTY, R. J. BING. 1965. Hemodynamic and metabolic effects of chronic alcoholism in man. Amer. J. Cardiol. 15: 175.
8. BING, R. J., C. WU & S. GUDBJARNASON. 1964. Mechanism of heart failure. Circ. Res. Suppl. II to 14–15: 64.
9. REGAN, T. J., G. KOROXENIDIS, C. B. MOSCHOS, H. A. OLDEWURTEL, P. H. LEHAN & H. K. HELLEMS. 1966. The acute metabolic and hemodynamic responses of the left ventricle to ethanol. J. Clin. Invest. 45: 270.
10. MARCINIAK, M., S. GUDBJARNASON & T. A. BRUCE. 1968. The effect of chronic alcohol administration on enzyme profile and glyceride content of heart muscle, brain, and liver. Proc. Soc. Exp. Biol. Med. 128: 1021.
11. HASSELBACH, W. & M. MAKINOSE. 1961. Die Calciumpumpe der "Erschlaffungsgrana" des Muskels und ihre Abhängigkeit von der ATP-Spaltung. Biochem. Z. 333: 518.
12. EBASHI, S. & F. LIPMANN. 1962. Adenosine triphosphate-linked concentration of calcium ions in a particulate fraction of rabbit muscle. J. Cell. Biol. 14: 389.
13. WEBER, A. 1959. On the role of calcium in the activity of adenosine-5'-triphosphate hydrolysis by actomyosin. J. Biol. Chem. 234: 2764.
14. OLSON, R. E. 1971. *In* Calcium and the Heart. P. Harris & L. H. Opie, Eds.: 1 Academic Press. New York, N.Y.
15. SCHWARTZ, A. 1971. Calcium and the sarcoplasmic reticulum. *In* Calcium and the Heart. P. Harris & L. H. Opie, Eds.: 66. Academic Press. New York, N.Y.
16. CARAFOLI, E., R. TIOZZO, C. S. ROSSI & G. LUGLI. 1971, 1972. Mitochondrial Ca^{++} uptake and heart relaxation. *In* Role of Membranes in Secretory Processes. Proceedings of the International Conference on Biology Membranes, Gargano, Italy. L. Bolis & R. D. Keynes, Eds.: 175–181. North Holland Publishing Co. Amsterdam, The Netherlands.
17. BING, R. J. & H. TILLMANNS. Cardiac Metabolism. V. Puddu & A. B. Anguissola, Eds. Cardiology Today. Torino, Italy. In press.
18. FLECKENSTEIN, A. 1971. Specific inhibitors and promoters of calcium action in the excitation-contraction coupling of heart muscle and their role in the prevention or production of myocardial lesions. *In* Calcium and the Heart. P. Harris & L. H. Opie, Eds.: 135. Academic Press. New York, N.Y.
19. RONA, G., C. I. CHAPPEL, T. BALAZS & R. GAUDRY. 1959. An infarct-like myocardial lesion and other toxic manifestations produced by isoproterenol in the rat. A.M.A. Arch. Path. 67: 443.
20. BAJUSZ, E. & G. JASMIN. 1973. Prevention of myocardial degeneration in hamsters with hereditary cardiomyopathy. *In* Myocardial Cell Damage. VI. Annual Meeting of the International Study Group for Research in Cardiac Metabolism. Abstracts.

21. HEBERDEN, W. 1786. Some account of a disorder of the breast. Med. Trans. Roy. Coll. Physicians 2: 59.
22. GOODMAN, L. & A. GILLMAN. 1941. The pharmacological basis of therapeutics. The Macmillan Co. New York, N.Y.
23. WHITE, P. D. 1931. Heart Disease: 436. The Macmillan Co. New York, N.Y.
24. LEVINE, S. A. 1940. Clinical Heart Disease. W. B. Saunders Co. Philadelphia, Pa. page 116.
25. LASKER, N., T. R. SHERROD & K. F. KILLAM. 1955. Alcohol on the coronary circulation of the dog. J. Pharmacol. Exp. Therap. 113: 414.
26. GANZ, V. 1963. The acute effect of alcohol on the circulation and on the oxygen metabolism of the heart. Amer. Heart J. 66: 494.
27. LOCHNER, A., R. COWLEY & A. J. BRINK. 1969. Effect of ethanol on metabolism function of perfused rat heart. Amer. Heart J. 78: 770.
28. SULZER, R. 1924. The influence of alcohol on the isolated mammalian heart. Heart 11: 141.
29. LEIGHNINGER, D. S., R. RUEGER & C. S. BECK. 1961. Effect of pentaerythritol tetranitrate, amyl nitrite and alcohol on arterial blood supply to ischemic myocardium. Amer. J. Cardiol. 7: 533.
30. WEBB, W. R. & I. U. DEGERLI. 1965. Ethyl alcohol and the cardiovascular system. J.A.M.A. 191: 1055.
31. WAKIM, K. G. 1946. The effects of ethyl alcohol on the isolated heart. Fed. Proc. 5: 109.
32. HAGGARD, H. W. 1941. Studies on the absorption, distribution and elimination of alcohol. IX. The concentration of alcohol in the blood causing primary cardiac failure. J. Pharmacol. Exp. Therap. 71: 358.
33. LOOMIS, T. A. 1962. Effect of alcohol on myocardial and respiratory function. The influence of modified respiratory function on the cardiac toxicity of alcohol. Quart. J. Studies Alcohol. 13: 461.
34. LOEB, O. 1905. Die Wirking des Alkohols auf das Warmblüterherz. Arch. Exp. Path. Pharmakol. 52: 459.
35. DIXON, W. E. 1907. Action of alcohol on circulation. J. Physiol. 35: 346.
36. BACHEM, C. 1905. Über die Blutdruckwirkung kleiner Alkoholgaben bei intravenöser Injektion. Arch. Int. Pharmacodyn. Ther. 14: 437.
37. MENDOZA, L. C., K. HELLBERG, A. RICKART, G. TILLICH & R. J. BING. 1971. The effect of intravenous ethyl alcohol on the coronary circulation and myocardial contractility of the human and canine heart. J. Clin. Pharmacol. 11: 165.
38. GILBERT, N. C. & C. K. FENN. 1929. The effect of purine base diuretics on the coronary flow. Arch. Int. Med. 44: 118.
39. SCHMITTHENER, J. E., J. H. HAFKENSCHIEL, I. FORTE, A. J. WILLIAMS & C. RIEGEL. 1958. Does alcohol increase coronary blood flow and cardiac work? Circulation 18: 778.
40. PACHINGER, O. M., H. TILLMANNS, J. C. MAO, J. M. FAUVEL & R. J. BING. 1973. The effect of prolonged administration of ethanol on cardiac metabolism and performance in the dog. J. Clin. Invest. 52: 2690.
41. BING, R. J., H. TILLMANNS, J. M. FAUVEL, K. SEELER & J. C. MAO. 1974. The effect of prolonged alcohol administration on calcium transport in heart muscle of the dog. Circulation Res. In press.
42. REGAN, T. J. 1971. Ethyl alcohol and the heart. Circulation 44: 957.
43. COHN, P. F., A. J. LIEDTKE, J. SERUR, E. H. SONNENBLICK & C. W. URSCHEL. 1972. Maximal rate of pressure fall (peak negative dp/dt) during ventricular relaxation. Cardiov. Res. 6: 263.
44. SORDAHL, L. A., W. B. McCOLLUM, W. G. WOOD & A. SCHWARTZ. 1973. Mitochondria and sarcoplasmic reticulum function in cardiac hypertrophy and failure. Amer. J. Physiol. 224: 497.
45. LINDENMAYER, G. E., S. HARIGAYA, E. BAJUSZ & A. SCHWARTZ. 1970. Oxidative phosphorylation and calcium transport of mitochondria isolated from cardiomyopathic hamster hearts. J. Mol. Cell. Cardiol. 1: 249.

46. SCHWARTZ, A., J. M. WOOD, J. C. ALLEN, E. P. BORNET, M. L. ENTMAN, M. A. GOLDSTEIN, L. A. SORDAHL & M. SUZUKI. 1973. Biochemical and morphologic correlates of cardiac ischemia. Amer. J. Cardiol. **32**: 46.
47. LEE, K. S., H. LADINSKY & J. H. STUCKEY. 1967. Decreased Ca^{++} uptake by sarcoplasmic reticulum after coronary artery occlusion for 60 and 90 minutes. Circulation Res. **21**: 439.
48. McCOLLUM, W. B., C. CROW, S. HARIGAYA, E. BAJUSZ & A. SCHWARTZ. 1970. Calcium binding by cardiac relaxing system isolated from myopathic syrian hamsters (strains 14.6, 82.62 and 40.54) J. Mol. Cell Cardiol. **1**: 445.
49. SULAKHE, P. V. and N. S. DHALLA. 1970. Excitation-contraction coupling in heart. VII. Calcium accumulation in subcellular particles in congestive heart failure. J. Clin. Invest. **50**: 1019.

HEART CELL RESPONSES TO ETHANOL*

Timothy J. Regan, Philip O. Ettinger, Henry A. Oldewurtel, and
Bunyad Haider

Department of Medicine
College of Medicine and Dentistry
New Jersey Medical School
Newark, New Jersey 07103

In considering the effects of ethyl alcohol on the heart, a determination of the acute responses may aid in the delineation of the influence of chronic usage. At blood levels that may be considered mildly to moderately intoxicating, ranging from 75 to 230 mg %, several investigators have indicated that function of the left ventricle may be depressed.[1-7] This is, in part, dependent upon the basal state of the heart. Persons who are addicted but do not have clinical evidence of heart disease appear to have some resistance to this effect when compared to normals.[4-6] However, the same oral dose given to patients with severe cardiac disease may elicit marked depression of the myocardium.[8] Supportive evidence for this effect is provided by studies in which ethanol was dialyzed from the blood.[9] Abnormal myocardial function was rapidly returned to control values after 15 to 30 minutes of hemodialysis.

The ultimate mechanism of the observed myocardial response is not due to altered preload or afterload and is presumed related to an action on excitation-contraction coupling and cell calcium transport, but this has yet to be delineated. Some information concerning more proximal steps in the metabolic responses to ethanol is available. A mechanism involving an osmolar gradient, which is known to depress cardiac contractility,[10] has been postulated as a possible mode of action.[11] This is based on the finding of a substantial rise of serum osmolality by the freezing-point depression method and a net plasma volume increase of 18% (^{131}I-labeled albumin) after the onset of ethanol infusion.[2] That a real increment in the osmotic activity of plasma was present is supported by the fact that the maximal expansion of plasma volume was present by 30 minutes, with a subsequent decline to a level of 5% above control when the 2-hour infusion was terminated. The transient nature of this phenomenon is consistent with a delayed equilibration of extravascular osmolality with the osmolar activity of the vascular compartment.

Contrary evidence on the role of osmolality in the function of the acute depressant effect of ethanol has been provided by Nakano.[12] In short-term studies of isolated ventricular strips using alcohols of different chain length, it was observed that the magnitude of myocardial depression was proportional to the length of the carbon chains. The author postulated that the shorter-carbon-chain alcohols have greater affinity for hydrogen bonding in the water phase, whereas the longer carbon chain of pentanol interacts with the lipid phase of the membrane and thus may have greater cell penetration. These responses in tissue slices may differ from those in which physiologic vascular perfusion is main-

*This investigation was supported in part by the National Institute on Alcohol Abuse and Alcoholism Research Grant No. AA00242 and the National Heart and Lung Institute Postgraduate Training Grant No. HL 05510.

tained, since large increases in osmolality did not alter contractility of the tissue slices, in contrast to the response of perfused heart.[10]

Since the vascular effects of hyperosmolar solutions have been reduced by sympathectomy,[13] the evidence advanced for sympathetic stimulation after ethanol[14] may be related to its osmotic effect. Unless the cardiac manifestations of a catecholamine influence are inhibited by ethanol, however, a relatively small sympathetic stimulus must be present in view of the lack of expected increments in heart rate, contractility, and coronary blood flow.[15] The diphasic response of the myocardial RQ and the increment in triglyceride uptake, with eventual accumulation in left ventricular tissue, do resemble the metabolic responses to catecholamine infusion.[16,17]

The sympathetic nervous system is known to have an important role in regulating cardiac contractility. While it has not been conclusively shown that inhibition of the sympathetic nervous system is not operative in ethanol's depressant action, it would appear that normal activity of the cardiac sympathetic nerves during the depressant response are required to partially maintain cardiac function. Thus, the use of beta adrenergic blockade has been shown to produce greater depression of left ventricular function during ethanol administration.[7] In addition, disulfiram is known to be an effective inhibitor of beta hydroxylation and thus diminishes the levels of endogenous norepinephrine in the rat heart.[18] The intensification of the cardiovascular response to ethanol in animals treated with disulfiram may well occur on this basis.[19] It is noteworthy that the adrenal gland does not appear to respond with greater secretion of epinephrine or norepinephrine, at least in response to moderately intoxicating blood levels,[20] so that cardiac catecholamine stores appear to be a major factor modifying the response to acute ethanol intake.

Accumulation of triglyceride in the left ventricle has been found in various pathological situations, but a direct role for this metabolic aberration in modifying ventricular function has yet to be established. One possible mechanism for the acute myocardial lipid accumulation observed after ethanol might be inhibition of oxidation of the free fatty acid entering the cardiac cell,[21] resulting in a tissue triglyceride increment through esterification with glycerol phosphate. This seems unlikely in view of the substantial reduction of free fatty acid uptake in the presence of a respiratory quotient, after 90 minutes of ethanol infusion, which indicated predominant dependence upon lipid for oxidative needs. The mechanism for the reduced extraction of free fatty acid may be related to reduced arterial levels of this substrate as well as competitive inhibition during increased extraction of acetate.[22] A similar competitive inhibition may be ascribed to lactate and glucose, which are extracted in increased amounts early in the course of ethanol infusion.[4] However, the persistence of diminished fatty acid extraction, when the extraction of these latter substrates and the RQ have reverted to near control levels, suggests another mechanism, possibly related to the enhanced triglyceride uptake. The apparent enhanced uptake of triglyceride after ethanol may itself account in large measure for the tissue increment of triglyceride. This implies a limit to the oxidative capacity of the myocardium when substantial uptake of triglyceride occurs. Whether this is absolute or conditioned by the increased uptake of carbohydrate substrate remains to be determined. It is noteworthy that the triglyceride changes were not dependent on an elevated arterial concentration of this lipid, a frequent consequence after ethanol infusion in man.[23]

In terms of the mechanism of lipid accumulation on acute exposure to ethanol, it is noteworthy that Kikuchi has observed that, in contrast to a response to a moderate dose of ethanol, plasma free fatty acids are increased in the case of large ethanol challenge.[24] Free fatty acid uptake may not be reduced and triglyceride extraction may remain unaltered from that of controls. Under this circumstance, a reduced oxidation of ^{14}C fatty acid and enhanced esterification of triglyceride appear to be the prevailing mechanism for lipid accumulation. The failure to observe a change in lipoprotein lipase activity, in contrast to the studies of Mallov,[25] may be attributed to the fact that free fatty acid rather than triglyceride was the predominant lipid extracted by heart muscle after large doses of ethanol.

In the acute canine studies the evidence of cardiac muscle damage suggests a direct effect of ethanol, which may be related to the decline in contractility. Selective release of ions and proteins has been described early in the course of injury in noncardiac tissue. The pattern of ion and enzyme release from the myocardium after ethanol is similar to that occurring during ischemic necrosis, but appears to be shorter in duration, presumably a reflection of altered cell permeability that is reversible at this dosage level.

CHRONIC EFFECTS OF ETHANOL ON MYOCARDIUM

Several clinical studies have suggested that chronic use of ethyl alcohol in large quantities is associated with disease of cardiac muscle.[27,28] While histologic abnormalities have been observed in 90% of unselected alcoholics at postmortem,[29] uncertainty as to the quantity of ethanol intake, the nutritional status of the patient including electrolye deficits, and the possibility of heart disease from other causes have obscured an understanding of the pathogenesis of this cardiomyopathy. Previous chronic experiments with ethanol have yielded conflicting data in terms of the production of a functional deficit,[30,31] but the negative study used smaller quantities.

To eliminate some of the above variables, a group of young adult male dogs were maintained in a relatively normal nutritional state while receiving up to 36% of calories as ethanol, approximating the quantity reported in a population of human alcoholics.[32] After an average of 18 months they were found to have maintained weight, hematocrit, serum proteins, vitamins, and electrolytes to a similar extent as the normal controls. They were anesthetized to permit determination of left ventricular performance, conduction, morphology, and metabolism using methods previously described.[33]

Mean heart rate and aortic pressure were similar in both groups. However, in the chronic ethanol animals there was a significantly higher end-diastolic pressure despite a lower level of end-diastolic volume. Assessment of left ventricular function was undertaken during afterload increments with angiotensin of similar extent in both groups. Stroke output increased moderately but significantly in the controls, while no such increment occurred in the alcoholic animals. Ejection fraction was similar in both groups before and after angiotensin. A rise of stroke work in the normals from 1.39 ± 0.23 to 1.81 ± 0.21 g-m/kg was significantly less in the experimental group ($P < 0.01$), 1.03 ± 0.04 to 1.11 ± 0.07 g-m/kg (FIGURE 1). The normal controls exhibited a moderate rise of end-diastolic pressure and end-diastolic volume during angiotensin infusion. However, a significantly larger rise of end-diastolic pressure occurred in the ethanol group, while the end-diastolic volume response was significantly less than in controls. This is presumably the basis for the reduced stroke volume.

To further analyze the apparent altered stiffness of the ventricle, 6 of the normal animals and 6 of the ethanol group were infused with normal saline via a catheter in the left ventricle. At an infusion rate of 50 ml/min for 3 to 4 minutes, the normals generally exhibited a proportionate rise of left ventricular end-diastolic pressure and volume. In the ethanol group, there was a significantly higher rise of end-diastolic pressure than in the normal ($P < 0.01$), despite an elevation of end-diastolic volume proportionate to that of controls. Heart rate declined and stroke volume rose similarly in both groups without a change in

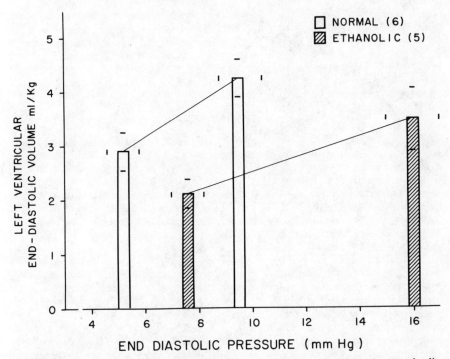

FIGURE 1. The response of the left ventricle to volume increments with normal saline was marked by a significantly higher end-diastolic pressure rise in animals on the chronic ethanol regimen, without significant differences in heart rate, aortic pressure, or stroke volume.

afterload, so that the significantly higher end-diastolic pressure in the experimental group does not appear to be related to these variables.

To examine a potential morphologic basis for the altered diastolic pressure-volume relations attributed to enhanced wall stiffness, apical sections of the left ventricle were examined histochemically. Staining with Alcian Blue showed distinct accumulation of a glycoproteinlike material in the interstitium of the left ventricular wall in the ethanol group (FIGURE 2). The degree of staining ranged from 2 to 3+ on a scale of 0 to 4. There was virtually no staining in the normal controls. Periodic acid-Schiff staining was slightly positive in the ethanol group.

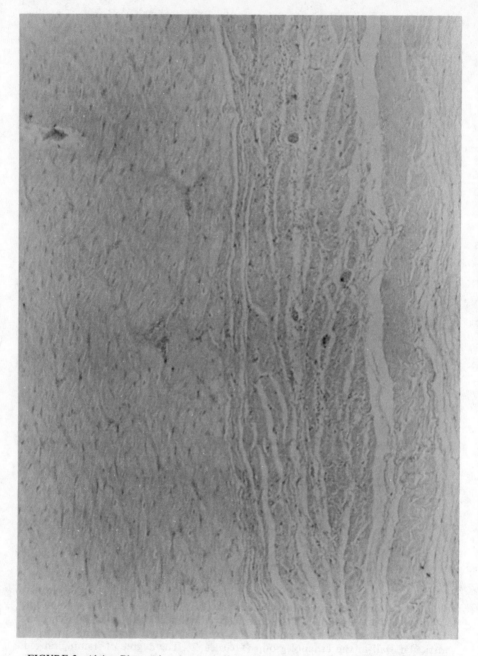

FIGURE 2. Alcian Blue stain of myocardium shows accumulation of glycoprotein material between muscle fibers. × 220.

As a further functional assessment of the myocardium in alcoholic animals, high-speed, high-frequency electrocardiograms were obtained. As noted in FIGURE 3, QRS time was distinctly abnormal in the longer-term animals. Similarly, the conduction time from the His bundle to the onset of ventricular depolarization was significantly prolonged.

METABOLIC STUDIES

Analyses of left ventricular lipids revealed an increment of triglyceride in the ethanol group, which appeared as fine cytoplasmic droplets in Oil Red 0 stain. Cholesterol, phospholipid, and free fatty acid levels were not significantly altered in the three layers of myocardium compared to those of the control group. It is noteworthy that at this stage of chronic alcoholism, the plasma lipid concentrations did not differ from control lipid levels, although transient increases of plasma triglyceride and cholesterol levels were present during the earlier months of the chronic ethanol period.

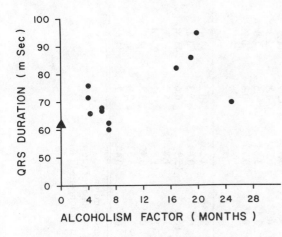

FIGURE 3. Triangle on vertical represents the mean QRS duration in controls. The individual alcoholic animals are plotted by duration of ingestion with a correction factor for those that did not consume 100% of the ethanol ration.

There was no significant extraction of triglyceride, phospholipid, or cholesterol by the myocardium in the anesthetized state by controls or chronic ethanol animals. In addition to comparable arterial levels of blood glucose, myocardial uptake of glucose did not differ between the groups; 0.44 ± 0.06 mM/g/min in controls and 0.50 ± 0.04 mM/g/min in the ethanol group.

To explore the metabolic basis for these lipid alterations, ^{14}C-1-oleic acid was administered by continuous infusion into the inferior vena cava. During the latter half of the 20-minute infusion period, when radioactivity in plasma had reached a plateau, the specific activity remained relatively constant in each dog.

Free fatty acid uptake was calculated from the product of arterial and coronary venous plasma concentration differences and coronary plasma flow, and was similar in both groups. Determinations of $^{14}CO_2$ production showed a significant difference between the ethanol ($12,438 \pm 2880$ cpm/g/min) and the normal group ($21,240 \pm 1917$ cpm/g/min). The total ^{14}C-oleic acid incorporated into lipid of the ventricle was higher in the ethanol group but was not significant, because of a large variance.

TABLE 1
Lipid Content and ^{14}C-Oleic Distribution in Left Ventricle

	Lipids (μM/g)			% ^{14}C Oleic Acid			Specific Activity (cpm/μM)		
	Epi*	Mid	Endo	Epi	Mid	Endo	Epi	Mid	Endo
Controls (N = 10)									
Triglyceride	2.07	1.98	2.08	24.8	25.1	25.7	9468	11034	11067
±	0.24	0.33	0.30	1.6	2.1	1.8	2463	2031	1587
Phospholipid	15.9	16.2	16.0	61.5	62.0	60.5	4977	4692	5283
±	2.3	1.9	1.7	5.9	6.2	5.1	1353	1155	1008
Free fatty acid	9.8	9.3	9.7	12.2	11.9	12.5	3276	3648	3537
±	0.63	0.78	0.66	1.8	2.3	2.5	1584	1632	1572
Cholesterol	3.50	3.42	3.63	1.5	1.0	1.3	774	591	696
±	0.49	0.56	0.70	0.3	0.2	0.2	75	69	91
Chronic Ethanol Group (N = 6)									
Triglyceride	3.80†	3.64†	4.50‡	40.2‡	33.6†	41.2†	9249	10911	12816
±	0.81	0.67	0.83	5.3	3.2	6.1	3051	4146	5466
Phospholipid	16.2	15.5	15.1	36.6‡	41.8†	37.2†	2028†	2100†	2022‡
±	1.7	1.4	1.8	5.2	5.3	5.5	588	528	492
Free fatty acid	11.5	11.3	11.8	21.2‡	23.0†	19.8†	1608	1677	1578
±	0.95	0.49	0.40	3.9	4.7	3.0	846	675	825
Cholesterol	3.18	3.35	3.33	2.0	1.6	1.8	453	495	480
±	0.38	0.37	0.40	1.2	1.6	1.1	306	114	105

*Epi = epicardium; mid = middle layers; endo = endocardium.
†Significantly different from control at $P < 0.01$ in nonpaired t test.
‡Significantly different from control at $P < 0.001$ in nonpaired t test.

Analysis of myocardium for distribution of the isotope in lipid classes indicated a shift from the normal (TABLE 1) in that there was a significant reduction in the percent of incorporation and specific activity of phospholipid. A greater incorporation of labeled fatty acid into triglyceride was associated with a specific activity unaltered from that of controls. In addition, the percent isotope in the free fatty acid fraction was enhanced, but specific activity had large statistical variation and was not significant. Incorporation of isotope in the cholesterol fraction was small and did not differ in the two groups.

Morphologic studies revealed no inflammatory response in heart muscle to complicate the assessment of chemical composition. The changes in lipid metabolism were not accompanied by unequivocal abnormalities of mitochondrial structure on electron micrographs, but accumulation of glycogen-type particles was evident (FIGURE 4). Lysosomal structures were relatively infrequent in both groups. Dilatation of the sarcoplasmic reticulum was a prominent feature in all animals receiving ethanol; the undifferentiated portion of the intercalated disc was similarly affected.

FIGURE 4. The electron micrograph from an alcoholic animal demonstrates the dilated sarcoplasmic reticulum and accumulation of glycogen particles. Original magnification × 40,850; final magnification × 22,825.

The distribution of potassium and sodium across the myocardial wall was found to be uniform in the control group from the outer to the inner layers. However, in the ethanol group there was a significant transmural gradient of potassium ion, with reduction of approximately 10% in the endocardium. A gain of sodium by left ventricular tissue was observed, but a transmural gradient of this cation was less evident. Coronary blood flow by the ^{85}Kr clearance method in paired determinations was 94 ± 5 ml/100 g/min in the controls and 91.4 ± 4.9 ml/100 g/min in the experimental group, so that ischemia did not appear to be the basis for the cation alteration. In addition, longitudinal dissection of the left coronary arteries revealed no detectable encroachment on the arterial lumen or visible lesions of the endocardial surface. At the conclusion of the study, the wieght of the left ventricle and septum in g/kg of total body weight was 4.7 ± 0.19 in the normals and 4.47 ± 0.17 in the ethanol group.

DISCUSSION OF THE MYOCARDIUM IN ALCOHOLISM

A previous study of chronic ethanol administration in the rat has shown a significant decrease in ventricular force development.[30] In contrast, a definite abnormality of ventricular function was not found in the same species fed less ethanol, 15% by volume,[31] as against 25% in the previous series. In addition, an important methodologic difference existed, in that ventricular function was tested at the upmost segment of the ascending portion of the function curve, so that the ventricle was not stressed to the same extent. Since caloric equivalents were not provided, it is difficult to compare these data with the present study; in addition, at least quantitative differences may exist between species.

However, it is noteworthy that this canine model receiving ethanol in a similar proportion of total calories as reported in humans[32] exhibits a preclinical malfunction similar to that seen in the latter species.[4] During increased afterload in dogs on the chronic ethanol regimen, the elevation of filling pressure was significantly higher than in control animals.

The lack of end-diastolic volume increment in animals receiving ethanol may be explicable on the basis of altered wall compliance or impaired ventricular relaxation. The latter must be considered, particularly in view of the apparent reduction of end-diastolic volume seen in some of the animals during increased afterload. However, during volume expansion with saline, a significantly greater rise of end-diastolic pressure was observed in the animals on ethanol than in normal controls, supporting the interpretation of increased diastolic stiffness of left ventricular muscle in the experimental group.

Since left ventricular weights were similar to control hearts, hypertrophy does not seem to contribute to this functional abnormality. Interstitial fibrosis was not evident on light microscopy; its frequent presence in the heart of the human alcoholic may be related to a longer duration of alcoholism.[29] However, the interstitium was altered by the presence of Alcian Blue staining material (FIGURE 2). While chemical assays are required for quantitation, this accumulation was apparently sufficient to alter the diastolic pressure-volume relations of the ventricle. Accumulation of Alcian positive material, also reported in the myocardium of human alcoholics[34] may well be related to the preclinical malfunction of the ventricle described in man.[4]

It seems reasonable to take the position that the relative prominence of glycoprotein in the interstitium suggests a basis for the diminished diastolic compliance. Elasticity of muscle at normal sarcomere lengths in isolated muscle preparations has been attributed to extracellular structures,[37] but the relative importance of collagen and glycoprotein in this regard is unknown. The former did not appear to be present in alcoholic animals in increased quantity on trichrome staining, but chemical assays are required to support this conclusion. Alterations of the extracellular space in the first few days of acute ischemia before new collagen is formed[38] is also associated with diminished compliance,[39] so that enhanced quantities of this fibrous protein are not essential to affect this property of myocardium. Moreover, the interstitium in experimental diabetes mellitus is marked by the presence of periodic acid-Schiff staining and glycoprotein and is also associated with diminished compliance.

Analysis of lipid classes in the myocardium after chronic ethanol ingestion revealed a substantial elevation of triglyceride content, in accord with a previous study in the dog after 10 weeks of ethanol.[38] Accumulation of this lipid is also observed up to 6 hours after acute ethanol administration in intoxicating quantities.[2,40] However, the acute response is marked by increased extraction of plasma triglyceride in the myocardium, associated with a decline of free fatty acid uptake[2] and oxidation.[24] By contrast, in the chronic alcohol state no significant uptake of triglyceride was observed and free fatty acid uptake did not differ significantly from that of controls.

Comparison of the myocardial metabolism of ^{14}C-1-oleic acid with that of controls during a steady state was facilitated by the comparability of the plasma specific activity, indicating that labeled oleate was diluted in a similar-size plasma free fatty acid pool in the control and experimental groups. While neither free fatty acid uptake nor oxidation was significantly altered by the chronic use of ethanol, the distribution of isotopically labeled oleic acid between phospholipid and triglyceride was substantially altered. As the dominant free fatty acid in canine plasma,[41] this would have quantitative importance even if the myocardial distribution of another fatty acid derived from plasma was unaffected. The lower fatty acid incorporation and specific activity of phospholipid in the presence of normal concentrations of this lipid suggests diminished esterification rather than enhanced hydrolysis as the dominant factor. This may result from diminished activity of an acyl transferase involved in phospholipid synthesis or may be an indirect effect of enhanced activity of a triglyceride-synthesizing transferase, as described in the liver of ethanol-fed animals.[42] The diversion of fatty acid through the latter pathway could then account for diminished phospholipid synthesis. A recent report of diminished arachidonate in cardiac phospholipids of ethanol-treated animals,[43] presumably through inhibition of the chain elongation-desaturation system, suggests substantial fatty acid compositional changes in phospholipids after chronic ethanol use.

Enhanced synthesis by esterification appears to be the major factor in triglyceride accumulation, since specific activity is not diminished. However, a reduced activity of the hormone-sensitive triglyceride lipase may be contributory. Triglyceride accumulation in myocardium exposed to diphtheria toxin has been attributed to diminished activity of the carnitine system.[44] Since the diphtheritic heart has impaired fatty acid oxidation without a change in phospholipid synthesis, this system does not appear to be abnormal in chronic ethanol animals with unaltered fatty acid oxidation.

In view of the substantial change of oleic acid incorporation, it is perhaps unnecessary to invoke a major role for enhanced *de novo* synthesis of triglyceride in this metabolic abnormality. Studies of acetate incorporation have indicated that this metabolic pathway contributes only in a minor way to triglyceride synthesis in normal myocardium.[45] Further, in other disease states associated with triglyceride accumulation the *de novo* route has not been found to be contributory.[45,46]

The relative prominence of lipid abnormalities in the myocardium has suggested that the toxic effects of chronic ethanol use on the cardiac cell may be related to this metabolic aberration. Whether mediated by the primary agent or its first metabolite, acetaldehyde, impaired lipid assembly in cardiac membranes if long sustained could represent an important mechanism of injury. Additionally, a major role for triglyceride accumulation in the pathogenesis of the intracellular alterations cannot be excluded. Periods of rapid hydrolysis, with free fatty acid liberation exceeding the capacity of protein binding sites, may result in cell injury.[47]

The cardiac cell abnormalities observed on electron microscopy included dilatation or swelling of the sarcoplasmic reticulum and intercalated disc as well as exaggeration of the sarcolemmal folds. While these changes have been observed in the cardiomyopathy of human alcoholics,[48,49] they do not appear to be specific. From this canine model we may conclude that these alterations can antedate hypertrophy and heart failure and may occur without clear-cut morphologic abnormalities of mitochondria and sarcomere units. The electron micrographic abnormalities of these latter organelles described after ethanol feeding in mice[50] may be the result of a relatively larger ethanol intake or attendant fluid and electrolyte disorders. In the human alcoholic with heart failure,[51] abnormalities of mitochondria and sarcomere units may also be effected by a longer duration of alcohol ingestion; a time-dependent relationship of ventricular conduction abnormalities has been observed in experimental alcoholism.[52] Alternatively, other variables, such as trace metal excess, nutrient deficit, electrolyte depletion, and tobacco use, may modify or exacerbate the underlying abnormality due to ethanol.[28]

Accumulation of glycogen-type particles was observed in the cardiac cells and has been described in the human disease.[48,49] This could result from impaired glycogenolysis if skeletal muscle responses to ethanol are analogous, since reduced phosphorylase levels and impaired lactate production occur in some human alcoholics.[53] Of interest is the contrast with the glycogen depletion associated with myocardial ischemia. The absence of obstructive lesions in the large coronary arteries or intramural vessels, as well as the normal coronary blood flow levels and appearance of the mitochondria, also tends to exclude ischemia as a contributory factor.

The reduction of myocardial potassium and gain of sodium appears to be based on changes in cell cation composition, since tissue water was not increased, as would be expected if interstitial edema were responsible; the latter was also not evident by light and electron microscopy. Moreover, the endocardium exhibited the largest cation change and tended to larger triglyceride increments and phospholipid reduction. This suggests that the metabolic abnormality is more pronounced in the endocardium, as has been observed in another type of myocardial injury without ischemia.[54] Whether the altered cardiac lipid metabolism contributes to the abnormal cation gradients remains to be determined.

Acknowledgment

The authors gratefully acknowledge the secretarial services rendered by Mrs. Anne Binetti and Mrs. Audrey Brown.

REFERENCES

1. GIMENO, A. L., M. F. GIMENO & J. L. WEBB. 1962. Effects of ethanol on cellular membrane potentials and contractility of isolated rat atrium. Amer. J. Physiol. **203:** 194.
2. REGAN, T. J., G. T. KOROXENIDIS, C. B. MOSCHOS, H. A. OLDEWURTEL, P. A. LEHAN & H. K. HELLEMS. 1966. The acute metabolic and hemodynamic response of the left ventricle to ethanol. J. Clin. Invest. **45:** 270.
3. WENDT, V. E., R. AJLUNI, T. A. BRUCE, A. S. PRASAD & R. J. BING. 1966. Acute effects of alcohol on the human myocardium. Amer. J. Cardiol. **17:** 804.
4. REGAN, T. J., G. E. LEVINSON, H. A. OLDEWURTEL, M. J. FRANK, A. B. WEISSE & C. B. MOSCHOS. 1969. Ventricular function in noncardiacs with alcoholic fatty liver: Role of ethanol in the production of cardiomyopathy. J. Clin. Invest. **48:** 397.
5. NEWMAN, W. H. & J. F. VALICENTI, JR. 1971. Ventricular function following acute alcohol administration: A strain-gauge analysis of depressed ventricular dynamics. Amer. Heart J. **81:** 61.
6. AHMED, S. S., G. E. LEVINSON & T. J. REGAN. 1973. Depression of myocardial contractility with low doses of ethanol in normal man. Circulation **48:** 378.
7. WONG, M. 1973. Depression of cardiac performance by ethanol unmasked during autonomic blockade. Amer. Heart J. **86** (4): 508.
8. REGAN, T. J. 1971. Ethyl alcohol and the heart. Circulation **44:** 957.
9. SYMBAS, P. N., D. H. TYRAS, R. E. WARE & B. J. BALDWIN. 1972. Alteration of cardiac function by hemodialysis during experimental alcohol intoxication. Circulation **45, 46:** II-227.
10. KOCH-WESER, J. 1963. Influence of osmolarity of perfusate on contractility of mammalian myocardium. Amer. J. Physiol. **204:** 957.
11. REGAN, T. J., A. B. WEISSE, H. A. OLDEWURTEL & H. K. HELLEMS. 1964. The hyperosmotic effects of ethanol and sucrose on the left ventricle. J. Clin. Invest. **43:** 1289.
12. NAKANO, J. & S. E. MOORE. 1972. Effect of different alcohols on the contractile force of the isolated guinea-pig myocardium. Europ. J. Pharmacol. **20:** 266.
13. LASSER, R. P., M. R. SCHOENFELD, D. F. ALLEN & C. K. FRIEDBERG. 1960. Reflex circulatory effects elicited by hypertonic and hypotonic solutions injected into femoral and brachial arteries of dogs. Circ. Res. **8:** 913.
14. SIEGEL, J. H. 1964. The effect of enteric ethanol on arterial and portal venous catecholamines. Clin. Res. **12:** 213.
15. REGAN, T. J., P. H. LEHAN, D. H. HENNEMAN, A. BEHAR & H. K. HELLEMS. 1964. Myocardial metabolic and contractile response to glucagon and epinephrine. J. Lab. Clin. Med. **63:** 638.
16. REGAN, T. J., L. TROUM, P. H. LEHAN & H. K. HELLEMS. 1962. Myocardial metabolism during epinephrine-induced necrosis. J. Clin. Invest. **42:** 1393.
17. MALING, H. M., B. HIGHMAN & E. C. THOMPSON. 1960. Some similar effects after large doses of catecholamines and myocardial infarction in dogs. Amer. J. Cardiol. **5:** 628.
18. MUSACCHIO, J., I. J. KOPIN & S. SNYDER. 1964. Effects of disulfiram on tissue norepinephrine content and subcellular distribution of dopamine, tyramine and their β-hydroxylated metabolites. Life Sci. **3:** 769.
19. NAKANO, J., J. E. HOLLOWAY & J. S. SCHACKFORD. 1969. Effects of disulfiram on the cardiovascular responses to ethanol in dogs and guinea pigs. Toxicol. Appl. Pharmacol. **14:** 439.
20. HIROSE, T., R. HIGASHI, H. IDEDA, K. TAMURA & T. SUZUKI. 1973. Effect of ethanol on adrenaline and nonadrenaline secretion of the adrenal gland in the dog. Tohoku J. Exp. Med. **109:** 85.
21. WITTELS, B. & R. BRESSLER. 1964. Biochemical lesion of diphtheria toxin in the heart. J. Clin. Invest. **43:** 630.
22. LINDENEG, O., K. MELLEMGAARD, J. FABRICIUS & F. LUNDQUIST. 1964. Myo-

cardial utilization of acetate, lactate and free fatty acids after ingestion of ethanol. Clin. Sci. **27:** 427.

23. JONES, D. P., M. S. LOSOWSKY, C. S. DAVIDSON & C. S. LIEBER. 1962. Effect of ethanol on plasma lipids in man. J. Lab. Clin. Med. **60:** 888.

24. KIKUCHI, T. & K. J. KAKO. 1970. Metabolic effects of ethanol on the rabbit heart. Circ. Res. **26:** 625.

25. MALLOV, S. & F. CERRA. 1967. Effect of ethanol intoxication and catecholamines on cardiac lipoprotein lipase activity in rats. J. Pharmacol. Exp. Therap. **156:** 426.

26. WOODIN, A. M. & A. A. WIENEKE. 1964. Cellular Injury. Ciba Symposium. Little, Brown. Boston, Mass.

27. FERRANS, V. J. 1966. Alcoholic cardiomyopathy. Amer. J. Med. Sci. **252:** 89.

28. REGAN, T. J. 1973. Alcoholic cardiomyopathy. *In* Myocardial Disease. N. O. Fowler, Ed.: 23 Grune & Stratton, Inc. New York, N. Y.

29. SCHENK, E. A. & J. COHEN. 1970. The heart in chronic alcoholism. Pathol. Microbiol. (Basel) **35:** 96.

30. MAINES, J. E. & E. E. ALDINGER. 1967. Myocardial depression accompanying chronic consumption of alcohol. Amer. Heart J. **73:** 55.

31. LOCHNER, A., R. COWLEY & A. J. BRINK. 1969. Effect of ethanol on metabolism and function of perfused rat heart. Amer. Heart J. **78:** 770.

32. NEVILLE, J. N., J. A. EAGLES, G. SAMPSON & R. E. OLSON. 1968. The nutritional status of alcoholics. Amer. J. Clin. Nutr. **21:** 1329.

33. REGAN, T. J., P. O. ETTINGER, M. I. KAHN, M. U. JESRANI, M. M. LYONS & H. A. OLDEWURTEL. 1974. Altered myocardial function and metabolism in chronic diabetes mellitus without ischemia. Circ. Res. In press.

34. REGAN, T. J., C. F. WU, A. B. WEISSE, B. HAIDER, S. S. AHMED, H. A. OLDE-WURTEL & M. M. LYONS. (Introduced by F. P. Chinard). 1974. Acute myocardial infarction in toxic cardiomyopathy without coronary obstruction. Trans. Assoc. Amer. Phys. **86:** 193.

35. GOULD, L. 1969. Cardiac hemodynamics in alcoholic patients with chronic liver disease and presystolic gallop. J. Clin. Invest. **48:** 860.

36. SPODICK, D. H., V. M. PIGOTT & R. CHIRIFE. 1972. Preclinical cardiac malfunction in chronic alcoholism. Comparison with matched normal controls and with alcoholic cardiomyopathy. New Eng. J. Med. **287** (14): 677.

37. BRADY, A. J. 1968. Active state in cardiac muscle. Physiol. Rev. **48** (3): 570.

38. HEGGTVEIT, H. A. 1971/72. Morphological alterations in the ischaemic heart. Cardiology **56:** 284.

39. HOOD, W. B. JR., J. S. BIANCO, R. KUMAR & R. B. WHITING. 1970. Experimental myocardial infarction. IV. Reduction of left ventricular compliance in the healing phase. J. Clin. Invest. **49:** 1316.

40. WONG, M. 1974. In vivo sampling of cardiac triglyceride from dogs during ethanol infusion. J. Lipid Res. **15:** 50.

41. ROTHLIN, M. E., C. B. ROTHLIN & V. E. WENDT. 1962. Free fatty acid concentration and composition in arterial blood. Amer. J. Physiol. **203** (2): 306.

42. JOLY, J-G., L. FEINMAN, H. ISHII & C. S. LIEBER. 1973. Effect of chronic ethanol feeding on hepatic microsomal glycerophosphate acyl transferase activity. J. Lipid Res. **14** (3): 337.

43. REITZ, R. C., E. HELSABECK & D. P. MASON. 1973. Effects of chronic alcohol ingestion on the fatty acid composition of the heart. Lipids **8** (2): 80.

44. WITTELS, B. & R. BRESSLER. 1964. Biochemical lesion of diphtheria toxin in the heart. J. Clin. Invest. **43:** 630.

45. WHEREAT, A. F. & M. W. ORISHIMO. 1969. Effects of fasting and diabetes on fatty acid synthesis by heart mitochondria. Amer. J. Physiol. **217:** 998.

46. REGAN, T. J., M. I. KAHN, M. U. JESRANI, H. A. OLDEWURTEL & P. O. ETTINGER. 1973. Alterations of myocardial function and metabolism in chronic diabetes mellitus. *In* Myocradial Metabolism: Recent Advances in Studies on Cardiac Structure and Metabolism. N. S. Dhalla, Ed. **3:** 169, University Park Press. Baltimore, Md.

47. BOIME, L., E. E. SMITH & F. E. HUNTER, JR. 1970. The role of fatty acids in mitochondrial changes during liver ischemia. Arch. Biochem. Biophys. **139**: 425.
48. BULLOCH, R. T., M. B. PEARCE, M. L. MURPHY, B. J. JENKINS & J. L. DAVIS. 1972. Myocardial lesions in idiopathic and alcoholic cardiomyopathy. Amer. J. Cardiol. **29**: 15.
49. FERRANS, V. J., W. C. ROBERTS, G. I. SHUGOLL, R. A. MASSUMI & N. ALI. 1972. Plasma membrane extension in intercalated discs of human myocardium and their relationship to partial dissociation of the discs. J. Molec. Cell. Cardiol. **5**: 161.
50. BURCH, G. E., H. L. COLCOLOUGH, J. M. HARB & C. Y. TSUI. 1971. The effects of ingestion of ethyl alcohol, wine and beer on the myocardium of mice. Amer. J. Cardiol. **27**: 522.
51. ALEXANDER, C. S. 1968. The concept of alcoholic myocardiopathy. Med. Clin. N. Amer. **42** (5): 1183.
52. ETTINGER, P. O., M. I. KAHN, H. A. OLDEWURTEL & T. J. REGAN. 1970. Left ventricular conduction abnormalities in chronic alcoholism. Circulation **42** (3): 98.
53. PERKOFF, G. T., P. HARDY & E. VELEZ-GRACIA. 1966. Reversible acute muscular syndrome in chronic alcoholism. New Eng. J. Med. **274**: 1277.
54. REGAN, T. J., A. MARKOV, M. I. KAHN, M. U. JESRANI, H. A. OLDEWURTEL & P. O. ETTINGER. 1972. Myocardial ion and lipid changes during ischemia and catecholamine induced necrosis: Relation to regional blood flow. *In* Myocardiology: Recent Advances in Studies on Cardiac Structure and Metabolism. E. Bajusz & G. Rona, Eds. **1**: 656. University Park Press. Baltimore, Md.

CLINICAL SIGNS AND NATURAL HISTORY OF ALCOHOLIC HEART DISEASE*

Rolf M. Gunnar

Section of Cardiology
Loyola University Stritch School of Medicine
Maywood, Illinois 60153 and Section of Cardiology
Veterans Administration Hospital
Hines, Illinois 60141

John Demakis

Loyola University Stritch School of Medicine
Maywood, Illinois 60153 and Veterans Administration Hospital
Hines, Illinois 60141

Shahbudin H. Rahimtoola

University of Oregon Medical School
Portland, Oregon 97201

Mohamed Ziad Sinno

Loyola University Stritch School of Medicine
Maywood, Illinois 60153 and Veterans Administration Hospital
Hines, Illinois 60141

John R. Tobin, Jr.

Department of Medicine
Loyola University Stritch School of Medicine
Maywood, Illinois 60153

Shortly after Walsh's description of localized cirrhosis of the heart in patients dying of chronic alcoholism,[1] Maguire reported to the Clinical Society of London 2 alcoholic patients who manifested acute dilatation of the heart, small pulses, and congestive heart failure.[2] Both patients improved with abstinence from alcohol, and Maguire attributed the heart disease to poisoning of the myocardium by alcohol. In the discussion that followed Maguire's paper doubt was expressed that alcohol was the offending agent, and other features of alcoholism including dietary deficiency and inflammatory disease were proposed as contributing or primary factors to the cardiac failure. This controversy then continued until the 1960s, when it was demonstrated that alcohol, of itself, can cause myocardial damage. In 1941 Haggard et al.[3] postulated that alcohol in high concentrations has a direct toxic effect on the myocardium, and this was based on their demonstration of production of cardiac failure in the experimental animal. Degerli and Webb[4] observed a decrease in myocardial contractile force as measured by strain gauges attached to the myocardium during

*Supported in part by Chicago Heart Association Grant RN 63-24 and National Heart and Lung Institute HE9666.

alcohol infusion in dogs. Regan et al. used longer periods of alcohol infusion and were able to demonstrate a decrease in cardiac output and left ventricular function at moderate levels of intoxication averaging 110 mg of alcohol per 100 ml of blood.[5] Mierzwyak et al.,[6] using a dog preparation in studying cardiac output, heart rate, left ventricular pressures, and first derivative of left ventricular pressure, demonstrated no change in left ventricular function when blood levels of alcohol were maintained at 100 mg/100 cc, while at levels of 300 mg of alcohol per 100 cc there was a demonstrable depression of ventricular function as manifested by an increase in left ventricular end-diastolic pressure with a decrease in stroke power and a fall in maximum rate of left ventricular pressure rise.

Using an isolated papillary muscle, Spann et al.[7] were able to demonstrate depression of the force volocity relationship at alcohol levels of 100 mg/100 cc. Wendt et al. studied alcoholic patients during rest and exercise and demonstrated a disproportionate loss of myocardial enzymes in the alcoholic patient.[8] Regan et al.[9] assayed ventricular function by increasing afterload with angiotensin infusion and demonstrated a marked rise in left ventricular end-diastolic pressure during afterload in alcoholic patients with liver disease but with no overt evidence of cardiac disease. Control patients demonstrated little change in end-diastolic pressure with similar increments in stroke work. After ingestion of 12 ounces of Scotch whiskey there was a progressive rise in left ventricular end-diastolic pressure and a decrease in stroke volume and stroke work. There was also a loss of myocardial enzymes during this level of alcohol ingestion. In one patient they were able to demonstrate the appearance of cardiac failure during long-term ingestion of 16 ounces of Scotch whiskey per day. After 12 weeks the heart rate, circulation time, and venous pressure had all increased and the cardiothoracic ratio had increased. By the 16th week a ventricular diastolic gallop appeared. Three to 4 weeks after discontinuance of the alcohol ingestion the patients findings' returned to normal without other forms of cardiac medication.

Thus, it appears that there is ample evidence to support the thesis that alcohol of itself will cause myocardial damage in the human and that at least some of the effects of alcoholic heart damage can be reversed by abstinence.

In the early phases of alcoholic heart disease the patient may have no symptom other than palpitations due to ventricular ectopic beats or paroxysmal atrial fibrillation. The patient may first be seen because of some intercurrent illness and recognized as having heart disease on the basis of persistent tachycardia and an atrial gallop sound. At this stage the heart size will be normal and it will be difficult to classify the patient as having heart disease. The electrocardiogram may show nondiagnostic S-T- and T-wave abnormalities and may show early evidence of left ventricular hypertrophy.[10,14]

As the disease progresses, left ventricular hypertrophy becomes clinically apparent. An atrial gallop sound is usually present and a ventricular gallop may occasionally be heard. The electrocardiogram will demonstrate left ventricular hypertrophy in almost all patients, and abnormal T waves will be present in more than half. Occasionally conduction disturbances such as left bundle branch block, right bundle branch block, or left anterior hemiblock will be present.[10] Arrhythmias have been less common in our series than in series reported by Evans[11] or Brigdon and Robinson.[12]

As the disease continues to progress, the heart dilates and the apical impulse becomes more diffuse, and evidence of atrioventricular valvular insufficiency is not infrequently present. During this phase the ventricular gallop sound is usually

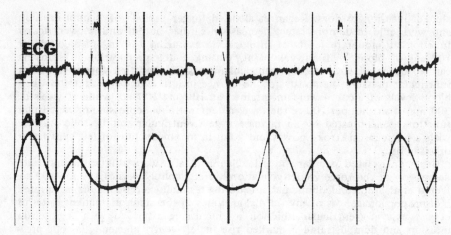

FIGURE 1. Dicrotic pulse in patient with alcoholic cardiomyopathy. Arterial pressure (AP) was recorded through a needle in the brachial artery. (From Gunnar et al.[14] By permission of *Disease-a-Month*.)

present. A dicrotic pulse is not uncommon in the young individual (FIGURE 1). In this late stage of the disease, electrocardiographic evidence of left ventricular hypertrophy frequently persists, bundle branch block patterns are more frequent, and atrial fibrillation may lead to sudden clinical deterioration of the patient.[10,14]

Electrocardiographic T-wave changes have been emphasized by Evans, and he has described dimpled, spinous, and blunted T waves that he originally felt were characteristic of alcoholic heart disease.[13] Occasionally inverted symmetrical T waves suggestive of acute ischemia are seen[14] (FIGURE 2). None of the T-wave changes is specific for the disease. The QRS changes include left ventricular hypertrophy and, later in the disease, some loss of the initial anterior forces that may suggest the presence of myocardial infarction.

It is probable, as proposed by Tobin et al.,[10] that the differences in presentation of patients just exemplify a spectrum of the same disease with varying findings based mostly on duration of the disease (length of symptoms) and continuance on or abstinence from alcohol (FIGURE 3).

Although malnutrition may play a role in development of the cardiomyopathy, it has been difficult to document such a factor. Of the 39 patients described by Tobin et al., 30 had dietary histories suggesting poor nutrition but none had overt evidence of vitamin deficiency and most did not appear malnourished. Twenty-two had major complications of alcoholism, including a history of delirium tremens in 12 and peripheral neuropathy in 2.

In 1971 we began an analysis of the patients with alcoholic cardiomyopathy who had been followed in a special cardiomyopathy clinic at Cook County Hospital during the years 1962 through 1970. The results of this analysis have recently been published by Demakis et al.[15] Of 133 patients who fulfilled the criteria for alcoholic cardiomyopathy, 57 returned for subsequent visits and became the subjects of the study. Duration of follow-up averaged 40.5 months.

The patients met the diagnostic criteria of alcoholic cardiomyopathy in having congestive heart failure as evidence of heart disease, but in the absence of other causes of heart disease such as hypertension, valvular disease, or coronary disease to explain the congestive heart failure. Alcoholism was defined in these patients as use of more than 8 ounces of whiskey or gin, 1 quart of wine, or 2 quarts of beer per day for a period of 5 years or more. In actuality, the majority of the patients were far more dedicated to their alcoholism than the minimal requirements to meet the criteria. All patients were under 50 years of age, the older group excluded to minimize confusion with arteriosclerotic heart disease. None of the patients was treated with prolonged bed rest, but they were followed in a special clinic and encouraged to return to that clinic for long-term follow-up. Follow-up of these patients ranged between 4 months and 8 years. The clinical characteristics of these patients are outlined in TABLE 1. The patients were divided into 3 groups on the basis of the follow-up evaluation of their clinical status. Patients in group A showed an improvement in their functional classification. Patients in group B had no change in their functional classification during the follow-up period, and patients in

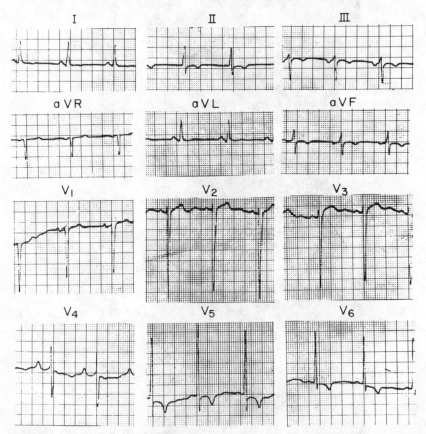

FIGURE 2. Electrocardiogram of patient with alcoholic cardiomyopathy demonstrating deeply inverted T waves and left ventricular hypertrophy. (From Gunnar et al.[14] By permission of *Disease-a-Month*.)

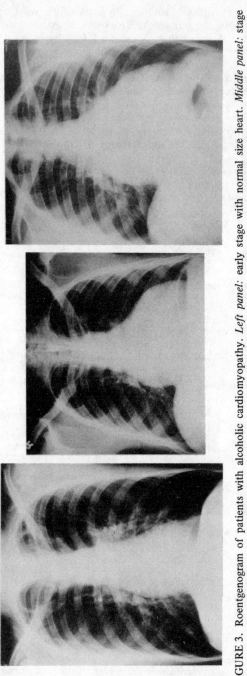

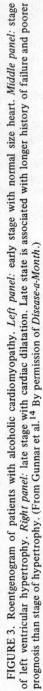

FIGURE 3. Roentgenogram of patients with alcoholic cardiomyopathy. *Left panel:* early stage with normal size heart. *Middle panel:* stage of left ventricular hypertrophy. *Right panel:* late stage with cardiac dilatation. Late state is associated with longer history of failure and poorer prognosis than stage of hypertrophy. (From Gunnar et al.[14] By permission of *Disease-a-Month.*)

TABLE 1
Symptoms and Signs at Time of Initial
Clinical Presentation

	Number of Patients
Symptoms	
Dyspnea on exertion	55
Paroxysmal nocturnal dyspnea	30
Orthopnea	25
Ankle swelling	39
Cough	14
Chest pain (nonspecific)	10
Fatigue	6
Palpitations	3
Hemoptysis	3
Signs	
Cardiomegaly	57
Rales	55
Edema	40
Hepatomegaly	33
S_3 heart sound	57
S_4 heart sound	47
Holosystolic murmur at cardiac apex	13
Ejection systolic murmur	11

group C showed definite deterioration of their cardiac functional classification. There were no differences between the 3 groups with respect to race, age, blood pressure, liver function, or alcohol intake prior to entrance into the series. As can be seen in TABLE 2, there were 15 patients who showed marked improve-

TABLE 2
Follow-Up Data

	Group A	Group B	Group C
	No.		
Patients	15	12	30
Mean length of follow-up*	45	44	37
Clinical features			
Persistent cardiomegaly	5	12	30
CCF†	0	0	22
Pulmonary emboli	0	2	10
Death	0	0	24
Electrocardiogram			
Normal	5	0	0
Abnormal	10	10	30
Mean duration of symptoms before therapy*	4.2	17	11.1
Pattern of drinking			
Abstained	11	3	4
Continued	4	9	26

*Measured in months.
†Congestive cardiac failure.

TABLE 3

Results of Exploratory Mediastinotomy and Myocardial Biopsy

Patient No.	Duration of Congestive Heart Failure (Months)	Stage	Gross Appearance	Histological Abnormalities in Myocardium*					
				Interstitial Fibrosis	Hypertrophy	Inflammation	Fatty Infiltration	Edema	Replacement Fibrosis
21	1	I	Normal	+	0	+	0	++	0
12	3	I	Normal	++	0	0	0	+	0
40	2	II	Left vent. hypertrophy	+	+	+	0	0	0
18	2	II	Left vent. hypertrophy	+	+	0	0	0	0
8	3	II	Left vent. hypertrophy	++	+	+/-	++	0	0
7	14	III	Left vent. dilatation	+	+	+/-	+	0	0
16	18	III	Left vent. dilatation	++	++	0	0	0	0
32	18	III	Left vent. dilatation	+++	+	0	0	0	0

*0 = absent; + = mild; ++ = moderate; +++ = severe; and +/- = scattered and mild.

ment in their functional classification. Ten of these patients had a return of heart size to normal, and 5 had a return of electrocardiogram to normal. The mean duration of symptoms in this group prior to the onset of treatment was 4.2 months, and of the 15 patients 11 abstained or seriously curtailed their drinking during the follow-up periods. Twelve patients showed no change in their functional classification. All continued to have cardiomegaly and abnormal electrocardiograph changes. Of these 12 patients, only 3 have abstained from alcohol, and as a group the mean duration of symptoms prior to onset of therapy was 17 months. There were 30 patients who deteriorated in their functional classification during the follow-up period. The cardiomegaly tended to increase or at least remain, and the electrocardiographic abnormalities persisted. Twenty-four of the 30 patients in this group died. Twenty-two died within the first 5 years, and 13 of these died within the first 3 years of follow-up. Twenty-two of the deaths were due to congestive heart failure. Of these 30 patients, 26 continued to drink heavily while only 4 abstained. The duration of symptoms prior to the onset of therapy for this group was 11.1 months.

It is concluded from this series that patients with cardiomyopathy due to alcoholism are more likely to improve if they abstain from alcohol and if the onset of treatment, which included abstinence, is begun shortly after the onset of symptoms. Although there was no attempt to compare patients treated with prolonged bed rest, it is of interest to note that the patients in the series reported by McDonald et al.,[16] who were treated with prolonged bed rest, had an improvement rate and a mortality similar to our own studies.

Pathologic studies of hearts from patients with alcoholism reveal evidence of interstitial fibrosis in 90%, and myocardial hypertrophy is not infrequent despite absence of clinical evidence of heart disease in these patients.[17] Myocardial biopsies of patients with the diagnosis of alcoholic cardiomyopathy reveal interstitial fibrosis in all and myocardial hypertrophy in most[10] (TABLE 3). Electron-microscopic studies reveal mitochondrial proliferation and disruption as well as dilatation of the sarcoplasmic reticulum and although these changes can be reproduced in the rat by ingestion of alcohol, they are not specific to this type of intoxication.[18,19]

It is disappointing that histologic studies have not been of more benefit in this disease. Although viruslike particles have been described in at least 1 patient,[20] it is unlikely that viral disease plays any significant role in this illness. A few patients with the diagnosis of alcoholic cardiomyopathy, however, could have viral cardiomyopathy.

The diagnosis of alcoholic cardiomyopathy is one of exclusion after the severity of the alcohol abuse has been established. If such a patient has evidence of disease of the heart muscle and if there is no evidence of valvular, congenital, hypertensive, or arteriosclerotic heart disease, and coronary angiography reveals normal coronary arteries, then one must conclude at this state of our knowledge that the myocardial disease is due to heavy alcohol intake.

SUMMARY

Chronic dedicated alcohol ingestion leads to myocardial fibrosis and hypertrophy and can eventuate in congestive heart failure and cardiac death. This process can be reversed by early detection and abstinence from alcohol. Although the exact biochemical sequence has not been agreed on, it is the consensus that alcohol is the common denominator and cardiac damage cannot be prevented by vitamins or attention to nutrition—only by elimination of alcohol from the diet.

REFERENCES

1. WALSHE, W. H. 1873. Diseases of the Heart and Great Vessels: 359. Smith, Elder & Company. London, England.
2. MAGUIRE, R. 1887. Acute dilatation of the heart produced by alcoholism. Brit. Med. J. 1: 1215.
3. HAGGARD, H. W., L. A. GREENBURG, L. H. COHEN & N. J. RAKIETEN. 1941. Studies on the absorption, distribution and elimination of alcohol. IX. The concentration of alcohol in the blood causing primary cardiac failure. J. Pharmacol. Exp. Ther. 71: 358.
4. DEGERLI, I. H. & W. R. WEBB. 1964. Cardiac effects of alcohol, digitalis and corticoids. Clin. Res. 12: 26.
5. REGAN, T. J., G. KOROXENIDIS, C. B. MOSCHOS, H. A. OLDEWURTEL, P. H. LEHAN & H. K. HELLEMS. 1966. The acute metabolic and hemodynamic responses of the left ventricle to ethanol. J. Clin. Invest. 45: 270.
6. MIERZWIAK, D. S., C. K. WILDENTHAL, A. M. SMITH & J. H. MITCHELL. 1967. Ethanol and left ventricular contractility in the dog. Clin. Res. 15: 215.
7. SPANN, J. F., JR., D. T. MASON, G. D. BEISER & H. K. GOLD. 1968. Actions of ethanol on the contractile state of the normal and failing cat papillary muscle. Clin. Res. 16: 249.
8. WENDT, V. E., C. WU, R. BALSON, G. DOTY & R. J. BING. 1965. Hemodynamic and metabolic effects of chronic alcoholism in man. Amer. J. Cardiol. 15: 175.
9. REGAN, T. J., G. E. LEVINSON, H. A. OLDEWURTEL, M. J. FRANK, A. B. WEISSE & C. B. MOSCHOS. 1969. Ventricular function in noncardiacs with alcoholic fatty liver: Role of ethanol in the production of cardiomyopathy. J. Clin. Invest. 48: 397.
10. TOBIN, J. R., JR., J. F. DRISCOLL, M. T. LIM, G. C. SUTTON, P. B. SZANTO & R. M. GUNNAR. 1967. Primary myocardial disease and alcoholism. Circulation 35: 754.
11. EVANS, W. 1961. Alcoholic cardiomyopathy. Amer. Heart J. 61: 556.
12. BRIGDEN, W. & J. ROBINSON. 1964. Alcoholic heart disease. Brit. Med. J. 2: 1283.
13. EVANS, W. 1959. The electrocardiogram of alcoholic cardiomyopathy. Brit. Heart J. 21: 445.
14. GUNNAR, R. M., G. C. SUTTON, R. J. PIETRAS & J. R. TOBIN, JR. 1971. Alcoholic cardiomyopathy. D. M. Sept. 1971.
15. DEMAKIS, J. G., S. H. RAHIMTOOLA, G. C. SUTTON & R. M. GUNNAR. 1974. The natural course of alcoholic cardiomyopathy. Ann. Int. Med. 80: 293.
16. McDONALD, C. D., G. E. BURCH & J. J. WALSH. 1971. Alcoholic cardiomyopathy managed with prolonged bed rest. Ann Int. Med. 74: 681.
17. SCHENK, E. A. & J. COHEN. 1970. The heart in chronic alcoholism. Pathl. Microbiol. (Basel) 35: 96.
18. ALEXANDER, C. S. 1967. Electron microscopic observations in alcoholic heart disease. Brit. Heart J. 29: 200.
19. SZANTO, P. B., K. LARSEN, B. MILES, G. C. SUTTON, R. M. GUNNAR & J. R. TOBIN, JR. 1967. Ultrastructural alterations in human and experimental "alcoholic cardiomyopathy." (abst.) Sc. Proc. Amer. Sco. Path. Bacteriol. 117: 55.
20. HIBBS, R. G., V. J. FERRANS, W. C. BLACK, D. G. WEILBAECHER, J. J. WALSH & G. E. BURCH. 1965. Alcoholic cardiomyopathy. An electron microscopic study. Amer. Heart J. 69: 766.

INTRODUCTION

Kenneth Williams

Diseases of skeletal muscle, bone, and skin related to alcohol abuse are grouped together in this section. The association between diseases of these organs and alcohol consumption has been recognized only relatively recently. While pain and some degree of disability may result, none of these disease entities are life-threatening.

Alcoholic myopathy, first described in 1955, is the best studied of these disease problems. Dr. Knochel's paper summarizes the categorization of the 3 types of alcoholic myopathy and reviews the mechanisms postulated as causing the muscle injury. He then presents his own argument that acute alcoholic myopathy may be induced by acute hypophosphatemia. He suggests that, in the alcoholic experiencing the alcohol-withdrawal syndrome, acute hypophosphatemia and its attendant complications might be avoided by phosphate supplementation.

The most common bone lesion in alcoholics is traumatic fracture experienced during inebriation. Certainly the alcoholic must be seen as being at high risk of experiencing trauma in automobile accidents, falls, etc.

Dr. Saville's paper reviews the mechanisms probably operative in producing prematurely developed osteoporosis. This condition would place the alcoholic at increased risk of fracture of hip, wrist, humerus, and spine from less than usual trauma. Proceeding to a description of "nontraumatic osteonecrosis of the hip" (also called avascular necrosis of the femoral head), he reviews the important clinical considerations.

A clinical categorization and review of common skin problems seen in the alcoholic person is found in Dr. Woeber's paper. He suggests that the alert practitioner should suspect underlying alcoholism when confronted with certain dermatologic problems.

THE MUSCLE CELL IN CHRONIC ALCOHOLISM:
THE POSSIBLE ROLE OF PHOSPHATE
DEPLETION IN ALCOHOLIC MYOPATHY*

James P. Knochel, Gordon L. Bilbrey,

Thomas J. Fuller, and Norman W. Carter

*Veterans Administration Hospital and University of
Texas Health Science Center
Dallas, Texas 75216*

The observation that acute muscular tenderness, swelling, pain, and myoglobinuria may occur in some patients with chronic, severe alcoholism was made by Hed et al. in 1955.[1] This was confirmed[2,3] and subsequently subjected to detailed study by Perkoff et al.[4-7] Alcoholic myopathy has thus been subdivided into 3 categories. Type I refers to the subclinical form manifesting only biochemical changes. These changes consist of elevated activity of enzymes in serum derived from skeletal muscle cells such as creatine phosphokinase (CPK). Type II alcoholic myopathy refers to the acute variety, characterized by muscle cramps, diffuse muscle weakness, frank rhabdomyolysis, and myoglobinuria. Type III alcoholic myopathy is the chronic form that resembles certain forms of long-standing muscular dystrophy demonstrating proximal muscle wasting and variable degrees of muscular weakness.

The criteria for identification of clinically evident alcoholic myopathy have recently been reviewed.[8,9]

PATHOGENESIS OF ALCOHOLIC MYOPATHY

In general, seven mechanisms have been cited as possible causes for injury to muscle cells in patients with chronic alcoholism.

1. *Prolonged ischemia* has been considered based upon evidence that intra-arterial administration of ethanol produced vasoconstriction and decreased muscle perfusion.[10,11] In criticism, it must be stated that this effect was not pronounced. In the single patient with myoglobinuria and 8 normal subjects, forearm flow fell equally and averaged 29%. This is not a dramatic effect if one considers actual values for muscle blood flow. It is well known, for example, that resting skeletal muscle is one of the most poorly perfused tissues in the body. Thus, even under normal conditions, muscle blood flow ranges between 2–4 ml/100 g/min. Of most importance, they showed in their 1 patient with myopathy that muscle blood flow rose with exercise.[9] Normally, blood flow may rise 20–40-fold above resting values.[12] The suggestion that ethanol induces myopathy by means of ischemia has little substantiating evidence.

2. The second mechanism given consideration is that of *direct injury to the sarcolemmal membrane*. It has been shown by several investigators that when exposed to concentrations of ethanol that prevail in clinical intoxication,

*Work supported by designated funds from the Veterans Administration and USPHS, NIH grant no. 2 PO1 HL11662.

membrane permeability to certain ions, determined *in vitro*, is generally increased.[13] Furthermore, following sufficiently prolonged ingestion of ethanol, or in patients with chronic alcoholic myopathy, electron microscopy has demonstrated intracellular edema[6] and mitochondrial damage,[14] both suggestive of direct toxic injury.

3. The third mechanism concerns *toxic inhibition of active transport* by the muscle cell. Many investigators have clearly shown that sodium and potassium transport, mediated by the enzyme Na^+, K^+-ATPase, are impaired in human red cells,[15] frog skin[16] and the rat and guinea pig cerebral cortex.[17,18] Such defects can be demonstrated acutely in the rat *in vitro* as well as *in vivo* following chronic administration of ethanol. If the mechanism by which Na^+ is transported from the skeletal muscle cell is electrogenic and its energy is also provided by the action of Na^+, K^+-ATPase on ATP, it might be predicted that the resting muscle membrane potential would become less negative if the enzyme is inhibited by ethanol. Support for this notion has been obtained by Mayer,[19] who has shown that the resting muscle membrane potential indeed becomes abnormally low in rats, following chronic administration of ethanol.

4. The fourth consideration is that of *nutritional deficiency*.[20] It is well appreciated that starvation and/or protein-calorie malnutrition in children may be associated with abnormal depression of glycolytic enzymes in muscle and abnormalities of muscle electrolyte composition.[21] Whether these events occur in adults has not been completely elucidated. Even in experimental animals such changes are difficult to identify but can be readily reproduced in the growing animal. The repeated demonstration that alcoholic myopathy may exist in the absence of apparent nutritional deficiency[7] and damage of skeletal muscle occurs in normal human volunteers after consumption of ethanol despite a very adequate dietary intake[14] suggests that nutrition *per se* plays no more than a contributory role.

5. The fifth mechanism given consideration is that of *depressed glycolytic enzyme activity*. In his studies of patients with overt alcoholic myopathy, Perkoff[4] showed that the activity of muscle phosphorylase was abnormally low. This did not occur in all patients with alcoholic myopathy. However, when it was abnormal, it was corrected following abstinence from ethanol for a sufficient period of time.

6. The sixth consideration has concerned *direct inhibition of muscle carbohydrate metabolism*. Chronic administration of ethanol to rats for 9 months resulted in a decrease of muscle lactate content and increased citrate, malate, fumarate, and isocitrate, but no change in ATP, ADP, AMP, or phosphocreatine. Animals pair-fed with glucose demonstrated higher content of glycolytic intermediate compounds.[4]

7. The seventh consideration is *potassium deficiency*. Myopathy and myoglobinuria may occur in some patients with potassium deficiency.[12] Martin,[22] noting that hypokalemia occurs commonly in alcoholics, examined muscle content of K in patients with alcoholic myopathy. Since they were subnormal, he proposed that K deficiency may have been responsible for their myopathy.

EVIDENCE THAT ACUTE MYOPATHY MAY BE INDUCED IN
ALCOHOLICS BY ACUTE HYPOPHOSPHATEMIA

At this point, evidence will be offered suggesting that acute myopathy may often be inadvertently induced or seriously aggravated by well-intentioned refeeding of the chronic alcoholic.

The nutritional status of many chronic alcoholics is tenuous. Consequently, besides possible cellular injury resulting from ethanol per se, these patients commonly have protein-calorie malnutrition, which may at least contribute to a subtle myopathy.

It has been known for many years that patients suffering from severe malnutrition or starvation, if refed overzealously, may become extremely ill and die. Thus, administration of large carbohydrate loads may precipitate acute thiamine deficiency, massive fluid retention, and depression of serum potassium concentration, with consequent cardiac arrhythmias. Such complications are well recognized and appropriately prevented by simultaneous treatment with KCl and vitamins.

In a large number of patients with severe alcoholism and inadequate nutrition, we have repeatedly observed that serum inorganic phosphorus concentration is commonly normal or only slightly depressed at the time of their admission to the hospital but falls sharply within the first 1 to 3 days during the refeeding period. During this time, the urine is virtually phosphorus-free. Of great interest, the precipitous fall of phosphate concentration is commonly associated with

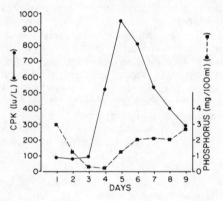

FIGURE 1. Comparison of serial values for serum creatine phosphokinase activity and serum inorganic phosphorus concentration in a chronic alcoholic.

a sharp rise in serum creatine phosphokinase activity. In many of these patients serum CPK activity is also normal at the time of admission. This typical and common pattern is illustrated in FIGURE 1. In this patient, serum phosphorus concentration measured 2.9 mg/100 ml on the day of admission. On day 2 it had fallen to 1.2 mg/100 ml and on day 3 to 0.3 mg/100 ml. Serum CPK activity was 100 international units per liter on the day of admission and remained normal until the fourth day, when it rose and peaked at nearly 1000 units in day 5. The peak value for CPK generally occurs at or immediately after the serum phosphorus falls to its lowest concentration. As apparent muscle injury occurs, phosphorus is released from the cells and the serum phosphorus concentration returns to normal.

MECHANISMS OF ACUTE HYPOPHOSPHATEMIA AND HYPOPHOSPHATURIA

There are 4 mechanisms whereby acute hypophosphatemia may occur.

1. *Rapid cellular uptake* may occur under conditions of starvation following provision of a stimulus for cellular anabolism such as refeeding. Thereby,

phosphate and potassium ions are rapidly taken up by the cell, leading to a sharp decrease in their serum concentration. Such events are not limited to starving alcoholics who are refed but have also been commonly observed in patients recovering from severe protein-calorie malnutrition or diabetic keto-acidosis and those receiving hyperalimentation.

2. *Acute respiratory or metabolic alkalosis* promotes movement of inorganic phosphate into cells. However, it is most unusual to observe a decline of serum phosphorus concentration to values less than 2.0 ml/100 ml as a result of alkalosis per se.

3. *Phosphate trapping* within cells of certain tissues such as the liver, renal cortex, or intestinal epithelium may occur under certain conditions,[23] especially following infusions of fructose.[24] Since those tissues contain fructokinase, fructose is rapidly phosphorylated to fructose phosphates. Phosphate trapping occurs because phosphorylation proceeds at a rate much faster than the phosphorylated intermediates can be utilized.

4. Utilized as an experimental tool, hypophosphatemia may occur in association with *formation of phosphate compounds that cannot be metabolized* by the cell, such as 6-methylglucose.[23]

When the concentration of inorganic phosphate within the cell becomes sufficiently low and occurs in the presence of severe hypophosphatemia, phosphate ions are no longer available to replenish supplies of ATP from ADP. A good amount of evidence indicates that when the concentration of cellular ATP falls below a critical level, structural abnormalities may occur.[23]

THE PATHOPHYSIOLOGY OF ACUTE HYPOPHOSPHATEMIA

During the past 6 years a number of clinical and experimental studies have at least partially characterized the pathophysiology of acute hypophosphatemia. Essentially, 6 major consequences have been described:

1. *Hemolysis.* By and large, this has occurred in malnourished patients receiving hyperalimentation with nutrients containing inadequate phosphate.[25,26] Under these conditions, the cellular content of ATP has been shown to fall markedly and the red cells undergo a series of changes in membrane structure, become smaller and finally hemolyze.

2. *Heart failure.* It is known that acute hypophosphatemia is generally associated with a rapid, sharp fall of red cell 2,3-diphosphoglycerate (2,3-DPG).[25] This decreases the cells' ability to release oxygen to peripheral tissues and in effect creates a state of anoxia. In patients experiencing alcoholic withdrawal who tend to become alkalotic, release of oxygen may be further impaired. Under such conditions, when energy demands are high, anoxia would prevent resynthesis of ATP. The circulatory response to this situation may be one of high output cardiac failure.

3. *Impaired phagocytosis by leukocytes.* This has been described by Jacob et al.[27] Thus, white blood cells must undergo mechanical movement in order to engulf bacteria. This movement is mediated by contractile elements within the cell and requires ATP for its proper function. When ATP supplies are exhausted, both chemotaxis and phagocytosis are impaired and infection occurs.

4. *Hemorrhage.* This has been ascribed to acute impairment of platelet function. Release of platelet factor 3 requires adequate supplies of high-energy phosphates. When these stores within platelets fall, platelet factor 3 cannot be released and normal clotting cannot occur.[27]

5. *Hepatic Anoxia*. Decreased oxygen uptake by the liver has been demonstrated in acute hypophosphatemia by Leevy et al.[28] and has been ascribed to the acute fall in erythrocyte 2,3-DPG content, with consequent hepatocellular anoxia. They suggested that this abnormality could be an important cause of progressive cellular injury in patients with liver disease. This defect is promptly reversed in patients with acute hypophosphatemia by administration of phosphate.

6. *Seizures and Coma*. Coma is preceded by weakness, paresthesia, ataxia, obtundation, and disorientation. Seizures also occur.[29] Autopsy of experimental animals with hypophosphatemia discloses a shrunken brain, similar to the diminution of red cell size before hemolysis.

It is to be emphasized that the foregoing comments do not necessarily refer to depletion but rather a major shift in inorganic phosphate of serum to organic phosphate compounds within the cell contents. Thus, the problem is one of acute *hypophosphatemia* and not total body depletion of phosphorus. However, a state of phosphate depletion could eventually occur following rapid cellular anabolism if adequate dietary phosphate were not provided to subjects rapidly building tissue. However the point must be made that, at least under the initial circumstances, total body phosphorus stores are not necessarily deficient.

EXPERIMENTAL METHODS

Patients admitted to the hospital with a diagnosis of acute alcoholism were screened for increased serum concentrations of CPK and aldolase. Seven noncirrhotic male patients were identified by these criteria and studied within 3 to 7 days after admission. The nature, purpose, and possible risks of the study were explained to all patients and control subjects prior to obtaining their voluntary consent to participate.

Skeletal muscle (10 to 20 mg wet weight) samples were obtained from all patients and control subjects by percutaneous needle biopsy of the right lateral thigh under local anesthesia according to the method described by Nichols et al.[30] Muscle samples were then processed for determination of water and electrolyte content in the manner previously described.[31] The supernatant of the digested sample was also analyzed for inorganic phosphate concentration by the method adapted to the Technicon Autoanalyzer. A second biopsy of skeletal muscle was obtained, immediately frozen in dry ice and acetone, and stored at $-20°C$ for subsequent analysis of skeletal muscle glycogen content by the method described by Lowry et al.[32] Measurements of resting skeletal muscle membrane potential (Em) were obtained by puncturing muscle cells of the right anterior tibial compartment with Ling-type electrodes, using the technique previously reported from this laboratory.[33] This value was used to partition extracellular (ECW) and intracellular (ICW) water compartments according to the passive distribution of chloride by equations previously published.[33] Electrolyte concentrations in ECW were calculated by the use of Donnan factors of 0.96 for cations and 1.04 for anions.

To avoid concentrative changes incident to protein binding, all samples for measurement of blood lactate, serum CPK, and aldolase activity and serum concentrations of sodium, potassium, chloride, phosphate, magnesium, total protein, and albumin were obtained under conditions of free flow. To assess glycogen utilization under anaerobic conditions, an indwelling needle was placed in a large antecubital vein and blood samples for lactate were collected before and at intervals after 1 minute of forearm exercise while arterial flow was occluded by a sphygmomanometer cuff. Lactate was measured by the enzymatic procedure.

RESULTS

Pertinent biochemical details on each patient are presented in TABLE 1. The normal range for CPK activity is 25 to 145 units. It is obvious that CPK activity in serum from patients 2 and 7 was only marginally elevated. Aldolase activity, normally ranging between 0 and 6 milliunits per ml, was elevated in each patient. When these studies were done, serum inorganic phosphorus concentration was below normal in 4 of the 7 patients. In those demonstrating normal serum phosphorus values, CPK values were also higher, suggesting that muscle necrosis had already occurred, thus liberating phosphate from muscle. All patients gave a history of heavy ethanol consumption over many years. Muscle weakness, weight loss, and gastrointestinal upset manifested by anorexia, nausea, and vomiting were prominent symptoms at the time of hospital admission. Muscle cramping and tenderness were present in 3 patients. None of our

TABLE 1
Biochemical Disturbances of Alcoholic Myopathy

Patient	CPK IU/liter	Aldolase mU/ml	Pi mg%	Albumin g%
1.	800	34.0	3.3	3.4
2.	187	34.0	1.0	2.9
3.	208	13.2	0.8	2.3
4.	1924	30.5	3.1	4.0
5.	2470	47.0	2.9	3.5
6.	550	18.2	1.9	2.4
7.	148	19.2	1.8	2.0
Normal Range	25–145	0–6	2.5–4.5	3.5–5.0

patients showed overt myoglobinuria or renal failure. Evidence of hepatic injury was minimal or absent. Six patients recovered and 1 (patient no. 1) unexpectedly died without apparent cause.

MUSCLE COMPOSITION

Muscle swelling in alcoholic myopathy has been observed by physical examination,[1] and electron microscopic studies have suggested that most of the fluid accumulation is intracellular.[6,14]

In agreement, we found that the mean total water content of skeletal muscle was $79.3 \pm 2.1\%$ (S.D.), or 410 ± 47 ml per 100 g fat-free dry weight (FFDW). The mean value in the alcoholic patients was higher than that for control subjects ($p < 0.001$, TABLE 2). Extracellular water was clearly increased in only 3 of 6 patients. Intracellular water was increased in 5 of 6 patients ($p < 0.02$). Potassium content (mEq per 100 g FFDW) of skeletal muscle was clearly normal. In contrast, muscle sodium content was abnormally elevated in 5 of 7 patients ($p < 0.001$). Muscle chloride content was abnormally elevated in 6 of 7 patients ($p < 0.001$). The increased ICW probably had a dilutional

TABLE 2

Skeletal Muscle Composition and Em in Alcoholic and Normal Subjects*

	$\%H_2O$	Na_m^+	Cl_m^-	K_m^+	$PO_{4\,m}$	TW	ECW	ICW
Alcoholic Patients								
1.	81.0	30.0	29.5	43.9	10.5	441	–	–
2.	81.1	22.1	17.0	54.6	18.7	453	120	333
3.	81.8	16.3	12.8	49.5	15.3	451	53	398
4.	76.3	10.8	7.1	44.3	12.4	327	38	289
5.	79.0	21.0	16.5	44.1	10.9	429	104	325
6.	78.8	10.9	9.1	50.0	9.7	378	61	317
7.	77.2	14.4	9.7	45.4	8.4	390	77	313
Mean	79.3	17.9	14.5	47.4	12.3	410	76	329
SD	2.1	6.9	7.6	4.1	3.6	47	31	37
Normal Subjects								
Mean	76.0	9.9	6.4	44.1	24.6	327	50	276
SD	1.6	1.5	1.4	2.8	7.0	32	13	34
p value	<0.01	<0.001	<0.001	N.S.	<0.001	<0.005	N.S.	<0.02

	$[Na^+]i$	$[Cl^-]i$	$[K^+]i$	$\dfrac{[K^+]ECW}{[Na^+]ECW}$	Goldman Em(–mv)	Measured Em(–mv)
Alcoholic Patients						
1.	–	–	–	3.5/140	–	–
2.	14.7	7.3	164	4.8/143	87.3	73.7
3.	23.9	13.3	124	4.4/129	82.3	57.9
4.	18.8	7.4	135	3.8/143	86.8	72.2
5.	17.5	10.6	136	5.5/147	79.3	63.7
6.	7.9	6.9	158	3.5/137	92.9	74.7
7.	14.0	5.2	145	4.0/130	88.4	80.0
Mean	16.1	8.4	144	4.2/138	86.2	70.4
SD	5.4	3.0	15	0.7/7	4.8	8.1
Normal Subjects						
Mean	11.4	4.4	155	4.4/146	87.5	86.7
SD	4.9	0.5	15	0.2/3	3.5	3.1
p value	N.S.	<0.005	N.S.	N.S./<0.02	N.S.	<0.001

*Definition of terms: Na_m^+, Cl_m^-, K_m^+, = mEg per 100 gram fat-free weight (FFDW); PO_4 = millimoles of phosphate per 100 g FFDW; TW, ECW, and ICW = total, extracellular, and intracellular water as ml per 100 g FFDW; $[Na^+]i$, $[Cl^-]i$, $[K^+]i$ = mEg per liter of ICW.

$$\text{Goldman Em} = -61.5 \log \frac{[K^+]i}{[K^+]0 + 0.01\,[Na^+]i}$$

effect on intracellular electrolyte concentrations. Thus, of the 6 values, intracellular potassium concentration was slightly depressed in 2 patients, clearly depressed in 1, and normal in 3. Hypokalemia was not observed. Intracellular sodium concentration was increased in 3 of 6 measurements. Intracellular chloride concentration was increased in all patients ($p < 0.005$). Muscle phosphate content was 12.3 ± 3.6 millimoles, a 50% decrease from normal ($p < 0.001$). Muscle glycogen content in alcoholic myopathy has been reported as normal

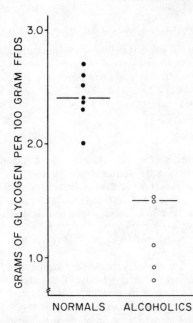

FIGURE 2. Muscle glycogen content in alcoholics and normal subjects.

or decreased.[4] Muscle glycogen content measured in 6 of our patients (FIGURE 2) was markedly depressed in 5, with a mean value of 0.015 ± 0.009 SD gm/gm FFDW. The mean value in 6 control subjects was 0.024 ± 0.002 ($p < 0.05$). Although muscle glycogen content was decreased, ischemic forearm exercise showed a normal lactate response (FIGURE 3).

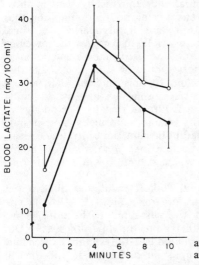

FIGURE 3. Venous blood lactate concentration after ischemic exercise of forearm in alcoholics and normal subjects.

MEMBRANE POTENTIAL

Skeletal muscle Em was abnormally low in all patients. The mean measured Em (TABLE 2) was -70.4 ± 8.1 SD millivolts, significantly lower than the mean control Em of -86.7 ± 3.1 SD mv (p < 0.001). In contrast, the predicted Em, calculated from the Goldman-Hodgkin-Katz equation,[34] was -86.2 ± 4.8 mv, a value not significantly different from that of controls.

DISCUSSION

The studies presented herein show that malnourished, chronic alcoholics with only minimal to moderate evidence of myopathy demonstrated a host of compositional and functional abnormalities of skeletal muscle. With respect to muscle composition, the content of sodium, chloride, and extracellular and intracellular water was commonly elevated. Intracellular edema was first noted as a prominent electron microscopic feature of alcoholic myopathy by Klinker-fuss et al.[6] and was recently confirmed by Song and Rubin.[14] Our studies support their observations of increased ICW.

As in findings reported by Mayer[19] in rats following prolonged administration of ethanol, resting membrane potential in our patients was also abnormally low. Experimental studies have shown that ethanol in concentrations comparable to those found in clinical intoxication decreases the active transport of sodium across cell membranes[18] and increases muscle membrane permeability to sodium.[19] Although muscle sodium content was abnormally high in our patients, average intracellular sodium concentration was higher but not statistically different from normal. However, it is of interest that the 2 patients (no. 4 and 5, TABLE 1) with the highest CPK values also had unquestionably elevated muscle intracellular sodium concentration. In previous studies of uremic[35] or seriously ill patients[33] and potassium-deficient dogs[31] from this laboratory, we postulated that increased membrane permeability to sodium could account for the decreased resting membrane potential characteristically seen in those illnesses. Alternatively, impairment of the electrogenic sodium pump and thus sodium extrusion from skeletal muscle cells in alcoholic myopathy could raise intracellular sodium concentration and be responsible, in part, for the increased water content of the intracellular compartment. The resting membrane potential is thought to be influenced by the concentration ratio of K in the cell and that prevailing in extracellular water. However, our findings indicate that, except for 3 patients, intracellular K concentration was normal. We have made similar observations on patients with chronic renal failure treated by hemodialysis— namely, that resting membrane potential remains abnormally low despite correction of intracellular and extracellular potassium concentration. As an alternative, it might be postulated that potassium ions were somehow bound inside the cell and thereby the ratio Ki/Ko would remain low despite a normal intracellular concentration of K.

In the mild form of alcoholic myopathy, Perkoff et al. described a flat blood-lactate curve in response to ischemic forearm exercise.[4] A low lactate response was confirmed by Nygren[36] but was suspected to be nonspecific, since a similar response was observed in other nonmyopathic illnesses.[37] Our results are different from theirs in that the blood-lactate response to ischemic forearm exercise was clearly normal. An important difference in the time at which the studies were conducted possibly explains this descrepancy. In the studies of Perkoff et al.[4] and Nygren,[37] the ischemic exercise study was performed within 48 hours of admission, whereas our studies were not done until 2–5 days after hospital admission. Also, there is a possibility that the rise of blood lactate concentration to normal values during ischemic exercise does not indicate normal lactate production. Thus, if muscle blood flow during exercise were subnormal, net production—i.e. the product of flow and venoarterial concentration difference—would be subnormal. In these studies, such a possibility was not excluded, since muscle blood flow and simultaneous measurements of lactate in venous and arterial blood were not performed.

Few measurements of muscle glycogen have been made in alcoholic myopathy. In 2 patients with hypokalemic alcoholic myopathy studied by Martin et al., skeletal muscle glycogen content was normal.[22] Experimentally, studies in our own laboratory have shown that K deficiency causes a marked decrease in skeletal muscle glycogen content even in the face of an adequate, balanced caloric intake.[38] Thus, it is rather surprising that glycogen content was normal in the report by Martin et al.[22] One of 3 patients reported by Perkoff et al. had a low muscle glycogen content.[4] In those studies,[4,22] skeletal muscle glycogen content was measured as glucose after acid hydrolysis by nonspecific colorimetric methods and thus may have been spuriously elevated. In the studies reported herein, glycogen was measured by a more specific fluorometric method for glucose after enzymatic hydrolysis of glycogen.[32] In the present study, only 1 of 6 patients had a normal skeletal muscle glycogen content. Our findings would appear consistent with those described in the other forms of myopathy in which glycogen content is often low.[41] Finally, many alcoholic patients suffer from malnutrition, and this per se may be associated with a subnormal muscle glycogen content.[39]

One of the most interesting and perhaps most important findings in this study relates to the abnormally low values for serum phosphorus concentration and muscle phosphate content. The latter finding and the observation that profound hypophosphatemia precedes a rise of CPK activity in such patients suggest that hypophosphatemia could play a role in precipitating a myopathy that before its occurrence was only subtle. The inference is made that a subtle myopathy had already existed, since there is no current evidence to suggest that glucose infusions and hypophosphatemia induce elevation of CPK in normal subjects. Moreover, there is inferential evidence that acute hypophosphatemia could precipitate release of CPK in other conditions in which nutritional disturbances and possibly subtle myopathy could preexist. Thus, in patients treated with insulin for diabetic ketoacidosis, marked hypophosphatemia commonly occurs on the second, third, or fourth day as hyperglycemia comes under control.[40,41] In a report from Perkoff's laboratory,[42] it was observed that 9 of 13 randomly selected patients undergoing treatment for diabetic ketoacidosis showed a rise of serum CPK activity between the 24th and 72nd hours after initiating treatment with insulin. Although serum phosphorus concentration was not measured in those patients, the rise in CPK activity coincides exactly with the most pronounced hypophosphatemia noted by others. The identical observations on CPK activity during treatment for diabetic ketoacidosis were recently confirmed.[43]

Examining the pattern of CPK activity in 50 consecutive patients following a heavy drinking spree, Lafair and Myerson[44] found that typically there was a lag of 24–48 hours after hospital admission before CPK began to rise. Thereafter it rose rapidly and peaked on the 4th or 5th day. They did not measure serum phosphorus concentration. However, this pattern is identical to the one observed by us and coincides with the most pronounced hypophosphatemia.

Observations by others suggesting that acute hypophosphatemia may induce structural damage in other tissues[25,27-29] suggests that it may exert similar effects on skeletal muscle. Although not examined as yet, acute hypophosphatemia could limit the supply of phosphate ions that otherwise passively diffuse into muscle cells and permit regeneration of ATP from ADP. This would be especially likely if there had occurred a stimulus toward increased formation of organic phosphates inside the cell. Indeed, Krebs[45] has stated that within the organism the immediate source of phosphate for cellular nucleotides is the extracellular inorganic $PO_4^=$; therefore profound depletion of inorganic $PO_4^=$ in the extracellular fluids may be a limiting factor in high-energy phosphate synthesis in mammalian cells. Evidence has already been cited to suggest that, at least in the liver,[28] erythrocytes, and brain,[25] depletion of ATP may be responsible for cellular destruction.

From these observations it would appear that attempts to provide calories by means of glucose or fructose infusion or carbohydrate feeding to patients undergoing ethanol withdrawal might be responsible for acute hypophosphatemia. This in turn may precipitate a host of complications that could possibly be averted by phosphate supplementation.

ACKNOWLEDGMENTS

The assistance of Julio Borroto, R.N., Patsy Robinson, James Long, D. L. Morris, and Carol Krumme is gratefully acknowledged.

REFERENCES

1. HED, R., H. LARSSON & F. WAHLGREN. 1955. Acute myoglobinuria, report of a case with a fatal outcome. Acta Med. Scan. 152: 459–462.
2. HED, R. 1955. Three cases of non-familial myoglobinuria. Acta Med. Scan. Suppl. 303: 86–97.
3. FAHLGREN, H., R. HED & C. LUNDMARK. 1957. Myonecrosis and myoglobinuria in alcohol and barbiturate intoxication. Acta Med. Scan. 158: 405–412.
4. PERKOFF, G. T., P. HARDY & E. VÉLEZ-GARCIA. 1966. Reversible acute muscular syndrome in chronic alcoholism. New Eng. J. Med. 274: 1277–1285.
5. PERKOFF, G. T., M. M. DIOSO, V. BLEISCH & G. KLINKERFUSS. 1967. A spectrum of myopathy associated with alcoholism. I. Clinical and laboratory features. Ann. Int. Med. 67: 481–492.
6. KLINKERFUSS, G., V. BLEISCH, M. M. DIOSO & G. T. PERKOFF. 1967. A spectrum of myopathy associated with alcoholism. II. Light and electronmicroscopic observations. Ann. Int. Med. 67: 493–510.
7. PERKOFF, G. 1971. Alcoholic myopathy. Ann. Rev. Med. 22: 125–132.
8. OH, S. J. 1972. Alcoholic myopathy, a critical review. Ala. J. Med. Sci. 9: 79–95.
9. MAYER, R. F. & R. FARCIA-MULLIN. 1972. Peripheral nerve and muscle disorders associated with alcoholism. In The Biology of Alcoholism. B. Kissin & H. Begleiter, Eds. 2: 21–65. Plenum Press. New York, N.Y.
10. DOUGLAS, R. M., J. D. FEWINGS, CASLEY-SMITH, JR. & R. F. WEST. 1966. Recurrent rhabdomyolysis precipitated by alcohol: A case report with physiological and electronmicroscopic studies of skeletal muscles. Aust. Ann. Med. 15: 251–261.
11. FEWINGS, J. D., M. J. D. HANNA, J. A. WALSH & R. H. WHELAN. 1966. The effects of ethyl alcohol on the blood vessels of the hand and forearm in man. Brit. J. Pharmacol. 27: 93–106.
12. KNOCHEL, J. P. & E. M. SCHLEIN. 1972. On the mechanism of rhabdomyolysis in potassium depletion. J. Clin. Invest. 51: 1750–1758.
13. KNUTSSON, E. & S. KATZ. 1967. The effect of ethanol on the membrane perme-

ability to sodium and potassium ions in frog muscle fibres. Acta Pharmacol. Toxical. **25**: 54–64.

14. SONG, S. K. & E. RUBIN. 1972. Ethanol produces muscle damage in human volunteers. Science **175**: 327–328.

15. STREETEN, D. H. P. & A. K. SOLOMON. 1954. Effect of ACTH and adrenal steroids on K transport in human erythrocytes. J. Gen. Physiol. **37**: 643–661.

16. ISRAEL, Y. & H. KALANT. 1963. Effect of ethanol on the transport of sodium in frog skin. Nature (London) **200**: 476–478.

17. ISRAEL-JACARD, Y. & H. KALANT. 1965. Effect of ethanol on electrolyte transport and electrogenesis in animal tissues. J. Cell. Comp. Physiol. **65**: 127–132.

18. ISRAEL, Y., H. KALANT & I. LAUFER. 1965. Effects of ethanol on Na, K. Mg-stimulated microsomal ATPase activity. Biochem. Pharmacol. **14**: 1803–1814.

19. MAYER, R. F. 1973. Recent studies in man and animal of peripheral nerve and muscle dysfunction associated with chronic alcoholism. Ann. N.Y. Acad. Sci. **215**: 370–372.

20. HED, R., C. LUNDMARK, H. FAHLGREN & S. ORELL. 1962. Acute muscular syndrome in chronic alcoholism. Acta Med. Scand. **171**: 585–599.

21. METCOFF, J., S. FRENK, T. YOSHIDA, R. T. PINEDO, E. KAISER & J. D. L. HANSEN. 1966. Cell composition and metabolism kwashiorkor (severe protein-calorie malnutrition in children). Medicine **45**: 365–388.

22. MARTIN, J. B., J. W. CRAIG, R. E. ECKEL & J. MUNGER. 1971. Hypokalemic myopathy in chronic alcoholism. Neurology **21**: 1160–1168.

23. FARBER, F. 1973. ATP and cell integrity. Fed. Proc. **32**: 1534–1539.

24. WOODS, H. F., L. V. EGGLESTON & H. A. KREBS. 1970. The cause of hepatic accumulation of fructose 1-phosphate on fructose loading. Biochem. J. **119**: 501–510.

25. JACOB, H. S. & T. A. AMSDEN. 1971. Acute hemolytic anemia with rigid red cells in hypophosphatemia. New Eng. J. Med. **285**: 1446–1450.

26. LICHTMAN, M. A., D. R. MILLER & R. B. FREEMAN. 1969. Erythrocyte adenosine triphosphate depletion during hypophosphatemia in a uremic subject New Eng. J. Med. **280**: 240–244.

27. YAWATA, Y., P. CRADDOCK, R. HEBBEL, R. HOWE, S. SILVIS & H. JACOB. 1973. Hyperalimentation hypophosphatemia: Hematologic-neurologic dysfunction due to ATP depletion. (abst.). Clin. Res. **21**: 729.

28. RAJAN, K. S., R. LEVINSON & C. M. LEEVY. 1973. Hepatic hypoxia secondary to hypophosphatemia. (abst.). Clin. Res. **21**: 521.

29. SILVIS, S. E. & P. D. PARAGAS, JR. 1973. Paresthesias, weakness, seizures and hypophosphatemia in patients receiving hyperalimentation. Gastroenterology **62**: 513–520.

30. NICHOLS, B. L., C. F. HAZELWOOD & D. J. BARNES. 1968. Percutaneous needle biopsy of quadriceps muscle: Potassium analysis in normal children. J. Pediat. **72**: 840–852.

31. BILBREY, G. L., L. HERBIN, N. W. CARTER & J. P. KNOCHEL. 1973. Skeletal muscle resting membrane potential in potassium deficiency. J. Clin. Invest. **52**: 3011–3018.

32. LOWRY, O. H., R. R. NIRA & J. I. KAPPHAHN. 1957. The fluorometric measurement of pyridine nucleotides. J. Biol. Chem. **224**: 1047–1064.

33. CUNNINGHAM, J. N., N. W. CARTER, F. C. RECTOR & D. W. SELDIN. 1971. Resting transmembrane potential difference of skeletal muscle in normal subjects and severely ill patients. J. Clin. Invest. **50**: 49–59.

34. GOLDMAN, D. E. 1943. Potential impedance and rectification in membranes. J. Gen. Physiol. **27**: 37–60.

35. BILBREY, G. L., N. W. CARTER, M. G. WHITE, J. F. SCHILLING & J. P. KNOCHEL. 1973. Potassium deficiency in chronic renal failure. Kidney Int. **4**: 423–430.

36. NYGREN, A. 1966. Serum creatine phosphokinase activity in chronic alcoholism, in connection with acute alcohol intoxication. Acta Med. Scand. **179**: 623–630.

37. NYGREN, A. 1971. The ischemic lactic acid response and the muscle LDH-isoenzyme pattern in alcoholics. Acta Med. Scand. **190**: 283–285.

38. BLACHLEY, J., J. LONG & J. P. KNOCHEL. 1974. The effect of potassium deficiency on resting muscle glycogen content and its response to exercise. (abst.). Clin. Res. **22:** 39A.
39. VIGNOS, P. J. & J. L. WARNER. 1963. Glycogen, creatine, and high energy phosphate in human muscle disease. J. Lab. Clin. Med. **62:** 579–590.
40. GUEST, G. M. & S. RAPOPORT. 1939. Role of acid soluble phosphorus compounds in red blood cells. Amer. J. Dis. Child. **58:** 1072–1089.
41. DITZEL, J. 1973. Importance of plasma inorganic phosphate on tissue oxygenation during recovery from diabetic ketoacidosis. Horm. Metab. Res. **5:** 471–472.
42. VÉLEZ-GARCIA, E., P. HARDY, M. DIOSO & G. T. PERKOFF. 1966. Cysteine-stimulated serum creatine phosphokinase: Unexpected results. J. Lab. Clin. Med. **68:** 636–645.
43. KNIGHT, A. H., D. N. WILLIAMS, R. J. SPOONER & D. M. GOLDBERG. 1974. Serum enzyme changes in diabetic ketoacidosis. Diabetes **23:** 126–131.
44. LAFAIR, J. S. & R. M. MYERSON. 1968. Alcoholic myopathy, with special reference to the significance of creatine phosphokinase. Arch. Int. Med. **122:** 417–422.
45. KREBS, H. 1959. Rate limiting factors in cell respiration. In Ciba Foundation Symposium on the Regulation of Cell Metabolism: 1–10. Little, Brown. Boston, Mass.

ALCOHOL-RELATED SKELETAL DISORDERS

Paul D. Saville

Creighton University School of Medicine
Omaha, Nebraska 68108

Throughout life, the skeleton is constantly remodeling. Somewhere bone is being torn down by osteoclasts, only to be rebuilt again by osteoblasts. The sequence of events is repeated again and again throughout the skeleton, starting with division of progenitor cells giving rise to daughter cells and the daughter cells giving rise to osteoclasts which resorb bone.

The osteoclasts die off in about 1 month, and osteoblasts now appear formed from the same daughter cells that had originally given rise to osteoclasts. The osteoblasts lay down bone matrix in the resorption cavities or on bone surfaces, and the matrix is 80% calcified within 48 hours, the remaining 20% calcification occurring more slowly. Now the osteoblasts die off within 2 months while a few of them become trapped by mineralized bone, and they become osteocytes in their lacunae. Osteocytes can, under some conditions, effect the release of calcium from their immediate vicinity. There are various factors, such as trauma, which will "turn on" progenitor cells to start off the intense cycle of bone resorption and new bone formation. Even a crack of the lateral malleolus at the ankle will stimulate intense bone activity, not only in the fibula but in the tibia, the femur, and even the iliac bone on the same side. Parathyroid hormone stimulates production of new osteoclasts and, in addition, stimulates osteoclasts to greater activity, thus resorbing and releasing bone mineral. Alcohol may interact with these complex homeostatic relations in a variety of ways. In 1963, Kalbfleish observed that 30 ml of ethanol given to controls and to alcoholics had a similar effect; within 20 minutes there was very nearly 100% increase in urinary calcium excretion and a 167% increase in magnesium excretion, lasting for about 2 hours.[1]

This calcium diuresis tends to lower serum calcium, thus stimulating parathyroid hormone release, which in turn stimulates osteoclasts and osteocytes to resorb calcium from the skeleton. Persistently increased parathyroid hormone stimulates progenitor cells to produce extra osteoclasts.

In the absence of an adequate calcium dietary intake or in the presence of intestinal disease or lack of vitamin D, bone resorption predominates and the skeleton would be expected to become less dense. In the presence of a high calcium diet and a healthy intestinal mucosa, increased calcium absorption should compensate for the increased urinary excretion.

BONE DENSITY CHANGES IN ALCOHOLICS

Standard bone plugs were taken from the left iliac crest of subjects who had died suddenly and unexpectedly in Manhattan and had come to autopsy by the medical examiner. No one with chronic diseases was examined. Among the nonalcoholic subjects, bone density decreased after 50 years of age in women and after 70 years of age in men. Among the alcoholics, all of whom were under 45 years of age, bone density was about the same as that of nonalcoholic men and women over the age of 70.[2] (FIGURE 1).

When fractures occur because of osteoporosis, they are usually found at the

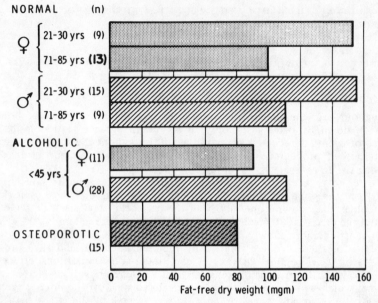

FIGURE 1. Comparison of fat-free dry weights of bones from normal alcoholic and osteoporotic human beings.

hip, the wrist, the upper humerus, and the vertebrae. It is known that the factors that contribute to the production of femoral neck fractures include increasing age, the female sex, and disease. The femoral neck fractures are uncommon in younger men with only mild or moderate trauma. Nilsson compared 70 men under the age of 70 with fractures of the hip due to mild or moderate trauma with 125 aged matched controls.[3] In this series, if subjects with obvious causes for fracture, such as paralysis, epilepsy, multiple sclerosis, and polio, were excluded, about half of the remainder of men with fractured hips had either sustained partial gastrectomy or were chronic alcoholics.[3] This was significantly different from the case of the controls.

Nilsson and Westlin measured bone density at the lower end of the femur using a photon absorption method. They compared a group of control men with a group of chronic alcoholic men as well as a third group of alcoholic men who had sustained fractures. TABLE 1 shows the bone mass in the three groups. There

TABLE 1
Bone Mass in the Forearm of Alcoholics and Controls

| | Number | Age | Bone Mass mg/cm^2 (mean + SD) | |
			Proximal	Distal
Control	56	45 ± 11	708 ± 69	459 ± 87
			0.02 > P > 0.01	0.01 > P > 0.001
Alc. Dept.	58	45 ± 11	675 ± 78	408 ± 84
			P < 0.001	0.1 > P > 0.05
Orthop. Dept.	35	52 ± 9		375 ± 90

were significant differences among them, and these differences increased with increasing age.[4] Alcoholism as a contributing cause to the so-called postmenopausal osteoporosis has not been investigated at this time. It is apparent, however, that under certain conditions, such as those pertaining in the New York study, excessive alcohol consumption can lead to decreasing bone density (osteoporosis) and to metabolic types of fracture, such as that of hip, wrist, humerus, and spine.

ANIMAL STUDY

To further investigate the relationship between alcohol consumption and osteoporosis, a group of rats was fed a nutritionally adequate diet but with ethanol isocalorically replacing sucrose. The ethanol-fed rats developed fatty liver, and although the growth constant was unchanged, it was calculated that the maximal weight they could attain if time were extended indefinitely was less than that of controls. The density of the tibia and femora was found to be a linear function of the animal's weight, and the decrease in density of these bones in the ethanol-fed animals could be explained by the difference in weight between the two groups of animals. Muscle magnesium was not significantly different in the ethanol-fed and control animals.[5]

Subsequent studies, however, might cast a different light on this conclusion. When we compared a group of normal rats to their littermates fed the same diet but restricted to $\frac{2}{3}$ of the quantity so that growth was retarded, the undernourished animals had *more* total body calcium at any given body weight than the controls. The long bones were of the same volume as the controls but had thicker cortices and appeared to sustain a greater load in compression. Thus, rats fed a well-balanced, nutritious diet but restricted in total amount and containing no alcohol grew more slowly but had a superior skeletal mass and increased physical characteristics. On the other hand, the rats whose growth was retarded because alcohol partially replaced sucrose calories did not benefit from their slower growth by having stronger, denser skeletons. Thus, the nature of the growth retardation and the skeletal changes that occur with alcohol consumption has not yet been fully explained. Alcohol consumption may cause osteoporosis in one of several ways: We have mentioned calcium diuresis, which could lead to osteoporosis provided that the subject consumed a diet marginal in calcium content or if alcohol imparied intestinal transport of calcium or if it had a harmful effect on vitamin D metabolism. Alcohol consumption causes a brisk magnesium diuresis, and there is some evidence to show that the parathyroid glands are sensitive to the ionic concentrations of both magnesium and calcium.[6] Thus, alcohol-induced hypomagnesemia could cause chronic stimulation of the parathyroid gland and bone resorption. A third possible mechanism by which alcohol could lead to osteoporosis is through alcohol-stimulated corticosteroid secretion by the adrenal glands and hence to the well-known demineralizing effect of Cushingism on the skeleton.[7]

NONTRAUMATIC OSTEONECROSIS OF BONE

Osteonecrosis of bone may be defined as death of a volume of bone tissue within an anatomical bone. Osteonecrosis is referred to commonly in the English literature as aseptic necrosis or avascular necrosis of bone. Since there is no counterpart to the descriptive adjective avascular, while septic necrosis of bone is now hardly ever seen, these terms should be dropped. Osteonecrosis is classified as either posttraumatic or nontraumatic. The disease occurs most commonly in the head of the femur but may occur elsewhere, such as in the humeral head or in the medial femoral condyle.

We are concerned with the nontraumatic syndrome. This may occur from obstruction to the vascular supply of the femoral head by air emboli in caisson workers; from macrophages in Gaucher's disease; by clumped red cells in sickle cell anemia, but in most cases none of these conditions is present. In about half the patients with osteonecrosis of the nontraumatic variety the patient is an alcoholic or at least a heavy drinker of alcohol. About $\frac{2}{3}$ of these patients are men, and the disease occurs bilaterally in over 50% of cases. Symptoms consist of severe pain in the hip. Pain frequently starts quite suddenly and radiographs reveal no abnormality for at least 2 months. Early radiographic lesion appears as a subchondral lucency followed some time later by increased density within the head of the femur. Increased density results from attempts of living bone surrounding the infarcted area to repair the damage and lay down new bone on the dead bone. Much dead bone is resorbed, and at this stage of the disease the mechanical integrity of the femoral head may be jeopardized, and it may partially collapse under weight bearing. When the femoral head no longer fits the acetabulum, serious disability and restriction of motion results. Sometimes there is destruction of articular cartilage and a severe form of osteoarthritis of the hip develops.

In 30 patients with osteonecrosis of the hip, Jones et al.[8] found lipuria in 9, and intravascular fat globules were seen within 2 resected femoral heads. Liver disease was demonstrated in 87% of patients; and they speculated that showers of fat emboli were released by the liver, some obstructing the blood supply to the femoral head. It is well known that alcoholics do develop fat emboli; for example, Lynch et al. examined 268 consecutive autopsy cases, and $\frac{3}{4}$ of chronic alcoholics with liver disease had demonstrable fat emboli in lungs, brain, and other tissues.[9] Jones injected lipidol into 26 rabbits and found microemboli concentrated in the metaphysis of the proximal and distal femur and tibia. After 24 hours, emboli were found in the subchondral capillaries of the femoral head.

Alcohol consumption, even in moderate amounts, has recently been shown to cause marked hyperlypemia in susceptible persons. This could explain why the disease does not occur in more than a small fraction of alcoholics and also would help to explain why the disease is seen much more frequently in men. Osteonecrosis will also occur spontaneously in nonalcoholics who are hyperlypemic, with or without the presence of pancreatitis.

DIAGNOSIS

Osteonecrosis should be suspected when severe hip pain unaccompanied by other evidence of arthritis occurs in middle-aged or older subjects especially men who are heavy drinkers. At first, physical examination will reveal limitation of movement in all directions because of pain. The patient will walk with a limp, and pain may be referred to the knee on the same side. A radiograph will reveal no significant abnormality for at least 2 months after the onset of the condition, but radioisotopic bone scans will usually show an abnormality in the head of the femur at this early stage. At this time, and before any deformities have occurred, the patient should be taken off weight bearing. He should also stop drinking. Radiographs should be repeated after about 2 months. For severe disease some authorities recommend the insertion of a bone graft up the femoral neck and into the head so as to speed repair. When articular cartilage is involved, a rapid onset of secondary arthritis will occur and a total hip prosthesis becomes necessary, since the natural repair process cannot result in a painless, functioning hip.

SUMMARY

Alcohol consumption has been shown to cause osteoporosis and an increased risk of fracture from mild to moderate trauma to the hip, the wrist, the upper humerus, and the spine. A syndrome of nontraumatic osteonecrosis of the hip is being recognized with increased frequency. A high porportion of these individuals regularly consume large quantities of alcohol, which may cause ostenecrosis through the blockage of end arteries by fat emboli. This hip disease may cause prolonged and severe disability, especially in men. If excessive alcohol consumption is a common problem in the Western world, it is likely to contribute significantly to disabling skeletal disease in older persons.

REFERENCES

1. KALBFLEISH, J. M., R. D. LINDEMANN, H. E. GINN & W. O. SMITH. 1963. Effects of ethanol administration on urinary excretion of magnesium and other electrolytes in alcoholic and normal subjects. J. Clin. Invest. **42:** 1471–1475.
2. SAVILLE, P. D. 1965. Changes in bone mass with age and alcoholism. J. Bone Joint Surg. **47-A:** 492–499.
3. NILSSON, B. E. 1970. Conditions contributing to fracture of the femoral neck. Acta Chir. Scand. **136**
4. NILSSON, B. E. & N. E. WESTLIN. 1973. Changes in bone mass in alcoholics, Clin. Orthop. Related Res. **90:** 229.
5. SAVILLE, P. D. & C. S. LIEBER. 1965. The effect of alcoholism on growth, bone density and muscle magnesium in the rat. J. Nutr. **87:** 477.
6. TARGOVNIK, J. H. & L. M. SHERWOOD. 1969. Regulation by calcium and magnesium of parathyroid hormone production in vitro. 51st Meeting of the American Endocrine Society. New York, N.Y.
7. SANTISTEBAN, G. A. & C. A. SWINYARD. 1956. The effect of ethyl alcohol on adrenal cortical activity in mice. Endocrinology **59:** 391–397.
8. JONES, J. P., R. M. JAMESON & E. P. ENGLMAN. 1968. Alcoholism, fat embolism, and avascular necrosis. J. Bone Joint Surg. **50-A:** 1065–1968.
9. LYNCH, M. J. G., F. S. RAPHAEL & T. P. DIXEON. 1959. Fat embolism in chronic alcoholism. Arch. Pathol. **67:** 68.

THE SKIN IN DIAGNOSIS OF ALCOHOLISM

Karlheinz Woeber

Medical Faculty
University of Bonn
Bonn
and Department of Dermatology
Luisen-Hospital
51 Aachen
Federal Republic of Germany

Studying the latest literature on chronic alcoholism and its effects on the human body, one sees that the skin, as the largest organ, plays no special part, mainly because there are more serious diseases to be expected in the internal organs. On the other hand, the public opinion that alcoholism has a direct visible effect on the body's surface—i.e., the skin and the mucous membranes—has not yet been refuted, and even today such symptoms are believed to indicate alcohol abuse. The "drinker's nose," the rosacea, or the rhinophyma are an indication for some that the bearer has a chronic preference for alcohol. It would make things much easier if by such simple external signs we could avoid tiresome investigations. But research has found that there are primary causes for these dermatoses, as will be shown later. Nevertheless, it does not seem meaningless to examine the reality and value of skin changes caused by the chronic use of alcohol and therewith perhaps aid the physician working in this field.

Dermatologists generally examine the entire skin and mucous membranes, as in the eyes, anal region, and, especially, the mouth cavity. Since chronic alcohol consumption influences noticeably the metabolism of the liver, changes of the skin that indicate liver affections can be expected.

PRURITUS GENARALISATUS

This primary invisible dermatosis, to be noticed only by scratch marks as a single symptom, appears quite frequently along with abnormalities of the liver. This itching of the skin can exist as the only symptom up to 2 years before cirrhosis of the liver can be proved by laboratory or clinical examination. According to Wust, itching should be present in 40% of liver diseases, accompanied in 80% by cell necrosis and round-cell infiltration. The reason for this dermatosis is not yet clear. Increase in bile acids or histamine, presence of toxic liver substances, potentiation of the autonomic nervous system, appearance of vasoactive substances are mentioned as being responsible. Sometimes a so-called lichenification of the skin follows this skin disease, a result of numerous and ever returning scratch marks.

PIGMENTATION

Liver cirrhosis patients are known for their dirty-gray skin color, the biliary melanodermia, which also can be identified on the mucous membranes of the mouth and on the face (chloasma faciei). Here we are dealing with different shades of color corresponding with the seriousness of the liver disease. It is possible that an increased secretion of indole is responsible in this case. Formation of N-acetylserotonine is greatly reduced, so that various enzymatic processes may cause an unrestricted pigmentation of the skin. Copper will accumulate in the liver and is co-responsible for the skin pigmentation. We will discuss the metabolism of iron later.

ALTERATIONS OF THE NAILS AND FINGERS

We will not discuss these changes here, even though they are observable, because their appearance is not typical enough to be diagnosed or considered as a symptom by an untrained person.

CHANGES OF THE HAIR

With chronic liver diseases it seems to be of interest to observe the alteration of the hairs in the axillary and pubic regions. The hair of the axillary region is reduced, while the pubic hair becomes more feminine and less kinky. This symptom, which in older patients is often only a result of decreased production of hormones, is significant in human beings of middle age suffering from liver disease and may precede any laboratory findings.

CHANGES IN THE MOUTH CAVITY

It is worthwhile to notice the purple-cyanosed discoloration of the tongue and its vertical furrow (split) on the upper surface caused by the chronically congested liver. Besides this we can observe the smooth red surface of the tongue and the so-called lacquered lips. The tongue appears extraordinarily smooth but moist with an atrophic appearance. Its color is red as far as it is not altered by a coating. These changes of the tongue are reversible and can well be used as an indicator in therapy of liver disease.

VASCULAR CHANGES OF THE SKIN

In the German literature Martini mentioned this symptom for the first time around 1950, whereas in 1886 Bouchard already considered the spider nevus as an indication of a liver disease. This term was derived from the New York underworld, where barmaids estimated the degree of their customers' liver cirrhosis by this symptom. It is remarkable that nevi aranei chiefly appear on the regions of the skin exposed to sunlight. From the point of view of pathology we are dealing with dilated arteries of the subcutaneous arterial net, which extends into subepidernal spider-ampullae but never forms an arteriovenous anastomosis.

These skin-vascular changes that occur with cirrhosis of the liver are also noticeable in pregnant women and in adolescents, but only temporarily, during this specific period. I should mention the palmar erythema, a spotlike redness of the skin of the thumb and the ball of the little finger. The erythema is most visible when the hand is stretched. In pregnant women the same temporary findings are observed, too. The erythema is probably due to the expansion of the arterioles and capillary vessels, which are permeated by arteriovenous anastomoses.

Besides the spider nevi we often find in the same patients the so-called white spot disease, which according to Martini stands in close connection and relationship to spider nevi. It occurs mostly after cooling of the skin and is serious only when found in areas of predilection and in correlation with spider nevi. The white spots occur mostly on the arterial supply regions of the skin and consequently can be seen on the forearms, the upper thighs, the buttocks, and the sacral area. The spots vary between pinpoints and peas in size. In the center of the spots the above-mentioned spider nevi are frequently present. According to Martini, white-spotting and spider nevi are, in the view of pathophysiology, joint phenomena of a neurovascular alteration. There are different theories for the cause of vasodilatation. Some consider bile acids as vasoactive substances; others mention a depressor or excitor mechanism. Also, hepatic metabolic products are thought responsible for these vascular changes.

PORPHYRIA CUTANEA TARDA

A very interesting and characteristic disease is porphyria cutanea tarda, and dermatologists have mentioned it for many years as occuring in connection with liver diseases. Recent research has shown that a hereditary latent enzyme deficiency is the most likely basis for this disease, which under the influence of UV-light causes an increased rate of change of amino-levulinic-acid into uroporphyrin and increased new growth of protoporphyrin stages in the liver. Moreover, the siderosis of the liver, which is very pronounced in the course of a cirrhosis, has a specific pathogenetic meaning, because there is in most patients an increased absorption of iron in the liver cells. The erythrocytes of these patients are believed to have an increased sensitivity to light. Because of the increased deposit of iron in the liver cells, blocking of the enzymes may occur at the mitochondria. According to Heilmeyer, this explains sufficiently the impairment of the enzyme function.

The influence of alcohol so often mentioned in the personal history of the tarda patients—this disease mostly strikes masons and carpenters working in the open air—must be considered under the aspect of the latent enzyme deficiency. Apparently both factors of alcohol and UV-light coincide here and lead to the recurrent attacks of erythematous, vascular, and blisterlike changes of the skin in light-exposed areas.

The iron-metabolism disturbance can be diagnosed easily by laboratory determination of the serum iron, which will be increased, like the porphyrin in the urine.

ROSACEA

As mentioned before, rosacea appears in close relation with chronic alcohol abuse, as has often been noted. There are, however, many causes for this disease. There is no question that, besides gastrointestinal disturbances, liver disease is responsible. Yet it would be wrong to cite alcoholic effects in all cases of this affliction, even though this would be correct in specific cases. The doctor not fully trained in the dermatological field might remember that the spider nevus also occurs mainly around the nose and could thus give the impression that the patient is suffering from rosacea, so that after this detour we are again talking about "the drinker's nose."

SKIN ASPECT

Here it seems correct to mention the visible skin in general in cases of chronic alcoholics. The rubefacience of skin through alcohol is well known. It localizes mainly in the center of the face. The outlines seem emphasized and the skin appears more oily and shiny. A conjuctivitis and a thickening of the margin of the eyelid occurs, and the skin appears puffed and swollen. This stage changes drastically with further alcohol abuse. The skin looks wrinkled, flabby, and corrugated. Its color turns grayish-blue. The patients look older and wear a dull expression.

ANDROLOGICAL QUESTIONS

Before I come to the end I would like to mention quite another aspect, andrology. As shown above, certain liver diseases that occur with endocrine disturbances explain the rise of certain skin syndromes. The diseased liver cannot inactivate estrogenic substances, so that the pituitary gland's function is inhibited. An imbalance of estrogen-androgenic hormones is caused by this and gynecomastia hepatica may occur. This is connected with a testicular atrophy and regressive symptoms, with diminishing of libido and the appearance of impotence. Gynecomastia will often be seen in countries where alcohol has an important place in everyday social life. Here it would be too far-fetched, though very interesting, to talk about the influence of alcohol on sperm and spermatogenesis.

This brief survey of alcohol and its effects on the skin, which is certainly incomplete, may show that none of the discussed phenomena is proof of alcoholic abuse or an alcoholic disease. Yet there are quite a number of symptoms, characteristic enough for the practitioner and especially for the specialist, so that he cannot avoid thinking or if necessary speaking of a chronic alcoholic damage when he observes changes of the skin in connection with other characteristic hints. This is true even if as primarily a dermatologist he is not expected to treat alcoholics, except when called on to do so in his special field. The skin may thus be a guide to those colleagues who deal intensively with the overall problem of the diagnosis and therapy of the chronic alcoholic.

INTRODUCTION

Kenneth Williams

Alcoholics often are found to have an abnormal hemogram. Until recently, the frequently coexisting chronic infection, liver disease, and malnutrition have been thought to be the primary causes. Increasingly, it has been appreciated that alcohol alone is capable of producing several types of hematologic abnormalities. Disease of the red blood cells, white blood cells, and platelets attributable to alcohol have now been described.

The red blood cell is pathologically affected at nearly every stage of its cycle in the body by the toxic effect of alcohol. Dr. Hillman's paper describes the impairment of red blood cell production in the bone marrow by alcohol, which also has a dramatic effect on the erythrocyte's maturation, delivery, and life span.

Alcohol is now recognized as a folic acid antagonist, blocking the effect of this vitamin at several levels, including: producing a malabsorption of folate and decreasing serum and liver folate levels. Folate deficiency may be the key hematologic abnormality in alcoholic liver disease. Folic acid deficiency anemia, almost invariably secondary to alcoholism, may be the most common type of anemia seen in university medical centers.

A possible mechanism for the development of cellular depletion of folate in alcoholic subjects is described in Dr. Hines's paper. His study also suggests a direct pathologic effect of excess alcoholic intake on vitamin B_6 metabolism. This would produce defective heme production by affecting the coenzyme system. Erythrocyte abnormalities can also occur from a pathologic effect of alcohol on iron metabolism. Thus, a sideroblastic, hypochromic anemia in which the red blood cells appear similar to that seen in iron deficiency is found in alcoholism. Further effect on red blood cell survival is seen by an effect of alcohol in producing several types of hemolytic syndromes.

The clinical picture of lead poisoning with anemia, abdominal pain, vomiting, delirium, and convulsions can be produced in alcoholics by the ingestion of illicitly distilled alcoholic beverages containing methanol. In addition, the alcoholic frequently has increased loss of red blood cells through bleeding from a number of potential sites, especially in the gastrointestinal tract or because of thrombocytopemia.

Transient depression of the platelet count in association with heavy consumption of alcohol has been recognized as a relatively common clinical entity. In addition, the structure and functioning of platelets in alcoholics appears to be impaired and their life span shortened. Dr. Cowan's paper reviews our current state of knowledge of the mechanisms involved.

ALCOHOL AND HEMATOPOIESIS

Robert S. Hillman

Division of Hematology
University of Washington Medical School
Seattle, Washington 98195

The adverse effects of alcohol on hematopoiesis have been well documented. While anemia is perhaps the most common manifestation of alcohol toxicity, abnormalities in platelet and white blood cell production and function may also be appreciated. The clinical incidence and characteristics of these hematological abnormalities have only recently been the subject of 2 excellent reviews.[1,2] This discussion will not attempt, therefore, to review all the clinical aspects of alcohol-induced hematological disorders. Rather, it will direct primary attention to new information accumulating as to the biochemical and physiological mechanisms involved in the alcohol effect.

BACKGROUND

The hematopoietic system is an excellent model for the study of any potential toxin. Because of the high level of specialization of individual cell lines and the rapid turnover of cells, the parent hematopoietic organ, the bone marrow, must maintain an ideal environment for cell proliferation, maturation, and daily delivery of a large number of new cells to circulation. In the case of red cell production, this involves the stimulation and proliferation of erythropoietin-sensitive stem cells, maturation of committed erythroblasts with synthesis of a large amount of hemoglobin, and then denucleation and delivery of adult erythrocytes of normal size, shape, and pliability. As for the white blood cell and platelet, a similar proliferation and maturation sequence is required, although along different, highly specialized functional lines. In each situation, any toxin that can interfere with the mechanisms required for stimulation of stem cells, the proliferative-mitotic cell cycle, the synthesis of specialized proteins, or the development of a normal cell membrane and intracellular metabolic machinery will have a dramatic effect on the ability of the bone marrow to provide the number and type of cells required for cell replacement. In addition, abnormalities within the vascular compartment, reticuloendothelial system, or individual organs can lead to marked changes in cell life span and function, increasing the demand on the marrow. This puts a further burden on the hematopoietic system, often demanding 3–6 times normal rates of cell production to maintain a normal circulating cell level. Obviously, the marrow must be capable of providing the increased level of substrate nutrients and maturation environment that can support this marked expansion of cell production. Borderline deficiencies of major substrates or a relatively minor effect of a toxin will be uncovered and magnified with this demand for higher levels of cell production.

From clinical studies, alcohol has now been implicated as a toxin at nearly every step of this cell proliferation, maturation, delivery, and life-span sequence. Direct suppression of megakaryocytopoiesis has been suggested by several investigators.[3–8] A similar mechanism has been considered in explaining the appearance of leukopenia in alcoholic subjects. While a direct toxic effect of alcohol on red cell proliferation has not been clearly documented, erythropoietin stimulation and cell proliferation may be suppressed as a part of tissue inflammation secondary to alcohol damage. Thus, subjects with alcoholic hepatitis generally demonstrate an anemia characteristic of inflammatory hypoproliferation. Perhaps the most frequent and dramatic toxic effect of alcohol is towards the maturation sequence of cell production. This is related primarily to interference with the availability of folic acid, pyridoxal-5-phosphate, and, in the case of the erythrocytic series, iron. Here, all of the potential adverse effects of alcohol come to bear. Not only is there an apparent inhibition of the metabolic pathways that rely on folic acid and pyridoxal-5-phosphate, but also the mere act of alcohol ingestion requires a major decrease in the dietary intake of these essential vitamins. The importance of this dietary deprivation in the face of a relatively high caloric intake has been repeatedly emphasized in clinical studies.[3,9-13] As so nicely demonstrated by Lindenbaum and Lieber,[14] alcoholics maintained on an excellent intake of protein, vitamins, and minerals during long periods of alcohol ingestion do not demonstrate the same high incidence of anemia, leukopenia, and thrombocytopenia apparent in alcoholics admitted to hospitals for complications of alcoholism. At the same time, all of the alcohol effect on folic acid metabolism cannot be attributed to associated dietary restriction. As first shown by Sullivan and Herbert,[4] alcohol will still interfere with cell maturation and production despite the intake of the apparent minimum daily requirement of folic acid. Thus, a specific blocking effect of alcohol on the internal kinetics of folic acid has been suggested.

Recently, a great deal of attention has also been directed towards pyridoxal-5-phosphate (PLP) metabolism and its relationship to abnormal cell maturation and the appearance of abnormal, iron-laden mitochondria in the marrows of alcoholic individuals. Several clinical studies have demonstrated a high incidence of abnormal and ring sideroblasts in chronic alcoholic patients admitted to hospitals for the complications of alcoholism.[10,15] Inasmuch as PLP plays a major role in mitochondrial porphyrin and heme formation, the same questions raised for folic acid metabolism must also be asked concerning the dietary availability and internal kinetics of pyridoxine. Moreover, because of the close association of the two defects in alcoholic patients, possible interrelationships between the two vitamins must be considered.

Prolonged alcohol ingestion can also effect adult red cell, white cell, and platelet life span and function. Hepatic dysfunction, reticuloendothelial hypertrophy (hypersplenism) and alterations in the plasma environment can interact with abnormalities of adult cell structure and function to result in a hemolytic anemia, leukopenia, or thrombocytopenia. Variations in demand, cell turnover, and cell type tend to influence the apparent severity of this form of alcohol toxicity. Marked leukopenia is most common in patients demonstrating a combination of prolonged alcohol ingestion, marked folate deficiency, and ongoing infection, while more subtle changes in leukocyte function may occur without an associated fall in the number of circulating cells.[16-20] Changes in platelet life span and organ distribution have been demonstrated as an almost immediate effect of alcohol ingestion.[6,22] Severe hemolysis requires a combination of hypersplenism and a change in red cell shape and perhaps pliability. Thus, markedly shortened life spans are usually associated with the appearance in circulation of spur cells (acanthocytes) or stomatocytes.[23-27] Moreover, major abnormalities in the plasma environment, especially the composition and concentration of lipids, often accompany the appearance of severe hemolysis.[28-36]

BIOCHEMICAL AND PHYSIOLOGICAL MECHANISMS

The biochemical and physiological mechanisms underlying the cellular toxicity of alcohol are best understood for the disturbances of red cell production, maturation, and life span. While many of the same principles should apply to white cell and platelet abnormalities, detailed studies of these areas have yet to be carried out. Four major metabolic abnormalities may be identified. These are (1) the restriction of cell production secondary to tissue inflammation, (2) interference with folic acid absorption and metabolism, (3) disruption of mitochondrial function, normal PLP metabolism, and heme synthesis, and (4) the development of membrane abnormalities which shorten cell life span.

INFLAMMATORY SUPPRESSION OF CELL PRODUCTION

Inherent in prolonged alcohol exposure with dietary restriction is the development of tissue damage, especially to liver parenchyma. As a part of this process, it is common to see associated inflammation, for the alcoholic is prone to repeated episodes of hepatitis and pancreatitis as well as complicating bacterial infections. This then sets the stage for the development of a hypoproliferative anemia. The presence of acute and/or chronic inflammation leads to a reduction in both erythropoietin stimulation and the availability of iron to maturing normoblasts.[37-39] This results in a suppression of the normal proliferative response to anemia and, in situations of prolonged, severe anemia, the production of a poorly hemoglobinized adult erythrocyte. In the evolution of this abnormality, the erythroid marrow is the victim. The defect in cell proliferation is not related to any direct alcohol effect on stem cells but rather reflects the inflammatory suppression of erythropoietin release and blockade of iron delivery from reticuloendothelial cells to normoblasts. When inflammation is not present, alcohol per se has no obvious effect on erythropoietin stimulation or the availability of iron, other than perhaps to slightly increase the serum iron and the potential level of iron supply.[14]

INTERFERENCE WITH FOLIC ACID ABSORPTION AND METABOLISM

In 1962, Herbert[40] performed the first study of the daily requirements for folic acid in normal man and the rate of induction of megaloblastic erythropoiesis with dietary deprivation. This demonstrated the importance of normal stores as a buffer against inadequate dietary intake. Subsequently, Sullivan and Herbert,[4] in a series of studies of severe alcoholic patients with major disruptions of normal dietary pattern, reported a high incidence of folic acid deficiency and associated hematological abnormalities. Moreover, they demonstrated a potential inhibitory effect of continued alcohol ingestion on the hematological recovery of these patients. This has since led to a number of studies of the potential toxicity of alcohol on folate uptake by the gut, absorption and storage in hepatic tissue, and, more recently, the kinetics of folic acid turnover in serum and storage sites.

Despite many studies of alcohol toxicity on folic acid absorption from the gut, results have been variable and inconclusive.[41-44] Certainly, alcohol has major adverse effects on gut function, including interference with the absorption of some dietary constituents.[45,46] However, it has been difficult to show a specific site and magnitude of blockade of folate absorption. This has led to consideration of other potential sites of alcohol toxicity in the internal metabolism of folic acid (FIGURE 1). Following ingestion, both methylated and non-

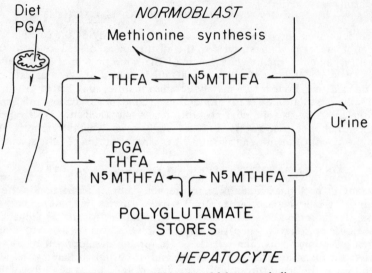

FIGURE 1. Internal kinetics of folate metabolism.

methylated mono and diglutamates are absorbed by the small intestine, transferred to plasma, and delivered to tissue for utilization or storage. Hepatic and renal tissue are apparently the most avid sites for folate storage, with the liver also acting as an important resource for reduction and methylation of pteroylglutamic acid (PGA) and tetrahydrofolic acid (THFA) to form N-5-methyltetrahydrofolic acid (N-5-MTHFA). As a storage site, the liver has the enzymatic mechanisms for the development and breakdown of polyglutamate forms of both nonmethylated and methylated folate congeners. According to need, polyglutamate stores are deconjugated, and the monoglutamate form of N-5-MTHFA (as well as other reduced and methylated folates) is delivered to serum for transport to end organs, for participation in DNA and protein synthesis. In the case of N-5-MTHFA, this participation involves methyl group transfer with subsequent recycling of the THFA for remethylation.

Since each of the several steps of this postulated folic acid cycle is a potential site for alcohol toxicity, detailed studies of alcohol effect on serum and tissue levels of folic acid have recently been attempted.[47,48] Perhaps the most striking finding from this work has been the demonstration of a rapid suppression of circulation N-5-MTHFA levels with alcohol ingestion (FIGURE 2). Within 6–8 hours of receiving oral or intravenous doses of alcohol, normal individuals will show a dramatic fall in the serum levels of N-5-MTHFA. With continued ingestion and dietary restriction, the serum level will fall into the deficient range within the next 24–72 hours and the induction of megaloblastic erythropoiesis be accelerated.[10,47] This phenomenon cannot be explained as either an effect of dietary restriction alone, an increased propensity for renal excretion of the vitamin, or a specific alcohol-induced artifact in the bacteriological (L. casei) assay. The urinary output of N-5-MTHFA, as shown for the subject studied in FIGURE 2, remains constant throughout the period of serum N-5-MTHFA depression. Extensive studies of the L. casei assay technique have failed to demonstrate any inhibitory effect of alcohol or alcohol metabolic products on the assay procedure, and recent work with nonbacteriological assays have confirmed the serum fall.[47,49] Attention must be directed, therefore, toward tissue mechanisms for the support of the serum level, specifically the rate of folate uptake into tissue stores, metabolic conversions to methylated congeners, storage patterns as polyglutamates, and the rate of transfer of methylated forms such as N-5-MTHFA from liver and tissue stores to serum.

Only rudimentary investigations in this area are presently available. Studies of nonmethylated folate uptake, using unlabeled and isotopic forms of PGA, have now been performed in normal, folate-deficient, and alcoholic individuals.[48,50-56] While these studies have failed to demonstrate any immediate defect in the rate of tissue uptake or the subsequent conversion to tissue-bound and methylated forms with acute alcohol ingestion, severe, prolonged alcoholism with cirrhosis has been shown to interfere with PGA uptake and storage in liver tissue.[56] In the latter situation, therefore, the normal mechanism for tissue storage of folate would be in part unavailable for the support of serum N-5-MTHFA levels and delivery. This could well explain a more rapid decline in serum N-5-MTHFA levels in chronic alcoholic and cirrhotic patients with even brief episodes of dietary deprivation and alcohol ingestion. However, the observed, rapid suppression of serum N-5-MTHFA levels in normal volunteers with normal folate stores is not so easily explained. To fully understand the acute toxicity of alcohol, future attention must be directed at the complex conversions of folates to storage forms, the role of conjugation and deconjugation enzymes, and pool kinetics of methylated folates and their transport to serum.

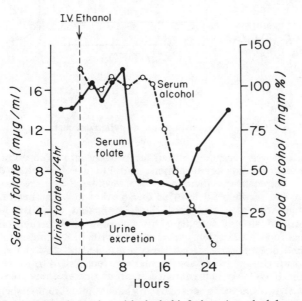

FIGURE 2. Serum folate depression with alcohol infusion: A marked depression of serum N-5-MTHFA occurs 6–8 hours after the initiation of an infusion of ethanol sufficient to raise blood alcohol levels to 100 mg per 100 ml. This effect clears soon after the return of alcohol levels to normal.

MITOCHONDRIAL DYSFUNCTION AND ABNORMAL PLP METABOLISM

With the demonstration of a high incidence of ring sideroblasts in the marrows of alcoholic patients, considerable interest has been generated in the study of the effects of alcohol on mitochondrial structure and function. In the latter category, the kinetics of pyridoxine uptake and intracellular conversion to pyridoxal-5-phosphate (PLP) for subsequent utilization in porphyrin and heme production, has received the most attention (FIGURE 3). Though understanding of the internal metabolic sequences of pyridoxine is still rather unsophisticated, it appears that the major portion of individual cell PLP is generated from dietary pyridoxine by way of intracellular kinase and oxidase enzymes. While tissue storage of pyridoxine and/or PLP for periods of dietary lack is probable, a specific remote storage site with subsequent transport of PLP to end organs has not been documented. Thus. recent studies have looked primarily at the steps leading to intracellular PLP generation as they might be affected by alcohol. Hines and Cowan have carried out several studies of ring-sideroblastic

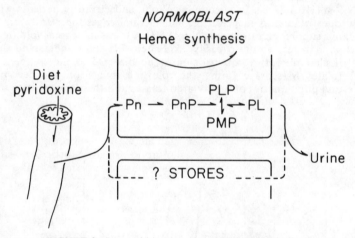

FIGURE 3. Internal kinetics of pyridoxine metabolism.

alcoholic patients with respect to their levels of serum PLP and their responsiveness to therapeutic trials of pyridoxine and PLP.[15,57,58] They demonstrated a correlation between the incidence of sideroblastic manifestations and the depression of the serum PLP level, a finding that now has been confirmed by other investigators.[59] In addition, they implicated pyridoxine kinase as a potential point of alcohol toxicity. This was supported in their clinical studies by the eradication of the sideroblastic defect with PLP administration, whereas pyridoxine had no apparent effect. However, in recent studies by Lu-Meng and Li,[59] *in vitro* measurements of enzyme activity have failed to show any decrease in pyridoxine kinase or oxidase activity in circulating erythrocytes of alcoholics. Instead, these authors have postulated that a membrane-associated neutral phosphatase is responsible for an increased intracellular hydrolysis of PLP and subsequent reduction in the serum PLP level.

At the same time, a direct toxic effect of alcohol on mitochondrial structure can not be ignored. Electron-microscopy studies have shown major distortions of mitochondrial anatomy in alcoholic marrows. This is reminiscent of the effect of other toxins, such as lead, in which mitochondrial distortion and iron deposition, with formation of ring sideroblasts, is also a common finding. This fact, that disruption of mitochondria with the formation of ring sideroblasts is not specific for alcohol toxicity, must be recognized before all investigations are directed at defects in PLP metabolism. Moreover, it is also important to be aware of the potential close relationships of folic acid deficiency, megaloblastic erythropoiesis, and the defects within the mitochondria. As part of the megaloblastic erythropoietic state, serum iron levels rise sharply, providing an increase in iron supply to maturing normoblasts. Together with the prolonged intermitotic time and potential increase in absorption of iron into the developing cell, this can lead to an accumulation of iron within cell structure in excess of that needed for hemoglobin production. Thus, the propensity to develop ring sideroblasts or abnormal sideroblast forms may be greatly encouraged by the megaloblastic state. The importance of this relationship is further emphasized by the relative frequency of both the megaloblastic and sideroblastic defects in the same patient. In fact, Eichner and Hillman[10] demonstrated in their clinical survey that virtually all sideroblastic patients were also markedly megaloblastic and that ring sideroblasts did not develop until marrow morphology is clearly megaloblastic in subjects maintained on abnormal diets and alcohol for prolonged periods.

MEMBRANE ABNORMALITIES WITH SHORTENED CELL LIFE SPAN

In contrast to the sudden depression of circulating platelets in patients acutely ingesting alcohol, there appears to be little toxic effect of alcohol on the life span of normal adult erythrocytes. At the same time, several types of hemolytic anemia have been described with prolonged alcohol ingestion. In these situations, there appears to be a combination of morphological distortions of circulating erythrocytes and major changes in plasma environment and reticuloendothelial cell activity. Most recently, a hemolytic syndrome associated with the appearance on smear of stomatocytes has been described.[23] In contrast to the reports on patients with acanthocytosis, the stomatocytosis patients showed a relatively mild hemolytic anemia and virtually no change in plasma environment. Acanthocytic patients (spur-cell subjects) usually show marked hypersplenism, severe liver disease, and changes in the cholesterol-to-phospholipid ratio in the cell membrane.[24-28] This has led to studies of the hepatic synthesis of lecithin-cholesterol acyltransferase. When this enzyme is deficient, free cholesterol accumulates in plasma and on the cell membrane, with subsequent formation of spur-cell morphology.[29-31] A similar mechanism has been implicated in the development of target cells in patients with marked liver disease.[31,60] In both circumstances, the change in shape and membrane structure may influence cell life span by changing the pliability of the cell and, therefore, the rate of cell removal by the reticuloendothelial system.

Finally, changes in plasma environment have been implicated in a transient hemolytic anemia associated with jaundice, hyperlipidemia, and marked cirrhosis, as first described by Zieve.[32] An exact causal relationship between the hyperlipidemia and a circulating hemolysin has not been documented for this syndrome; rather it is now thought that some other changes in environment or in reticuloendothelial system must be responsible for the marked increase in hemolysis. In the determination and investigation of hemolysis in the alcoholic, it is always important to recognize that high levels of red cell production may not necessarily imply ongoing hemolysis but rather reflect the response to alcoholic withdrawal and the reinstitution of dietary folate input. As described by Eichner and Hillman,[10] the rapid reversion of megaloblastic to normoblastic erythropoiesis and effective red cell output can mimic the picture of a hemolytic anemia in hospitalized alcoholic patients.

In summary, the adverse effects of alcohol on hematopoiesis may be on several physiological and biochemical mechanisms. In the case of the mega-karyocyte, alcohol can be a direct toxin to stem cell proliferation. In the area of red cell production, alcohol may affect cell proliferation and, by inflammatory inhibition of erythropoietin, the level of iron supply. The maturation sequence of all hematopoietic cells is especially vulnerable to alcohol toxicity because of the need for folic acid and pyridoxal-5-phosphate for cell DNA metabolism replication and maturation with synthesis of specialized proteins. Finally, alcohol may affect the membrane or function of the cell in such a way as to shorten cell life span or interfere with normal cellular activities and distribution.

REFERENCES

1. STRAUS, D. J. 1973. Hematologic aspects of alcoholism. Seminars in Hematology 10: 183.
2. EICHNER, E. R. 1973. The hematologic disorders of alcoholism. Amer. J. Med. 54: 621.
3. LINDENBAUM, J. & R. L. HARGROVE. 1968. Thrombocytopenia in alcoholics. Ann. Intern. Med. 68: 526.
4. SULLIVAN, L. W. & V. HERBERT. 1964. Suppression of hematopoiesis by ethanol. J. Clin. Invest. 43: 2048.
5. POST, R. M. & J. F. DESFORGES. 1968. Thombocytopenia and alcoholism. Ann. Intern. Med. 68: 1230.
6. POST, R. M. & J. F. DESFORGES. 1968. Thrombocytopenic effect of ethanol infusion. Blood 31: 344.
7. SULLIVAN, L. W., Y. K. LIU, L. TALARICO & C. P. EMERSON. 1968. Alcohol-induced thrombocytopenia in man. J. Clin. Invest. 47: 95a.
8. COWAN, D. H. & J. D. HINES. 1971. Thrombocytopenia of severe alcoholism. Ann. Intern. Med. 74: 37.
9. SULLIVAN, L. W. & V. HERBERT. 1964. Mechanism of hematosuppression by ethanol. Amer. J. Clin. Nutr. 14: 238.
10. EICHNER, E. R. & R. S. HILLMAN. 1971. The evolution of anemia in alcoholic patients. Amer. J. Med. 50: 218.
11. EICHNER, E. R., H. I. PIERCE, R. S. HILLMAN. 1971. Folate balance in dietary-induced megaloblastic anemia. New. Eng. J. Med. 284: 933.
12. HERBERT, V., R. ZALUSKY & C. S. DAVIDSON. 1963. Correlation of folate deficiency with alcoholism and associated macrocytosis, anemia and liver disease. Ann. Intern. Med. 58: 977.
13. EICHNER, E. R., B. BUCHANAN, J. W. SMITH & R. S. HILLMAN. 1972. Variations in the hematologic and medical status of alcoholics. Amer. J. Med. Sci. 263: 35.
14. LINDENBAUM, J. & C. S. LIEBER. 1969. Hematologic effects of alcohol in man in the absence of nutritional deficiency. New Eng. J. Med. 281: 333.
15. HINES, J. D. 1969. Reversible megaloblastic and sideroblastic marrow abnormalities in alcoholic patients. Brit. J. Haemat. 16: 87.
16. CHOMET B. & B. M. BACH. 1967. Lobar pneumonia and alcoholism: an analysis of thirty-seven cases. Amer. J. Med. Sci. 253: 300.
17. McFARLAND, W. & E. P. LIBRE. 1963. Abnormal leukocyte response in alcoholism. Ann. Intern. Med. 59: 865.
18. JOHNSON, W. D., P. STOKES & D. KAYE. 1969. The effect of intravenous ethanol on the bactericidal activity of human serum. Yale J. Bio. Med. 42: 71.

19. BRAYTON, R. G., P. E. STOKES, M. S. SCHWARTZ & D. B. LOURIA. 1970. Effect of alcohol and various diseases on leukocyte mobilization, phagocytosis and intracellular bacterial killing. New Eng. J. Med 282: 123.
20. CROWLEY, J. P. & N. ABRAMSON. 1971. Effect of ethanol on complement-mediated chemotaxis. Clin. Res. 19: 415.
21. DeMEO, A. N. & B. R. ANDERSON. 1972. Defective chemotaxis associated with a serum inhibitor in cirrhotic patients. New Eng. J. Med. 286: 735.
22. RYBACK, R. & J. F. DESFORGES. 1970. Alcoholic thrombocytopenia in three inpatient drinking alcoholics. Arch. Intern. Med. (Chicago) 125: 475.
23. DOUGLASS, C. C. & J. J. TWOMEY. 1970. Transient stomatocytosis with hemolysis: a previously unrecognized complication of alcoholism. Ann. Intern. Med. 72: 159.
24. SMITH, J. A., E. T. LONERGAN & K. STERLING. 1964. Spur-cell anemia. New Eng. J. Med. 271: 396.
25. SILBER, R., E. AMOROSI, J. LHOWE & H. J. KAYDEN. 1966. Spur-shaped erythrocytes in Laennec's cirrhosis. New Eng. J. Med. 275: 639.
26. GRAHN, E. P., A. A. DIETZ, S. S. STEFANI & W. J. DONNELLY. 1968. Burr cells, hemolytic anemia and cirrhosis. Amer. J. Med. 45: 78.
27. DOUGLASS, C. C., M. S. McCALL & E. P. FRENKEL. 1968. The acanthocyte in cirrhosis with hemolytic anemia. Ann. Intern. Med. 68: 390.
28. MARTINEZ-MALDONADO, M. 1968. Role of lipoproteins in the formation of spur cell anemia. J. Clin. Path. 21: 620.
29. COOPER, R. A. 1969. Anemia with spur cells. A red cell defect acquired in serum and modified in the circulation. J. Clin. Invest. 48: 1820.
30. SIMON, J. B. & SCHEIG, R. 1970. Serum cholesterol esterification in liver disease. Importance of lecithin-cholesterol acyltransferase. New Eng. J. Med. 283: 841.
31. McBRIDE, J. A. & H. S. JACOB. 1970. Abnormal kinetics of red cell membrane cholesterol in acanthocytes: studies in genetic and experimental abetalipoproteinemia and in spur-cell anemia. Brit. J. Haemat. 18: 383.
32. ZIEVE, L. 1958. Jaundice, hyperlipemia and hemolytic anemia: a heretofore unrecognized syndrome associated with alcoholic fatty liver and cirrhosis. Ann. Intern. Med. 48: 471.
33. LOSOWKSY, M. S., D. P. JONES, C. D. DAVIDSON & C. S. LIEBER. 1963. Studies of alcoholic hyperlipemia and its mechanism. Amer. J. Med. 35: 794.
34. BLASS, J. P. & H. M. DEAN. 1966. The relation of hyperlipemia to hemolytic anemia in an alcoholic patient. Amer. J. Med. 40: 283.
35. BALCERZAK, S. P., M. P. WESTERMAN & E. W. HEINIE. 1968. Mechanism of anemia in Zieve's syndrome. Amer. J. Med. Sci. 255: 277.
36. SHOHET, S. B. 1972. Hemolysis and changes in erythrocyte membrane lipids. II. New Eng. J. Med. 286: 638.
37. BAINTON, D. F. & C. A. FINCH. 1964. The diagnosis of iron deficiency anemia. Amer. J. Med. 37: 62.
38. HILLMAN, R. S. & P. A. HENDERSON. 1969. Control of marrow production by the level of iron supply. J. Clin. Invest. 48: 443.
39. ZUCKER, S., S. FRIEDMAN & R. M. LYSIK. 1974. Bone marrow erythropoiesis in the anemia of infection, inflammation, and malignancy. J. Clin. Invest. 53: 1132.
40. HERBERT, V. 1962. Experimental nutritional folate deficiency in man. Trans. Assn. Amer. Physicians 75: 307.
41. HALSTED, C. H., R. C. GRIGGS & J. W. HARRIS. 1967. The effect of alcoholism on the absorption of folic acid (H³PGA) evaluated by plasma levels and urine excretion. J. Lab. Clin. Med. 69: 116.
42. HALSTED, C. H., E. A. ROBLES & E. MEZEY. 1971. Decreased jejunal uptake of labeled folic acid (³H-PGA) in alcoholic patients: Roles of alcohol and nutrition. New Eng. J. Med. 285: 701.
43. HALSTED, C. H., E. A. ROBLES & E. MEZEY. 1972. Intestinal malabsorption induced by feeding a folate-deficient diet and ethanol to alcoholic patients. Amer. J. Clin. Nutr. 25: 449.
44. HERMOS, J. A., W. H. ADAMS, K. L. YONG, L. W. SULLIVAN & J. S. TRIER. 1972.

Mucosa of the small intestine in folate-deficient alcoholics. Ann. Intern. Med. **76:** 957.

45. LINDENBAUM, J. & C. S. LIEBER. 1969. Alcohol-induced malabsorption of vitamin B_{12} in man. Nature (London) **224:** 806.

46. THOMSON, A. D., H. BAKER & C. M. LEEVY. 1970. Patterns of ^{35}S-thiamine hydrochloride absorption in the malnourished alcoholic patient. J. Lab. Clin. Med. **76:** 34.

47. EICHNER, E. R. & R. S. HILLMAN. 1973. Effect of Alcohol on Serum Folate Level. J. Clin. Invest. **52:** 584.

48. LANE, F., P. GOFF, R. McGUFFIN & R. S. HILLMAN. 1973. Influence of ethanol on folate metabolism. (abst.). Blood **42:** 998.

49. EICHNER, E. R. 1974. Personal communication.

50. CHANARIN, I., D. L. MOLLIN & B. B. ANDERSON. 1958. The clearance from the plasma of folic acid injected intravenously in normal subjects and patients with megaloblastic anemia. Brit. J. Haemat. **4:** 435.

51. HERBERT, V. & R. ZALUSKY. 1962. Interrelations of vitamin B_{12} and folic acid metabolism: folic acid clearance studies. J. Clin. Invest. **41:** 1263.

52. CHANARIN, I. & M. C. BENNETT. 1962. The disposal of small doses of intravenously injected folic acid. Brit. J. Haemat. **8:** 28.

53. JOHNS, D. G., S. SPERTI & A. S. V. BURGEN. 1961. The metabolism of tritiated folic acid in man. J. Clin. Invest. **40:** 1684.

54. CHANARIN, I., E. H. BELCHER & V. BERRY. 1963. The utilization of Tritium-labelled folic acid in megaloblastic anemia. Brit. J. Haemat. **9:** 456.

55. YOSHINO, T. 1968. The clinical and experimental studies on the metabolism of folic acid using tritiated folic acid. III. Plasma clearance in man and organ distribution in rat following intravenous administration of tritiated folic acid. J. Vitamin. **14:** 49.

56. BAKER, H., O. FRANK, S. GEINGOLD, H. ZIFFER, R. A. GELLENE, C. M. LEEVY & H. SOBOTKA. 1965. The fate of orally and parenterally administered folates. Amer. J. Clin. Nutr. **17:** 88.

57. HINES, J. D. & D. H. COWAN. 1970. Studies on the pathogenesis of alcohol-induced sideroblastic bone-marrow abnormalities. New Eng. J. Med. **283:** 441.

58. HINES, J. 1969. Altered phosphorylation of vitamin B_6 in alcoholic patients induced by oral administration of alcohol. J. Lab. Clin. Med. **74:** 882.

59. LU-MENG, L. & TING-KAI LI. 1974. Vitamin B_6 metabolism in chronic alcohol abuse. Pyridoxal phosphate levels in plasma and the effects of acetaldehyde on pyridoxal phosphate synthesis and degradation in human erythrocytes. J. Clin. Invest. **53:** 693.

60. COOPER, R. A. & S. J. SHATTIL. 1971. Mechanisms of hemolysis—the minimal red-cell defect. New Eng. J. Med. **285:** 1514.

HEMATOLOGIC EFFECTS OF ALCOHOL*

Victor Herbert and Glenn Tisman

Department of Pathology
Columbia University College of Physicians & Surgeons
New York, New York 10032
and
Veterans Administration Hospital
Bronx, New York 10468

Perhaps one of the earliest evidences of the ability of ethanol to interfere in cellular metabolism was the observation by Gram in 1884 of macrocytosis in association with cirrhosis.[1] The nutritional deficits associated with alcoholism were suspected in 1938 by Bianco and Jolliffe,[2] who, noting no correlation between macrocytosis and severity of liver damage, concluded, "In view of these findings, we are inclined to regard the macrocytosis of the alcohol addict not as a manifestation of inability on the part of the liver to store a hematopoietic principle, but as an extrinsic deficiency of some necessary hematopoietic substance required to maintain normocytosis."

Burgeoning research into the hematologic effects of alcohol has led to recognition that among these effects are:

1. Nutritional deficiencies due to inadequate ingestion of other foods because of alcohol addiction and "empty alcohol calories" supplying caloric need;
2. Alcohol-induced malabsorption of other nutrients;
3. Ethanol-induced interference with cellular metabolism.

Elsewhere in this monograph, Dr. Lindenbaum[3] deals with alcohol and vitamin B_{12} malabsorption and Dr. Hines[4] deals with alcohol-induced abnormalities of folic acid and vitamin B_6 metabolism. Dr. Cowan[5] deals with the mechanism of ethanol-related thrombocytopenia and thrombocytopathy, and Dr. Leevy[6] deals with the lymphocyte and alcoholism. Particularly useful recent reviews of hematologic aspects of alcoholism have been published by Straus[7] and by Hines and Cowan.[8,9] The current report will therefore focus particularly on those facets of the subject in which our laboratory has been most interested.

FOLATE DEFICIENCY

Folate deficiency appears to be the rule in association with alcoholism rather than the exception.[10,11] A decade ago it was noted that, of 70 alcoholic subjects, 65 (93%) had serum folate activity below normal, 56 (86%) of the concentrations being below 5 ng/ml. In 1974, it was reported[8] that of 70 patients admitted to hospital for acute alcoholic withdrawal symptoms, serum folate was subnormal in 61 and erythrocyte folate subnormal in 30.

Although the high incidence of folate deficiency is due in large measure to inadequate dietary intake of folate,[10,12] other factors also play a role.[12a]

*Supported in part by United States Public Health Service Grant NIAMDD 15163, by Health Research Council of the City of New York Career Scientist Award I-683, and a Veterans Administration Medical Investigatorship (Project 3570-01 and 02) to the senior author.

Gastrointestinal bleeding, hypersplenism, and hemolysis that occur in cirrhosis tend to induce hyperactivity in the bone marrow, resulting in an increased demand for folate.[11] When the folate supply is marginal, this increased demand may result in overt folate deficiency, with its associated megaloblastic anemia. Such marginal folate supply is the rule in "hard liquor" alcoholics, since hard liquor contains no folate. Wine contains a variable (but usually low) amount of folate, and beer contains a substantial amount of the vitamin, usually present in a poorly absorbable form.

Among the many facets of the interference of ethanol in cellular metabolism appears to be an effect on folate metabolism. A decade ago, it was demonstrated[13] that ethanol, in amounts readily consumed by "heavy drinkers," suppresses the hematopoietic response of anemic, folate-deficient patients to doses of folic acid in the range of the minimal daily adult folate requirement of 50 μg. It was demonstrated that this suppression could be overcome, either with larger doses of folic acid or by cessation of alcohol. Thus, the "spontaneous" hematologic improvement seen in alcoholic subjects after hospitalization appeared due not only to ingestion of folate-containing food but also to cessation of alcohol ingestion. In that study,[13] it was demonstrated that ethanol not only could convert bone marrow morphology from normoblastic to megaloblastic within 10 days but could also suppress erythropoiesis, leukopoiesis, and thrombopoiesis, as well as cause sharp elevation of serum iron concentration and saturation of iron-binding capacity. To this day, the mechanisms whereby ethanol interferes with folate metabolism remain unknown but include the possible stimulation by ethanol of liver alcohol dehydrogenase, which can then combine with folate,[14] and a possible effect of ethanol on the intermediary enzymes in folate metabolism.[15]

There is some evidence that ethanol diminishes the absorbability of folate,[16] although this is not yet unequivocally established.[17] Additionally, once alcoholism has produced a damaged liver, diminished ability of the liver to store folate[18] may contribute to the folate deficiency. Eichner and Hillman[19] have noted that ethanol sharply drives down serum folate level, and this has been confirmed.[8] The meaning of this phenomenon in terms of folate metabolism awaits elucidation.

A decade ago it was postulated[11,20] that the damaged liver may release a folate-binding protein that irreversibly ties up folate in the serum, resulting in a normal serum folate level but tissue folate deficiency, producing megaloblastosis. Recent support for this concept[21,22] suggests that further study may prove it to be of importance. In our further studies in this area, measurement of *red cell* folate as an index of tissue stores is proving of great value, as is measurement of biochemical megaloblastosis by the "dU suppression test."[21]

VITAMIN B$_{12}$ DEFICIENCY

As indicated above, although there are many factors at work in the high frequency of folate deficiency in association with alcoholism, inadequate dietary intake of the vitamin appears to be a dominant influence. Since hard liquor contains no vitamin B$_{12}$, as well as no folate, it might be expected that chronic alcoholics would gradually develop deficiency of this vitamin, as well as of folate. This could be expected to be a very slowly developing process, because body stores of vitamin B$_{12}$ ordinarily will last for a number of years.[23] However, body stores of vitamin B$_{12}$ are much more rapidly exhausted when the normal high enterohepatic circulation of vitamin B_{12}[24] is interrupted by vitamin B_{12} malabsorption,[24] such as ethanol may produce.[3]

The liver disease frequently associated with alcoholism tends to confuse the picture with respect to the vitamin B_{12} nutritional state because, with chronic liver disease, although serum vitamin B_{12} levels tend to be normal or elevated,[25,26] liver stores of vitamin B_{12}[26-28] as well as of other vitamins,[28] tend to be sharply reduced. Furthermore, much of the vitamin B_{12} in serum may not be available for hematopoiesis in chronic liver disease, since it may be attached to an abnormal protein released from the damaged liver,[29] and this complex may be unable to deliver its load of vitamin B_{12} to hematopoietic cells for use in blood formation.[30] Four patients with liver disease in association with alcoholism were reported to have megaloblastic anemia despite normal serum levels of vitamin B_{12} and folate, and the megaloblastosis was corrected by a normal hospital diet.[20]

The most recent supporting evidence for the concept that in the alcoholic with chronic liver disease the serum vitamin B_{12} level may be misleading (i.e., vitamin B_{12} deficiency may be present despite a normal to elevated serum vitamin level)[11] is the finding[21] that biochemical megaloblastosis may be demonstrated *in vitro*, and may be improved by the addition of vitamin B_{12} *in vitro*, in the bone marrow of an alcoholic patient with a megaloblastic bone marrow morphology but an elevated serum vitamin B_{12} level (and a normal serum folate level). In fact, it may well be that those alcoholic patients with folate deficiency who respond to therapy with a large "pharmacologic" dose of vitamin B_{12}[31] may in fact have true vitamin B_{12} deficiency demonstrable by the "dU suppression test" measurement of biochemical megaloblastosis despite normal serum vitamin B_{12} levels.[32]

DIRECT TOXICITY OF ETHANOL TO HEMATOPOIETIC CELLS

McCurdy et al.[33] reported a direct toxicity of ethanol on hematopoietic cells manifested by development of vacuoles in hematopoietic stem cells similar to the vacuoles associated with toxic effects of chloramphenicol. These findings have been confirmed in relation to quantity and recency of alcohol intake.[34-37] Corcino et al.[38] found that ethanol, in concentrations within the range observed in the plasma of intoxicated humans, appeared to selectively suppress incorporation of radioactive uridine into RNA, and they suggested impairment of RNA synthesis may be the basis for the vacuolization. Their studies did not make clear whether the ethanol effect constituted interference with uptake rather than, or in addition to, interference with incorporation of radioactive uridine into RNA of hematopoietic cells, and further elucidation awaits future studies.

McFarland and Libre[39] described a leukopenic response to infection in alcoholic patients, and Brayton et al.[40] observed a similar leukopenic response to inflammation in patients receiving intravenous infusions of ethanol. To determine whether these phenomena represented ethanol interference with production of granulocytes, and also whether ethanol can also interfere with lymphocyte proliferation, we have been carrying out a number of *in vitro* studies.[41] These studies will be reviewed below.

IN VITRO MYELOSUPPRESSION AND IMMUNOSUPPRESSION BY ETHANOL

Significant inhibition by ethanol of ^{3}H-TdR incorporation into DNA of bone marrow cells incubated *in vitro* for 4 hours occurred only with large concen-

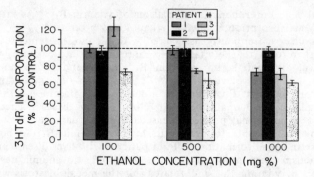

FIGURE 1. Effect of various concentrations of ethanol on incorporation of ^{3}HTdR into bone marrow DNA. Vertical lines = ±1 S.D. Diagnosis: patients 1 and 2, iron deficiency anemia; 3, rheumatoid arthritis; patient 4, diabetes mellitus. From Tisman & Herbert.[41] By permission of the publisher of the Journal of Clinical Investigation.

trations of ethanol (FIGURE 1). However, *in vitro* concentrations of ethanol in the range of 200–300 mg/100 ml, concentrations that occur in heavily intoxicated individuals, depress both the ability of bone marrow colonies to grow (FIGURE 2) and the ability of mitogens to stimulate lymphocyte transformation (FIGURES 3–5).

Under the proposed National Uniform Act Regulating Traffic on Highways, the presence of 150 mg or more of ethanol/100 ml blood is the minimum standard for presuming drunkenness from blood ethanol evidence.[42] The *in vitro* data summarized in FIGURES 1–5 suggest that alcohol may both inhibit myeloid tissue growth and suppress immunocompetence when the alcohol is present in concentrations found in the blood of acute and chronic alcoholics. Furthermore, this suppression was not overcome by enriching the incubation medium with large quantities of folic acid, vitamin B_{12}, and vitamin B_6.[41]

The immediate question is whether these suppressive effects of alcohol on

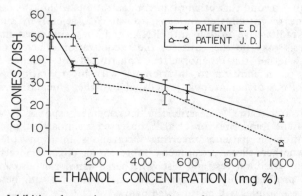

FIGURE 2. Inhibition by various concentrations of ethanol of bone marrow colony growth in soft agar of 2 other patients than those in FIGURE 1. Diagnosis: patient E. D., pancreatic carcinoma; patient J. D., diabetes mellitus. Underlay leukocytes were from each patient studied. Colony counts are the average of 3 dishes. Vertical lines = ±1 S.D. From Tisman & Herbert.[41] By permission of the publisher of the Journal of Clinical Investigation.

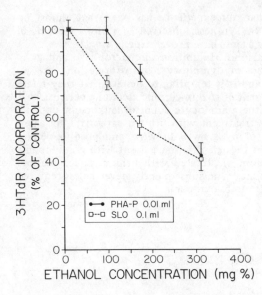

FIGURE 3. Ethanol inhibition of SLO- and PHA-P-induced lymphocyte transformation as measured by incorporation of ^{3}HTdR into lymphocyte DNA. Patient had diabetes mellitus. Culture medium was THAA plus 10% autologous serum. Vertical lines = ±1 S.D. From Tisman & Herbert.[41] By permission of the publisher of the Journal of Clinical Investigation.

granulocytes (and possibly macrophages), and on lymphocytes, occur *in vivo*. In preliminary studies, Dr. E. Straus[43] has evidence suggesting that when blood is obtained from an alcoholic who comes in with a blood alcohol level in the range of 200 mg/100 ml blood, the ability of those lymphocytes to be transformed by mitogen is retarded. Should this preliminary observation hold up, we will have the *in vivo* substantiation for the *in vitro* observation. In this

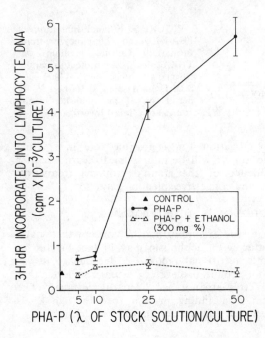

FIGURE 4. Ethanol inhibition of lymphocyte transformation induced by varying concentrations of PHA-P. Normal volunteer. Culture medium was RPMI 1640 plus 200 ml/liter L-glutamine plus 0.6 M Tris buffer pH 7.4, plus 10% fetal calf serum. Vertical lines = ±1 S.D. From Tisman & Herbert.[41] By permission of the publisher of the Journal of Clinical Investigation.

connection, it should be noted that our experience has been that almost in-variably suppressive effects on DNA synthesis observed in various systems *in vitro* by addition of various noxious agents have proved true *in vivo*.[44-49]

These three *in vitro* effects of alcohol (inhibition of macrophage and gran-ulocyte production and inhibition of lymphocyte transformation) are all directed against immune defense, and it is tempting to believe that they relate to the susceptibility to infection present *in vivo* in chronic alcoholic patients.[50,51]

Recent studies[52,53] suggest that the granulocyte count of leukopenic patients with alcoholism may be raised by treatment with lithium carbonate, an agent known to stimulate granulocyte colony growth *in vitro* and produce leuko-cytosis *in vivo*.[54,55] However, even though the first patient with granulopenia in association with alcoholism whom we treated with lithium had a marked improvement in his granulocyte count,[52] he subsequently nevertheless required splenectomy because of persistent thrombocytopenia.

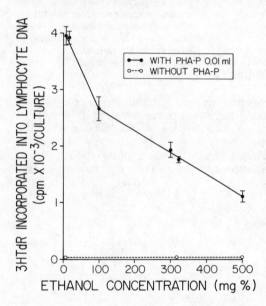

FIGURE 5. Ethanol inhibition of PHA-P-induced lymphocyte trans-formation. Culture medium was THAA plus 10% autologous serum. Normal volunteer. Vertical lines = ± 1 S.D. From Tisman & Herbert.[41] By permission of the publisher of the Journal of Clinical Investigation.

Currently, lithium is under investigation for a possible role in treating emotional states underlying alcoholism. It will be interesting to learn whether such treatment reduces the incidence of the granulocytopenia frequently observed in alcoholics with cirrhosis and congestive splenomegaly.

EFFECTS OF ALCOHOL ON IRON METABOLISM

Straus[7] has recently reviewed the studies supporting the concept that much of the "hemochromatosis" associated with alcoholism may in fact be due to the combination of alcoholism and nutritional factors. A decade ago it was reported[13] that ingestion of ethanol produced elevated serum iron levels that remained high until 24–72 hours after ethanol had been discontinued. The percentage of saturation of serum iron-binding protein rose to high levels within 72 hours after beginning ethanol administration and fell to normal or low values within 48 hours after cessation thereof. Reticulocytosis occurring during alcohol ingestion was not accompanied in 2 patients by either a fall in serum iron or a fall in the percentage saturation of iron-binding protein, until after cessation of alcohol. This dissociation of the changes in serum iron and saturation of iron-binding capacity from the reticulocyte response suggested an effect of alcohol on iron metabolism separate and distinct from the changes secondary to increased or decreased hematopoiesis.

Because this interference of alcohol with iron metabolism could be of significance in the pathogenesis of iron overload in alcoholic subjects, the admonition stated a decade ago[13] remains valid: "The diagnosis of idiopathic hemochromatosis should probably not be made in alcoholic patients until it has been shown that the excessive iron stores in the liver are not due to deficiencies of these factors (folate, vitamin B_{12}, pyridoxine) and cannot be reduced by cessation of alcohol and long-term therapy with folic acid, vitamin B_{12}, and pyridoxine."[56]

References

1. GRAM, C. 1884. Untersuchungen über die grösse der roten Blutkorperchen im Normalzustande und bei verschiedenen Krankheiten. Fortschr. Med. **2:** 33.
2. BIANCO, A. & N. JOLLIFFE. 1938. The anemia of alcohol addicts. Observations as to the role of liver disease, achlorhydria, nutritional factors and alcohol on its production. Amer. J. Med. Sci. **196:** 414.
3. LINDENBAUM, J. & C. S. LIEBER. 1974. Effects of chronic ethanol administration on intestinal absorption in man in the absence of nutritional deficiency. This monograph.
4. HINES, J. D. 1974. Hematologic abnormalities involving vitamin B_6 and folate metabolism in alcoholic subjects. This monograph.
5. COWAN, D. H. & R. C. GRAHAM, JR. 1974. The platelet defect in alcoholism. This monograph.
6. LEEVY, C. M., T. CHEN & R. ZETTERMAN. 1974. Alcoholic hepatitis, cirrhosis, and immunologic reactivity. This monograph.
7. STRAUS, D. J. 1973. Hematologic aspects of alcoholism. Sem. Hemat. **10:** 183–194.
8. HINES, J. D. & D. H. COWAN. 1974. Anemia in alcoholism. *In* Drugs and Hematologic Reactions. N. V. Dimitrov & J. H. Nodine, Eds.: 141–153. Grune & Stratton. New York, N.Y.
9. COWAN, D. H. & J. D. HINES. 1974. Alcohol, vitamins, and platelets. *In* Drugs and Hematologic Reactions. N. V. Dimitrov & J. H. Nodine, Eds.: 283–295. Grune & Stratton. New York, N.Y.
10. HERBERT, V., R. ZALUSKY, C. S. DAVIDSON. 1963. Correlation of folate deficiency with alcoholism and associated macrocytosis, anemia, and liver disease. Ann. Intern. Med. **58:** 977–988.
11. HERBERT, V. 1965. Hematopoietic factors in liver disease. *In* Progress in Liver Diseases. H. Popper & F. Schaffner, Eds.: 57–68. Grune & Stratton. New York, N.Y.
12. KLIPSTEIN, F. A. & J. LINDENBAUM. 1965. Folate deficiency in chronic liver disease. Blood **25:** 443.
12a. STEBBINS, R., J. SCOTT & V. HERBERT. 1973. Drug-induced megaloblastic anemias. Sem. Hemat. **10:** 235–251.
13. SULLIVAN, L. W. & V. HERBERT. 1964. Suppression of hematopoiesis by ethanol. J. Clin. Invest. **43:** 2048–2062.
14. SNYDER, R., W. H. VOGEL & M. P. SHULMAN. 1963. Inhibition of liver alcohol dehydrogenase by folic acid. Fed. Proc. **22:** 183.
15. BERTINO, J. R., J. WARD, A. C. SARTORELLI & R. SILBER. 1965. An effect of ethanol on folate metabolism. J. Clin. Invest. **44:** 1028.
16. HALSTED, C. H., E. A. ROBLES & E. MEZEY. 1973. Intestinal malabsorption in folate-deficient alcoholics. Gastroenterol. **64:** 526.

17. KLIPSTEIN, F. A. 1972. Intoxicated enterocytes? New Eng. J. Med. **286:** 161.
18. CHERRICK, G. R., H. BAKER, O. FRANK & C. M. LEEVY. 1965. Observations on hepatic avidity for folate in Laennec's cirrhosis. J. Lab. Clin. Med. **66:** 446.
19. EICHNER, E. R. & R. S. HILLMAN. 1971. The evolution of anemia in alcoholic patients. Amer. J. Med. **50:** 218.
20. HERBERT, V., R. R. STREIFF, L. W. SULLIVAN & P. L. McGEER. 1964. Deranged purine metabolism manifested by aminoimidazole carboxamide excretion in megaloblastic anemias, hemolytic anemia, and liver disease. Lancet **2:** 45–46.
21. HERBERT, V., G. TISMAN, L. T. GO & L. BRENNER. 1973. The dU suppression test using ^{125}IUdR to define biochemical megaloblastosis. Brit. J. Haematol. **24:** 713–723.
22. ROTHENBERG, S. P. 1973. Application of competitive ligand binding for the radioassay of vitamin B_{12} and folic acid. Metabolism **22:** 1075.
23. HERBERT, V. 1970. Drugs effective in megaloblastic anemias. In The Pharmacologic Basis of Therapeutics. 4th edit. L. S. Goodman & A. Gilman, Eds.: 1414–1444. Macmillan. New York, N.Y.
24. HERBERT, V. 1975. Megaloblastic anemias. In Cecil-Loeb Textbook of Medicine, 14th edit. P. B. Beeson & W. McDermott, Eds. W. B. Saunders Co. Philadelphia, Pa.
25. STEVENSON, T. D. & M. BEARD. 1959. Serum vitamin B_{12} content in liver disease. New Eng. J. Med. **260:** 206.
26. HALSTED, J. A., J. CARROLL & S. RUBERT. 1959. Serum and tissue concentrations of vitamin B_{12} in certain pathologic states. New Eng. J. Med. **260:** 575.
27. JOSKE, R. A. 1963. The vitamin B_{12} content of human liver tissue obtained by aspiration biopsy. Gut **4:** 231.
28. BAKER, H., O. FRANK, H. ZIFFER, S. GOLDFARB, C. M. LEEVY & H. SOBOTKA. 1964. Effect of hepatic disease on liver B-complex vitamin titers. Amer. J. Clin. Nutr. **14:** 1.
29. RACHMILEWITZ, M., B. MOSHKOWITZ, B. RACHMILEWITZ, N. GROSSOWICZ & J. GROSS. 1972. Serum vitamin B_{12} binding proteins in viral hepatitis. Europ. J. Clin. Invest. **2:** 239–242.
30. HERBERT, V., N. DAWBER & S. H. INGBAR. 1964. Vitamin B_{12} binding protein in human serum. Clin. Res. **12:** 223.
31. ZALUSKY, R., V. HERBERT & W. B. CASTLE. 1962. Cyanocobalamin therapy effect in folic acid deficiency. Arch. Intern. Med. **109:** 545–554.
32. VAN DER WEYDEN, M. B., M. ROTHER & B. G. FIRKIN. 1972. The metabolic significance of reduced serum B_{12} in folate deficiency. Blood **40:** 23.
33. McCURDY, P. R., L. E. PIERCE & C. E. RATH. 1962. Abnormal bone marrow morphology in acute alcoholism. New Eng. J. Med. **266:** 505.
34. JARROLD, T., J. J. WILL, A. R. DAVIES, P. H. DUFFEY & J. L. BRAMSCHREIBER. 1967. Bone marrow-erythroid morphology in alcoholic patients. Amer. J. Clin. Nutr. **20:** 716.
35. LINDENBAUM, J. & C. S. LIEBER. 1969. Hematological effects of alcohol in man in the absence of nutritional deficiency. New Eng. J. Med. **281:** 333.
36. GREENBERG, M. S., G. STROHMEYER, G. J. HINE, W. R. KEENE, G. CURTIS & T. C. CHALMERS. 1964. Studies in iron absorption. III. Body radioactivity measurements of patients with liver disease. Gastroenterology **46:** 651.
37. WATERS, A. H., A. A. MORLEY & J. G. RANKIN. 1966. Effect of alcohol on haemopoiesis. Brit. Med. J. **2:** 1565.
38. CORCINO, J., S. WAXMAN, A. RUBIN & V. HERBERT. 1970. Selective suppression by ethanol of RNA synthesis in human hematopoietic cells in vitro: fact or artifact? J. Clin. Invest. **49:** 22a.
39. McFARLAND, W., & E. P. LIBRE. 1963. Abnormal leukocyte response in alcoholism. Ann. Intern. Med. **59:** 865.
40. BRAYTON, R. G., P. E. STOKES, M. S. SCHWARTZ & D. B. LOURIA. 1970. Effect of alcohol and various diseases on leukocyte function. New Eng. J. Med. **282:** 123.
41. TISMAN, G. & V. HERBERT. 1973. In vitro myelosuppression and immunosuppression by ethanol. J. Clin. Invest. **52:** 1410–1414.

42. ERWIN, R. E. 1971. Defense of drunk driving cases. 3rd edit. Matthew Bender, New York, N.Y.
43. STRAUS, E. 1974. Personal communication.
44. HERBERT, V., G. TISMAN & H. EDLIS. 1973. Determination of therapeutic index of drugs by *in vitro* sensitivity tests using human host and tumor cell suspensions. Cancer Chemother. Rep. 57: 11–19.
45. TISMAN, G., V. HERBERT, H. EDLIS, L. T. GO & L. BRENNER. 1972. Differences in DNA metabolism in tumor vs. host cells; predicting patient response to chemotherapy. J. Clin. Invest. 51: 98a.
46. WAXMAN, S., J. J. CORCINO & V. HERBERT. 1970. Drugs, toxins and dietary amino acids affecting vitamin B_{12} or folic acid absorption or utilization. Amer. J. Med. 48: 599–608.
47. SIVE, J., R. GREEN & J. METZ. 1972. Effect of trimethoprim on folate-dependent DNA synthesis in human bone marrow. J. Clin. Pathol. 25: 194–197.
48. TISMAN, G., V. HERBERT & S. ROSENBLATT. 1973. Evidence that lithium produces human granulocyte proliferation. Brit. J. Haematol. 24: 767–771.
49. TISMAN, G. & V. HERBERT. 1973. Selective kill of lymphocyte subpopulations by varying concentrations of immunosuppressive drugs. Blood 40: 958.
50. BRAYTON, R. G., P. STOKES & D. B. LOURIA. 1965. The effects of alcohol on host defenses. J. Clin. Invest. 44: 1030.
51. GUARNERI, J. J. & G. A. LAURENZI. 1968. Effect of alcohol on the mobilization of alveolar macrophages. J. Lab. Clin. Med. 72: 40.
52. JACOB, E. & V. HERBERT. 1974. Lithium therapy for neutropenias. J. Clin. Invest. 53: 35a.
53. TISMAN, G. Unpublished data.
54. TISMAN, G., V. HERBERT & S. ROSENBLATT. 1973. Evidence that lithium induces human granulocyte proliferation: elevated serum vitamin B_{12} binding capacity *in vivo* and granulocyte colony proliferation *in vitro*. Brit. J. Haematol. 24: 767–771.
55. CLARKSON, D. R., J. W. ATHENS, G. ROTHSTEIN & H. ASHENBRUCKER. 1974. DF^{32}P leukokinetic studies of lithium-induced neutrophilia. Clin. Res. 22: 386A.
56. SULLIVAN, L. W. & V. HERBERT. 1964. Macrocytic anemia (other than pernicious anemia). *In* Current Therapy. H. F. Conn, Ed.: 185. W. B. Saunders Co. Philadelphia, Pa.

HEMATOLOGIC ABNORMALITIES INVOLVING VITAMIN B₆ AND FOLATE METABOLISM IN ALCOHOLIC SUBJECTS*

John D. Hines

Department of Medicine
Case Western Reserve University School of Medicine
at Cleveland Metropolitan General Hospital
Cleveland, Ohio 44109

INTRODUCTION

Certain abnormalities in folate and vitamin B_6 metabolism have been well documented in chronic alcoholic subjects.[1-13] Studies on the effect of alcohol on folate metabolism were stimulated by the suggestion of Jandl[14] that excessive alcohol ingestion per se could cause a direct hemosuppressive effect in certain subjects. Subsequent studies conducted by Sullivan and Herbert[1,2] illustrated the frequent association of megaloblastic anemia in such subjects and provided conclusive evidence that excessive alcohol ingestion caused impaired cellular utilization of folate in selected patients. This effect of alcohol on folate utilization was further shown to be overcome with administration of pharmacologic amounts of folic or folinic acid. Additional predisposing factors leading to folate deficiency in chronic alcoholics include poor dietary intake, altered absorption, and defective hepatic storage of folate in patients with liver disease.

Indirect evidence that abnormalities in vitamin B_6 metabolism were associated with chronic alcohol abuse were provided by the observations of Hines,[8] documenting a relatively high incidence of marrow sideroblastic abnormalities in patients admitted for alcohol withdrawal that reverted rapidly after cessation of alcohol intake. These findings were confirmed by other investigators.[4,5] Grasso and Hines[9] demonstrated that the iron in these abnormal sideroblasts was deposited within the mitochondria (FIGURE 1), suggesting heme synthesis, possibly as a result of cellular deprivation of pyridoxal phosphate (PLP), the coenzyme for the rate-limiting enzyme for heme biosynthesis (delta amino-levulinic acid synthetase).

The purpose of this paper is to review and extend observations that demonstrate specific abnormalities in vitamin B_6 metabolism in subjects ingesting excessive alcohol and to describe another mechanism that creates impaired folate utilization in alcoholic patients.

PATIENTS

The subjects comprising these studies were chronic alcoholics admitted to the hospital with acute withdrawal symptoms. There was no clinical or biochemical evidence of liver disease in subjects selected for investigation. The criteria for eligibility for investigation have been previously described.[6,10] The patients were investigated on the Metabolic Unit and received a standard hospital diet containing approximately 1500 µg of total folate and 5–6 mg of pyridoxine. In selecting instances folic acid and pyridoxine supplementation were employed

*This project is supported by National Institute on Alcohol Abuse and Alcoholism grant number AA-00225-07.

(*vida infra*). Ethanol in the form of 86-proof bar whiskey was administered in graded amounts up to 900–1000 ml per day as previously described[10] and was isocalorically substituted for carbohydrate. Serum levels of ethanol in excess of 300 mg/100 ml were achieved in every subject. All investigations were performed in accordance with the Helsinki Declaration for Human Investigation and were approved by the Hospital Committee on Investigation in Humans.

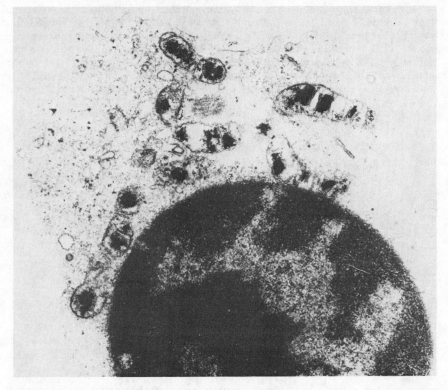

FIGURE 1. Electron photomicrograph of abnormal sideroblast of alcoholic patient with vitamin B$_6$ deficiency. There are numerous abnormal mitochondria above the nucleus with iron-loading and distorted cristae.

MATERIALS AND METHODS

Routine hematologic studies were performed according to standard methods.[15] Serum and erythrocyte folate were assayed by both *Lactobacilius casei*[16,17] and a radiochemical method employing partially purified hog kidney folate binder.[18] Serum hepatic and erythrocyte pyridoxal phosphate (PLP) levels were assayed by the method of Hines and Love.[19] Erythrocyte and hepatic pyridoxal phosphokinase estimations were performed by the method previously described.[6] Serum vitamin B$_{12}$ levels were determined with *Euglena gracilis*.[20] Serum iron and total iron-binding capacity were measured by the method of Shade et al.[21] Estimation of the *in vivo* conversion of intravenous pyridoxine to PLP was performed by the method of Hines and Cowan.[6]

RESULTS

Effect of Alcohol on Vitamin B_6 Metabolism

Previous experience in this laboratory has illustrated that the majority of chronic alcoholic subjects admitted for acute withdrawal symptoms have subnormal serum folate and PLP levels.

FIGURE 2 illustrates the serum PLP values in 16 alcoholic subjects at the time of admission compared with those of age-matched, nonalcoholic, hospital control patients. None of these alcoholic patients had any clinical or biochemical evidence of liver disease. A similar, though not strictly comparable, decrease in serum PLP levels in alcoholic subjects has been reported by other investigators.[4,13] The measurements of whole blood PLP levels in the same 16 alcoholics contrasted to age-matched, nonalcoholic control subjects are illustrated in FIGURE 3. The results are expressed in ng/ml of an adjusted packed red cell

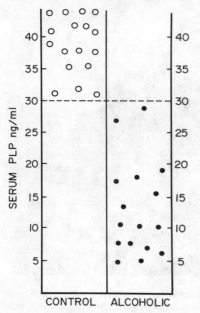

FIGURE 2. Serum PLP levels in age-matched controls and alcoholic subjects. (Normal 30–60 ng/ml).

volume of 50%. The alcoholic subjects with marrow sideroblastic abnormalities exhibited the lowest values. An additional 30 chronic alcoholic patients admitted to the hospital for acute alcoholic withdrawal were investigated. None had clinical or biochemical evidence of liver disease; however, 17 of 30 were anemic (Hct < 40% male, < 38% female). Folate deficiency as defined by subnormal serum and erythrocyte folate (*L. casei*) was present in 16 of the 30 subjects. Bone marrow sideroblastic abnormalities were present in 13 of the 30 subjects. The mean serum PLP levels in the nonsideroblastic group were 24.5 ng/ml, as contrasted to the mean of the sideroblastic subjects of 9.2 ng/ml, a statistically significant difference (P < 0.01). These findings illustrated that chronic alcohol abuse is associated with abnormal vitamin B_6 metabolism. In order to further delineate the effect of excessive alcohol intake on vitamin B_6 metabolism, 6 chronic alcoholic volunteer subjects, without clinical or biochemical evidence of liver or renal

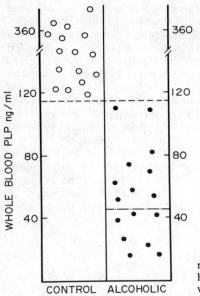

FIGURE 3. Whole-blood PLP levels in age-matched, nonalcoholic controls and chronic alcoholic subjects. (Normal > 115 ng/ml). The lowest values are for alcoholic-sideroblastic patients.

disease, were investigated on the Metabolic Unit. The hematological status of all subjects was normal, and all had been hospitalized without receiving alcohol for 3 weeks prior to investigation. Graded amounts of 86-proof bar whiskey of to 900 ml per day were administered with a standard hospital diet (*vida supra*). After receiving the alcohol for 2 weeks, each subject received a 20-mg intravenous injection of pyridoxine, and serum PLP levels were determined at 30, 120, and 240 minutes following the injection. These results are depicted in FIGURE 4. Prior to

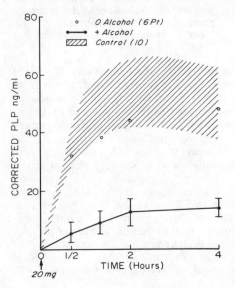

FIGURE 4. *In vivo* pyridoxine loading in controls, alcoholics receiving alcohol (solid line) and alcoholics abstaining from alcohol (open circles).

the administration of alcohol the identical procedure was performed and the net increase in PLP levels in these subjects was normal, as against the marked reduction in generation of PLP during alcohol administration. These results further illustrated the adverse effect of alcohol on vitamin B_6 metabolism and implied that alcohol impaired the oxidation and/or phosphorylation of pyridoxine to PLP. In 3 subjects a single intravenous injection of 20 mg of PLP was administered and the serum PLP levels were monitored in the same fashion. In all 3 there was a prompt increase in serum PLP levels of from 30 to 70 ng/ml, which was sustained for 2 hours in a manner not different from age-matched controls not receiving alcohol (not illustrated). This finding ruled out an accelerated egress of PLP from the circulation in the alcoholic subjects receiving alcohol.

In order to determine, more precisely the effect of alcohol on conversion of pyridoxine to PLP, an assessment of erythrocyte hemolysate pyridoxal phosphokinase was made on 4 chronic alcoholic volunteer subjects before and after administration of alcohol on the Metabolic Unit. This method of assessment of erythrocyte PL-kinase has been previously reported.[6] The results of these studies

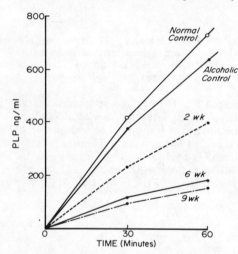

FIGURE 5. Red cell PL-kinase studies in normal, alcoholic control (0 alcohol), and alcoholic subjects receiving 900 ml/day of 86-proof bar whiskey from 2–9 weeks.

are summarized in FIGURE 5. The mean erythrocyte hemolysate PL-kinase activities of the alcoholic volunteer subjects were not significantly different from 4 age-matched control, nonalcoholic subjects prior to the administration of alcohol. However, in marked contrast were the progressive reduction in PL-kinase activity sequentially determined up to 9 weeks of alcohol ingestion. This is in contrast to the report of Lemeng and Li,[13] who were unable to discern any significance in PL-kinase activities of intact erythrocytes of controls and chronic alcoholics. However, none of their alcoholic subjects were receiving alcohol at the time of study.

It was next decided to test whether or not a circulating factor (or factors) was present in alcoholic subjects that might be inhibitory to the PL-kinase enzyme system. The results of such an experiment are illustrated in FIGURE 6. Erythrocyte hemolysates of an alcoholic volunteer prior to administration of alcohol were not significantly different from an age-matched, nonalcoholic control subject. After 4 weeks of receiving 900 ml of 86-proof bar whiskey per day with a standard hospital diet, a marked impairment of erythrocyte hemolysate PL-

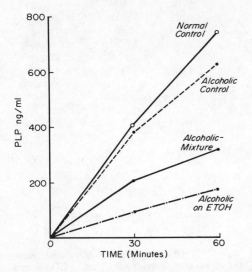

FIGURE 6. Red cell PL-kinase levels in normal, alcoholic control (0 alcohol), alcoholic mixture (plasma from alcoholic on 900 ml 86-proof bar whiskey/day mixed with normal red cells), and alcoholic subjects receiving alcohol (patient's own red cells).

kinase was observed. Equal amounts of plasma from the alcoholic subject were admixed with normal erythrocyte hemolysate, and this caused a greater than 50% reduction in enzyme activity by 60 minutes of incubation, confirming the possibility that some circulating factor(s) were present in plasma from the alcoholic on ethanol that were inhibitory to the PL-kinase enzyme system. In order to confirm this observation, an equal volume of plasma from age-matched control subjects and 6 alcoholic volunteer subjects was incubated with normal human hepatic tissue along with optimal amounts of magnesium, pyridoxine, and pyridoxal and ATP in a 0.05-M glycerol phosphate buffer. The amounts of pyridoxine and pyridoxal were adjusted to avoid substrate inhibition. The results are illustrated in FIGURE 7. There was a statistically significant reduction in hepatic PL-kinase

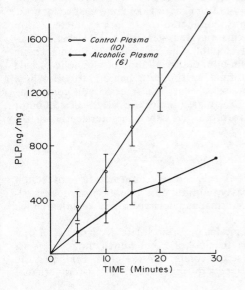

FIGURE 7. Hepatic PL-kinase levels in control vs. alcoholic subjects.

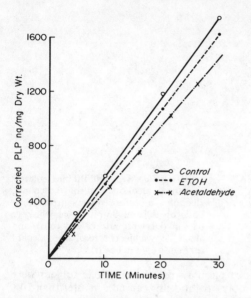

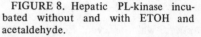

FIGURE 8. Hepatic PL-kinase incubated without and with ETOH and acetaldehyde.

activity in the specimens incubated with alcoholic plasma as compared to controls ($P < 0.001$). These results raised the obvious question as to whether or not the plasma ethanol or acetaldehyde present in alcoholic plasma was responsible for the observed inhibition of PL-kinase activity demonstrated in these studies. In order to test this possibility, ethanol (300 mg%), acetaldehyde (2 mM), and normal saline (control) were incubated with normal human hepatic specimens under the same conditions as described above and the net synthesis of PLP was assessed from 0 to 30 minutes. These results are illustrated in FIGURE 8. No significant change in hepatic PL-kinase activity could be demonstrated with the addition of either ethanol or acetaldehyde from that of the control specimen.

Several experiments were subsequently conducted to attempt characterization of the inhibitory factor(s) of the PL-kinase system generated in plasma of alcoholics ingesting excessive amounts of alcohol. The factor(s) are nondialyzable and, therefore, were felt to be protein-bound. An aliquot of alcoholic plasma demonstrated to be inhibitory to normal erythrocyte hemolysate PL-kinase activity was placed on a G-100 Sephadex column. The fraction still containing an inhibitory factor(s) was present in a calculated molecular weight of 35,000 or less. Further studies are in progress to more precisely characterize this factor (or factors).

Effect of Alcohol on Folate Metabolism

Eichner and coworkers demonstrated that precise interpretation of serum folate employing *Lactobacillus casei* assay required determination of blood alcohol levels in alcoholic subjects and in normal subjects given oral or intravenous ethanol.[4,22]

These investigators demonstrated a rapid fall in serum folate occurring after oral or intravenous ethanol administration to alcoholic and nonalcoholic subjects. Subsequently, using a radioassay for serum folate,[23] Paine et al. compared the serum folate in 3 normal volunteer subjects during and after short-term ethanol ingestion and compared these results with those of control regimens containing no ethanol.[24] The degree of the observed fall in serum folate as determined by both radioassay and *L. casei* seemed to correlate with the amount of ethanol consumed. The results of the radioassay essentially paralleled the *L. casei* assay results, suggesting that the observed decrease in serum folate activity was not an artifact of the microbiological assay.

Recently, Hines et al.[25] illustrated a significant difference in "free" and "bound" folate in serum obtained from patients with chronic renal insufficiency with the use of a newly developed radiochemical folate assay described by Kamen and Caston.[18] It was noted that although the total ("bound" and "free") serum folate of these subjects was normal and parallel to *L. casei* values, the "free" folate was subnormal in all subjects tested. Moreover, all subjects exhibited morphologic evidence of folate deficiency in peripheral blood and bone marrow. Following administration of pharmacologic amounts of pteroylglutamic acid (P6A) 5 mg/day, the morphologic signs of folate deficiency disappeared. The authors postulated that in certain of these patients the "bound" folate was apparently not available for cellular utilization.

A similar finding was noted in certain chronic alcoholic patients admitted for intoxication or acute withdrawal symptoms who had elevated blood alcohol levels on admission.[26] This finding prompted investigation of serum folate levels in alcoholic subjects assayed by both *L. casei* and the radioassay of Kamen and Caston. The results of the radioassay for serum folate performed in a chronic alcoholic volunteer subject investigated on the Metabolic Unit are illustrated in FIGURE 9. The patient was a 40-year-old white male who had an elevated blood alcohol on hospital admission (210 mg%). There was no clinical or biochemical evidence of liver or renal disease, and the patient was clinically well nourished. The "free" serum folate was less than 2 ng/ml, while the "bound" plus "free" level was nearly 8 ng/ml, as contrasted to the *L. casei* level of 2.8 ng/ml. Al-

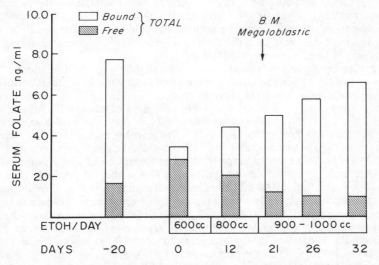

FIGURE 9. Serum folate data on alcoholic volunteer subject employing radiochemical assay before and during alcohol administration. Note the increase in "bound" folate and decrease in "free" folate on alcohol.

though he was not anemic, the patient's peripheral blood smear contained hyper-segmented neutrophiles and occasional ovalomacrocytic erythrocytes. After 3 weeks of hospitalization, while ingesting a standard hospital diet and requiring no medication, the patient was started on a regimen of 86-proof bar whiskey and standard diet. As is illustrated, the "bound" and "free" serum folate had re-turned to a normal concentration before alcohol ingestion, and thereafter the "free" serum folate dropped progressively to less than 1 ng/ml while the "bound" folate fraction increased to abnormally high levels. The *L. casei* folate values (not illustrated) closely paralleled the "free" serum folate. Bone marrow aspiration performed on the 21st day of the alcohol regimen revealed definite megaloblastic alterations in the erythroid and myeloid series despite a normal "total" serum folate (by radioassay). These results illustrate that the "bound" folate in alcoholic serum as detected by this assay system is apparently not available for cellular utilization and are very similar to the data previously reported in certain patients with chronic renal insufficiency.[25]

DISCUSSION

Pyridoxal phosphate constitutes the major fraction of vitamin B_6 congeners in human serum, and reduction in serum and whole blood (or erythrocyte) is con-sidered to be a reliable indicator of the status of vitamin B_6 nutrition in man.[19,27] The assay system for PLP assay employed in this laboratory employs rabbit skele-tal muscle apophosphorylase *b*, and the results for normal controls, irrespective of age, are higher than those reported by other investigators, using other enzy-matic assays.[13,28-30]

The present studies demonstrate that altered vitamin B_6 metabolism occurs relatively soon after excessive alcohol ingestion occurs and in the absence of clinical and/or biochemical evidence of liver disease. However, the studies re-ported by Lieber and Rubin[31,32] have clearly shown a reversible, altered hepatic histologic change may occur after several days of alcohol abuse even in nonalco-holic subjects. Although vitamin B_6-induced deficiency is associated with altered hepatic architectural changes in the rat and monkey,[33-35] no such causal relation-ship has as yet been documented in man.

The precise mechanism whereby excessive alcohol ingestion in conjunction with a nutritionally adequate diet produces abnormal vitamin B_6 metabolism has not been completely unraveled. Studies reported herein strongly support a pos-sible mechanism, which is interference of conversion of vitamin B_6 (pyridoxine, pyridoxal) to the active major coenzyme form PLP. Both the *in vivo* and *in vitro* studies support this possibility. An alternative possible mechanism has been re-cently reported by Lemeng and Li.[13] These investigators demonstrated that acetaldehyde, but not ethanol, impaired the net formation of PLP from substrate pyridoxine and pyridoxal in erythrocytes. This effect of acetaldehyde was abolished by addition of 80 mM phosphate ostensibly because of inhibition of B_6-phosphate phosphatase. By employing disrupted erythrocyte preparations, the authors demonstrated that the action of acetaldehyde was mediated by the membrane-bound phosphatase, resulting in accelerated degradation of phos-phorylated B_6 congeners in erythrocytes. In contrast to the studies reported herein, these authors did not detect decreased PL-kinase activity in erythrocytes from alcoholic patients with subnormal serum PLP levels; however, none of their study subjects were receiving ethanol at the time of investigation, and their studies were performed on intact erythrocytes.

Unpublished observations in this laboratory have failed to detect any decrease in PLP concentration in erythrocyte hemolysates when incubated with 1.0 mM acetaldehyde for up to 30 minutes of incubation at 37°C. This may represent a difference in our observed higher initial concentration in erythrocyte PLP content from that found by Lemeng and Li[13] or result partially from the fact that we employ a glycerol phosphate buffer system in our assay procedure.[19] The studies reported herein clearly show no effect of acetaldehyde on erythrocyte or hepatic PL-kinase activity. Regulation of erythrocyte PLP concentration depends upon pyridoxine phosphate oxidase, pyridoxal phosphokinase, and B$_6$-phosphate phosphatase.[13,36] The major body site for PLP synthesis is the liver. Unfortunately, little is known regarding the role, if any, of B$_6$-phosphate phosphatase activity in regulation of hepatic PLP synthesis. The studies reported herein have demonstrated that certain healthy, well-nourished, chronic alcoholic subjects, when ingesting excessive alcohol, generate a protein-bound plasma inhibitor for both erythrocyte and hepatic PL-kinase. The precise physiochemical properties of this factor(s) remain to be elicited.

As discussed previously, folate deficiency is a well-recognized complication of chronic alcoholic abuse.[1-5] The mechanisms for the evolution of folate deficiency in chronic alcoholic subjects include marginal or suboptimal intake, reduced hepatic storage,[37] altered intestinal absorption,[38] or altered cellular utilization.[1,2] Recently, Wu et al.[39] described macrocytic erythrocyte changes in 89% of 63 chronic alcoholic subjects consuming nearly 80 g of ethanol per day for at least several years. Rather surprisingly, these investigators found low serum folate levels as assayed by *L. casei* in only one-third of these patients. These authors postulated that ethanol ingestion per se caused the abnormal erythrocytic maturation independently of folate status. Studies reported herein employing a radiochemical assay for serum folate illustrated that although the "bound" plus "free" serum folate ("total" serum folate) remained normal in an alcoholic volunteer subject ingesting excessive amounts of alcohol, the "free" folate fraction decreased below normal and was associated with megaloblastic marrow maturation. The latter observations suggest that in this subject the "bound" folate was not available for marrow utilization, somewhat analogous to the reported studies from this laboratory in certain patients with chronic renal disease.[25] An alternative possibility explaining the findings of Wu et al.[39] is that their strain of *L. casei* was capable of growth with "free" and "bound" folate, in contrast to the *L. casei* results observed in our subject.

SUMMARY

The studies described here illustrate that chronic alcohol abuse frequently results in deranged vitamin B$_6$ metabolism, often resulting in deficiency of the coenzyme form PLP. Subsequent studies in this laboratory point to a direct effect of excess alcohol intake on generation of PLP from other vitamin B$_6$ congeners, specifically on the enzyme system pyridoxal phosphokinase. Studies reported by other investigators[13] suggest that acetaldehyde formation increases erythrocyte membrane-bound B$_6$-phosphate phosphatase, which results in defective synthesis of intracellular PLP and accelerated degradation of PLP within the erythrocyte.

Another possible mechanism for development of cellular depletion of folate in alcoholic subjects is described in 1 patient investigated with metabolic balance studies. This mechanism would appear to depend on the generation of folic-acid-binding substance(s) within the plasma of the patient when ingesting excess alcohol occurring while the "free" folate plasma levels fall to subnormal levels. This phenomenon was associated with the development of megaloblastic marrow abnormalities.

REFERENCES

1. SULLIVAN, L. W. & V. HERBERT. 1964. Suppression of hematopoiesis by ethanol. J. Clin. Invest. 43: 2048.
2. SULLIVAN, L. W. & V. HERBERT. 1964. Mechanism of hematosuppression by ethanol. Amer. J. Clin. Nutr. 14: 238.
3. HERBERT, V., R. ZALUSKY & C. S. DAVIDSON. 1963. Correlation of folate deficiency with alcoholism and associated macrocytosis, anemia, and liver disease. Ann. Int. Med. 58: 977.
4. EICHNER, E. R. & R. S. HILLMAN. 1971. The evolution of anemia in alcoholic patients. Amer. J. Med. 50: 218.
5. EICHNER, E. R., B. BUCHANAN & J. W. SMITH. 1972. Variations in the hematologic and medical status of alcoholics. Amer. J. Med. Sci. 263: 35.
6. HINES, J. D. & D. H. COWAN. 1974. Anemia in alcoholism. In Drugs and Hematologic Reactions. The Twenty-Ninth Hahnemann Symposium. N. V. Dimitrov & J. H. Nodine, Eds.: 148. Grune and Stratton. New York, N.Y.
7. WILLIAMS, J. R. & R. H. GIRDWOOD. 1970. The folate status of alcoholics. Scot. Med. J. 15: 285.
8. HINES, J. D. 1969. Reversible megaloblastic and sideroblastic marrow abnormalities in alcoholic patients. Brit. J. Haemat. 16: 87.
9. GRASSO, J. & J. D. HINES. 1969. A comparative electron microscopic study of refractory and alcoholic sideroblastic anaemias. Brit. J. Haemat. 17: 35.
10. HINES, J. D. & D. H. COWAN. 1970. Studies on the pathogenesis of alcohol-induced sideroblastic bone marrow abnormalities. New Eng. J. Med. 283: 441.
11. WATERS, A. H., A. A. MORLEY & J. G. RANKIN. 1966. Effect of alcohol on haemopoiesis. Brit. Med. J. 2: 1565.
12. HOURIHANE, D. O'B. & D. G. WEIR. 1970. Suppression of erythropoiesis by alcohol. Brit. Med. J. 1: 86.
13. LUMENG, L. & T. K. LI. 1974. Vitamin B_6 metabolism in chronic alcohol abuse. J. Clin. Invest. 53: 698.
14. JANDL, J. H. 1958. Hematologic changes in chronic liver disease. Amer. J. Gast. 30: 46.
15. Page, L. B. & P. J. Culver, Eds. 1960. A Syllabus of Laboratory Examinations in Clinical Diagnosis. Harvard University Press, Cambridge, Mass.
16. HERBERT, V. 1966. Aseptic addition method for Lactobacillus casei assay of folate activity in human serum. J. Clin. Pathol. 19: 12.
17. HOFFBRAND, A. V., B. F. A. NEWCOMBE & D. L. MOLLIN. 1966. Method of assay of red cell folate activity in the value of the assay as a test for folate deficiency. J. Clin. Pathol. 19: 17.
18. KAMEN, B. & D. CASTON. 1974. Direct radio chemical assay for serum folate: competition between folic acid and 5-methyl tetrahydrofolate for a folate binder. J. Lab. Clin. Med. 83: 164.
19. HINES, J. D. & D. S. LOVE. 1969. Determination of serum and blood pyridoxal phosphate concentrations with purified rabbit skeletal muscle phosphorylast b. J. Lab. Clin. Med. 73: 343.
20. ANDERSON, B. B. 1964. Investigations into the Euglena methods for the assay of vitamin B_{12} in serum. J. Clin. Pathol. 17: 14.
21. SCHADE, A. L., J. OYAMA & R. W. REINHART. 1954. Bound iron and unsaturated iron-binding capacity of serum: rapid and reliable quantitative determination. Proc. Soc. Exp. Biol. Med. 87: 443.
22. EICHNER, E. R. & R. S. HILLMAN. 1973. Effect of alcohol on serum folate level. J. Clin. Invest. 52: 584.
23. WASMAN, S., C. SCHREIBER & V. HERBERT. 1971. Radioisotopic assay for measurement of serum folate levels. Blood 38: 219.

24. PAINE, C. J., E. R. EICHNER & V. DICKSON. 1973. Concordance of radio assay and microbiological assay in the study of the ethanol-induced fall in serum folate level. Amer. J. Med. Sci. 266(2): 135.
25. HINES, J. D., B. KAMEN & D. CASTON. 1973. Abnormal folate binding protein(s) in azotemic patients. (abstr.). Blood 42: 997.
26. HINES, J. D. 1974. Unpublished observations.
27. SAUBERLICH, H. E., E. M. CANHAM, N. BAUER, J. RAICA & Y. F. HERMAN. 1972. Biochemical assessment of the nutritional status of vitamin B$_6$ in the human. Amer. J. Clin. Nutri. 25: 629.
28. CHABNER, B. & D. LIVINGSTON. 1970. A simple enzymatic assay for pyridoxal phosphate. Anal. Biochem. 34: 413.
29. HAMFELT, A. 1966. Age variation in vitamin B$_6$ metabolism in man. Clin. Chim. Acta 10: 48.
30. WALSH, M. P. 1966. Determination of plasma pyridoxal phosphate with wheat germ glutamic-aspartic apotransaminase. Amer. J. Clin. Pathol. 46: 282.
31. LIEBER, C. S. & E. RUBIN. 1968. Alcoholic fatty liver in man on a high protein and low fat diet. Amer. J. Med. 44: 200.
32. RUBIN, E. & C. S. LIEBER. 1968. Alcohol-induced hepatic injury in nonalcoholic volunteers. New Eng. J. Med. 278: 869.
33. FRENCH, S. W. & J. CASTAGNA. 1967. Some effects of chronic ethanol feeding on vitamin B$_6$ deficiency in the rat. Lab. Invest. 16: 526.
34. OKODA, M. & A. OCHI. 1971. The effect of diet protein level on transaminase activities and fat deposition in the vitamin B$_6$-depleted rat. J. Biochem. (Tokyo) 70: 581.
35. GREENBERG, L. D. 1964. Arteriosclerotic dental and hepatic lesions in pyridoxine deficient monkeys. Vitamins Horm. 22: 677.
36. ANDERSON, B. B., C. E. FULFORD-JONES, J. A. CHILD, M. E. J. BEARD & C. J. T. BATEMAN. 1971. Conversion of vitamin B$_6$ compounds to active forms in the red blood cell. J. Clin. Invest. 50: 1901.
37. CHERRICK, G. R., H. BAUER, O. FRANK & C. M. LEEVY. 1965. Observation on hepatic activity for folate in Laennec's cirrhosis. J. Lab. Clin. Med. 66: 446.
38. HALSTED, C. H., R. C. GRIGGS & J. W. HARRIS. 1967. The effect of alcoholism on the absorption of folic acid (H[3] P6A) evaluated by plasma levels and urine excretion. J. Lab. Clin. Med. 69: 116.
39. WU, A., I. CHARARIN & A. J. LEVI. 1974. Macrocytosis of chronic alcoholism. Lancet 1: 829.

THE PLATELET DEFECT IN ALCOHOLISM*

Dale H. Cowan

Department of Medicine
Case Western Reserve University at Cleveland
Metropolitan General Hospital
Cleveland, Ohio 44109

The occurrence of thrombocytopenia in persons ingesting large quantities of alcohol has been well documented by a number of investigators.[1-6] No apparent relationship exists between the development of thrombocytopenia and that of anemia or leukopenia.[6,7] Additionally, the reduction in the number of circulating platelets in patients ingesting ethanol is not dependent on the presence of concomitant nutritional deprivation, in particular folate deficiency.[4,6] Rather, several investigators have shown that thrombocytopenia may be a direct toxic effect of high concentrations of ethanol per se.[4,8] It has recently been shown that ethanol can also impair the function of circulating platelets both *in vivo* and *in vitro*.[9] The extent of the impairment in platelet function induced by ethanol is greater in patients with ethanol-related thrombocytopenia than in patients consuming ethanol in whom thrombocytopenia does not supervene.[9]

These observations raise a number of questions regarding the cellular kinetics underlying the development of thrombocytopenia in individuals ingesting large quantities of ethanol, the mechanism underlying the disturbances in platelet function in alcoholic subjects, and the apparent parallelism between the extent of impairment of platelet survival and platelet function in alcoholism. This report will focus on these questions by reviewing the results of studies of platelet production, survival, and function in alcoholic patients. In addition, the results of recent experiments examining both intracorpuscular and extracorpuscular factors affecting platelets in alcoholic patients will be summarized.

PATIENTS

The subjects comprising these studies were chronic alcoholic patients who were initially admitted to hospital for treatment of acute intoxication or alcohol withdrawal syndrome. The criteria used to select patients for study have been described previously.[8,9] The patients were housed on a metabolic ward and fed either folate-deficient or standard hospital diets. The standard hospital diet contains approximately 1500 μg of "total folate." Patients receiving this diet received a daily oral 200-μg supplement of pteroylglutamic acid (PGA) during abstinence and a 5-mg supplement of PGA during periods of ethanol ingestion. Ethanol in the form of 86-proof whiskey was administered in graded amounts to a maximum of 900 to 990 ml per day as described previously.[8,9] Levels of blood ethanol in excess of 300 mg/100 ml were achieved in each subject receiving this amount of ethanol. All studies were done in accordance with the Helsinki Declaration for Human Research and were approved by the hospital Committee on Investigation in Humans.

*Supported by Grant No. AA-00272 from the National Institute of Alcohol Abuse and Alcoholism.

MATERIALS AND METHODS

Thrombopoiesis and Platelet Survival

The total platelet-producing capacity of the marrow was measured by a modification[8] of the method for quantitating megakaryocytes described by Harker.[10] Platelet survival studies were done by a minor modification[8] of the acid-citrate method of Aster and Jandl.[11] Intravenous administration of ethanol was performed using the method of Post and Desforges.[3]

Platelet Function

Bleeding times were determined by the template method of Mielke et al.[12] Platelet aggregation was measured in citrated platelet-rich plasma (PRP) by the turbidometric method of Born and Cross.[13] Measurements using normal control PRP were done in parallel with those using patient PRP. The concentration of platelets in control and patient PRPs were adjusted to similar values in autologous platelet-poor plasma (PPP).[9] Platelet factor 3 (PF 3) availability was measured by the method of Spaet and Cintron.[14] The release of platelet adenine nucleotides from washed platelets in Tris buffer (pH 7.4) following thrombin stimulation was measured using a modification[15] of the method of Mürer.[16] Serotonin release was measured by a minor modification of the method of Valdorf-Hansen and Zucker.[17]

Biochemistry

The carbohydrate metabolism of platelets was studied using a modification[18,19] of the methods described by Stjernholm.[20] Platelet protein content was determined by the method of Lowry et al.[21] The metabolism of adenine nucleotides was studied with a modification[22] of the method of Holmsen and Weiss.[23]

Immunology

The presence of antiplatelet antibodies was determined with use of the platelet factor 3 immuno-injury assay of Karpatkin et al.[24]

Ultrastructure

The fine structure of citrated platelets was studied by the methods of White.[25]

RESULTS

Effect of Ethanol on Thrombopoiesis

The effect of ethanol on platelet production was assessed by determining the total megakaryocyte mass from sections of bone marrow biopsies. The results of these studies are listed in TABLE 1, in which the patients are grouped according to whether they were (1) ingesting ethanol, (2) folate-deficient, and (3) thrombocytopenic. The marrows from patients with folate deficiency showed classic changes of megaloblastic maturation: increases in size and relative numbers of basophilic and polychromatophilic erythroblasts; less compact chromatin network; and giant myelocytes, metamyelocytes and bands. Significant increases over normal in the total mass of megakaryocytes occurred in patients who were folate-deficient. The increases in the total mass of megakaryocytes in folate-

TABLE 1
The Effect of Ethanol on Platelet Production*

Patient Group	Ingest-ing Ethanol	Folate-Deficient	Thrombo-cytopenia	Megakaryocyte		
				Number ($\times 10^6$/ KgBW)	Volume (μ^3)	Mass ($\times 10^{10}\mu^3$/ KgBW)
Normal (9)†	0	0	0	13.0 ± 4.3‡	3982 ±253	5.1 ± 1.0
I (7)	0	+	0	40.6	3762	15.2
II (2)	+	+	0	35.5	2750	9.5
III (3)	+	+	+	57.2	3347	18.6
IV (3)	0	0	0	14.1	4136	5.4
V (1)	+	0	0	25.0	3050	7.6
VI (2)	+	0	+	20.8	3627	7.7

*Data from references 8 and 26.
†Numbers in parentheses denote number of subjects.
‡Denotes ±1 SEM.

deficient patients were due to increases in the numbers of megakaryocytes. These increases were not dependent on concomitant ethanol ingestion or the development of thrombocytopenia. However, the largest increases in mega-karyocyte number and total mass occurred in folate-deficient patients who developed thrombocytopenia with ethanol ingestion. The mean megakaryo-cyte volume was reduced in folate-deficient patients who were ingesting ethanol.

The finding of increased numbers of megakaryocytes in megaloblastic marrows by this technique is at variance with the common observation that megakaryo-cytes are reduced in number in marrow aspirates from patients with megalo-blastic maturation defects. This discrepancy may be attributed to a relatively greater degree of hyperplasia of erythroid elements as compared to megakaryo-cytes in megaloblastic marrows. This results in an apparent (relative) reduction in the numbers of megakaryocytes. The administration of ethanol to folate-supplemented patients was associated with increases in the numbers of megakaryocytes that were appreciably less than the increases observed in folate-deficient patients. The total mass of megakaryocytes was not significantly in-

TABLE 2
Results of Survival Studies Using Autologous Platelets*

Patient Group†	Life Span (Days)	Recovery (%)	Turnover (Platelets/μl/Day)
Normal	8.5 ± 0.2‡	62 ± 3	$49,200 \pm 3600$
I	8.6	52	62,000
II	6.5	73	58,700
III	2.7	55	37,600
IV	8.7	58	51,300
V	6.6	65	69,200
VI	3.8	61	25,700

*Data from references 8 and 26.
†The patients are grouped as indicated in TABLE 1.
‡Denotes ±1 SEM.

creased over normal and was similar in both thrombocytopenic and non-thrombocytopenic patients.

The results of survival studies using autologous platelets are listed in TABLE 2. Patients are grouped as indicated in TABLE 1. Folate deficiency alone was not associated with a reduction from normal in the survival of circulating, autologous platelets. In contrast, the survival of autologous platelets was significantly reduced in patients ingesting large amounts of ethanol. The extent of the decrease was markedly greater in patients who were thrombocytopenic. The presence of

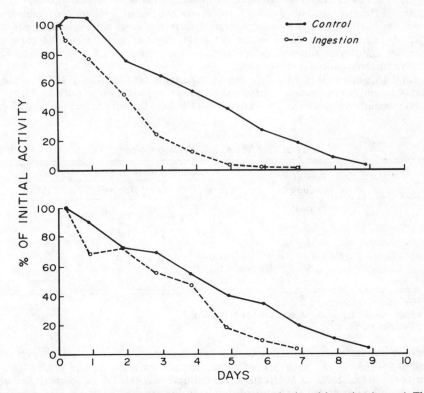

FIGURE 1. Platelet survival during abstinence (●——●) and ethanol ingestion (○– – –○). The upper portion of the figure depicts results in a patient who developed thrombocytopenia with alcohol ingestion. The lower portion presents results in a patient in whom thrombocytopenia did not develop. From Cowan.[8] By permission of the publisher of the Journal of Laboratory of Clinical Medicine.

concomitant folate deficiency in patients ingesting ethanol had no appreciable additive effect on the results of the life span determinations.

The morphology of the platelet survival curves observed in thrombocytopenic and nonthrombocytopenic patients ingesting ethanol is depicted in FIGURE 1. In each instance, the initial portion of the disappearance curve was linear. After approximately one-half the life span, the curves "tail off," suggesting the presence of a subpopulation of somewhat longer-lived cells. The recovery of labeled platelets, calculated at time zero after their infusion, was normal in each of the groups of patients. The platelet turnover—i.e., the number of platelets per unit volume entering and leaving the circulation per day—was greater than normal in those patients ingesting ethanol who were not thrombocytopenic and was subnormal in those patients in whom thrombocytopenia supervened.

These data indicate that a major reason for the development of thrombocytopenia in patients ingesting large quantities of ethanol is a reduction in platelet life span. An additional reason may be discerned from examination of TABLE 3. The term "total thrombopoiesis" refers to the total platelet-producing capacity of the marrow as determined from the measurements of total megakaryocyte mass. "Effective thrombopoiesis" refers to the actual delivery of platelets from the marrow to the bloodstream as determined from the measurements of platelet turnover. The mean values for total megakaryocyte mass and platelet turnover in normal subjects define the control values of 1.0 for total and effective thrombopoiesis, respectively.

Total thrombopoiesis in folate-deficient patients ranged from 1.9–3.6 × normal. In contrast, effective thrombopoiesis was approximately normal. Hence, total thrombopoiesis was in excess of effective thrombopoiesis—a situation

TABLE 3
"Total" and "Effective" Thrombopoiesis*

Patient Group†	Thrombopoiesis	
	Total	Effective
Normal	1.0 ± 0.2‡	1.0 ± 0.1
I	3.0	1.2
II	1.9	1.2
III	3.6	0.8
IV	1.0	1.0
V	1.5	1.4
VI	1.5	0.6

*Data from references 8 and 26.
†The patients are grouped as indicated in TABLE 1.
‡Denotes ±1 SEM.

defined as ineffective thrombopoiesis. This is analogous to ineffective erythropoiesis, which is the hallmark of megaloblastic maturation. The greatest disparity between total and effective thrombopoiesis existed in folate-deficient patients who developed thrombocytopenia during ethanol ingestion.

The increases over normal in total thrombopoiesis in patients ingesting ethanol were substantially less in folate-supplemented patients than in folate-deficient patients. Administration of ethanol was not associated with ineffective thrombopoiesis in folate-supplemented patients who were not thrombocytopenic. In contrast, the development of thrombocytopenia in the course of ethanol ingestion by folate-supplemented patients was associated with a degree of ineffective thrombopoiesis similar to that seen in nonthrombocytopenic, non–alcohol-ingesting folate-deficient patients. Consequently, an additional reason for the development of thrombocytopenia is reduced effective platelet production due to the ineffective marrow response. When the marrows of patients ingesting ethanol are unable adequately to compensate for the accelerated rate of destruction of circulating platelets, thrombocytopenia supervenes.

Mechanisms for Altered Thrombokinetics

The possible mechanisms underlying the observed alterations in thrombopoiesis and platelet survival may be considered on the basis of whether they are due primarily to extracellular or intracellular factors.

Extracellular Factors

Among the possible extracellular factors are (1) ethanol per se or metabolites of ethanol, (2) ethanol-induced antiplatelet antibodies, and (3) ethanol-induced fibrinolysis. The possibility of ethanol's producing platelet sequestration and/or destruction by a direct toxic action was assessed by determining the platelet counts in patients before, during, and after finite intervals (3 hours) of intravenous ethanol administration. Post and Desforges[3] reported that administration of ethanol intravenously produced decreases in platelet counts of 10%, 25%, and 40% on 3 separate occasions in 1 of 3 patients. No changes were observed in the other 2 patients. Decreases in platelet counts of 20% below the preinfusion control values were detected in 2 of 8 patients receiving intravenous ethanol in our laboratory.[8] Blood ethanol levels during the infusions were 190–210 mg/100 ml in each of the patients. The average of the results in the 8 patients showed no detectable change in the concentration of circulating platelets. It may be concluded that transient increases in blood ethanol concentration to levels in the range of 200 mg/100 ml are not associated with a significant degree of platelet sequestration or destruction.

It is possible that ethanol per se may damage platelets sufficiently to impair their function and that the impairment in function may lead to premature cellular destruction. To determine this, the function of platelets from patients receiving intravenous administration of ethanol and of normal platelets exposed to ethanol *in vitro* in concentrations detected in the patients ingesting ethanol was measured. Intravenous administration of ethanol to 3 patients produced partial impairment in secondary platelet aggregation, 10 to 15% impairment in the release of adenine nucleotides, no impairment in primary aggregation, and no decrease in PF 3 availability.[9]

Exposure of normal platelets to ethanol *in vitro* produced no impairment in primary aggregation. A reduction in secondary aggregation occurred that was greater with lower concentrations of aggregating agents and higher concentrations of ethanol.[9] Additionally, *in vitro* exposure to ethanol caused reduced PF 3 availability from platelets stimulated by kaolin or by ADP and a decrease in the rate of nucleotide release.[9] *In vitro* exposure of normal platelets to concentrations of ethanol similar to those observed in study patients also caused significant impairment in the release of ^{14}C-serotonin (FIGURE 2), a phenomenon analogous to nucleotide release. These findings indicate that ethanol per se can alter the behavior of circulating platelets primarily by impairing the release reaction.

The possibility that ethanol ingestion might lead to the production of antiplatelet antibodies was studied by testing the plasma of patients ingesting ethanol for antiplatelet antibody. Using the PF 3 immunoinjury assay, the studies failed to detect any evidence for antiplatelet antibodies in this clinical setting.

The possibility that excessive ethanol consumption might produce disseminated intravascular coagulation (DIC) was studied by testing the serum of the patients for fibrinogen-related antigens (FRA) using the method of Rabaa et al.[27] FRA were not detected in any of the patients.[9]

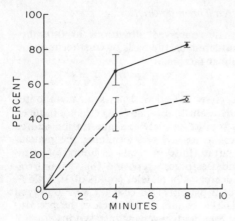

FIGURE 2. Release of ^{14}C-serotonin by normal platelets incubated with ethanol for 5 minutes prior to stimulation with collagen. The closed circles (solid line) denote results in control platelets. The open circles (interrupted line) denote results with use of ethanol-treated cells. The 4-minute and 8-minute points are the means of 4 and 2 determinations, respectively, done in duplicate. The vertical bars denote ±1 S.D.

The data suggest that ethanol per se may affect the circulating platelet directly but provide no support for a role by other humoral factors.

Intracellular Factors

Intracellular abnormalities capable of affecting platelet kinetics might be expected to alter the structure, function, and/or metabolism of the circulating platelets. To interpret results of studies of platelet structure and behavior, it is necessary to consider first the average age and size of the platelets in patients ingesting ethanol as compared with that seen in normal subjects. The subnormal platelet survival observed in alcoholic patients could reflect destruction of newly formed, "young" platelets or, alternatively, the terminal portion of the survival of platelets sequestered early in their life cycle and released to the circulation as "older" platelets. Based on the studies of Karpatkin,[28] the cell population in the former instance would be larger, heavier, and functionally and metabolically more active than normal, whereas in the latter instance the opposite would be the case. Karpatkin and coworkers[29] have shown further that the percentage of large platelets, termed megathrombocytes, is increased in patients with disorders causing increased platelet destruction.

Fifty to 100% increases in the protein content were observed in platelets from patients ingesting alcohol as compared with platelets from the same subjects during abstinence.[8] Increased numbers of giant platelets, as seen by both light and electron microscopy, were present in the blood of patients ingesting ethanol who were thrombocytopenic.[22] The utilization of ^{14}C-glucose and the production of ^{14}C-lactate, when determined on a per-platelet basis, were increased in nonstimulated platelets from patients with alcohol-related thrombocytopenia.[19] The extent of the increases in these activities was commensurate with the increases in protein content of the platelets. These findings support the contention that the reduced platelet survival in alcoholic patients represents the premature destruction of newly formed platelets.

On the basis of this interpretation and Karpatkin's observations,[28] it would be expected that the functional activity of the "young" platelets circulating in alcoholic patients would be greater than normal. A finding of subnormal functional activity would then be indicative of substantial cellular derangement and would imply that ethanol ingestion produces intracellular abnormalities in platelets.

Platelet Function

The bleeding time in 1 patient with a normal platelet count $(300,000/\mu 1)$ during ethanol ingestion was twice that observed during the control period of abstinence.[9] The development of thrombocytopenia with ethanol ingestion was associated with 4- to 5-fold increases in bleeding times over control values in each of 3 patients.[9]

The aggregation of platelets in response to adenosine $5'$-diphosphate (ADP), epinephrine, thrombin, and collagen was reduced in each of 5 patients ingesting ethanol.[9] Representative tracings of the aggregation responses are depicted in FIGURE 3. Impairment of aggregation was evident when platelet counts were normal and became more profound when thrombocytopenia supervened. Additionally, the impairment in the aggregation responses was greater with lower concentrations of aggregating agents. Both primary aggregation, induced by low concentrations of ADP and epinephrine, and secondary aggregation, in-

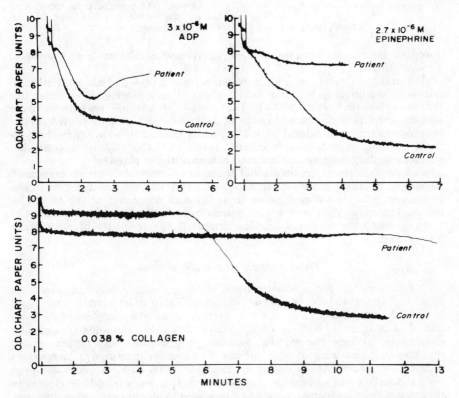

FIGURE 3. Aggregation of citrated PRP obtained from a patient ingesting ethanol and having a blood ethanol concentration of 430 mg/100 ml. Platelet count in patient was $210\,000/\mu l$. The concentration of platelets in the PRP from both patient and control was adjusted to $200\,000/\mu l$ with autologous PPP. Final concentrations of aggregating agents are shown. The results are representative of those obtained in patients during ethanol ingestion. From Haut & Cowan.[9] By permission of the authors and the publisher of the American Journal of Medicine.

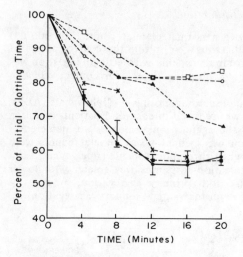

FIGURE 4. Effect of ethanol ingestion on PF 3 availability from platelets stimulated with 5% kaolin. The concentration of platelets in the PRP was 200 000/μl. The mean of 20 determinations done in duplicate using normal platelets is depicted by the uninterrupted line (●——●). The vertical bars denote ±1 SEM. The results using patients' platelets are depicted by the interrupted lines (———). The abscissa indicates the time elapsed after addition of kaolin to PRP. The clotting times are expressed as percent of initial clotting time. From Haut & Cowan.[9] By permission of the authors and the publisher of the American Journal of Medicine.

duced by high concentrations of these agents and by thrombin and collagen, were impaired.

PF 3 availability was impaired in platelets from 2 of 4 patients with ethanol-related thrombocytopenia and in 1 patient ingesting ethanol who was not thrombocytopenic[9] (FIGURE 4). The release of adenine nucleotides from washed platelets was reduced in each of 2 patients with ethanol-related thrombocytopenia and was normal in the 1 patient studied in whom thrombocytopenia did not supervene with ethanol ingestion.[9] The findings suggest that ethanol ingestion produces intracellular abnormalities in platelets.

In contrast to the effect on platelet function of intravenous administration of ethanol or of ethanol added *in vitro* to normal platelets, ethanol ingestion causes impairment of primary aggregation in addition to depression of the release reaction. This may indicate that one consequence of ethanol ingestion, but not of transient exposure to ethanol, is impairment in the reactivity of the platelet membrane.

Platelet Structure and Metabolism

To determine whether ethanol-induced platelet dysfunction is associated with structural and metabolic abnormalities, studies of platelet ultrastructure, carbohydrate metabolism, and adenine nucleotide metabolism were done with use of cells in both resting and stimulated states. Studies using transmission electron microscopy showed that platelets from patients with ethanol-related thrombocytopenia vary greatly in size.[22] As noted previously, many giant platelets were seen. Additionally, the circumferential band of microtubules in resting platelets was missing or fragmented.[22] This was particularly evident in the large platelets. Granules were often increased in number and unusually large. Several rodlike structures were seen in many of the larger platelets. The open-channel system was often dilated. After collagen stimulation, the centripetal migration of granules was characteristically retarded and incomplete and the platelet aggregates were smaller and less compact than normal.[22]

Reference was made earlier to the finding that the utilization of ^{14}C-glucose and production of ^{14}C-lactate by resting platelets from patients ingesting ethanol were increased over normal to an extent commensurate with the increase in protein content of the cells. The rates of oxidation of carbons 1 and 6 of glucose to $^{14}CO_2$ were also greater than normal. The increases over resting levels in the rates of ^{14}C-glucose utilization and ^{14}C-lactate production associated with thrombin stimulation of platelets from patients ingesting ethanol were significantly less than those observed in normal platelets[19] (TABLE 4). Thrombin-related increases in glucose oxidation by "alcoholic" platelets were normal. In contrast, stimulation with epinephrine of platelets from patients ingesting ethanol was associated with normal increases above resting values in ^{14}C-glucose utilization and ^{14}C-lactate production, but significantly subnormal increases in oxidation of ^{14}C-glucose to CO_2. Despite the subnormal net increases in glycolysis or glucose oxidation, it seems evident that the capacity of platelets from patients with alcohol-related thrombocytopenia to increase energy production following stimulation is not markedly impaired. Ethanol ingestion appears to inhibit platelet function more than it inhibits the metabolic reactions that provide the energy for the functional activities.

Ethanol ingestion also affects adenine nucleotide metabolism in platelets.[22] As depicted in FIGURE 5, the intracellular concentration of ADP and the amount of ADP released to plasma after collagen stimulation are significantly reduced with the development of thrombocytopenia during ethanol ingestion. The intracellular concentration of ATP is normal or minimally subnormal and the amount of ATP released is normal. The ratio ATP/ADP is, therefore, increased. The specific radioactivity of ATP and ADP in nonstimulated platelets, determined after incubation of platelets with ^{14}C-adenine, is increased in the presence of alcohol-related thrombocytopenia to levels equal to or greater than those found in stimulated normal platelets.[22] The formation of ^{14}C-hypoxanthine is similarly increased. These results are interpreted as indicating that there is relative depletion of ADP in the storage pool of adenine nucleotides in addi-

TABLE 4

Effect of Thrombin and Epinephrine on Utilization and Oxidation of
^{14}C-Glucose and on Production of ^{14}C-Lactate

	Mean Net Increase with	
	Thrombin	Epinephrine
	(Micromoles per 10^9 platelets per hour)	
^{14}C-Glucose Utilization		
Normal	1.00 ± 0.08†	0.53 ± 0.09
Alcoholic	0.73 ± 0.11	0.44 ± 0.08
^{14}C-Lactate Production		
Normal	1.98 ± 0.15	0.87 ± 0.15
Alcoholic	1.43 ± 0.22	0.86 ± 0.14
	(Nanomoles per 10^9 platelets per hour)	
$^{14}C_1 \longrightarrow {}^{14}CO_2$		
Normal	7.4 ± 1.3	30.3 ± 4.4
Alcoholic	7.5 ± 2.9	8.9 ± 4.2
$^{14}C_6 \longrightarrow {}^{14}CO_2$		
Normal	1.66 ± 0.33	4.08 ± 1.20
Alcoholic	1.74 ± 0.68	0.89 ± 0.29

*Data derived from reference 19.
† Denotes ±1 SEM.

tion to an absolute reduction in total cellular ADP. The depletion of storage pool ADP results in the subnormal release of ADP with stimulation. The increase over normal in the amount of hypoxanthine formed suggests that an increased amount of ATP is catabolized to provide energy for the release reaction.

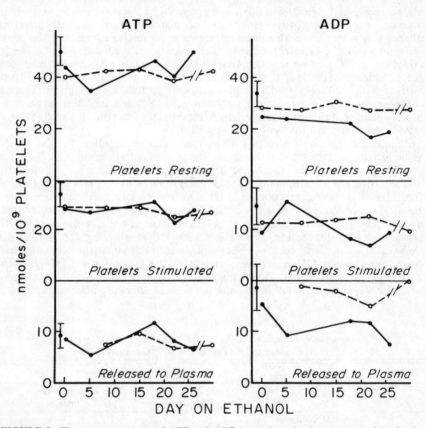

FIGURE 5. The concentrations of ATP and ADP in resting platelets (top panels), platelets stimulated with collagen (center panels), and released from platelets to plasma after collagen stimulation (bottom panels). The solid line (●——●) denotes results in a patient who developed thrombocytopenia with ethanol ingestion and the interrupted line (○---○) denotes results in a non-thrombocytopenic patient. The vertical bars to the left of each panel denote the mean ±1 SD in platelets from 7 normal subjects.

Significant disturbances in adenine nucleotide metabolism were not observed when thrombocytopenia failed to develop during ingestion.[22] This finding, together with the observation that the impairment in platelet function was appreciably more severe in thrombocytopenic than in nonthrombocytopenic patients, suggests that some of the platelet abnormalities in patients with ethanol-related thrombocytopenia occur during megakaryocyte maturation.

DISCUSSION

The nature and mechanism of production of ethanol-induced defects in platelets are presently unknown. One possible cause is suggested by the observation made earlier in this report that the pattern of cellular kinetics in folate-replete patients with ethanol-related thrombocytopenia is similar to that seen in folate-deficient patients, i.e. ineffective thrombopoiesis. Hines[30] has observed the appearance of folate-binding protein in the blood of patients ingesting large amounts of ethanol. Conceivably, the presence of a folate-binding protein may interfere with the utilization of folate in patients who otherwise have adequate tissue stores of this essential nutrient. Such an event would likely impair normal protein synthesis in rapidly proliferating cells and might result in structural and/or metabolic abnormalities in the developing cells.

Blood ethanol concentrations in excess of 300 mg/100 ml are associated with marked increases in plasma osmolarity.[31] Studies in our laboratory assessing the effect of hyperosmolarity on platelet function have shown that choline chloride, sorbitol, sodium chloride, and urea in concentrations sufficient to raise the osmolarity of plasma to levels seen in patients ingesting large amounts of ethanol depress collagen- and epinephrine-induced platelet aggregation.[32] Sorbitol and urea also impair the release of ^{14}C-serotonin. These results suggest that ethanol-related platelet dysfunction may be due in part to ethanol-induced hyperosmolarity.

Greene and coworkers[33] showed that ethanol stimulates the activity of the enzyme adenylate cyclase in intestinal tissue from rats and humans. Preliminary studies in our laboratory indicate that the level of cyclic AMP in platelets is increased in patients ingesting large amounts of ethanol. There are considerable data to indicate that agents that produce increased levels of platelet cyclic AMP inhibit platelet aggregation.[34] It is possible, therefore, that ethanol-induced changes in cyclic nucleotide metabolism may constitute another mechanism for the alterations in platelet behavior observed in alcoholism.

It is possible that ethanol may alter the reactivity of platelet membranes by acting as a local anesthetic.[35,36] Local anesthetic agents appear able to "stabilize" membranes,[37] and drugs which act as stabilizers of biologic membranes inhibit the secondary phase of ADP-induced platelet aggregation.[38] The local anesthetics cocaine and tetracaine also inhibit ADP-induced aggregation.[39,40]

Recent observations of Lumeng and Li[41] raise the possibility that acetaldehyde, the major metabolite of ethanol, may also affect the platelet membrane. These authors reported that acetaldehyde decreased the net synthesis of pyridoxal-5'phosphate by enhancing the activity of the membrane associated enzyme B_6-phosphate phosphatase. Ethanol itself had no effect. Conceivably, acetaldehyde or another metabolite of ethanol may affect a membrane-bound protein on platelets and thereby alter the reactivity of the membrane by a mechanism different from that proposed for ethanol per se.

Whatever the mechanism, it is probable that the presence of functional disturbances in platelets from patients ingesting ethanol contributes to the observed reductions in platelet survival. Some controversy still prevails regarding the mechanism by which platelets normally leave the circulation. The weight of evidence suggests, however, that the survival of a given platelet is a function of both a predetermined finite life span and the number of interactions between the platelet and other surfaces. It is probable that the ability of a cell to participate in and survive these interactions is dependent in large measure upon its functional capacity and its regenerative metabolic activities. Cells having metabolic and functional defects may be less able to survive or recover from damage sustained in the course of normal activities and thus may be destroyed prematurely. Hence, cells with severely impaired function are likely to have short life spans.

SUMMARY

The studies described here indicate that ingestion of large amounts of ethanol is associated with multiple abnormalities in platelet production, survival, structure, function, and metabolism. The severity of the abnormalities is greater in patients who develop thrombocytopenia. Both the presence of ethanol in the plasma and intracellular defects contribute to the production of the platelet abnormalities observed. It is expected that greater understanding of the ethanol-induced defects in platelets will advance our understanding of the toxic effect of ethanol on other cell systems in the body.

REFERENCES

1. SULLIVAN, L. W. & V. HERBERT. 1964. Suppression of hematopoiesis by ethanol. J. Clin. Invest. 43: 2048.
2. LINDENBAUM, J. & R. L. HARGROVE. 1968. Thrombocytopenia in alcoholics. Ann. Intern. Med. 68: 526.
3. POST, R. M. & J. F. DESFORGES. 1968. Thrombocytopenia and alcoholism. Ann. Intern. Med. 68: 1230.
4. LINDENBAUM, J. & C. S. LIEBER. 1969. Hematologic effects of alcohol in man in the absence of nutritional deficiency. New Eng. J. Med. 281: 33.
5. RYBACK, R. & J. F. DESFORGES. 1970. Alcoholic thrombocytopenia in three inpatient drinking alcoholics. Arch. Intern. Med. 125: 475.
6. COWAN, D. H. & J. D. HINES. 1971. Thrombocytopenia of severe alcoholism. 74: 37.
7. EICHNER, E. R. & R. S. HILLMAN. 1971. The evolution of anemia in alcoholic patients. Amer. J. Med. 50: 218.
8. COWAN, D. H. 1973. Thrombokinetic studies in alcohol-related thrombocytopenia. J. Lab. Clin. Med. 81: 64.
9. HAUT, M. J. & D. H. COWAN. 1974. The effect of ethanol on hemostatic properties of human blood platelets. Amer. J. Med. 56: 22.
10. HARKER, L. A. 1968. Megakaryocyte quantitation. J. Clin. Invest. 47: 452.
11. ASTER, R. H. & J. H. JANDL. 1964. Platelet sequestration in man. I. Methods. J. Clin. Invest. 43: 843.
12. MIELKE, C. H., JR., M. M. KANESHIRO, I. A. MAHER, M. J. WEINER & S. I. RAPAPORT. 1969. The standardized normal Ivy bleeding time and its prolongation by aspirin. Blood 34: 204.
13. BORN, G. V. R. & M. J. CROSS. 1963. The aggregation of blood platelets. J. Physiol. (London) 168: 178.
14. SPAET, T. H. & J. CINTRON. 1965. Studies of platelet factor-3 availability. Brit. J. Haematol. 11: 269.
15. COWAN, D. H. & M. J. HAUT. 1972. Platelet function in acute leukemia. J. Lab. Clin. Med. 79: 893.
16. MÜRER, E. H. 1968. Release reaction and energy metabolism in blood platelets with special reference to the burst in oxygen uptake. Biochim. Biophys. Acta 162: 320.
17. VALDORF-HANSEN, J. F. & M. B. ZUCKER. 1971. Effect of temperature and inhibitors on serotonin-^{14}C release from human platelets. Amer. J. Physiol. 220: 105.
18. COWAN, D. H. 1973. Platelet metabolism in acute leukemia. J. Lab. Clin. Med. 82: 54.
19. COWAN, D. H. 1974. Platelet metabolism in alcohol-related thrombocytopenia. Thrombos. Diathes. Haemorrh. 31: 149.
20. STJERNHOLM, R. L. 1967. Metabolism of glucose, acetate, and propionate by human plasma cells, J. Bacteriol. 93: 1657.

21. LOWRY, O. H., N. J. ROSEBROUGH, A. L. FARR & R. J. RANDALL. 1951. Protein measurement with the Folin phenol reagent. J. Biol. Chem. **193:** 265.
22. COWAN, D. H. & R. C. GRAHAM, JR. Studies on the platelet defect in alcoholism. Submitted for publication.
23. HOLMSEN, H. & H. J. WEISS. 1972. Further evidence for a deficient storage pool of adenine nucleotides in platelets from patients with thrombocytopenia—"storage pool disease." Blood. **39:** 197.
24. KARPATKIN, S. & G. W. SISKIND. 1969. In vitro detection of platelet antibody in patients with idiopathic thrombocytopenic purpura and systemic lupus erythematosus. Blood **33:** 795.
25. WHITE, J. G. 1968. Fine structural alterations induced in platelets by adenosine diphosphate. Blood **31:** 604.
26. COWAN, D. H. & J. D. HINES. 1973. Thrombokinetics in dietary-induced folate deficiency in human subjects. J. Lab. Clin. Med. **81:** 577.
27. RABAA, M. S., G. M. BERNIER & O. D. RATNOFF. 1973. Rapid detection of fibrinogen-related antigens in serum. J. Lab. Clin. Med. **81:** 476.
28. KARPATKIN, S. 1969. Heterogeneity of human platelets. I. Metabolic and kinetic evidence suggestive of young and old platelets. J. Clin. Invest. **48:** 1073.
29. GARG, S. K., E. L. AMOROSI & S. KARPATKIN. 1971. Use of the megathrombocyte as an index of megakaryocyte number. New Eng. J. Med. **284:** 11.
30. HINES, J. D. 1975. Hematologic abnormalities involving vitamin B_6 and folate metabolism in alcoholic subjects. This monograph.
31. ROBINSON, A. G. & J. N. LOEB. 1971. Ethanol ingestion—commonest cause of elevated plasma osmolality? New Eng. J. Med. **284:** 1253.
32. COWAN, D. H., P. J. SHOOK & R. C. GRAHAM, JR. 1974. Hyperosmolality, effect on platelet function and ultrastructure. (abstr.). Clin. Res. **22:** 386A.
33. GREENE, H. C., R. H. HERMAN & S. KRAEMER. 1971. Stimulation of jejunal adenyl cyclase by ethanol. J. Lab. Clin. Med. **78:** 336.
34. SALZMAN, E. W. 1972. Cyclic AMP and platelet function. New Eng. J. Med. **286:** 358.
35. MOORE, J. W., W. ULBRICHT & M. TAKATA. 1964. Effect of ethanol on the sodium and potassium conductances of the squid axon membrane. J. Gen Physiol. **48:** 279.
36. ARMSTRONG, C. M. & L. BINSTOCK. 1964. The effects of several alcohols on the properties of the squid giant axon. J. Gen. Physiol. **48:** 265.
37. SEEMAN, P., W. O. KWANT, T. SANKS & W. ARGENT. 1969. Membrane expansion of intact erythrocytes by anesthetics. Biochim. Biophys. Acta **183:** 490.
38. MILLS, D. C. B. & G. C. K. ROBERTS. 1967. Membrane active drugs and the aggregation of human blood platelets. Nature (London) **213:** 35.
39. O'BRIEN, J. R. 1964. A comparison of platelet aggregation produced by seven compounds and a comparison of their inhibitors. J. Clin. Pathol. **17:** 275.
40. ALEDORT, L. M. & J. NIEMETZ. 1968. Dissociation of platelet aggregation from clot retraction, potassium loss, and adenosine triphosphatase activity. Proc. Soc. Exp. Biol. Med. **128:** 658.
41. LUMENG, L. & T.-K. LI. 1974. Vitamin B_6 metabolism in chronic alcohol abuse. J. Clin. Invest. **53:** 693.

INTRODUCTION

Kenneth Williams

In the 1800s, Robert Koch found that alcohol ingestion increased the susceptibility of guinea pigs to infection with the cholera bacillus. Clinically, the alcoholic is found to frequently experience infections, especially of the lung. For example, newly acquired cases of pulmonary tuberculosis in this country are found today almost exclusively in the alcoholic population. Pneumococcal and gram-negative pneumonias are also recognized to occur more frequently and resolve more slowly in the alcoholic.

Dr. Johnson's paper presents a review of studies relating to impaired host defense mechanisms against infection (glottis closure, ciliary activity, lung bacterial clearance, polymorphonuclear leucocyte mobilization, leucocyte chemotaxis and function, and serum bactericidal activity) found in acute intoxication. Even mildly intoxicating doses of alcohol have been shown to be associated with impaired mobilization of polymorphonuclear leucocytes and decreased serum bactericidal activity against *E. coli* and *H. influenzae*. However, the mechanisms by which alcohol produce these changes are unknown.

Dr. Andersen's paper presents an overview of research relating to impaired defense mechanisms to infection in patients with Laennec's cirrhosis. Concluding his remarks with a discussion of his own research, Dr. Andersen describes what he believes to be an inhibitor of chemotaxis found in the serum of his cirrhotic patients.

Dr. Hudolin begins his paper by reviewing previous publications on alcoholism and tuberculosis. Progressing to a discussion of his own experiences in Yugoslavia, he presents his data showing the frequent coexistence of pulmonary tuberculosis and alcoholism. In his country, patients with both diseases are being found with increased frequency. Dr. Hudolin has found tuberculosis in alcoholics to be particularly severe and resistant. Studies in his country have revealed that recurrence of TB in those who continue to drink is 4 times greater than in those who abstain. Such evidence gives added weight to the argument that both the alcoholism and tuberculosis must be treated if there is to be a favorable outcome. Dr. Hudolin ends with a special call to form an international committee of interested health professionals to address themselves to the special problem of pulmonary tuberculosis in alcoholics.

IMPAIRED DEFENSE MECHANISMS ASSOCIATED
WITH ACUTE ALCOHOLISM

Warren D. Johnson, Jr.

Cornell University Medical College
New York, New York 10021

It has generally been assumed that alcohol increases host susceptibility to infection.[1-4] This assumption is correct in the presence of profound intoxication with stupor or coma, where aspiration of oropharyngeal contents may lead to the development of pneumonia.[5,6] However, there is little evidence to suggest that nonpulmonary infections are more common in healthy subjects who are acutely intoxicated. In some experimental studies it is difficult to distinguish between the effects of alcohol per se and those of chronic alcoholism and its associated problems. For this reason, the present report will be restricted to acute alcohol intoxication and will rely on studies that determined the effects of single doses of ethanol in healthy volunteers or animals.

The effect of ethanol on numerous pulmonary and systemic defense mechanisms has been experimentally determined (TABLE 1). These include nonimmunologic mechanisms, such as glottis closure or tracheal ciliary activity, as well as immunologic mechanisms such as leukocyte mobilization, chemotaxis, and function, and serum bactericidal activity. The influence of ethanol on these defense mechanisms will be reviewed.

PULMONARY DEFENSE MECHANISMS

Glottis Closure

Glottis closure is an important mechanism in preventing the entrance of foreign particles, including infectious agents, into the lung. It has been shown that rats are unable to effect glottis closure after receiving large doses of ethanol.[5] The impairment of this mechanism by ethanol facilitated the aspiration of intranasal pneumococci and mucin and the subsequent development of pneumonia. However, there was no specificity in the action of ethanol. Similar results were obtained in animals subjected to either deep ether anesthesia, exposure to cold, or local benzocaine anesthesia of the epiglottis region. An impairment of this mechanical barrier to infection is undoubtedly the major reason for an increased incidence of pneumonia in the setting of profound alcohol intoxication and other conditions such as shock or coma.

Ciliary Activity

Ciliary activity was not inhibited by the amounts of ethanol that impaired glottis closure in the aforementioned studies.[5] Serum ethanol levels of 600 to 1000 mg% were required to depress the ciliary activity of the cat trachea.[7] Since these concentrations of ethanol are potentially lethal in man, it is very unlikely that an impairment of ciliary activity predisposes to pulmonary infections.

Lung Bacterial Clearance

The pulmonary clearance of infectious agents has recently been reviewed.[8] There has been considerable interest during the past decade on the effects of ethanol on this mechanism. Green and Kass demonstrated that intoxication of mice with ethanol decreased the rate at which inhaled staphylococci were cleared from the lung.[9] In their study, animals made ataxic or stuporous with ethanol and then exposed to aerosolized staphylococci had twice as many bacteria recovered from their lungs 4 hours later than did control animals. This inhibitory effect of ethanol was dose-related. A similar depressant effect on bacterial clearance was also observed in animals subjected to either severe hypoxia or acute starvation. Animals receiving large doses of ethanol had altered patterns of respiration; hypoxia produced by this respiratory depression seemed a plausible explanation for the ethanol effect. However, attempts to reverse the effects of ethanol by placing the mice in increased concentrations of oxygen after the aerosolized pulmonary infections were unsuccessful.

TABLE 1

Host Defense Mechanisms Experimentally Evaluated Following
Acute Administration of Ethanol

Pulmonary Defense Mechanisms
  Glottis Closure
  Ciliary Activity
  Lung Bacterial Clearance
  Alveolar Macrophage
    Mobilization
    Function
Systemic Defense Mechanisms
  Polymorphonuclear Leukocyte
    Mobilization
    Chemotaxis
    Function
  Peritoneal Macrophage
  Serum Bactericidal Activity

Alveolar Macrophage

Mobilization: A possible mechanism for the observed ethanol-induced decrease in pulmonary clearance was offered by Guarneri and Laurenzi.[10] They utilized a similar experimental model to demonstrate that mice given ethanol had a decrease in the number of alveolar macrophages that could be recovered by lavage of the lungs after a pulmonary bacterial challenge. However, when these studies were repeated in the rabbit, they were unable to demonstrate any adverse effect of ethanol on alveolar macrophage mobilization. The variability in the response of different species to ethanol indicates the potential danger in extrapolating from animal experiments to man.

Function: Gee et al. have studied the effect of ethanol on the phagocytic and antistaphylococcal activity of isolated rabbit alveolar macrophages.[11] They were unable to demonstrate any impairment in the phagocytosis and killing of *S. aureus* by macrophages exposed to ethanol *in vitro*.

SYSTEMIC DEFENSE MECHANISMS

Polymorphonuclear Leukocyte

Mobilization: The accumulation of polymorphonuclear leukocytes at sites of induced infection or trauma is decreased in animals and man following ethanol administration. Pickrell demonstrated that rabbits made stuporous with large amounts of ethanol (blood ethanol levels of 550–700 mg%) had fewer polymorphonuclear leukocytes in experimental pneumococcal infections of skin, lung, and pleural spaces than did control animals.[6] However, ether anesthesia had as marked an inhibitory effect on the inflammatory response as did ethanol intoxication. Louria confirmed these observations in mice given a single injection of 0.5 ml of 30% ethanol subcutaneously and then challenged with 10^8 coagulase-negative staphylococci intraperitoneally.[12] The number of polymorphonuclear leukocytes in peritoneal washouts 4 hours later was significantly lower than in saline-injected mice or animals rendered comatose with barbiturates and was inversely related to the blood ethanol concentrations. Peripheral blood leukocyte counts did not differ in control and alcohol-treated mice. Moses et al. reported that alcohol also diminished leukocyte mobilization into the suprapatellar bursa of rabbits following the local injection of a "stimulating substance" obtained from rabbit granulocytes.[13] This was attributed to a defect in vascular permeability and could be partially corrected by increasing the skin temperature. No abnormalities in leukocyte margination or stickiness were observed following ethanol administration in studies utilizing a rabbit ear chamber model.

A leukocyte mobilization defect has also been documented in man with the Rebuck skin window technique.[14] Human volunteers were given 50–75 ml of 95% ethanol intravenously over a 30-minute period. Immediately before injecting the alcohol a 1-cm^2 area of the volunteers' forearm was abraded to the point of uniform redness and then covered with a siliconized glass cup, which was then filled with isotonic saline. The contents of the cup were evacuated at multiple time points and the numbers of polymorphonuclear leukocytes counted. A marked reduction in the leukocyte counts occurred during the first 4 hours after ethanol infusion. Similar findings were observed in volunteers given ethanol by mouth. However, a comparable degree of impaired leukocyte mobilization was observed in patients with profound terminal shock. Diabetic patients showed a less marked decrease in mobilization. No significant depression of mobilization was observed in patients with cirrhosis, uremia, or coma, or in patients undergoing prolonged general anesthesia for major surgery. The mechanisms responsible for these observations were not defined. There was no clinical evidence of intoxication in the volunteers, nor was there hypotension, perceptible skin cooling, or changes in peripheral blood leukocyte counts. The investigators emphasized that "failure of emigration of leukocytes into the skin does not necessarily mean that alcohol will induce a similar abnormality in the lung parenchyma, the only site in which alcohol ingestion is clearly associated with increased proclivity to and severity of infection."

Chemotaxis: The effect of ethanol on leukocyte chemotaxis was first studied in the 1930s by Klepser and Nungester.[15] They measured the movement of human leukocytes toward pneumococci on glass slides after exposure of the leukocytes to ethanol *in vitro*. The chemotactic response of the leukocytes was diminished by as little as 100 mg% of ethanol. Leukocytes from "deeply intoxicated" rats also had a diminished chemotactic response.

A recent report has confirmed that exposure of human leukocytes to ethanol *in vitro* will impair their chemotactic response, but only at ethanol concentrations of 800–1600 mg%.[16]

Function: Animal studies initially suggested that polymorphonuclear leukocyte phagocytic capacity and ability to effect intracellular killing was impaired by ethanol.[12] These observations have not been confirmed by more recent studies utilizing quantitative measures of leukocyte function. Brayton et al.[14] utilized a modification of the technique of Maaloe to gauge phagocytosis and intracellular killing of coagulase-negative staphylococci by human polymorphonuclear leukocytes. They were unable to demonstrate any impairment of these functions in leukocytes exposed to 200 to 400 mg% of ethanol *in vitro* or in leukocytes obtained from volunteers receiving infusions of ethanol.

Peritoneal Macrophages

Louria reported a decrease in the clearance of staphylococci from the peritoneal cavity of mice rendered comatose or ataxic with ethanol.[12] Seventy-seven percent of control animals reduced peritoneal bacterial populations at least 10-fold during a 1-hour period following intraperitoneal infection. In contrast, only 47% of ataxic mice and 21% of comatose animals effected similar reductions in bacterial counts. *In vitro* studies suggested that peritoneal macrophages from comatose animals had a reduction in their phagocytic ability and perhaps impaired intracellular killing. Macrophages from ataxic animals had variable and often normal phagocytic and intracellular killing activity.

Serum Bactericidal Activity

Studies by Kaplan and Brande on 2 human volunteers suggested that the bactericidal activity of serum was decreased against a strain of *Escherichia coli* and a strain of *Hemophilus influenzae* following ingestion of ethanol.[17] This observation was confirmed and extended in subsequent studies in which normal volunteers received intravenous infusions of 50–75 ml of absolute ethanol.[18] Serum bactericidal activity against strains of *E. coli* and *H. influenzae* type B were transiently decreased but near normal 5 hours after the ethanol infusion. The decrease in bactericidal activity was demonstrated by testing diluted serum. The decrease in bactericidal activity was not related to the presence of ethanol or acetaldehyde in the serum per se and could not be attributed to changes in serum lysozyme or electrolytes or to alterations of bactericidal antibody or complement levels. There was no correlation between the serum ethanol level of the degree to which bactericidal activity was decreased.

A preliminary report on the bactericidal activity of dog serum following ethanol infusion suggests that the effect of ethanol might be to impair the *in vivo* production of complement.[19]

SUMMARY

Ethanol administered to animals in large amounts sufficient to produce coma and occasionally death will impair glottis closure, ciliary activity, lung and peritoneal bacterial clearance, mobilization of macrophages, and polymorphonuclear leukocytes and leukocyte chemotaxis. There is little or no impairment of these pulmonary and systemic host defense mechanisms in experimental studies employing amounts of ethanol that produce serum concentrations likely to be encountered in an intoxicated human. Modest amounts of ethanol in man, sufficient to produce minimal euphoria to mild intoxication, are associated with impaired mobilization of polymorphonuclear leukocytes into skin and decreased serum bactericidal activity against certain gram-negative bacteria. The mechanism by which ethanol impairs these latter defense mechanisms has not been clearly defined.

REFERENCES

1. RUSH, B. 1943. An inquiry into the effects of ardent spirits upon the human body and mind with an account of the means of preventing and of the remedies for curing them. (1785). Reprinted in Quart. J. Stud. Alcohol **4:** 321–341.
2. PERLA, D. & J. MARMORSTON. 1941. Alcohol and resistance. *In* Natural Resistance and Clinical Medicine. 1153–1161. Little, Brown and Co. Boston, Mass.
3. EICHNER, E. R. 1973. The hematologic disorders of alcoholism. Amer. J. Med. **54:** 621–630.
4. LOURIA, D. B. 1973. The infectious complications of alcohol ingestion. Rev. Environ. Health **1:** 175–184.
5. NUNGESTER, W. J. & R. G. KLEPSER. 1938. A possible mechanism of lowered resistance to pneumonia. J. Infect. Dis. **63:** 94–102.
6. PICKRELL, K. L. 1938. Effect of alcoholic intoxication and ether anesthesia on resistance to pneumococcic infection. Bull. Johns Hopkins Hosp. **63:** 238–260.
7. LAURENZI, G. A. & J. J. GUARNERI. 1966. A study of the mechanisms of pulmonary resistance to infection: the relationship of bacterial clearance to ciliary activity and alveolar macrophage function. Amer. Rev. Resp. Dis. **93:** 134–141. (Supplement)
8. GREEN, G. 1968. Pulmonary clearance of infectious agents. Ann. Rev. Med. **19:** 315–336.
9. GREEN, G. M. & E. H. KASS. 1964. Factors influencing the clearance of bacteria by the lung. J. Clin. Invest. **43:** 769–776.
10. GUARNERI, J. J. & G. A. LAURENZI. 1968. Effect of alcohol on the mobilization of alveolar macrophages. J. Lab. Clin. Med. **72:** 40–51.
11. GEE, J. B. L., J. KASKIN, M. P. DUNCOMBE & C. L. VASSALLO. 1974. The effects of ethanol on some metabolic features of phagocytosis in the alveolar macrophage. J. Reticuloendothel. Soc. **15:** 61–68.
12. LOURIA, D. B. 1963. Susceptibility to infection during experimental alcohol intoxication. Trans. Ass. Amer. Physicians **76:** 102–112.
13. MOSES, J. M., E. H. GESCHICKTER & R. H. EBERT. 1968. Pathogenesis of inflammation. The relationship of enhanced permeability to leukocyte mobilization in delayed inflammation. Brit. J. Exp. Path. **49:** 385–394.
14. BRAYTON, R. G., P. E. STOKES, M. S. SCHWARTZ & D. B. LOURIA. 1970. Effect of alcohol and various diseases on leukocyte mobilization, phagocytosis and intracellular bacterial killing. New Eng. J. Med. **282:** 123–128.
15. KLEPSER, R. G. & W. J. NUNGESTER. 1939. The effect of alcohol upon the chemotactic response of leukocytes. J. Infect. Dis. **65:** 196–199.
16. CROWLEY, J. P. & N. ABRAMSON. 1971. Effect of ethanol on complement-mediated chemotaxis. Clin. Res. **19:** 415.
17. KAPLAN, N. M. & A. I. BRANDE. 1958. Hemophilus influenzae infection in adults: observations on the immune disturbance. Arch. Intern. Med. **101:** 515–523.
18. JOHNSON, W. D. Jr., P. STOKES & D. KAYE. 1969. The effect of intravenous ethanol on the bactericidal activity of human serum. Yale J. Biol. Med. **42:** 71–85.
19. MARR, J. J. & I. SPILBERG. 1973. A mechanism for infection by gram-negative bacteria in acute alcohol intoxication. Clin. Res. **22:** 449a.

HOST FACTORS CAUSING INCREASED SUSCEPTIBILITY
TO INFECTION IN PATIENTS WITH LAENNEC'S CIRRHOSIS

Burton R. Andersen

Departments of Medicine and Microbiology
Abraham Lincoln School of Medicine
University of Illinois
and
West Side Veterans Administration Hospital
Chicago, Illinois 60612

Infection is one of the common precipitating factors of hepatic coma in patients with cirrhosis. It is also the immediate cause of death of about $\frac{1}{4}$ of the patients with Laennec's cirrhosis.[1] This paper will deal with the effects of cirrhosis on host-defense mechanisms that increase the risk of infection, but it will not cover the influences of acute alcoholic intoxication on these mechanisms.

The types of infections found in cirrhotics are many, but pyogenic bacterial infections as a group tend to predominate. Organisms arising from the gastrointestinal tract, such as gram-negative bacilli and anaerobes, are most common, but pneumococcal, staphylococcal, and streptococcal infections frequently occur.[1-4] Pneumonia, peritonitis, bacteremia, and pyelonephritis are the most common sites of these infections. The facets of the host-defense mechanisms that appear to be most important in preventing pyogenic infections are (1) the reticuloendothelial system (fixed macrophages), (2) antibodies, (3) complement, and (4) neutrophilic granulocytes. The major steps in the prevention of pyogenic infections are the phagocytosis of bacteria by granulocytes and fixed macrophages and the subsequent intracellular killing of these organisms. The serum factors primarily serve to facilitate these activities. Current knowledge about the functional capacity of these systems in cirrhotics will be reviewed individually.

The reticuloendothelial system is important for clearing organisms from the blood that enter from the gastrointestinal tract, lungs, skin, and other sites. Since the liver is the major organ of the reticuloendothelial system, it would not be surprising if function were abnormal in cirrhotic patients. In a study of cirrhotic rats, Rutenberg et al.,[5] demonstrated that intravenously injected bacteria were normally cleared from the blood; however, there was a delay in bacterial killing in these animals. As cirrhosis progresses, additional difficulty probably results from shunting of blood around the cirrhotic liver and thereby bypassing this very important reticuloendothelial organ.

Antibodies function as opsonins to facilitate phagocytosis of bacteria by granulocytes and to initiate the inflammatory process that ultimately limits and controls the infection. The antibody-forming ability of the cirrhotic does not appear to be deficient and may even be greater than normal. Cirrhotic patients commonly have a polyclonal hypergammaglobulinemia.[6] Triger et al.[7] found increased levels of antibodies to *E. coli* in patients with liver disease; however, the antibody levels to *Hemophilus influenzae* were within the normal range. They concluded that patients with liver disease are unable to degrade the antigen from bacterial products that arise in the gastrointestinal tract and consequently make antibodies to this increased level of bacterial antigen. Since *Hemophilus influenzae* is not a normal inhabitant of the gastrointestinal tract, it would not be ex-

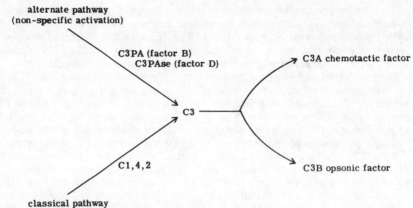
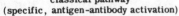

FIGURE 1. Pathways of C3 activation.

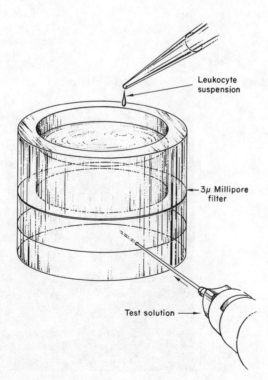

FIGURE 2. The chamber used in determining the chemotactic ability of granulocytes and the chemotactic activity of serum.

pected to be present in increased amounts. Havens,[8] however, reported an increased secondary immunologic response in patients with alcoholic cirrhosis who were immunized with tetanus toxoid. The cause of the increased antibody response is unclear at the present time, but for the purposes of this discussion, there is clearly no deficiency in this facet of the host-defense mechanisms.

The importance of the complement system in pyogenic infections is that, with appropriate activation, factors will be produced that attract granulocytes to the site of an infection and will increase the rate of phagocytosis of bacteria by the granulocytes. They are referred to as chemotactic and opsonic factors, respectively. The complement system may be activated either by the classic route with bacterial antigens and their antibodies or by the nonspecific alternate pathway (FIGURE 1). The alternate pathway is particularly important in the early phases of an infection before the host has had time to mount an immunologic response to the invading organism. In a study of 12 cirrhotic patients at the West Side VA Hospital, a number of the complement components were found to be decreased.[6] Seven of the 12 patients had levels of C3 well below the normal range. Half of the patients had decreased C4 levels, while only 3 patients had reduced levels of the C5 component. Four of 12 patients had C3 proactivator (C3PA) levels that were depressed, and among 11 patients who had total hemolytic complement assays performed, 8 had levels that were below the normal range. These comple-

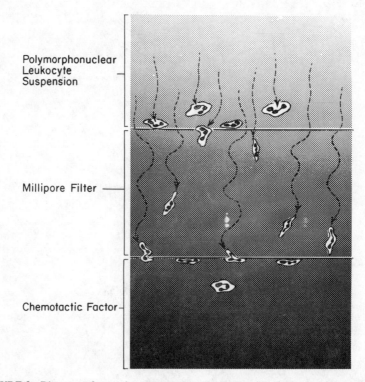

Polymorphonuclear Leukocyte Suspension

Millipore Filter

Chemotactic Factor

FIGURE 3. Diagram of granulocytes moving through a micropore membrane toward a chemotactic factor diffusing up from the lower compartment of a chemotaxis chamber.

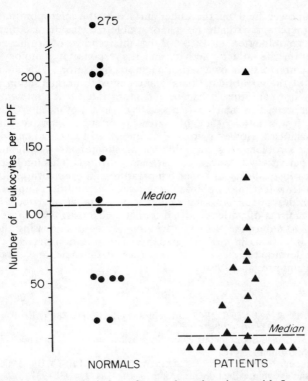

FIGURE 4. The chemotactic index of normals and patients with Laennec's cirrhosis. Serum (as the source of chemotactic factors) and granulocytes from the same individual were used in this chemotaxis assay.

ment deficiencies, therefore, may serve to provide a less than optimal chemotactic and phagocytic stimulus for the granulocytes of the cirrhotic patient.

Evidence to date does not seem to indicate that granulocytes of cirrhotic patients have any significant functional defect. In an earlier study,[6] 2 important functional characteristics of granulocytes were observed, namely chemotactic capacity and the intracellular killing ability of granulocytes. The chemotactic ability of the cirrhotic's granulocytes when exposed to an active chemotactic attractant was entirely normal in most cases. When the intracellular killing ability was tested with *Candida albicans* as the test organism, there was no evidence that the granulocytes from these patients had any difficulty in killing the *Candida albicans*. Occasionally cirrhotic patients have granulocytopenia as an additional defect in host defense.

It was apparent from an earlier study[6] that the cirrhotic patients' granulocytes demonstrated a poor chemotactic response to their own serum. The ability of a patient's serum to attract normal and his own granulocytes was tested using a chemotaxis chamber requiring only small volumes of serum and granulocytes (FIGURE 2). The granulocytes that moved through the micropore membrane (FIGURE 3) toward the serum chemotactic factors in the lower chamber were counted following staining with hematoxylin. The degree of chemotactic response was determined by calculating the average number of granulocytes present per high-power field on the under surface of the micropore membrane. In many cases there was virtually no demonstrable movement of either normal or the patients' granulocytes. FIGURE 4 shows the response of normal granulocytes to normal serum chemotactic activity and the response of granulocytes from 22 cirrhotic patients to their own serum chemotactic factors. The chemotactic responsiveness of the cirrhotic patients' granulocytes to normal serum was in most cases entirely normal. Since it had been demonstrated that complement components were depressed in many patients with cirrhosis, especially C3, C4, and C3 proactivator, it was initially thought that the poor chemotactic response was due to these deficiencies. However, normal serum added to the patients serum failed to correct the problem. A serum inhibitor of chemotaxis was demonstrated in most of the patients with advanced Laennec's cirrhosis. This inhibitor was quite labile and was lost quickly at room temperature and even with prolonged freezing. Some patients lost the inhibitor as their clinical condition improved.

The studies described above have identified a number of defects in the host-defense mechanisms of patients with Laennec's cirrhosis. At the present time it is impossible to determine their relative importance in increasing the incidence of pyogenic infections in cirrhotic patients. This question probably will be answered as we develop the means to correct these deficiencies and observe changes in the course and prognosis of the disease.

REFERENCES

1. RATNOFF, O. & A. PATEK. 1942. Intercurrent infection in 386 patients with cirrhosis. Medicine (Balt.) **21**: 207–268.
2. TISDALE, W. 1961. Spontaneous colon bacillus bacteremia in Laennec's cirrhosis. Gastroenterology **40**: 141–148.
3. LUFKIN, E., M. SILVERMAN, J. CALLAWAY & H. GLENCHUR. 1966. Mixed septicemias and gastrointestinal disease. Amer. J. Dig. Dis. **11**: 930–937.
4. GINSBERG, M. D. 1968. Spontaneous group B streptococcal bacteremia complicating hepatic cirrhosis. Amer. J. Dig. Dis. **13**: 1065–1071.
5. RUTENBURG, A., E. SONNENBLICK, I. KOVEN, F. SCHWEINBURG & J. FINE. 1959. Comparative response of normal and cirrhotic rats to intravenously injected bacteria. Proc. Soc. Exp. Biol. Med. **101**: 279–281.
6. DEMEO, A. & B. R. ANDERSEN. 1972. Defective chemotaxis associated with a serum inhibitor in cirrhotic patients. New Eng. J. Med. **286**: 735–740.
7. TRIGER, D. R., M. H. ALP & R. WRIGHT. 1972. Bacterial and dietary antibodies in liver disease. Lancet **1**: 60–63.
8. HAVENS, W. P. 1959. Liver disease and antibody formation. Int. Arch. Allerg. (Suppl.) **14**: 75–83.

TUBERCULOSIS AND ALCOHOLISM

Vladimir Hudolin

Center for Study and Control of Alcoholism and Other Dependencies
Zagreb, Yugoslavia

There have always been theories in existence that would relate alcoholism and tuberculosis to poverty, and generally to a low socioeconomic status. However, until alcoholism was more generally accepted as a medical problem and a disease, after World War II, the combination alcoholism-tuberculosis was not held to be of major significance either. In the meantime there had occurred a rise of the living standard in numerous countries, the discovery of efficient methods of treatment of tuberculosis, and a general acceptance of alcoholism as a disease. Also, numerous more successful therapeutic methods were introduced in the treatment of alcoholics. Nevertheless, there exist still today a certain number of alcoholic and tuberculous patients whose condition can be alleviated only with difficulty. The general impression is that in their severest forms the course of these diseases often runs relatively concurrently. Although numbers of theories have so far been advanced on the genesis of this frequent association of alcoholism and tuberculosis, the correct interpretation is still beyond our reach. The time has come when we should pay greater attention to this problem.

After World War II several papers were published endeavoring to establish the effect of alcoholism on the function of the lungs, the causes of the association between alcoholism and tuberculosis, and the personality of the tuberculous alcoholic, etc. Regrettably, it would not be feasible here to deal with such investigations. There have been also many practical and epidemiologic descriptions of combined cases. It becomes apparent ever more frequently that such cases as these would necessitate special institutions for the parallel treatment of both diseases. In the majority of cases the authors advocate treatment in hospitals for respiratory tuberculosis, with the understanding that a psychiatrist should be consulted whenever the severity of a case would demand it. Despite the fact that the number of tuberculous patients has experienced a rapid decline, there have occurred combined cases ever more frequently, especially in cases with severe respiratory tuberculosis.

Kok-Jensen[15] describes 428 males who had been discharged from tuberculosis departments in Copenhagen (1958–1960). Eighty-nine were alcoholics as well. Both the alcoholics and nonalcoholics from this group were dying 3 times more frequently than the normal population. Bacillarity and recurrences of tuberculosis were much more severe and frequent in the alcoholics. Among the tuberculous, alcoholism is a frequent occurrence (20%), according to the authors, most likely owing to diminished resistance of alcoholics to infections.

H. Massé[17] finds in France that correlation of alcoholism and tuberculosis as the cause of death is very high, actually much higher than for many other diseases. Wessely and Pernhaupt[18] describe a phenomenon which has been observed by everybody concerned with alcoholism—namely, that alcoholics commencing abstinence smoke much more. Levendel et al.[10] state that as far back as 1961 a special department for tuberculous alcoholics was opened at the State Institute for Tuberculosis in Budapest. This department was established for the purpose of investigating this problem. The authors believe that in spite of the difficulties produced by the combination alcoholism-tuberculosis, one ought not to be overpessimistic.

On the basis of experience in Hungary, Levendel et al.[4] demand that in hospitals for tuberculosis, alcoholism be tackled from the medical aspect, and not administratively (disciplinarily). They find among their combined cases almost always psychic disorders (neurosis, psychopathy, etc.).

Levendel et al.[2] describe the treating of 180 tuberculous alcoholics (26 women among them) in Hungary. Treatment was performed by psychotherapy, tranquilizers, and disulfiram. The results of treatment of tuberculosis in their cases were as good as in nonalcoholics: the results of treatment of alcoholism were less discussed in their paper. Yershov,[3] concerned with experience in the Soviet Union, states that treatment of combined cases is hard, not only because of disciplinary difficulties but also because alcoholics exhibit a low tolerance for antituberculosis drugs. According to him, active tuberculosis is no contra-indication for treatment with emetic preparations or disulfiram. A total of 100 persons suffering from both tuberculosis and alcoholism were treated. Out of this number only 7 had abstained for longer than 11 months. Dzyak and Bezborodko[9] state that alcoholics exhibit a tendency to a decrease in oxygen utilization, vital capacity, and maximal ventilation of the lungs.

Rainaut[11] and Righini[12] recommend that some of the existing departments for the treatment of tuberculosis should be transformed into special institutions for the treatment of tuberculous alcoholics. Tuberculous alcoholics exhibit a poor motivation for treating tuberculosis, while the results in such special institutions are better.

According to Smith and Demone,[1] in Massachusetts in 1958, the prevalence of alcoholism among tuberculous patients admitted to institutional treatment amounted to 28%, while alcoholism in the general population was assessed as 5.3%. Other authors[15] also note a great percentage of alcoholics among tuberculous patients.

Gerardi and Mazzola[6] deal with the very bad results of treatment. Certain drugs are likely to lead to difficulties in alcoholics with a damaged liver[12] or other damage (polyneuropathy[16]). Krstić et al.[8] are in favor of simultaneous treatment of the diseases. Hoff and Kryspin-Exner[7] recommend special hospitals for combined cases. Cheung[5] also deals with the difficulties in treating combined cases.

Although the number of cases of tuberculosis diminished after World War II, the number of tuberculous alcoholics has risen, and in this category very severe cases of tuberculosis are relatively the highest in number. Moreover, combined cases are the severest ones also from both the phthisiologic and alcoholic aspects.

EXPERIMENTAL STUDIES

We, too, noticed such combinations in our cases, so we decided to explore this problem in greater depth. As far back as 1964 we have been conducting a research center for alcoholism with the possibility of institutional treatment in a day hospital, partial hospitalization, and outpatient treatment of alcoholics. We have formed clubs of treated alcoholics all over Croatia and also in the other Yugoslav Republics. We are conducting a survey of institutionally treated alcoholics, registering all persons in the Republic who have been referred to a Commission for an evaluation of working ability as affected by alcoholism. In studying these materials we were able to notice the relatively frequent combina-

TABLE 1
Registered Cases of Active Tuberculosis in Croatia, December 31, 1972

Disease	No.	Patients per 100 000 population
Tb of all organs	25 156	565
M.	16 342 (65%)	M. 765
F.	8814 (35%)	F. 381
Tb of respiratory organs	23 253	523
Tb of extrarespiratory organs	1903	43
Tb of respiratory organs culture-positive	4425 (19%)	99

tion of pulmonary disease and alcoholism. We started in collaboration with phthisiologists, to pay more attention to the problem. The latter began, through the medium of their specific services, to follow up and record this problem ever more intensively (TABLE 1).

A large number of patients, up to 40%, with alcoholism and tuberculosis were disciplinarily discharged; almost none abstained after hospitalization was terminated.

In 1972, 523 cases of respiratory tuberculosis per 100 000 of population, were registered in Croatia (males almost double in ratio), of which 19%, or 99/100 000, were bacillary cases. In 1972, as well as in previous years, the percent of resistant cases of tuberculous alcoholics among all categories of patients was higher than was the average for all patients. Among patients with

TABLE 2
Registered Patients with Active Tuberculosis of Respiratory Organs by
Age and Sex, December 31, 1972

Age Groups	No.			Per 100 000		
	M	F	Total	M	F	Total
0–4	35	31	66	22	27	24
5–9	129	106	235	75	64	70
10–14	113	105	218	61	59	60
15–19	294	284	578	146	147	146
20–24	762	489	1251	401	279	343
25–29	736	495	1231	512	361	438
30–34	1065	591	1656	633	368	503
35–39	1498	675	2173	833	383	611
40–44	1910	773	2683	1145	452	794
45–49	1665	741	2406	1145	454	837
50–54	1470	652	2122	1832	616	1140
55–59	1293	505	1798	1383	421	842
60–64	1674	752	2426	1630	586	1050
65–69	1432	696	2128	1819	674	1169
70+	1466	816	2282	1550	524	912
Total	15 542	7711	23 253	728	333	523

TABLE 3

Pattern of New Admissions to Register in Chest Clinics, 1972

	No.	%000
New admissions	6187	139
Respiratory	5645	127
Respiratory culture +	2253	51
Extrarespiratory	542	12
Newly detected	4758	107
Respiratory	4272	96
Respiratory culture +	1777	40
Extrarespiratory	486	11
Relapses	780	18
Respiratory	746	17
Respiratory culture +	413	9.3
Extrarespiratory	34	0.8
Immigrated	649	15
Respiratory	627	14
Respiratory culture +	63	1.4
Extrarespiratory	22	0.5
New admissions, total	6187	
Of which		
newly detected	4758 (76.9%)	
relapses	780 (12.6%)	
immigrated	649 (10.5%)	

respiratory tuberculosis the ratio of alcoholics has somewhat increased, amounting to 8.4%, but among bacillary cases it is 32.7% (TABLES 2–7).

On the basis of these data, which had confirmed our impression, we organized a collaboration between the Hospital for Pulmonary Diseases and Pulmonary Tuberculosis at Klenovnik, and the Center for Study and Control of Alcoholism and other dependencies in Zagreb, opening a department with about 100 beds for combined cases—that is, patients suffering at the same time from alcoholism and tuberculosis. At the same department in the hospital we organized complete

TABLE 4

New Cases and Relapses with Active Tuberculosis in Croatia, 1972

	Patients			
Tuberculosis	No.		Per 100 000 population	
Tb of all organs		5538		124
	M	3613 (65%)	M	169
	F	1925 (35%)	F	83
Tb of respiratory organs		5018		113
Tb of extrarespiratory organs		520		12
Tb of respiratory organs culture-positive		2190 (43.6%)		49

TABLE 5

Incidence of Active Respiratory Tuberculosis by Spread of Lesions,
by Age Groups, 1972

Age Groups	Patient Total	Minimal		Moderately Advanced		Far-Advanced	
		No.	%	No.	%	No.	%
0–4	36	33	91.6	2	5.6	1	2.8
5–9	56	54	96.4	2	3.6	–	–
10–14	51	35	68.6	16	31.4	–	–
15–19	255	123	48.2	115	45.1	17	6.7
20–24	360	161	44.7	165	45.9	34	9.4
25–29	261	94	36.1	137	52.4	30	11.5
30–34	359	137	38.2	173	48.2	49	13.6
35–39	489	183	37.4	240	49.1	66	13.5
40–44	580	196	33.8	297	51.2	87	15.0
45–49	511	174	34.1	262	51.2	75	14.7
50–54	418	139	33.3	219	52.3	60	14.4
55–59	324	94	29.0	166	51.2	64	19.8
60–64	438	152	34.7	212	48.4	74	16.9
65–69	419	140	33.4	211	50.4	68	16.2
70+	461	152	33.0	218	47.3	91	19.7
Total	5018	1867	37.2	2435	48.5	716	14.3

TABLE 6

Deaths from Tuberculosis of Respiratory Organs by Age and Sex, 1971

Age Groups	Males		Females		Total	
	No.	%000	No.	%000	No.	%000
0–4	1	0.6	–	–	1	0.3
5–9	–	–	–	–	–	–
10–14	–	–	–	–	–	–
15–19	1	0.5	–	–	1	0.3
20–24	–	–	1	0.5	1	0.3
25–29	5	3.4	1	0.7	6	2.0
30–34	14	8.4	1	0.6	15	4.6
35–39	28	15.9	4	2.3	32	9.1
40–44	45	27.3	13	7.6	58	17.3
45–49	41	33.3	8	4.9	49	17.1
50–54	28	34.9	10	9.5	38	20.5
55–59	50	53.7	4	3.3	54	25.4
60–64	86	83.3	21	16.5	107	46.4
65–69	81	102.0	24	23.4	105	57.7
70–74	67	125.7	17	22.4	84	65.1
75–79	23	93.0	16	38.2	39	58.5
80+	16	99.9	7	21.2	23	46.9
Total	486	22.8	127	5.5	613	13.8

TABLE 7

Prevalence and Incidence (New Cases and Relapses) or Bacillary Cases

	Prevalence				Incidence			
	Total		Culture-positive		Total		Culture-positive	
Year	No.	%000	No.	%000	No.	%000	No.	%000
1966	34 458	799	6798	158	6117	142	2155	50
1967	31 730	731	5934	138	5472	126	2000	46
1968	29 479	676	5841	134	5501	126	2085	48
1969	29 002	662	5766	132	6046	138	2220	51
1970	27 286	620	5406	123	5766	131	2099	48
1971	25 628	579	4605	104	4952	112	1923	43
1972	23 253	523	4425	99	5018	113	2190	49

treatment of both diseases. After 2 years of work we compiled an assessment of the work done, which we present here.

A therapeutic community was introduced into this part of the hospital. All physicians, social workers, and medical nurses had additional training in social psychiatry and alcoholism at the Center for Study and Control of Alcoholism and other dependencies in Zagreb, 130 km away. The Director of the Center in Zagreb inspected the hospital once a month. A team from the Center (physician, social worker, medical nurse) visited the hospital once a week. The patients were divided into groups of 15 patients each, which held at least 2 group meetings every day with medical nurse, physician, or social worker. All patients and staff met once a day. The Department was operated as a self-management community. In the evenings there was a joint social program. Tuberculosis treatment was also begun, thereafter to be performed in group, and the patients were given education in alcoholism and tuberculosis, and after a time would take an examination on the knowledge acquired.

Patients' families were asked to visit the hospital and study the problem of alcoholism and tuberculosis and take an examination on the subject. During treatment the patients were allowed to visit home and recruit their spouses into their local Club of Treated Alcoholics. A Club of Treated Alcoholics was also instituted in the hospital. One hundred fourteen field visits were made over a wide area of the Republic of Croatia, covering almost all patients treated in 1973. The 114 patients comprised 74% out of a total of 143 patients treated. In 29 cases (26%) no control was possible.

Investigations were performed on the basis of an especially composed questionnaire, and patients found at home were medically examined. We were unable to examine 24 patients, some of whom were repeatedly being treated in various inpatient institutions. Nevertheless, we were able to collect data

TABLE 8

Total Number of Alcoholics Called Upon at Home

Sex	Alive	%	Dead	%	Total	%
Males	103	90.2	6	5.3	109	95.5
Females	5	4.5	–	–	5	4.5
Total	108	94.7	6	5.3	114	100.0

TABLE 9

Examined Patients Categorized by Occupation

Occupation	Number of Patients	%
Laborers	33	30.5
Employees	4	3.7
Agriculturalists	14	13.0
Retired	33	30.5
Socially imperiled	18	17.3
Unemployed	6	5.6
Total	108	100.0

from members of their families, in some cases also from neighbors or from members of clubs of treated alcoholics to which they belonged. A few tables demonstrate the results of our follow-up (TABLES 8–10).

Our checkups embraced 114 patients, 95.5% males and 4.5% female. One of the 5 females is abstaining and visits the Club of Treated Alcoholics regularly. After discharge from the hospital 6 patients died (5.3%). One of them had committed suicide. None of the deceased had achieved abstinence (TABLE 11).

Approximately one out of three patients is retired, mostly for disability; 34.2% are employed, mainly as laborers (30.5%).

The average age of the examinees is 47.61 years, while almost 80% of the patients are younger than 35.

On discharge during examination almost 32% of the patients abstained. The average duration of abstinence on discharge from the hospital in this group amounts to about 9 months. On examination it was established that after discharge 34 patients (31.4%) had not abstained at all. The average abstinence in the group of those who on the occasion of the checkup consumed alcohol lasted about 2 months. Twelve were subsequently treated for alcoholic recurrence, 8 as inpatients and 4 as outpatients. The majority relapsed immediately on leaving the hospital. The results are worst where there is no organized acceptance of the patient and in cases with marked dementia. On account of the extraordinary difficulties encountered in treating combined cases, we organized at the beginning of this year in Zagreb a club of treated tuberculous alcoholics, the task of which is to deal with all combined cases in Croatia.

In 75% of the abstainers the pulmonary finding is improved or there has been a cure, while improvement was found in approximately 42% of those in a state of alcoholic recurrence. An unchanged or aggravated pulmonary

TABLE 10

Age Groups of Examined Patients

Age Groups	Number of Patients	%
20–35	10	9.2
36–45	41	38.0
46–55	35	32.4
56+	22	20.4
Total	108	100.0

TABLE 11

Results of Treatment as Determined by Abstention

Success in Treatment of Alcoholism	Number of Patients	%
Abstaining	36	31.6
Not abstaining	78	68.4
Total	114	100.0

finding was found in 22.2% of the abstainers and in 56.9% of those continuing to consume alcohol (TABLE 12).

The statistically most significant difference is to be noticed in the aggravation of the pulmonary findings. While in the abstainers the aggravation of respiratory tuberculosis had occurred in 8.3% of the patients, the aggravation was found in 34.7% of those consuming alcohol. These data point to the well-known fact that tuberculous alcoholics are not properly treated and that they do not present themselves for checkups. However, when there does occur an improvement in alcoholic disease, their attitude in regard to tuberculosis also improves (TABLES 13 & 14).

Because of worsening of pulmonary findings, 12% of the patients were re-hospitalized, that is, a little less than one-half of the total number of patients with an aggravated pulmonary finding (26%). Outpatient treatment was given to 20.4%.

Almost all abstainers present themselves for regular pulmonary checkups, which suggests that the alcoholic in a state of abstinence takes better care of his health than the alcoholic in recurrence.

Posthospital treatment ought to be organized so that checkup and treatment of tuberculosis and alcoholism are carried out simultaneously. We firmly believe that a permanent close collaboration between the Club of Treated Alcoholics and the outpatient institution for respiratory tuberculosis is necessary. It is evident that the patient should be actively included in the therapeutic procedure.

In the group of abstainers, 83.3% visit regularly the Club of Treated Alcoholics. In the absence of a collaboration with the Club of Treated Alcoholics, 16.7% are able to abstain from alcohol. Patients who have stopped going to the Club or those who live far from it relapse very soon. There is no doubt

TABLE 12

Results of Treatment of Tuberculosis

Pulmonary Finding	Abstainers		Recurrences		Total	
	No.	%	No.	%	No.	%
Cured	5	13.9	7	9.7	12	11.1
Improved	22	61.1	23	31.9	45	41.7
Unchanged	5	13.9	16	22.2	21	19.4
Aggravated	3	8.3	25	34.8	28	26.0
Unknown	1	2.8	1	1.4	2	1.8
Total	36	100.0	72	100.0	108	100.0

TABLE 13
Subsequent Treatment Conditioned by Pulmonary Recurrence

Subsequently Treated	Abstainers		Recurrences		Total	
	No.	%	No.	%	No.	%
As inpatients	1	2.8	12	16.7	13	12.0
As out-patients in dispensary	8	22.2	14	19.6	22	20.4
Untreated	27	75.0	46	63.9	73	67.6
Total	36	100.0	72	100.0	108	100.0

TABLE 14
Followup Regularity

Patients Treated	Presenting Themselves		Not Presenting Themselves		Total	
	No.	%	No.	%	No.	%
Abstainers	34	94.4	2	5.6	36	100.0
Recurrences	47	65.3	25	34.7	72	100.0
Total	81	75.0	27	25.0	108	100.0

TABLE 15
Relation to the Club of Treated Alcoholics

Patients Treated	Member of Club of Treated Alcoholics		Not Member of Club of Treated Alcoholics		Total	
	No.	%	No.	%	No.	%
Abstainers	30	83.3	6	16.7	36	100.0
Recurrences	1	1.3	71	98.6	72	100.0
Total	31	28.7	77	71.3	108	100.0

TABLE 16
Activities by Family Members in Club for Treated Alcoholics

Family Member	Visits to Club of Treated Alcoholics		No Visits to Club of Treated Alcoholics		Total	
	No.	%	No.	%	No.	%
Abstainers	10	27.8	26	72.2	36	100.0
Recurrences	–	–	72	100.0	72	100.0
Total	10	9.2	98	90.8	108	100.0

TABLE 17
Liver Disease in Checkup Cases

Liver Disease	Abstainers		Recurrences		Total	
	No.	%	No.	%	No.	%
Present	7	19.4	30	41.7	37	34.2
Absent	19	52.8	26	36.1	45	41.7
Unknown	10	27.8	16	22.2	26	24.1
Total	36	100.0	72	100.0	108	100.0

that patients are inclined to consider tuberculosis their disease rather than alcoholism: more than 65% of those who drink are likely to present themselves to the antituberculosis dispensary for checkups and treatment, while only about 29% visit the Club of Treated Alcoholics for control and treatment (TABLES 15 & 16).

Our experience shows that a favorable issue of treatment may in the main be expected only in those patients whose family members or neighbors and workfellows participate in the Club's activities. Insufficient collaboration in the Club of Treated Alcoholics on the part of families is evident. Families of only 26% of the abstainers visit the Club of Treated Alcoholics, while no family member of recurrent drinkers visits it. This implies sometimes that the respective family has completely disintegrated or that the patient is in the skid-row group. In medical examination we tried to gauge the amount of liver damage, polyneuropathy, and the economic psycho-organic syndrome in the group of abstainers and those who continue drinking, and we obtained the following results:

Liver damage occurs approximately twice as frequently in those who do not abstain. Liver disorders as well as other complications due to alcoholism are the reason why these patients frequently seek medical care (TABLE 17).

Examinations have shown that approximately every other patient suffers from polyneuropathic disorders. The aforementioned disorders occur in 28% of abstainers, and in 61% of those that continue drinking (TABLE 18).

Examinations have demonstrated that the pattern of the chronic psycho-organic syndrome is marked in 38.9%. This percentage is 25 in the group of examined abstainers, and 45.8 in the recurrent drinkers. This might partially explain the fact that a large part of patients in a state of recurrence are entirely noncritical in regard to their alcoholism and refuse to consider a need for continuous treatment of their alcoholism. Some in this group had abandoned treatment and did not abstain on leaving the hospital (TABLE 19).

TABLE 18
Polyneuropathy in Checkup Cases

Polyneu-ropathy	Abstainers		Recurrences		Total	
	No.	%	No.	%	No.	%
Present	10	27.8	44	61.0	54	50.0
Absent	16	44.4	12	16.7	28	25.9
Unknown	10	27.8	16	22.2	26	24.1
Total	36	100.0	72	100.0	108	100.0

TABLE 19
Psycho-Organic Syndrome with Symptoms of Dementia

Psycho-organic Syndrome	Abstainers		Recurrences		Total	
	No.	%	No.	%	No.	%
Present	9	25.0	33	45.8	42	38.9
Absent	17	47.2	23	31.9	40	37.0
Unknown	10	37.8	16	22.2	26	24.1
Total	36	100.0	72	100.0	108	100.0

CONCLUSIONS

Our studies and followups clearly show that the combination pulmonary tuberculosis and alcoholism is relatively frequent. Moreover, today, when the number of cases of respiratory tuberculosis is on the decline, the number of tuberculous alcoholics is relatively on the rise. In combined cases we are usually concerned with severe cases of both tuberculosis and alcoholism. As regards alcoholism, these are mainly cases with very frequent liver damage, polyneuropathy, psycho-organic lesions, and grave social circumstances. In regard to tuberculosis, bacillary, resistant, chronically Koch-positive cases are frequently noted.

Almost all the combined cases were treated on several occasions with no success against one disease separately from the other, which would favor the assertion that these 2 diseases should be submitted to a systematic therapeutic procedure.

In the majority of cases, treatment in institutions for pulmonary diseases was discontinued on account of lack of discipline or by premature choice. If both these diseases are concurrently treated in a therapeutic community, disciplinary violation and discharge can be eliminated. The patients themselves start participating in their own treatment.

In over 30% of the cases our treatment gave good results.

In treating tuberculosis and alcoholism we should not ignore the fact that in such combined cases there frequently exist liver lesions, toxic neuropathy, and other organic complications.

In our experience, treatment can be performed only by engaging the patient himself in the therapeutic procedure and setting up associations of treated alcoholics, in which members of the families of treated alcoholics should also take part.

In conclusion, especial attention will have to be paid to the habit of smoking, notably to the intensive smoking during abstinence. We are currently making efforts to introduce a special plan of treatment of the smoking habit into the program. Everyone working on this problem is now only too well aware of the difficulty of such a task.

We firmly believe that it would be worth while trying to organize a special international committee to meet such combined cases.

ACKNOWLEDGMENTS

Thanks are due to Drs. M. Pavlović, S. Sakoman, and S. Nikolić, of the Hospital Klenovnik, for participation in this work.

REFERENCES

1. SMITH, J. C. & H. W. DEMONE, JR. 1961. Measurement of tuberculosis in Massachusetts and steps to combat it. Amer. Rev. Resp. Dis. **84**: 263–267.
2. LEVENDEL, L., T. VARADY, L. BEDE & A. KAROLYI. 1963. Über die Behandlung und ihre Ergebnisse von 180 lungentuberkulösen Patienten mit chronischen Alkoholismus. (On treatment and its results in 180 pulmonary tuberculosis patients with chronic alcoholism.) Beitr. Klin. Tuberk. **126**: 303–317.
3. YERSHOV, A. I. 1963. Lecheniye bol'nykh tuberkulyozom legkikh, stradayushchikh alkogolizmom. (Treatment of patients with pulmonary tuberculosis associated with alcoholism.) Sovet. Med. **26** (3): 89–94.
4. LEVENDEL, L., A. MEZEI, L. NEMES & T. VARADY. 1964. Über die Persönlichkeit der Alkoholiker und ihre Führung in der Tuberkulose-Heilanstalt. (On the personality of alcoholics and their management in the tuberculosis sanitarium.) Beitr. Klin. Erforsch. Tuberk. **128**: 131–145.
5. CHEUNG, O. T. 1965. Some difficulties in the treatment of tuberculous alcoholics. Canad. J. Public Health, **56**: 281–284.
6. GERARDI, A. & S. MAZZOLA. 1965. La tubercolosi polmonare nell'alcoolismo: studio clinico-radiologico su 49 soggeti. (Pulmonary tuberculosis in alcoholism. Clinical-radiological study of 49 subjects.) Lotta Tuberc. **35**: 420–426.
7. HOFF, H. & K. KRYSPIN-EXNER. 1966. Der tuberkulöse Alkoholkranke. (The tuberculous alcoholic.) Wien. Med. Wschr. **116**: 17–20.
8. KRSTIĆ, S., R. PARDON & J. BURGAR. 1967. Alkoholizam kao uzrok kroničnosti tuberkuloze. (Alcoholism as the cause of chronicity of tuberculosis.) Tuberkuloza, Beograd **19**: 597–599.
9. DZYAK, V. N. & B. N. BEZBORODKO. 1968. Vneshneye dykhaniyu pri khronicheskom alkogolizme. (External respiration in chronic alcoholism.) Vrach. Delo (1): 86–88.
10. LEVENDEL, L., D. KOZMA & A. MEZEI. 1968. Rezultati i poteškoće u lečenju tuberkuloznih alkoholičara. Tuberkuloza, Beograd: 33.
11. RAINAUT, J. 1968. L'établissement pour alcoolique tuberculeux; utopie ou progrès? (The institution for tuberculous alcoholics; utopia or progress?) Rev. Alcsme **14**: 79–81.
12. RIGHINI, C. L. 1968. L'alcoolisme dans les services de phtisiologie et en sanatorium. (Alcoholism in the phthisiology services and in the sanitarium.) Rev. Alcsme **14**: 75–76.
13. GRYMINSKI, J., J. LYCZEWSKA, H. STYSZEWSKA & J. WALCZAK. 1969. Ocena hepatoksycznego dzialania lekow przeciwpratkowych u chrorych na gruzlice pluc naduzywajacych alkoholu. (Assessment of hepatotoxicity of antitubercular drugs in patients with pulmonary tuberculosis who abuse alcohol.) Gružlica, Wars. **37**: 749–757.
14. KOK-JENSEN, A. 1970. The prognosis of pulmonary tuberculosis in patients with abuse of alcohol. Scand. J. Resp. Dis. **51**: 42–48.
15. LENNON, B. E., J. H. REKOSH, V. D. PATCH & L. P. HOWE. 1970. Self-reports of drunkenness arrests; assessing drinking problems among men hospitalized for tuberculosis. Quart. J. Stud. Alcohol **31**: 90–96.
16. LEVIĆ, Z. 1970. Alkohol, tuberkuloza i izonijazid u etiologiji polineuropatija. (Alcohol, tuberculosis and isoniazid in the etiology of polyneuropathy.) Alkoholizam, Beograd **10** (3–4): 19–26.
17. MASSÉ, H. 1972. L'alcoolisme facteur de mortalité; son incidence sur les principales de décès. (Alcoholism as a cause in mortality; its effect on the main causes of death.) Nouv. Presse Méd. (Paris) **1**: 1857–1860.
18. WESSELY, P. & G. PERNHAUPT. 1972. Suchttransposition; zur Frage von Rauchgewohnheiten bei Alkoholikern. (Transference of addiction; smoking habits in alcoholics.) Suchtgefahren, Hamburg **18** (3): 1–9.

INTRODUCTION

Kenneth Williams

In 1952 Ledermann pointed out the increased incidence of cancers in alcoholics. Subsequent more sophisticated epidemiologic studies have identified the bodily location of such cancers and have attempted to delineate the specific carcinogenic effect of alcohol usage. The following papers review the pertinent, mostly epidemiologic, evidence that there is an association between chronic consumption of large amounts of alcoholic beverages and cancers of the head and neck (hypopharynx, larynx, esophagus, oropharynx, tongue), and discuss the possible mechanisms in which heavy drinking might predispose to the development of cancer.

Dr. Lowenfels' paper reviews the evidence supporting a link between alcoholism and cancer of the cardiac portion of the stomach, the liver, the pancreas, and the prostate. The possibility that concomitant heavy smoking and/or malnutrition in the alcoholic adds to his risk of cancer development is discussed.

Dr. Kissin's paper presents preliminary data from an ongoing epidemiologic study linking alcohol consumption to cancer of the head and neck. His findings suggest that alcohol might play a greater role in development of cancers of those parts of the upper gastrointestinal tract in which ingested alcohol typically comes into direct contact—i.e., the floor of the mouth, hypopharynx, and esophagus.

ALCOHOLISM AND THE RISK OF CANCER*

Albert B. Lowenfels

*New York Medical College
and
Grasslands Hospital
Valhalla, New York 10595*

A large number of human and experimental noeplasms are thought to be related to contact with a carcinogen, and even weakly carcinogenic substances may induce tumors if contact is prolonged. A large portion of our population is exposed to alcohol, and this has led to a review of the accumulated evidence linking alcohol and cancer. In what ways might heavy drinking predispose to subsequent formation of neoplasms?

(1) Alcohol by itself might be carcinogenic. However, this seems unlikely in view of the simple, uncomplicated molecular structure of ethanol. Furthermore, prolonged exposure of mice to 20% alcohol in their drinking water does not induce tumors.[1]

(2) Contamination of alcoholic beverages during or after production. Potential sites for contamination could include the initial carbohydrate, the water, the production equipment, or the storage vessels.

(3) Damage to the mucus membranes from alcohol might increase susceptibility to another carcinogen. This would be consistent with the experimental observation that alcohol enhances the action of 7,12,-dimethylbenz-(a)-anthracene (DMBA) in the production of intraoral and skin tumors.[2]

(4) Alcohol might enhance the carcinogenic effect of smoking. Heavy drinkers are nearly always heavy smokers, and to date it has proved difficult to study a population of drinkers who do not smoke.

(5) An associated nutritional defect in the alcoholic might predispose to cancer.

At present we cannot tell which mode of action of alcohol leads to cancer. The clinical association seems strongest where there is direct contact of tissues with alcohol (oropharynx, larynx, esophagus) or where there is serious organ damage (liver). Alcoholism apparently has no influence on the major forms of cancer in Westernized countries: namely, cancer of the breast, lung, colon, or cervix.

HEAD AND NECK TUMORS

Heavy smoking and heavy drinking accompany each other, making it difficult to study the separate effects of these two agents. Nevertheless, there is inescapable evidence that alcoholics have a greatly increased risk of cancer in this region.

Tumors of the Oropharynx

Numerous reports underscore the strong relation between alcohol and oropharyngeal tumors: the incidence is almost 6 times greater than in comparable nondrinkers.[3-6] Tumors are more likely to follow exposure to "hard liquor" than beer or wine, and, as might be expected, those patients who drink enough to

*This work was supported by a grant from the Christopher D. Smithers Foundation.

develop cirrhosis of the liver have an especially high risk of oropharyngeal tumors. Careful examination of the oropharynx (FIGURE 1) should be an essential part of the work-up of all alcoholics. Mandel and associates[7] have noted an elevation of salivary immunoglobulins (especially IgA) in patients with oropharyngeal cancer and also in tumor-free patients who smoke and drink heavily. These intriguing findings are as yet unexplained.

Cancer of the Larynx

This form of cancer is also associated with consumption of whiskey, and the location of the tumor is most likely to be extrinsic rather than intrinsic.[8] The symptoms of hoarseness or voice change in an alcoholic should make the clinician suspicious about an underlying cancer of the larynx, and, when present, these symptoms should lead to prompt visualization of the larynx.

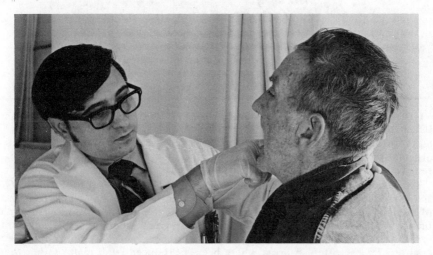

FIGURE 1. Alcoholics have a high incidence of oropharyngeal cancer. Intraoral palpation may be rewarding. (From Lowenfels.[54] By permission of the Williams & Wilkins Co.)

Parotid Tumors

Excess drinking does not lead to parotid tumors.[9] However, chronic alcoholism is the commonest cause of parotid enlargement in adults, and this has led to confusion and unnecessary biopsy.[10] Excess fat in the gland produces the enlargement, and the swelling subsides when the patient's nutritional status improves (FIGURE 2).

CANCER OF THE ESOPHAGUS

Heavy drinkers run the risk of developing esophageal cancer, and in America a plot of alcohol consumption by state shows a strong correlation with the incidence of esophageal cancer.[11,12] In our country the disease is increasing in frequency, especially in the nonwhite urban population.[13] Smoking is another causative factor, and it is entirely possible that the 2 agents work synergisti-

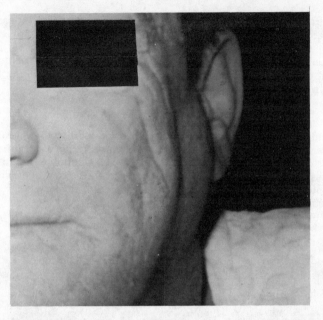

FIGURE 2. Painless parotid enlargement accompanies some cases of advanced alcoholism. Usually bilateral. (From Lowenfels.[54] By permission of the Williams & Wilkins Co.)

cally.[14] However, alcohol alone was implicated long before cigarette smoking became widespread.[15]

The type of beverage and the source of carbohydrate are probably related to the subsequent development of esophageal tumors. France has a high incidence of tumors in the Northwest, where the main alcoholic drink produced is apple brandy.[16] Eastern and southern Africa are regions where there is an extraordinarily high incidence of cancer of the esophagus, and here the tumor is encountered most often in areas where beer is produced from maize rather than other carbohydrate sources.[17] Home-processed rum has been implicated as a cause of esophageal cancer in Puerto Rico.[18]

Dimethyl nitrosamine, a known site-specific carcinogen, was originally suspected to be related to the induction of esophageal cancer because traces of the substance were discovered in samples of "home brew" collected in Zambia.[19] However, more sensitive methods have cast doubt on the role of nitrosamines in the genesis of human esophageal cancer.[20] Alcohol is probably only one of several factors capable of inducing this tumor; the highest known incidence of esophageal cancer is in Iran, where there is no evidence to implicate alcohol.[21]

STOMACH CANCER

Does alcoholism lead to gastric cancer? World cancer statistics do show that the frequency of stomach cancer is closely related to the frequency of esophageal cancer.[22] (FIGURE 3). The cardiac portion of the stomach is subject to the same undiluted alcohol as is the esophagus, and in one study there did seem to be an excessive incidence of alcoholism in patients with cancer of the cardia.[23] Furthermore, the large number of male patients with cancer of the cardia would be consistent with the known higher frequency of alcoholism in males.[24] The role of alcohol must be minor because gastric cancer has been decreasing dramatically[25] while consumption of alcohol is increasing.

LIVER TUMORS AND ALCOHOLISM

Hepatomas almost always arise in a previously damaged liver, and in Westernized countries the commonest antecedent disease is alcoholic cirrhosis.[26] The chance that a patient with alcoholic cirrhosis will subsequently develop a hepatoma has been reported to range from 8 to 30% and the longer the cirrhotic patient lives the greater is the risk of this tumor.[27–30] Nonalcoholic cirrhosis appears to have less risk of leading to hepatoma. It is unclear what role malnutrition plays in the development of this tumor, since many of these patients are chronically malnourished and it is known that in many parts of the world this is a common tumor in abstinent but poorly nourished subjects.[31]

Diagnostic Aids

There is no single symptom, sign, or diagnostic procedure that enables the clinician to make an early diagnosis with surety, and in many instances the tumor is found only at autopsy (FIGURE 4). Males are afflicted more than females, probably reflecting the higher incidence of cirrhosis in males. One should suspect

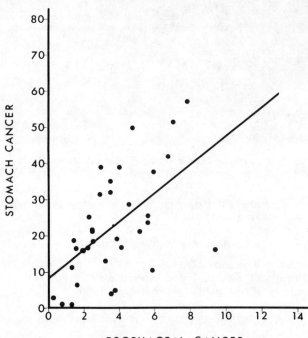

FIGURE 3. Frequency (per 100 000 population) of stomach cancer plotted against frequency of esophageal cancer. Each point represents data from a different country or region. Males and females combined. (R = 0.57, P = 0.001 or less). From Doll.[22]

this tumor in any alcoholic patient with weakness, jaundice, ascites, and an enlarging liver. Liver biopsy and liver scans are helpful procedures, and if the alpha fetoprotein levels are elevated the patient almost certainly has a hepatoma.[32] The great majority of these tumors are hepatocellular in type rather than being cholangiocarcinomas.

Cirrhosis and Metastatic Liver Cancer

Many clinicians believe that metastatic tumors do not grow in a cirrhotic liver, and this idea may have originated from early studies of groups of cirrhotic patients with a preponderance of head and neck cancer. Such tumors are known to metastasize only rarely to the liver; more recent studies show no difference in

FIGURE 4. Massive hemorrhage from an unsuspected hepatoma was the cause of death in this alcoholic patient. (From Lowenfels.[54] By permission of the Williams & Wilkins Co.)

the incidence of secondary liver cancer in patients with or without portal hypertension and alcoholic cirrhosis.[33]

Cirrhosis and Diffuse Lipomatosis

This rare syndrome is characterized by multiple nonencapsulated lipomas distributed throughout the trunk and cervical regions. For some unexplained reason, the majority of such patients have been cirrhotic.[34]

ALCOHOL AND CANCER OF THE PANCREAS

For the past few decades there has been a rapid and dramatic increase in the incidence of pancreatic cancer.[35,36] Does alcohol play a role in explaining this remarkable increase? We do know that chronic pancreatitis, a frequent disease in alcoholics, is a common finding in patients with pancreatic cancer, but in most instances this association can be explained by obstruction of ducts by the neoplasm.

Burch and Ansari[37] discovered a significantly greater incidence of alcoholics in a group of patients dying from pancreatic cancer than in a comparable control group, and on the basis of this they postulated that alcohol was an important factor. Ishii et al.[38] drew the same conclusions from a study of Japanese patients, since the risk of cancer was found to be twice as great for males who drank every day as for nondrinkers. On the other hand, Wynder et al.[39] failed to find any link between alcoholism and subsequent death from cancer of the pancreas, but they did feel that smoking was implicated.

Part of the confusion arises from the elusive nature of this disease, which makes histologic confirmation a requirement for accurate diagnosis. However, unlike head-and-neck or esophageal cancer, in which biopsy can be obtained with relative ease, an exploratory laparotomy or an autopsy is necessary to obtain pancreatic tissue for the pathologist, and recent statistics point out that such confirmation was obtained only in about half of all suspected cases.[40]

Pancreatic Calcification

In general, when calcification is present in the pancreas it is a sign of chronic pancreatitis.[41] However, cancer of the pancreas has been found on many occasions in patients with diffuse pancreatic calcification.[42,43] It is unwise for the clinician to exclude the diagnosis of cancer when the abdominal X-ray discloses calcification because the incidence of cancer in such patients may be as high as 10%.[44]

CANCER OF THE PROSTATE

Small amounts of alcohol are excreted in the urine, and this might explain why several studies[45,46] have shown a relation between alcoholism and prostatic cancer. However, neither Wynder et al.[47] nor Schoones et al.[48] found any significant correlation between alcoholism and cancer of the prostate. The incidence of this tumor is low in alcoholics, so that large groups must be studied to obtain meaningful data. Once again, the smoking factor makes firm conclusions difficult, because smoking is known to lead to genitourinary cancer.

ALCOHOL INTOLERANCE IN CANCER PATIENTS

This is a poorly understood but occasionally helpful clinical finding and may provide a clue to an underlying neoplasm. Patients with this syndrome complain of pain, discomfort, or burning after ingestion of alcohol, and in many instances the patient notices that the symptoms are most prominent in an area of tumor growth. The syndrome is seen mostly in patients with Hodgkin's disease and lymphomas, but it has been reported with a wide variety of tumors.[49-52] The reason for this unusual phenomenon is unknown, but it may be related to the vasodilating effects of alcohol. Another explanation might be that ingestion of alcohol causes release of a hormone such as calcitonin.[53] Women are more likely to be troubled by the syndrome than men.

CLINICAL IMPLICATIONS

When an alcoholic patient does develop a cancer he is likely to seek help only when the tumor has reached an advanced stage, and then there is often further delay if the physician attributes the symptoms to underlying alcoholism as in the following case report:

> Case Report: A middle-aged alcoholic noted difficulty in swallowing, mild pain, and a "sticking" sensation in the lower chest. He assumed his symptoms were caused by heartburn, and he attempted to modify his diet and alter his drinking habits. The swallowing problem worsened until he was limited to liquids.
>
> At this point he sought medical attention, and the first physician who treated him felt that he had alcoholic gastritis, for which he was told to take antacids and stop drinking. Much later, when the symptoms persisted, the patient consulted a second physician, who obtained a barium swallow which revealed a large cancer of the lower esophagus.

The lesson is clear—any somatic complaint in an alcoholic must be given close attention. It is dangerous to assume that such symptoms as sore throat, hoarseness, difficulty in swallowing, and weight loss are solely related to alcoholism. In addition to treatment delays, the alcoholic patient often neglects to return for regular followup visits, and this is another factor that makes it difficult to achieve a successful result.

SUMMARY

Heavy drinking increases the risk of head, neck, oropharyngeal, esophageal, and liver cancer; it may possibly be implicated in the genesis of pancreatic and prostatic cancer. By itself ethanol has not proved to be an experimental carcinogen, so that one must postulate some other mode of action for alcohol in the production of human tumors. Heavy smoking and malnutrition often accompany alcoholism, and these factors may increase the risk of cancer in certain organs. When tumors appear in alcoholics they are often late in stage and originate in such organs as the esophagus, extrinsic larynx and liver—locations where treatment is notoriously difficult. Although we should continue to strive for earlier diagnosis and more effective treatment methods, it would appear that decreased exposure to alcohol will be the most effective method to achieve a significant decrease in cancer deaths.

ACKNOWLEDGMENT

I thank Dr. B. J. Sobol for help in preparing FIGURE 3.

REFERENCES

1. KETCHAM, A. S., H. WEXLER & N. MANTEL. 1963. Cancer Res. 23: 667–670.
2. ELZAY, R. P. 1969. J Dent. Res. 48: 1200–1205.
3. WYNDER, E. L., I. J. BROSS & R. M. FELDMAN. 1957. Cancer 10: 1300–1323.
4. NELSON, J. F. & I. I. SHIP. 1971. J. Amer. Dent. Assoc. 82: 564–568.
5. FARR, H. W. & K. ARTHUR. 1972. J. Laryngol. Otol. 86: 243–253.
6. KISSIN, B., M. M. KALEY, W. HUEY-SU & R. LERNER. 1973. J.A.M.A. 224: 1174–1175.
7. MANDEL, M. A., K. DVORAK, & J. J. DECOSSE. 1973. Cancer 31: 1408–1413.
8. WYNDER, E. L., I. J. BROSS, & E. DAY. 1956. Cancer 9: 86–110.
9. KELLER, A. Z. 1969. Amer. J. Epidem. 90: 269–277.
10. DUGGAN, J. J. & E. N. ROTHBELL. 1957. New Eng. J. Med. 257: 1262–1267.
11. WYNDER, E. L. & I. J. BROSS. 1961. Cancer 14: 389–413.
12. SCHOENBERG, B. S., J. C. BAILAR III & J. F. FRAUMENI, JR. 1971. J. Nat. Cancer Inst. 46: 63–73.

13. BURBANK, F. & J. F. FRAUMENI, JR. 1972. J Nat. Cancer Inst. **49**: 649.
14. JUSSAWALLA, D. J. 1972. Int. J. Cancer **10**: 436–441.
15. LAMU, L. 1910. Arch. Mal. Appar. Dig. **4**: 451–475.
16. TUYNS, A. J. 1970. Int. J. Cancer. **5**: 152–156.
17. COOK, P. 1971. Brit. J. Cancer. **25**: 853–880.
18. MARTINEZ, I. 1969. J. Nat. Cancer Inst. **42**: 1069–1094.
19. McGLASHAN, N. D. 1969. Gut **10**: 643–650.
20. COLLIS, C. H., J. J. COOK, J. K. FOREMAN & J. F. PALFRAMAN. 1972. Lancet **1**: 441.
21. KMET, J. & E. MAHBOUBI. 1972. Science **175**: 846–853.
22. DOLL, R., P. PAYNE & J. WATERHOUSE, Eds. 1966. *In* Cancer Incidence in Five Continents. Vol 1. International Union Against Cancer. Geneva, Switzerland.
23. MACDONALD, W. C. 1972. Cancer **29**: 724–732.
24. FLAMANT, R., O. LASSERRE, R. LAZAR, J. LEGUERINAIS, P. DENOIX & D. SCHWARTZ. 1964. J. Nat. Cancer Inst. **32**: 1309–1316.
25. LOWENFELS, A. B. 1973. Surg. Gynec. Obstet. **137**: 291–298.
26. HIGGINSON, J. 1969. Gastroenterology **57**: 587–598.
27. LEEVY, C. M., R. GELLENE & M. NING. 1964. Ann. N. Y. Acad. Sci. **114**: 1026–1040.
28. SUNDBY, P. 1967. Alcoholism and Mortality. Publication 6, National Institute for Alcohol Research: 106.
29. PARKER, R. G. F. 1957. Proc. Roy. Soc. Med. **50**: 145–147.
30. LEE, F. I. 1966. Gut **7**: 77–85.
31. DAVIDSON, C. S. 1970. Amer. J. Clin. Nutr. **23**: 427–436.
32. ALPERT, M. E., J. URIEL & B. DENECHAUD. 1968. New Eng. J. Med. **278**: 984–986.
33. GOLDSTEIN, M. J., W. J. FRABLE & P. SHERLOCK. 1966. Amer. J. M. Sci. **252**: 26–30.
34. HELLER, R. F., I. A. ALAVI & G. DUNEA. 1971. Amer. J. Dig. Dis. **16**: 333–336.
35. STEPHENSON, H. E. JR. 1972. Surgery **71**: 307–308.
36. KRAIN, L. S. 1973. Geriatrics **28**: 140–145.
37. BURCH, G. E. & A. ANSARI. 1968. Arch. Int. Med. **122**: 273–275.
38. ISHII, K., K. NAKAMURA, H. OZAKI, N. YAMATA & T. TAKEYUCHI. 1968. Jap. J. Clin, Med. **26**: 1839–1842.
39. WYNDER, E. L., K. MABUCHI, N. MARUCHI & J. G. FORTNER. 1973. J. Nat. Cancer Inst. **50**: 645–667.
40. LEVIN, D. L. & R. R. CONNELLY. 1973. Cancer **31**: 1231–1236.
41. RING, E. J., S. B. EATON, JR., J. T. FERRUCCI, JR. & W. F. SHORT. 1973. Amer. J. Roentgen. **117**: 446–452.
42. JOHNSON, J. R. & H. A. ZINTEL. 1963. Surg. Gynec. Obstet. **117**: 585–588.
43. PAULINO-NETTO, A., D. A. DREILING & I. P. BARONOFSKY. 1960. Ann. Surg. **151**: 530–537.
44. TUCKER, D. H. & I. B. MORE. 1963. New Eng. J. Med. **268**: 31–33.
45. PELL, S. & C. A. D'ALONZO. 1973. J. Occup. Med. **15**: 120–125.
46. SCHMIDT, W. & J. DE LINT. 1972. Quart. J. Stud. Alcohol **33**: 171–185.
47. WYNDER, E. L., K. MABUCHI & W. F. WHITMORE, JR. 1971. Cancer **28**: 344–360.
48. SCHOONEES, R., L. DIPALMA, J. F. GAETA, R. H. MOORE & G. P. MURPHY. 1972. New York J. Med. **72**: 1021–1027.
49. JAMES, A. H. 1960. Quart. J. Med. **29**: 47.
50. BREWIN, T. B. 1966. Brit Med. J. **2**: 437–441.
51. ADAMSON, A. R., D. G. GRAHAME-SMITH, W. S. PEART & M. STARR. 1969. Lancet **2**: 293.
52. PERKIN, G. D. 1973. Brit Med. J. **3**: 478.
53. COHEN, S. L., D. GRAHAME-SMITH, D. MacINTYRE & J. G. WALKER. 1973. Lancet **2**: 1172–1173.
54. LOWENFELS, A. B. 1971. The Alcoholic Patient in Surgery: 172, 234, 237. Williams & Wilkins. Baltimore, Md.

EPIDEMIOLOGIC INVESTIGATIONS OF POSSIBLE BIOLOGICAL INTERACTIONS OF ALCOHOL AND CANCER OF THE HEAD AND NECK

Benjamin Kissin

State University of New York
Downstate Medical Center
Brooklyn, New York 11203

The close clinical association between the heavy ingestion of alcohol and cancer of the head and neck has long been recognized and has been thoroughly documented.[4] Despite this suggestion of causal relationship, no direct experimental evidence that ethanol is in itself a carcinogenic agent has been developed.[3] Consequently, the major hypotheses that have evolved relating alcohol to cancer usually invoke some intermediary mechanism. Among those suggested are (a) the presence of alcohol-related malnutrition, (b) the presence in alcoholic beverages of carcinogenic congeners, (c) the possible augmenting action of ethanol on concomitantly administered true carcinogenic substances, such as specific congeners, tobacco tars, environmental chemicals, (d) the direct or indirect irritating effect of ethanol on the affected tissues—direct as in cancer of the head and neck, indirect as in hepatomas in cirrhotic livers. These and similar hypotheses are open to experimental study but are perhaps more easily, if less definitely, explored by epidemiologic research. The present epidemiologic study was undertaken in an attempt to provide hypotheses that could ultimately be tested through more direct biological experimentation.

There is already a substantial epidemiologic literature[4] on the relationship of alcohol to cancer of the head and neck, and from this, many hypotheses, such as those previously described, have been generated. The major defects in most of these studies have been of two kinds: (a) most studies have been retrospective rather than prospective and (b) most retrospective studies have been only roughly quantitative. Our approach in the present study has been directed toward attempting to improve the quality of retrospective studies through the development of a more quantitative instrument. Toward that end, a carefully designed interview has been developed that generates more reliable data relative to the drinking, smoking, and eating habits of patients with cancer of the head and neck as well as of suitable control groups. These questionnaires are directed toward establishing the smoking, drinking, and eating patterns of subjects during the 5-year period prior to the development of the specific lesion. On the basis of these data, we hope to be able to validate hypotheses that have been developed from existing epidemiologic data. The present report is a preliminary one, based on approximately $\frac{1}{2}$ of our total sample. It is directed more toward an exploration of methodology and to a description of trends rather than to the report of a definitive or conclusive study. Nevertheless, we trust that it will be of interest.

The specific hypotheses we set out to test were, as stated, derived from existing epidemiologic data. The remainder of this report will deal with several specific hypotheses, the existing epidemiologic data on which they are based, and the indicated trend in our present studies tending to support or contradict these hypotheses.

1. Patients with head and neck cancer should show a higher incidence of heavy drinking, heavy smoking, and malnutrition than other control groups, with the probable exception of known alcoholics.

This hypothesis is based on the classic studies of Wynder et al.,[7,8] of Keller and Terris,[2] of Martinez,[6] and of Flamant et al.[1] All these authors found significantly higher patterns of alcohol ingestion and tobacco use in the cancer groups than in control groups. Wynder et al.[7] and Martinez[6] found marked malnutrition in their cancer groups but, surprisingly enough, this was not significantly different from their control groups that were matched on socio-economic parameters.

Our preliminary results tend to support all of these conclusions. It would appear that head and neck cancer patients did smoke and drink more heavily than control groups for the 5-year period prior to the development of their lesions. However, at this point, we have not found any significant difference in the eating patterns during that period in the 2 groups. On the other hand, in a routine head-and-neck survey of 3000 alcoholics carried out in our program,[5] 8 subjects were found to have early cancer of the head and neck against an expected incidence of one per 3000 ($p < 0.01$). Those 8 patients did have lower vitamin and serum albumin levels than did the other alcoholics without cancer, suggesting that malnutrition might still play a pertinent role. Accordingly, the possible role of malnutrition in the pathogenesis of head and neck cancer requires further exploration.

2. Patients with head and neck cancer should have a longer history of heavy drinking and smoking than should control populations. This hypothesis is a commonsense one stemming from the clinical observations that the development of cancer seems to be related not only to the severity of a specific irritating influence but to the length of time that influence is in effect. It was supported by our just described "head and neck cancer in alcoholics" study[5] in that the alcoholics in whom we discovered cancer had been drinking and smoking for a significantly longer period of time than had alcoholics of equal age in whom no cancer was found. This was true even though the total amount of drinking and smoking in the two groups was not significantly different. In our present study, we find, too, that patients with cancer of the head and neck appear to have adopted a heavier pattern of drinking and smoking earlier in life than did most control groups and tended to maintain that pattern for a longer period of time.

3. In cancer of the head and neck, smoking might play a greater role in those areas where tobacco smoke would make most direct contact—the roof of the mouth, nasopharynx, larynx, and lungs. On the other hand, alcohol might play a greater role in those areas where alcohol would make most direct contact—the floor of the mouth, the hypopharynx, and the esophagus. If this were true, one would expect to find a greater smoking/drinking ratio in those individuals with cancer of the "inhalation" tract and a greater drinking/smoking ratio in those individuals with cancer of the "ingestion" tract.

These hypotheses stem mainly from the work of Flamant et al.,[1] who found a particularly high pattern of alcohol intake associated with cancers of the hypopharynx, larynx, esophagus, and tongue, and particularly high patterns of smoking associated with cancers of the nasopharynx, larynx, lung, and oropharynx. We have modified the hypothesis to attempt to relate more directly the smoking/drinking ratio to the specific sites of contact. It is obviously impossible to separate completely the sites of contact of alcohol and tobacco smoke. Nevertheless, on the basis of the concepts of an "inhalation" tract as opposed to an "ingestion" tract, we compared the smoking/drinking ratios for individuals with cancers of these two tracts.

The results are illustrated in FIGURE 1. Although the differences between the two slopes do not reach significance, it can be seen that the nicotine vs. ethyl

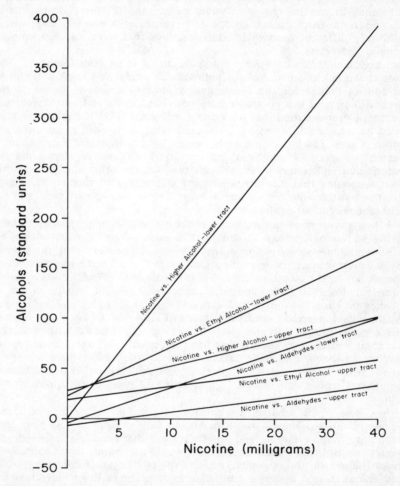

FIGURE 1. Regression equations for nicotine and the three types of alcohol and cancers of the upper and lower tract. Upper tract consists of the roof of the mouth, nasopharynx, and larynx; lower tract of the floor of the mouth, hypopharynx, and esophagus.

alcohol–lower tract (that is, "ingestion" tract) ratio inclines more to the alcohol side while the line nicotine vs. ethyl alcohol–upper tract (i.e., "inhalation" tract) inclines more heavily to the nicotine side. These data tend to support the specific hypothesis that the site of development of cancer is related to the directness of contact of either alcohol or tobacco smoke.

4. As a corollary of the last hypothesis, it would seem plausible that hard whiskey, which contains both a higher concentration of ethyl alcohol and a higher content of higher alcohols, would be more intimately associated with cancers of the "ingestion" tract than with cancers of the "inhalation" tract. This is a commonsense hypothesis based on the concept that if direct contact with ethanol plays a significant role in carcinogenesis, then the higher the concentration of ethanol and the higher the content of higher alcohols that are even stronger than ethanol, the greater the effect should be. This hypothesis is further supported by the findings of Wynder and his group[7,8] that cancer of the mouth, pharynx, and larynx was associated with a higher level of whiskey ingestion than of wine or beer.

These relationships are explored in FIGURE 1, again in a comparison of the nicotine vs. higher alcohol–lower tract slope and the nicotine vs. higher alcohol–upper tract slope. One can see that they are even more widely divergent than the slopes involving ethyl alcohol, with the lower tract ("ingestion" tract) inclining much more heavily to the alcohol side, and the upper tract (the "inhalation" tract) inclining more heavily toward the smoking side.

In summary, we have presented preliminary data that suggest certain pathogenetic mechanisms through which the heavy chronic ingestion of alcoholic beverages may contribute to the development of cancer of the head and neck. Most of these preliminary findings did not quite reach statistical levels of significance. We have hopes that when the study is complete they may. In any event, these data are presented here not so much as a report of conclusive findings as an indication that epidemiologic techniques can be of value in generating hypotheses that may form the basis of biological research.

REFERENCES

1. FLAMANT, R., O. LASSERRE, R. LAZAR, J. LEQUERINAIS, P. DENOIX & D. SCHWARTZ. 1964. Differences in sex ratio according to cancer site and possible relationship with use of tobacco and alcohol. Review of 65,000 cases, J. of Nat. Cancer Inst. 32: 1309–1316.
2. KELLER, A. Z. & M. TERRIS. 1965. The association of alcohol and tobacco with cancer of the mouth and pharynx, Amer. J. Public Health 55: 1578–1586.
3. KETCHAM, A. S., H. WEXLER & N. MANTEL. 1963. Effects of alcohol in mouse neoplasia. Cancer Res. 23: 667.
4. KISSIN, B. & M. M. KALEY. 1974. Alcohol and cancer. In Biology of Alcoholism 3. Clinical Pathology. B. Kissin and H. Begleiter, Eds.: 481–511. Plenum Press. New York, N.Y.
5. KISSIN, B., M. M. KALEY, W. H. SU & R. LERNER. 1973. Head and neck cancer in alcoholics. J.A.M.A. 224: 1174.
6. MARTINEZ, I. 1969. Factors associated with cancer of the esophagus, mouth and pharynx in Puerto Rico. J. Nat. Cancer Inst. 42: 1069–1099.
7. WYNDER, E. L., I. J. BROSS & E. DAY. 1956. Epidemiological approach to etiology of cancer of the larynx. J.A.M.A. 160: 1384–1391.
8. WYNDER, E. L., I. J. BROSS & R. M. FELDMAN. 1957. A study of etiological factors in cancer of the mouth. Cancer 10: 1300–1323.

INTRODUCTION

Kenneth Williams

A large volume of literature has been written on prescribing medications for the outpatient treatment of alcoholics. In comparing the efficacy of one drug with another, most have not provided scientific rigor in experimental design, having failed to randomize patients, or to utilize the double-blind trial. The papers that follow provide a thoughtful discussion on the role of sedatives, especially minor tranquilizers, in the long-term, outpatient treatment of alcoholism. The authors had been preselected for their known opposing views. Dr. Kissin was selected because of his use of sedatives in outpatient management, Dr. Bissell because of her known opposition to their use. Dr. Becker was known to espouse a middle-of-the-road position.

The papers are most notable for the agreement reached: (1) the ideal treatment for alcoholism, a form of drug abuse, would involve no psychoactive medication; (2) the indiscriminate prescribing of minor tranquilizers to alcoholics is too common, and to be condemned; (3) diazepam, the most frequently prescribed drug in this country, has a high abuse potential in the alcoholic. The authors have noted the large increase in alcoholics coming into treatment who have abused minor tranquilizers. Some treatment centers have declared that the "virgin" alcoholic, with no significant exposure to prescribed sedatives, is dead. In some areas 70–80% of the alcoholics entering into treatment have been found to have abused other sedatives as well as alcohol.

Dr. Kissin, in outlining his indications for the use of psychoactive drugs in the ambulatory care of the alcoholic, warned against reducing the most powerful motivating force for recovery, the anxiety and depressive symptoms of withdrawal with medication, and making the alcoholic dependant on the medication. He emphasized that the medication was not the treatment itself, but merely the "handle" to maintain the alcoholic in treatment. Dr. Kissin presents his evidence that chloridazepoxide is effective in keeping some alcoholics in treatment. However, he warned that this medication is indicated for only about 20–30% of the patients seen at his center, and advised that the lowest possible dosage be used for the shortest possible time (usually not over 6 months). He believes that these patients should be given nonrefillable prescriptions and should be seen at least weekly.

Dr. Becker took a strong position against any outpatient use of tranquilizing medication. However, he brought up a positive experience in using placebos as an anxiety-relieving mechanism for the alcoholic patient subsequent to withdrawal.

Dr. Bissell, in emphasizing the addictive potential of the minor tranquilizers, concludes that there is no convincing evidence that the advantages of prescribing them outweigh the hazards. She criticizes the common practice of prescribing drugs for the patient essentially because the doctor has been trained how to do it and the patient desires it. She suggests that rather than substitute another sedative for alcohol, the therapist attempt to substitute a caring, interpersonal involvement with people.

RATIONAL DRUG THERAPY OF ALCOHOLISM WITH SEDATIVE HYPNOTIC DRUGS! IS THIS POSSIBLE?

Charles E. Becker, Robert Roe, Robert Scott, Theodore Tong,
Udo Boerner, and Judith Luce

Division of Clinical Pharmacology
Department of Medicine
San Francisco General Hospital
San Francisco, California 94110

Rational drug therapy with sedative hypnotic drugs of the complicated medical condition known as alcoholism is exceedingly difficult. By far the most difficult problem entails interpreting the previously reported studies that have suggested therapeutic benefits. "Alcoholism" is a heterogenous diagnosis covering a broad spectrum of diseases for which some definite diagnostic criteria have been proposed.[1] Treatment groups of alcoholics are rarely homogenous, and fixed dosages of sedative hypnotic drugs have often been administered to these non-homogenous groups. It is widely recognized that the "alcoholic patient" is a highly complex subject who may have subtle but real organ pathology. In view of the complexity of the entity and its complications, it must be recognized how difficult it is to ensure that the addition of drug therapy alone is the sole factor responsible for improvement.

It is well known that patients in general, and alcoholic patients in particular, often do not comply with the therapeutic regimen. Although compliance with drup therapy may be anticipated by the physician, the patient in fact may not take the medication.[2] Few of the sedative hypnotic drugs that might be useful in the treatment of alcoholism are easily measured in biologic fluids to ensure compliance. Sedative hypnotic drugs as a class also have a strong placebo effect that can account for at least 30% of any therapeutic effect.[3] The therapeutic end point selected for the use of the sedative hypnotic drug is often difficult to define. The concept of "cure" of the withdrawal syndrome or "cure" for alcoholism may be only relative, in that the background of spontaneous remission or of gradual spontaneous improvement is not carefully defined.

In spite of all of these reservations, we still have a few controlled studies and some clinical experiences as a guide in using these medications. The Division of Clinical Pharmacology at the San Francisco General Hospital has had clinical experience in dealing directly with approximately 10,000 alcoholic and drug-abuse patients. Although it has been difficult to control all the therapeutic decisions on these patients, certain general comments can be made concerning the treatment with sedative hypnotic drugs of the alcoholic patient.

It can be said with some assurance that patient discomfort during the alcoholic-withdrawal syndrome may be treated by substituting long-acting sedative hypnotic drugs for the short-acting drug alcohol and then tapering these longer-acting drugs. This process, known as detoxification, can be managed effectively with the use of several different sedative hypnotic drugs. This statement does not exclude the possibility that some of the patients' discomfort could also be managed without drug therapy in a carefully controlled environment. If drugs are used, exactly which sedative hypnotic drug is most effective is probably best determined by the clinical criteria of overall safety, lack of adverse drug reaction, lack of detectable drug interactions, and conveniency of administration route. In our clinical experience the benzodiazepine drugs are useful, and the drug diazepam (Valium®) seems to be most useful. Associated major medical or surgical conditions tend to make the withdrawal syndrome much more severe and may modify the drug therapy.

There are several clinical factors during detoxification that have been reported in the literature and confirmed by us that may complicate therapeutic decision-making. Many, if not most, alcoholic patients smoke, and it has been recognized in the Boston Drug Surveillance Program that smoking decreases the therapeutic effects of the benzodiazepine drugs but not other sedative hypnotic drugs.[4] It is also clear that since most alcoholic patients smoke there is probably a high incidence of lung disease in alcoholic patients, which may increase the risk of respiratory depression when sedative hypnotic drugs are administered. In a nonspecific way, age and the serum albumin level have also been suggested as key factors for predicting dangers with these medicines; our clinical experience supports these observations. Although it is difficult to quantitate, we believe that the environment has some effect on the symptomatology and drug effects in treating the alcoholic-withdrawal syndrome. Although hard to define, a sympathetic, understanding staff, quiet surroundings, and judicious nutritional and psychological support are adjuncts to pharmacological manipulations.

Once the detoxification process is completed, there are few studies that definitely document that the long-term behavioral modifications so necessary for the alcoholic patient can be accomplished by the administration of any sedative hypnotic drugs. One of the biggest problems that confront the physician in deciding whether sedative hypnotic drugs are useful in alcoholic patients concerns the clinical recognition of drug tolerance. Tolerance develops to all sedative hypnotic drugs. When these drugs are given in divided doses and over long periods, it is clear that the therapeutic efficacy is compromised to some degree and that higher doses are required for the same effects. Our clinical

TABLE 1

Alcohol Intake History of 147 Patients Interviewed in Utilization Study

1. Frequency	
"Never drank alcohol"	11%
"Occasional drinker"	32%
"Daily drinker"	44%
"Binge drinker"	5%
"Variable"	5%
Unknown	3%
2. Amount	
"Less than 2 drinks"	20%
"2–5"	26%
"Greater than 2"	40%
"Variable"	4%
Unknown	4%
3. Duration of Alcohol Intake History	
"0–1 year"	3%
"Less than 5 years"	12%
"More than 5 years"	82%
Unknown	3%

TABLE 2

Summary of Utilization Review of Antianxiety Drugs

1. Number of patients surveyed	226
2. Percent of patients receiving antianxiety drugs	69%
3. Percent of "PRN" orders for antianxiety drugs	52%
4. Percent of patients who receive combined daytime and bedtime anti-anxiety drugs	24%
5. Percent of patients receiving combined antianxiety drugs with other drugs causing central nervous system depression	27%
6. Number of surveyed patients who were interviewed	147
7. Percent of patients who responded "no" when asked if they *need* "something" for restlessness, etc. during the day or for sleeplessness at bedtime	35%
8. Percent of the "no" responders who were documented to be receiving one or more antianxiety drug at the time.	45%
9. Percent of patients who responded "no" when asked if they were *receiving* "something" for restlessness, etc. during the day or for sleeplessness at bedtime.	40%
10. Percent of the "no" responders who were documented to be receiving one or more antianxiety drug at the time.	37%

experience also suggests that the usual timing of the alcoholic withdrawal may be delayed many hours if the patient has simultaneously ingested alcohol and longer acting sedative hypnotic drugs prior to admission. The physician may thus become confused concerning the time of the symptoms' occurence and miss the basic causative factor.

It is clear that anxiety reactions can be modified by acute doses of some sedative hypnotic medications, but in fact each of the sedative hypnotic drugs themselves has a potential for addiction, and to initiate chronic administration leads to drug tolerance, with less therapeutic effects. One could argue that progress has been made by addicting the patient to the benzodiazepine drugs or other sedative hypnotic drugs in lieu of alcohol, for this might lessen the risks of the organ complications of chronic alcohol abuse, much as methadone administration eliminates the complications of intravenous use of heroin. This is a fine hypothesis—but totally unproved!

When one attempts to use the sedative hypnotic drugs in a rational fashion for purposes of alleviating the anxiety and sleep disorders that so frequently are associated with alcoholism, one is faced with a formidable, difficult task. At San Francisco General Hospital, where chronic alcoholism is a major problem among the patients admitted (TABLE 1), a sedative-hypnotic-drug utilization review was recently conducted for purposes of examining the extent of their use and the events that precipitated the decision to use them. Over a 21-day period, the treatment records of 226 hospitalized patients were monitored (TABLE 2) and it was found that 158 (69%) of the patients received 1 or more barbiturate, nonbarbiturate, or benzodiazepine-type agents for purposes of relieving restlessness, anxiety, or agitation or for promoting sleep. One hundred eight (52%) of the total number of those drugs were prescribed on a "PRN" or as-needed basis. Twenty-four percent of the patients surveyed received antianxiety medication (usually diazepam) during the day and at bedtime (usually flurazepam). Twenty-seven percent of the patients received antianxiety agents concurrently with narcotics or antihistamines, agents that are capable of prolonging sedation by producing additive central nervous system depression.

There were ward differences in the utilization of antianxiety drugs ranging from 40% to 94% of the total number of patients on the ward. Common dosages prescribed were not unusual. Regimens of diazepam (5–10 mg) 3 to 4 times daily and flurazepam (30 mg) at bedtime were most frequently prescribed either alone or in combination. Secobarbital (100 mg) was the barbiturate sedative most frequently prescribed for bedtime use. Although most of the patients surveyed were hospitalized for conditions other than acute alcohol intoxification, a history of alcohol abuse and of medical complications associated with alcoholism was a common occurrence. By self-admission, 62 (44%) of the patients interviewed gave a history of daily alcohol ingestion of 5 years or more (82%) and drinking more than 5 drinks (40%) daily.

The patients surveyed were interviewed in an attempt to explore and possibly to identify factors that might be responsible for the apparent widespread use of these antianxiety agents. Patients were asked if they were receiving "anything" for restlessness during the day or sleeplessness at bedtime. Eighty-six (60%) responded in the affirmative while 59 (40%) in the negative. Seventy-eight (89%) patients who responded "yes" were in fact receiving antianxiety agents, while 22 (37%) of the 59 who responded "no" were documented (in the patient chart) to have been given 1 or more antianxiety agents. Patients were asked if they were in need of "something" for restlessness or agitation during the day or for sleeplessness at bedtime. Ninety-six (75%) of the patients responded in the affirmative and 51 (25%) replied in the negative. Only 20% of the patients who answered affirmatively were *not* receiving any antianxiety agents; 23 (45%) of the 51 who said they did not need any antianxiety agents received one or more.

These data raise several questions concerning the use of these agents. Are patients aware of what medications they are receiving? In the interaction between the patient, physician, and nurse, where does the responsibility lie for making a decision to either administer or receive antianxiety agents that have been prescribed on an "as needed" basis? It was observed in an earlier study on hypnotic drug usage in this hospital that it was the usual procedure on some wards to administer sedative hypnotics "PRN" to patients who were still awake at 10 or 11 P.M. We also found this to be routine practice on several wards during our survey. Whether this practice can account for our observation that some patients who claim they did not need any medications for anxiety or sleeplessness but were in fact being administered them is worth considering. An obvious problem in a survey such as this is the question of patient reliability and the role the patient's manipulative behavior may play in response to inquiries made in an interview. Patients who were in delirium or stupor or who were agitated or incoherent were not interviewed.

Recently increased interest and concern have been expressed for the cause-and-effect relationship of hospital noise and its potential hazards to health.[6] In patient interviews conducted during our utilization of sedative hypnotic drugs, the number of complaints registered by the patients of the bothersome noise and activity on the ward was most striking. While it is known that excessive exposure to noise can interfere with sleep, speech communication, and so on, nothing is known about its influence on the utilization of drugs for purposes of relieving anxiety and sleeplessness in ward environment, where noise is a constant annoyance.

The relationship between noise exposure and performance of staff caring for patients in a hospital is a subject that needs to be explored. Since the utilization review of sedative hypnotic drugs in our present study suggests that approximately 70% of the patients surveyed received these medications often on an "as needed" basis, it should be determined whether the excessive exposure of the staff and patient to noise on the ward contributed to the pattern of use. We subsequently conducted 2 surveys in attempts to assess patient and staff attitudes and opinions about their ward environment. Interestingly, the majority of ward staff personnel surveyed (80%) felt the noise and activity contributed to their patients' difficulty in getting rest or sleep, while responses from the patients indicate this to be a lesser problem (40%). The number of patients who indicated that they needed "something" for sleep was in the majority (56%) in the subsequent study. More objective studies to assess the association of noise levels and ward activity to the utilization of sedative hypnotic drugs and patient response to the drugs would certainly be worthwhile.

Another area that deserves mention is the difficulty of treating alcoholic patients in outpatient mental health clinics, a setting to which they often present themselves and one in which it may be impossible to distinguish an organic from a functional brain syndrome. Although some alcoholic patients may also have a major thought disorder, there is no evidence that the syndrome of alcoholism per se is amenable to phenothiazine pharmacotherapy. We recently conducted a drug surveillance study in the San Francisco Mental Health Centers and found that a variety of sedative hypnotic drugs are being used for alcoholic patients in Mental Health Centers without apparent awareness of the tolerance factors, drug reactions, or toxic side effects. The most important finding of this study was that 1 health center, which turned its therapeutic decision making over to a clinical pharmacist working with the physicians, used fewer drugs, had much better monitoring of compliance and better observation and control over side effects. The better control permitted both use of higher and perhaps more clinically effective doses of drugs in the more severely ill population as well as supervised drug withdrawal in a few patients, some of whom had been taking a host of psychopharmacologic agents for most of their lives. It seemed clear that the clinical pharmacist, working closely with physicians, was able to dramatically improve health-care delivery that included psychopharmacologic agents. Clinical pharmacists have been shown to markedly improve health care delivery to hypertensive patients.[5]

These data suggest a greater role for the clinical pharmacist in the treatment of alcoholic patients, not only in the areas of compliance assessment and drug interactions but also in increasing community awareness of the problems of alcoholism.

We have also been impressed with the usefulness of the medical audit as an index to the therapeutic decisions for alcoholic patients. A medical audit was conducted on alcoholism and pancreatitis at the San Francisco General Hospital. Although this audit turned up very few instances of sedative hypnotic or other drug abuse in our particular population, it did uncover a striking clinical association of recurrent pancreatitis with alcoholism. Although the problem-oriented record format of our records suggested that physicians recognize alcoholism as a precipating event for the pancreatitis, no long-term referral for any follow-up for the alcoholism was established. Since the medical audit procedure is required now for hospital accreditation, it may in the future prove to be a powerful tool to draw a profile of the use of sedative hypnotic drugs in the care of alcoholic patients, thus forming a baseline for judging therapeutic efficacy.

Clinical experience with over 7500 alcoholic patients in a county hospital setting and several drug surveillance studies and a medical audit has led us to believe that the rational role of sedative hypnotic drugs in alcoholism today is speculative. We have become very much interested in the efforts of groups such as the Boston Collaborative Drug Surveillance Program and hope to participate in studying the possibility that data collected through such a program could yield clinically important associations between alcoholism and the response to sedative hypnotic therapy. For drug surveillance and medical audit procedures to be successful we feel it is imperative that some ongoing definition of the process of alcoholism be developed such as the National Council on Alcoholism's Criteria for Alcoholism. It would be useful to have an ongoing review committee for these criteria, bringing them up to date and then applying them as part of a national computerized system concerning both drug therapy and medical complications in alcoholism. Certainly we have been impressed with the idea that drug surveillance studies and medical audit procedures are essential before we can make definitive statements concerning the efficacy of drugs in alcohol abuse. When this is accomplished, we could more rationally approach the role of placebo therapy, noise levels, and compliance in alcoholic patients.

Individual clinical experience will give us only a small piece of the puzzle. We need extensive surveillance to find small but perhaps significant differences in patient responses to drugs if we are to ensure maximum therapeutic efficacy. We must also be willing to judge the overall effectiveness of our therapy in terms of both cost and improved patient function. "Alcoholics," after all, are first "people" with problems, and it is quite possible that the overall effect of sedative hypnotic drugs might not be beneficial. The whole theme of this conference is accumulative toxicity of the excessive amounts of alcohol; we must also consider the accumulative effects of the drug used in the treatment of this condition. I am unable to answer with certainty whether the sedative hypnotic drugs are definitely rational in the treatment of alcoholism. We need more scientific pharmacologic data to make this determination.

REFERENCES

1. NATIONAL COUNCIL ON ALCOHOLISM. 1972. Criteria for the diagnosis of alcoholism. Ann. Intern. Med. 77: 249–258.
2. BLACKWELL, B. 1973. Patient Compliance. New Eng. J. Med. 289: 249–252.
3. BEECHER, H. K. 1955. The powerful placebo. JAMA 159: 1602–1606.
4. BOSTON COLLABORATIVE DRUG SURVEILLANCE PROGRAM. 1973. Clinical depression of the central nervous system due to diazepam and chlordiazepoxide in relation to cigarette smoking and age. New Eng. J. Med. 288: 277–280.
5. MCKENNEY, J. M., J. M. SLINING, H. R. HENDERSON, D. DEVINS & M. BARR. 1973. The effect of clinical pharmacy services on patients with essential hypertension. Circulation 43: 1104–1111.
6. FALK, S. A. & N. F. WOODS. 1973. Hospital noise-levels and potential health hazards. New Eng. J. Med. 289: 774–781.

THE USE OF PSYCHOACTIVE DRUGS IN THE LONG-TERM TREATMENT OF CHRONIC ALCOHOLICS

Benjamin Kissin

State University of New York
Downstate Medical Center
Brooklyn, New York 11203

The question of the use of psychoactive drugs is a sensitive one, not only in the treatment of alcoholism and other forms of drug dependency but in the treatment of neurotic symptoms in the general public as well. The problem lies in the fact that tranquilizers do effectively reduce anxiety; in turn, the overly anxious person comes to depend upon the tranquilizer as the ultimate solution to all of his difficulties. Where the "addictive" cycle has already been established, as in alcoholism or drug addiction, the danger of tranquilizer abuse is even greater and must be guarded against even more assiduously.

Given this demonstrated tendency, there has developed an understandable position in many quarters that psychoactive drugs should never be used in the long-term treatment of chronic alcoholics. But this may be throwing away the baby with the bath water. There appears to be a reasonable rationale for the use of psychoactive drugs in the long-term treatment of some chronic alcoholics and reasonable evidence to support that rationale. The rationale is based on our present understanding of the dynamics of alcoholism and the evidence is based on clinical studies measuring the effectiveness of psychoactive drug treatment in chronic alcoholics.

FIGURE 1 illustrates schematically our present conceptualization of the development of alcoholism. The susceptible person with predisposing tendencies, which may be biological, psychological, social, or any combination thereof, experiences alcohol and finds the experience rewarding. This reward may be a direct euphoriant effect or an indirect effect through the reduction of underlying tension or anxiety. Each subsequent exposure reinforces the alcohol-seeking behavior in a positive-conditioning paradigm, and primary psychological dependence ultimately develops.

Subsequently, as tolerance occurs, the person finds it necessary to ingest ever larger amounts of alcohol to secure the desired effect and an entirely new sequence of events associated with physical dependence develops. This consists chiefly of the insidious onset of withdrawal symptoms, mainly tremulousness, anxiety, depression, and insomnia, for which the only immediate relief is more alcohol. The gradually accelerating spiral of drinking to relieve withdrawal symptoms, which return shortly in an aggravated form, requiring still more alcohol with still greater subsequent withdrawal symptomatology, is the classic "addictive" cycle. As the addiction becomes more firmly entrenched, there are the associated psychological and social disruptions that still further reduce the human resources of the alcoholic and reinforce the vicious cycle.

Parenthetically, this scheme helps clarify the controversy as to whether alcoholism is a "symptom" or a "disease." In the early phases, when alcohol is utilized to help cope with some underlying predisposing tensions, whatever they might be—biological, psychological, or social—alcoholism may be viewed as a "symptom." At this stage, alcohol is being used to remedy a variety of underlying discomforts in the individual. At the end stage, when alcohol is not only the remedy but also the cause of the discomfort, alcoholism may be viewed as a distinct disease entity of which alcohol is the specific causative agent. This view of physical dependence as the dominant element in "addiction" has been presented most strongly by Dole[3] in his conceptualization of heroin addiction and as a rationale for methadone maintenance to control what he has called "tissue craving." Although other workers[17] feel that this position overemphasizes the role of physical dependence and underestimates the importance of psychological dependence even in heroin addiction, few challenge the importance of the physical dependency mechanism in perpetuating the addictive cycle. Physical dependency mechanisms are slower to develop in alcoholism; they are nevertheless probably of equal significance to those in heroin addiction, since alcohol withdrawal symptoms are so much greater and more severe and persist so much longer than those of heroin withdrawal.

Accordingly, in the alcoholic in whom significant physical dependence has developed—and this probably occurs in the great majority of severe chronic alcoholics—persistent withdrawal symptoms characterized by tremulousness,

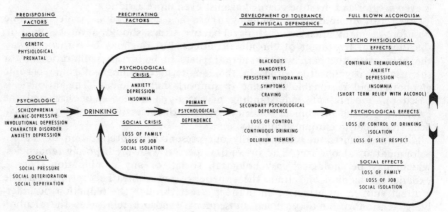

FIGURE 1. Alcoholism as symptom and disease.

anxiety, depression, and insomnia persist for periods of up to 6 months or more after the cessation of drinking. This symptom complex, which the alcoholic knows can be at least temporarily relieved by alcohol, acts as a constant reinforcement to the underlying predisposing pathology that drove him to drink in the first place. Accordingly, it would seem rational—and experimental evidence tends to support this view—that to the extent that one can help to control these withdrawal symptoms, one can help the alcoholic achieve and maintain sobriety.

However, this apparently commonsense conclusion needs strong qualification. On one hand we have the fact that severe withdrawal symptoms lead to serious discomfort, which, in turn, may lead to more drinking. On the other hand we have the paradoxically opposite but apparently equally true finding that often severe withdrawal symptoms accompanied by psychological and social disruption are the only sufficient stimulus to motivate the alcoholic to stop drinking. This is the time-honored observation that the alcoholic has to "hit bottom" before he will be willing to begin the long, hard road to rehabilitation. How, then, is one to deal with this apparent contradiction?

The answer, if there is one, seems to be that, as in so many other situations, one cannot generalize. Some chronic alcoholics, if they have sufficient internal and external resources, when they hit bottom bounce back, and are on the road to recovery. Others, with less internal and external resources, hit bottom and stay there. For those who have made the recovery without the need of medication, it is often difficult to understand why others should need it. But for those who are mired in the quicksands of the vicious cycle of addiction and are unable to extricate themselves, it is no consolation that others have been more successful.

In either event, the vicious cycle must be broken either by sheer will power, by strong psychological and social support, or, when these are not successful, through the discriminate use of medication. Breaking the cycle means abstinence from drinking and is the first step in the recovery phase. But if medication is used to combat the symptoms of withdrawal—the tremulousness, anxiety, depression, and insomnia—it should be used to reduce these to manageable proportions and not to remove them totally. Because to remove them totally is not only to remove the most powerful motivation for recovery; it is also to make the alcoholic totally dependent upon the drug.

This, then, is, in our opinion, a major indication for the use of psychoactive drugs in the long-term treatment of chronic alcoholism—to reduce withdrawal symptoms to a level low enough to permit the alcoholic to achieve abstinence but high enough to motivate him to maintain abstinence. Implicit in this concept is the position that the medication is not a treatment in itself. It is merely the handle by which one gets hold of the alcoholic to maintain him in the real treatment process, which is psychological and social rehabilitation. Goldstein[6] has stated that even in methadone maintenance the medication is not the treatment; it is merely a device for holding the patient in treatment. Similarly, when psychoactive medication is being used to control withdrawal symptoms, it is not the treatment itself but merely an adjunct for holding the patient in treatment.

How successful are tranquilizers in holding alcoholics in treatment? Recently Rosenberg[15] in a double-blind study randomly assigned new patients to one of 4 treatment conditions: disulfiram, chlordiazepoxide, multivitamins, or no medication. Since only 44% of those assigned to disulfiram accepted that treatment, the other 56% were randomly assigned to the other 3 conditions. All patients were given group therapy as the major therapeutic intervention. Using persistence in treatment as his criterion, Rosenberg found that those taking chlordiazepoxide tended most to remain in treatment, followed, in order, by those taking disulfiram, multivitamins, and no medication. The chlordiazepoxide group retention rate was significantly greater than that for the no-medication group. The disulfiram group, despite the fact that it was self-selected and hence presumably better motivated, had a more rapid dropout rate than did the chlordiazepoxide group, although the difference was not statistically significant. The patients on chlordiazepoxide showed a greater reduction in anxiety and depression than did any of the other groups. Rosenberg concludes that chlordiazepoxide appears to be effective in helping to retain alcoholics in a long-term outpatient treatment setting. This conclusion is similar to that reached by Ditman,[2] who found that unselected and mostly skid-row alcoholics on chlordiazepoxide had a lower short-term dropout rate than those on placebo, imipramine, thioridazine, or diethylpropion.

A recent study[1] in our own program tends further to support this conclusion. In one of our outpatient clinics where there is a single physician, each patient was assayed on admission on a scale of 0 to 3 for anxiety, depression, insomnia, and drinking status. The physician then prescribed medication according to his assessment, usually prescribing phenothiazines for severe agitation, chlordiazepoxide for moderate anxiety, and multivitamins when there was little evidence of agitation or anxiety. TABLE 1 illustrates relative levels of anxiety, depression, and insomnia in the 3 groups and also the 6-month retention rates. What we termed the "Librium" group was mostly on chlordiazepoxide, although there were also a few patients on diazepam (Valium®), while the phenothiazine group was mainly on either chlorpromazine (Thorazine®) or thioridazine (Mellaril®). As one can see, the levels of anxiety, depression, and insomnia, and also the drinking status, were significantly higher in the Librium and phenothiazine groups than in the no-medication group. The retention rates for the Librium and no-medication groups were both significantly higher than those for the phenothiazine group. The retention rate for the Librium group was about the same as for the no-medication group (45% to 43%). However, one would have expected the Librium group to have had a higher dropout rate than the no-medication group, since several studies[1] have shown that highly anxious and depressed patients tend to drop out of treatment more rapidly than those less so. Of further interest is the fact that among those patients with previous histories of hospitalization for delirium tremens, the retention rate in the Librium group was 48%, as against 40% in the no-medication group. It is in the DT's group that persistent withdrawal symptoms should presumably be most apparent.

Consequently, both Rosenberg's study and our own appear to support the conclusion that chlordiazepoxide is effective in keeping alcoholics in treatment in an outpatient clinic setting. The question is, how long should patients be maintained on the medication? The answer would seem to be: as long as necessary and as short as possible. Possibly because of the widespread attitude that alcoholics are particularly susceptible to become addicted to tranquilizers, many alcoholics themselves ask to have their medication first reduced and then removed. These subjects should be strongly encouraged in their resolution. With other alcoholics the trend is in the opposite direction, and one finds them gradually stepping up the use of medication. These persons must be carefully observed and strongly discouraged. However, in our own program, in which chlordiazepoxide is widely used, we have been struck by how many more there are of the first type than of the second.

If withdrawal symptoms are a rational indication for the use of chlordiazepoxide, it would seem that after 3 to 6 months of medication treatment, even in the most severe instances of persistent withdrawal symptoms, medication should be discontinued. But this line of reasoning ignores another aspect of the pathogenesis of alcoholism. Returning to FIGURE 1, we see that an important predisposing element to the development of alcoholism is a specific psychopathology. Two studies on alcoholic populations show surprisingly similar breakdowns. In a psychiatric study of 161 alcoholics Sherfey[16] found approximately 19% to be schizoid or schizophrenic, about 21% to show a severe depressive disorder, and about 41% to have psychoneurotic personality disorders. In a similar psychiatric survey of 340 alcoholics, Panepinto et al.[14] found about 18% to be schizoid or schizophrenic, about 15% to have a severe depressive disorder, and about 40% to show personality disorders. In both schizophrenia and, particularly, the depressive disorders, marked anxiety and depression were outstanding symptoms. If some form of preexisting psychopathology exists in up to $\frac{1}{3}$ of alcoholics, these patients may require chemotherapeutic intervention

TABLE 1

Patient Characteristics on Admission and Retention Rates in 3 Treatment Conditions*

	Lib vs. No Med	Librium Group (n = 129)	No Medication (n = 51)	Thorazine Group (n = 66)	No Med vs. Thor
Initial Drinking Status	$p < 0.01$	1.28 ± 1.03	0.79 ± 0.92	1.38 ± 0.96	$p < 0.001$
Anxiety	$p < 0.01$	1.40 ± 0.88	0.98 ± 0.85	1.45 ± 0.80	$p < 0.001$
Depression	$p < 0.02$	1.27 ± 0.87	0.95 ± 0.88	1.35 ± 0.77	$p < 0.01$
Sleep Disturbance	$p < 0.02$	1.15 ± 1.01	0.79 ± 0.86	1.08 ± 1.00	$p < 0.10$
Final Drinking Status	$p < 0.01$	0.76 ± 0.87	0.41 ± 0.69	0.94 ± 0.94	$p < 0.001$
Retention Rate	n.s.	45%	43%	19%	$p < 0.005$

$p < 0.005$

*Patient characteristics rated on a scale of 0–3.

entirely apart from their alcoholism. If they were not alcoholics, surely we would not withhold medication. In a sense, these persons have been medicating themselves with alcohol for their severe underlying agitation and depression; are we to deny them the more specific tranquilizers and antidepressants which they need merely because they are alcoholics?

This position highlights the importance of a careful psychiatric assay of every alcoholic to uncover any specific psychopathology for which specific chemo-therapy is indicated. The use of phenothiazines for psychotic agitation, of tri-cyclic antidepressants for retarded depressions, and possibly of lithium for manic-depressive disorders must be more extensively explored. Similarly, when the underlying psychopathology incorporates a high level of anxiety with or without depression, the use of chlordiazepoxide with or without tricyclic anti-depressants may be indicated. If the underlying psychopathology is such that in the absence of alcoholism it would require chemotherapeutic intervention, the presence of alcoholism is in itself not sufficient to contraindicate the use of psychoactive medication.

What is the overall effectiveness of this approach to the treatment of chronic alcoholism? We have recently completed a study of the drinking status of our 2 outpatient clinics, the Kings County Hospital Alcohol Clinic and the Sunset Park Alcohol Clinic. The first clinic draws from a predominantly inner-city area where 65% of the population is black and over 80% is indigent. The Sunset Park Clinic draws from a predominantly white lower middle class area. That clinic population is about 70% white and 20% Puerto Rican, but also about 65% indigent. The Kings County Clinic has about 800 patients in active treat-ment, the Sunset Park Clinic about 400. The treatment approaches in both clinics are similar; the results, not surprisingly, are also similar, although perhaps a little better at the Sunset Park Clinic, where the overall socioeconomic level is a little higher.

All patients are registered at their first visit even if they are intoxicated. At both clinics, about 35% of all registrants remain in treatment 6 months or longer. On the basis of previous experience[10] we consider all patients who leave treatment before 6 months as failures. Of those remaining in treatment 6 months or longer, approximately 45% achieve total or near total abstinence and an additional 25% achieve "limited improvement."

"Limited improvement" means a marked reduction in the amount and pattern of drinking, associated with improvement in social, family, and job status. It is usually achieved by patients who previously had patterns of totally uncon-trolled drinking, through the use of chlordiazepoxide to control withdrawal symptoms. The subject who previously entered the vicious cycle of binge drinking on every occasion can, and often does, stop at an early phase when he can control the withdrawal symptoms with chlordiazepoxide. This results in fewer binges, absence of hospitalization for detoxification, a markedly reduced alcohol intake, and often a definite improvement in social and family relationships. There is an unquestionable improvement over their original pattern of drinking and social behavior.

The "limited improvement" category has, in addition to its overall benefit, certain specific advantages and disadvantages. The advantages are apparent. It involves an interruption of the previous pattern of uncontrolled drinking. It retains people in treatment who previously would have left. It is often an intermediary stepping stone to full abstinence. In our program we never make "limited improvement" a therapeutic goal. We do accept it, however, as a real improvement on the road to "recovery." But at all times total abstinence remains the therapeutic goal of our program.

The disadvantages of the "limited improvement" category are more subtle. For one thing, the fact that the alcoholic can more or less control the pattern of his drinking paradoxically reduces his motivation to stop drinking. Secondly, to an extent, his dependence on alcohol is transferred to chlordiazepoxide. Thirdly, some alcoholics prefer to believe that this situation has permitted them to become "social" drinkers, an obvious self-delusion. Consequently, although the improvement in drinking and social adjustment in this situation is real, both in our therapeutic approach and in our overall evaluation, we consider this success as "limited," and only as a way station on the road to full abstinence.

Of the 1200 patients in the 2 outpatient clinics, approximately 80%, or about 1000, have been in treatment for 6 months or longer. Of these, 70%, or 700, have now been abstinent or "improved" alcoholics for at least 6 months. All of them were uncontrolled drinkers at registration. Since approximately $\frac{1}{3}$ of all patients presenting themselves to our clinics remain in treatment 6 months or longer and about 70% achieve some improvement, we calculate approximately a 23% overall improvement rate for all persons coming to our clinic even once.

This present improvement rate in our program, in which chlordiazepoxide alone or combined with imipramine is the chief chemotherapeutic modality, is almost identical to that found in 2 previous studies conducted by us under similar circumstances.[10, 11] Although our program began in 1957, the patient population did not assume its present characteristics, i.e., predominantly black, inner-city, and indigent, until 1962. Between 1962 and 1964 we ran a double-blind study[10] on 292 patients using emylcamate (a meprobamate derivative), amitriptyline, and placebo. The overall improvement rate, with our present criteria, was 8%. In 1964, we changed to a study[10] using our present treatment regimen—chlordiazepoxide alone or combined with imipramine—in 112 patients. The overall improvement rate was 21%. Between 1965 and 1966 we switched back to a double-blind study[10] using Prozine (a combination of promazine and meprobamate), amitriptyline, and placebo. The overall improvement rate again fell to 8%. In summary, in that study[10] the overall improvement rate for placebo in 234 patients was 9%; for amitriptyline, meprobamate and its derivatives, or metronidazole in 342 patients the rate was 7%; while for chlordiazepoxide alone or with imipramine the rate was 21%.

On the basis of this experience, in 1967 we switched to our present regimen of chlordiazepoxide alone or combined with imipramine as our predominant chemotherapeutic modality. In a study run between 1967 and 1970,[11] a careful follow-up on 497 patients 1 year after their admission revealed an overall improvement rate of 23.6%. Accordingly, over a period of 12 years, in 3 separate studies in 3 separate populations, we have found an overall improvement of about 23% in an outpatient setting using predominantly a chlordiazepoxide regimen. This is opposed to an average of about 8% in our own programs when we used placebo or other medication. This latter figure is of interest, since Gerard and Saenger[4] using similar criteria of improvement and a similar critical severity (i.e., counting all patients who come even once) found an overall improvement rate of about 10% in their survey of several outpatient clinics with population characteristics similar to those of our own.

Our overall treatment philosophy with special reference to the specific role of chemotherapy is schematically represented in FIGURE 2. We believe that the core problem in alcoholism is essentially a psychological one and that the path from alcoholic to ex-alcoholic is the one from emotional immaturity to emotional maturity. However, before one can—to use drug addiction parlance—"turn the alcoholic's head around," it is essential to remove those additional obstacles that stand between the alcoholic and his ability to obtain insight. First and foremost is the alcoholism itself. The first step in interrupting the vicious cycle of addiction is complete and adequate detoxification. This does not mean 3 or 4 days on chlordiazepoxide but rather sufficiently sustained treatment till withdrawal symptomatology has subsided to a tolerable level. Then there must be adequate medical and psychiatric care to provide for those complications and adequate social intervention to provide the basic human needs in these areas. For the inner-city alcoholic derelict who has no home, no food, no education, no job, and no vocation, group therapy is relatively meaningless. Only after the basic social supports have been provided for this individual can the "core" process of rehabilitation begin.

The core process is the process of emotional growth and reconstruction. It is at this level that the traditional treatments—AA, individual therapy, group therapy, behavioral therapy, disulfiram—are most effective, and it is at this level that ultimately the long-term treatment of alcoholism rests. Alcoholics who are fortunate enough not to have the biological and social complications of alcoholism need only these essentially psychological experiences. For them, psychoactive drugs are specifically contraindicated. For the alcoholics who have even the biological and social sequelae of alcoholism but have sufficient internal and external resources to hit bottom and bounce back, psychoactive drugs are also unnecessary. But for those less fortuante persons who have neither the internal nor the external resources to bounce back when they hit bottom, the judicious use of psychoactive drugs associated with strong psychosocial support may be essential for their ultimate recovery.

There is, finally, the question of risk. What are the dangers of using psycho-active medication in the treatment of alcoholism? This is a highly significant

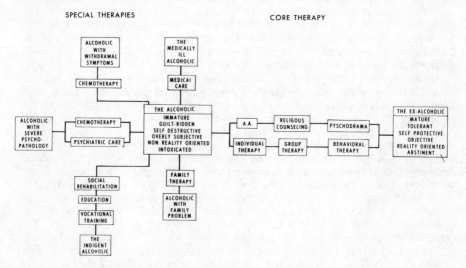

FIGURE 2. Core and special therapies of chronic alcoholism.

TABLE 2

Drugs in Order of Diminishing Hazard (with Maximum Chronic Abuse)

Drugs	I/S*	Hazard
†Alcohol		
distilled spirits (45%)	81/79	
wines (12%)	77/79	
Secobarbital	65/83	very high
Methamphetamine	63/69	
Cocaine	61/69	
†Food	‡53/16	
Diazepam (Valium)	42/69	high
Δ9-THC	40/55	
Hashish	39/50	
Heroin	§48/47	
Methylphenidate (Ritalin®)	37/48	
Methadone	§40/44	
†Cigarettes	‡37/0	intermediate
LSD-25	§31/41	
Codeine	§29/41	
Opium	§28/40	
Beer (6%)	27/42	
Chlordiazepoxide (Librium)	21/37	
Marijuana (1.2%)	25/29	low
Caffeine	23/22	
†Cigars	‡13/0	
Coffee	10/9	very low

*% of maximum possible score (100%). Individual harmfulness vs. social harmfulness.
† Significant tissue damage.
‡ High individual hazard scores only with prolonged abuse.
§ Much lower hazard with continuous use because of tolerance development (6/6).

question, since in a recent survey by Jones and Helrich[8] of some 15 000 physicians in the United States, approximately 60% prescribed chlordiazepoxide at one time or another in the treatment of chronic alcoholism, about 45% chose diazepam, and about 35% gave phenothiazines. These were the 3 tranquilizing drugs most commonly used. What can we say about them?

To be used at all in the treatment of chronic alcoholism a tranquilizing drug should have 3 qualities: (1) it should be effective in maintaining individuals in treatment, (2) it should have a low abuse potential, and (3) because of the danger of fatal interaction with alcohol, it should not potentiate the effects of alcohol. On the first issue, the effectiveness in keeping patients in treatment, our results (TABLE 1) and those of Rosenberg[15] and Ditman[2] demonstrate that the benzodiazepine drugs (chlordiazepoxide and diazepam) are more effective than the phenothiazines. In the area of drug-abuse potential, the benzodiazepines appear to have a higher abuse potential than do the phenothiazines. On the other hand, there appears to be a much higher abuse potential for diazepam than for chlordiazepoxide. This is indicated in TABLE 2, which is based on a report by Irwin.[7] That investigator grouped the estimates of 7 experts in the field of psychopharmacology on the potential harm of various drugs, the I/S heading standing for individual harmfulness vs social harmfulness. As may be seen, in this scale diazepam is a drug of high individual and social hazard, while chlordiazepoxide is one of markedly lesser hazard. In our own drug program, in which there are many polydrug abusers, diazepam is a frequent drug of abuse, chlordiazepoxide a very infrequent one. This clinical impression is supported by the study of Kokoski et al.,[12] who, studying benzodiazepine abuse in narcotic addicts through urine examination, found diazepam 5 or 6 times more frequently than chlordiazepoxide.

Finally, on the question of potentiating the effects of alcohol, available evidence suggests that of these 3 groups of drugs, phenothiazines are most potentiating, diazepam intermediate, and chlordiazepoxide least so.[9] In fact, Goldberg[5] has suggested that not only is chlordiazepoxide not potentiating, in many respects it appears to antagonize the depressant effects of alcohol. These relationships tend to be supported by the toxicologic data (TABLE 3) from the New York City Medical Examiner's Office[13] in which phenothiazine

TABLE 3

Toxicologic Findings in 2874 Cases
New York City Medical Examiner's Office
January–June, 1973

Drug	Number of Cases	Percent
Alcohol	961	33%
Methadone	379	13%
Quinine	277	10%
Barbiturates	214	$7\frac{1}{2}$%
Morphine	173	7%
Phenothiazines	120	4%
Salicylates	113	4%
Propoxyphene	79	3%
Methaqualone	63	2%
Lidocaine	28	1%
Meprobamate	26	1%
Amitriptyline	18	<1%
Benzodiazepines	18	<1%
Meperidine	11	<0.5%
Glutethimide	10	<0.5%
Ethylchlorvynol	10	<0.5%
Cocaine	9	<0.5%
Imipramine	8	<0.5%

was found in sudden deaths approximately 7 times more frequently than the benzodiazepines. Unfortunately, the latter group was not broken down into its components, but if we extrapolate the 5-6 to 1 ratio of diazepam to chlordiazepoxide found in the general abuse population, the number for the latter drug would be relatively small. Accordingly, chlordiazepoxide appears to be the drug of choice in the outpatient treatment of alcoholism. It is significantly more effective than the phenothiazines in keeping anxious and agitated patients in treatment. It has a much lower drug abuse potential than diazepam. Finally, it appears to potentiate the effects of alcohol to a lesser extent than either diazepam or the phenothiazines.

In conclusion, we believe that alcoholism, like any other form of drug dependence, is best treated without the use of any psychoactive drugs. Unfortunately, as with heroin addiction, drug-free treatment is most desirable but not always effective. For those persons who cannot make it without pharmacologic assistance, many alcoholics who would otherwise be doomed to failure can be helped by the judicious use of psychoactive medications.

REFERENCES

1. BAEKELAND, F., B. KISSIN & L. LUNDWALL. 1975. The influence of medication on outcome in the outpatient treatment of chronic alcoholics. In preparation.
2. DITMAN, K. S. 1961. Evaluation of drugs in the treatment of alcoholics. Quart. J. Stud. Alcohol (Suppl. 1): 107–116.
3. DOLE, V. P. & N. E. NYSWANDER. 1966. A medical treatment for diacetyl morphine (heroin) addiction. J.A.M.A. 195: 972.
4. GERARD, D. L. & G. SAENGER. 1966. In Outpatient Treatment of Alcoholism. Univ. of Toronto Press, Toronto, Canada.
5. GOLDBERG, L. 1970. Effects of ethanol in the central nervous system. In Alcohol and Alcoholism. R. E. Popham, Ed.: 42–56. Univ. of Toronto Press, Toronto, Canada.
6. GOLDSTEIN, A. 1974. Understanding narcotic addiction. J. Addiction Res. Foundation. 3: 7.
7. IRWIN, S. 1973. A rational approach to drug abuse prevention. Contemporary Drug Problems 2 (1): 3–46.
8. JONES, R. W. & A. R. HELRICH. 1972. Treatment of alcoholism by physicians in private practice. Quart. J. Stud. Alcohol 33: 117–131.
9. KISSIN, B. 1974. Interactions of ethyl alcohol and other drugs. In Biology of Alcoholism. 3, Clinical Pathology. B. Kissin & H. Begleiter, Eds.: 109–161. Plenum Press. New York, N.Y.
10. KISSIN, B. & A. PLATZ. 1968. The use of drugs in the long term rehabilitation of chronic alcoholics. In Psychopharmacology—A Review of Progress, 1957–1967. D. H. Efron, Ed.: 835–852. P.H.S. Publication 1836. Washington, D.C.
11. KISSIN, B., A. PLATZ & W. H. SU. 1971. Selective factors in treatment choice and outcome in alcoholics. In Recent Advances in Studies of Alcoholism. N. K. Mello, & J. H. Mendelson, Eds.: 781–802. HEW publication 71-9045.
12. KOKOSKI, R. J., S. HAMMER & M. SHIPLET. 1974. Benzodiazepine abuse in narcotic addict treatment programs: urinalysis as a detection and control measure. 36th Annual Scientific Meeting Committee on Problems of Drug Dependence. Mexico City, March 10–14, 1974.
13. NEW YORK CITY MEDICAL EXAMINER'S OFFICE STATISTICS. 1973. Courtesy of Dr. Dominick J. DiMaio, Acting Chief Medical Examiner.
14. PANEPINTO, W. C., M. J. HIGGINS, W. Y. KEANE-DAWES & D. SMITH. 1970. Underlying psychiatric diagnosis as an indicator of participation in alcoholism therapy. Quart. J. Stud. Alcohol 31: 950–956.
15. ROSENBERG, C. M. 1974. Drug maintanance in the outpatient treatment of chronic alcoholism. Arch. Gen. Psychiat. 30: 373–377.
16. SHERFEY, M. J. 1955. Psychopathology and character structure in chronic alcoholism. In Etiology of Chronic Alcoholism. O. Diethelm, Ed.: 16–42, Charles C. Thomas, Springfield, Ill.
17. WIKLER, A. 1972. Theories related to physical dependence. In Chemical and Biological Aspects of Drug Dependence. S. J. Mule & H. Brill, Eds.: 359–387. CRC Press. Cleveland, Ohio.

THE TREATMENT OF ALCOHOLISM:
WHAT DO WE DO ABOUT LONG-TERM SEDATIVES?

LeClair Bissell

Smithers Alcoholism Treatment and Training Center
The Roosevelt Hospital
New York, New York 10019

Before discussing the more controversial aspects of long-term use of sedative drugs in the treatment of the alcoholic, it is helpful to acknowledge those areas that are relatively free from debate. A variety of soporifics and minor tranquilizers is helpful in treating acute withdrawal states when the intake of these drugs can be adequately controlled. This, of course, is not long-term use.

Because a patient happens to be alcoholic, there is no guarantee that he may not also suffer from an emotional illness for which phenothiazines are needed. They should be given to alcoholics thoughtfully and carefully, and only in those situations where they are truly indicated, but this is true for any patient, not just the alcoholic. The stronger soporific drugs have resulted in so many deaths among alcoholics, either when used alone or in combination with alcohol, that only the foolhardy would continue to prescribe them, particularly now that evidence is mounting that they are ineffective in treating insomnia for more than a few days and in fact, if used regularly, may soon make the insomnia worse.[1]

The real storm center of the sedative controversy is the long-term use of the "minor" tranquilizers. Chlordiazepoxide (Librium®) and diazepam (Valium®) are the most widely used and are therefore the ones we might most profitably examine. Librium was first marketed in 1960. That same year, Leo Hollister of the Palo Alto VA Hospital gave very large doses of this drug to 11 psychiatric inpatients for several months and then withdrew them abruptly by switching to placebos. He was able to demonstrate withdrawal reactions in 10 of them. Three had seizures while others suffered insomnia, loss of appetite, nausea, agitation, and/or depression.[2]

In 1963 Valium was marketed, too late to be included in Carl Essig's 1964 paper, in which he reported on 6 new depressant drugs that he felt to be potentially hazardous and addicting. These were meprobamate, chlordiazepoxide, methyprylon (Noludar®), glutethimide (Doriden®), ethinamate (Valmid®), and ethchlorvynol (Placidyl®). He noted that these 6 bore a "striking resemblance" to barbiturates in their major signs of intoxication and withdrawal symptoms. He stated that the withdrawal effects of chlordiazepoxide were less acute than meprobamate or barbiturates but did occur.[3]

In 1966 the federal government attempted to include chlordiazepoxide and diazepam in the Drug Abuse Control Amendments. Hollister and Harris Isbell, among many others, testified before examiner Edgar Buttle. After some 5000 pages of testimony, Buttle recommended to FDA Commissioner Goddard that these drugs be included. Goddard temporized on the grounds that since the FDA and the Treasury Department were on the verge of transferring their enforcement responsibilities to the Justice Department, it would be unfair for him to decide the matter. In April of 1968, the Bureau of Narcotics and Dangerous Drugs was formed, and in May 1969, its director, Ingersole, ordered that these drugs be federally controlled. Roche Laboratories objected.

In April of 1970, a new set of hearings began. By this time chlordiazepoxide and diazepam sales had reached $200 million per year, or about 45% of the U.S. tranquilizer market, now glutted with some 700 varieties of tranquilizers and tranquilizer combinations. Meanwhile reports were coming in from Los Angeles County—U. of Southern California Medical Center—implicating the 2 in widespread drug misuse. They, together with secobarbitol (Seconal®), chloral hydrate, and dextropropoxyphene (Darvon®), were the drugs most often prescribed in "excessive quantities." By 1970, worldwide sales of these two drugs had come to $2 billion from the time they were introduced.[4]

In early June of 1970, 14 days of hearings again produced testimony of widespread abuse of both drugs. On November 16, 1970, examiner Buttle again ruled for the government, saying the 2 drugs had a "substantial" potential for abuse. By October, the Comprehensive Drug Abuse Prevention and Control Act passed the House and went on to the Senate. Chlordiazepoxide and diazepam had not been included. Senator Dodd succeeded in having them included in the Senate version. Since the 2 versions now differed, the bills went into committee. The story of what went on in that committee is a fascinating account of the art of lobbying. The final version of the bill emerged with both drugs uncontrolled.

Finally, in February, 1971, BNDD ordered that the 2 drugs be included in the new law. Roche appealed and in April, 1971, was granted a stay by federal court, which meant that they would not be controlled until the appeal process was finished. In 1971, Roche sold 50 million Valium prescriptions and 24 million Librium, a sales volume of just under 3.6 billion pills.[4]

On March 28, 1973, the 3rd District U.S. Court of Appeals in Philadelphia issued a 44-page decision on these 2 drugs. In it the court noted that evidence was ample that both produce euphoria, tolerance, withdrawal, and sometimes paradoxical rage, are illegally diverted, and have a substantial potential for abuse. However, on the technicality that in 1966 the FDA counsel, James Phelps, did not submit a certain report to Roche Labs and, therefore, had denied them due process, both drugs in fact escaped regulation. That same month saw Valium the number-one prescription drug in the United States, followed by Darvon and Librium.

In view of the above history, one could well question the use of these drugs, particularly in an alcoholic population who come to us for treatment because of their inability to control another sedative drug, ethyl alcohol. Alcoholics are people prone to seek a chemical solution to human problems. Why then would anyone want to risk compounding their difficulties by giving them yet another addicting drug?

I have been struck repeatedly by the fact that whenever I lecture to a physician audience about disulfiram (Antabuse®), there are almost always questions raised about potential hazards to the patient. There is immediate concern about the risk in an alcohol-disulfiram reaction. Rarely does a similar audience raise such questions about chlordiazepoxide and diazepam.

Suppose the question is asked: Do these drugs do harm? I would have to answer yes; they do.[5-7] The week that I was asked to deliver this paper, I was asked to consult in the case of a New York businessman. He is an alcoholic who has done no drinking for 3 years but has been given diazepam on a regular basis by his internist. Complaints by his wife and business associates about his altered personality, slurred speech, and unsteady gait had forced him to confess to getting diazepam from 4 different doctors and taking it in excessive amounts. Several attempts to cut down on his intake had been unsuccessful. He is now undergoing inpatient treatment in Minnesota for his addiction. He faces the expense and inconvenience of several weeks away from job and family as well as whatever effect his behavior has had on his wife and children.

Also, during that same week, I watched a respected colleague attempt to chair a meeting. Usually meticulous, this physician was rather disheveled. To the embarrassment of some of his staff, his behavior was grandiose and inappropriate; he stumbled over his words, spilled his coffee, and was obviously under the influence of drugs. He, too, is alcoholic and has not, as best I can ascertain, been drinking. However, he is a chlordiazepoxide abuser who frequently uses over 400 mg/day. He, too, has had to be hospitalized for this problem in the past.

My original plan for this paper was to review the literature, to collect statistical evidence and the opinions of others to support my own point of view, and to avoid at all costs the impressionistic and anecdotal approach. However, as I went through the process of reading, duplicating articles, and quarreling with research design, I became increasingly aware that this was not very productive. My thinking about this issue has not come from orderly columns of figures. Rather it has come from the experience of living for 21 years as a sober alcoholic observing and sharing experience with other alcoholics and from the clinical experience of working in this field. I do not believe in chlordiazepoxide and diazepam maintenance programs, and I do not prescribe long-term sedative drugs. I have not encountered any convincing evidence that their benefits outweigh their hazards.

Some of these hazards are the obvious ones of cross-addiction, but there are other problems, too. A pragmatic one is that many AA members also disapprove of these drugs and will exert a subtle or not so subtle group pressure on the sedative user. This tends to separate him from other group members and to place him in conflict between his need to win acceptance from his fellows and his desire to trust in his physician. These drugs, therefore, serve to isolate him from an important source of help.

Another consideration is that anxiety itself and its attendant discomfort may provide motivation for change. While drugs may keep a patient comfortable, they may simultaneously make it harder to convince him of the need to alter his patterns of behaving and reacting. Most psychiatrists admit that organic brain syndromes are difficult to treat. A patient who has been drinking or is otherwise sedated is harder to reach than one whose brain is free of chemicals.

Often we delude ourselves that we have the option of attempting to substitute drugs for the patient's alcohol, as if this possibility had never occurred to the patient. Careful questioning will often reveal that the alcoholic has already been using them and, in fact, is already taking them in combination with his alcohol. This attempted solution, then, is frequently one the alcoholic has tried and which has failed before he comes to us for treatment.

One wonders, then, why physicians are so stubbornly insistent on prescribing these drugs. Part of the story is probably that we have moved from the old tradition of taking the badness out of patients by bleeding or purging them to the era of putting the goodness in. Patients expect to be given drugs, and we in turn feel obliged to meet their expectations. Giving medicine is what most of us are taught to do. Deprived of our prescription pads and expected to treat only with ourselves, we are facing a much more difficult situation.

I think physicians often resist giving disulfiram not because of the handful of patients who have died but because giving this particular drug means depriving him of alcohol, of saying no to something. I think we like to give sedatives because we are gratifying the patient, giving him something he wants or that we feel he ought to want that is a substitute for the alcohol we're taking away from him. It is much quicker and easier to give a drug for insomnia than it is to spend an hour exploring with a patient the ways of dealing with the discomfort of not sleeping.

Keith Ditman has said that "Drugs, to be of benefit for the alcoholic, must be significantly better than a placebo. Unfortunately, although drugs are widely prescribed there is little evidence to support the use of very many. Since they are more widely used than evidence warrants, one can only conclude that they are used in ignorance or desperation which in effect is treating the doctor and not the patient."[8]

Arguments are still advanced at times that, if one does not prescribe sedatives for a highly manipulative patient, he will simply get his drugs from another doctor and fall into hands less expert than ours. The same reasoning could be applied whenever one is asked to give penicillin for a viral pharyngitis, but that does not justify our doing so. It is also agreed that giving drugs makes the patient more likely to keep coming back to us. Many a street-corner drug pusher would agree.

I do think we need to give our patients a substitute for alcohol, but I don't think that substitute can be another sedative. I think it has to be our concern, our time, our caring, and ourselves.

REFERENCES

1. KALES, ANTHONY, E. O. BIXLER, T-L. TAN & M. B. SCHARF. 1974. Chronic hypnotic-drug use, ineffectiveness, drug-withdrawal insomnia, and dependence. J.A.M.A. 227: 513.
2. HOLLISTER, LEO E., F. P. MOTZENBECKER & R. O. DEGAN. 1961. Withdrawal reactions from chlordiazepoxide ("Librium"). Psychopharmacologia 2: 63–68.
3. ESSIG, CARL. 1964. Addiction to non-barbiturate sedative and tranquilizing drugs. Clin. Pharmacol. Ther. 5: 334.
4. PEKKANEN, JOHN. 1973. The American Connection. Follett Pub. Co. Chicago, Ill.
5. BARTEN, HARVEY H. 1965. Toxic psychosis with transient dysmnestic syndrome following withdrawal from Valium. Amer. J. Psychiat. 121: 1210–1211.
6. RELKIN, RICHARD. 1966. Death following withdrawal of diazepam. New York J. Med. 66: 1770–1772.
7. PATCH, VERNON D. 1974. The dangers of diazepam, a street drug. N. Eng. J. Med. 290: 807.
8. DITMAN, KEITH S. 1966. Review and evaluation of current drug therapies in alcoholism. Psychosom. Med. 28 (4) Part II: 667–677.